UK COMPETITION PROCEDURE

The Modernised Regime

ELIZABETH O'NEILL

Barrister, Treasury Solicitor's Department

EMMA SANDERS (née SCAIFE)

*Solicitor of the Supreme Court of England and Wales, Barrister and Solicitor
of the Supreme Courts of Western Australia and Victoria*

Consultant Editors

ANNELI HOWARD

Barrister, Monckton Chambers

MARGARET BLOOM

*Senior Consultant, Freshfields Bruckhaus Deringer, London,
and Visiting Professor, King's College, London*

OXFORD
UNIVERSITY PRESS

OXFORD
UNIVERSITY PRESS

Great Clarendon Street, Oxford OX2 6DP

Oxford University Press is a department of the University of Oxford.
It furthers the University's objective of excellence in research, scholarship,
and education by publishing worldwide in

Oxford New York

Auckland Cape Town Dar es Salaam Hong Kong Karachi
Kuala Lumpur Madrid Melbourne Mexico City Nairobi
New Delhi Shanghai Taipei Toronto

With offices in

Argentina Austria Brazil Chile Czech Republic France Greece
Guatemala Hungary Italy Japan Poland Portugal Singapore
South Korea Switzerland Thailand Turkey Ukraine Vietnam

Oxford is a registered trade mark of Oxford University Press
in the UK and in certain other countries

Published in the United States
by Oxford University Press Inc., New York

Crown copyright material is reproduced under Class Licence
Number C01P0000148 with the permission of OPSI
and the Queen's Printer for Scotland

First published 2007

British Library Cataloguing in Publication Data
Data available

Library of Congress Cataloging in Publication Data
Data available

Typeset by RefineCatch Limited, Bungay, Suffolk
Printed in Great Britain
on acid-free paper by
Antony Rowe, Chippenham

ISBN 978–0–19–928427–6

1 3 5 7 9 10 8 6 4 2

UK COMPETITION PROCEDURE

The Modernised Regime

This book is dedicated to

Terry Butler, Victoria Butler, Anne Clayton, Neil Feinson, Mark Haskew,
Georgina Laverack, Sophie Mitchell (née Gregg), Sejual Shah,
and Jonathan Spence.

FOREWORD

'May you live in interesting times' is said to be an ancient Chinese curse. Although, the nearest real Chinese proverb is probably 'It's better to be a dog in a peaceful time than be a man in a chaotic period'. The past seven years have certainly been an interesting time for competition law as the competition framework facing firms in the United Kingdom has completely changed. The key changes are outlined below. Some may even have considered this was a chaotic period. Hence, the need for a user-friendly book that explains the extensive competition procedure and practice that now applies.

In March 2000, the Competition Act 1998 came into force introducing prohibitions on anti-competitive agreements and abuses of a dominant position, modelled on the EC Articles 81 and 82. This dramatically changed the role and increased the resources of the Office of Fair Trading (OFT) which, for the first time, had strong powers of investigation—including dawn raids—and the ability to impose substantial fines for any breaches of the prohibitions. These new powers required completely new procedures at the OFT. The Sectoral Regulators for the communications, energy, rail and water industries (now called Ofcom, Ofgem, Ofreg NI, ORR and Ofwat) obtained concurrent competition powers with the OFT which they can apply in their particular sectors. A new appeal tribunal—now called the Competition Appeal Tribunal (CAT)—was established with its own procedure.

Only three years later, in mid-2003, the Enterprise Act 2002 came into force. Apart from a new merger regime (which is not discussed in this book) other important changes introduced by this Act include OFT market studies, a new market investigation regime at the Competition Commission (CC), super-complaints, company director disqualification following competition infringements and a criminal cartel offence. This again dramatically changed the role and increased the resources of the OFT. The Regulators also obtained some of these new powers.

The Competition and Enterprise Acts together provide the UK competition authorities—the OFT, the CC and the Regulators—with one of the most extensive sets of competition powers in the world. This will deliver real benefits for consumers if the powers are used to ensure markets work well. But the implications for business are significant, whether as a defendant, a complainant to a competition authority, or a claimant in a private action in a court.

It was not just the UK government that introduced new competition laws in this period—an important new European Union Regulation was also introduced. Hard on the heels of the Enterprise Act, the procedures for applying Articles 81 and 82 throughout the European Union were revolutionised by the Modernisation Council Regulation 1/2003 which came into force in May 2004. This Regulation gives the Member States a new major role in applying the competition prohibitions. The Member States, together with the European Commission, set up the European Competition Network (ECN) in order to work more closely together under the new Regulation. Prior to Modernisation, the Community competition rules were almost entirely applied by the European Commission, while national authorities worked largely independently of each other using their various national laws. Today, Community and national competition rules are frequently applied simultaneously, national laws have generally been aligned with Community law and the authorities cooperate extensively. The overlap and interaction of these regimes can have significant implications for business as is explained by Elizabeth O'Neill and Emma Sanders, the authors of this book.

Clearly, there has been a dramatic rate of change since 2000—and particularly so compared with the past. The previous major reform in competition law in the United Kingdom was over 25 years earlier when the Fair Trading Act of 1973 established the OFT. Although it may be a rash prediction, it seems to me that further dramatic changes in competition procedure are unlikely over the next few years. Hence, this is an excellent time to publish a guide to the procedure and practice of UK competition authorities in enforcing competition laws.

The book will enable practitioners, in-house counsel, students and others working in competition law to cope more effectively with the demands of the regulatory regime—and to benefit from the new regime. Not only does this work capture the experience gained from Competition Act cases since 2000 (and some recent Enterprise Act cases), but it is also the first book to concentrate on procedure in the modern competition regime. This allows a comprehensive coverage of the extensive practice and procedure of UK competition authorities in applying the prohibitions in the Competition Act and Article 81 and 82, as well as of that for Enterprise Act market studies, market investigations, super-complaints, director disqualification and the criminal cartel offence. Elizabeth and Emma explain the bodies involved in the United Kingdom (including the European Commission), the investigatory and decision processes and appeals. Substantive competition law is only considered briefly, by way of background.

Elizabeth and Emma are in a unique position to write this book. After a period working in contentious and non-contentious competition law in city law firms, they joined the OFT to lead the introduction of the EC Modernisation changes in the UK. They worked together in the OFT's modernisation team during the preparation for the new regime on 1 May 2004. They led in introducing the necessary changes to the OFT's practice and procedure for the proper implementation of Regulation 1/2003. Their role included leading in the drafting of revised OFT guidelines, commenting on the draft revisions to the Competition Act 1998 (and suggesting alternative drafting), and liaising with the European Commission (and the other members of the ECN) on issues relating to the implementation of Regulation 1/2003,

Anneli Howard has contributed generously to this book in her editorial role. A former solicitor and référendaire at the ECJ, Anneli is a barrister specialising in European law, human rights and competition law. She has extensive experience of UK competition practice and procedure, whether during administrative proceedings before the regulators or trial litigation before the courts. She has participated in some of the most important recent competition cases, such as the Replica Kits price fixing appeals (*Allsports and JJB v OFT*) before the CAT and the Court of Appeal and *Inntrepreneur v Crehan* before the House of Lords. She acts for private undertakings (for example she represented Visa in the *Master-Card v OFT* interchange appeals) and competition authorities (*Floe v Ofcom, Brannigan v OFT* and *E.On v ORR*). Her practical experience as a barrister specialised in competition law gives her a unique insight into how the modernised competition regime works in the real world.

Lastly, the subject matter of this book is of great interest to me. As Director of Competition Enforcement at the Office of Fair Trading until summer 2003, I was responsible for the implementation of the Competition Act 1998 and the Enterprise Act 2002, and began the process of implementing Regulation 1/2003. Since then I have seen the impact of these changes as a practitioner and academic. It was therefore with great interest that I accepted the role of consultant editor. In discussing draft chapters it was notable that Emma, Elizabeth, Anneli and I sometimes had different opinions as to the appropriate stance to adopt towards some of the more contentious issues. This reflects our different but complementary experiences of competition law and practice which are very real strengths for producing a well-balanced book in this novel and important area.

Today there are over 100 jurisdictions in the world with some competition laws and a quarter of these are in the European Union. Twenty-five years ago there were around 30 jurisdictions with some competition laws but very few European countries had enforcement authorities with powers to prohibit anti-competitive agreements or unilateral conduct. It is increasingly important for business to be aware of competition law, but this is becoming a real challenge because of the increasing complexity of the regulatory regimes. The UK regime is arguably one of the most complex—at least in terms of the variety of powers. This unique book should be the answer for those who need a clear picture of it.

Margaret Bloom

PREFACE

Piglet was so excited at the idea of being Useful that he forgot to be frightened any more . . .

Winnie-the-Pooh, chapter 7[1]

We (Elizabeth and Emma) first worked together on the 'modernisation' project at the Office of Fair Trading, where we were tasked with bringing into effect in the UK the changes resulting from Regulation 1/2003. Despite being under constant pressure, the project team we worked with managed to make the entire process remarkably enjoyable—so much so that we jumped at the chance to continue the project by writing this book on UK competition procedure. The book draws from much of the effort of the modernisation team and is dedicated to our OFT colleagues, whom we thank for providing us with sufficient enthusiasm to take on this project. Of course, the views expressed in this book are ours and do not represent the views of the OFT, Treasury Solicitors or any law firm, or other organisation.

The final product is also the result of a great deal of work on the part of many individuals who provided input or assistance in the process. We wish to thank in particular our consultant editors, Margaret Bloom and Anneli Howard, whose contributions surpassed all expectations and vastly improved the end product. We are also indebted to Claudia Mercer, Carrie Orr, and Sulema Jahangir for their invaluable research and assistance; and we are grateful to Tabitha Bonney, James Aitken, Chris Mayock, Bea Tormey, and Nicholas Gibson for their helpful comments and insights which found their way into various chapters.

When we began writing, we envisaged a shorter book and a rather shorter time frame. Not only did the scope of the book expand inexorably over time but we and our consultant editors have, collectively, experienced two weddings, the birth of two children and two grandchildren, and three job changes in the past two years. It is perhaps unsurprising that this project has taken a little longer to complete than we originally intended.

This book would not have been possible without the support and encouragement of our families, friends and, in particular, our partners. Although it cannot

[1] From Winnie the Pooh © A A Milne. Published by Egmont UK Limited, London and used with permission.

possibly make up for the experience we have put them through, we do wish to express here our gratitude for our partners' patience and good humour in allowing this book to take over much of our lives for such an extended period of time. Thus we thank Michael Sanders and Philippe Carré.

Lastly, having overcome our initial trepidation, we very much hope that someone, somewhere, finds this book to be Useful.

Emma and Elizabeth
March 2007

CONTENTS—SUMMARY

CONTENTS

4. Exemptions and Exclusions

6. Starting an Investigation in the United Kingdom

Contents

TABLES OF UK CASES

COMPETITION COMMISSION REPORTS

INFORMATION COMMISSIONER

OFFICE OF COMMUNICATIONS

OFFICE OF FAIR TRADING DECISIONS

TABLES OF EUROPEAN CASES

EUROPEAN COURT OF JUSTICE (numerical/chronological)

EUROPEAN COURT OF FIRST INSTANCE (numerical/chronological)

EUROPEAN COMMISSION DECISIONS (alphabetical)

EUROPEAN COMMISSION DECISIONS (numerical/chronological)

TABLES OF UK LEGISLATION

STATUTORY INSTRUMENTS

TABLES OF EU TREATIES AND LEGISLATION

REGULATIONS

TABLE OF INTERNATIONAL TREATIES AND AGREEMENTS

LIST OF ABBREVIATIONS

CAA	Civil Aviation Authority
CAT	Competition Appeal Tribunal
CC	Competition Commission
CDO	Competition Disqualification Order
CDU	Competition Disqualification Undertaking
CFI	Court of First Instance
the Commission	European Commission
ECHR	European Convention on Human Rights
ECJ	European Court of Justice
ECN	European Competition Network
ECtHR	European Court of Human Rights
FSA	Financial Services Authority
LME	London Metal Exchange
Ofcom	Office of Communications
Ofgem	Gas and Electricity Markets Authority
Ofreg NI	Northern Ireland Authority for Energy Regulation
OFT	Office of Fair Trading
Ofwat	Water Services Regulation Authority
ORR	Office of Rail Regulation
SFO	Serious Fraud Office

1

COMPETITION RULES APPLICABLE IN THE UNITED KINGDOM

A. Introduction

1.01 Over the past seven years, there has been a significant increase in competition law regulation at both national and international levels.[1] Any undertaking currently active in the United Kingdom is subject to a complex and jurisdictionally diverse regulatory regime. Anti-competitive behaviour in the United Kingdom is potentially caught by diverse prohibitions of domestic and European provenance, each carrying its own enforcement procedure and each leading to different civil and/or criminal sanctions.

1.02 In such a complex regulatory environment (which carries significant penalties), there is a need for a textbook to examine the practice and procedure of competition law enforcement in the United Kingdom. It is the aim of this book to undertake this examination, in order to facilitate the orientation of undertakings, practitioners, and students interested in this area. This book considers the practice and procedure relating to the enforcement of competition measures applicable in the United Kingdom, and in particular focuses on procedures applied by UK based competition authorities in relation to the following: Article 81 and Article 82 of the Treaty of Rome, the Chapter I and Chapter II prohibitions contained in the Competition Act 1998, the market investigation regime contained in the Enterprise Act 2002, the criminal cartel offence, and director disqualification following breach of competition law.

1.03 Further, as one undertaking's behaviour can be simultaneously investigated by more than one competition authority (or alternatively, the undertaking's behaviour can be investigated by one authority exercising different powers), this book also examines the legal and practical problems that arise from the overlap and interaction between the various procedural regimes mentioned above.

1.04 As the focus of this book is on the procedure for the enforcement of competition law in the United Kingdom, substantive competition law is only considered briefly, by way of background (see paras 1.21 et seq below). Further, the main focus is on the application of competition law by domestic competition authorities such as the Office of Fair Trading (**OFT**), Sectoral Regulators, and the Competition Commission (**CC**), although authorities outside the United Kingdom (such as the European Commission (**the Commission**) and national competition authorities of other Member States) that are able to take action relating to behaviour in the United Kingdom are mentioned and discussed where relevant.

---

[1] To name but a few measures that have been introduced: the Competition Act 1998, the Enterprise Act 2002, Council Regulation (EC) 1/2003 of 16 December 2002 on the implementation of the rules on competition laid down in Articles 81 and 82 of the Treaty [2003] OJ L1/1.

This book only considers in passing the private enforcement of competition **1.05** rules by means of civil litigation before the courts. It does not consider the procedure relating to merger control in the United Kingdom, nor does it look at the application of sectoral legislation regulating the utilities in regulated sectors such as communications matters, gas, electricity, water and sewerage, railway and traffic services, although there is some discussion of competition aspects of such legislation.

B. The EC Treaty

The Treaty of Rome 1957[2] (**the EC Treaty**) established a common market **1.06** within which people, goods, services, and capital could move freely. From the very outset, competition rules formed an integral part of the common market scheme devised by the EC Treaty. The rules were included in the EC Treaty in order to facilitate the achievement of market integration: they prevented private undertakings from erecting barriers to trade between Member States by means of anti-competitive conduct. Today, in addition to contributing to the single market enterprise, the same EC competition rules are valued because of their contribution to achieving broader social objectives such as the development of a stable economy, the enhancement of efficiency, and the protection of consumers.[3]

The EC rules on competition are contained in Chapter 1, Title VI, Pt III of the **1.07** EC Treaty (Articles 81 to 89 EC).[4] The EC Treaty contains two substantive antitrust prohibitions aimed at deterring anti-competitive agreements and conduct by undertakings: Article 81, which prohibits anti-competitive agreements between undertakings; and Article 82, which prohibits dominant undertakings from abusing their position of dominance on the market.

Council Regulation 1/2003 on the implementation of the rules on competition **1.08** laid down in Articles 81 and 82 of the Treaty[5] (**Regulation 1/2003**) gives effect

---

[2] As amended by the Single European Act (1986), the Treaty of Maastricht (1992), the Treaty of Amsterdam (1997), and the Treaty of Nice (2000).

[3] Commission Notice, *Guidelines on the application of Article 81(3) of the Treaty* [2004] OJ C101/97, para 13 provides: 'The objective of Article 81 is to protect competition on the market as a means of enhancing consumer welfare and of ensuring an efficient allocation of resources.'

[4] For further reading on substantive EC competition law the following texts are recommended: *Faull & Nikpay: The EC Law of Competition* (Oxford University Press, 1999); *Bellamy & Child: European Community Law of Competition* (5th edn, Sweet & Maxwell, 2001); R Whish, *Competition Law* (5th edn, LexisNexis Butterworths, 2003).

[5] Council Regulation (EC) 1/2003 of 16 December 2002 on the implementation of the rules on competition laid down in Articles 82 and 82 of the Treaty [2003] OJ L1/1.

to Article 81 and Article 82. It provides the procedural framework for the enforcement of Article 81 and Article 82 across the European Community. Before examining Regulation 1/2003 and Articles 81 and 82, it is worth considering how these measures take effect in the United Kingdom.

(a) Effects of European competition provisions in the United Kingdom

1.09 The provisions of the EC Treaty, including Articles 81 and 82 EC, are part of the law of the United Kingdom and are enforced as such by UK courts.[6] They take effect according to their terms, as interpreted by the European Court of Justice (**ECJ**).[7]

(i) Direct effect

1.10 The ECJ has held that the prohibitions contained in Article 81(1) and Article 82 EC are directly applicable provisions of European law.[8] This means that they create rights for individuals and, conversely, impose obligations on them:

> Article 85(1) of the Treaty [now Article 81(1)EC] and Article 86 of the EC Treaty (now Article 82EC) produce direct effects in relations between individuals and create rights for the individuals concerned which the national courts must safeguard (judgments in Case 127/73 BRT and SABAM [1974] ECR 51, paragraph 16, (BRT I) and Case C-282/95 P Guérin Automobiles v Commission [1997] ECR I-1503, paragraph 39).

> It follows from the foregoing considerations that any individual can rely on a breach of Article 85(1) of the Treaty before a national court even where he is a party to a contract that is liable to restrict or distort competition within the meaning of that provision.[9]

1.11 In addition to the Treaty provisions themselves, Article 81 and Article 82 are given effect by means of directly applicable regulations (such as block exemption regulations) and Commission Notices. Block exemption regulations and other relevant European regulations adopted in the competition field, such as Regulation 1/2003, are directly applicable by their very nature and therefore, provided they are sufficiently clear, can be relied upon by individuals.[10] Commission Notices are non-binding instruments (although they may bind the Commission itself), but UK courts and authorities have regard to them in

---

[6] By virtue of European Communities Act 1972, s 2(1).   [7] ibid, s 3(1).
[8] The provision for exemption contained in Art 81(3) EC has only recently become directly applicable, under Art 1(2) of Regulation 1/2003.
[9] Case C-453/99 *Courage Ltd v Crehan* [2001] ECR I-6297, paras 23 and 24.
[10] Art 249 EC provides: 'A regulation shall have general application. It shall be binding in its entirety and directly applicable in all Member States.' See also Case C-253/00 *Antonio Munoz y Cia SA v Frumar Ltd* [2002] ECR I-7289.

applying Article 81 and Article 82 EC and the Chapter I and Chapter II prohibitions in the Competition Act 1998.[11]

National courts are under an obligation to safeguard the effectiveness of **1.12** Article 81 and Article 82. This obligation extends to creating a right to damages or other relief for those harmed by a breach of the competition rules:

> The full effectiveness of Article 85 of the Treaty and, in particular, the practical effect of the prohibition laid down in Article 85(1) would be put at risk if it were not open to any individual to claim damages for loss caused to him by a contract or by conduct liable to restrict or distort competition.[12]

(ii) Supremacy

Further, by virtue of the supremacy of EC law,[13] Article 81 and Article 82 EC **1.13** (as well as any EU regulations or directives) take precedence over any contrary provision of national law. National courts and national competition authorities must, if necessary, decline to give effect to inconsistent domestic law.[14] The ECJ has elaborated how the principle of primacy takes effect in the competition field in the case law.[15] In *Ahmed Saeed Flugreisen* it held:

> [I]t should be borne in mind in the first place that, as the Court has consistently held, while it is true that the competition rules set out in Articles 85 and 86 concern the conduct of undertakings and not measures of the authorities in the Member States, Article 5 [now Article 10] of the Treaty nevertheless imposes a duty on those authorities not to adopt or maintain in force any measure which could deprive those competition rules of their effectiveness.[16]

Further discussion of this issue, and an examination of the interaction between domestic competition law provisions and European law provisions can be found in Chapters 3, 13 and 14.

(b) Regulation 1/2003

Council Regulation 1/2003 on the implementation of the rules on competition **1.14** laid down in Article 81 and 82 of the Treaty (Regulation 1/2003) provides the

---

[11] By virtue (respectively) of their obligation of loyal cooperation under Art 10 EC and s 60 of the Competition Act 1998.

[12] Case C-453/99 *Courage Ltd v Crehan* [2001] ECR I-6297, para 26.

[13] Case 26/62 *NV Algemene Transport- en Expeditie Onderneming van Gend en Loos v Nederlandse Administratie der Belastingen* [1963] ECR 1; Case 6/64 *Costa v ENEL* [1964] ECR 585.

[14] Case 106/77 *Simmenthal (No 2)* [1978] ECR 629; Case C-198/01 *Consorzio Industrie Fiammiferi v Autorita Garante della Concorrenza e del Mercato* [2003] ECR I-8055.

[15] Case 14/68 *Wilhelm v Bundeskartellamt* [1969] ECR 1.

[16] Case 66/86 *Ahmed Saeed Flugreisen v Zentrale zur Bekampfung unlauteren Wettbewerbs eV* [1989] ECR 803, para 48.

framework for the procedure and enforcement of Article 81 and Article 82.[17] Regulation 1/2003 came into force on 1 May 2004 and replaced Regulation 17/62, First Regulation implementing Articles [81] and [82] of the Treaty (**Regulation 17**).[18] It substantially changed the procedure for the enforcement of Article 81 and Article 82 and applies to all sectors.[19]

1.15 Regulation 17 provided a centralised system of competition enforcement. The overwhelming majority of the enforcement burden lay with the Commission. In particular, the Commission was the sole authority empowered to apply Article 81(3) to agreements. For an agreement to escape the prohibition in Article 81(1), it either had to be notified to the Commission for the Commission to grant it an individual exemption decision, or it had to fall within the terms of the few block exemption regulations by which the Commission exempted categories of agreements.

1.16 The centralised system of competition enforcement established under Regulation 17 gave rise to an extremely heavy administrative burden for the Commission, which was unable to address the thousands of individual agreements notified for exemption. As the preambles to Regulation 1/2003 acknowledge, such a system 'hampers application of the Community competition rules by the courts and competition authorities of the Member States, and the system of notification it involves prevents the Commission from concentrating its resources on curbing the most serious infringements. It also imposes considerable costs on undertakings.'[20]

1.17 Regulation 1/2003 revolutionised the procedure for the enforcement of Article 81 and Article 82 by introducing the following key changes:

- It removed the Commission monopoly on the application of Article 81(3) by empowering national courts and national competition authorities to apply

---

[17] The legal basis for the regulation is Art 83(1) EC, which empowers the Council to legislate to give effect to the principles set out in Arts 81 and 82.

[18] [1962] OJ 13/204.

[19] Initially, Regulation 1/2003 did not implement Arts 81 and 82 EC in respect of all sectors (see Art 32 thereof). Regulation 1/2003 did not apply to (1) international tramp vessel services as defined in Art 1(3)(a) of Regulation (EEC) 4056/86, (2) maritime transport service that takes place exclusively between the ports in one and the same Member State as foreseen in Art 1(2) of Regulation (EEC) 4056/86, and (3) air transport between Community airports. These exclusions have since been removed by Council Regulation (EC) 1419/2006 of 25 September 2006 and Council Regulation (EC) 411/2004 of 26 February 2004, so that all these sectors now fall within the remit of the European Commission and the national competition authority's powers of investigation and enforcement with regard to infringements of Arts 81 and 82 EC. Previously, enforcement procedures in these sectors were provided by the EC Competition Law (Articles 84 and 85) Enforcement Regulations 2001, SI 2001/2916.

[20] Regulation 1/2003, Preamble 3.

Article 81(3).[21] Individuals can now rely on Article 81(3) before the national courts and in proceedings before the domestic regulatory authorities.

- It abolished the system of notification and exemption and allowed undertakings to rely directly on Article 81(3), no prior decision by the European Commission (or any other authority) to that effect being required.[22]

- It decentralised the enforcement of Article 81 and Article 82 by, in certain circumstances, obliging national competition authorities to apply Article 81 and Article 82.[23]

- It obliged the Commission and the competition authorities of the Member States to apply Article 81 and Article 82 in close cooperation.[24] Simultaneously, the Member States' competition authorities and the Commission established the European Competition Network of National Competition Authorities (**ECN**) in order to facilitate this cooperation.[25]

- It gave national competition authorities extensive powers (such as information exchange, investigating on each others' behalf) to enable their cooperation in ensuring the effective application of Article 81 and Article 82 in the context of the ECN.

In the United Kingdom, the following authorities have been designated as **1.18** national competition authorities for the purposes of Regulation 1/2003:[26] the OFT, the Office of Communications (**Ofcom**), the Office of Rail Regulation (**ORR**), the Gas and Electricity Markets Authority (**Ofgem**), the Northern Ireland Authority for Energy Regulation (**Ofreg NI**), the Water Services Regulation Authority (**Ofwat**), and the Civil Aviation Authority (**CAA**). These authorities, in addition to their powers to apply Chapter I and Chapter II, are thereby additionally empowered (and occasionally obliged) to apply Articles 81 and 82

---

[21] See Chapter 4.

[22] Regulation 1/2003, Art 1(2) provides: 'Agreements, decisions and concerted practices caught by Article 81(1) of the Treaty which satisfy the conditions of Article 81(3) of the Treaty shall not be prohibited, no prior decision to that effect being required.'

[23] ibid, Art 3(1) provides: 'Where the competition authorities of the Member States or national courts apply national competition law to agreements, decisions by associations of undertakings or concerted practices within the meaning of Article 81(1) of the Treaty which may affect trade between Member States within the meaning of that provision, they shall also apply Article 81 of the Treaty to such agreements, decisions or concerted practices. Where the competition authorities of the Member States or national courts apply national competition law to any abuse prohibited by Article 82 of the Treaty, they shall also apply Article 82 of the Treaty.'

[24] ibid, Art 11(1) provides: 'The Commission and the competition authorities of the Member States shall apply the Community competition rules in close cooperation.' See Chapter 3 generally.

[25] See the *Joint Statement of the Council and the Commission on the functioning of the Network of Competition Authorities*, document 15435/02 ADD1, available at <http://register.consilium.eu.int>.

[26] Pursuant to Competition Act 1998 and Other Enactments (Amendment) Regulations 2004, SI 2004/1261, reg 3.

EC in the United Kingdom in those sectors of the economy where they have jurisdiction.

1.19 Regulation 1/2003 does not seek to harmonise the procedures by which Article 81 and Article 82 are enforced in the Member States. These are provided under national law. The Competition Act was amended with the introduction of Regulation 1/2003 to extend the designated authorities' powers of investigation and enforcement in relation to Chapter I and Chapter II cases to Article 81 and Article 82 cases.

1.20 Shortly before Regulation 1/2003 came into effect, the Commission published the following Notices aimed at clarifying the practice and procedure under Regulation 1/2003:[27]

- Commission Notice on cooperation within the Network of Competition Authorities (2004/C 101/03) (**Network Notice**);
- Commission Notice on the cooperation between the Commission and the courts of the EU Member States in the application of Articles 81 and 82 EC (2004/C 101/04) (**Courts Cooperation Notice**);
- Commission Notice on the handling of complaints by the Commission under Articles 81 and 82 of the EC Treaty (2004/C 101/05) (**Complaints Notice**);
- Commission Notice on informal guidance relating to novel questions concerning Articles 81 and 82 of the EC Treaty that arise in individual cases (guidance letters) (2004/C 101/06) (**Informal Guidance Notice**);
- Guidelines on the effect on trade concept contained in Articles 81 and 82 of the Treaty (2004/C 101/07) (**Effect on Trade Notice**);
- Guidelines on the application of Article 81(3) of the Treaty (2004/C 101/08) (**Article 81(3) Notice**).

(c) **Article 81 of the EC Treaty**

1.21 Article 81 of the EC Treaty is made up of three parts:

1.22 First, the prohibition: Article 81(1) of the EC Treaty prohibits all agreements between undertakings, decisions by associations of undertakings, and concerted practices which may affect trade between Member States and which have as their object or effect the prevention, restriction, or distortion of competition within the common market.[28] Non-exhaustive examples of anti-competitive conduct caught by Article 81(1) are provided in the text of Article 81(1). These

---

[27] Although Commission Notices are non-binding, they provide a valuable source of guidance and UK courts and competition authorities have regard to them, where relevant, by virtue of s 60 of the Competition Act and Article 10 EC.
[28] The full text of Art 81 EC is at Annex 1 to this chapter.

include: directly or indirectly fixing prices, limiting or controlling production, and sharing markets or sources of supply.

Secondly, the consequences of breaching the prohibition: Article 81(2) provides **1.23** that where an agreement falls within the prohibition of Article 81(1), it shall automatically be void.[29] However, there are additional consequences that follow from breaching the prohibition that are not expressly set out in the text of the EC Treaty. Undertakings breaching Article 81(1) may be susceptible, inter alia, to regulatory fines by the Commission and/or the national competition authorities and to civil actions for damages before the courts of the Member States.[30] In some Member States, such as the Republic of Ireland, criminal charges may follow. In the United Kingdom, the breach of Article 81 may also indirectly lead, for certain individuals involved, to criminal cartel proceedings or director disqualification proceedings.

Thirdly, Article 81(3) provides a possible 'defence' to infringement of Article **1.24** 81(1) for certain agreements that are deemed to have the redeeming pro-competitive features it identifies. Agreements satisfying the conditions set out in Article 81(3) have a defence to a finding of infringement of Article 81(1). Those agreements are accordingly valid and enforceable, despite falling within the prohibition of Article 81(1).

The application of Article 81 is a two-step process. First, assessing whether an **1.25** agreement falls within the Article 81(1) prohibition. Only if the agreement falls within the prohibition in Article 81(1) does it become relevant to undertake the second step, which is to apply Article 81(3) to determine whether the pro-competitive benefits produced by the agreement outweigh the anti-competitive effects.[31] Each of these steps is considered in turn below.

(i) *The prohibition in Article 81(1)*

The prohibition contained in Article 81(1) can be broken down into four **1.26** constitutive elements:

- agreements, decisions by associations of undertakings and concerted practices
- between undertakings
- which may affect trade between Member States
- which have as their object or effect the prevention, restriction or distortion of competition within the common market.

---

[29] Case C-126/97 *Eco Swiss China Time Ltd v Benetton* [1999] ECR I-3055, paras 36 and 37; Case C-453/99 *Courage Ltd v Crehan* [2001] ECR I-6297, paras 21 and 22.
[30] On the consequences that flow from breach of the Art 81(1) prohibition, see Chapter 10. See Case C-453/99 *Courage Ltd v Crehan* [2001] ECR I-6297 on the right to damages.
[31] Commission Notice, *Guidelines on the application of Article 81(3) of the Treaty* [2004] OJ C101/97, para 11.

The legal burden of establishing that an agreement falls within Article 81(1) and satisfies each of the elements above lies on the party or authority alleging the infringement of Article 81.[32] Each of these elements to the Article 81(1) prohibition has, over time, acquired a distinct and autonomous definition in the jurisprudence of the ECJ and the European Court of First Instance (**CFI**) as well as in decisions taken by the European Commission.[33] The section below discusses the four key elements to the prohibition in Article 81(1) identified above. Further, it considers two additional elements that are relevant to determining whether an agreement falls within Article 81(1). The case law has established that, in certain circumstances, an agreement will not fall within Article 81(1) either if ancillary restrictions contained therein are necessary to the agreement (the concept of 'necessity') or alternatively if the agreements themselves do not sufficiently affect competition—known as 'appreciability' or 'de minimis' thresholds.

1.27 **Agreements, decisions by associations of undertakings, and concerted practices**   The terms 'agreement', 'decisions by associations of undertakings', and 'concerted practice' have each acquired a conceptually distinct meaning.[34] However, it is important to note at the outset that the boundaries between the concepts are imprecise and that the definitions are not necessarily mutually exclusive: it is possible, on the particular facts of a case, that a decision by associations of undertakings also amounts to an 'agreement' or that 'an agreement and/or a concerted practice' can be held to arise from the same facts.[35] The regulator need not characterise an infringement as either an agreement or a concerted practice, it is sufficient that the conduct amounts to one or the other.[36]

1.28 *Agreements*   The ECJ has given the term 'agreement' a broad definition, which is aimed at capturing the various means by which an anti-competitive course of behaviour can be agreed upon between undertakings. Accordingly, there are no requirements as to form: the definition extends from binding written agreements[37] between undertakings to informal, oral, non-binding 'gentlemen's agreements'.[38]

1.29 Further, there is no need for the agreement actually to have been put into effect.[39] The fact that certain parties to a cartel may have participated ineffectually,

---

[32] Regulation 1/2003, Art 2.

[33] See Chapter 3 for a discussion of the roles of the ECJ, the CFI, and the European Commission and the extent of any obligation on UK courts and competition authorities with regard to the case law emanating from these bodies.

[34] For an in-depth discussion of these concepts see Whish (n 4 above) 91 et seq.

[35] Case C-49/92 P *Commission v ANIC Partecipazioni SpA* [1999] ECR I-4125.

[36] See *JJB Sports v OFT* [2004] CAT 17, judgment on liability, para 174.

[37] Joined Cases 41, 44 & 45/69 *ACF Chemiefarma NV v Commission* [1970] ECR 661.

[38] Cases 41, 44 & 45/69 *ACF Chemiefarma NV v Commission* [1970] ECR 661.

[39] Case T-7/89 *Hercules Chemicals NV v Commission* [1991] ECR II-1711.

reluctantly, or intermittently is not sufficient to negate the existence of the anti-competitive agreement or to excuse the conduct of those undertakings.[40]

However, for there to be an agreement there has to be a concurrence of **1.30** wills between two or more distinct undertakings. There is a fine and difficult line to draw between situations in which one undertaking unilaterally takes anti-competitive action (which are excluded from the remit of Article 81) and situations where one undertaking tacitly acquiesces in practices and measures adopted by another (which amount to an agreement for the purposes of Article 81).[41]

The following extract from *Volkswagen v Commission*[42] provides a useful **1.31** indication of the breadth of the concept of an 'agreement':

> According to settled case-law, in order for there to be agreement within the meaning of Article 81(1) EC it is sufficient that the undertakings in question should have expressed their joint intention to conduct themselves on the market in a specific way . . . As regards the form in which that common intention is expressed, it is sufficient for a stipulation to be the expression of the parties' intention to behave on the market in accordance with its terms . . .
>
> It follows that the concept of agreement within the meaning of Article 81(1) EC, as interpreted by the case-law, centres around the existence of a concurrence of wills between at least two parties, the form in which it is manifested being unimportant so long as it constitutes the faithful expression of the parties' intention (the Bayer judgment, paragraph 69).

Decisions by associations of undertakings   Trade associations may serve as the **1.32** fora for anti-competitive collusive behaviour. Accordingly, their constitutions, regulations and recommendations can all amount to decisions for the purposes of Article 81(1).[43] Alternatively they may be construed as an agreement between all the members of the association.

Concerted practices   A concerted practice is a loose, informal understanding **1.33** between undertakings to limit competition that falls short of an agreement or a decision. The ECJ defined a concerted practice as follows in *ICI v Commission*:[44]

---

[40] ibid.

[41] Case T-41/96 *BayerAG v Commission* [2000] ECR II-3383 and Joined Cases C 2/01 & 3/01 P *Bundesverband der Arzneimittel-Importeure eV v Bayer AG* [2004] ECR I-23.

[42] Case T-208/01 [2003] ECR II-5141, paras 30 and 33. Approved on appeal to the ECJ in Case C-74/04 P *Commission v Volkswagen*, judgment of 13 July 2006, para 37: 'in order to constitute an agreement within the meaning of Article 81(1) EC, it is sufficient that an act or conduct which is apparently unilateral be the expression of the concurrence of wills of at least two parties, the form in which that concurrence is expressed not being by itself decisive'. See also *Argos, Littlewoods and JJB v OFT* [2006] EWCA Civ 1318.

[43] *Re National Sulphuric Acid Association Ltd* [1980] OJ L260/24.

[44] Case 48/69 [1972] ECR 619, para 64.

> . . . the object is to bring within the prohibition of that Article [Article 81] a form of coordination between undertakings which, without having reached the stage where an agreement properly so-called has been concluded, knowingly substitutes practical cooperation between them for the risks of competition.

1.34 There is no need for a verbal expression of this consensus: parties may signal their intention to cooperate with each other by means of their conduct.[45] Accordingly (and controversially),[46] the existence of a concerted practice may be inferred from the conduct of the parties:[47]

> By its very nature, then, a concerted practice does not have all the elements of a contract but may inter alia arise out of a coordination which becomes apparent from the behaviour of the participants.

> Although parallel behaviour may not by itself be identified with a concerted practice, it may however amount to strong evidence of such practice if it leads to conditions of competition which do not correspond to the normal conditions of the market, having regard to the nature of the products, the size and number of the undertakings and the volume of the said market.

In *JJB Sports Plc v OFT*,[48] the Competition Appeal Tribunal (**CAT**) found that two undertakings at the same level in the market had reached an agreement or formed a concerted practice with one another and a third party (the intermediary) by indicating their future pricing intentions to the third party (who was not at the same level in the market).[49]

1.35 **Between undertakings** By their terms, Article 81 and Article 82 only apply to anti-competitive conduct by undertakings. The term 'undertaking' has accordingly been broadly defined by the ECJ, expanding the scope of Article 81 and Article 82. The basic definition of the concept is provided in *Hofner and Elser v Macrotron GmbH*:[50]

> [T]he concept of an undertaking encompasses every entity engaged in an economic activity regardless of the legal status of the entity and the way in which it is financed.

1.36 The presentation or form of the entity is accordingly irrelevant: individuals, partnerships, clubs, associations, charities, all can qualify as undertakings providing they carry on an 'economic activity'. The concept of an economic activity, which is the substantive concept at the heart of the definition of an undertaking, is broad. The ECJ recently confirmed, in its judgment in *FENIN*,[51] that it is the

---

[45] Case 40/73 *Cooperatieve Vereniging Suiker Unie UA v Commission* [1975] ECR 1663.
[46] See Whish (n 4 above) 514–516.
[47] Case 48/69 *ICI v Commission* [1972] ECR 619, paras 65–66.   [48] [2004] CAT 17.
[49] Upheld on appeal to the Court of Appeal in *Argos, Littlewoods and JJB v OFT* [2006] EWCA Civ 1318, para 103.
[50] Case C-41/90 [1991] ECR I-1979, para 21.
[51] Case C-205/03 P, judgment of 11 July 2006.

activity consisting in offering goods and services on a given market that is the characteristic feature of an economic activity. It endorsed the CFI's finding in *FENIN v Commission*[52] that, despite wielding significant purchasing power, the organisations managing the Spanish Health Service did not act as undertakings, as they were operated according to the principle of solidarity (funded from social security contributions and other state funding) and provided services free of charge.

An agreement within the meaning of Article 81(1) can only be reached if there is **1.37** an anti-competitive coordination between two or more independent undertakings: Article 81(1) does not apply to agreements reached between entities that are part of the same undertaking.[53] In determining whether entities are part of the same undertaking, so that Article 81 may apply to an agreement reached between these entities, European case law does not consider the legal personality of the entities, but the degree to which the entities are economically dependent on each other. Entities will be considered part of a 'single economic unit' where one controls the behaviour of the other (for example, parent-subsidiary) so that the latter does not enjoy real autonomy in determining its course of action on the market.[54]

Which may affect trade between Member States The effect on trade test is an **1.38** essential element of both Articles 81 and 82: Article 81(1) and Article 82 only apply where the agreement or the conduct at issue 'may affect trade between Member States'. The notion of effect on trade is therefore the jurisdictional criterion that determines whether EC competition law applies to any one case.[55]

In an oft-cited case, the ECJ has defined the test for effect on trade as follows **1.39** (STM test):

> . . . it must be possible to foresee with a sufficient degree of probability on the basis of a set of objective factors of law or of fact that the agreement [or conduct] in question may have an influence, direct or indirect, actual or potential, on the pattern of trade between Member States.[56]

The ECJ has confirmed that there is no need for the restrictions of competition in the agreement to affect trade, as long as the agreement *as a whole* may do so.[57]

---

[52] Case T-319/99 *Federacion Nacional de Empresas de Instrumentacion Cientifica Medica Tecnica y Dental (FENIN) v Commission* [2003] ECR II-357.

[53] Case 15/74 *Centrafarm BV v Sterling Drug Inc* [1974] ECR 1147.

[54] Case T-102/92 *Viho v Commission* [1995] ECR II-17.

[55] Joined Cases 56 & 58/64 *Etablissements Consten Sarl and Grundig-Verkaufs GmbH v Commission* [1966] ECR 299; see also Regulation 1/2003, Art 3(1).

[56] *Société Technique Minière v Maschinenbau Ulm* [1966] ECR 235.

[57] See to this effect, Case 193/83 *Windsurfing International Inc v Commission* [1986] ECR 611, para 96.

As the above definition makes clear, there is no need for an actual effect on trade to be established; the mere potential for an agreement to do so suffices.

1.40　An alternative test has also been applied occasionally, which relates to a change in the structure of competition in the relevant market, as opposed to an influence on the pattern of trade.[58] This alternative test is usually more helpful in the Article 82 context of assessing whether particular *conduct* may have an effect on trade between Member States, although it has also occasionally been applied to *agreements* as well.[59]

1.41　*The European Commission Notice*　The European Commission has provided guidance in applying the effect on trade test by publishing a notice on the test— the Effect on Trade Notice. The Notice is not intended to be exhaustive. It summarises the basic principles developed by the EC courts on the effect on trade test, and provides examples of the application of these principles in various scenarios. The Effect on Trade Notice also sets out a new trade de minimis or appreciability threshold test. The Effect on Trade Notice is not binding on the ECJ, national courts, or national competition authorities, but provides guidance on the methodology recommended by the Commission.[60] It is, however, binding on the European Commission by virtue of principles of fair administration and legitimate expectations, subject to any future developments in the Community case law.[61] UK courts and authorities have regard to the Effect on Trade Notice.[62]

1.42　*What is 'trade'?*　Trade is a broad concept covering all economic activity, including activity relating to the exchange of goods and services, and the establishment of corporate entities.[63] The effect on trade test is not applied by reference to any effect on competition, since this would be part of the substantive application of competition law, which is irrelevant to the application of the jurisdictional test. Further, it is irrelevant whether any effect on trade is positive or negative: the test merely requires that there may be an effect on trade.[64] Evidence of an increase in cross-border trade will not mean that the test is not satisfied.

1.43　*What is 'between Member States'?*　This can cover agreements and undertakings which originate from or exist outside the European Union, as well as agreements

---

[58] Case T-228/97 *Irish Sugar Plc v Commission* [1999] ECR II-2969, para 169.
[59] Case C-306/96 *Yves Saint Laurent Parfums SA v Javico International* [1998] ECR I-1983.
[60] Except where they have agreed to be so bound. Note also that para 3 of the Effect on Trade Notice states that it is also 'intended to give guidance to the courts and authorities of the Member States in their application of the effect on trade concept'.
[61] Effect on Trade Notice, para 5.
[62] Competition Act 1998, s 60, see also OFT442, *Modernisation* (December 2004) para 4.6.
[63] See further Effect on Trade Notice, paras 19–20.
[64] Case T-141/89 *Trefileurope* [1995] ECR II-791 and Effect on Trade Notice, paras 34–35.

and undertakings which operate purely within one Member State.[65] Factors relevant to this assessment are the geographic extent of the agreement(s) or conduct, the location of the relevant undertaking(s), the place where the agreement is implemented, and the place where its effects are felt. There will not be any effect on trade between Member States where the effect or possible effect of the agreement or conduct is too removed from the European Union. This would occur where the agreement or undertaking was entirely outside the European Union and the agreement has at most a very limited effect on any market within the European Union. There will also not be any effect on trade between Member States where the effects or possible effects of the agreement or conduct are purely regional or local within one Member State.

Assessment by reference to the agreement or conduct   The application of the **1.44** effect on trade test is examined by reference to the agreement or conduct in question. The agreement or conduct is assessed as a whole. This means the test is applied by reference to a network of agreements, or a pattern of conduct, rather than simply reviewing the individual act or agreement in isolation.[66] It also means that, in relation to agreements, the extent of the involvement of a particular party to the agreement is entirely irrelevant to the application of this test.[67]

Potential and indirect effects   The STM test is not confined to actual and direct **1.45** effects but extends to an indirect or potential influence on trade as well. Direct effects occur in relation to products covered by the agreement or conduct in question whereas indirect effects extend to related products such as raw materials, intermediate products, and spare parts. It is not required that an agreement or conduct has actual effect on trade between Member States.

The words 'may affect' have been interpreted by the ECJ to require that the **1.46** agreement or conduct must be *capable* of having such an effect, even if that is an indirect effect, or a potential effect at some stage in the future. In some cases, the implementation of the agreement will not necessarily result in immediate effects on trade but may do so at some point in the future, if foreseeable market developments are taken into account.[68] This interpretation has significantly widened the test, and reduced the evidential requirements which might otherwise apply for establishing an effect on trade between Member States. Nevertheless there is a limit to this interpretation: the potential or indirect effects must not be

---

[65] See further Effect on Trade Notice, paras 21–22.

[66] Case 193/83 *Windsurfing International Inc v Commission* [1986] ECR 611, para 96; Effect on Trade Notice, paras 14 and 17.

[67] Case T-2/89 *Petrofina SA v Commission* [1991] ECR II-1087, para 226; Effect on Trade Notice, para 15.

[68] Case 107/82 *AEG Telefunken AG v Commission* [1983] ECR 3151, para 60.

hypothetical or speculative, as this will mean they are too remote to establish a link between the (possible) effects of the conduct or the agreement and trade between Member States.[69] There must be a *sufficient degree of probability*, established by a set of objective factors viewed as a whole. Such factors may be factual or legal in nature, including, but not limited to, the nature of the agreement or practice, the market position of the undertakings concerned, and the relevant legal and economic context.[70]

1.47 *'By nature' effect on trade* In some cases the ECJ has found that particular types of agreement or conduct are by their very nature capable of having an effect on trade between Member States. This includes cross-border cartel agreements, agreements between undertakings in two or more Member States that concern imports and exports, agreements and practices covering or implemented in several Member States, and agreements extending over the whole territory of a single Member State.[71]

1.48 *Appreciable effect on trade* The ECJ's jurisprudence to date has focused on the positive conditions for there to be an effect on trade. There is little guidance as to what characterises a situation where there is no such effect. However, the jurisprudence has defined a quantitative element to the effect on trade test: certain agreements have been held to fall outside of the scope of Article 81 and Article 82 by reason of their insignificant effect on trade.[72] According to the case law, when, having regard to the weak position of the undertakings on the relevant market, the agreements do not have the capacity to affect trade appreciably between Member States, the criterion of effect on trade is not satisfied and Article 81(1) does not apply.[73] For most small or medium sized enterprises, the most important aspect of the effect on trade test is to consider whether or not any relevant effect on trade of an agreement falls below the appreciability threshold.

1.49 The case law does not identify clear thresholds below which an agreement can be considered not to have an appreciable effect on trade, but the European Commission Notice spells out a rule, based on the ECJ jurisprudence on appreciability, which provides certain minimum thresholds for agreements,

---

[69] Effect on Trade Notice, para 43.
[70] Case C-306/96 *Yves Saint Laurent Parfums SA v Javico International* [1998] ECR I-1983, para 17; Effect on Trade Notice, paras 28–32.
[71] Effect on Trade Notice, paras 29–30.
[72] The concept should be distinguished from 'appreciable effect on competition' which applies an appreciability threshold in relation to the anti-competitive effects of an agreement: see the Commission's Notice on agreements of minor importance [2001] OJ C368/07.
[73] Case 5/69 *Volk v Ets Vervaecke SPRL* [1969] ECR 295, para 7.

below which the European Commission considers that it can be assumed there is 'no appreciable affectation of trade' (**the NAAT rule**).[74]

The NAAT rule imposes a minimum floor, below which there is a rebuttable **1.50** presumption that there is no appreciable effect on trade. In essence, it requires that two cumulative conditions be satisfied:

(1) the aggregate market share of the parties does not exceed 5 per cent; and
(2) the annual turnover of the relevant party or parties[75] does not exceed 40 million euros.

The Effect on Trade Notice at paragraphs 54 to 57 sets out further details of **1.51** how the factors relevant to this appreciability threshold test will be measured and assessed by the European Commission. Significantly, even if an agreement is such that by its very nature it is capable of affecting trade, it will not be viewed as being capable of affecting trade if it falls below the appreciability threshold.[76] In other words, the appreciability threshold takes precedence over the nature of the agreement.

Falling below the threshold provisions does not mean that an agreement is *not* **1.52** conclusively capable of having an appreciable effect on trade between Member States: it only gives rise to a rebuttable presumption to this effect. Relevantly, the European Commission has stated that where undertakings assume in good faith that an agreement falls below the trade appreciability threshold, it will not impose fines.[77] The OFT has to the authors' knowledge not taken this stance, presumably because an agreement falling below the threshold may fall within the Competition Act prohibitions.

---

[74] Effect on Trade Notice, para 52 sets out the NAAT rule (so-called by the European Commission but a better description may be the Trade de Minimis rule).

[75] For horizontal agreements, the turnover threshold applies to the aggregate annual Community turnover of the undertakings concerned, and where the agreements concern the joint buying of products the relevant turnover is the parties' combined purchases of the products covered by the agreement(s). For vertical agreements, the turnover threshold applies to the aggregate annual Community turnover of the supplier, and for licence agreements the relevant turnover is the aggregate turnover of the licensees in the products incorporating the licensed technology and the licensor's own turnover in such products. In cases concerning vertical agreements between a buyer and several suppliers the relevant turnover is the buyer's combined purchases of the products covered by the agreement(s). (Effect on Trade Notice, para 52.)

[76] Effect on Trade Notice, para 50. See also para 53, which states that the European Commission will also hold the view that where an agreement by its very nature is capable of affecting trade between Member States, there is a rebuttable *positive* presumption that such effects on trade are appreciable when the turnover of the parties in the products covered by the agreement exceeds 40 million euros. A similar positive presumption applies where the parties' market share exceeds 5% unless the agreement covers only part of a Member State.

[77] ibid, para 50.

1.53   Conversely, if the agreement is above the appreciability threshold, there is no automatic presumption that it necessarily affects trade to an appreciable extent. The Commission will assess qualitative elements, such as the nature of the agreement and the nature of products concerned on a case by case basis.[78]

1.54   Although the Commission Notice only represents the Commission's view, and is accordingly not binding on the European courts or on other courts or competition authorities that may apply Article 81(1), the NAAT rule can assist in ruling out an appreciable effect on trade in respect of a small category of agreements that satisfy the thresholds set out in the rule.

Which have as their object or effect the prevention, restriction or distortion of competition within the common market

1.55   *Prevention, restriction or distortion of competition*   The concept of prevention, restriction or distortion of competition is not a reference to contractual restrictions. It relates to whether the agreement, viewed in its economic context, and from an economic perspective, interferes with competition.[79] One of the fundamental premises underlying Article 81(1) is that each economic operator must independently determine the policy that it intends to adopt on the market.[80]

1.56   *Object or effect*   Agreements will fall foul of Article 81(1) where either their object or their effect is anti-competitive, as emphasised by the ECJ in *Société Technique Minière v Maschinenbau Ulm*: 'The fact that these are not cumulative but alternative requirements [is] indicated by the conjunction "or" . . .'.[81]

1.57   Where an agreement can be identified as having an anti-competitive object, there is no need to go on and establish that it has an anti-competitive effect:[82]

> [T]here is no need to take account of the concrete effects of an agreement once it appears that it has as its object the prevention, restriction or distortion of competition.

1.58   The object of an agreement is not determined by reference to the intention of the parties to the agreement, but by considering the terms of the agreement in their economic context.[83] Only some types of anti-competitive conduct are

---

[78]   ibid, paras 51 and 59; see discussion of various types of agreements and practices at ibid, paras 61 et seq.

[79]   *Société Technique Minière v Maschinenbau Ulm* [1966] ECR 235.

[80]   Joined Cases 40–48/73 *Cooperatieve Vereniging Suiker Unie UA v Commission* [1975] ECR 1663, para 173.

[81]   Case 56/65 [1966] ECR 235.

[82]   Joined Cases 56 & 58/64 *Etablissements Consten Sarl and Grundig-Verkaufs GmbH v Commission* [1966] ECR 299, 342.

[83]   *Société Technique Minière v Maschinenbau Ulm* [1966] ECR 235.

considered so serious and obviously damaging to competition that any agreement providing for such conduct is considered anti-competitive by its very object. Examples of such 'per se' or 'hard-core' anti-competitive conduct include: horizontal price fixing, limiting production, market sharing, and market partitioning.[84] Where the terms of an agreement do not provide for the narrow category of identified conduct that is considered particularly anti-competitive, the agreement does not have an anti-competitive object as such.

Agreements that do not have an anti-competitive object will nonetheless be caught by the prohibition in Article 81(1) if they have anti-competitive effects. In order to determine whether an agreement has anti-competitive effects, one must consider the effects of the agreement at issue on the market in which the agreement operates. Market definition is discussed at paras 1.77–1.81. An in-depth economic analysis of the agreement is required—not only considering its effects, but also weighing these effects against the competition that would exist on the market absent the agreement: 'The competition in question must be understood within the actual context on which it would occur in the absence of the agreement in dispute.'[85] This is known in economic terms as 'the counterfactual'.[86] **1.59**

Necessity Although the ECJ and CFI have expressly ruled out adopting a 'rule of reason' approach (involving weighing the pro-competitive effects of the agreement against its anti-competitive effects) to the application of Article 81,[87] there are a number of cases in which these courts have considered that a restriction contained in an agreement did not fall within Article 81(1), because the restriction was necessary to achieve the legitimate objectives of the agreement.[88] The 'ancillary restraints' test applies only in cases where the main transaction is not restrictive of competition.[89] In *Métropole Télévision*,[90] the CFI rejected **1.60**

---

[84] Case 27/87 *Louis Erauw Jacquery Sprl v La Hesbignonne Société Coopérative* [1988] ECR 1919. For further discussion relating to these concepts, see *Competition Law* by R.Whish (n 4 above) 109–115 and *Bellamy & Child* (n 4 above) 2.056–2.122.

[85] *Société Technique Minière v Maschinenbau Ulm* [1966] ECR 235. See Article 81(3) Notice, para 17.

[86] Case T-328/03 *O2 v Commission*, judgment of 2 May 2006.

[87] ibid, para 69: 'Such a method of analysis does not amount to carrying out an assessment of the pro- and anti-competitive effects of the agreement and thus to applying a rule of reason, which the Community judicature has not deemed to have its place under Article 81(1) EC (Case C-235/92 P *Montecatini v Commission* [1999] ECR I-4539, paragraph 133; *M6 and others v Commission*, paragraphs 72 to 77; and Case T-65/98 *Van den Bergh Foods v Commission* [2002] ECR II-4653, paragraphs 106 and 107)'.

[88] Case 26/76 *Metro SB-Grossmärkte v Commission* [1977] ECR 1875 (selective distribution agreements); Case 161/84 *Pronuptia de Paris v Schillgalis* [1986] ECR 353 (franchising agreements).

[89] See Commission Notice, *Guidelines on the Application of Article 81(3) of the Treaty* [2004] OJ C101/97, para 29.

[90] Case T-112/99 *Métropole Télévision (M6) v Commission* [2001] ECR II-2459.

a wholesale evaluation of the pro- as against anti-competitive effects of the agreements for the purposes of determining whether Article 81(1) applied. But it accepted that an ancillary restriction directly related and necessary to the main agreement could fall outside Article 81(1). The evaluation carried out for these purposes involves determining whether, in the specific context of the agreement, the restriction is necessary to implement it. If, without the restriction, the agreement is difficult or even impossible to implement, the restriction may be regarded as objectively necessary for its implementation.[91] In *Wouters v Algemene Raad van de Nederlandsche Orde van Advocaten*,[92] the ECJ accepted that a restriction of competition which is necessary to achieve a non-economic objective (in that case, the restriction was regulatory in nature and aimed at ensuring the integrity and experience of the legal profession) could reasonably be considered to be necessary in order to ensure the proper practice of the legal profession and hence fell outside Article 81(1).

1.61 **Appreciability or de minimis**   The case law has established that certain agreements which have an anti-competitive object or effect may nonetheless fall outside the prohibition in Article 81(1) because, given the relative unimportance of the parties to the agreement, the effect of the agreement on the market is not appreciable.[93]

1.62 Those agreements that do not appreciably affect competition (otherwise known as agreements that are 'de minimis') may therefore escape the prohibition. There is accordingly a requirement that the agreements have as their object or effect the *appreciable* restriction, distortion, or prevention of competition in order to fall within the prohibition in Article 81(1).

1.63 There is not much case law on the 'de minimis' concept, because most instances of such cases are settled informally by the European Commission and do not give rise to litigation. However the EC Commission has published a Notice on agreements of minor importance[94] (**De Minimis Notice**) in order to give guidance on what type of agreements it considers to be 'de minimis'. In brief, agreements do not, in the Commission's view,[95] appreciably restrict competition if:

---

[91] ibid, para 109.   [92] Case C-309/99 [2002] ECR I-1577.

[93] Case 5/69 *Volk v Ets Vervaecke SPRL* [1969] ECR 295.

[94] *Commission Notice on agreements of minor importance which do not appreciably restrict competition under Article 81(1) of the Treaty (de minimis)* [2001] OJ C368/07.

[95] On the status of Commission Notices in the UK and on other courts and authorities that may apply Art 81(1), see paras 1.54 above and 1.64 below.

- where the parties to the agreement are actual or potential competitors[96] on any of the relevant markets affected by the agreement, their aggregate market share does not exceed 10 per cent on any of the markets affected by the agreement;
- where the parties are not potential competitors on any of the relevant markets affected by the agreement, the individual market share of each party does not exceed 15 per cent on any of the markets affected by the agreement.

The De Minimis Notice does not apply to agreements that contain restrictions **1.64** that the Commission has defined as 'hard-core' such as agreements fixing prices, market sharing, and limiting production.[97] The De Minimis Notice only represents the Commission's view on appreciability, and is not binding on the European courts or on other courts or competition authorities that may apply Article 81(1). However, these authorities—certainly in the United Kingdom—will have regard to the Notice when applying Article 81(1).[98]

(ii) Article 81(3)

Article 81(3) provides that the prohibition contained in Article 81(1) may be **1.65** declared inapplicable in case of agreements that satisfy two positive conditions:

- they contribute to improving the production or distribution of goods or to promoting technical or economic progress,
- while allowing consumers a fair share of the resulting benefits,

and two negative conditions:

- they do not impose restrictions which are not indispensable to the attainment of these objectives,
- they do not afford the undertakings the possibility of eliminating competition in respect of a substantial part of the products concerned.

---

[96] The De Minimis Notice clarifies: 'A firm is treated as an actual competitor if it is either active on the same relevant market or if, in the absence of the agreement, it is able to switch production to the relevant products and market them in the short term without incurring significant additional costs or risks in response to a small and permanent increase in relative prices (immediate supply-side substitutability). A firm is treated as a potential competitor if there is evidence that, absent the agreement, this firm could and would be likely to undertake the necessary additional investments or other necessary switching costs so that it could enter the relevant market in response to a small and permanent increase in relative prices.'

[97] *Commission Notice on agreements of minor importance*, para 11.

[98] See Competition Act 1998, s 60 and OFT401, *Agreements and concerted practices* (December 2004) para 2.18: 'In determining whether an agreement has an appreciable effect on competition for the purposes of Article 81 and/or the Chapter 1 prohibition the OFT will have regard to the European Commission's approach as set out in the Notice on Agreements of Minor Importance.'

1.66   All four conditions have to be satisfied for the defence to apply, and the burden of proof of establishing if each of the conditions applies is on the undertaking seeking to benefit from the exception conditions.[99]

1.67   Although the text of Article 81(3) refers to the prohibition in Article 81(1) being 'declared inapplicable', until 1 May 2004, when Regulation 1/2003 came into effect, the Commission was the only body (subject to review by the European courts) that was empowered to apply Article 81(3). The only way to protect an agreement from the prohibition in Article 81 was therefore to obtain a European Commission 'exemption' decision in relation to the agreement. There were two routes by which an agreement could benefit from an Article 81(3) exemption decision. First, the agreement could be notified to the European Commission for an individual exemption decision. Alternatively, it could fall under a European Commission 'block' exemption regulation, by which the Commission applied Article 81(3) to categories of agreements defined in the block exemption regulation.

1.68   Since 1 May 2004 there is now no need—and it is not possible—for an undertaking to obtain a prior declaration to that effect in order to benefit from the defence: undertakings rely on Article 81(3) without prior decision or declaration from the courts or competition authorities.[100] This is known as the legal exception regime.

1.69   The European Commission published a Notice entitled Guidelines on the application of Article 81(3) of the Treaty[101] that sets out the European Commission's interpretation of the conditions for the exception contained in Article 81(3). The Notice draws on the jurisprudence of the European Courts and the European Commission's experience in applying Article 81(3). Although this Notice is not binding on the courts and competition authorities of the Member States, it will certainly guide them in their application of Article 81(3).[102] Like the European Commission, the OFT no longer makes individual exemption decisions.

1.70   On how Article 81 is applied and enforced in practice, see Chapters 6, 7, and 9.

(d) Article 82 of the EC Treaty

1.71   Article 82 of the EC Treaty addresses unilateral anti-competitive conduct. It prohibits the abuse by one or more undertakings of a dominant position held within the common market (or in a substantial part of it) in so far as it

---

[99]   Regulation 1/2003, Art 2.   [100]   See Article 1(2) of Regulation 1/2003.
[101]   [2004] OJ C101/97.
[102]   s 60 of the Competition Act 1998. See also OFT401, *Agreements and concerted practices* (December 2004) para 5.5: 'The OFT will have regard to this Notice in considering the application of Article 81(3) and section 9(1) of the Act.'

may affect trade between Member States.[103] The prohibition in Article 82 can be broken down into four components parts, each of which is considered individually below:

- dominance by one or more undertakings
- within the common market or a substantial part of it
- abuse
- that may affect trade between Member States.

In addition, this section will consider the informal 'defences' to Article 82 claims **1.72** that have been developed in the jurisprudence. The discussion below is based on the relevant jurisprudence of the European courts and the decisional practice of the Commission to date. It should be noted that in December 2005 the Commission launched a review of the concept of abuse under Article 82, which considers adopting a more 'effects-based' approach than has been the practice to date. Discussion on reform of Article 82 is still ongoing at the time of writing.

(i) Dominance by one or more undertakings

Undertaking   Article 82 prohibits the abuse of dominance by one or more **1.73** undertakings. Although the term 'undertaking' is not defined in the EC Treaty, it has acquired an autonomous definition in the jurisprudence of the ECJ. For a discussion on the definition of undertaking, see paras 1.35–1.37 above.

Dominance   Dominance as such is not prohibited by Article 82; rather it is **1.74** the abuse of a position of dominance that is prohibited.

Dominance was defined in *United Brands Co v Commission*[104] as: **1.75**

> [A] position of economic strength enjoyed by an undertaking which enables it to prevent effective competition being maintained on the relevant market by giving it the power to behave to an appreciable extent independently of its competitors, customers and ultimately of its consumers.

In order to establish whether an undertaking is dominant, it is necessary to **1.76** follow a two-step process. First, one must define the relevant market on which the undertaking is allegedly dominant. Secondly, one must assess the undertaking's position on that market.

Step one: defining the market   Market definition is not an end in itself, but **1.77** rather a step which helps in the process of determining whether an undertaking or undertakings possess market power, through identifying in a systematic way the constraints the undertaking(s) face. The defined market also provides a useful analytical framework for the analysis of the effects of the agreement (for

---

[103] The full text of Art 82 EC is provided in Annex 1 to this chapter.
[104] Case 27/76 [1978] ECR 207, para 65.

Article 81) or conduct (for Article 82). Market definition is primarily a matter of economic analysis. It involves gathering economic evidence in order to assess the market on which the undertaking is active. The discussion below provides a very brief description of the main elements involved in market definition. A fuller description of the process by which the European Commission defines the market, is provided in its Notice on the definition of the relevant market for the purposes of Community competition law (**the Commission Notice**).[105] The OFT has published a similar guideline entitled *Market Definition*.[106]

1.78 The definition of the market involves gauging two dimensions of the market,[107] the product market and the geographic market. The Commission explains that:

> The objective of defining a market in both its product and geographic dimension is to identify those actual competitors of the undertakings involved that are capable of constraining their behaviour and of preventing them from behaving independently of an effective competitive pressure. It is from this perspective, that the market definition makes it possible, inter alia, to calculate market shares that would convey meaningful information regarding market power for the purposes of assessing dominance or for the purposes of applying Article 8[2].[108]

1.79 First, one defines the product market. The main analytical tools used with which to define the product market are:

- identifying which products may readily be substituted with the product investigation if prices were increased above (or quality decreased below) competitive levels (demand-side substitutability). This must be approached with caution where prices are substantially different from competitive levels—as will often be the case in markets with dominant undertakings;

- identifying which undertakings (currently not supplying the product under investigation) could relatively easily and swiftly switch production to produce the product (supply-side substitutability).

1.80 This requires diverse evidence from different sources ranging from statistical analyses on price movements and patterns to direct evidence from customers relating to the characteristics of the product and its intended use.

1.81 Secondly, one defines the geographical market. The geographic market was defined in *United Brands* as a geographic area 'where the conditions are sufficiently homogeneous'.[109] The Commission's Notice provides:

---

[105] [1997] OJ C372/5.   [106] December 2004.

[107] Occasionally, one must have regard to the temporal market. See OFT403, *Market definition* (December 2004) paras 5.1–5.3.

[108] Commission Notice on the definition of the relevant market, para 2.

[109] Case 27/76 *United Brands Co v Commission* [1978] ECR 207.

The relevant geographic market comprises the area in which the undertakings concerned are involved in the supply and demand of products or services, in which the conditions of competition are sufficiently homogeneous and which can be distinguished from neighbouring areas because the conditions of competition are appreciably different in those areas.[110]

Step two: assessing dominance on the market as defined   Once the product **1.82** and geographic dimensions of the market have been defined, the next step is to gauge whether the undertaking holds sufficient market power as to be dominant on that market. The OFT has published guidance on this issue entitled *Assessment of market power*.[111] An undertaking will not be dominant unless it has substantial market power. There are several indicators of dominance:

- **Market shares**: In *Hoffmann-La Roche & Co AG v Commission*[112] the ECJ held that 'very large shares are in themselves, and save in exceptional circumstances, evidence of the existence of a dominant position'. The case law has defined certain market share thresholds at which presumptions of dominance arise: in *AKZO Chemie BV v Commission*,[113] the ECJ held that dominance can be presumed, in the absence of evidence to the contrary, if an undertaking constantly holds a market share that is above 50 per cent.

- **Barriers to entry**: Market shares are not conclusive. For example, a firm may have a high market share, but not enjoy any true market power because of competitive pressure exerted on it by potential market entry by undertakings as yet not active in the market. It is necessary therefore to have regard to whether there are any barriers to entry that protect the incumbent/s by deterring market entry. The presence of such a barrier to entry favours a conclusion of dominance. The concept of barriers to entry in European law jurisprudence is broad. To give a few examples of factors that have been viewed as barriers to entry by the ECJ or CFI: legal provisions such as intellectual property rights (*Hugin*,[114] *Hilti*[115]), superior technology (*United Brands*,[116] *Hoffmann-La Roche*), deep pockets (*United Brands*), economies of scale (*United Brands*), vertical integration (*United Brands*), and, controversially, the conduct of the dominant undertaking itself (*Michelin*[117]).

- **Buyer power**: Another constraint on a firm with a high market share could be its buyers where they have a strong negotiating position.

[110] Commission Notice on the definition of the relevant market, heading II.
[111] December 2004.   [112] Case 85/76 [1979] ECR 461, para 41.
[113] Case C-62/86 [1991] ECR I-3359.
[114] Case 22/78 *Hugin Kassaregister AB v Commission* [1979] ECR 1869.
[115] Case T-30/89 *Hilti AG v Commission* [1990] ECR II-163.
[116] Case 27/76 *United Brands Co v Commission* [1978] ECR 207.
[117] Case 322/81 *Nederlandsche Banden Industrie Michelin NV v Commission* [1983] ECR 3461.

1.83 **Collective dominance** Article 82 applies to '[a]ny abuse by one or more undertakings of a dominant position'. Although the wording seems to envisage that several undertakings may jointly hold a dominant position, collective dominance has only relatively recently been defined under European law. In *Italian Flat Glass*,[118] the CFI confirmed that: 'There is nothing, in principle, to prevent two or more independent economic entities from being, on a specific market, united by such economic links that, by virtue of that fact, together they hold a dominant position vis a vis the other operators on the same market.'[119] In *Compagnie Maritime Belge*,[120] the ECJ explained that the link between collectively dominant undertakings need not be structural; it suffices that 'from an economic point of view they present themselves or act together on a particular market as a collective entity'.[121]

(ii) Within the common market or a substantial part of it

1.84 The undertaking must be dominant 'within the common market or a substantial part of it' for Article 82 to apply. Dominance within a Member State will generally suffice to meet the requirement of a 'substantial' part of the common market, and sometimes even a region may qualify.[122] In some cases, rather than considering the geographic scope of the relevant market, to determine whether it is 'substantial', it may be more appropriate to determine the economic significance of the market relative to the European Union.[123]

(iii) Abuse

1.85 The fact that an undertaking may hold a dominant position is not itself a ground of criticism.[124] However, Article 82 prohibits dominant undertakings from abusing their privileged position. It is difficult to provide a comprehensive definition of what behaviour amounts to an abuse for the purposes of Article 82. Article 82 provides the following examples of 'abuse':

(a) directly or indirectly imposing unfair purchase or selling prices or other unfair trading conditions;[125]

---

[118] Case T-68/89 *Societa Italiano Vetro SpA v Commission* [1992] ECR II-1403.
[119] ibid, para 358.   [120] Joined Cases C 395 & 396/96 P [2000] ECR I-1365.
[121] ibid, para 36.
[122] Case C-179/90 *Merci Convenzionali Porto di Genova SpA v Siderurgica Gabriella SpA* [1991] ECR I-5899.
[123] Case 40/73 *Cooperatieve Vereniging Suiker Unie UA v Commission* [1975] ECR 1663.
[124] Joined Cases C 395 & 396/96 P *Compagnie Maritime Belge Transports SA v Commission* [2000] ECR I-1365, para 37.
[125] eg, in Case 26/76 *United Brands Co v Commission* [1978] ECR 207, United Brands was held to have infringed Art 82 by imposing excessively high prices. In Case 62/86 *AKZO Chemie BV v Commission* [1991] ECR I-3359, AKZO was held to have infringed Art 82 by reason of its predatory prices.

(b) limiting production, markets, or technical development to the prejudice of consumers;[126]

(c) applying dissimilar conditions to equivalent transactions with other trading parties, thereby placing them at a competitive disadvantage;[127]

(d) making the conclusion of contracts subject to acceptance by the other parties of supplementary obligations which, by their nature or according to commercial usage, have no connection with the subject of such contracts.[128]

These examples provide a good indication of the conduct that may fall foul of Article 82, but they are not exhaustive. In *Hoffmann-La Roche & Co AG v Commission*, the ECJ defined abuse as follows: **1.86**

> The concept of abuse is an objective concept relating to the behaviour of an undertaking in a dominant position which is such as to influence the structure of a market where, as a result of the very presence of the undertaking in question, the degree of competition is weakened and which, through recourse to methods different from those which condition normal competition in products or services on the basis of the transactions of commercial operators, has the effect of hindering the maintenance of the degree of competition still existing in the market or the growth of that competition.[129]

The above extract, with its emphasis on objectivity and 'recourse to methods different from those which condition normal competition', would seem to indicate that dominant undertakings remain free to compete on the merits, providing their behaviour falls within the boundaries of 'normal competition'. However, subsequent cases have emphasised that dominant undertakings have a 'special responsibility' not to impair competition further in the markets in which they are dominant. In *Michelin* the ECJ held: **1.87**

> A finding that an undertaking has a dominant position is not in itself a recrimination but simply means that, irrespective of the reasons for which it has such a dominant position, the undertaking concerned has a special responsibility not to allow its conduct to impair genuine undistorted competition on the common market.[130]

Accordingly, in evaluating whether conduct is an abuse, the effect of the conduct on the structure of the market, and in particular on competitors, has taken **1.88**

---

[126] In *United Brands*, one of the abuses consisted in discontinuing the supply to a Danish banana distributor and ripener, thus limiting the development of markets.

[127] Another abuse in *United Brands* consisted in the discriminatory pricing policy pursued by United Brands in different Member States.

[128] In Case T-30/89 *Hilti AG v Commission* [1990] ECR II-163, the dominant undertaking abused its position by 'tying' the supply of the product in relation to which it was dominant to several other products.

[129] Case 85/76 [1979] ECR 461, para 91.

[130] Case 322/81 *Nederlandsche Banden Industrie Michelin NV v Commission* [1983] ECR 3461, para 57. See also Joined Cases C 395 & 396/96 P *Compagnie Maritime Belge Transports SA v Commission* [2000] ECR I-1365, para 37.

on increasing importance. The difficulty with this is that, sometimes, a dominant undertaking's conduct will have the effect of driving competitors out of the market because of its superior efficiency, rather than through recourse to 'different' methods. Superior efficiency with lower prices is likely to increase consumer welfare—at least in the shorter term—and the objective of competition law is to enhance consumer welfare.

1.89 Broadly speaking, abuse can be divided into two categories. There are exploitative abuses, which are aimed at exploiting customers, such as excessive pricing. On the other hand, there are exclusionary abuses, which are aimed at removing or weakening competitors, such as predatory pricing. Some of the more controversial decisions on what amounts to abuse have been in the latter category, where the Commission has qualified as an abuse behaviour that does not seem, to all commentators, to amount to 'recourse to methods different from those which condition normal competition', but rather an example of superior efficiency on the part of the dominant undertaking. In *ITT Promedia*,[131] the CFI appeared to accept that the initiation of legal proceedings against a competitor could, in certain circumstances, amount to an abuse.

1.90 In view of the tension between allowing dominant undertakings to compete on the merits and subjecting them to a 'special responsibility', it is difficult, in practice, to distinguish between legitimate commercial behaviour of dominant undertakings and abusive behaviour that should be prohibited. The jurisprudence of the European courts and the decision-making practice of the Commission takes a mixed approach to the issue of abuse. It has taken a form-based approach to the issue of abuse: for example, the form of a price rebate (for example whether it is conditional or non-conditional, whether it is on all purchases or just on incremental ones) is considered rather than the overall economic effects of the rebates at issue. Another example is the emphasis on the structure of the market rather than on whether any foreclosure of competitors is likely to have a harmful effect on consumer welfare. However, the Commission is showing increased willingness to take an effects-based approach and is reviewing its practice with respect to exclusionary practices under Article 82 as this is written.

1.91 It is not always necessary for the abuse (or its effects) to be in the same market in which the undertaking is dominant. Article 82 can apply to prohibit an abuse in a different, but closely related market.[132] Typically, this is where an undertaking is dominant in one market, and leverages on this strength to commit an abuse in the neighbouring market, where it is not dominant.[133]

---

[131] Case T-111/96 *ITT Promedia NV v Commission* [1998] ECR II-2937.
[132] Case T-83/91 *Tetra Pak International SA v Commission* [1994] ECR II-755, confirmed on appeal before the ECJ in Case C-333/94 P [1996] ECR I-5951.
[133] eg, in Case 6/73 *Commercial Solvents Corp v Commission* [1974] ECR 223.

(iv) Effect on trade between Member States

The concept of effect on trade is discussed at paras 1.38–1.54 above. **1.92**

(v) Possible defences to Article 82 claims

Article 82 does not contain a 'saving' provision equivalent to Article 81(3) **1.93**
which permits consideration of the benefits of the conduct under scrutiny in
the evaluation of the abuse. In practice, however, the Commission and the
European courts, in considering whether conduct amounts to an abuse, have
tended to consider two types of defence, both of which build on the notion that
dominant firms should be free to compete on the merits.

Objective justification   The most prevalent defence is for the undertaking to **1.94**
provide 'objective justification' for conduct that is allegedly abusive.[134] If there
is a legitimate reason for the conduct, then it may not amount to an abuse.
The OFT provides, as an example of objective justification, the situation in
which a refusal to supply by a dominant undertaking is justified by poor
creditworthiness.[135]

The European Commission Green Paper on exclusionary abuse of dominance[136] **1.95**
identifies two trends of objective justification. First, where the dominant company is able to show that the otherwise abusive conduct is actually necessary on
the basis of objective factors external to the parties involved and in particular
external to the dominant company ('objective necessity defence').

The second type (also known as the 'meeting competition defence') is where the **1.96**
dominant company is able to show that the conduct is a loss-minimising
response to competition from others. This would usually apply in the context of
allegedly abusing pricing practices.

Efficiency defence   A more recent concept to emerge is the 'efficiency defence'. **1.97**
It allows a defence for a dominant undertaking if the undertaking can demonstrate that the efficiencies brought about by its conduct outweigh the likely
negative effects on competition. It may become relevant in the context of
pricing abuses, if the dominant undertaking can establish that its behaviour
enhances consumer welfare. According to the European Commission in its
Green Paper, the dominant undertaking must establish the following:

i)   that efficiencies are realised or likely to be realised as a result of the conduct
concerned;

---

[134] Case T-30/89 *Hilti AG v Commission* [1990] ECR II-163.
[135] OFT402, *Abuse of a Dominant Position* (December 2004) para 5.3.
[136] *DG Competition discussion paper on the application of Article 82 of the Treaty to
exclusionary abuses*, December 2005, <http://ec.europa.eu/comm/competition/antitrust/others/
discpaper2005.pdf>.

ii) that the conduct concerned is indispensable to realise these efficiencies;

iii) that the efficiencies benefit consumers;

iv) that competition in respect of a substantial part of the products concerned is not eliminated.[137]

(vi) Consequences of breach

1.98 An undertaking that breaches Article 82 EC may be fined by the European Commission for up to 10 per cent of its worldwide turnover, and national competition authorities may also fine for breaches of Article 82 under national law. Further, following the ECJ's judgment in *Courage Ltd v Crehan*,[138] it may be susceptible to civil claims for damages or for other appropriate relief before the national courts of the Member States, brought by those whom its conduct has affected.

C. The Competition Act 1998

1.99 The Competition Act 1998 introduced a competition regime under domestic law that was closely modelled on Article 81 and Article 82 of the EC Treaty. The intention of the government was to introduce a system that was consistent with the EC Treaty. The Competition Act's close links with Article 81 and Article 82 would ensure that businesses did not face the burdens of two divergent regimes of competition law addressing similar practices, whilst establishing the government's commitment to building a strong competition regime.

1.100 To avoid repetition, the aim of this section is to focus on the relevant differences between the competition prohibitions in the Competition Act 1998 and Articles 81 and 82. Where concepts arising under the Competition Act are identical to those concepts under Article 81 and Article 82, this section will refer the reader to the relevant discussion above.

1.101 The Competition Act applies to the United Kingdom. This means Great Britain (England, Wales and the subsidiary Islands, excluding the Isle of Man and the Channel Islands) and Northern Ireland.[139]

(a) The Chapter I prohibition

(i) The prohibition

1.102 Section 2(1) of the Competition Act is known as the Chapter I prohibition. It is closely modelled on Article 81(1) EC. It provides that:

---

[137] ibid, para 84.

[138] Case C-453/99 *Courage Ltd v Crehan* [2001] ECR I-6297, paras 23 and 24.

[139] OFT401, *Agreements and concerted practices* (December 2004) para 2.27.

. . . agreements between undertakings, decisions by associations of undertakings or concerted practices which—

(a) may affect trade within the United Kingdom, and
(b) have as their object or effect the prevention, restriction or distortion of competition within the United Kingdom,

are prohibited unless they are exempt in accordance with the provisions of this Part.

Section 2(2) of the Competition Act provides a non-exhaustive list of examples **1.103** of prohibited agreements (such as price-fixing etc) that is identical to that provided in Article 81(1).

The Chapter I prohibition can be broken down into four constitutive elements: **1.104**

- agreements, decisions by associations of undertakings, and concerted practices (see paras 1.27–1.34 above)
- between undertakings (see paras 1.35–1.37 above)
- which may affect trade within the United Kingdom
- which have as their object or effect the prevention, restriction or distortion of competition within the United Kingdom (see paras 1.55–1.59 above for the meaning of 'object or effect' and 'prevention, restriction or distortion of competition').

The differences with Article 81(1) turn on the geographic scope and application **1.105** of the prohibition:

- First, the Chapter I prohibition will only apply if the agreement, decision or practice is, or is intended to be, implemented in the United Kingdom,[140] or part of it.[141]
- Secondly, Chapter I prohibits agreements that *may affect trade within the United Kingdom*, whereas Article 81 prohibits those that may affect trade between Member States. These concepts are not mutually exclusive; it is possible (and indeed likely, given the breadth of the concept of effect on trade between Member States)[142] that agreements that may affect trade within the United Kingdom also satisfy the test of effect on trade for the purposes of Article 81. The threshold for affecting trade within the United Kingdom is low. The CAT held in *Aberdeen Journals Ltd v OFT*[143] that, in relation to Chapter II, the appreciability test that applies to 'effect on trade between Member States' in European law (discussed at paras 1.48–1.54 above) does not apply to the 'effect on trade in the United Kingdom'. It is questionable

---

[140] Competition Act 1998, s 2(3).   [141] ibid, s 2(7).
[142] See paras 1.38–1.54 above for a discussion of this concept.   [143] [2003] CAT 11.

whether, in practice, the requirement that trade be affected within the United Kingdom brings an additional element to the Chapter I prohibition. The OFT's view is that: 'In practice, it is very unlikely that an agreement which appreciably restricts competition within the United Kingdom does not also affect trade within the United Kingdom. So, in applying the Chapter I prohibition the OFT's focus will be on the effect that an agreement has on competition.'[144]

• Thirdly, Chapter I requires the agreements to have as their object or effect the distortion of competition within *the United Kingdom*, where Article 81 requires such object or effect within *the common market*. As with its European counterpart, Chapter I contains an unexpressed 'appreciability' threshold, so that only agreements which have as their object or effect the *appreciable* distortion of competition within the United Kingdom are caught within the prohibition. To assess appreciability, the OFT will define the relevant market and consider the position that is held by the infringing undertakings on that market.[145] The OFT has indicated that it will have regard to the factors and thresholds set out in the Commission's De Minimis Notice in determining whether there is an appreciable restriction on competition,[146] see paras 1.62–1.63 for a brief explanation of this.

(ii) Exemption

1.106 The Chapter I prohibition does not apply to agreements that meet four cumulative conditions. Section 9(1) of the Competition Act 1998 provides that:

> An agreement is exempt from the Chapter I prohibition if it—
> (a) contributes to—
>   (i) improving production or distribution, or
>   (ii) promoting technical or economic progress,
> while allowing consumers a fair share of the resulting benefit; and
> (b) does not—
>   (i) impose on the undertakings concerned restrictions which are not indispensable to the attainment of those objectives; or
>   (ii) afford the undertakings concerned the possibility of eliminating competition in respect of a substantial part of the products in question.

1.107 The wording in s 9(1) is modelled on that in Article 81(3), which provides an exemption from Article 81(1) for agreements meeting essentially the same four

---

[144] OFT401, *Agreements and concerted practices* (December 2004) para 2.25.
[145] OFT403, *Market definition* (December 2004) para 2.2 and OFT415, *Assessment of market power* (December 2004) para 2.2.
[146] OFT401, *Agreements and concerted practices* (December 2004) para 2.18. See also Competition Act 1998, s 60.

conditions.[147] The OFT has indicated that, in considering the application of s 9(1) of the Competition Act it will have regard to the Commission Notice on this issue, entitled *Guidelines on the application of Article 81(3) of the Treaty*.[148] As under Article 81(3), the burden of establishing that an agreement satisfies the conditions for exemption set out in s 9(1) falls on the party seeking to benefit from the exemption.[149]

To ensure consistency with the system of legal exception under Article 81(3) (see para 1.68 above), the Competition Act has been amended so as to introduce a system of legal exception and to remove the possibility of notifying agreements for individual exemption by the competition authorities.[150] Any individual exemptions granted prior to 1 May 2004 remain effective until their expiry. The OFT is not itself empowered to exempt categories of agreements from Chapter I. However, it may, under s 6 of the Competition Act, propose that the Secretary of State make a Block Exemption Order.[151] **1.108**

Section 10 of the Competition Act ensures there is consistency with respect to exemptions under Article 81 and Chapter I by granting a parallel exemption from Chapter I for agreements that fall within (or would fall within, if there was an effect on trade) an EC Block Exemption Regulation or would benefit from a declaration of inapplicability made by the Commission under Article 10 of Regulation 1/2003. **1.109**

(iii) Exclusions from the Chapter I prohibition

Unlike Article 81(1), from which there are no express exclusions, the Competition Act provides for exclusions from the Chapter I prohibition. An exclusion differs from an exemption in that excluded agreements do not fall within the Chapter I prohibition at all. Exempted agreements fall within the Chapter I prohibition, but are exempt under s 9(1) until the exemption expires. An exclusion from the Competition Act will not protect an agreement from the application of Article 81. **1.110**

Section 3 and Schs 1–3 of the Competition Act introduce a number of exclusions from Chapter I, and s 50 empowers the Secretary of State to provide for **1.111**

---

[147] The only difference in wording is that Art 81(1) refers to 'improving the production or distribution of goods'. The reference to 'goods' was not transposed in s 9(1) to clarify that the exemption also applies to improving the production and distribution of services. This is consistent with the practice that has developed with respect to Art 81(3), see Commission Notice, *Guidelines on the application of Article 81(3) of the Treaty* [2004] OJ C101/97, para 48.

[148] [2004] OJ C101/97.   [149] Competition Act 1998, s 9(2).

[150] See paras 4.10–4.15 below.

[151] eg, Competition Act 1998 (Public Transport Ticketing Schemes Block Exemption) Order 2001, SI 2001/319 and the amendment thereto in Competition Act 1998 (Public Transport Ticketing Schemes Block Exemption) (Amendment) Order 2005, SI 2005/3347.

exclusions in respect of vertical agreements and land agreements. Certain of these exclusions, such as the exclusion of mergers falling under the EC Merger Regulation, are no more than codification of exclusions from Article 81 that have been developed with practice. Others, however, give rise to a substantive difference with Article 81.

1.112 The most significant exclusion from Chapter I is that relating to land agreements as defined in the Competition Act 1998 (Land Agreements Exclusion and Revocation) Order 2004.[152] Exclusions are discussed in detail in Chapter 4.

(b) The Chapter II Prohibition

(i) The prohibition

1.113 Section 18(1) of the Competition Act provides: 'any conduct on the part of one or more undertakings which amounts to the abuse of a dominant position in a market is prohibited if it may affect trade within the United Kingdom'.

1.114 The Chapter II prohibition is closely modelled on Article 82 EC. Like Article 82, it can be broken down into four component parts:

- dominance by one or more undertakings (see paras 1.82–1.83 above)
- abuse (see paras 1.85–1.90 above)
- within a market
- may affect trade within the United Kingdom.

1.115 Unlike Article 82, which requires that the undertaking hold a dominant position 'within the common market or in a substantial part of it', the requirement under Chapter II is that the undertaking should hold a dominant position in the United Kingdom or any part of it.[153] This may or may not also amount to a dominant position in the common market, depending on the facts of the case, but it is clear that the two prohibitions may apply simultaneously.

1.116 Unlike Article 82 which requires an effect on trade between Member States, Chapter II requires an effect on trade within the United Kingdom. The threshold as to what affects trade is low. The CAT held in *Aberdeen Journals Ltd v OFT*[154] that the de minimis test that applies to 'effect on trade between Member States' in European law (discussed at paras 1.48–1.54 above) could not be

---

[152] SI 2004/1260.

[153] s 18(3) provides that 'dominant position' means a dominant position within the UK; and 'the United Kingdom' means the UK or any part of it.

[154] [2003] CAT 11.

applied to the 'effect on trade in the United Kingdom' under the Chapter II prohibition.[155]

(ii) Exclusions

Unlike Article 82 EC, there are a number of exclusions from the Chapter II **1.117** prohibition. The exclusions are set out in Schs 1 and 3 to the Competition Act and are discussed in Chapter 4. An exclusion will not prevent the application of Article 82.

(c) Consequences of breach of the prohibitions

An agreement that falls within Chapter I is void and unenforceable.[156]   **1.118**

An undertaking that has intentionally or negligently committed an infringe-   **1.119** ment may be fined by the OFT up to a limit of 10 per cent of the undertaking's worldwide turnover. Chapter 10 discusses the method by which the penalties are calculated, and any immunities that may apply in relation to penalties under the Competition Act.

A finding of infringement may also give rise to civil actions for damages or **1.120** other relief. The CAT has been specifically empowered, in addition to the High Court, to hear civil actions for damages following on from a finding of infringement of the Competition Act prohibitions or Article 81 or 82 by the OFT or the European Commission.[157] Further, a finding of infringement by the OFT or by the CAT will bind a court in an action for civil damages, providing that the appeal period has lapsed or any appeals have been concluded.[158]

(d) Interaction with Article 81 and Article 82: a very brief overview

(i) Jurisdiction

It is readily apparent that, by their terms, the Competition Act prohibitions **1.121** overlap with Article 81 and Article 82. There is not only a substantive overlap in respect of key elements of the prohibitions, but also a very considerable jurisdictional overlap. Chapter I and Chapter II apply wherever there may be an effect on trade within the United Kingdom. They do not, however, cease to apply wherever the agreements or conduct at issue may affect trade between Member States. Given the breadth of the effect on Member States criterion, as

---

[155] 'We accept the Director's submission that, since we are already dealing, under domestic law, with conduct which takes place within the United Kingdom, there is no need to import into section 18(1) of the 1998 Act the rule of "appreciability" under Community law, the essential purpose of which is to demarcate the fields of Community law and domestic law respectively.' Ibid, para 460.
[156] Competition Act 1998, s 2(4).   [157] ibid, s 47A.   [158] ibid, s 58A.

interpreted by the ECJ, it is likely that many cases that are investigated under Chapter I and Chapter II also potentially give rise to the application of Article 81 and Article 82.

1.122 In such cases, as mandated by Article 3(1) of Regulation 1/2003, the OFT will apply both the relevant prohibition under the Competition Act and Article 81 or Article 82 as relevant. The interaction of European law with domestic law is considered in depth in Chapter 3. The practical and theoretical difficulties that arise from this dual application of domestic and European competition law are considered in Chapter 11.

(ii) Section 60

1.123 We have seen above that the Chapter I and Chapter II prohibitions are closely modelled on Articles 81 and 82 EC. The relationship between the Competition Act and EC law does not stop there. Section 60(1) of the Competition Act provides:

> The purpose of this section is to ensure that so far as is possible (having regard to any relevant differences between the provisions concerned), questions arising under this Part in relation to competition within the United Kingdom are dealt with in a manner which is consistent with the treatment of corresponding questions arising in Community law in relation to competition within the Community.

1.124 Section 60 imposes an obligation on courts and tribunals and the OFT to apply Chapter I and Chapter II consistently with relevant Community precedent. The precise ambit of this obligation is considered in Chapter 3, which addresses the relationship between national law and Community law.

D. Enterprise Act 2002

1.125 The Enterprise Act 2002 introduced a number of measures to strengthen the United Kingdom's competition law framework.[159] The following features of the UK competition regime established under the Enterprise Act are of particular interest:

- **cartel offence**: the creation of a criminal offence for individuals who dishonestly participate in hardcore cartels;
- **director disqualification**: the introduction of director disqualification for company directors of undertakings involved in competition infringements;

---

[159] The competition measures are but one aspect of the Enterprise Act 2002, which also reformed corporate insolvency and bankruptcy law and enhanced consumer protection.

- **market studies**: the introduction of a general power for the OFT to conduct market studies;
- **market investigations**: a new market investigation regime to replace the previous regime under the Fair Trading Act 1973;
- **super complaints**: a new 'fast-track' complaint system for consumer associations to bring competition complaints to regulators.

(a) The cartel offence

(i) Definition

Sections 188 and 189 of the Enterprise Act 2002 define the cartel offence. In essence, these provide that it is an offence for an individual to agree dishonestly with one or more other persons that two or more undertakings will engage in one of the prohibited cartel activities. The cartel offence only applies to natural persons. **1.126**

The prohibited cartel activities are: **1.127**

- price-fixing arrangements;
- arrangements limiting supply or production;
- market-sharing arrangements; and
- bid-rigging arrangements.

The offence only applies if the cartel arrangements are between undertakings operating at the same level in the supply chain—so-called 'horizontal' arrangements.[160] The offence is committed irrespective of whether the agreement reached is implemented. **1.128**

(ii) Dishonesty

The criminal test for dishonesty was set out by the Court of Appeal in *R v Ghosh* as follows: **1.129**

> In determining whether the prosecution has proved that the defendant was acting dishonestly, a jury must first of all decide whether according to the ordinary standards of reasonable and honest people what was done was dishonest. If it was not dishonest by those standards, that is the end of the matter and the prosecution fails.
>
> If it was dishonest by those standards, then the jury must consider whether the defendant himself must have realised that what he was doing was by those standards dishonest. In most cases, where the actions are obviously dishonest by ordinary standards, there will be no doubt about it. It will be obvious that the defendant himself knew that he was acting dishonestly. It is dishonest for a defendant to act in a way which he knows ordinary people consider to be dishonest, even if he asserts or genuinely believes that he is morally justified in acting as he did.[161]

---

[160] Enterprise Act 2002, s 189.   [161] [1982] QB 1053, 1064.

(iii) Interaction with Article 81/Chapter I

1.130 The White Paper that introduced the Enterprise Act 2002[162] considered two very different approaches to the criminalisation of cartels. The first was to define the criminal offence by reference to Article 81 EC, the second was to create a stand-alone offence that centred on an element of dishonesty. The Enterprise Act has taken the second approach. The language used to describe the offence very deliberately differs from that used in Article 81—for example there is no reference to 'agreements' between undertakings, but 'arrangements'. Unlike Article 81, the offence only applies to individuals, and undertakings are not subject to the criminalisation provisions. Most substantively, the focal point of the offence is the mental element—the element of dishonesty of the individual concerned.

(iv) Investigation

1.131 Two authorities, the OFT and the Serious Fraud Office (**SFO**), are empowered to investigate and prosecute suspected cartels. Sections 193–200 of the Enterprise Act provide the OFT with wide-ranging powers to investigate suspected cartels. These powers include compelling persons to answer questions or otherwise provide information and entering premises under warrant. The OFT also has powers of intrusive (covert) surveillance and property interference for the purpose of covert installation of surveillance devices. These powers must be exercised in accordance with the Regulation of Investigatory Powers Act 2000 and the Police Act 1997. See Chapter 7 for further discussion of these powers. Chapter 8 on information exchange considers to what extent the OFT may rely on information obtained using other powers (for example under the Competition Act) in the prosecution of the cartel offence.

1.132 The SFO is tasked, along with the OFT, to act as prosecutor for the cartel offence under the Enterprise Act 2002.[163] Further, the SFO may, under the Criminal Justice Act 1987, investigate any suspected criminal offence that appears to involve serious or complex fraud. Its powers include obtaining search warrants and requiring persons to answer questions or otherwise furnish information.[164] A Memorandum of Understanding[165] sets out how the OFT and SFO will cooperate in the investigation and prosecution of cartels. It is envisaged that the OFT is more likely to carry out preliminary investigations into the cartel offence; the SFO may, at a later stage in the investigation, lead the

---

[162] *Productivity and Enterprise: A World Class Competition Regime*, Cm 5223 (July 2001) paras 7.28–7.32.

[163] Enterprise Act 2002, s 190.   [164] Criminal Justice Act 1987, s 2.

[165] OFT547, *Memorandum of Understanding between the Office of Fair Trading and the Director of the Serious Fraud Office* (October 2003).

investigation using its powers under s 2 of the Criminal Justice Act 1987, where the case meets its acceptance criteria.

(v) Penalties

The cartel offence is triable either way. Before the magistrates, a convicted offender may receive a six month term of imprisonment and/or a fine up to the statutory maximum. On conviction on indictment, an offender may receive a maximum of five years' imprisonment and/or an unlimited fine.[166] In England, Wales and Northern Ireland, prosecutions may be undertaken by the SFO and the OFT. In Scotland, prosecutions will be brought by the Lord Advocate.[167]   **1.133**

(vi) No-action letters

The OFT has the power, under s 190(4) of the Enterprise Act 2002, to issue written notices confirming that a particular individual will not be prosecuted for the offence in England, Wales, and Northern Ireland. No-action letters are given to individuals who have participated in a cartel but go on to cooperate with the OFT to facilitate its prosecution. The OFT has set out the conditions that must be satisfied to qualify for a no-action letter in its guideline *The cartel offence: guidance on the issue of no-action letters for individuals*;[168] see further Chapter 5.   **1.134**

(vii) Extradition

Extradition is now governed by the Extradition Act 2003.[169] In general terms,[170] the cartel offence is an offence which may give rise to a request for extradition under the Extradition Act 2003. The Extradition Act 2003 provides, broadly, for two categories of extradition procedure, depending on the territory to which extradition is sought: **1.135**

- Part 1 of the Extradition Act provides a fast track system of extradition for those countries falling within 'Category 1'. To date, these are the EU Member States that have implemented the European Arrest Warrant.[171] For an offence to give rise to extradition in relation to Pt 1 territories, it must fall within the European framework list of extraditable crimes, listed in Sch 2 to the Act. This list is quite vague and generic, but includes 'fraud' as one of the categories of offences giving rise to extradition under Pt 1—it has yet to be determined

---

[166] Enterprise Act 2002, s 190(1).   [167] ibid, s 190(2).   [168] April 2003.

[169] Extradition Act 2003, Sch 4 repeals Enterprise Act 2002, s 191.

[170] The procedures governing extradition are complex, and readers are referred to textbooks dealing specifically with this subject in more depth, such as Arvinder Sambei and John RWD Jones, *Extradition Law Handbook* (Oxford University Press, 2005).

[171] 2002/584/JHA: Council Framework Decision of 13 June 2002 on the European arrest warrant and the surrender procedures between Member States—Statements made by certain Member States on the adoption of the Framework Decision [2002] OJ L190/1.

whether the cartel offence would qualify under this heading. If the cartel offence falls outside this category, extradition to a Pt 1 territory would still be possible subject to the requirement of dual criminality (ie the conduct amounts to an offence in both territories).

- If extradition is sought from a territory that is not designated as a Pt 1 territory, extradition remains possible under Pt 2 of the Extradition Act 2003 (extradition to Category 2 Territories), provided (in essence) that:
  — the United Kingdom has signed a bilateral extradition treaty with the country;
  — the requirement of dual criminality is satisfied. A request for extradition may therefore only ever be made by a country that has criminal penalties for the same activity. As at the time of writing, the United States is seeking the extradition of Ian Norris, the former CEO of Morgan Crucible, in relation to alleged price fixing of carbon related products in the United States. This is the first extradition sought in relation to a competition law offence.

(b) Director disqualification

1.136 Section 204 of the Enterprise Act 2002 amended the Company Directors Disqualification Act 1986 to provide for disqualification of directors for breach of competition law infringements.

(i) *The test for disqualification*

1.137 Under s 9A of the Company Directors Disqualification Act 1986 (as amended), the court must make a Competition Disqualification Order (**CDO**) against a person if it is satisfied that:

(a) an undertaking which is a company of which that person is a director commits a breach of competition law, and
(b) the court considers that person's conduct as a director makes him or her unfit to be concerned in the management of a company.

1.138 A breach of competition law for the purposes of s 9A(1) of the Company Directors Disqualification Act 1986 is a breach of any of Chapter I, Chapter II, Article 81, or Article 82. When deciding whether the director's conduct makes him or her unfit to be concerned in the management of a company, the court must consider whether the director contributed to the breach, failed to take steps to prevent it, or ought to have known that the conduct breached competition law.[172] The maximum period of disqualification under a CDO is 15 years.[173] It is a criminal offence for a person subject to a CDO to be a director of a

---

[172] Company Directors Disqualification Act 1986, s 9A(6).   [173] ibid, s 9A(9).

company or to take on certain other roles relating to company management for the duration of the CDO.

(ii) Process

The OFT and the 'specified regulators' under s 9E(2) of the Company Directors **1.139** Disqualification Act 1986[174] are empowered to apply to the court for a CDO. The OFT and the specified regulators have extensive powers of investigation to enable them to decide whether to make a disqualification application order, as the powers provided are the same as those available for an investigation into a suspected infringement of the Competition Act.[175] Prior to making the application to the court for a CDO, the OFT and the specified regulators are obliged to give notice to the director and to give him or her an opportunity to make representations.[176] The OFT has indicated it will only apply for CDOs in respect of breaches of competition law that have been proven in decisions or judgments (see para 3.40 below).[177]

(iii) Competition Disqualification Undertakings

The OFT is empowered, under s 9B, instead of applying for a CDO, to accept a **1.140** Competition Disqualification Undertaking (**CDU**) from a person. This has the same effect as a CDO, but is a binding commitment given on a voluntary basis to the OFT by the director in question.

The OFT has published a guideline setting out its approach to CDOs entitled **1.141** *Competition disqualification orders*.[178] Since the introduction of the power, the OFT has not yet applied for a CDO.

(c) Market studies

(i) What is a market study?

Market studies are pro-active general exploratory studies undertaken by the **1.142** OFT into markets that do not appear to be working well for consumers but in respect of which it is not immediately apparent what action—whether consumer regulation or competition enforcement—is appropriate. They are carried out under s 5 of the Enterprise Act 2002 (although sometimes the OFT additionally relies on ss 6–8 of the Act which cover providing information to the public and to Ministers as well as promoting good consumer practice). Section 5 provides that, in order to ensure that the OFT has sufficient information to make informed decisions and carry out its competition and consumer functions

---

[174] Ofcom, Ofgem, Ofwat, ORR and CAA.   [175] ibid, s 9C(2).
[176] ibid, s 9C(4).
[177] OFT510, *Competition disqualification orders: Guidance* (May 2003) para 4.6.
[178] OFT510 (May 2003).

effectively, one of the functions of the OFT is to obtain information on matters relating to carrying out its functions. The sectoral regulators do not have this function under s 5 of the Enterprise Act, but in effect have similar powers in the sectors they regulate as part of their general regulatory powers.

(ii) Triggers

1.143 The OFT guideline, *Market studies: guidance on the OFT approach*,[179] indicates that its decision to begin a market study may be triggered by the receipt of the following:

- information acquired in the course of its own competition or consumer enforcement work
- evidence from enquiries and complaints to the OFT
- suggestions from other interested parties, such as businesses, trade associations or consumer groups
- suggestions made by other government departments, trading standards departments, and regulatory bodies, and
- internal OFT research.[180]

Additionally, some market studies are initiated following a super-complaint made by a designated consumer body or after a complaint made under the Competition Act.[181]

(iii) Short and long studies

1.144 There are two types of market study, a short study lasting three to six months (such as the Public Sector Procurement study[182]) and a full study (approximately one year) (for example, private dentistry[183]).

1.145 Depending on the study undertaken, the OFT may decide to initiate a long study at the outset. Alternatively, at the conclusion of a short study, it may decide to extend the study to a long study. The OFT determines whether to undertake a full study on the basis of the following considerations:

- the nature and significance of the competition problems that the OFT suspects may exist in the market concerned;

---

[179] OFT519 (November 2004).   [180] ibid, para 2.1.

[181] The OFT announced the launch of its market study into the private dentistry market in January 2002 in response to a super-complaint from the Consumers' Association made in October 2001. Since then so far three other market studies have led to market studies; doorstep selling, care homes, and payment protection insurance.

[182] OFT press release 16/04, 'OFT to review public sector procurement', 5 February 2004.

[183] OFT630, *The private dentistry market in the UK* (March 2003). This super-complaint was actually made before Enterprise Act 2002, s 11 came into operation, but was treated by the OFT as if s 11 had taken effect. The market study was carried out under the now-repealed s 2 of the Fair Trading Act 1973, which empowered the then Director General of Fair Trading to keep markets under review and collate information thereto.

- whether a reference to the CC for a market investigation would be a proportionate response to the scale of the competition problems identified;
- whether remedies are likely to be available or whether a CC market investigation report might provide a useful contribution; and
- whether the OFT is in a position to address the concerns fully itself.[184]

(iv) Powers

Although s 5(1) and (3) of the Enterprise Act authorises the OFT to request **1.146** information and to carry out, commission, or support (financially or otherwise) research, no express investigatory powers are provided to the OFT to enable it to carry out market studies. There is no obligation on those consulted to provide the information requested. There are no sanctions for failure to comply or for providing misleading information. It relies on its informal fact-finding powers such as consulting consumers, competitors and undertakings operating in the market concerned, and may carry out 'mystery shopping' exercises in order to understand the market at first hand.

(v) Outcomes

Market studies may have a number of different outcomes including: **1.147**

- OFT enforcement action under the Competition Act;
- OFT enforcement action under Pt 8 of the Enterprise Act 2002 (consumer provisions);
- a market investigation reference to the CC;
- proposals for changes to laws, regulations and self-regulation;
- publishing better information for consumers; or
- giving the market in question a clean bill of health.[185]

Undertakings that are consulted by the OFT and receive a request for informa- **1.148** tion will want to bear in mind the open-ended nature of market studies. At the conclusion of a market study, it is open to the OFT to exercise a number of statutory powers, including commencing formal Chapter I, Chapter II, Article 81 or Article 82 investigations under the Competition Act, or making a market investigation reference.

(d) Market investigation references

The market investigation regime contained in Pt 4 of the Enterprise Act 2002 **1.149** replaces and modernises the provisions on complex and scale monopolies contained in the Fair Trading Act 1973. Market investigations are broad

---

[184] OFT519, *Market studies: Guidance on the OFT approach* (November 2004) para 3.35.
[185] ibid, para 1.10.

investigations that are conducted into how markets function as a whole, as opposed to the conduct of individual undertakings.[186] They are aimed at identifying how the market is working, what (if any) the problems might be, and how to solve these problems for the future, without attaching any blame to the undertakings active in that market. This is an additional tool that permits the resolution of competition issues that do not readily fit within the parameters of prohibited behaviour under the EC Treaty or the Competition Act.

1.150 The market investigation regime consists of two distinct stages, each of which is undertaken by a different competition authority. In brief (and simplifying the process), the OFT undertakes a preliminary stage investigation to determine whether a particular market warrants further investigation.[187] If so, it refers the market to the CC to undertake an in-depth investigation. The CC is a specialist second stage competition authority. It has no power to initiate its own investigations. On receipt of the reference from the OFT, the CC investigates the market referred to it and must, within two years of the reference,[188] publish a report containing its findings and the recommended remedies in relation to any problems it has identified.[189]

1.151 Under s 131(1) of the Enterprise Act 2002:

> The OFT may . . . make a reference to the Commission if the OFT has reasonable grounds for suspecting that any feature, or combination of features, of a market in the United Kingdom for goods or services prevents, restricts or distorts competition in connection with the supply or acquisition of any goods or services in the United Kingdom or a part of the United Kingdom.

A 'feature of the market' is a broadly defined concept[190] that includes both behavioural issues (such as the conduct of those supplying or purchasing goods in the market concerned) as well as structural issues (barriers to entry, information asymmetries). Section 131(1) thus enables the OFT to refer a wide range of issues to the CC, even where there are no behavioural issues. The OFT's power to make a reference is discretionary. Factors that are relevant to the exercise of its discretion to make a reference, and the test for reference itself, are discussed in more detail in Chapter 13.

1.152 On receipt of the reference, the CC must, under s 136 of the Enterprise Act

---

[186] Market investigations are addressed in Chapter 14.

[187] Useful information is provided on the OFT's role in making references in OFT511, *Market investigation references: Guidance about the making of references under Part 4 of the Enterprise Act* (March 2006).

[188] Enterprise Act 2002, s 137(1).

[189] ibid, s 136. The CC provides guidance on its market investigation functions, see *Market Investigation References: CC Guidelines* (June 2003).

[190] ibid, s 131(2).

2002, prepare and publish a report on the issues referred. The CC's investigation leading to the publication of its report proceeds in two distinct stages.

(i) Competition analysis

First, it decides whether any feature, or combination of features of the market(s) referred, restricts or distorts competition in connection with the supply or acquisition of any goods or services in the United Kingdom or a part of the United Kingdom.[191] This involves defining what market or markets exist in connection with the supply or acquisition of the goods or services described in the reference. Market definition for the purposes of a market investigation under the Enterprise Act is similar to that described in paras 1.77–1.81. Its main purpose, as under the competition prohibitions, is to serve as a framework for the competition analysis. The CC's guidelines on *Market Investigation References* provide: **1.153**

> There are normally two dimensions to the definition of a market: a product dimension and a geographical dimension. The products that should be included in the relevant market, and the geographic boundaries of that market, are determined by the extent to which customers can readily switch between substitute products, or suppliers can readily switch their facilities between the supply of alternative products. The key to market definition is substitutability.[192]

The CC's approach to market definition is described in detail in the guideline.

Once it has defined the market(s), the CC considers whether any feature or combination of features of the markets identified prevents, restricts or distorts competition in connection with the supply or acquisition of goods or services in the United Kingdom. The concept of 'prevention, restriction and distortion of competition' is considered above in relation to Article 81. The CC has indicated that it: **1.154**

> . . . will interpret this phrase broadly using its ordinary and natural meaning so as to include any adverse effect on actual or potential competition. In particular, the Commission will interpret this phrase to include one circumstance in which several features create a situation in which the suppliers do not compete to the extent they would in a fully competitive market.

(ii) Remedies

In the second stage, where the CC has identified one or more adverse effects on competition, s 134(4) of the Enterprise Act 2002 requires it to decide whether, and what, action should be taken by it or by others to remedy, mitigate, or prevent the adverse effects on competition or any 'detrimental effects on **1.155**

---

[191] ibid, s 134(1).
[192] *Market Investigation References: CC Guidelines* (June 2003) para 2.1.

customers' (in the form of higher prices, lower quality or less choice of goods or services, or less innovation in relation to goods or services in any UK market[193]) in so far as they have resulted from, or may be expected to result from, any adverse effect on competition that it has identified.

1.156 The CC can take extremely broad remedial action. Action can be taken by the CC itself through exercising its own extensive remedial powers or by accepting undertakings from the parties. Alternatively, it may make (non-binding) recommendations that remedial action should be taken by others, such as government, regulators, and public authorities, to remedy the adverse effects on competition or any detrimental effect on customers resulting from the adverse effect on competition.

1.157 The CC's own remedial powers include behavioural remedies (such as imposing price caps), but also extend to imposing significant structural remedies, such as ordering divestiture.[194] The CC guidelines on *Market Investigation References* provide:

> Except for the statutory limits on the content of orders, there are no formal restrictions on the remedial action that the Commission can take or recommend. However, possible remedies can be categorised as follows:
>
> (a) remedies designed to make a significant and direct change to the structure of a market by a requirement, for example, to divest a business or assets to a newcomer to the market or to an existing, perhaps smaller, competitor;
>
> (b) remedies designed to change the structure of a market less directly by reducing entry barriers or switching costs, for example, by requiring the licensing of know-how or intellectual property rights or by extending the compatibility of products through industry-wide technical standards;
>
> (c) as a particular category of (b), recommendations for changes to regulations found to have adverse effects on competition or detrimental effects on customers, for example, by limiting entry to a market;
>
> (d) remedies directing firms (whether sellers or buyers) to discontinue certain behaviour (for example, giving advance notice of price changes) or to adopt certain behaviour (for example, more prominently displaying prices and other terms and conditions of sale);
>
> (e) remedies designed to restrain the way in which firms would otherwise behave, for example, the imposition of a price cap.[195]

1.158 Where the CC publishes a report that identifies an adverse effect on competition, it is obliged under s 138(2) of the Enterprise Act 2002 to take action that it considers reasonable and practicable to remedy, mitigate, or prevent the adverse effect on competition and any detriment to consumers. Section 138(3) requires that the CC's remedial decision should be consistent with its decisions as

---

[193] Enterprise Act 2002, s 134(5).   [194] ibid, ss 138(2), 161 and Sch 8.
[195] *Market Investigation References: CC Guidelines* (June 2003) para 4.18.

included in its report by virtue of s 134(4), unless there has been a material change of circumstances since the preparation of the report or the CC has a special reason for deciding differently.

(e) Super-complaints

Section 11 of the Enterprise Act 2002 empowers designated consumer bodies **1.159** to make super-complaints to the OFT or concurrent regulators[196] where a feature or features of a market allegedly result in 'significant harm to consumers'.[197] The OFT explains that 'one or more features of the market' may be:

- the structure of the market concerned or any aspect of that structure;
- any conduct (whether or not in the market concerned) of one or more than one person who supplies or acquires goods or services in the market concerned; or
- any conduct relating to the market concerned of customers of any person who supplies or acquires goods or services.[198]

Only consumer bodies designated by the Secretary of State for Trade and Industry **1.160** can make a super-complaint. To date the following consumer organisations have been designated: the Campaign for Real Ale Ltd, the Consumers' Association (now known as Which), the Gas and Electricity Consumer Council, the General Consumer Council for Northern Ireland, the National Association of Citizens Advice Bureaux, the National Consumer Council, the Consumer Council for Postal Services, the WaterVoice Council.[199]

The OFT has set out its approach to super-complaints in a guideline titled **1.161** *Super-complaints: guidance for designated consumer bodies.*[200] Complainants are requested to submit a reasoned complaint setting out reasons for further investigation. The Annex to the OFT's guideline sets out the kind of evidence that designated consumer bodies should consider providing when deciding whether to make a super-complaint.

No formal investigatory powers are provided to the OFT to collect information **1.162** in the 90 day period available to it before responding to a super-complaint. As with market studies, the OFT relies on its informal powers to gather information.

---

[196] In 2003, the ability to receive super-complaints was extended to the concurrent regulators (see Enterprise Act 2002, s 205 and Enterprise Act (Super-complaints to Regulators) Order 2003, SI 2003/1368).

[197] See Chapter 11 for more information on super-complaints.

[198] OFT504, *Super-complaints: guidance for designated consumer bodies* (August 2002) para 2.3.

[199] Enterprise Act 2002 (Bodies Designated to make Supercomplaints) (Amendment) Order 2005, SI 2005/2340.

[200] OFT504, *Super-complaints: guidance for designated consumer bodies* (August 2002).

1.163 Within 90 days of the super-complaint, the OFT is required to publish a considered response to a super-complaint, setting out what action, if any, it proposes to take under its competition or consumer powers.[201] There are many possible outcomes to a super-complaint, which include:

- enforcement action by the OFT under the Competition Act or the OFT's consumer powers;

- launching a market study into the issue (for example, the OFT announced the launch of its market study into car homes in June 2004 in response to a super-complaint from the Consumers' Association made in October 2003);

- making a market investigation reference to the CC (for example, in both its *Response to the super-complaint on personal current account banking in Northern Ireland made by Which? and the General Consumer Council for Northern Ireland*[202] and in its *Response to the super-complaint on home credit made by the National Consumer Council*,[203] the OFT found that the test for a market investigation reference to the CC was satisfied);

- finding that another authority with concurrent duties is better placed to deal with the complaint;

- referring the complaint to another consumer enforcement body; for example, following a super-complaint from Postwatch on mail consolidation, the OFT and Postcomm agreed the latter would look at this issue, with OFT liaising with Postcomm as necessary;

- finding the complaint requires no action;

- finding the complaint to be unfounded.[204]

Annex 1:
Article 81 EC

1.164 (1) The following shall be prohibited as incompatible with the common market: all agreements between undertakings, decisions by associations of undertakings and concerted practices which may affect trade between Member States and which have as their object or effect the prevention, restriction or distortion of competition within the common market, and in particular those which:
(a) directly or indirectly fix purchase or selling prices or any other trading conditions;
(b) limit or control production, markets, technical development, or investment;
(c) share markets or sources of supply;
(d) apply dissimilar conditions to equivalent transactions with other trading parties, thereby placing them at a competitive disadvantage;

---

[201] Enterprise Act 2002, s 11(2). [202] OFT771a (11 February 2005).
[203] OFT747a (10 September 2004).
[204] OFT504, *Super-complaints: guidance for designated consumer bodies* (August 2002) para 2.25.

(e) make the conclusion of contracts subject to acceptance by the other parties of supplementary obligations which, by their nature or according to commercial usage, have no connection with the subject of such contracts.

(2) Any agreements or decisions prohibited pursuant to this Article shall be automatically void.

(3) The provisions of paragraph 1 may, however, be declared inapplicable in the case of:
— any agreement or category of agreements between undertakings;
— any decision or category of decisions by associations of undertakings;
— any concerted practice or category of concerted practices,

which contributes to improving the production or distribution of goods or to promoting technical or economic progress, while allowing consumers a fair share of the resulting benefit, and which does not:
(a) impose on the undertakings concerned restrictions which are not indispensable to the attainment of these objectives;
(b) afford such undertakings the possibility of eliminating competition in respect of a substantial part of the products in question.

Annex 2:
Article 82 EC

Any abuse by one or more undertakings of a dominant position within the common market or in a substantial part of it shall be prohibited as incompatible with the common market insofar as it may affect trade between Member States. **1.165**

Such abuse may, in particular, consist in:
(a) directly or indirectly imposing unfair purchase or selling prices or other unfair trading conditions;
(b) limiting production, markets or technical development to the prejudice of consumers;
(c) applying dissimilar conditions to equivalent transactions with other trading parties, thereby placing them at a competitive disadvantage;
(d) making the conclusion of contracts subject to acceptance by the other parties of supplementary obligations which, by their nature or according to commercial usage, have no connection with the subject of such contracts.

2

ENFORCEMENT BODIES IN THE UNITED KINGDOM

A. The Office of Fair Trading

(a) History of the Office of Fair Trading

The Office of Fair Trading (**OFT**) was established pursuant to the Fair Trading **2.01**
Act 1973 as a non-ministerial government department to support the Director
General of Fair Trading. Following the commencement of the Enterprise Act
2002, the role of the Director General of Fair Trading was abolished and the
OFT became a corporate body. The OFT now has a board consisting of a
Chairman, Chief Executive and, at the time of writing, five non-executive

members.[1] They are all appointed by the Secretary of State for Trade and Industry.

(b) Functions

2.02 The OFT's stated goal is to make markets work well for consumers. To this end, the OFT's activities involve enforcement of competition and consumer protection rules, studies into how markets are working, and communication to explain and improve both awareness and understanding.[2] In relation to enforcement of competition rules, the OFT's functions include investigating and applying penalties for breaches of the Competition Act and/or Articles 81 and 82 of the EC Treaty. The OFT also has a joint role together with the Serious Fraud Office (**SFO**) (and the Crown Office in Scotland) to investigate and prosecute criminal cartel offences.[3] The OFT's functions in relation to competition enforcement also extend to investigation of mergers and, where necessary, referral to the Competition Commission[4] (**CC**) where there is or may be expected to be a substantial lessening of competition in a UK market. The OFT may refer markets to the CC for investigation where it has reasonable grounds for suspecting any feature, or combination of features, prevents, restricts, or distorts competition.[5]

2.03 In addition to its enforcement of competition rules, the OFT has significant functions in relation to the enforcement of consumer protection rules.[6] The OFT also has a key role in undertaking and publishing market studies which may lead to use of its competition and consumer enforcement functions. The OFT's communication responsibilities include explaining its decisions transparently and promoting compliance by explaining to business what the law is and how the OFT will apply it.[7]

(c) Organisation

2.04 The OFT Board is responsible for the OFT's strategic direction, priorities, plans and performance. The OFT Board is likely to be directly involved in decisions on individual market studies and market investigations. It may take

---

[1] Information about the OFT Board and its members may be found at <http://www.oft.gov.uk/About/oft+board/default.htm>.
[2] <http://www.oft.gov.uk/About/Aims+and+objectives/default.htm>.
[3] See paras 1.127–1.133 above.   [4] See Chapter 13.
[5] In relation to market investigations, see Chapters 13 and 14 below.
[6] In accordance with its responsibilities pursuant to a myriad of legislative provisions including the Consumer Credit Act 1974, the Estate Agents Act 1979, and the Unfair Terms in Consumer Contracts Regulations 1999 to name but a few.
[7] <http://www.oft.gov.uk/About/Aims+and+objectives/default.htm>.

enforcement decisions in important individual cases. The minutes of the OFT Board are published.[8]

The OFT is arranged into three main market-facing areas: Policy and Strategy; **2.05** Markets and Projects; and Consumer Advice and Trading Standards. The three main operational areas are supported by central services: the Executive Office; Operations; and Communications.

The Markets and Projects division of the OFT is arranged into three market **2.06** groupings, dealing with services, goods, and infrastructure respectively. In addition, it has a 'front end/preliminary investigation' section, and two separate sections dealing with mergers and cartels respectively.

The aim of the OFT organisational structure is to arrange its work by market **2.07** rather than by legislation. The OFT has stated that it intends to use consumer and competition enforcement, market studies and market investigation references, education and communication in whatever combination is appropriate. The OFT's current organisational structure has been prompted, at least in part, by the criticisms of the National Audit Office in its 2005 report on the OFT, *Enforcing Competition in Markets* (see para 2.13 below). The effectiveness of this structure is likely to rely heavily on the prioritisation of markets and cases as determined by the Board.

(d) Statistics about the OFT

The OFT spent approximately £16 million on competition enforcement **2.08** activities in 2005–06. In the same year, the average number of full-time staff employed by the OFT was 696, of which competition enforcement comprised 232. In competition enforcement in 2005–06, the OFT opened 1,195 cases under the Competition Act, launched 18 formal investigations, and made six formal decisions and one interim measures decision. The OFT imposed total fines of £4,696,305 (reduced to £1,864,305 after leniency).[9] Funds received by the OFT in respect of penalty payments are recorded in the OFT's annual accounts and are paid into the Consolidated Fund, which is a general fund kept by the Treasury at the Bank of England.

The OFT is situated at Fleetbank House, 2–4 Salisbury Square, London, EC4Y **2.09** 8JX. The web address is <http://www.oft.gov.uk> and the general telephone number is +44 (0)20 7211 8000.

---

[8] <http://www.oft.gov.uk/About/oft+board/default.htm>.
[9] OFT's Annual Report and Resource Accounts 2005–06.

(e) Publications

(i) Rules and guidance

2.10 The OFT is required to publish procedural rules and guidance relating to commitments and penalties, which publications must be approved by the Secretary of State. Accordingly, the OFT must abide by the Competition Act 1998 (Office of Fair Trading's Rules),[10] penalties guidance, and guidance on accepting commitments.[11]

(ii) Guidelines

2.11 OFT guidelines are published in relation to a variety of topics, to explain how the OFT goes about fulfilling its functions and using its powers. The OFT has published numerous guidelines covering a wide variety of topics, which are also updated from time to time. Although the OFT is obliged to take its guidelines into account in making decisions, the guidelines do not have the same binding status as Secretary of State approved guidance, as noted above. An up-to-date list of the OFT's publications may be found at the OFT website.[12]

(iii) Annual reports

2.12 The OFT is required to prepare an annual plan, for consultation, containing its

---

[10] SI 2004/2751. The OFT's Rules are set out in full at Appendix 3.

[11] *Guidance as to the appropriate amount of a penalty* (December 2004); and *Enforcement* (December 2004).

[12] <http://www.oft.gov.uk/News/Publications/Leaflet+Ordering.htm>. Currently, the OFT guidelines relating to competition enforcement comprise: **Mini guides:** *Competing fairly* (March 2005); *How your business can achieve compliance* (March 2005); *Under investigation?* (March 2005); *How to make a complaint* (February 2000); *Cartels and the Competition Act 1998* (March 2005); *Leniency in cartel cases* (March 2005); *Public sector bodies and the Competition Act 1998* (April 2001); *The OFT and the bus industry* (February 2003). **Competition law guidelines:** *Modernisation* (December 2004); *Agreements and concerted practices* (December 2004); *Abuse of a dominant position* (December 2004); *Market definition* (December 2004); *Powers of investigation* (December 2004); *Concurrent application to regulated industries* (December 2004); *Enforcement* (December 2004); *Trade associations, professions and self-regulating bodies* (December 2004); *Assessment of market power* (December 2004); *Exclusion for mergers and ancillary restrictions* (September 1999); *Application in the water and sewerage sectors* (February 2000); *Vertical agreements and restraints* (December 2004); *Land agreements* (December 2004); *Services of general economic interest exclusion* (December 2004); *Application in the telecommunications sector* (January 2005); *Application to the Northern Ireland energy sectors* (July 2001); *Public transport ticketing schemes block exemption* (August 2002); *Application to the railway services* (November 2002). **Draft competition law guidelines:** *Assessment of conduct* (Consultation draft version, December 2004); *Intellectual property rights* (Draft November 2001). **Enterprise Act guidelines:** *Practical information* (March 2005); *How will the Enterprise Act 2002 change the Competition Act 1998 regime?* (June 2003); *Overview of the Enterprise Act—The competition and consumer provisions* (June 2003); *Market investigation references (March 2003); Market studies—guidance on the OFT approach* (November 2004); *The cartel offence (April 2003); Competition disqualification orders* (May 2003); *Enforcement of consumer protection legislation* (March 2005); *Super-complaints* (July 2003); *Powers for investigating criminal cartels* (January 2004).

main objectives and priorities for the year. The OFT must also prepare an annual report, which among other aspects, must state the extent to which it has met the objectives and priorities in its annual plan. The OFT is required to publish its annual plans and annual reports, as well as a response to the consultation, and these may be found on the OFT's website.

(iv) National Audit Office reports

The Comptroller and Auditor General, as the head of the National Audit **2.13** Office, certifies the accounts of all government departments and a wide range of other public sector bodies including the OFT. The Comptroller also has statutory authority to report to Parliament on the economy, efficiency, and effectiveness with which departments and other bodies have used their resources. The National Audit Office has published two full reports in relation to the OFT: *Progress in Protecting Consumers' Interests* (6 March 2003); and *Enforcing Competition in Markets* (17 November 2005). Copies of these reports are available on the National Audit Office website at <http://www.nao.org.uk>.

B. Concurrent Regulators

(a) The concurrent regulators

In the United Kingdom, there are a number of economic regulatory bodies **2.14** responsible for specific regulated sectors. In relation to competition matters in each of their regulated sectors, these sector regulators have largely the same powers as the OFT to apply and enforce the Competition Act, Articles 81 and 82 EC, and the Enterprise Act market investigation powers. The concurrent regulators (**Regulators**) and their areas of responsibility are:

(1) the Office of Communications (**Ofcom**),[13] responsible for agreements or conduct relating to activities connected with communications matters in television, radio, telecommunications, and wireless communications services;[14]
(2) the Gas and Electricity Markets Authority (**Ofgem**),[15] with responsibility for agreements or conduct relating to the shipping, conveyance, or supply of gas and ancillary activities;[16]
(3) the Northern Ireland Authority for Energy Regulation (**Ofreg NI**),[17] with responsibility for agreements and conduct relating to commercial activities

---

[13] Communications Act 2003.   [14] <http://www.ofcom.org.uk>.
[15] Gas Act 1986 and Electricity Act 1989.   [16] <http://www.ofgem.gov.uk>.
[17] Electricity (Northern Ireland) Order 1992, SI 1992/231 (NI 1) and Gas (Northern Ireland) Order 1996, SI 1996/275 (NI 2).

connected with the generation, transmission, or supply of electricity in Northern Ireland and the conveyance, storage or supply of gas in Northern Ireland;[18]

(4) the Water Services Regulation Authority (**Ofwat**),[19] with responsibility for agreements or conduct relating to commercial activities connected with the supply of water or with the provision or securing of sewerage services in England and Wales;[20]

(5) the Office of Rail Regulation (**ORR**),[21] with responsibility for agreements or conduct relating to the supply of services relating to railways;[22] and

(6) the Civil Aviation Authority (**CAA**),[23] with responsibility for agreements or conduct relating to the supply of air traffic services.[24]

2.15 Each of the Regulators is independently a member of the European Competition Network (**ECN**) and is a signatory to the joint ECN statement in relation to the exchange of information and in particular in relation to the exchange of information provided by a leniency application.

(b) Concurrent enforcement of the Competition Act prohibitions

2.16 While each Regulator has concurrent powers in relation to a specific industry sector (or a part thereof), the OFT may enforce competition law provisions in relation to any sector, including any one within which a Regulator operates. The powers of the Regulators to apply and enforce competition law concurrently with the OFT are provided under s 54 of and Sch 10 to the Competition Act 1998. The division of cases between each of the Regulators and the OFT is governed by regulations made under the Competition Act concerning concurrency[25] (**Concurrency Regulations**). The OFT has published a guideline providing information about how the OFT and the Regulators with concurrent competition powers under the Competition Act work together to enforce competition law in the United Kingdom (**Concurrency Guideline**).[26] The Department of Trade and Industry and HM Treasury published a report in 2006 considering the application of the competition rules by the OFT and the Regulators.[27]

---

[18] <http://www.ofregni.gov.uk>.   [19] Water Industry Act 1991.
[20] <http://www.ofwat.gov.uk>.
[21] Railways Act 1993 (as amended by Transport Act 2000).
[22] <http://www.rail-reg.gov.uk>.   [23] Transport Act 2000.
[24] <http://www.caa.co.uk>.
[25] Competition Act 1998 (Concurrency) Regulations 2004, SI 2004/1077.
[26] OFT405, *Concurrent application to regulated industries* (December 2004).
[27] *Concurrent competition powers in sectoral regulation* (May 2006), URN 06/1244.

The Concurrency Regulations require the OFT and the Regulators to consult **2.17**
with each other before acting on a case where it appears they may have concurrent jurisdiction. Cases are allocated to a Regulator or the OFT according to
specific criteria, which are set out in the Concurrency Guideline. These criteria
include the sectoral knowledge of the Regulator, whether the case affects more
than one regulatory sector, any previous contacts between the parties or complainants and a Regulator or the OFT, and any recent experience in dealing with
any of the undertakings or similar issues which may be involved in the proceedings. Until it has been decided which authority will conduct a particular case, no
UK authority may take any investigative action or make any appealable decisions
in relation to the case.[28] The general policy is that the Regulators will act rather
than the OFT—and this has been the normal practice to date. For more detail
on the concurrent enforcement of the Competition Act, see Chapter 11.

(c) Concurrent enforcement of Articles 81 and 82 within the United Kingdom

The same sector divisions between the OFT and each of the Regulators noted **2.18**
above apply in respect of the enforcement of Articles 81 and 82 EC in the
United Kingdom, with each Regulator and the OFT being a designated competition authority for the purposes of Regulation 1/2003.[29] The Concurrency
Regulations have been updated to reflect the additional enforcement role of the
Regulators. In relation to some ECN functions, the OFT acts as a central body
for all of the Regulators, conducting certain activities on their behalf. For
example, the transmission of information to and from the ECN is in practice
done via a central point within the OFT. Representation at most ECN meetings
is also usually carried out by the OFT on behalf of all the relevant UK designated competition authorities. However, the relevant Regulator will usually
attend meetings (with or without the OFT) on its sector. This does not reflect
any reduction in the Regulators' powers in relation to the enforcement of
Articles 81 and 82: these measures are in place only for practical efficiency.

C. Competition Commission

The CC is an independent public body established by s 45 of the Competition **2.19**
Act 1998.[30] The CC's role is to conduct in-depth inquiries into mergers,

---

[28] Concurrency Regulations, reg 6(1).
[29] Council Regulation (EC) 1/2003 of 16 December 2002 on the implementation of the rules
on competition laid down in Articles 81 and 82 of the Treaty [2003] OJ L1/1.
[30] The CC replaced the Monopolies and Mergers Commission (**MMC**) on 1 April 1999. The
MMC itself was established in 1949.

markets and the regulation of the major regulated industries. All inquiries are undertaken following a reference made to the CC by another authority.[31] The CC does not have any power to conduct inquiries on its own initiative.

2.20 The CC comprises approximately 50 members appointed by the Secretary of State for Trade and Industry. The Chairman and Deputy Chairmen of the Commission are also members of the Commission. For each inquiry, the Chairman appoints a group of members (usually four or five) to undertake the inquiry. There are specialist panels for utilities, telecommunications, water, and newspapers. The utilities panel is the specialist panel for electricity and gas inquiries. Where an inquiry relates to one of these areas, the group of members undertaking it will have at least one member from the appropriate panel.

2.21 In addition to the members of the CC, there is a staff of approximately 150 people engaged to support the members.

2.22 The CC is an executive non-departmental public body, independent from government, though wholly funded through the Department of Trade and Industry.

2.23 Each financial year, the CC provides a rolling corporate and business plan to the Department of Trade and Industry. Progress against qualitative and quantitative key performance indicators is reviewed in the annual review of the CC's work. The CC's corporate plan for the coming year is published on its website.[32]

2.24 The Department of Trade and Industry is to commission a comprehensive review of the CC at least once every five years. The next review of the CC is scheduled to take place by 1 April 2008.

2.25 The CC's work in relation to market investigations is set out in detail in Chapters 13 and 14 below.

D. Competition Appeal Tribunal

(a) Functions of the Competition Appeal Tribunal

(i) Overview

2.26 The Competition Appeal Tribunal (**CAT**) was created by s 12 of and Sch 2 to the Enterprise Act 2002, which came into force on 1 April 2003. Prior to

---

[31] The OFT, the Secretary of State, or the Regulators.
[32] <http://www.competition-commission.org.uk>.

that date, the Competition Commission Appeals Tribunal[33] held many of the functions of the CAT.

In essence, the functions of the CAT are:　　　　　　　　　　　　　　　　　**2.27**

- to hear appeals on the merits in respect of decisions made under the Competition Act by the OFT and the Regulators;
- to hear actions for damages and other monetary claims under the Competition Act;
- to review decisions made by the Secretary of State, the OFT, and the CC in respect of merger and market references or possible references under the Enterprise Act;
- to hear appeals against certain decisions made by OFCOM and the Secretary of State relating to the exercise by OFCOM of its functions under certain provisions of the Communications Act 2003.[34]

Cases are heard before a panel consisting of three members: either the President **2.28** or a member of the panel of chairmen and two ordinary members. The members of the panel of chairmen are judges of the Chancery Division of the High Court and other senior lawyers. The ordinary members have expertise in law and/or related fields. The CAT's jurisdiction extends to the whole of the United Kingdom. The President and chairmen are appointed by the Lord Chancellor (following selection by the Judicial Appointments Commission), and the ordinary members by the Secretary of State for Trade and Industry.

(ii) Competition Act appeals

Under ss 46 and 47 of the Competition Act 1998, certain decisions taken by the **2.29** OFT or the Regulators may be appealed to the CAT. The CAT may confirm, set aside, or vary the OFT's decision, or remit the matter to the OFT, or make any other decision that the OFT could have made. Further information on who may appeal, and the types of decisions which may be appealed to the CAT, is set out in Chapter 12.

In respect of appeals concerning the acceptance, release, non-release, or variation **2.30** of commitments,[35] the CAT has power to determine such appeals in accordance with judicial review principles.

Except in the case of an appeal against the imposition or the amount of a **2.31**

---

[33] The CCAT was established under the Competition Act 1998.
[34] Communications Act 2003, Pt 2 (networks, services and the radio spectrum) and ss 290–294 and Sch 11 (networking arrangements for Channel 3). For more details on the CAT's functions, see Chapter 12.
[35] See paras 10.28 et seq for a discussion of the OFT's power to accept binding commitments.

penalty, the making of an appeal to the CAT does not suspend the effect of the decision to which the appeal relates, unless the CAT orders otherwise.

(iii) Competition Act damages claims

2.32 Under s 47A of the Competition Act 1998 (inserted by s 18 of the Enterprise Act 2002) any person who has suffered loss or damage as a result of an infringement of either UK or EC competition law may bring a claim for damages or for a sum of money before the CAT in respect of that loss or damage.

2.33 Such claims may only be brought in relation to loss or damage suffered as a result of infringement of the following prohibitions:

- the Chapter I and Chapter II prohibitions;
- Articles 81(1) and 82 of the EC Treaty;
- Articles 65(1) and 66(7) of the ECSC Treaty.[36]

2.34 In general claims may only be brought before the CAT when the relevant competition authority (namely the OFT or a Regulator or the European Commission) has made a decision establishing that one of the relevant prohibitions has been infringed, and any appeal from such decision has been finally determined.

2.35 Under s 47B of the Competition Act 1998 (inserted by s 19 of the Enterprise Act 2002), claims under s 47A may be brought by certain specified bodies on behalf of consumers.

(iv) Review of merger and market reference decisions

2.36 Under ss 120 (mergers) and 179 (market investigations) of the Enterprise Act 2002, any person aggrieved by a decision of the OFT, the Secretary of State or the CC in connection with a reference or possible reference, may apply to the CAT for a review of that decision.

2.37 In addition, under s 114, the imposition of a penalty by the CC for a person's failure to comply with a notice to provide evidence may be appealed to the CAT.

2.38 In relation to these reviews, the CAT applies the same principles as would be applied by a court on an application for judicial review.

(v) Appeals under the Communications Act 2003

2.39 Part 2 of the Communications Act 2003 confers power on OFCOM to regulate electronic communications networks and services by the setting, modification, or revocation of general or specific conditions of entitlement to provide such

---

[36] Note the ECSC Treaty expired on 23 July 2002.

networks or services in accordance with s 45 of that Act. Part 2 also confers power on OFCOM relating to the use of the radio spectrum. Decisions made by OFCOM under Pt 2 of the Communications Act 2003 that may be appealed (by a person affected) to the CAT are set out in s 192 of the Communications Act 2003.

Section 192 also applies to certain decisions made by the Secretary of State made **2.40** under certain provisions of the Communications Act.[37]

Appeals may also be brought by a Channel 3 licence holder against a deci- **2.41** sion made by OFCOM pursuant to ss 290–294 and Sch 11 concerning the competition aspects of networking arrangements (arrangements which allow programmes made, commissioned or acquired by a Channel 3 licensee to be made available to all other regional Channel 3 licensees).

Decisions that may not be appealed to the CAT are specified in Sch 8 to the **2.42** Communications Act 2003, including decisions to institute, bring, or carry on any criminal or civil proceedings, or to carry out any preliminary steps towards instituting such proceedings.

The CAT must decide the appeal on the merits and by reference to the grounds **2.43** of appeal set out in the notice of appeal (s 195(2)).

(b) CAT procedures

CAT procedures are governed by the Competition Appeal Tribunal Rules[38] **2.44** (**CAT Rules**). The CAT Rules were amended by the Competition Appeal Tribunal (Amendment and Communications Act Appeals) Rules 2004,[39] which primarily added new procedures relevant to the Communications Act 2003, and also made some minor amendments to the CAT Rules. The CAT Rules cover all aspects of procedure before the CAT, from case management to settlement offers.

The CAT has also published a detailed guide to its procedures[40] which contains **2.45** useful information in relation to matters such as commencing proceedings, pleadings, dealing with case management issues, evidence, confidentiality, the hearing, and costs issues.

(c) Appeals from the CAT's decisions

A further appeal lies from decisions of the CAT either on a point of law or, in **2.46** penalty cases, as to the amount of any penalty.

---

[37] ss 5, 156, 109, and 132.
[38] Competition Appeal Tribunal Rules 2003, SI 2003/1372.   [39] SI 2004/2068.
[40] Competition Appeal Tribunal, *Guide to Proceedings*, October 2005.

2.47   Such appeals lie to the Court of Appeal in relation to CAT proceedings in England and Wales; in relation to CAT proceedings in Scotland, to the Court of Session; and in relation to CAT proceedings in Northern Ireland to the Court of Appeal in Northern Ireland. An appeal may only be made with the permission of the CAT or the relevant appellate court. Further appeals (from a decision of the Court of Appeal) lie to the House of Lords, which may only be brought with the permission of the Court of Appeal or the House of Lords.

2.48   Specific questions on a point of European law may be the subject of a reference under Article 234 of the EC Treaty, whereby questions are referred to the European Court of Justice (**ECJ**).[41]

E. Serious Fraud Office

2.49   The SFO is an independent government department that investigates and prosecutes serious or complex fraud, and is part of the UK criminal justice system. The SFO has jurisdiction over England, Wales and Northern Ireland, but not over Scotland, the Isle of Man, or the Channel Islands. The SFO has concurrent powers alongside the OFT to prosecute individuals under the criminal cartel offence established by s 188 of the Enterprise Act 2002.[42] Prosecutions will generally be undertaken by the SFO, although the OFT also has the power to prosecute. In Scotland, prosecutions will be brought by the Lord Advocate.[43] The SFO and its powers were created by the Criminal Justice Act 1987 (as amended).

2.50   The SFO's powers of investigation and the ways in which the OFT and SFO work together are discussed in Chapter 7. There is also a discussion of the SFO's powers in relation to bringing prosecutions and seeking the imposition of fines and imprisonment in Chapter 10.

F. European Commission

2.51   The European Commission is one of the three main institutions carrying out the functions of the European Union, and is the enforcement body seen to uphold the interests of the European Union as a whole. The other two main institutions are the European Parliament, which represents the European

---

[41] The CAT may make a preliminary reference to the ECJ under Art 234 EC, pursuant to r 60 of the CAT's rules of procedure. For further information, see paras 10.143 and 12.48.

[42] For further information, see <http://www.sfo.gov.uk>.

[43] OFT518, *Overview of the Enterprise Act* (June 2003) para 6.8.

Union's citizens and is directly elected by them, and the Council of the European Union which represents the individual Member States that make up the European Union.

In addition, the ECJ and the Court of First Instance (**CFI**) uphold the rule of **2.52** European law, and the Court of Auditors checks the financing of the European Union's activities. Appeals from decisions of the European Commission are heard at first instance by the CFI, and further appeals on issues of law are heard by the ECJ.

The European Commission's role in enforcing European law includes the **2.53** enforcement of Articles 81 and 82 of the EC Treaty, alongside the national competition authorities of each Member State. The way in which the concurrent powers of the national competition authorities and the European Commission are used is discussed in Chapter 6, in the context of starting an investigation.

One of the European Commission's directorates is the Directorate for Com- **2.54** petition (also known as **DG COMP**). DG COMP is responsible for policy and enforcement of the European competition rules, and covers five main policy areas: Antitrust, Mergers, Liberalisation, State Aid, and International.

Under the authority of the Commissioner responsible for competition policy, **2.55** DG COMP is tasked with establishing and implementing a coherent competition policy for the European Union. DG COMP is headed by a Director General, who is supported by a Chief Competition Economist reporting directly to the Director General to provide independent economic advice on cases and policy.

There are also two independent Hearing Officers.[44] The Hearing Officers **2.56** are independent of the Directorate General for Competition and report directly to the Competition Commissioner. They are tasked with ensuring due process, safe-guarding the parties' procedural rights, and contributing to the quality of the decision-making in antitrust and merger proceedings. The organisation of DG COMP into a number of sub-directorates may be viewed on its website.[45] As at December 2005, the staff of DG COMP numbered approximately 600, with almost one-third of staff working in antitrust and cartel investigations.[46]

---

[44] The Hearing Officers' email address is: ec.external.hearing-officer@cec.eu.int. The Hearing Officers also have a webpage with details on their role and information about the two current Hearing Officers: <http://ec.europa.eu/comm/competition/hearings/officers/index_new.html>.

[45] <http://www.europa.eu.int/comm/dgs/competition/directory/organi_en.pdf>.

[46] <http://www.europa.eu.int/comm/dgs/competition/directory/staff.pdf>.

2.57 For policy enforcement in respect of antitrust matters, the European Commission's powers are set out in Regulation 1/2003 and in the implementing regulation, Commission Regulation (EC) 773/2004,[47] which relates to the conduct of proceedings by the European Commission pursuant to Articles 81 and 82.

2.58 In addition, the European Commission has published seven notices intended to provide guidance to businesses affected by the European competition rules.[48] The relevant legislation and decisions are set out on the DG COMP website.[49]

G. National Competition Authorities within Europe

2.59 From 1 May 2004, national competition authorities within the European Community are obliged to apply Articles 81 and 82 EC where they apply national competition law to agreements and practices which may affect trade between Member States.[50] In addition, the national authorities are given the power to apply not only Articles 81(1) and 82 EC, which have direct applicability by virtue of the case law of the ECJ, but also Article 81(3) EC.[51]

2.60 This power, which sits alongside the power of the European Commission to apply Articles 81 and 82 EC, is not limited under Regulation 1/2003 to the application of Articles 81 and 82 only in relation to the particular Member State that a national competition authority serves. As a consequence, it is possible in theory that any national competition authority in the European Community could exercise jurisdiction and impose penalties in relation to an infringement connected with the United Kingdom. But without the cooperation of the OFT, it is highly unlikely that another authority could obtain the information necessary for an infringement decision.

2.61 The national competition authorities and the European Commission have formed a network called the European Competition Network. Amongst other things, the ECN is intended to provide a framework for the cooperation of the national authorities and the European Commission in cases where Articles 81

---

[47] [2004] OJ L123/18.

[48] The notices are: Cooperation within the network, Cooperation with the courts, Handling of complaints, Informal guidance, Effect on trade, Application of Art 81(3) TEC, and Access to file. See Chapter 1 for more detail.

[49] <http://www.europa.eu.int/comm/competition/antitrust/legislation>.

[50] Regulation 1/2003, Art 3. For further information on the relationship between EC and national law, see Chapter 3.

[51] ibid, Arts 1 and 2.

and 82 EC are applied.[52] Apart from Regulation 1/2003, there are two primary documents which govern the operation of the ECN. These are the Joint Statement of the Council and the European Commission on the Functioning of the ECN (**Joint Statement**), and the Commission Notice on Cooperation within the Network of Competition Authority's (**Network Notice**).[53] The Joint Statement sets out high level principles for cooperation between the ECN members. The Network Notice sets out the basic principles covering the division of work and principles of case allocation, agreed principles relating to consistent application of EC Competition Rules, and the role and functioning of the Advisory Committee in the new system. The Network Notice also attaches a list of those national competition authorities which have signed the statement acknowledging the principles in the Network Notice and declaring that the national competition authority in question will abide by those principles. All the authorities from the current 25 Member States have signed the statement. The Notice is also binding on the European Commission. The principles in relation to case allocation and the division of work generally are discussed in Chapter 6, in relation to starting an investigation.

H. National Courts

(a) Civil courts

Under Article 3 of Regulation 1/2003, national courts have the same obligation as national competition authorities to apply Articles 81 and 82 EC wherever domestic competition law is applied.[54] In the United Kingdom, civil actions for damages or other remedies relating to breaches of the prohibitions in the Competition Act or Articles 81 or 82 must be commenced either in the CAT (see above) or in the Chancery Division of the High Court at the Royal Courts of Justice.[55] In an important decision in relation to jurisdiction, the High Court held in 2003 that, where a subsidiary of a cartelist has implemented a cartel in England, the English High Court has jurisdiction to hear claims by other European claimants against the English subsidiary, even if there was no contractual relationship between the claimant and the English subsidiary.[56] Although

2.62

---

[52] Commission notice on cooperation within the network of competition authorities (2004/C 101/03) [2004] OJ C101/43, para 1.

[53] ibid.

[54] For further information on the relationship between EC and national law, see Chapter 3.

[55] Civil Procedure Rules, *Practice Direction (Competition law—Claims relating to the application of Articles 81 and 82 of the EC Treaty and Chapters 1 and 2 of Part 1 of the Competition Act 1998)*, para 2.1(a). Note, in Scotland, the relevant court is the Court of Session.

[56] *Provimi Ltd v Aventis Animal Nutrition SA* [2003] EWHC 961 (Comm), [2003] 2 All ER (Comm) 683.

this decision was made on a strike-out application and was not therefore a final ruling, this decision is likely to be highly persuasive should the issue arise again before the English courts.

2.63 In certain circumstances, the CAT also has jurisdiction to hear civil actions in relation to breaches of Articles 81 or 82 or under the Competition Act.[57] Such issues may arise in appeals from decisions of the OFT or a Regulator, or in self-standing claims for damages. Claims before the CAT must relate to monetary claims, for damages or any other sum of money. They must also be follow-on claims where a finding of infringement has already been made. The Competition Appeal Tribunal Rules set out various matters in relation to such claims.[58] In future, it is possible that the CAT will play a greater role: the Enterprise Act provides for regulations to be made by the Lord Chancellor for cases to be transferred between the courts and the CAT.[59] At the time of writing, no such regulations have been made.

2.64 The applicable procedures and remedies which may be obtained in relation to actions in the UK courts are set out further in Chapter 10.

(b) Criminal courts

2.65 The Competition Act creates a number of offences relating to obstruction of the OFT in fulfilling its enforcement functions. These criminal offences are required to be tried before UK criminal courts. The Enterprise Act 2002 also created the cartel offence, which must be prosecuted (by the OFT or the SFO) before a national criminal court. As to whether the national courts, in applying the cartel offence, are also obliged to apply Articles 81 or 82 pursuant to Article 3 of Regulation 1/2003, see the discussion below at paras 3.32–3.36. At the time of writing, no prosecutions in relation to the cartel offence have been brought.

---

[57] Competition Act 1998, s 47A.
[58] Competition Appeal Tribunal Rules 2003, SI 2003/1372, Pt IV.
[59] Enterprise Act 2002, s 16.

3

THE RELATIONSHIP BETWEEN EUROPEAN COMPETITION LAW AND NATIONAL COMPETITION LAW

A. Introduction

By entrusting national authorities and courts with a key role in the enforce- **3.01** ment of Articles 81 and Article 82 EC, Regulation 1/2003 places additional emphasis on the relationship between European competition law and national competition law. Since 1 May 2004, each competition case initiated by the domestic competition authorities or disputed before the national courts potentially gives rise to the application of either (or both) European and national competition law.[1]

3.02 The interaction between European competition law and UK national competition law is particularly critical at three stages of competition proceedings. First, at the outset of every case, it is necessary to determine which law should be applied to the case (see Article 3(1) of Regulation 1/2003). Secondly, in the substantive evaluation of the case, it is necessary to resolve any conflict between European and UK national law: see Article 3(2) of Regulation 1/2003. Thirdly, even where a case is governed purely by domestic law in the form of the Chapter I or Chapter II prohibitions, s 60 of the Competition Act 1998 obliges the Office of Fair Trading (**OFT**) and the national courts to deal with questions arising under Pt I of the Competition Act in a manner that is consistent with the treatment of corresponding questions arising in European law. Additionally, where an undertaking is subject to investigation, the relationship between European competition law enforcement procedure and the domestic procedures for enforcement adopted under s 51 of the Competition Act may be relevant in determining the extent of that undertaking's procedural rights.[2]

B. The Supremacy of Community Competition Law

(a) General principles

3.03 The jurisprudence of the European Court of Justice (**ECJ**) has established, as a fundamental principle of European law, that Community law takes precedence over any conflicting measure of national law.[3] In *Simmenthal*,[4] the ECJ held:

> . . . the relationship between provisions of the Treaty and directly applicable measures of the institutions on the one hand and the national law of the Member States on the other is such that those provisions and measures not only by their entry into force render automatically inapplicable any conflicting provision of current national law but—in so far as they are an integral part of, and take precedence in, the legal order applicable in the territory of each of the member states—also preclude the valid adoption of new national legislative measures to the extent

---

[1] Council Regulation (EC) 1/2003 of 16 December 2002 on the implementation of the rules on competition laid down in Articles 81 and 82 of the Treaty [2003] OJ L1/1, Art 3(1). The simultaneous application of EC and national competition law and the problem of double jeopardy are considered in Chapter 11.

[2] *Pernod-Ricard SA v OFT* [2004] CAT 10.

[3] Case 6/64 *Costa v ENEL* [1964] ECR 585.

[4] Case 106/77 *Amministrazione delle Finanze del Stato v Simmenthal SpA* [1978] ECR 629.

to which they would be incompatible with community provisions. [Accordingly] . . . [i]t follows from the foregoing that every national court must, in a case within its jurisdiction, apply Community law in its entirety and protect rights which the latter confers on individuals and must accordingly set aside any provision of national law which may conflict with it, whether prior or subsequent to the Community rule.[5]

Articles 81 and 82 of the EC Treaty are directly applicable provisions of **3.04** European law,[6] and all block exemption and other European regulations adopted in the competition field are directly applicable by their very nature[7] and take precedence over any conflicting provision of national law. The obligation to disapply conflicting measures of national law applies to all state authorities, including the national courts and the competition authorities:

> The duty to disapply national legislation which contravenes Community law applies not only to national courts but also to all organs of the State, including administrative authorities (see, to that effect, Case 103/88 Fratelli Costanzo [1989] ECR 1839, paragraph 31), which entails, if the circumstances so require, the obligation to take all appropriate measures to enable Community law to be fully applied (see Case 48/71 Commission v Italy [1972] ECR 527, paragraph 7).

> Since a national competition authority such as the Authority is responsible for ensuring, inter alia, that Article 81 EC is observed and that provision, in conjunction with Article 10 EC, imposes a duty on Member States to refrain from introducing measures contrary to the Community competition rules, those rules would be rendered less effective if, in the course of an investigation under Article 81 EC into the conduct of undertakings, the authority were not able to declare a national measure contrary to the combined provisions of Articles 10 EC and 81 EC and if, consequently, it failed to disapply it.[8]

What is a conflicting measure of national law? The ECJ considered the oper- **3.05** ation of the principle of primacy in the competition field in *Wilhelm*.[9] This case establishes that where the conduct or agreements subject to scrutiny by national

---

[5] ibid, paras 17 and 22.

[6] Case 127/73 *BRT v SABAM* [1974] ECR 51, para 16.

[7] Art 249 EC provides 'A regulation shall have general application. It shall be binding in its entirety and directly applicable in all Member States'. See also Case C-253/00 *Antonio Munoz y Cia SA v Frumar Ltd* [2002] ECR I-7289 for an example of the horizontal enforcement of a regulation between private parties.

[8] Case C-198/01 *Industrie Fiammiferi (CIF) v Autorità Garante della Concorrenza e del Mercato* [2003] ECR I-8055.

[9] Case 14/68 *Wilhelm v Bundeskartellamt* [1969] ECR 1. See also Case 66/86 *Ahmed Saeed Flugreisen v Zentrale zur Bekampfung unlauteren Wettbewerbs eV* [1989] ECR 803, para 48: 'In that connection it should be borne in mind in the first place that, as the Court has consistently held, while it is true that the competition rules set out in Articles 85 and 86 concern the conduct of undertakings and not measures of the authorities in the Member States, Article 5 of the Treaty nevertheless imposes a duty on those authorities not to adopt or maintain in force any measure which could deprive those competition rules of their effectiveness. That would be the case, in particular, if a Member State were to require or favour the adoption of agreements, decisions or concerted practices contrary to Article 85 or reinforce their effects.'

authorities may affect trade between Member States, the parallel application of national competition law by the national authorities is allowed only in so far as it does not prejudice the uniform application of Community competition rules and the measures adopted in implementation thereof. Accordingly, Member States courts and authorities cannot authorise under national law agreements or practices that are prohibited by Article 81 or Article 82. Further, according to the ECJ in *Wilhelm*, the uniform interpretation of Community law would also be compromised if national courts and authorities were free to prohibit agreements benefiting from an individual exemption or clearance decision by the European Commission. However, supremacy as enunciated in *Wilhelm* does not require that Member States should refrain from prohibiting behaviour not prohibited under European law. Member States are therefore free to apply stricter national law[10] (note however that Regulation 1/2003 has expanded the obligations of consistency, as is discussed below).

3.06   Supremacy (as enunciated in the jurisprudence) therefore demands that where European law applies to prohibit anti-competitive behaviour, it will take precedence over any conflicting evaluation of the behaviour under national law.[11] Further, where European law specifically upholds an agreement (that is, where the European Commission has specifically cleared an agreement or given it an exemption by individual decision) the Member State authorities, pursuant to *Wilhelm*, are obliged to avoid decisions that conflict with the Commission's decision. The obligation to avoid decisions that conflict with decisions of the European Commission is but one aspect of the broader principle of supremacy.[12] It extends to national competition authorities and national courts:[13]

> [W]here a national court is ruling on an agreement or practice the compatibility of which with Articles 85(1) and 86 of the Treaty is already the subject of a Commission decision, it cannot take a decision running counter to that of the Commission, even if the latter's decision conflicts with a decision given by a national court of first instance.[14]

3.07   The principle of supremacy is central to the success of Regulation 1/2003 and the decentralised enforcement of Articles 81 and 82 EC. First, it gives Article 3(1) of Regulation 1/2003 (which defines when the obligation to apply Articles

---

[10] Note, however, to contrary effect, the Opinions of AG Tesauro in Case C-266/93 *Bundeskartellant v Volkswagen* [1995] ECR I-3477 and Case C-70/93 *BMW* [1995] ECR I-3439. The ECJ did not address the issue in either case.

[11] See the Courts Cooperation Notice and the Network Notice (see para 1.20 above).

[12] The House of Lords considered the ambit of the obligation to avoid decisions that conflict with those of the European Commission in *Inntrepreneur Pub Co (CPC) v Crehan* [2006] UKHL 38, [2006] 3 WLR 148.

[13] Regulation 1/2003, Art 16.

[14] Case C-344/98 *Masterfoods Ltd (t/a Mars Ireland) v HB Ice Cream Ltd* [2000] ECR I-11369.

81 and 82 arises) precedence over national law. Supremacy thereby contributes to effectiveness, by increasing the application of Articles 81 and 82 by national competition authorities and courts. Secondly, supremacy plays a critical role in reducing the scope for inconsistent decisions by national competition authorities and courts either under national law or Community law. Article 3(2) of Regulation 1/2003 restates and extends the principle of supremacy as applied to competition matters by the ECJ in *Wilhelm*.

C. The Scope of 'National Competition Law'

Article 3(1) of Regulation 1/2003 makes the obligation to apply Articles 81 and **3.08** 82 conditional upon the application of 'national competition law'. Article 3(2) prohibits, in certain circumstances, the application of stricter 'national competition law'. This begs the question: of the many legislative provisions that potentially apply to agreements and conduct in the United Kingdom, which of these would be considered to be 'national competition law' for the purposes of Article 3?

(a) Article 3(3)

Article 3(3) of Regulation 1/2003 provides us with clues as to what should **3.09** be considered national competition law for the purposes of Articles 3(1) and 3(2):

> Without prejudice to general principles and other provisions of Community law, paragraphs 1 and 2 do not . . . preclude the application of provisions of national law that *predominantly pursue an objective different from that pursued by Articles 81 and 82 of the Treaty.* [emphasis added]

The derogation in Article 3(3) is a double. It enables Member States authorities **3.10** both:

• to apply certain provisions of national law that are not deemed to be 'national competition law' (such as consumer protection law) without having to apply European competition law;[15] and
• to prohibit agreements under national law even if the agreement would not be prohibited under Article 81.[16]

Article 3(3) therefore provides some guidance as to what is *not* to be considered **3.11** national competition law for the purposes of Article 3(1) and (2) of Regulation 1/2003.

---

[15] As would otherwise be required by Regulation 1/2003, Art 3(1).
[16] As would otherwise be prohibited by Regulation 1/2003, Art 3(2).

(i) How broad is the derogation contained in Article 3(3)?

3.12   Article 3(3) provides for a derogation for national measures that might perhaps otherwise be considered national competition law under the domestic regime. It is clear from its terms that national authorities applying national merger control are not applying 'national competition law' for the purposes of Article 3(1) and (2). But what other national laws predominantly pursue an objective different from that pursued by Articles 81 and 82 EC?

3.13   Article 3(3) identifies the defining factor as to whether national law is competition law as the extent to which that law shares the same objectives as Articles 81 and 82. That this constitutes the critical distinguishing factor is reinforced in Recital 9 to Regulation 1/2003:

> Articles 81 and 82 of the Treaty have as their objective the protection of competition on the market. *This Regulation, which is adopted for the implementation of these Treaty provisions, does not preclude Member States from implementing on their territory national legislation, which protects other legitimate interests provided that such legislation is compatible with general principles and other provisions of Community law. In so far as such national legislation pursues predominantly an objective different from that of protecting competition on the market, the competition authorities and courts of the Member States may apply such legislation on their territory.* Accordingly, Member States may under this Regulation implement on their territory national legislation that prohibits or imposes sanctions on acts of unfair trading practice, be they unilateral or contractual. Such legislation pursues a specific objective, irrespective of the actual or presumed effects of such acts on competition on the market. This is particularly the case of legislation which prohibits undertakings from imposing on their trading partners, obtaining or attempting to obtain from them terms and conditions that are unjustified, disproportionate or without consideration. [Emphasis added]

3.14   At one extreme, it is clear that the Chapter I and II prohibitions in the Competition Act 1998 (which mirror the wording of Articles 81 and 82) are national competition law, given that they share with Articles 81 and 82 the respective objectives of preventing agreements that restrict, distort, or prevent competition and any abuse of dominance.

3.15   At the other extreme, Recital 9 indicates that laws such as unfair trading laws and consumer protection laws are clearly amongst those laws 'pursuing a different objective'. This merely reflects European case law preceding Regulation 1/2003: for example, national legislation generally prohibiting resale at a loss was not considered to fall foul of the Treaty rules on free movement in *Keck* (that case also raised the question whether the national provisions may be considered to have anti-competitive effect, but the ECJ did not answer the question).[17] European case law preceding Regulation 1/2003 provides further

---

[17]   Joined Cases C 267 & 268/91 *Keck and Mithouard* [1993] ECR I-6097.

indices as to what is the pursuit of a different objective: for example, Member States would appear to retain their ability to establish bodies to regulate the market environment in the public interest.[18]

With these clues to assist, let us turn to evaluate various provisions of UK law that might potentially be considered national competition law: market investigation references; sectoral rules; the cartel offence; director disqualification for competition law infringements; and the Financial Services and Markets Act 2000. Aside from the extremes discussed above, which could clearly be included or excluded from the concept of 'national competition law', it is hard to determine with any certainty to what extent the provisions discussed below can be said to share or not to share the objectives of Articles 81 and 82 in the absence of any case law defining the concept further.   **3.16**

Market investigation references   Under s 131 of the Enterprise Act 2002, the OFT may make a market investigation reference to the Competition Commission (**CC**) where it has reasonable grounds for suspecting that any feature, or combination of features, of a market in the United Kingdom for goods or services prevents, restricts, or distorts competition in connection with the supply or acquisition of any goods or services in the United Kingdom or a part of the United Kingdom. Section 134 of the Enterprise Act provides that, on receipt of a reference, the CC shall decide whether any feature, or combination of features, of each relevant market prevents, restricts, or distorts competition in connection with the supply or acquisition of any goods or services in the United Kingdom or a part of the United Kingdom.   **3.17**

Ex ante *or* ex post?   There has been some debate[19] as to whether the UK market investigation regime, and other *ex ante* competition scrutiny provisions aimed at 'promoting' competition could be said to pursue a different objective from *ex post* punitive competition provisions aimed at 'protecting' competition (see the first sentence of Recital 9 above). However, this is a tenuous distinction. It is difficult to maintain that the objective of Articles 81 and 82 is limited solely to *ex post* protection of competition: the case law establishes that they apply to agreements and conduct that prevent potential competition from developing.[20]   **3.18**

It is also difficult to see how a competition regime aimed at 'promoting' competition is not also aimed at protecting competition: these are far from mutually   **3.19**

---

[18] Case 231/83 *Cullet v Centre Leclerc* [1985] ECR 305, para 18: 'Article 5, in conjunction with Articles 3(f) and 85 of the Treaty, does not prohibit the Member States from regulating, in the manner laid down by the rules contested in the main proceedings, the fixing of the retail selling price of goods'.

[19] FIDE conference, Dublin, June 2004.

[20] See Joined Cases C 241 & 242/91 P *RTE v Commission* [1991] ECR I-743 and Case C-234/89 *Delimitis v Henninger Brau AG* [1991] ECR I-935.

exclusive objectives. This is highlighted by the language of the market investigation reference provisions, which closely shadows that of Article 81 EC. The key determination made by both the OFT and the CC is 'whether any feature, or combination of features, of each relevant market prevents, restricts or distorts competition'. It is not sustainable to argue that this is a different objective from Article 81, which is aimed at agreements that have as 'their object or effect the prevention, restriction or distortion of competition'.

3.20 Despite the fact that market investigations focus on a market as a whole as opposed to individual undertakings, so that undertakings that are active in the market subject to investigation are not 'in the dock' as they are in the context of a Competition Act investigation, at heart the market investigation reference provisions focus on establishing whether competition is prevented, restricted or distorted—effectively the same objectives that are pursued by Articles 81 and 82.

3.21 *OFT and CC position* It is clear from the following passage of its guidance (upon which it consulted the CC) that the OFT has accepted that the market investigation reference regime amounts to 'national competition law' for Regulation 1/2003:

> When the modernisation regulation comes into force, where the OFT applies national competition law such as the Enterprise Act to agreements, decisions or concerted practices within the meaning of Article 81(1) which may affect trade between Member States it must also apply Article 81 . . . In the context of a market investigation by the CC, the obligation to apply Articles 81 or 82 in parallel with national competition law will arise only at the stage where remedies are imposed by the CC following a reference.[21]

3.22 The CC's Market Investigation Guidelines make a similar acknowledgement:[22]

> In the context of a market investigation, the obligation to apply Articles 81 and 82 in parallel with national competition law will arise only at the stage where remedies are imposed by the Commission. The obligation does not affect the exercise by the Commission of its powers of investigation.

3.23 For a discussion as to how the obligation to apply Articles 81 and 82 can be accommodated in the context of the market investigation regime, see Chapter 13.

3.24 **Sectoral rules** The Regulators (as defined in paras 2.14–2.18 above) have powers under sectoral legislation listed at paragraph 2.14 above. These statutes provide the Regulators with a broad spectrum of powers. Some of these powers

---

[21] OFT511, *Market investigation references: Guidance about the making of references under Part 4 of the Enterprise Act* (March 2006) paras 2.12 and 2.13.
[22] CC3, *Market Investigation References: Competition Commission Guidelines* (June 2003) para 1.13.

pursue objectives that are obviously different to those pursued by Articles 81 and 82: for example, ensuring that there is sufficient provision of the regulated service throughout the United Kingdom; and ensuring that licence holders are able to finance those activities which they are authorised by their licences to carry out.[23] Sectoral regulators may also have social or environmental duties and powers.

In the context of exercising these powers, the Regulators may adopt measures or regulate undertakings' behaviour (for example, by fixing prices) in a manner which may appear to be at odds with Articles 81 and 82. It has however been established that where Member States are acting in the public interest, and are subject to the rules on free movement and to Article 86(2) EC, they are not precluded by Articles 81 and 82 from fixing prices directly or establishing bodies that regulate prices in the public interest[24]—precisely because in so doing they are pursuing different objectives to the protection of competition. **3.25**

The exercise of these powers will accordingly not trigger the obligations contained in Article 3(1) and (2). As stated in the OFT's guidance:[25] **3.26**

> Article 3 does, however, not preclude the application of national law that predominantly pursues objectives different from those pursued by Articles 81 and 82. This means that the Regulators may still apply powers set out in their sector-specific legislation to agreements which are compatible with Community competition law provided they do so predominantly in pursuit of objectives different from that pursued by Article 81 and Article 82 of the Treaty (the protection of competition on the market).

However, most of the Regulators are also entrusted with powers, separate from their prescribed functions under the Competition Act 1998, to promote or facilitate competition. These powers were originally introduced as a temporary measure to ensure the protection of consumers pending the development of real competition in the regulated sectors. For the reasons provided at para 3.19 above in relation to the market investigation regime, no meaningful distinction can be drawn between the objective of protecting competition that is pursued by Articles 81 and 82, and the objective of promoting or facilitating competition under sectoral regulation. The following extract from DTI and HM Treasury's *Report on Concurrent Competition Powers in Sectoral Regulation*[26] emphasises the closeness of certain sectoral powers to competition powers: **3.27**

---

[23] eg, see the CAA's general duty under Transport Act 2000, s 2, Water Industry Act 1991, s 2(2) and Electricity Act 1989, s 3.

[24] Case 231/83 *Cullet v Centre Leclerc Toulouse* [1983] ECR 305.

[25] OFT405, *Concurrent application to regulated industries* (December 2004) para 4.8. This is published after consultation with the Regulators under Competition Act 1998, s 52.

[26] May 2006, URN 06/1244.

A distinctive feature of the concurrency regime is that it allows the regulators to use both sector-specific regulatory powers and general competition powers to regulate markets. Indeed, sectoral regulation has played a key role in opening up markets and stimulating market development, removing barriers to entry, regulating dominant players and ensuring fair, transparent pricing.[27]

3.28 It is clear from the OFT's guidance[28] that the OFT and Regulators recognise that the exercise of some sectoral powers can trigger the obligation to apply Articles 81 and 82:

> To the extent that some of the Regulators' sectoral powers may, as set out above, in certain circumstances be capable of being used to pursue the same objective as that of Articles 81 and 82, i.e. the protection of competition on the market, the use of these powers would be considered the application of national competition law for the purposes of Article 3.

3.29 The above quotation implies that the use that is made of a particular power in an individual instance will determine whether the national law at issue pursues similar objectives to Articles 81 and 82. This is at odds with the wording of Article 3 of Regulation 1/2003 which indicates that one must consider the objective pursued by the national provision at issue, and not its exercise in an individual case, in order to determine whether the law is 'national competition law'.

3.30 The issue is difficult in the context of the powers of Regulators because protection of competition is often formulated as a power that is available to Regulators *as a means* of achieving consumer protection,[29] for example, as in s 3(1) of the Communications Act 2003:

> It shall be the principal duty of Ofcom, in carrying out their functions;
> (a) to further the interests of citizens in relation to communications matters; and
> (b) to further the interests of consumers in relevant markets, where appropriate by promoting competition.

3.31 Although the general objectives entrusted to Regulators frequently intertwine competition and non-competition objectives, individual provisions that are aimed at promoting competition are already identifiable and constitute in the authors' view, national competition law.[30] The closeness between these provisions and their competition powers under the Competition Act has meant that sectoral regulators frequently tackle competition powers under sectoral legislation rather than under the Competition Act. The *Report on Concurrent*

---

[27] ibid, para 7.
[28] OFT405, *Concurrent application to regulated industries* (December 2004) para 4.4.
[29] See also the electricity, gas and water sectors, eg the Water Act 2003 introduces a new duty for Ofwat to further the consumer objective by protecting the interests of consumers, wherever appropriate, by promoting effective competition in the provision of water and sewerage services.
[30] Communications Act 2003, ss 316, 217, and 318.

Competition Powers in Sectoral Regulation notes: 'Regulators have a degree of discretion over whether to tackle potential competition concerns through their concurrent powers [ie competition powers] under the Competition Act or through other means . . .'. Further, it finds that 'where regulators have a choice, they usually choose to use their regulatory powers and do not use their concurrent competition powers [under the Competition Act]'.[31] It is not clear whether, going forward, the Regulators will be compelled by Article 3(1) to apply Articles 81 and 82 EC (and hence the Competition Act) somewhat more frequently whenever they address competition patterns.

The cartel offence   Under the Enterprise Act 2002 it is a criminal offence if **3.32** an individual dishonestly agrees with one or more other persons to make or implement, or to cause to be made or implemented, arrangements relating to at least two undertakings involving the following prohibited cartel activities: price-fixing, market sharing, limitation production, or supply and bid-rigging.

Although the language used is different to that in Article 81 or Chapter I, the **3.33** offence is obviously aimed at deterring hard-core cartel activities. Further, the UK government introduced the offence to strengthen the UK competition regime:

> But for the most damaging form of anti-competitive behaviour engaging in a 'hard-core' cartel the Government believes that there is a strong case for strengthening the penalties, with the introduction of criminal sanctions against individuals. A new criminal regime would work alongside the existing civil regime.[32]

This has led certain commentators to the conclusion that the cartel offence is **3.34** indeed a provision of national competition law that triggers the obligations in Article 3 of Regulation 1/2003.[33]

OFT's position   The OFT's position is that the cartel offence is not a provision **3.35** of national competition law for the purposes of Article 3 of Regulation 1/2003. The rationale for this is as follows:

(1) The cartel offence is a stand-alone offence, which in essence turns on dishonesty (a well-defined concept in UK criminal law[34]) as opposed to competition-based elements. The offence is not dependent upon any prior finding of a competition law breach. The legal issues for determination by the courts are different to those in Article 81 cases, as they do not comprise

---

[31] May 2006, URN 06/1244, para 6.4. The Report notes that between January 2001 and September 2005, the sectoral regulators did not make one infringement decision.

[32] DTI White Paper, *A World Class Competition Regime* Cm 5233 (July 2001) para 7.2

[33] See, eg, Dr Wouter Wils, 'European Union and European Competition Law and Policy: The Reform of Competition Law Enforcement—will it work?', Community Report, FIDE XXI Congress Dublin, para 162, fn 239.

[34] *R v Ghosh* [1982] QB 1053.

any element of economic analysis and focus instead on the issue of the individual's dishonesty. At the time of drafting, there was a choice as to whether the offence would be formulated as a criminal offence that 'attached' to a competition law infringement,[35] as in the Irish Competition Act 2002, or whether it would not be better to define it as dishonest participation in an agreement which has one of four prohibited purposes. The latter was chosen, partially because of the complexity of putting a competition-based offence raising complex economic issues before a jury, and also because there was a wish to distance the offence from any competition-based 'exemption' defence.[36]

(2) The cartel offence is a national law aimed solely at punishing individuals, as opposed to undertakings (which are more usually the subject of competition law).[37]

(3) The final sentence of Recital 8 (which relates to Article 3 of Regulation 1/2003) provides that 'this Regulation does not apply to national laws which impose criminal sanctions on natural persons except to the extent that such sanctions are the means whereby competition rules applying to undertakings are enforced'. In the negotiations leading to the adoption of Regulation 1/2003, the United Kingdom specifically requested that this sentence be added to Recital 8 in order to clarify the status of the cartel offence. Unlike the Irish Competition Act 2002, which provides for criminal penalties for breaches of Articles 81 and 82 and their domestic equivalent,[38] the UK cartel offence is clearly not a means of enforcement of competition rules against undertakings: therefore, the language of Recital 8 lends support to the OFT's view that the cartel offence does not fall within national competition law within the meaning of Article 3.

3.36 Whilst it is true that the cartel offence is not, like Articles 81 and 82, aimed at identifying agreements or practices that prevent, restrict, or distort competition

---

[35] See DTI White Paper, *A World Class Competition Regime* Cm 5233 (July 2001) paras 7.28–7.31. 'We have identified two broad approaches to the offence itself, both of which involve setting out on the face of the statute the types of hard-core cartel activities identified above: price-fixing, market sharing and bid-rigging. . . . The first would make it unlawful for a person to participate in an agreement whose purpose is one or more of the hard-core cartel activities identified above, where the agreement also involves a breach of either Article 81 of the EC Treaty or the equivalent prohibition of the Competition Act 1998 (Chapter I) . . . This could require a lay jury with no competition expertise to consider potentially complex economic arguments. The second approach is to remove the direct link to a finding that an undertaking has breached Article 81 or Chapter I. Instead the offence would be defined as the dishonest participation in an agreement which has, as a purpose, one or more of the specified hard-core cartel activities. A jury would need to determine whether a defendant had acted dishonestly.'

[36] R Nazzini, 'Criminalisation of Cartels and concurrent proceedings' [2003] ECLR 483.

[37] See R Nazzini, *Concurrent Proceedings in Competition Law—procedure, evidence and remedies* (Oxford University Press, 2004) 90–3 and 285–7 for a general discussion on this topic.

[38] Irish Competition Act 2002, ss 4 and 5.

and therefore the offence is prosecuted without any such analysis being undertaken, the offence was introduced to deter the worst manifestations of anti-competitive behaviour. Ultimately, the question as to whether or not the cartel offence should be considered national competition law will depend very much on the stance adopted by the ECJ towards 'national competition law': it may be influenced by the wording in Recital 8 to take a narrow approach to the concept, as advocated by the OFT; on the other hand, a recital is not the strongest of grounds on which the OFT could build its case. An article in the Regulation would have been a stronger basis, but was not considered necessary by the United Kingdom when the Regulation was being negotiated.

Director disqualification   Unlike the cartel offence, director disqualification is   **3.37** closely tied to, and dependent upon, a prior finding of a competition law breach by the undertaking of which the individual to be disqualified is a director.

Under the Company Directors Disqualification Act 1986, as amended by the   **3.38** Enterprise Act 2002, the court must make a Competition Disqualification Order (**CDO**) against a person, if the court considers that the following two conditions are satisfied in relation to that person:

(1) an undertaking which is a company of which that person is a director commits a breach of competition law, and
(2) the court considers that that person's conduct as a director makes him or her unfit to be concerned in the management of a company.[39]

A breach of competition law for the purposes of s 9A(1) of the Company   **3.39** Directors Disqualification Act 1986 is a breach of any of Chapter I, Chapter II, Article 81, or Article 82.[40] Accordingly, it is clear that if a court is invited to make a finding relating to breaches of Chapter I or Chapter II, it will be applying 'national competition law' for the purposes of Article 3(1).

However, OFT guidance indicates that: **3.40**

> The OFT or Regulator only intends to apply for CDOs in respect of breaches of competition law that have been proven in decisions or judgments (as the case may be) of the OFT or a Regulator, European Commission, Competition Appeal Tribunal, or European Court.[41]

The OFT will therefore not be requesting the courts to make any findings that   **3.41** could be considered national competition law, without the benefit of a prior finding to that effect for the court to rely upon. This raises the question as to whether there is really a fresh application of national competition law in such a context:

---

[39] Company Directors Disqualification Act 1986, s 9A(2) and (3), referred to in Chapter 1.
[40] ibid, s 9A(4).
[41] OFT510, *Competition disqualification orders: Guidance* (May 2003) para 4.6.

(1) application of national competition law (in the shape of a finding of a breach of Chapter I and Chapter II) will already have occurred prior to the director disqualification proceedings, so that the obligation also to apply European competition law should already have been considered and complied with, where appropriate;

(2) the focus of the director disqualification proceedings will not be on determining whether there has been a restriction, distortion or prevention of competition but on determining whether a particular director's conduct renders him or her unfit to be concerned in the management of a company.

3.42 As against this, in the unlikely event that a court be requested to rely upon a prior finding of breach of Chapter I by the OFT, the facts of which clearly gave rise to an obligation also to apply Article 81, the court would probably, consistently with its obligations under Article 3(1), also apply Article 81 on the basis that the OFT should have done so, and did not.[42]

3.43 Certainly, even if director disqualification proceedings are to be considered 'national competition law', the scope for Article 3(1) and Article 3(2) to have any impact on such proceedings is much reduced by the OFT's policy of relying on previous findings before initiating proceedings. In most cases, any application of European competition law necessitated by Article 3(1) will already have taken place. As regards Article 3(2), it is unlikely that any such proceedings would involve the need to disapply any conflicting provisions of national competition law.

3.44 **Financial Services and Markets Act 2000** Chapter III of Pt X of the Financial Services and Markets Act 2000, entitled 'Competition Scrutiny', provides the OFT with powers to consider the Financial Services Authority's (FSA's) practices and regulating provisions in order to determine whether any of these has, alone or combined, a 'significantly adverse effect on competition'.

3.45 It is difficult to dispute that the significantly adverse effect on competition test is anything other than a provision of national competition law. However, although these provisions arguably share the same objective as Articles 81 and 82 (and are therefore national competition law), they are aimed at scrutinising one body's (the FSA) practices and regulating provisions. It is unclear whether the FSA amounts to an 'undertaking' for the purposes of Articles 81 and 82. The FSA, acting as a regulator, may not be acting as an undertaking within the meaning of Article 81 or Article 82, in view of the public law nature of its functions.[43] The consequences of this are that Articles 81 and 82 do not apply to the FSA where

---

[42] See paras 3.49 et seq on the obligation in Article 3(1).
[43] Case C-205/03 P *Fenin v Commission*, judgment of 11 July 2006. Case C-343/95 *Cali v Porto de Genoa* [1997] ELR 1547.

it is carrying out a public law function and there can accordingly be no obligation for the OFT to apply these provisions to the FSA under Article 3(1).

Chapter II of Pt XVIII of the Financial Services and Markets Act 2000 provides **3.46**
for two separate competition scrutiny provisions:

(1) an *ex ante* competition analysis by the OFT of regulatory provisions sub-
    mitted by any body that applies to the FSA for recognition under ss 287 or
    288 of the Financial Services and Markets Act;
(2) an ongoing obligation on the OFT, under s 304 of the Financial Services
    and Markets Act, to keep the regulatory provisions and practices of recog-
    nised bodies under review and to issue a report if at any time it concludes
    that any such regulatory provisions or practices (alone or in combination)
    has a significantly adverse effect on competition.

As discussed above at para 3.18, the *ex ante* nature of any competition provision **3.47**
is extremely unlikely to alter its fundamental nature as a provision of national
competition law, given that the substantive evaluation undertaken is aimed at
identifying and remedying significantly adverse effects on competition, be they
present or future. Further, both these provisions relate to the conduct of bodies
corporate or unincorporated associations which are either applying for, or have
been granted the status of recognised investment exchange or clearing house,
which would appear to qualify as undertakings for the purposes of Articles 81
and 82.[44] Accordingly, the OFT is bound under Article 3(1) and (2) in applying
these provisions.

Conclusion   It is unlikely that the issue of what amounts to 'national competi- **3.48**
tion law' for the purposes of Regulation 1/2003 will be determined by the ECJ
in the near future. From a practical perspective, it is unlikely that the Commission will devote much resources to taking enforcement action against Member
States on this issue, when the system of decentralised enforcement is still in
its infancy and there are issues of greater importance and priority, such as
addressing the need for consistent application of Articles 81 and 82. The High
Court briefly considered what amounts to national competition law under
Article 3 of Regulation 1/2003 in *Days Medical Aids Ltd v Pihsiang Machinery
Co Ltd & Ors*.[45] It look a fairly generous approach to the concept holding that
'Whatever characterisation may be given to the common law doctrine of
restraint of trade and despite Mr Beal's submission to the contrary I do not

---

[44] eg, the OFT imposed interim measures on the London Metal Exchange (LME) on
27 February 2006 to avoid further abusive conduct by the LME, contrary to Art 82 EC (the
direction was subsequently withdrawn, but not on the basis that the LME did not qualify as an
undertaking).
[45] [2004] EWHC 44 (Comm).

think it can be said predominantly to pursue an objective different from Articles 81 and 82.'

D. Which Law to Apply: Article 3(1) of Regulation 1/2003

3.49 Article 3(1) of Regulation 1/2003 does not merely empower national competition authorities and courts to apply Articles 81 and 82, it imposes a positive obligation on them to do so. The rationale for this obligation is set out in Recital 8 to Regulation 1/2003:

> In order *to ensure the effective enforcement of the Community competition rules* and the proper functioning of the cooperation mechanisms contained in this Regulation, *it is necessary to oblige the competition authorities and courts of the Member States to also apply Articles 81 and 82 of the EC Treaty* where they apply national competition law to agreements and practices which may affect trade between Member States. [Emphasis added]

3.50 However, Article 3(1) expresses the obligation to apply Article 81 separately from the obligation to apply Article 82, in different terms, and to different effect: the obligation on national authorities and courts to apply Article 81 is broader in scope than that to apply Article 82.

(a) Obligation to apply Article 81

3.51 The obligation to apply Article 81 is phrased as follows:

> Where the competition authorities of the Member States or national courts apply national competition law to agreements, decisions by associations of undertakings or concerted practices within the meaning of Article 81(1) of the Treaty which may affect trade between Member States within the meaning of that provision, they shall also apply Article 81 of the Treaty to such agreements, decisions or concerted practices.

(i) Conditions for obligation to apply Article 81 to arise

3.52 Article 3(1) provides for the fulfilment of several conditions before the obligation to apply Article 81 is triggered.

3.53 **The national competition authorities or courts must apply national competition law** The obligation to apply Article 81 only arises once national competition law is applied to the agreements at issue. The discretion currently enjoyed by national competition authorities in deciding whether or not to take a case forward is accordingly preserved: national competition authorities can decline to investigate a case, even where the agreements at issue would appear to affect trade between Member States, providing the authorities do not propose to apply national competition law to the matter.

The same logic applies to national courts: so long as the national court does not **3.54** propose applying national competition law to the agreements at issue, there is no obligation for it to consider the application of European competition law. However, if the national court (at whatever stage in the proceedings) proposes to make a finding concerning the application of national competition law to agreements within the meaning of Article 81(1), it will also, providing the other conditions set out in Article 3(1) are met, have to apply Article 81 to the agreements, if necessary of its own motion.[46]

Article 3(1) envisages that *both* European and domestic competition law should **3.55** be applied to agreements or conduct affecting trade between Member States. It does not draw a clear jurisdictional boundary, predicated on the exclusive application of Community law where there is an effect on trade on the one hand, and the exclusive application of national law where there is no such effect on the other. By mandating the application of European competition law wherever national law is applied to agreements that may affect trade, it is now more likely that both European and domestic competition law will be applied to agreements and conduct affecting trade. However, there is no obligation for national competition authorities and courts to continue applying their national competition law to conduct and agreements affecting trade. They are free to proceed solely under Article 81 and Article 82. The OFT like other national competition authorities generally proceeds against agreements and conduct affecting trade under both domestic legislation and Article 81/Article 82.[47] This raises the question of double jeopardy for the firms potentially subject to prosecution and penalty under both sets of provisions, as to which, see Chapter 11 below.

Agreements, decisions by associations of undertakings or concerted practices **3.56** **within the meaning of Article 81(1)**   The obligation is dependent on national competition law being applied to an 'agreement', 'decision by associations of undertakings' or 'concerted practice' 'within the meaning of Article 81(1)'. This reference is to the autonomous meaning that each of these terms have acquired in European case law relating to Article 81.[48] An agreement, decision or concerted practice only falls within Article 81(1) if reached between 'undertakings' as defined in the European case law.[49] The definition has been followed (and developed) by the Competition Appeal Tribunal (**CAT**) in *JJB Sports Plc v OFT*.[50]

---

[46] See Case C-234/04 *Kapferer v Schlank & Schick GmbH*, judgment of 16 March 2006.

[47] See eg the OFT's decision in the Investigation of multilateral interchange fees provided for in the UK domestic rules of MasterCard UK Members Forum Ltd, 6 September 2005, Case CP/0090/00/S (currently on appeal).

[48] See paras 1.28–1.34 above.

[49] See Chapter 1 above. Case C-41/90 *Hofner and Elser v Macrotron* [1991] ECR I-1979 and Case C-205/03 P *Fenin v Commission*, judgment of 11 July 2006.

[50] [2004] CAT 17. Upheld by the Court of Appeal in [2006] EWCA Civ 1318.

3.57 **Which may affect trade between Member States** Lastly, the national authorities and courts' obligation to apply Article 81 is dependent on whether the agreements at issue are capable of affecting trade between Member States. The concept of effect on trade pre-dates Regulation 1/2003 and has been addressed extensively in the case law as it is the jurisdictional criterion that indicates whether Article 81 and Article 82 can apply in any case. Where there is no effect on trade, Articles 81 and 82 do not apply and the matter is determined solely by application of national competition law.[51]

3.58 The European Commission has published a Notice to assist in assessing whether an agreement may affect trade between Member States.[52] The OFT will take account of the Commission Notice in its approach to effect on trade.[53] The concept is explained in more detail in Chapter 1 (at paras 1.38–1.54).

3.59 **No need for agreement to be anti-competitive** There is no need for the agreement, decision of an association of undertakings or concerted practice to be *prohibited* by Article 81 for the obligation to apply Article 81 to the agreement to be triggered. The obligation is triggered by the *application* of national law to an agreement within the meaning of Article 81(1) that may affect trade within the meaning of Article 81(1). This broad obligation to apply Article 81 means that the OFT or the court will be obliged to apply Article 81 to any agreements that may affect trade even in cases where they consider there are no grounds for action against the agreement under Article 81. This obligation is linked to the broad obligation on national competition authorities and courts to disapply conflicting national law relating to agreements: where an agreement is compatible with Article 81, no stricter national law may be applied (see paras 3.81 et seq below).

(b) Obligation to apply Article 82

3.60 The obligation to apply Article 82 is expressed as follows:

> Where the competition authorities of the Member States or national courts apply national competition law to any abuse prohibited by Article 82 of the Treaty, they shall also apply Article 82 of the Treaty.

(i) *Conditions for obligation to apply Article 82 to arise*

3.61 **The national competition authority or courts must apply national competition law** The same criterion applies in respect of the obligation to apply Article 81, and has been dealt with at paras 3.52–3.54 above.

---

[51] Case 56/65 *Société Technique Minière v Maschinenbau Ulm* [1966] ECR 235.
[52] Guidelines on the effect on trade concept contained in Articles 81 and 82 of the Treaty [2001] OJ C368/13; these are discussed at paras 1.38–1.54 above. This Notice represents the Commission's view of the law, and is not binding.
[53] See Competition Act 1998, s 60 and OFT442, *Modernisation* (December 2004) para 4.6.

An abuse that is prohibited by Article 82   The obligation to apply Article 82   **3.62**
is more narrowly drawn than that to apply Article 81. Unlike the broad obligation to apply Article 81 to any agreement capable of affecting trade between
Member States, irrespective of whether or not it has the object or effect of
restricting, preventing, or distorting competition, the obligation to apply
Article 82 is triggered only where the unilateral conduct at issue amounts to *an
abuse that is prohibited by Article 82 of the Treaty.* This means the obligation is
conditional on each of the substantive criteria of the Article 82 prohibition
being satisfied, namely:

- conduct which amounts to an abuse
- by one or more undertakings
- holding a dominant position
- in the common market (or a substantial part of it)
- which may affect trade between Member States.

This means, for example, that if the Chapter II prohibition is applied by a UK   **3.63**
national competition authority to an undertaking that is dominant in a small
part of the United Kingdom which does not amount to a substantial part of the
common market (such as abuse in local markets) the obligation to apply Article
82 is not triggered and the matter can be dealt with solely by reference to the
relevant provisions of the Competition Act 1998. Similarly, if national competition law is applied to a dominant undertaking within the common market in
respect of unilateral conduct that is not an 'abuse' within the meaning of Article
82, the obligation to apply Article 82 is not triggered.

In the United Kingdom, this ability to apply national competition law to   **3.64**
unilateral conduct without applying Article 82 where there is no abuse within
the meaning of Article 82 takes on great significance in the context of a market
investigation reference. The CC therefore remains free to examine and remedy
unilateral conduct, without being subject to any obligation to apply Article 82
so long as the conduct does not amount to abuse within the meaning of Article
82.[54]

The reason for the difference between the scope of the obligations to apply   **3.65**
Article 81 and Article 82 becomes clear when we turn to Article 3(2) (see
paras 3.81 et seq below). Article 3(2) similarly distinguishes between Article 81
and Article 82 in defining the ambit of national competition authorities and
courts' obligation to disapply conflicting national laws in the event of conflict
with European law.

---

[54] The CC is not designated as a national competition authority for the purposes of Regulation
1/2003 and cannot apply Article 81 or Article 82. See Chapters 13 and 14 for a discussion of the
relationship between market investigation and Articles 81 and 82 EC.

(c) Timing of the obligation to apply Community competition law

(i) Does Article 3(1) require simultaneous or parallel application of Articles 81 or 82?

3.66 Both OFT and CC guidelines occasionally refer to an obligation under Article 3(1) to apply Article 81 or 82 'in parallel with' national competition law.[55] However, the OFT's view is that such application need not be contemporaneous. Article 3(1) merely provides that *where* (and not when) national competition authorities and courts apply national competition law, they must *also apply* European competition law. Arguably, this leaves some room for the application of European competition law to be subsequent to that of national competition law.[56]

3.67 The reference to 'in parallel with' contained in the older OFT guidelines is a hangover from the draft wording of Regulation 1/2003. The initial wording for Article 3(1) proposed by the Commission in its White Paper did in fact contain the words 'in parallel with'. These words were dropped following negotiations, presumably for the purpose of removing the clear inference that application of European law had to be simultaneous with the application of national competition law.

3.68 This question is really of practical significance in the United Kingdom only in the context of market investigation references.[57] The CC is not a designated competition authority for the purposes of Regulation 1/2003, but (as discussed above) it applies national competition law. Accordingly, the obligation to apply Article 81 or Article 82 may potentially arise in the context of a market investigation by the CC. In such a situation, the CC cannot itself apply Article 81 or Article 82. The OFT, as the authority responsible for applying Article 81 or Article 82 as necessary, will generally do so after the market investigation reference has been completed. European competition law would therefore be applied *after* the application of national competition law. This issue is discussed further in Chapter 13.

3.69 In other cases, as a matter of practice, the OFT will apply both legal regimes simultaneously, given that to proceed otherwise would be a waste of resources.

3.70 The rest of this chapter will proceed on the assumption that the obligation to apply Articles 81 and 82 arises *simultaneously* with the relevant application of national competition law.

---

[55] CC3, *Market Investigation References: Competition Commission Guidelines* (June 2003) para 1.13; OFT511, *Market investigation references: Guidance about the making of references under Part 4 of the Enterprise Act* (March 2006) para 2.12.

[56] This is particularly important in the context of market investigation references, see Chapter 13 below.

[57] Upon which, see further Chapters 13 and 14.

(ii) When is national competition law 'applied' in the United Kingdom for the purposes of Article 3(1)?

It is important to determine exactly at what stage in the procedure competition **3.71** law is 'applied' to agreements or to an abuse prohibited by Article 82, in order to identify when the correlative duty to apply European competition law and to disapply conflicting provisions of national competition law arises for the national competition authorities and courts.

In the context of national court proceedings, it is relatively clear when law is **3.72** applied. There can be no application of national competition law until the court reaches a determination of some kind. It is submitted that even an interim order by a court, for example, an interim injunction preventing the further abuse of a dominant position in the United Kingdom under Chapter II, would amount to an application of national competition law for the purposes of Article 3(1), with the consequence that the court would be obliged to consider the application of Article 82 in making the interim order, if not raised by the parties themselves. Clearly, when a court reaches the stage at which it passes final judgment, it is applying national competition law.

The stage at which application of national competition law occurs in the con- **3.73** text of an investigatory process is more complicated. From the perspective of the undertakings subject to compulsory powers of investigation, it is clear that from the moment the OFT crosses the s 25 threshold initiating an investigation and exercises its formal powers of investigation under the Competition Act 1998, competition law is being 'applied' to those undertakings, as it is being used to compel them to behave in a certain manner (such as allowing access to premises, producing materials, etc).

However, the OFT has adopted the policy position that national competition law **3.74** is only applied at the culmination of the investigatory procedure when a decision is made applying remedies. Accordingly, the obligation to apply European competition law under Article 3(1) of Regulation 1/2003 only crystallises at the remedies stages. This policy position is apparent from the following.

In the context of market investigation references, the policy is overtly stated **3.75** both in OFT and CC guidelines on market investigation references. The OFT guidelines provide that:

> In the context of a market investigation by the CC, the obligation to apply Articles 81 or 82 in parallel with national competition law will arise only at the stage where remedies are imposed by the CC following a reference.[58]

---

[58] OFT511, *Market investigation references: Guidance about the making of references under Part 4 of the Enterprise Act* (March 2006) para 2.12.

CC market investigation guidelines contain near-identical wording.[59]

3.76 In the context of investigations conducted under the Competition Act 1998, the OFT is careful to reserve for itself the ability to apply European competition law at any stage in the process prior to making an infringement decision. The OFT's Procedural Rules, r 10 provides:

> (1) The OFT may, at any time prior to making an infringement decision, elect to apply to a case one or more of the Chapter I prohibition, the Chapter II prohibition, the prohibition in Article 81(1) and the prohibition in Article 82 (whether or not any such election has previously been made by the OFT in that case).

3.77 One can readily see why the OFT and other authorities exercising investigatory powers do not wish to equate the exercise of an investigatory power with the application of national competition law. To do so would mean that before the authority possesses sufficient information to determine the exact nature and scope of the competition problem at issue (especially as regards complex issues such as effect on trade and market definition), it may be compelled to apply European law. In the context of the market investigation regime, such an interpretation gives rise to distinct problems for the United Kingdom.[60]

3.78 In support of the OFT's position, one may distinguish between use of powers of investigation, which are not governed by Regulation 1/2003, and the application of the substantive prohibitions, which are so governed. Arguably it is only when a substantive decision is made that national law is applied in the sense of Regulation 1/2003. The difficulty with the OFT and the CC's position is that it identifies the application of remedies as the application of national law, rather than the application of the prohibitions. Such an interpretation allows the circumvention of the obligations in Article 3(1) and (2) in cases where the OFT does not apply a remedy. This issue is further discussed in Chapter 14.

E. Which Law Takes Precedence in Event of Conflict: Article 3(2)

3.79 The ECJ's decision in *Wilhelm*[61] which considers the issue of primacy in the competition context, leaves open several critical issues on the substantive interaction between European and national competition law, some of which only

---

[59] CC3, *Market Investigation References: Competition Commission Guidelines* (June 2003) para 1.13: 'In the context of a market investigation, the obligation to apply Articles 81 and 82 in parallel with national competition law will arise only at the stage where remedies are imposed by the Commission. The obligation does not affect the exercise by the Commission of its powers of investigation.'

[60] See further Chapter 14 below.

[61] Case 14/68 *Wilhelm v Bundeskartellamt* [1969] ECR 1, discussed at paras 3.05–3.06.

arise now that a legal exception regime has been introduced.[62] First, the judgment appears to allow national competition authorities and courts to prohibit, under national law, agreements that do not infringe Article 81. Secondly, as the European Commission was at the relevant time the sole authority empowered to apply Article 81(3) to exempt agreements, the judgment naturally does not consider the application of national competition law to agreements that meet the criteria in Article 81(3) but do not benefit from an individual or block exemption: this is logical because at the time such agreements would have been automatically void.[63] Lastly, it was unclear to what extent national authorities and courts were free to prohibit under national law agreements that fell under a block exemption regulation.[64]

All these issues are now addressed in Article 3(2) of Regulation 1/2003.   **3.80**

(a) Article 3(2)

Article 3(2) provides: **3.81**

> The application of national competition law may not lead to the prohibition of agreements, decisions by associations of undertakings or concerted practices which may affect trade between Member States but which do not restrict competition within the meaning of Article 81(1) of the Treaty, or which fulfil the conditions of Article 81(3) of the Treaty or which are covered by a Regulation for the application of Article 81(3) of the Treaty. Member States shall not under this Regulation be precluded from adopting and applying on their territory stricter national laws which prohibit or sanction unilateral conduct engaged in by undertakings.

On the one hand, this provision takes the principle of primacy elaborated in **3.82** *Wilhelm* one step further as regards Article 81, by preventing Member States from applying stricter national competition law to agreements affecting trade. Member States may not prohibit agreements affecting trade which either do not restrict competition within the meaning of Article 81(1) or which fulfil the conditions of Article 81(3). Accordingly, agreements affecting trade that do not fall foul of Article 81 are effectively 'protected' from the application of stricter national competition law by Article 81.

On the other hand, the Member States remain free to apply stricter national law **3.83** to unilateral conduct that is not prohibited under Article 82. The rationale for this distinction is partially explained in Recital 8 to Regulation 1/2003.[65] As

---

[62] See paras 1.65–1.69 above.   [63] See para 1.17 above.
[64] See R Whish, *Competition Law* (5th edn, LexisNexis Butterworths, 2003) 76.
[65] Recital 8 provides: 'In order to create a level playing field for agreements, decisions by associations of undertakings and concerted practices within the internal market, it is also necessary to determine pursuant to Article 83(2)(e) of the Treaty the relationship between national laws and Community competition law. To that effect it is necessary to provide that the application of

agreements operate across national borders, the view was taken that there could not be inconsistent treatment of the same agreement under the national laws of the Member States, without prejudicing the level playing field. This rationale does not apply to unilateral conduct in different Member States, although clearly a divergence in the national rules on unilateral conduct in each Member State must considerably augment burdens for business. Another reason for this provision is that it was introduced to allow Germany, France, Italy, and other relevant Member States to retain 'ordoliberal' laws against abuse of economic dependence, ie 'unfair' competition.

3.84 The difference in the scope of the obligation to disapply conflicting national laws under Article 3(2) is foreshadowed in Article 3(1). In order to ensure that no stricter national law should be applied to agreements irrespective of where they are prohibited by Article 81, Article 3(1) provides for a broad obligation to apply Article 81: it is triggered by the existence of an agreement that may affect trade, irrespective of whether it is prohibited by Article 81. Contrast this with the obligation to apply Article 82, which is not triggered under Article 3(1) unless the unilateral conduct is actually prohibited by Article 82: see paras 3.52 and 3.62 above.

(b) Potential impact of Article 3(3) on supremacy

3.85 Article 3(3) provides:

> Without prejudice to general principles and other provisions of Community law, *paragraphs 1 and 2 do not apply* when the competition authorities and the courts of the Member States apply national merger control laws nor do they preclude the application of provisions of national law that predominantly pursue an objective different from that pursued by Articles 81 and 82 of the Treaty. [emphasis added]

3.86 The precise interaction between Article 3(2) and (3) is unclear. In particular, does Article 3(3) allow national authorities and courts to *clear*, under national law that is not 'national competition law', agreements or conduct that would be *prohibited* if Articles 81 and 82 were applied?

3.87 On the one hand, Article 3(2) could be viewed as the legislative articulation of the principle of supremacy in a competition context, so that its express disapplication in Article 3(3) automatically precludes applying the underlying primacy case law, such as *Wilhelm*. The reference to general principles and other provisions of Community law in Article 3(3) would, on that view, be interpreted as intended to preserve more general principles of EC law.

---

national competition laws to agreements, decisions or concerted practices within the meaning of Article 81(1) of the Treaty may not lead to the prohibition of such agreements, decisions and concerted practices if they are not also prohibited under Community competition law.'

On the other hand, Article 3(3) is expressed to be '[w]ithout prejudice to **3.88** general principles and other provisions of Community law'. The fact that Article 3(3) expressly preserves general principles of European law means that the disapplication of Article 3(2) leaves in place the general (but narrower, see para 3.05 above) principle of supremacy as expressed in *Wilhelm* and the case law, which would continue to apply.[66] The application of that principle would prevent clearance under national law of agreements or conduct that are prohibited under European law. It appears that the OFT takes this approach.[67]

(c) Scope of protective effect of Article 81

Article 3(2) accords Article 81 a 'protective effect' over agreements that either are **3.89** not prohibited by Article 81(1) or which satisfy the conditions of Article 81(3): they cannot be prohibited under national competition law. Given that prohibiting a particular clause in an agreement amounts to prohibiting an agreement including such a clause, the 'protective effect' of Article 81 effectively means that there is no scope, under national competition law relating to anti-competitive agreements, either to prohibit, or to alter, such agreements. By way of example, parties to market investigation references are already raising arguments based on Article 3(2) to prevent the CC from imposing certain remedies in their agreements, as in *Domestic LPG*.[68]

The following paragraphs discuss possible inroads into the protective effect of **3.90** Article 81.

(i) Applying Article 82 to conduct related to agreements that do not infringe Article 81

Although Article 3(1) provides that *national competition law* may not lead to the **3.91** prohibition of agreements affecting trade which do not restrict competition within the meaning of Article 81(1) or which fulfil the conditions of Article 81(3), the protective effect of Article 81 does not prevent the application of Article 82 to dominant undertakings that enter into or operate certain agreements, even where the agreements are 'protected' under Article 81. This is because Articles 81 and 82 are independent and complementary provisions designed, in general, to regulate distinct situations by different rules. See the European Court of First Instance's (**CFI**) judgment in *Tetrapak Rausing SA v Commission*:[69]

---

[66] Supremacy as defined in *Wilhelm* allows national authorities to prohibit, under national law, agreements that do not breach Art 81. This is not the case under Art 3(2).
[67] OFT405, *Concurrent application to regulated industries* (December 2004), para 4.8.
[68] *Domestic LPG*, Final Report, para 7.114.
[69] Case T-51/89 [1990] ECR II-309, para 25.

> . . . in the scheme for the protection of competition established by the Treaty the
> grant of exemption, whether individual or block exemption, under Article 85(3)
> cannot be such as to render inapplicable the prohibition set out in Article 86 . . .
> this would be tantamount, in view of the non-retroactive nature of the withdrawal
> of exemption, to accepting that an exemption under Article 85(3) operates in reality
> as a concurrent exemption from the prohibition of abuse of a dominant position.

3.92 This case supports the proposition that national competition authorities and
courts remain free to apply Article 82 to conduct of dominant undertakings
comprising the conclusion of 'protected' agreements. However, the Commission
has recently, in the context of the Article 82 reform, indicated the contrary. Its
paper on the notion of exclusionary abuse under Article 82 EC proposes that
there should be consistency in the application of Articles 81 and 82, so that an
agreement that is found to meet the criteria in Article 81(3), should not fall foul
of Article 82.[70]

*(ii) Applying national law relating to unilateral conduct to agreements that do not
infringe Article 81*

3.93 Arguably, national competition authorities and courts are not only able to apply
Article 82, but can also apply *national law* relating to unilateral conduct to
undertakings entering or operating agreements protected under Article 81.
First, the language of Article 3(2) preserving Member States' ability to apply
stricter national law relating to unilateral action is very broad: 'Member States
shall not under this Regulation be precluded' from applying stricter national law
to unilateral conduct. Coming, as this does, immediately after the prohibition
on applying stricter national competition law to protected agreements, the fact
that the right to apply stricter national law to unilateral conduct is not expressed
as being 'subject to the above' and that it is preserved for the purposes of *the
Regulation as a whole* is significant. Secondly, the rationale adopted by the CFI
in *Tetrapak*, which was to distinguish between prohibition of the agreement
itself (which was not prohibited) and prohibiting an undertaking's unilateral
behaviour in entering and operating an agreement (which was prohibited), can
also be adopted to justify the application of national competition law relating to
unilateral conduct to the entering and operation of an agreement, as opposed to
the agreement itself. As discussed in Chapter 1, there is a very fine line, in some
factual contexts, between coordinated behaviour that amounts to an agreement
or a concerted practice, and unilateral action by various parties which lacks the

---

[70] '[I]f the conduct of a dominant company generates efficiencies and provided that all the
other conditions of Article 81(3) are satisfied . . ., such conduct should not be classified as an
abuse under Article 82 of the EC Treaty': *DG Competition discussion paper on the application of
Article 82 to exclusionary abuses*, para 8, <http://ec.europa.eu/comm/competition/antitrust/others/
discpaper2005.pdf>. The Commission relies on Case T-193/02 *Piau v Commission* [2005] ECR
II-209 in support of its position.

necessary consensus to amount to an agreement. The ability of Regulators to apply stricter national law to unilateral behaviour may therefore be significant in certain contexts.

F. Competition Act: The Obligation of Consistent Interpretation

The government's intention in introducing the Competition Act 1998 was to introduce a domestic regime closely modelled on the European regime that interacted with it in a seamless manner so as to reduce the regulatory burdens on business arising from the application of both domestic and EU competition rules.[71] To ensure that, as it develops, UK competition law remains tightly aligned and consistent with its European counterpart, the Competition Act 1998 includes a provision (s 60) that obliges the OFT and the national courts to deal with questions arising under the Act in a manner that is consistent with the treatment of corresponding questions arising in European law. **3.94**

Section 60 of the Competition Act 1998 takes the obligation to apply European law into a new domain—beyond the remit of the EC Treaty rules on competition themselves—namely cases that have no effect on trade between Member States and which fall to be determined solely on the basis of national competition law. As the then Director General of Fair Trading, John Bridgeman, explained on the introduction of the Competition Act:[72] 'the legislator has effectively dismantled our sea defences and invited the tide [of European competition law] to flow much further upstream'.[73] **3.95**

The adherence to European precedent brings with it the additional legal certainty that comes with a well-established body of jurisprudence. However, it should be borne in mind that the ECJ and the CFI do not share the same notion of legal precedent that is the hallmark of common law jurisdictions. This could expose those authorities and courts who slavishly follow their jurisprudence to some about-turns. **3.96**

---

[71] See the following statement made by Lord Simon of Highbury on the passage of the Competition Bill: 'The purpose of the governing principles clause is to ensure as far as possible that the UK and EC prohibitions are interpreted and develop consistently with the EC competition law system. This is of critical importance in minimising burdens on business. The problems for business in having two similar, but in their detail different, prohibitions interpreted according to two different bodies of case law could be very burdensome.' *Hansard*, HL col 960 (25 November 1997).

[72] John Bridgeman, 'The Competition Act 1998 and EC jurisprudence! Some questions answered', The Denning Lecture 1999.

[73] John Bridgeman was referring to Lord Denning's famous analogy: 'But when it comes to matters with a European element, the treaty is like an incoming tide, it flows into the estuaries and up the rivers. It cannot be held back.' *HP Bulmer Ltd v J Bollinger SA (No 2)* [1974] Ch 401.

3.97 It is universally agreed that s 60 gives rise to a considerably broader obligation to apply EU law than would be the case under EU law itself. However, the exact ambit of the obligation of consistency remains a matter of some dispute, as the terms of s 60 are somewhat ambiguous. The key subsections are s 60(1) to (3). Section 60(1) sets out the purpose of the section as a whole. It provides:

> (1) The purpose of this section is to ensure that so far as is possible (having regard to any relevant differences between the provisions concerned), questions arising under this Part in relation to competition within the United Kingdom are dealt with in a manner which is consistent with the treatment of corresponding questions arising in Community law in relation to competition within the Community.

3.98 The purpose of s 60, as set out in s 60(1), is not to give rise to an *absolute* obligation of consistency: the obligation is nuanced—'so far as possible' and 'having regard to any relevant differences between the provisions concerned'. Examples of relevant differences in the law applicable that were provided when the Competition Bill was debated in Parliament were the community objective of achieving a single internal market;[74] legal professional privilege[75] (the ambit of this privilege is defined in the Competition Act and is considerably broader than the equivalent privilege under European law[76]); and appeals processes[77] (these are defined under the Competition Act and differ from appeals to the European courts). Section 60(1) appears also to limit the quest for consistency to 'questions arising in relation to competition' and not other areas of substantive European law.

3.99 Section 60(2) and (3) defines the obligation of consistency:

> (2) At any time when the court determines a question arising under this Part, it must act (so far as is compatible with the provisions of this Part and whether or not it would otherwise be required to do so) with a view to securing that there is no inconsistency between—
>   (a) the principles applied, and decision reached, by the court in determining that question; and
>   (b) the principles laid down by the Treaty and the European Court, and any relevant decision of that Court, as applicable at that time in determining any corresponding question arising in Community law.
> (3) The court must, in addition, have regard to any relevant decision or statement of the Commission.

---

[74] *Hansard*, HL col 961 (25 November 1997).   [75] ibid, col 960.
[76] See paras 7.09 et seq and 8.188 et seq below for a discussion of the ambit of legal professional privilege under domestic and European law.
[77] *Hansard*, HL col 961 (25 November 1997).

(a) Who is bound by s 60?

The obligation in s 60 extends to the OFT, Regulators and any person acting **3.100** on behalf of the OFT or the Regulator, and any court or tribunal (such as the Court of Appeal and the CAT).[78]

(b) How broad is the obligation?

Two aspects of s 60(2) have led to difficulties in understanding the extent of the **3.101** obligation of consistency. The first issue concerns at what stage the obligation to have regard to EC law arises. The obligation arises when an authority 'determines a question arising under Part I' of the Competition Act 1998 which is not always clear. Clearly, in reaching substantive decisions applying the prohibitions in Pt I, regulators are determining questions arising under Pt I. And indeed, the CAT's and the Regulators' practice to date has been to draw heavily on relevant European jurisprudence in determining substantive questions relating to the application of the prohibitions such as what amounts to an undertaking,[79] what is an effect on trade, what is an abuse,[80] etc.

A range of additional decisions, some of them procedural, are taken by the **3.102** Regulators under powers provided to them under Pt I, such as decisions to initiate an investigation, to conduct on-site inspections, and to apply interim measures. There is also a third tier of procedural decisions that are not taken under Pt I as such, but under secondary legislation that Pt I permits, such as a decision refusing access to the file taken under the OFT's Rules of Procedure.[81] It is unclear whether such procedural questions amount to 'a question arising under this Part' for the purposes of s 60(2). Section 60(1) provides that the purpose of s 60 as a whole is to ensure consistent treatment of 'questions arising under this Part *in relation to competition*' (emphasis added). Do these issues amount to questions arising under Pt I in relation to competition? Section 60(1), by referring to 'having regard to any relevant differences between the provisions concerned', gives rise to the implication that the starting point for the evaluation for consistency consists of the provisions of Pt I themselves and there is no need to ensure consistency with respect to procedural rules not contained in this Part I. This is confirmed by the views expressed in Parliament: '[i]n making the procedural rules, the DGFT is not obliged to secure that there is no inconsistency with EC procedural law since he will not be "determining a question" under Part I'.[82] However, as will be seen below, there is now a real

---

[78] Competition Act 1998, s 60(4) and (5).
[79] *Bettercare v Director General of Fair Trading* [2002] CAT 7.
[80] eg *Napp Pharmaceutical Holdings Ltd v Director General of Fair Trading* [2002] CAT 1.
[81] Made under s 51 of the Competition Act 1998.
[82] Lord Simon of Highbury, *Hansard*, HL col 961 (25 November 1997).

question mark as to whether the obligation of consistency extends to procedural issues arising under the OFT's Rules of Procedure.

3.103 Secondly, the breadth of the material with respect to which consistency is to be sought is unclear. What is comprised by 'the principles laid down by the Treaty and the European Court'? Initially, it was widely understood that this concept was limited to substantive principles of competition law and the procedural safeguards defined by 'high-level' principles of Community law (such as the principles of non-discrimination, proportionality, etc) but that specific EC procedural rules were not relevant. The OFT's position on s 60 was expressed as follows:

> We must however, draw a clear distinction between procedure and fundamental procedural safeguards. It is not always possible completely to separate substance and procedure. Certain procedural safeguards are derived from general principles of Community law and include concepts such as fairness in administrative action. So while we are not bound to follow the Commission in drawing up our procedures, we must ensure that they are consistent with these procedural safeguards.[83]

3.104 Both the above issues were raised in *Pernod Ricard.*[84] The appeal related inter alia to the OFT's refusal to disclose the Rule 14 Notice issued to Bacardi to the complainant (Pernod) and its decision to close its file on Bacardi's conduct without consulting Pernod. Pernod pointed to rights enjoyed by complainants in EC law procedure under Regulation 17/62 and to s 60 of the Competition Act 1998 to argue that it should have been granted disclosure of the Rule 14 Notice and consulted by the OFT prior to closure of the file. The CAT, in considering whether s 60 applied to oblige the OFT to grant third parties equivalent procedural rights, stated:

> Although the question with which we are dealing does not relate directly to competition, it seems to us that the question at issue does arise 'in relation to competition' within the meaning of section 60(1), at least indirectly, since it concerns the procedural principles to be applied in the application and enforcement of the competition rules.[85]

3.105 As to the content of the 'principles' referred to in s 60(2), the CAT took note[86] of the parliamentary statements that had identified these as 'high level principles, such as proportionality, legal certainty and administrative fairness'. It emphasised that the complainant's right to be heard had stood for 40 years,

---

[83] John Bridgeman, 'The Competition Act 1998 and EC jurisprudence! Some questions answered', The Denning Lecture 1999. For a similar view from an academic commentator, see Shaun Goodman, 'The Competition Act, section 60—the governing principles clause' [1999] ECLR 73–7.

[84] *Pernod Ricard SA v OFT* [2004] CAT 10.   [85] ibid, para 229.

[86] *Pepper (Inspector of Taxes) v Hart* [1993] AC 593.

and that the principle of administrative fairness found its expression in the EC relevant procedural rules.

On the issue of relevant differences, the CAT did not hold much store by the **3.106** fact that OFT's Rules of Procedure differed from the Commission's by not providing for such rights. '[T]here is nothing in the Act or the Director's Rules which prevents the participation of the complainant in the ways indicated above.'[87]

Accordingly, the CAT found that the OFT should have granted disclosure of the **3.107** Rule 14 Notice and consulted Pernod prior to closing its file. The implications of this decision are potentially far-reaching. It would appear from this decision, first, that the CAT considers questions relating to procedure under the OFT's Rules to be 'a question arising in relation to competition', thus giving rise to an obligation of consistency. Secondly, it does not appear to consider the fact that there are no equivalent procedural provisions in the OFT's Procedural Rules as a 'relevant difference'. Potentially, this approach could lead to complete 'soft' convergence in UK and EC enforcement procedure, where the procedural rights at issue can be tied to general administrative fairness.

(i) Decisions or statements of the Commission

In addition to having regard to the EC Treaty and the case law of the ECJ and **3.108** CFI, s 60(3) of the Competition Act 1998 requires that regard should be had to 'any relevant decision or statement of the Commission'. This obligation argu-ably goes beyond what is required under Article 16 of Regulation 1/2003, in particular with regard to statements made by the Commission, which are not binding under European law.

---

[87] *Pernod Ricard SA v OFT* [2004] CAT 10, para 230.

4

EXEMPTIONS AND EXCLUSIONS

A. Introduction

(a) General

4.01 There is sometimes a tension between the desire to encourage certain types of agreements in pursuit of the wider objectives of society, and the aim of eliminating aspects of such agreements which are restrictive of competition. To address this tension, there are provisions which allow certain agreements to escape the application of the competition law prohibitions. Such provisions either disapply competition law from certain types of agreements or undertakings altogether (exclusions, and the doctrine of ancillary restraints), or conditionally exempt certain agreements or types of agreements from the competition law prohibitions which would otherwise act to invalidate them (exemptions).

4.02 These provisions operate in addition to and are separate from the general case law and construction surrounding the application of Article 81(1) and the Chapter I prohibition, which is discussed in Chapter 1, above.

(b) Exemptions

4.03 The prohibitions on anti-competitive agreements in both Article 81(1) and Chapter I of the Competition Act 1998 are sufficiently wide to capture agreements which may, on the whole, be useful to the economy and to society more generally. Examples include agreements which allow undertakings to combine resources to bring a new product to the market, or to create new efficiencies which could not be achieved individually. The application of an automatic prohibition to such agreements would not necessarily further the best interests of consumers. To address this, agreements which meet certain conditions are therefore exempt from the application of Article 81(1) and the Chapter I prohibition. The EC Treaty contains explicit legislative provisions setting out specific conditions which must be met for an exemption to apply.[1] Chapter I of the Competition Act similarly provides for specific exemption conditions (as well as separately providing for a number of exclusions from the Chapter I prohibition).

---

[1] Compare with the US system, where s 1 of the Sherman Act 1890 sets out the antitrust prohibition applicable in the US. There is no statutory possibility for exemption, which has resulted in a long line of case law based on the principle of the 'rule of reason' and involves the balancing of anti-competitive elements with other issues of importance to society in determining whether or not the prohibition itself catches the agreement in question. The CFI and the ECJ have repeatedly denied the existence of a rule of reason in Community competition law : see Case T-112/99 *Métropole télévision (M6) and Télévision française 1 SA (TF1) v Commission* [2001] ECR II-2459, paras 72–77 and Case T-65/98 *Van den Bergh Foods Ltd v Commission* [2003] ECR II-4653, para 106.

(i) Exemption from Article 81(1)

Article 81(3) provides expressly for the possibility of exemption from the **4.04** prohibition set out in Article 81(1). Article 81(3) states:

> The provisions of paragraph 1 may, however, be declared inapplicable in the case of:
>
> — any agreement or category of agreements between undertakings;
> — any decision or category of decisions by associations of undertakings;
> — any concerted practice or category of concerted practices;
>
> which contributes to improving the production or distribution of goods or to promoting technical or economic progress, while allowing consumers a fair share of the resulting benefit, and which does not:
>
> (a) impose on the undertakings concerned restrictions which are not indispensable to the attainment of those objectives;
> (b) afford such undertakings the possibility of eliminating competition in respect of a substantial part of the products in question.

The substantive terms of Article 81(3) did not change with the advent of **4.05** Regulation 1/2003.[2] However, its application may now change over time in light of the fact that the authorities responsible for applying Article 81(3) have multiplied, and the enhanced significance of businesses being able to self-determine the scope of their commercial agreements (these changes are discussed below). In addition, the guidance published by the European Commission in 2004 on the application of Article 81(3) (**Article 81(3) Notice**)[3] indicates a narrower approach to both Article 81(1) and (3). This implies that fewer agreements are likely to be caught by Article 81(1). On the other hand, if an agreement is considered to be restrictive of competition it may be tougher to satisfy Article 81(3). The European Commission is bound to follow the Article 81(3) Notice, but national competition authorities, national courts, and the European Court of Justice (**ECJ**) are not bound by the Article 81(3) Notice.[4] Nevertheless, most of these bodies would require some considerable persuasion before departing from the terms of the Notice. In particular, the Office of Fair Trading (**OFT**) has stated that in applying Article 81(3), it will 'have regard to this Notice in considering the application of Article 81(3) and section 9(1) of the [Competition Act]'.[5]

The Article 81(3) Notice is intended simply to re-state the existing case law, and **4.06** in general terms it does do this, making it a useful starting point for a basic

---

[2] Council Regulation (EC) 1/2003 of 16 December 2002 on the implementation of the rules on competition laid down in Articles 81 and 82 of the Treaty [2003] OJ L1/1.

[3] Article 81(3) Notice (see para 1.20).

[4] Save where they have agreed to be so bound.

[5] OFT401, *Agreements and concerted practices* (December 2004) para 5.5. Note also that s 60(3) of the Competition Act 1998 provides that courts must have regard to statements of the European Commission.

assessment of the Article 81(3) conditions. However, this area of law is exceptionally complex and in some instances contradictory or unresolved. The Article 81(3) Notice attempts to give clarity to these types of issues and in doing so it may occasionally set out the European Commission's interpretation of the applicable case law more definitively than the legal precedent properly supports. It also remains subject to the further interpretation of the ECJ. Thus practitioners should be cautious in relying solely upon the Article 81(3) Notice, particularly in proceedings before bodies other than the European Commission.

4.07 While the scope of this book does not extend to a full discussion of the legal interpretation of the Article 81(3) conditions, these conditions have traditionally been interpreted as involving a 'balancing exercise' weighing up pro-competitive and restrictive effects of an agreement.[6] However, on occasion the provision has been thought to extend to wider commercial and public interest benefits, such as environmental efficiencies, economic efficiencies, and the promotion of employment[7] and culture.[8] Thus it covers more than merely a balancing of pro- and anti-competitive effects. Arguably, the terms of the Article 81(3) Notice restrict the scope for this wider balancing exercise.

(ii) Exemption from the Chapter I prohibition

4.08 Chapter I of the Competition Act 1998, being based on the terms of Article 81, also provides for the possibility of exemption from the prohibition. This is set out in s 2(1) of the Act, which provides that anti-competitive agreements 'are prohibited unless they are exempt in accordance with the provisions of this Part'. The exemption conditions are contained in s 9 of the Competition Act as follows:

> (1) An agreement is exempt from the Chapter I prohibition if it—
>   (a) contributes to—
>   (i) improving production or distribution, or
>   (ii) promoting technical or economic progress,
>   while allowing consumers a fair share of the resulting benefit; and

---

[6] See, eg, Case T-65/98 *Van de Bergh Foods v Commission* [2003] ECR II-4653, para 107 (and the cases cited therein) and Case T-112/99 *Métropole télévision (M6) and Télévision française 1 SA (TF1) v Commission* [2001] ECR II-2459, para 74.

[7] Case 26/76 *Metro v Commission* [1977] ECR 1875, para 43. (See also para 21: 'The powers conferred upon the Commission under Article 85(3) show that the requirements for the maintenance of workable competition may be reconciled with the safeguarding of objectives of a different nature and that to this end certain restrictions on competition are permissible, provided that they are essential to the attainment of those objectives and that they do not result in the elimination of competition for a substantial part of the common market.')

[8] For a detailed discussion on the development of case law in this regard, see R Whish, *Competition Law* (5th edn, LexisNexis Butterworths, 2003) 152–156.

(b) does not—
    (i) impose on undertakings concerned restrictions which are not indispensable to the attainment of those objectives; or
    (ii) afford the undertakings concerned the possibility of eliminating competition in respect of a substantial part of the products in question.

The wording in s 9 is slightly different to the wording in Article 81(3), in that **4.09** the phrase 'of goods' is removed from the first condition. This is to reflect the position that the first condition may equally apply to services as well as goods.[9]

(c) Legal exception regime

(i) The procedural system for exemption

One of the most significant changes brought about by Regulation 1/2003 is the **4.10** abolition of the procedural system associated with exemption from Article 81(1) by the application of Article 81(3). Under the previous system, parties could notify their agreement to the European Commission or OFT to seek a formal exemption decision under EC or UK law respectively.[10] Notification has now been replaced with a new system known as a legal exception regime. 'Legal exception regime' is a term introduced by Regulation 1/2003 which is derived from French (*exception légale*) and describes the method by which agreements may be exempted from the effects of the application of Article 81(1) or the Chapter I prohibition.

Article 1(2) of Regulation 1/2003 is the basis of the legal exception regime: **4.11** 'Agreements, decisions and concerted practices caught by Article 81(1) of the Treaty which satisfy the conditions of Article 81(3) of the Treaty shall be prohibited, no prior decision to that effect being required'.

This new provision sits a little awkwardly with the wording of Article 81(3) **4.12** itself, with the reference to agreements being 'declared' exempt, but it seems unlikely that this could form the basis for a successful challenge to the vires of Article 1(2) of Regulation 1/2003, due to the tendency for broad interpretation of provisions of the EC Treaty.[11] Thus, Regulation 1/2003 enables undertakings to self-assess their agreements against the conditions of Article 81(3).

---

[9] In practical terms, Art 81(3) is also applied to both goods and services.
[10] See paras 4.16–4.21.
[11] Art 81(3) provides: 'The provisions of [Article 81(1)] may, however, be *declared* inapplicable in the case of . . .' [emphasis added]. It is thus apparent that Art 81(3) contemplates a system whereby some form of declaration is required before any agreement falling within Art 81(1) may be exempted from the effects of that article applying; namely, that the agreement would be void and the undertaking(s) potentially subject to fines and damages claims. This was how it was interpreted in the previous regime, pursuant to Regulation 17/62, where Art 4 stated that in order

4.13 Similarly, the Competition Act 1998 has been amended to repeal ss 4 and 5 which had set out the notification process. Section 9 has been amended to implement a legal exception regime in the United Kingdom. All the sections of the OFT's Procedural Rules which previously dealt with the notification system have also been removed. Thus all of the previous UK competition legislation associated with the notification system was repealed as of 1 May 2004 (for the Competition Act) and as of 17 November 2004 (for the OFT's Procedural Rules).

4.14 Regulation 1/2003 has also removed the European Commission's monopoly over the application of Article 81(3) and provided for Article 81(3) to be applied directly by national competition authorities and by national courts, as well as the European Commission. This is achieved in Regulation 1/2003 by specifying the powers of the national competition authorities and the national courts by reference to 'Article 81' as a whole, rather than limiting their powers to Article 81(1). Article 5 of Regulation 1/2003 provides that '[t]he competition authorities of the Member States shall have the power to apply Articles 81 and 82 of the Treaty in individual cases'. Article 6 sets out a similar provision in respect of national courts.[12]

4.15 The introduction of a legal exception regime gave rise to a number of issues in relation to the interaction between the old and the new systems—and the change was subject to much scrutiny as it appeared to remove the legal certainty associated with the previous system. In order to understand the following sections on procedure and block exemptions, it may be helpful to understand some of the history behind the exemption system for competition law in the EC.

(ii) The previous system of notification

4.16 In Regulation 17/62,[13] Article 4 stated that in order for an agreement to benefit from exemption under Article 81(3), it must first be notified to the European Commission and approved for exemption. This type of individual exemption would commence from the date the agreement was first submitted to the European Commission, and not any earlier.[14]

---

for an agreement to benefit from exemption under Art 81(3), it must first be notified to the European Commission and approved for exemption. On this basis, it is arguable that Art 1(2) of Regulation 1/2003 is ultra vires as it effectively seeks, as a piece of secondary legislation, to amend the EC Treaty.

[12] Under the old notification regime, national courts had no competence to determine whether Art 81(3) applied in a particular case, as their powers were limited to considering the application of Art 81(1)—unless the undertaking had received an exemption (very rare) or the agreement fitted clearly within one of the block exemptions.

[13] First Regulation implementing Articles [81] and [82] of the Treaty [1962] OJ 13/204.

[14] Regulation 17/62, Recital 3 and Art 4. Importantly, Art 4 allowed backdating for vertical agreements (and a few others) to the date of the agreements.

Vast numbers of agreements were notified to the European Commission— **4.17** particularly when Regulation 17/62 was introduced. These far outweighed the resources available to the Commission and were predominantly made up of agreements which had little or no anti-competitive effect. Thus the European Commission's resources were being directed at a task which was beyond its abilities to complete and which was, in any event, largely focused on the least problematic agreements in competition terms. This constrained the Commission from concentrating on its most important task in the field of competition regulation, namely detecting and eliminating anti-competitive practices.[15]

The aspiration of providing legal certainty for businesses was similarly **4.18** unachievable. The European Commission was unable to issue any more than three or four exemption approvals each year, and the cost of the notification system threatened to undermine effective enforcement.[16]

There were two key ways in which the European Commission dealt with this **4.19** unacceptable situation. The first and most useful was to create 'block exemptions'. These are regulations made by the Commission under the authority of a European Council Regulation on a specific topic or industry. Block exemptions provided for various common types of agreements—such as vertical agreements and technology transfer agreements—to be presumed exempt from Article 81(1) provided they met certain listed criteria.[17] The creation of block exemptions meant that large swathes of agreements no longer needed to be notified to the European Commission for exemption.

The second way in which the European Commission eased the burden on its **4.20** resources was to issue 'comfort letters'. These were letters stating that the Commission did not intend to conduct a full review of the agreement in question, but believed that the agreement would be exempt if such a review were to be conducted. Although a comfort letter did not provide an exemption at law it did provide some measure of comfort in respect of any future investigation or fine by the European Commission. Such comfort letters were also regarded as persuasive by national courts in relation to litigation to enforce contracts where a defendant might claim that the contract was in breach of competition law and therefore void, and thus had additional value for undertakings in seeking to enforce contracts, although comfort letters were neither reasoned nor published.

---

[15] The second recital to Regulation 17/62 stated: 'Whereas in establishing the rules for applying Article 85(3) account must be taken of the need to ensure effective supervision and to simplify administration to the greatest possible extent.'

[16] See, eg, the speech of Commissioner Mario Monti on Competition Law Reform, made at the CBI conference on competition law reform on 12 June 2000, published at <http://ec.europa.eu/comm/competition/speeches/text/sp2000_008_en.html>.

[17] See paras 4.52–4.77.

In many cases, the comfort letter was the highest degree of reassurance an undertaking could expect. Thus actual legal certainty was provided to very few undertakings as a result of notification, which was of concern in an area where private litigation was increasing.

4.21 The European Commission was unable to implement any solution involving the sharing of responsibility with other competition authorities for providing exemptions. This was because Regulation 17/62 clearly prohibited such a course of action[18]—the European Commission was the sole body responsible for administering the exemption system.

B. Procedure for Exemption or Exclusion

(a) Exemption decisions

4.22 Article 81(3) (set out at para 4.04 above) remains the substantive basis for the legal exception regime. However, rather than interpreting this to require some form of regulatory control over the application of the substantive provisions of Article 81(3), Regulation 1/2003 provides for the direct and immediate application of Article 81(3) to agreements, without the need for any prior approval or scrutiny to activate the application. Thus there is no requirement or ability for undertakings to notify their agreements.

4.23 Regulation 1/2003 and the amended Competition Act do not provide any regulatory means for businesses to be *certain* that their agreements are exempt from Article 81(1) or the Chapter I prohibition for all purposes. However, in practice, businesses and/or their legal advisers can normally assess whether an agreement will be caught by Article 81(1)—and if so, whether Article 81(3) or any block exemption will apply. However, for some agreements, exemption issues will only be resolved in the context of an infringement investigation by an authority, or in private litigation proceedings before the national courts.

---

[18] Regulation 17/62, Art 4(1). When this system came to be reformed, Commissioner Mario Monti stated: 'The Commission's monopoly on the application of Article 81(3) is a significant obstacle to the enforcement of EC competition law by national competition authorities and courts. This obstacle follows from the fact that companies alleged to be in breach of Article 81(1) quite naturally claim that their agreements meet the conditions of Article 81(3) and therefore are legal. As the national bodies have no power to apply Article 81(3), the continuation of their enforcement action is made very difficult. In most cases, the national action must be suspended pending the Commission's decision. This leads to unnecessary delays and creates a clear disincentive to apply EC competition law. In practice the Commission is virtually the only enforcer of EC competition law.' Speech on Competition Law Reform, made at the CBI conference on competition law reform on 12 June 2000, published at <http://ec.europa.eu/comm/competition/speeches/text/sp2000_008_en.html>.

(i) Power to make an exemption decision

The OFT   The OFT's decision-making power under the competition Act **4.24** extends to decisions 'as to whether [a competition law prohibition] has been infringed'.[19] This wording clearly encompasses a decision that a particular prohibition has not been infringed, for any reason, including a decision that the exemption conditions are satisfied, or that a UK exclusion applies.

As a result of the removal of the notification procedure, the only way a non- **4.25** infringement decision can be made by the OFT is in the context of an investigation (however that investigation is started).[20] This introduces a different process to that which previously existed, as an undertaking being investigated under Article 81(1) or the Chapter I prohibition now has an additional, complex defence based on proving that its agreement satisfies the exemption conditions.

The European Commission   The European Commission has retained a power **4.26** to make 'inapplicability' decisions despite the removal of the notification process:

> Where the Community public interest relating to the application of Articles 81 and 82 of the Treaty so requires, the Commission, acting on its own initiative, may by decision find that Article 81 of the Treaty is not applicable to an agreement, a decision by an association of undertakings or a concerted practice, either because the conditions of Article 81(1) are not fulfilled, or because the conditions of Article 81(3) are satisfied.

> The Commission may likewise make such a finding with reference to Article 82 of the Treaty.[21]

It is anticipated in Regulation 1/2003 that such inapplicability decisions will **4.27** only be made '[i]n exceptional cases where the public interest of the Community so requires . . . with a view to clarifying the law and ensuring its consistent application throughout the Community, in particular with regard to new types of agreements or practices that have not been settled in the existing case-law and administrative practice'.[22]

As with the OFT, the removal of the notification procedure means the only way **4.28** an inapplicability decision can be made by the European Commission is in the context of an investigation (however that investigation is started).

---

[19] Competition Act 1998, s 46(3).

[20] Note that where the OFT decides to close an investigation, under Article 81 or Article 82, it is arguable that the correct terminology for a case closure decision is not a 'non-infringement decision', but rather a decision that 'there are no grounds for action on its part'. This is because Article 5 of Regulation 1/2003 lists (arguably exhaustively) the decision-making powers of national competition authorities. It does not provide for non-infringement decisions, only 'no grounds for action' decisions.

[21] Regulation 1/2003, Art 10.

[22] ibid, Recital 14. As of October 2006, no Art 10 decisions had been made.

4.29 **National courts** In the United Kingdom, the High Court has a discretionary power to make binding declarations as to the rights of the parties and the application of the law. The civil procedure rules of court allow the High Court to make binding declarations whether or not any other remedy is claimed.[23] In the context of an alleged competition law infringement, this means that the High Court has the power to declare that the competition law prohibitions are not infringed in a particular case, and may make further declarations as to whether the exemption conditions are satisfied.

4.30 Declarations of non-liability are known as a 'negative declarations', which are to be scrutinised and their use rejected (at the court's discretion) where it would serve no useful purpose. It has been noted in a more recent judgment:

> While negative declarations can perform a positive role, they are an unusual remedy in so far as they reverse the more usual roles of the parties. The natural defendant becomes the claimant and vice versa. This can result in procedural complications and possible injustice to an unwilling 'defendant.' This in itself justifies caution in extending the circumstances where negative declarations are granted, but, subject to the exercise of appropriate circumspection, there should be no reluctance to their being granted when it is useful to do so.[24]

The courts will also generally not entertain any request for a remedy where the proceedings raise a purely hypothetical question and do not decide a dispute between the parties.[25]

4.31 Thus in competition law proceedings before the UK courts, an undertaking will generally only be able to seek an exemption decision (declaration of non-liability) in the context of a dispute with another party, and then only where that would serve a useful purpose.

(ii) Establishing an exemption: burden of proof

4.32 In order for an undertaking to establish that its agreement satisfies the exemption conditions, there must be clear rules on where the burden of proof lies in the assessment of the case by an authority or by a court. This allows each party to know what it is required to prove, and to which standard.

4.33 Regulation 1/2003 aims to regulate the burden of proof in relation to Article 81 and states that it is for the party or the authority alleging an infringement of Article 81(1) to prove its existence to the requisite legal standard.[26] Conversely, if an undertaking wishes to invoke the benefit of Article 81(3), it bears the legal burden of proving, to the requisite legal standard, that the conditions

---

[23] Civil Procedure Rules, r 40.20.
[24] *Messier-Dowty Ltd v Sabena SA* [2000] 1 WLR 2040 (CA) per Lord Woolf MR at para 42.
[25] *Ainsbury v Millington (Note)* [1987] 1 WLR 379 (HL).
[26] Regulation 1/2003, Art 2 and Recital 5.

of Article 81(3) are fulfilled.[27] The Competition Act sets out similar provisions in s 9(2).

In private litigation, Article 81(3) will normally be raised by way of defence **4.34** to a claim asserting the invalidity of a commercial agreement by reason of Article 81(1). In such cases, the claimant will have to establish the infringement before the burden 'switches' to the defendant of demonstrating that the agreement is exempt pursuant to Article 81(3) or s 9(1) of the Competition Act.

(iii) Establishing an exemption: standard of proof

Regulation 1/2003 is not intended to affect national rules governing the stand- **4.35** ard of proof nor the requirement of the national courts and competition authorities to establish the relevant facts of the case.[28] In the United Kingdom, the normal civil standard of proof on the balance of probabilities will apply where an undertaking seeks to establish that an agreement is exempt. In all cases, national procedural rules must also comply with the general principles of Community law, including the rights of defence in Article 6(1) of the European Convention on Human Rights.

Where an investigation is being conducted by a competition authority which **4.36** is, in effect, acting as both prosecutor and first instance judge with the potential of imposing fines and other sanctions, the issues associated with the standard of proof which the authority must apply are more complex. In the United Kingdom, the Competition Appeal Tribunal has held that the more serious the allegation of infringement, the more cogent the evidence must be to overcome the presumption of innocence in favour of the accused.[29] The changes to the Competition Act in this respect, coupled with the authority's duties under the Human Rights Act 1998, give undertakings more flexibility in defending their agreements by establishing an exemption than the previous notification system allowed.

(iv) Impact of a non-infringement decision on later cases

The impact of non-infringement decisions is the same as the impact of an **4.37** infringement decision.

Thus, an OFT non-infringement decision which is final (ie upheld on appeal or **4.38** not appealed) is binding on the addressee(s) and on courts in any private litigation based on the same facts, and will also be used as persuasive authority in any similar cases.[30] A decision of non-liability by a national court which is final (ie

---

[27] ibid.   [28] ibid, Recital 5.

[29] See *Allsports Ltd v OFT* [2004] CAT 1. See also paras 9.19–9.26.

[30] See *Inntrepreneur Pub Co (CPC) v Crehan* [2006] UKHL 38, [2006] 3 WLR 148, paras 6, 11 and 12.

upheld on appeal or not appealed) is binding on the parties in that case, and will be persuasive authority in similar cases.

(b) Self-assessment

4.39 Apart from the limited circumstances in which a decision may be made that the exemption conditions apply, as set out above, the legal exception regime results in undertakings taking the risk that their own assessment of the exemption conditions will be found to be incorrect. If so, they may be liable to a financial penalty or other enforcement measures, and damages. In addition, the agreement will be void and unenforceable. However, although there was originally concern from business over this aspect of the modernised regime, in practice it has not been a real issue. Self-assessment is the norm in most competition regimes outside the European Union. Even within the European Union, self-assessment applied under French national competition law.

4.40 There are effectively two options for businesses seeking certainty that an agreement satisfies Article 81(3) or s 9(1) without the expense, adversarial context, and uncertainty of legal or administrative proceedings. These are obtaining an opinion from a legal adviser, and obtaining guidance from a competition authority. Conducting a self-assessment of non-infringement in good faith could result in a reduced or no penalty in the event of an investigation. In addition, the block exemption system effectively provides immunity from penalties for agreements that fall within their terms (see paras 4.72–4.77 on withdrawal of block exemptions), and there is also limited protection for small businesses.

(i) Effect of self-assessment on penalties

4.41 For undertakings which do not benefit from the protections offered for small businesses, there is still some benefit to carrying out a self-assessment (in good faith). One of the criteria taken into account by the European Commission and the OFT in assessing the level of penalty to be imposed in the event of an infringement finding is whether an undertaking has conducted itself in good faith. In this way an undertaking's self-assessment of the exemption conditions may be relevant as a mitigating factor to reduce the amount of any eventual penalty. It may even be relevant to the first step, whereby fines may only be imposed where the undertaking has infringed competition law intentionally or negligently. There is a full discussion of penalties, including the ways in which a penalty may be waived or reduced, in Chapter 10 below.

(ii) Legal opinion

4.42 An independent legal opinion from a barrister or solicitor on the merits of a particular agreement does not have any legal effect on whether an authority or a court will find that Article 81(3) or s 9 of the Competition Act applies to a particular agreement. However, a legal opinion based on all relevant facts may be relevant in establishing whether an undertaking has conducted itself in good faith (although to use it in such a way will involve a waiver of any legal professional privilege which might otherwise attach to the legal opinion). Thus, although a legal opinion will have little or no bearing on a damages claim in private litigation, it may be relevant as a mitigating factor to reduce the amount of any eventual penalty in infringement proceedings.

(iii) Guidance from a competition authority

There are a number of ways in which competition authorities may be approached for guidance. Informal guidance is one way of obtaining some assistance with self-assessment from the regulatory authorities in the United Kingdom and from the European Commission.

4.43

Confidential, informal guidance   The OFT responds to requests for informal guidance in relation to competition enforcement as part of its general remit to provide guidance to businesses under its competition enforcement function. It is unlikely that the OFT would provide its advice to an undertaking in writing; it prefers to give informal advice in person or by telephone. The OFT may deal with requests for informal guidance and will endeavour to deal with such requests fairly quickly (usually within six weeks, depending on the complexity of the request). Informal guidance is provided on the basis of a submission of facts—and quite often a proposed assessment of the legal construction—by the undertaking concerned. This service is free (unlike the previous system of notifications), and the OFT encourages undertakings to seek informal guidance if they have any doubt as to the application of competition law to the agreement or conduct in question.

4.44

It should be borne in mind that, where the OFT provides informal advice regarding agreements, it is unlikely to give detailed advice. Since the OFT does not conduct any investigation itself into the facts surrounding the request, the guidance provided can only ever be given on the basis of the material and information provided by the undertaking itself. Further, any informal guidance provided by the OFT is not binding on it,[31] nor is the OFT prevented from commencing an investigation on the basis of material provided to it by an undertaking in the course of seeking informal guidance. However, the risk of such material being used to commence an investigation is probably quite low despite the OFT's ability to do so. Although informal guidance is not binding on the OFT, it will be taken into account in the conduct of any later investigation. This probably means that it would have the effect of supporting an undertaking's

4.45

---

[31] OFT442, *Modernisation* (December 2004) para 7.20.

case that it acted in good faith on the basis of the guidance provided, and may reduce any penalty in the unlikely event that a penalty is imposed.

4.46 Another useful aspect of seeking informal guidance from the OFT is the fact that it is a confidential process. It does not require any consultation with third parties, nor does it require any publication of the request or the guidance provided.

4.47 The European Commission does not specifically offer informal guidance, as in the past this function has been largely managed by the provision of comfort letters. With the abolition of the notification process, comfort letters have also been abolished. In order to provide a mechanism for undertakings to obtain some degree of certainty in the new system, the European Commission has a new power to provide guidance in the form of a published letter. This is described in further detail below. The European Commission has not created any system for the provision of informal guidance, although individual officials will provide informal advice as they consider appropriate.

4.48 **Published OFT opinions**   The OFT has stated that it will provide formal opinions in order to help undertakings make their own informed assessment of their agreements. The OFT views this type of assistance as having a wider benefit than simply helping the undertaking in question, and this view informs the OFT's criteria for deciding whether to provide an opinion as well as the procedure for doing so. The OFT has published its general procedure for requesting and providing a formal opinion, possibly the most important aspect of which is that the formal opinion will be published (albeit in redacted form). The OFT has also stated that it will not issue a formal opinion in hypothetical cases or where to do so may conflict with a case or request before another competition authority or national court. A formal opinion issued by the OFT is not binding, although the OFT has stated that it will have regard to its opinion when carrying out any subsequent assessment.[32] As at October 2006, one draft opinion had been issued by the OFT.[33]

4.49 **Published European Commission guidance letters**   The European Commission also offers guidance to undertakings in the form of guidance letters, and has published a notice setting out its proposed approach to providing such guidance.[34] The European Commission's approach is essentially founded on the

---

[32]   ibid, paras 7.4–7.19.

[33]   The OFT published a draft advisory opinion (for consultation) in relation to the compatibility of newspaper and magazine distribution agreements with competition law on 19 May 2005, which was followed by a fresh draft opinion for consultation published on 31 May 2006. The OFT indicated that a final opinion would be published in first quarter 2007.

[34]   Notice on informal guidance relating to novel questions concerning Articles 81 and 82 of the EC Treaty that arise in individual cases (guidance letters) [2004] OJ C101/78.

basis that it will provide guidance letters where a case gives rise to genuine uncertainty because it presents novel or unresolved questions for the application of the law. Like the OFT's opinions, such letters will be published (possibly in redacted form).[35] Further, guidance letters are not binding on the European Commission (but they will be taken into account in any later assessment) and are not binding on any other authority or court (although national competition authorities and courts would presumably be reluctant to make a decision conflicting with guidance issued by the European Commission).[36] The European Commission may also use any material submitted in relation to a guidance letter request in order to commence an investigation or use its other powers under Regulation 1/2003.[37] No guidance letters had been issued as at October 2006.

(iv) Protection for small businesses

It is worth noting, in relation to the cost and risk associated with self-assessment, that in the United Kingdom, small businesses are protected from penalties in respect of most competition law infringements. The protection is set out in ss 39 and 40 of the Competition Act and in the Competition Act 1998 (Small Agreements and Conduct of Minor Significance) Regulations 2000.[38] In relation to agreements which infringe the Chapter I prohibition, where an agreement is made between undertakings whose combined annual turnover is less than £20 million, those undertakings may qualify for immunity from fining. In respect of the conduct of an undertaking which infringes the Chapter II prohibition, where the undertaking's turnover is less than £50 million, that undertaking may qualify for immunity from fining. In addition to the turnover requirement, the OFT must also be satisfied that the undertaking or undertakings acted on the reasonable assumption that on the facts they qualified for the limited immunity.[39] This protection for small businesses does not cover price fixing agreements, nor does it cover any infringement of Article 81 or Article 82. Further, the OFT has the power to withdraw the immunity in particular cases, although this has not been done to date. This immunity does not protect undertakings from private damages actions.

4.50

Some protection for small businesses applies in relation to the application of Article 81 by virtue of the European Commission's Notice on Agreements of Minor Importance,[40] but it does not offer immunity where otherwise a fine could be imposed.

4.51

---

[35] ibid, para 21.   [36] ibid, para 25.   [37] ibid, paras 11 and 18.
[38] SI 2000/262.
[39] OFT401, *Agreements and concerted practices* (December 2004) para 7.4; and OFT402, *Abuse of a Dominant Position* (December 2004) para 2.14.
[40] [2001] OJ C368/13.

C. Block Exemptions and Exclusions

(a) Block exemptions

(i) EC block exemptions

4.52 Block exemptions (in the form of specific European Council and/or European Commission regulations) have been created from time to time. Some of the European Council regulations provide for block exemptions in themselves, and others empower the European Commission to create block exemptions in relation to a particular industry.[41] Although block exemptions were specifically introduced to address the problems associated with the old notification system,[42] they were not abolished with the advent of the new regime. However, their purpose has shifted in emphasis. Rather than reducing the need for notification, the function of block exemptions in the new system is to provide greater certainty in self-assessment of particular types of agreement. Where an agreement fits within the terms of a block exemption, it also provides for immunity from penalties up until the time the benefit of the block exemption is withdrawn.

4.53 Previously, several block exemptions contained 'opposition procedures', whereby an undertaking could notify its agreement to the European Commission for approval if it was unclear whether or not the agreement fell within the terms of the block exemption regulation. Such procedures were often used as a tactical weapon to stall private litigation claims, which would have to be suspended pending the Commission's determination. Regulation 1/2003 removed the opposition procedure in the block exemption regulations which contained such a procedure and thereby prevents the maintenance of a notification procedure 'by the back door'.

4.54 Under Regulation 1/2003, the European Commission has retained its power to create new block exemption regulations.

4.55 If an agreement does not fit within the terms of a block exemption, it may satisfy Article 81(3) or s 9(1). The ECJ has held that there is no category of agreement that cannot satisfy the exemption conditions. Even if the agreement is discriminatory or contains 'black-listed' clauses, it may still be justified in the specific context in which it is enforced.[43]

---

[41] The European Council's power is able to be conferred by virtue of Art 83(2)(b) EC.

[42] In the past, due to their original function, block exemptions were generally created to cover large numbers of relatively innocuous agreements, so that by the creation of a single block exemption, many agreements would be saved from the notification requirement.

[43] Case T-17/93 *Matra Hachette v Commission* [1994] ECR II-595; and *Visa International— Multilateral Interchange Fee* [2002] OJ L318/17.

In terms of practical guidance, it is likely that national courts will have regard to **4.56** the terms of the block exemption regulations when assessing the compatibility of particular types of agreement with Article 81(3).[44] It is therefore sound practice, where possible, to draft agreements along the lines of the block exemption even if, for example, one or two of the key criteria are not met.

It is also worth remembering that if an agreement does not comply with the **4.57** terms of a block exemption this does not mean that Article 81(1) automatically applies, as not every agreement infringes Article 81(1) in the first place. Nor does it mean that the agreement will not satisfy Article 81(3).

The types of agreements covered by EC block exemptions currently in force are **4.58** set out in summary form below. Given the complexity of many of the block exemptions, the following summaries should be taken only as a general guide to the types of agreements covered by EC block exemptions.

Vertical agreements[45]   This EC block exemption is one of the most important **4.59** exemptions, as it covers agreements between undertakings at different levels in the supply chain. It applies to agreements where the supplier's[46] market share does not exceed 30 per cent. This block exemption is supported by the European Commission's guidelines on vertical restraints which contain more detailed guidance on how the block exemption is to apply.[47]

Technology transfer agreements[48]   The block exemption covers agreements **4.60** concerning the licensing of technology, where a licensor permits a licensee to exploit the licensed technology for the production of goods or services. In addition, the European Commission's guideline on the application of Article 81 to technology transfer agreements provides guidance on the block exemption as well as on the application of Article 81 to technology transfer agreements that fall outside its scope.[49]

---

[44] Prior to modernisation, an agreement which fitted within a block exemption did not need to be notified to the European Commission. This was one of the main benefits of fitting within a block exemption. Now there is no need (or ability) to notify an agreement regardless of whether it fits within the terms of a block exemption, so this benefit no longer exists. This may mean that, over time, undertakings become less concerned about fitting exactly within the terms of a block exemption, and may treat them more as guidelines as to the application of the individual exemption criteria to particular types of agreement.
[45] Commission Regulation (EC) 2790/99 [1999] OJ L336/21.
[46] Or the buyer's market share, but only in limited circumstances where there is an exclusive supply obligation.
[47] Guidelines on Vertical Restraints [2000] OJ C291/1.
[48] Commission Regulation (EC) 772/2004 [2004] OJ L123/11.
[49] European Commission TTBER Guideline [2004] OJ C101/38.

4.61 **Motor vehicle distribution agreements**[50] This block exemption applies to cars and commercial vehicles. It deals with a range of agreements from the sale of new cars to the supply of spare parts, and sets out the key rules which such agreements must comply with in order to fall within the block exemption. In general terms, it seeks to increase the independence of car dealers from car manufacturers, and to improve consumer benefits in the after-sales markets of servicing and spare parts. Further guidance on this block exemption is set out in an explanatory brochure published by the European Commission.[51]

4.62 **Specialisation agreements**[52] This block exemption is limited to agreements between competing undertakings (other types of agreements will probably fall to be assessed under the vertical agreements block exemption). It covers one of the areas where consumers are seen to benefit from cooperation between competitors, and allows undertakings to enter into certain arrangements whereby they agree to specialise their production of goods or services in order to promote development and improve efficiency. The exemption applies to agreements where the combined market share of the parties does not exceed 20 per cent.

4.63 **Research and development agreements**[53] This block exemption covers agreements for joint research and development and, between the same parties, the joint exploitation of such research and development, in relation to goods or services. The block exemption imposes a market share cap of 25 per cent in certain circumstances and also imposes a time frame of seven years for the exploitation of the research and development.

4.64 **Inland transport agreements**[54] This block exemption applies to agreements relating to transport by rail, road, and inland waterway, and provides exemption for certain technical cooperation agreements and for small to medium sized enterprises.

4.65 **Liner conferences and maritime transport services agreements**[55] This block exemption has been repealed, subject to a transitional period of two years in relation to certain provisions. The block exemption only applied to international maritime transport services between Community ports, and does not

---

[50] Commission Regulation (EC) 1400/02 [2002] OJ L203/30.
[51] Explanatory Brochure, available at <http://ec.europa.eu/comm/competition/car_sector>.
[52] Commission Regulation (EC) 2658/2000 [2000] OJ L304/3.
[53] Commission Regulation (EC) 2659/2000 [2000] OJ L304/7.
[54] Council Regulation (EEC) 1017/68 [1968] OJ L175/1.
[55] Council Regulation (EEC) 4056/86 [1986] OJ L378/1. Note that this regulation was repealed on 25 September 2006 by Council Regulation (EC) 1419/2006 [2006] OJ L269/1. However, Art 1(3)(b) and (c), Arts 3–7, Art 8(2) and Art 26 of Regulation (EEC) 4056/86 shall continue to apply in respect of liner shipping conferences satisfying the requirements of Regulation (EEC) 4056/86 on 18 October 2006, for a transitional period of two years from that date.

apply where the services are between ports within a single Member State. It exempted agreements between carriers relating to the operation of scheduled maritime transport services, and agreements whose sole object and effect is to achieve technical improvements and cooperation. The European Commission repealed this block exemption on the basis that it was exceptionally generous and is no longer an effective means of ensuring quality and efficiency.[56] The European Commission does not propose to replace the block exemption.

Agreements between liner shipping undertakings[57]   This block exemption is **4.66** closely linked to the liner conferences block exemption, but there is no proposal to repeal this exemption at present. It covers liner shipping consortia (groups of shipping lines) which cooperate to provide joint maritime cargo transport services. It covers consortia having a market share of less than 30 per cent.[58] It does not cover passenger transport.

Insurance agreements[59]   This block exemption covers insurance agreements **4.67** for: the joint calculations of risks, and joint studies on future risks; the establishment of non-binding standard policy conditions; the establishment and management of insurance pools; and the testing and acceptance of security equipment.[60]

Air transport   The European Commission also has the power to grant block **4.68** exemptions for agreements in the air transport sector.[61] The block exemptions previously granted pursuant to this power have expired, and currently there are no such block exemptions in force.

*(ii)   Application of EC block exemptions in the United Kingdom
        (parallel exemptions)*

The power to create EC block exemption regulations remains with the European **4.69** Council and has not been devolved to the national competition authorities as part of the decentralisation process. Because EC block exemptions are EC regulations, they are directly applicable in the United Kingdom in relation to the application of Article 81 by the OFT.

By virtue of s 10 of the Competition Act 1998, EC block exemption regulations **4.70**

---

[56] European Commission, Proposal for a Council Regulation, 14 December 2005, COM(2005) 651, 2005/0264 (CNS).
[57] Commission Regulation (EC) 823/2000 [2000] OJ L100/24, as amended by Commission Regulation (EC) 611/2005 [2005] OJ L101/10.
[58] Or less than 35% in some cases.
[59] Commission Regulation (EC) 358/2003 [2003] OJ L53/8.
[60] European Commission press release IP/03/291, 'Commission adopts new Regulation exempting certain agreements in insurance sector', 27 February 2003.
[61] Council Regulation (EEC) 3976/87 [1987] OJ L374/9.

also apply in parallel to exempt an agreement from the application of the Chapter I prohibition. Where an agreement does not affect trade between Member States, but otherwise falls within a category of EC exempt agreements, it will also be exempt from the Chapter I prohibition.[62] This system of parallel exemption has existed since the Competition Act first came into force and was not changed with modernisation.[63]

(iii) UK-specific block exemptions

4.71 Under s 6 of the Competition Act 1998, the OFT has the power to make block exemptions applicable in the United Kingdom under the authority of the Secretary of State, in addition to the EC block exemptions which are automatically applicable in the United Kingdom. There has been one block exemption created by the OFT using this power, relating to bus ticketing schemes concerning joint travel-card and other similar arrangements.[64] This block exemption is not mirrored in EC law, but it is unlikely that any agreements covered by its terms would have an effect on trade between Member States and thereby cause a problem with the simultaneous application of UK and EC competition law.

(iv) Withdrawal of block exemptions

4.72 The European Commission has the power to remove the benefit of an EC block exemption in relation to a particular agreement 'when it finds that in any particular case an agreement, decision or concerted practice to which the exemption Regulation applies has certain effects which are incompatible with Article 81(3) of the Treaty'.[65] This power is also extended to the national competition authorities in their application of Article 81(1) in the United Kingdom.[66] The OFT has a similar power to cancel the application of a UK block exemption to a particular agreement, where that is provided for in the relevant block exemption order.[67] The UK courts do not have any power to withdraw the benefit of a block exemption.

4.73 The power to withdraw the benefit of a block exemption or exclusion is firmly linked to a situation where an agreement does not in fact satisfy the individual

---

[62] Competition Act 1998, s 10(2).

[63] See Chapter 1 for an explanation of the jurisdictional test for which regime applies, or whether both may apply.

[64] Competition Act 1998 (Public Transport Ticketing Schemes Block Exemption) Order 2001, SI 2001/319. This block exemption expired on 28 February 2006 but the OFT has recommended that it be extended for a further five years, with some minor changes. See also the Competition Act guideline, OFT439, *Public transport ticketing schemes block exemption* (August 2002). The OFT has indicated that a new draft guideline will be published for consultation.

[65] Regulation 1/2003, Art 29(1).

[66] ibid, Art 29(2) and Competition Act 1998, s 10(5)(d).

[67] Competition Act 1998, s 6(6)(c).

conditions despite fitting within the terms of a block exemption or exclusion. As block exemptions are generally crafted to capture agreements which largely fit the individual exemption conditions, this situation is likely to arise only in rare circumstances.[68]

Under the legal exception regime, the benefit of a block exemption is twofold. **4.74** First, it provides a general guideline for assessing the application of the exemption conditions. Secondly, each block exemption deems that agreements which fit within its terms will thereby automatically satisfy the individual exemption conditions. The procedures surrounding withdrawal of a block exemption preserve this second benefit as far as possible, since the agreement is technically not infringing the competition law prohibitions until the block exemption is withdrawn. Thus, where an agreement fits within the terms of a block exemption but in fact does not satisfy the individual exemption conditions, then even if the benefit of the block exemption is ultimately withdrawn from that agreement, the undertakings concerned are held immune from penalties up until the date on which the benefit is formally withdrawn.[69]

The OFT's procedure for removal of the benefit of a block exemption com- **4.75** mences with s 25(8) and (9) of the Competition Act. These subsections provide the OFT with the power to carry out an investigation in order to decide whether or not to remove the benefit of the block exemption. The OFT may use the same investigative powers for this purpose as it would for an infringement investigation. In practical terms, the OFT will only undertake one investigative procedure, during the course of which it will assess both whether the individual exemption conditions apply (ie whether the block exemption should be withdrawn) and whether there is an infringement of competition law. If the OFT then concludes that the block exemption should be removed, it can make that direction simultaneously with a decision that the agreement infringes Article 81(1) and/or the Chapter I prohibition. The OFT has also indicated that a reference to the CC may be appropriate where it is considering removing the benefit of a block exemption (see para 13.103 below).

Prior to making any direction to remove the benefit of a block exemption, the **4.76** OFT must comply with the provisions of r 13 of the OFT's Rules. This requires the OFT to give notice of its proposal to withdraw the benefit of the block exemption to each person whom the OFT considers is a party to the agreement. The notice must provide certain details and allow for inspection of documents, representations to be made on the treatment of confidential information, and for the persons addressed to submit written and oral representations.[70] This

---

[68] OFT401, *Agreements and concerted practices* (December 2004) para 5.9.
[69] ibid, para 5.11.　　　[70] OFT's Procedural Rules, rr 13 and 5.

notice is effectively the same as a Statement of Objections (as to which, see Chapter 9).

4.77 This procedure is similar to that of the European Commission, which also anticipates that the decision to remove the benefit of the block exemption will be simultaneous with any infringement decision.

(b) Exclusions

(i) *Exclusions relating to the Chapter I prohibition*

4.78 The Competition Act 1998 provides for certain agreements to be excluded from the application of the Chapter I prohibition and, in some cases, the Chapter II prohibition. These UK exclusions have no conceptual counterpart in EC law (although some UK exclusions reflect specific EC case law). UK exclusions were introduced when the Competition Act was first brought into force, as a way of promoting particular types of agreement or preserving legal certainty where such agreements are already governed by a separate legal regime. Exclusions operate in a different way to exemptions: they provide that certain classes of agreement are excluded from the application of the Chapter I prohibition altogether. Exclusions also operate regardless of any pro-competitive benefit conferred by the particular agreement.

4.79 The following paragraphs set out the types of agreements that are excluded from the Chapter I prohibition by UK exclusions. These are reasonably complex and are set out below in summary form only.

4.80 **Restrictive Trade Practices Act, s 21(2) approved agreements**[71] These are agreements which benefited from directions made by the Secretary of State under s 21(2) of the Restrictive Trade Practices Act 1976, whereby the provisions those agreements contained were not considered to be of such significance as to warrant an investigation.

4.81 **Investment exchanges approved rules**[72] This covers agreements and conduct relating to the constitution of (or compliance with) practices and regulatory provisions (ie rules and guidance) issued by FSA-recognised investment exchanges or clearing houses. The OFT is under a duty to review the regulating provisions and practices of such investment exchanges and clearing houses.

---

[71] The exclusion for agreements which have already been approved under s 21(2) of the Restrictive Trade Practices Act 1976 will be repealed with effect from 1 May 2007 (Competition Act 1998, Sch 3, para 2).

[72] The UK government has indicated that the FSMA and FSA exclusions will be considered for repeal in further reviews of financial services regulation in the UK (see the Explanatory Memorandum to the Competition Act 1998 (Office of Fair Trading's Rules) Order 2004, SI 2004/2751, para 2.17).

FSA approved rules[73] This exclusion covers agreements to the extent that they **4.82**
contain provisions encouraged by the regulating provisions (ie rules and guidance) issued by the Financial Services Authority (**FSA**) or the practices of the
FSA. The OFT is under a duty to review the regulating provisions and practices
of the FSA.

Mergers and concentrations[74] This exclusion covers agreements which com- **4.83**
prise merger situations (under Pt 3 of the Enterprise Act) or concentrations with
a Community dimension (under the EC Merger Regulation 4064/89[75] as
amended).

Services of general economic interest[76] This covers undertakings entrusted **4.84**
with the operation of services of general economic interest or having the character of a revenue-producing monopoly insofar as the prohibition would
obstruct the performance, in law or fact, of the particular tasks assigned to the
undertaking.

Land agreements These are agreements between undertakings which create, **4.85**
alter, transfer or terminate an interest in land, or agreements to enter into such
agreements, as well as obligations and restrictions which relate to relevant land.
To the extent that the agreement is a vertical agreement it is not a land
agreement.[77]

Agreements complying with planning obligations[78] These are agreements **4.86**
which are: planning obligations for the purposes of ss 106 or 299A of the Town
and Country Planning Act 1990; or made under ss 75 or 246 of the Town
and Country Planning (Scotland) Act 1997; or made under Article 40 of the
Planning (Northern Ireland) Order.[79]

EEA regulated financial markets[80] This exclusion covers certain agreements, **4.87**
decisions and practices of EEA regulated markets (being markets which are
listed by an EEA State other than the United Kingdom).

Agreements fulfilling international obligations of the United Kingdom[81] **4.88**
This exclusion allows the Secretary of State to make an order excluding a specific
agreement or conduct from the application of national competition law, in
order to avoid conflict between the provisions of the Competition Act and an

---

[73] Financial Services and Markets Act 2000, ss 159–164. See also n 71 above.
[74] Competition Act 1998, Sch 1, paras 1–6.   [75] [1990] OJ L257/13.
[76] Competition Act 1998, Sch 3, para 4. See also OFT421, *Services of general economic interest
exclusion* (December 2004).
[77] Competition Act (Land Agreements Exclusion and Revocation) Order 2004, SI 2004/1260.
Also see OFT420, *Land agreements* (December 2004).
[78] Competition Act 1998, Sch 3, para 1.   [79] SI 1991/1220 (NI 11) as amended.
[80] Competition Act 1998, Sch 3, para 3.   [81] ibid, Sch 3, para 6.

international obligation of the United Kingdom (including civil aviation arrangements).

4.89 **Compliance with legal requirements**[82]   This exclusion covers requirements imposed by or under any UK enactment, the EC Treaty or EEA Agreements, or a law in another Member State which has legal effect in the United Kingdom.[83]

4.90 **Agricultural products**[84]   This covers certain agreements relating to the production of or trade in an agricultural product listed in Annex II to the EC Treaty.[85]

4.91 **Accountancy bodies**[86]   This covers rules and guidance (and other incidental provisions) issued by accountancy bodies which are applying for or have been granted the status of 'recognised supervisory body' or 'recognised qualifying body'.

4.92 **Channel 3 news provision**[87]   This relates to agreements for securing the appointment by holders of Channel 3 licences of a single body corporate to be the appointed news provider for the purposes of s 31(2) of the Broadcasting Act 1990. It is subject to a declaration by the Secretary of State.

4.93 **Channel 3 networking arrangements**[88]   This covers networking agreements to the extent to which they are subject to the special competition regime in Sch 4 to the Broadcasting Act 1990 (a list of such agreements to be published by Ofcom).

4.94 **Environmental protection obligations**[89]   This exclusion allows regulations imposing producer responsibility obligations on prescribed persons to provide for the exclusion or modification of the Chapter I prohibition insofar as it would apply to exemption schemes.

4.95 **Public policy**[90]   This exclusion allows the Secretary of State by order to exclude any agreement or conduct from the application of the Chapter I or Chapter II prohibitions where he or she is satisfied that there are exceptional and compelling reasons of public policy to do so.

---

[82] ibid, Sch 3, para 5.
[83] For the equivalent EC 'exclusion', see Joined Cases C-359/95 P and C-379/95 P *Commission and France v Ladbroke Racing Limited* [1997] ECR I-6265.
[84] Competition Act 1998, Sch 3, para 9.
[85] An EC equivalent 'exclusion' applies by virtue of Regulation (EEC) 26/62 [1962] OJ 30/993.
[86] Competition Act 1998, Sch 2; Companies Act 1989, Sch 14; and Companies (Northern Ireland) Order 1990, SI 1990/593 NI5).
[87] Competition Act 1998, Sch 2; Broadcasting Act 1990, s 194A.
[88] Competition Act 1998, Sch 2; Broadcasting Act 1990, s 39 and Sch 4.
[89] Competition Act 1998, Sch 2; and Environment Act 1995, s 94.
[90] Competition Act 1998, Sch 3, para 7.

(ii) Exclusions relating to the Chapter II prohibition

Some of the UK exclusions listed above also exclude certain types of conduct **4.96** from the application of the Chapter II prohibition. The exclusions which allow for this are: financial services regulation; financial services investment exchanges; mergers and concentrations; services of general economic interest; compliance with legal requirements; international obligations; and public policy. The remaining exclusions do not contain any provisions allowing for excluding the operation of the Chapter II prohibition.

(iii) Withdrawal of a UK exclusion

The Secretary of State has a power to provide for the withdrawal of the **4.97** application of a UK exclusion from a particular agreement in certain circumstances.[91] The establishment of some of the UK exclusions included provision allowing for the OFT to direct that the exclusion does not apply to a particular agreement, where it considers that the agreement would fall within the Chapter I prohibition and that it would be unlikely to satisfy the conditions in s 9(1) of the Competition Act.[92] The UK courts do not have any power to withdraw the benefit of an exclusion.

The exclusions which the OFT may withdraw are the mergers exclusion,[93] the **4.98** agricultural products exclusion,[94] and the land agreements exclusion.[95]

In order to withdraw the application of an exclusion, the OFT must follow the **4.99** procedures set out in r 14 of the OFT's Rules. This requires the OFT to consult each person whom it considers is a party to the agreement. The OFT must also follow the required procedures for withdrawal as set out in the exclusion itself, which generally provide for notice of withdrawal to be in writing and not to have any retrospective effect.[96]

If the OFT is considering making a direction for withdrawal of an exclusion, it **4.100** may also seek the provision of information in connection with the agreement. Failure to comply with such a request allows the OFT to make the withdrawal direction without further consideration.[97] Otherwise, the OFT can only make a withdrawal direction, in the case of the mergers exclusion and the land agreements exclusion, if it considers that the agreement will, if not excluded, infringe the Chapter I prohibition, and the agreement is not a 'protected

---

[91] ibid, s 3(5).   [92] See OFT404, *Powers of investigation* (December 2004) para 8.2.
[93] Competition Act 1998, Sch 1   [94] ibid, Sch 3.
[95] Competition Act (Land Agreements Exclusion and Revocation) Order 2004, SI 2004/1260. Also see OFT420, *Land agreements* (December 2004).
[96] See eg, Competition Act 1998, Sch 1, para 4(7).
[97] ibid, Sch 1, para 4(2), (3) and (4); Sch 3, para 9(4), (5) and (6); and Competition Act (Land Agreements Exclusion and Revocation) Order 2004 (SI 2004/1260), art 6.

agreement',[98] or, in the case of the agricultural products exclusion, 'if it considers that an agreement . . . is likely, or is intended, substantially and unjustifiably to prevent, restrict or distort competition in relation to an agricultural
product'.[99]

4.101 Although no such direction has yet been made by the OFT, in practice, the
OFT would probably conduct a separate, initial investigation to decide whether
to withdraw the application of an exclusion. Such an investigation would be
based on its limited powers of investigation as specified in the exclusion itself.
Assuming the undertakings in question respond properly to the request for
information, the OFT would then need to make an initial determination that it
considers that the agreement will, if not excluded, infringe the Chapter I prohibition[100] (or, in the case of the agricultural products exclusion, be likely to distort
competition).

4.102 Directions withdrawing the benefit of an exclusion are not specifically included
in the list of appealable decisions in s 47 of the Competition Act 1998.
An aggrieved undertaking may only have judicial review as an option for disput-
ing the OFT's use of its power to withdraw an exclusion. This would be
a difficult task given that the wording of this requirement is subjective (the
OFT 'considers') and therefore would be given a broad interpretation by
a court.

4.103 Once the exclusion is withdrawn, the OFT would be able to commence a full
investigation under its Pt I powers.

(c) Effect of exclusions and block exemptions in the United Kingdom

(i) Effect of UK exclusions

4.104 Most of the UK exclusions listed above do not have an identical counterpart in
EC law. Where agreements covered by a UK exclusion also have (or may have)
an effect on trade between Member States, the protective effect of the UK
exclusion is therefore questionable. With the OFT applying Article 81(1) and
the Chapter I prohibition simultaneously, businesses do not have full protection
because the UK exclusions do not affect the full application of Article 81(1) to
such agreements. By retaining separate exclusions, the UK system creates an
additional layer of complexity, and cases may turn on the technical differences

---

[98] ibid, Sch 1, para 4(5). Protected agreements are defined in Sch 1, para 5 as, in essence,
agreements which are or have been the subject of a Competition Commission reference.
[99] ibid, Sch 3, para 9(7).
[100] This determination must include an assessment of the exemption conditions, because the
'Chapter I prohibition' is defined in s 2(8) of the Competition Act 1998 as the prohibition
imposed by s 2(1), which in turn includes the concept of exemption.

between the UK exclusion and the EC equivalent exemption, as well as the test of 'effect on trade', a notoriously difficult test to apply.[101]

(ii) *Effect on the cartel offence, director disqualification, and the market investigation regime*

There are no exemptions or exclusions applying to the other aspects of competition law applicable in the United Kingdom: the cartel offence, competition disqualification orders, or market investigations. Clearly, it is not possible for an agreement which satisfies the Article 81(3) and/or s 9(1) conditions to form a basis for a competition disqualification order as there would be no infringement. Nor would it form a basis for the cartel offence.   **4.105**

Categories of agreement/conduct which satisfy block exemption or exclusion	Chapter I exempt	Chapter II exempt	Article 81 exempt	Article 82 exempt[102]
EC				
Vertical agreements	Yes	No	Yes	No
Technology transfer	Yes	No	Yes	No
Motor vehicle distribution	Yes	No	Yes	No
Specialisation	Yes	No	Yes	No
Research and development	Yes	No	Yes	No
Inland transport	Yes	No	Yes	No
Maritime transport	Yes	No	Yes	No
Liner shipping	Yes	No	Yes	No
Insurance	Yes	No	Yes	No
UK				
Bus ticketing	Yes	No	No	No
Restrictive Trade Practices Act 1976, s 21(2)	Yes	No	No	No
Investment exchanges	Yes	Yes	No	No
FSA approved rules	Yes	Yes	No	No
Mergers and concentrations	Yes	Yes	No	No
Services of general economic interest	Yes	Yes	No	No
Land agreements	Yes	No	No	No
Planning obligations	Yes	No	No	No
EEA regulated markets	Yes	No	No	No
International obligations	Yes	Yes	No	No
Compliance with legal requirements	Yes	Yes	No	No
Agricultural products	Yes	No	No	No
Accountancy bodies	Yes	No	No	No
Channel 3 news	Yes	No	No	No
Channel 3 networking	Yes	No	No	No
Environmental protection	Yes	No	No	No
Public policy	Yes	Yes	No	No

---

[101] See Chapter 1 for a discussion of the application of this test.

[102] Even if an agreement benefits from a block exemption, a party to that agreement which is also a dominant undertaking may nevertheless be found to be in breach of Art 82 (or the Chapter II prohibition) by reason of its conduct in entering into that agreement: Case T-51/89 *Tetra Pak Rausing SA v Commission* [1990] II-ECR 309.

(iii) Summary table showing the effect of block exemptions and exclusions in the United Kingdom

4.106 The table set out above shows the protective effect of the EC and UK block exemptions and the UK exclusions in relation to the application of Articles 81 and 82, and the Chapter I and Chapter II prohibitions to an agreement which falls within the terms of the block exemption or exclusion.

D. Transitional Matters

(a) Individual exemptions granted by formal decision prior to 1 May 2004

4.107 Exemption decisions in relation to individual agreements made prior to 1 May 2004, whether by the European Commission or by the OFT, continue to be valid until their expiry (as specified by the terms of the decision).

4.108 Some individual exemption decisions provide for the exemption to be renewed for a further period of time upon its initial expiry. This type of provision was generally included to allow the authority to re-assess the market and the effect of the agreement on the relevant market at a later date. Thus any renewal is effectively a new exemption decision—which neither the OFT nor the European Commission has the power to make after 1 May 2004. Accordingly, individual exemption decisions will not be renewed once the initial expiry date has passed.

4.109 Individual exemption decisions now form a temporary exception to the new system of self-assessment. Where these are EC exemptions, by virtue of the supremacy of EC law and the fundamental requirements of legal certainty (see Chapter 3 on the relationship between EC and UK law) these agreements continue to be protected by the exemption decision against any contrary finding of infringement. By the same token, individual exemption decisions are also binding on national courts, so they also continue to afford effective protection against private damages claims, at least to the extent that the case involves the same parties and the same agreement.[103] The Commission is not technically bound by its own previous decisions,[104] however the principle of legal certainty means that the Commission cannot revoke or change its position without providing reasons justifying its change of approach.

4.110 The OFT is bound by an individual exemption decision issued by the European

---

[103] *Inntrepreneur Pub Co CPC v Crehan* [2006] UKHL 38, [2006] 3 WLR 148, paras 6, 11 and 12.

[104] Case T-210/01 *General Electric Co v Commission* [2006] 4 CMLR 15, para 120.

Commission in respect of a finding of infringement of Article 81(1).[105] By virtue of Article 3(2) of Regulation 1/2003, the OFT can no longer prohibit under national law an agreement that has been cleared under Article 81. It is questionable whether the OFT would be able to invoke a subsequent change of circumstances or different economic considerations, for example, a different market analysis in a related case, to distinguish the European Commission's decision. The status of a Commission exemption decision before national courts was considered by the House of Lords in *Inntrepreneur Pub Co (CPC) v Crehan*,[106] where it was held that such a decision was not binding in a related case which involved different parties. However, the House of Lords left open the question of how this related to national competition authorities, noting that the position may differ from national courts.

In theory, as a result of the doctrine of supremacy, the European Commission is **4.111** not bound by any decision of the OFT, whether an infringement or a prior exemption decision, even where the facts are identical.[107] However, in practice, the European Commission and the OFT are likely to work in close cooperation,[108] before any decision is adopted which should minimise the risk of future conflict. The authors consider that it would only be in very exceptional circumstances that the European Commission would make an infringement finding in a case where a fully reasoned exemption decision had already been issued by the OFT.

(b) European Commission comfort letters pre-dating 1 May 2004

As discussed earlier, for many years the European Commission pursued a policy **4.112** of providing undertakings with 'comfort letters' in respect of notified agreements rather than subjecting their terms to a full compliance assessment. For many undertakings, comfort letters were the highest level of protection from an infringement finding that they could obtain.

With the new legal exception regime in place, comfort letters carry no formal **4.113** legal authority after 1 May 2004. However, both the European Commission and the OFT have acknowledged that comfort letters will be taken into account in the event that an agreement, which has benefited from a comfort letter in the

---

[105] In the same way as national courts are bound by Commission decisions: Case C-344/98 *Masterfoods Ltd (t/a Mars Ireland) v HB Icecream Ltd* [2000] ECR I-11369. See also OFT401, *Agreements and concerted practices* (December 2004) para 5.18, and Regulation 1/2003, Art 16(2).
[106] [2006] UKHL 38, [2006] 3 WLR 148.
[107] Case 14/68 *Wilhelm v Bundeskartellamt* [1969] ECR 1. For a general discussion of the doctrine of supremacy, see paras 3.03–3.07.
[108] Regulation 1/2003, Art 11.

past, falls to be assessed by one of these authorities.[109] What this means in practice is something yet to be developed. The doctrine of legal certainty may foreclose the authority from imposing a penalty, but it will not prevent an authority from making an infringement decision altogether. Further, unlike a legal opinion, a comfort letter may have some bearing on a judge's decision in private litigation proceedings, since it is produced by an independent body rather than by the undertaking through its lawyers. The English courts may be receptive to arguments of legitimate expectation, estoppel and legal certainty, which would operate to prevent the imposition of a penalty in respect of any period prior to 1 May 2004, in circumstances where an undertaking had relied to its detriment on the apparent authority of the European Commission's comfort letter. To date, such concepts are relatively undeveloped in Community law and this area may be the subject of a reference to the ECJ at some stage, although the likelihood of this decreases as time passes and comfort letters become more dated.

(c) OFT guidance decisions pre-dating 1 May 2004

4.114 Prior to 1 May 2004, the OFT was able to issue guidance decisions, as well as individual exemption decisions. Guidance decisions were not published. A guidance decision carried less weight than an individual exemption decision, but in most cases it nevertheless involved a relatively thorough assessment of an agreement. From 1 May 2004, guidance decisions do not have any legal force, nor do they bind the OFT or any other body in future cases. However, the authors consider it most unlikely that the OFT would make an infringement finding in relation to an agreement which had previously been the subject of a guidance decision. Although guidance decisions have never been binding on the OFT, an undertaking would have strong arguments for contesting the imposition of a penalty in circumstances where it had actively taken steps in reliance on the guidance provided to it by the OFT. In practice, few guidance decisions were issued.

4.115 It is unlikely that a decision that an agreement satisfies Article 81(3) would be deemed to apply retrospectively where the agreement was not notified prior to 1 May 2004, as this is arguably contrary to the rights of third party claimants who would have been able to sue on non-notified agreements before modernisation.

---

[109] See OFT401, *Agreements and concerted practices* (December 2004) para 5.18 where it states that the OFT 'will consider comfort letters issued by the European Commission'; and see also the Commission notice on informal guidance relating to novel questions concerning Articles 81 and 82 of the EC Treaty that arise in individual cases (guidance letters) (2004/C 101/06) [2004] OJ C101/78, para 24.

(d) Transitional matters relating to exclusions

The UK exclusion for vertical agreements (but not land agreements) was **4.116** repealed with effect from 1 May 2005, from which date such agreements fall to be assessed under the equivalent (but not identical) EC block exemption or Article 81(3) or its domestic equivalent.[110]

The most striking tension between an EC block exemption and its UK equiv- **4.117** alent is shown by the application of the EC vertical agreements block exemption to agreements that would formerly have been covered by the UK verticals exclusion. The EC block exemption appears to cover the majority of agreements that would have been excluded under the domestic regime. However, as identified by the DTI consultation paper of June 2003,[111] there are 'gaps' between the two. In particular, there are clauses that would have been excluded by domestic law which will not be covered by the EC block exemption. The most important factor in this regard is the market share 'safe harbour' threshold which is set at 30 per cent in the EC vertical agreements block exemption, whereas the UK verticals exclusion did not have any threshold at all. The newspaper and magazine publishers, distributors and wholesalers expressed particular concern about the impact of the repeal of the verticals exclusion on their distribution agreements. They applied to the OFT for a published opinion. As at October 2006 the OFT was consulting on a draft opinion.[112]

---

[110] Competition Act 1998 (Land Agreements Exclusion and Revocation) Order 2004, SI 2004/1260. The transitional period of one year from 1 May 2004 was intended to allow businesses a period of time to assess their agreements for compliance. The application of the transitional period—and the exclusion itself—did not depend upon the date on which the agreement was made. The protection extended to all agreements falling within the terms of the UK verticals exclusion up until 1 May 2005.

[111] DTI, *UK Competition Law (Modernisation—a consultation on the Government's proposals for exclusions and exemptions from the Competition Act 1998 in light of Regulation 1/2003)* (June 2003) 21–32.

[112] OFT851, *Newspapers and magazine distribution—public consultation on the draft opinion of the Office of Fair Trading* (May 2006). The OFT anticipates publishing a final opinion in the first quarter of 2007.

5

LENIENCY

A. Making the Decision to Whistleblow

(a) Leniency programmes generally

5.01 Leniency (or immunity) programmes are an increasingly widely used operational tool for cartel enforcement worldwide. Leniency programmes are established by competition authorities and provide for a reduction in the level of a fine in return for an undertaking coming forward and producing evidence of a cartel. The granting of lenient treatment is not part of the substantive competition law; it is a procedural mechanism by which competition authorities address the most harmful competition law infringements. The aims of a leniency programme are deterrence and detection: to deter cartel activity by destabilising cartels, and to detect cartel activity by the voluntary submission of information from the undertaking(s) involved. Leniency programmes generally do not operate in respect of other types of infringements, such as less harmful agreements or infringements committed by a single undertaking.

5.02 As the aims are essentially the same with all programmes, the basic principles of leniency programmes worldwide also tend to be similar, although there are some important differences in the details of individual programmes. The best incentive is always offered to the first applicant 'through the door', as the first disclosure brings the infringement to the attention of the authorities. There are also usually incentives for subsequent applicants that cooperate generally, especially by providing inculpatory evidence of the extent of the cartel and its participants. Leniency programmes encourage cooperation as well as initial disclosure because once a cartel is uncovered, the authorities' next aim is usually to prosecute the participants as quickly and effectively as possible. The primary drawback of leniency programmes is that they cannot protect an applicant from private damages actions.[1]

5.03 Due to their common aims, leniency programmes are often similar in their effect, but rarely in their operation because of the different systems in which they operate.[2] There is no requirement for competition authorities to harmonise their leniency programmes, nor is there any obligation on any

---

[1] This was a particularly significant drawback in the US, where treble damages are awarded for competition law infringements in private suits. This drawback was recognised, and legislation was introduced in the US in 2004 to limit the liability of a cartel member to single damages where the cartel member turns itself in and cooperates with the plaintiff and the authorities (subject to other conditions): Antitrust Criminal Enhancement and Reform Act 2004, Pub L No 108–237, 118 Stat 661. See also para 5.58 in relation to confidentiality issues.

[2] For a discussion of the differences between leniency programmes operated by authorities within the ECN, see Margaret Bloom, 'Immunity/Leniency/Financial Incentives/Plea Bargaining', paper prepared for the 11th EUI Competition Law and Policy Workshop, June 2006. See also paras 5.106–5.131 below in relation to cross-border cartels.

competition authority to recognise any lenient treatment offered, promised, or granted by another competition authority.[3] It would be possible for competition authorities to cooperate and recognise leniency granted by each others' programmes, but this has not happened in any way other than on an ad hoc basis.[4]

In some jurisdictions, including the United Kingdom, there are criminal **5.04** offences related to the civil competition law enforcement system, which apply to *individuals* rather than to undertakings.[5] A civil leniency programme benefiting an undertaking would not be as effective without an ability for *individuals* to receive immunity from prosecution for any related criminal offences. In some jurisdictions where criminal sanctions apply there is no leniency protection available in relation to the related criminal offences. Some systems have criminal sanctions attached directly to a breach of competition law, without any additional element: in such cases, the civil leniency programme would deal with leniency in relation to the criminal sanctions so there is no need to provide for a separate leniency programme to operate in the criminal context.

(b) Leniency in the United Kingdom

The Office of Fair Trading (**OFT**) and the Regulators[6] operate a civil leniency **5.05** programme based on the principle that bringing a cartel to the attention of the authorities (and providing inculpatory evidence) is of paramount importance. The first applicant to make contact with the OFT—provided certain conditions are met—will receive total immunity from fines, whereas later applicants may only receive a reduction in fines. Further, the OFT is able to make a guarantee of lenient treatment very early in the process, although such a guarantee is still subject to on-going cooperation (amongst other conditions).

To deal with the UK operation of criminal offences associated with cartels, the **5.06**

---

[3] In the UK, this position may be changing in the light of the broad interpretation given by the CAT to s 60 of the Competition Act 1998 in *Pernod Ricard SA v OFT* [2004] CAT 10, paras 228–234. Essentially the CAT found that s 60 (which requires competition questions in the UK to be treated consistently with those in the European Community) could be extended to consistency in procedural matters as well. In that case, the application of s 60 related to the complaints procedure, but on the basis set out in that case, there may be some justification to applying a similar approach in relation to leniency. For further detail, see paras 3.94–3.107 above.

[4] eg, under the OFT's criminal leniency programme there is recognition of leniency granted under the European Commission's leniency programme as a basis upon which an applicant can secure a no-action letter: see OFT513, *The cartel offence: Guidance on the issue of no-action letters for individuals* (April 2003) para 3.6.

[5] This is not the case in all jurisdictions: eg, EC law does not provide for any criminal offences against individuals for competition law related offences.

[6] The OFT's civil leniency programme has been adopted by each of the sectoral Regulators in the UK.

OFT also has an ability to grant 'no-action' letters to individuals, as an adjunct to the civil programme, to ensure full cooperation where an individual may be involved in a separate criminal offence.[7]

(c) Critical factors in deciding whether to whistleblow

5.07 The decision to apply for leniency can be finely balanced and depends on the interaction of numerous commercial and strategic considerations. In many cases, the first time an undertaking considers making a leniency application is when the OFT's case officers arrive at its offices to conduct a dawn raid.[8] Given the race to be first in through the door, the decision and application may need to be made as quickly as possible: often in hours rather than days. Thus it may be necessary to make a rapid assessment based on the most significant factors. The most common critical factors in deciding whether to whistleblow are discussed below in the context of the OFT, but essentially these same factors will apply in respect of almost all leniency programmes.

5.08 One of the most important factors is whether the potential cartel has already been discovered by the OFT. If it has, then there is no room to consider whether the possible cartel will remain undiscovered, so any strategic considerations of this type are rendered irrelevant. In addition, there will be only a very short time to make a decision, because it is likely to be a race to be the first applicant and thereby obtain the possibility of full immunity from fines.[9] This can be an enormous financial incentive, depending on the level of fine which is likely to ensue.

5.09 Another crucial factor is whether another undertaking has already made a leniency application in the case. This factor is relevant regardless of whether the OFT has already conducted a dawn raid. This is important because the first applicant is almost always in the best position, even if it is the cartel ringleader. Where an undertaking is not the first applicant, it will only be entitled to a reduction of up to 50 per cent maximum in fines and not to full immunity.[10]

---

[7] No-action letters do not apply in Scotland—see the discussion on this at para 5.82 below.

[8] At this stage, it may well be too late to be the first applicant. Cartels may be unearthed as part of compliance training or due diligence on the sale of the business or simply by senior management being made aware of activities by staff at a junior level. In other cases, the undertaking may have been a minor player in a long-established cartel which wants to get out. However, where an undertaking is not the first to blow the whistle on a cartel, the usual situation involving applying for leniency is in reaction to a dawn raid.

[9] An application may be made even while the OFT is carrying out a dawn raid, so there is no need to wait until the conclusion to make the application.

[10] Note that the European Commission's programme is slightly different: although it does give priority to the first undertaking to apply for leniency by revealing the existence of an infringement, it also allows for the possibility of total immunity for an undertaking disclosing useful evidence, even if that undertaking did not bring the case to the attention of the European Commission.

With this reduced incentive, there may well be other matters of greater import-ance to consider before making an application for leniency. To allow an under-taking to discover whether it would be the first in the queue, the OFT will accept anonymous calls where the only information required to be provided is the relevant market, and the OFT will advise whether or not an application has been made in that market.

Another significant factor in deciding whether to whistleblow relates to the **5.10** possible sanctions which might be imposed on the individuals involved. In the United Kingdom, with cartels there is also a risk of criminal sanctions being imposed on individuals, or of competition disqualification orders banning indi-viduals from acting as directors for up to 15 years. The opportunity of obtaining a no-action letter from the OFT may be a strong incentive to approach the OFT with a civil leniency application, coupled with an application on behalf of the individuals involved for a no-action letter.

The above three factors are likely to be among the most important and **5.11** immediate considerations for any undertaking considering making a leniency application. Clearly, there are many other significant factors relevant to making a decision as to whether to apply for leniency. For example, an undertaking may first need to consider questions such as: Is a leniency application going to compromise the defence of the claim? Are there likely to be issues of negative publicity or matters for which it is crucial that confidentiality is maintained? Will the leniency application and ensuing obligations of cooperation comprom-ise commercial relations? What are the chances of a leniency application being successful? Does the undertaking have access to the best evidence?[11] What is the likely reduction in fines if the application is successful? What risks does the undertaking face if it makes an unsuccessful application? Is there likely to be a damages claim by way of private action? What is the likely extent of a fine or other order?

Another important question for undertakings considering making a leniency **5.12** application is *where* such an application should be made. Not all jurisdictions operate leniency programmes,[12] and there is currently no 'one stop shop' in the European Community.[13] The general advice given by authorities to undertakings

---

[11] The quality of evidence available is a criterion of particular importance where an undertak-ing is not the first leniency applicant, since the level of reduction may well depend upon the quality of the evidence the undertaking is able to supply to the authority.

[12] As at August 2006, 19 of the 25 Member States had competition authorities which oper-ate leniency programmes (and most of the remainder were progressing toward introducing a leniency programme). The European Commission maintains on its website a list of the national competition authorities which operate a leniency programme.

[13] This remains a regular topic for discussion, and is often raised by Neelie Kroes (the Member of the European Commission in charge of Competition Policy) as it could provide much clarity

is to apply for leniency in every jurisdiction where the cartel operates, provided it is possible to do so. In practical terms, the cost and resource burden of making multiple applications is likely to be considerable and for some undertakings this may outweigh the risk of the cartel being uncovered.

5.13 In the following sections of this chapter, these matters are discussed in the context of understanding the civil and criminal leniency programmes in the United Kingdom, and the interaction of these programmes with cases and competition authorities outside the United Kingdom.

(d) Alternatives to applying for leniency

5.14 Although leniency may be available and may be an attractive option in some circumstances, it may also be worth considering the alternatives available to an undertaking.

5.15 Although competition authorities are understandably reluctant to dwell on the point, it is possible that a cartel could remain undetected. For an undertaking, this chance may outweigh the significant risks associated with making a leniency application, such as the risk of the cartel becoming publicly known, or the risk of facing private damages claims after an infringement finding is made. Thus one clear alternative is to do nothing (although an undertaking would be well advised to cease its participation in the cartel). Once a cartel has ended, the progression of time may reduce the chance of an investigation, and in many cases may eventually eliminate any power of the competition authorities to impose a fine in respect of a cartel.[14]

5.16 Where the potential cartel is to be investigated, an undertaking may want to consider whether its defence strategy is best served by making a leniency application, especially in view of the extensive cooperation involved. The fact of having made a leniency application is tantamount to an admission of infringement by an undertaking. Although civil leniency applications to the OFT do not require such an admission, the perception and the practical effect

---

and certainty for undertakings. There is a working group within the ECN set up to establish a 'one-stop-shop' for leniency applicants within the EU. It is not clear what time frame is proposed for this initiative: it is likely to face practical difficulties as the various Member States have different priorities and enforcement systems, and such a system may go against the move to de-centralise enforcement processes. For a further recent discussion on this topic, see Bloom (n 2 above).

[14] In relation to the European Commission, there is a limitation period of five years before issuing a Statement of Objections or reaching a decision, but this limitation period only stops the Commission imposing a fine on undertakings—it may still consider that it has a legitimate interest in making an infringement decision. See *Vitamins* (Case COMP/E–1/37.512) Commission Decision 2003/2/EC, [2003] OJ L6/1, para 651. See also paras 6.79–6.95 below for a discussion of various time limitation periods.

in many ways is the same as if an admission of infringement had been made. In the criminal context, a recipient of a no-action letter may be required first to admit participation in a cartel activity, so this could require an actual admission of guilt. Thus if an undertaking intends to defend the allegation of infringement, making a leniency application or applying for a no-action letter for the individuals involved will be effectively inconsistent with any defence on liability, thus leaving less scope for appeal.[15] This may not be sufficient to outweigh the option of obtaining full immunity if that is still available. However, where full immunity is not available, simply cooperating with the authority outside the leniency regime could result in a reduction in fines equivalent to the lower reductions available through the leniency programme.[16] This avoids the undertaking having to make an effective admission, and also avoids the undertaking coming under a specific duty to cooperate during the process of the investigation. The usefulness of this approach will vary in each individual case and is unlikely to be attractive to an undertaking unless it is a third or subsequent prospective leniency applicant and therefore already facing a lower reduction in fines.

Reaching a direct settlement with an authority may be another option. This is **5.17** likely to be difficult because there is no technical procedure for settlements, as the provision for accepting commitments does not apply in the case of hard-core cartels.[17] The possibility of 'plea bargaining' (or direct settlements) has been raised by the European Commission as an alternative way of achieving swift anti-cartel enforcement.[18] Although plea bargaining is not technically offered by the OFT, there is a recent example of a cartel case conducted by the OFT which was concluded by the parties reaching a settlement with the OFT. This case concerned the OFT's investigation into the exchange of information about the fees charged by 50 independent schools in the United Kingdom. In the settlement the schools agreed to make a payment into a trust to benefit the students and made an admission that they had infringed the Chapter I prohibition, but they made no admission of liability as to the effect of the agreement. In return, the OFT agreed to end its investigation. This 'novel and exceptional' solution

---

[15] By contrast, the penalty (and/or percentage leniency reduction) imposed is almost always appealed by undertakings, usually resulting in a reduced penalty.

[16] The OFT is aware of this possibility and will use its discretion to avoid a situation where an undertaking achieves the same reduction for simple cooperation as it would have for a successful leniency application. See *Umbro Holdings Ltd v OFT* [2005] CAT 22, para 314 for a discussion of the difference between simple cooperation and cooperation in accordance with the conditions of leniency, where the CAT agreed with the OFT's submission that an undertaking ought not recover more for general cooperation than it would for participating in the leniency regime.

[17] This restriction applies under both the Competition Act 1998 and Regulation 1/2003.

[18] Neelie Kroes, Member of the European Commission in charge of Competition Policy, speech: 'The First Hundred Days', Brussels, 7 April 2005, SPEECH/05/205.

allowed the schools to resolve the OFT's concerns whilst not being fined: as
the settlement provided a fund for compensation rather than a fine, the schools
were not actually subject to a penalty. This settlement agreement also limited
the prospect of subsequent private damages actions since there was no pronouncement or finding by the OFT on the effect of the infringement upon
which to base a damages action.[19]

B. Civil Immunity and Leniency in the United Kingdom

5.18   This section deals with the immunity and leniency programme operated by the
OFT and the Regulators in the United Kingdom, in the context of the civil
competition law infringements applicable in the United Kingdom (referred to
hereafter as the 'OFT's leniency programme'). The immunity and leniency programme offered by the European Commission is referred to where appropriate
to demonstrate areas of contrast between the two programmes.[20]

5.19   The key publications by the OFT about the OFT's leniency programme are:

- *OFT's guidance as to the appropriate amount of a penalty* (**Penalties Guidance**);[21]
- *Leniency in Cartel Cases: A Guide to the leniency programme for cartels*;[22]
- *Leniency and no-action—OFT's draft final guidance note on the handling of applications*;[23]
- *Modernisation.*[24]

(a) Infringements covered by the OFT's leniency programme

5.20   The OFT's leniency programme only applies in relation to those types of
competition law infringements which may be described as 'cartel activities'.
Cartel activities are defined as 'agreements which infringe Article 81 and/or the
Chapter I prohibition and involve price fixing (including resale price maintenance), bid-rigging (collusive tendering), the establishment of output restrictions
or quotas and/or market-sharing or market-dividing'.[25]

---

[19] See OFT press release, 'Settlement proposed in independent schools investigation',
27 February 2006: <http://www.oft.gov.uk/News/Press+releases/Statements/2006/schools.htm>.
[20] For detailed information on the leniency programme offered by the European Commission,
see *Commission Notice on Immunity from fines and reduction of fines in cartel cases* (2006/
C 298/11) [2006] OJ 298/17, published 8 December 2006 (**Immunity Notice**).
[21] OFT423 (December 2004).   [22] Quick Guide published by the OFT in 2005.
[23] OFT803 (November 2006) (**Interim note**). This note sets out an interim policy being
'road-tested' by the OFT.
[24] OFT442 (December 2004).
[25] OFT423, *OFT's guidance as to the appropriate amount of a penalty* (December 2004) 3–4,
fn 8.

Leniency applies in relation to cartel activities under both EC and national **5.21** competition laws, when these laws are applied by the OFT. However, leniency is not available for Article 82 or Chapter II infringements.[26]

Although the OFT's leniency programme does cover resale price maintenance, **5.22** it is not intended to cover any other vertical arrangements except where the relevant vertical behaviour can be said to be facilitating horizontal collusion.[27]

By way of comparison, the infringements which are covered by the European **5.23** Commission's leniency programme are 'secret cartels . . . between two or more competitors aimed at coordinating their competitive behaviour on the market and/or influencing the relevant parameters of competition through practices such as the fixing or purchase or selling prices or other trading conditions, the allocation of production or sales quotas, the sharing of markets including bid-rigging, restrictions of imports or exports and/or anti-competitive actions against other competitors'.[28] The most notable difference is that the European Commission does not offer any leniency in respect of vertical cartels, even resale price maintenance, because the programme is restricted to cartels 'between competitors'.

(b) What is offered under the OFT's leniency programme

The OFT's leniency programme offers either total immunity from fines, or a **5.24** percentage reduction of fines, depending on various factors. Total immunity from fines is only available to one undertaking in each infringement.

(i) Total immunity ('Type A' immunity)

Total immunity, sometimes called 'Type A' immunity, is automatic if the **5.25** applicant is the first member of a cartel to come forward and provide information, as long as this is done before the OFT has gathered enough evidence on its own account to establish a case, and the OFT has not already started an investigation. The undertaking must also meet certain conditions.

The relevant paragraph of the OFT's Penalties Guidance states: **5.26**

> An undertaking *will* benefit from total immunity from financial penalties if the undertaking is the first to provide the OFT with evidence of cartel activity in a market before the OFT has commenced an investigation of the cartel activity, provided that the OFT does not already have sufficient information to establish

---

[26] To the extent that anti-competitive activity comprises both an infringement of Art 81/Chapter I and Art 82/Chapter II, leniency will only apply in respect of the Art 81/Chapter I infringements, and an undertaking may still be exposed to penalties in respect of Art 82/Chapter II infringements.

[27] Interim note, paras 6.13 and 6.14.   [28] Immunity Notice, para 1.

the existence of the alleged cartel activity, and conditions (a) to (d) below are satisfied.

The undertaking must:

(a) provide the OFT with all the information, documents and evidence available to it regarding the cartel activity

(b) maintain continuous and complete co-operation throughout the investigation and until the conclusion of any action by the OFT arising as a result of the investigation

(c) refrain from further participation in the cartel activity from the time of disclosure of the cartel activity to the OFT (except as may be directed by the OFT), and

(d) not have taken steps to coerce another undertaking to take part in the cartel activity.[29]

5.27 These conditions (relating to provision of information and cooperation etc) are discussed in the following section at paras 5.46–5.52.

5.28 When an undertaking makes a leniency application, it can at the same time apply for individual immunity for all current and former individual employees and directors. This type of immunity relates to the criminal cartel offence, and is discussed at paras 5.81–5.105 below. Where an undertaking is granted total immunity, it will automatically receive guaranteed immunity for all its current and former employees and directors (subject to their cooperation).

5.29 With this promise of total immunity, the OFT's objective is clearly to provide prospective leniency applicants with as much certainty as possible, and to demonstrate the importance attached to bringing cartel infringements to the attention of the OFT.

5.30 By contrast, the European Commission places greater significance on the quality of evidence provided by a leniency applicant. The European Commission's leniency programme thus provides that immunity from fines may be granted if the undertaking is the first to submit evidence which (in the European Commission's view) may enable it to adopt a decision to carry out an investigation in connection with an alleged cartel; or the undertaking is the first to submit evidence which (in the European Commission's view) may enable it to find an infringement of Article 81 in connection with an alleged cartel. In both cases, there is a condition that the European Commission does not already have sufficient evidence to adopt the relevant decision. There are also conditions attached to the granting of immunity by the European Commission, namely: that the undertaking cooperates genuinely, fully, and continually throughout the investigation; that it ends its involvement in the suspected

---

[29] OFT423, *OFT's guidance as to the appropriate amount of a penalty* (December 2004) para 3.9.

cartel; and that it did not take steps to coerce other undertakings to participate in the infringement.[30]

(ii) Reduction of up to 100 per cent ('Type B' immunity)

Where an undertaking applies for leniency *after* the OFT has started an investi- **5.31**
gation, but is the first undertaking to do so, up to 100 per cent reduction is available, on a discretionary basis. If granted at the level of 100 per cent, this is total immunity, sometimes called 'Type B' immunity. The OFT has indicated that it expects the grant of Type B immunity to be the norm rather than the exception.[31] The same four conditions applying to total immunity also attach to this type of reduction, as noted above. In order to exercise its discretion, the OFT must be satisfied 'that the undertaking should benefit from a reduction in the level of the financial penalty taking into account the stage at which the undertaking comes forward, the evidence in the OFT's possession and the evidence provided by the undertaking'.[32]

The provision of evidence in these circumstances needs to be over and above **5.32**
the ordinary level of cooperation required under the OFT's powers of investigation. The undertaking will need to proffer material which adds value, and may be described as 'information which genuinely advances the OFT's investigation'.[33]

The OFT also offers a further advantage in relation to a Type B immunity **5.33**
applicant. The OFT has stated that where an undertaking has been able to perfect a marker for Type B immunity the OFT will grant corporate immunity and will also grant individual immunity to criminal prosecution for all the current and former employees and directors.[34]

(iii) Reduction of up to 50 per cent ('Type C' leniency)

For undertakings not qualifying for total immunity, whether Type A or Type B, **5.34**
a reduction in fines is also available under the OFT's leniency programme. A reduction of up to 50 per cent of the amount of the fine is, in theory, available to all undertakings that have participated in the infringement (sometimes called 'Type C' leniency). A reduction in fines is offered by the OFT where the undertaking is not the first to come forward, but still does so before a statement of objections is issued. This type of reduction is also available to undertakings which coerced others to participate in the cartel. The conditions attaching to

---

[30] Immunity Notice, paras 12 and 13. [31] Interim note, para 2.29.
[32] OFT423, *OFT's guidance as to the appropriate amount of a penalty* (December 2004) paras 3.11 and 3.12.
[33] Interim note, para 2.35.
[34] ibid, para 4.15. In relation to the immunity for individuals, see paras 5.81–5.105 below.

the grant of a reduction are the same as the conditions attaching to total immunity as noted above, except that the final condition relating to coercion does not apply.

5.35 With Type C leniency, there is no guaranteed or automatic 'blanket' immunity against criminal prosecution for individual employees and directors. It is nevertheless possible for an undertaking to seek such immunity on behalf of individuals, or to discuss with the OFT whether there is in fact any criminal exposure for the undertaking's current and former employees and directors at all, and the OFT encourages exploring this option with it (including on a 'no names' basis). The granting of immunity against criminal prosecution will depend on an assessment of the overall value added by the Type C applicant and of whether such a grant would be in the public interest.[35]

(iv) Leniency plus

5.36 In the United Kingdom, lenient treatment once obtained will only apply to the particular case for which the lenient treatment was sought. Thus undertakings wanting to obtain leniency for more than one case will need to apply for leniency separately in respect of each case. This applies even where a second case is uncovered during the course of the investigation of the first case.

5.37 Where a leniency applicant applies for leniency in a second case, the OFT programme allows the applicant to receive a further reduction in the first case. This is known as 'leniency plus'. This further reduction in the first case is available even where the undertaking has not applied for leniency in the first case, but is cooperating with the OFT.[36]

5.38 By contrast, the European Commission's leniency programme does not provide for leniency plus.

(v) Competition Disqualification Orders

5.39 Pursuant to the Company Directors Disqualification Act 1996, the OFT and the Regulators may apply to the court for a Competition Disqualification Order (**CDO**) against a director of a company infringing competition law.[37] The OFT and the Regulators have stated that they will not apply for a CDO against a director of a company which benefits from leniency from either the

---

[35] ibid, paras 4.18–4.20.

[36] OFT423, *OFT's guidance as to the appropriate amount of a penalty* (December 2004) paras 3.16 and 3.17. For an example of leniency plus, see OFT decision CA98/01/2006 (Joined Cases CE/3123–03 and CE/3645–03), 'Collusive tendering for flat roof and car park surfacing contracts in England and Scotland', 22 February 2006, para 859 (where one of the undertakings, Pirie, was granted a reduction of 55% which included an additional reduction for leniency plus).

[37] See paras 1.136–1.141 above for a discussion on CDOs.

OFT, the Regulators, or the European Commission in respect of the relevant infringement. This statement is set out in the OFT's guideline on CDOs, as follows:

> The OFT or Regulator will not apply for a CDO against any current director of a company whose company benefited from leniency in respect of the activities to which the grant of leniency relates. Companies benefiting from leniency will receive confirmation of this policy.
>
> However, where a director has at any time been removed as a director of a company owing to his or her role in the breach of competition law in question and/or for opposing the relevant application for leniency, then the OFT or Regulator may still consider applying for a CDO against that person, irrespective of whether his or her former company has been granted leniency by the OFT or Regulator or European Commission.[38]

A CDO may still be made in respect of any other infringement by the company **5.40** where the company has not applied for leniency. Leniency in this context includes any leniency granted by the European Commission under its leniency programme, but does not include any mitigation of penalties other than through a leniency application.[39]

(vi) Case examples

Recent examples of reductions in fines for leniency include the OFT decisions **5.41** in relation to double glazing, roofing contractors, and stock check pads.

The double glazing cartel case concerned four double glazing industry firms. **5.42** The first undertaking to apply for leniency received a 100 per cent reduction in fines while the second was granted a 40 per cent reduction.[40]

The OFT's roofing contractors decision concerned collusion in setting tender **5.43** prices. The decision involved 13 companies. The first of these to apply for leniency was granted a 100 per cent reduction in fines, and a further six companies were also granted reductions of 55 per cent (this reduction included an uplift for leniency plus), 45 per cent, 40 per cent, 30 per cent, and two received reductions of 25 per cent respectively.[41]

In the OFT's stock check pads cartel decision of April 2006, which involved **5.44** two leniency applicants, the OFT granted full immunity to the first applicant

---

[38] OFT510, *Competition disqualification orders: Guidance* (May 2003) paras 4.12 and 4.13.
[39] ibid, paras 4.11 and 4.12.
[40] OFT decision CA98/04/2006, 'Agreement to fix prices and share the market for aluminium double glazing spacer bars', 28 June 2006.
[41] OFT decision CA98/01/2006 (Joined Cases CE/3123–03 and CE/3645–03), 'Collusive tendering for flat roof and car park surfacing contracts in England and Scotland', 22 February 2006.

and a 50 per cent reduction to the second leniency applicant. The third undertaking subject to the decision did not apply for leniency and accordingly did not receive any reduction for leniency.[42]

5.45 A recent example in the European context is the bleaching chemicals case. The leniency applicants in that case received reductions of 100 per cent, 40 per cent, 30 per cent, and 10 per cent respectively, dependent largely upon the value (and timing) of the information provided to the European Commission. In that case, the various leniency applications were made within a matter of hours and days from each other.[43]

(c) Conditions of leniency

(i) Ceasing participation in the cartel

5.46 The condition concerning ceasing participating in the cartel is a requirement in many leniency programmes. One exception to this requirement is where the OFT directs continued involvement. This may occur when the OFT wishes to use covert surveillance to obtain evidence of the cartel with the assistance of the leniency applicant, which is discussed in Chapter 7 below (see paras 7.186 et seq).

5.47 It can be difficult in practice to ensure that an undertaking ceases its participation in a cartel whilst not 'tipping off' the other participants indirectly, as the other participants may be alerted to a potential problem by the change in behaviour of the leniency applicant. The OFT is generally understanding about the practical difficulties involved and will discuss and agree proposed solutions.

(ii) No coercion

5.48 The requirement not to have coerced another undertaking to take part in the cartel activity only applies in respect of applications for total immunity (Type A or Type B). Thus even if an undertaking meets the test for coercion (as to which, see below), it may still apply for the lesser form of leniency—a reduction in fines of up to 50 per cent.

5.49 The test for coercion involves two elements: first, the coercion must have involved an unwilling cartel participant; and secondly, 'clear, positive and ultimately successful steps from a participant (that is, the coercer) to pressurise an unwilling participant to take part in the cartel'.[44] The OFT has been

---

[42] OFT decision CA98/03/2006, 'Price fixing and market sharing in stock check pads', 31 March 2006.

[43] *Hydrogen Peroxide and Perborate* (Case COMP/F/38.620) Commission Decision, 3 May 2006.

[44] Interim note, para 3.4.

concerned to make it clear that coercion is not likely to be a factor often used by the OFT to reject an application for immunity, and has provided examples of coercion (such as the use of physical violence) to demonstrate that the test for being a coercer will not often be met.[45]

(iii) Obligation to cooperate

The obligations on an undertaking to cooperate with the OFT under a leniency application are identical whether the undertaking obtains total immunity or a significant reduction in the fine. They are absolute and non-negotiable obligations. An undertaking cannot 'trade off' the amount of information it is willing to provide in exchange for an increased percentage in the reduction.[46]   **5.50**

The duties of complete and continuous cooperation are onerous and extend to providing the OFT with witness statements, feedback on oral and written submissions made by other parties during the course of the investigation, and even appearing as a witness for the OFT in any subsequent appeal proceedings. In certain cases, these obligations may disrupt the undertaking's commercial relationships with its suppliers, competitors, or customers. Failure to comply with the cooperation obligations at any stage jeopardises the leniency award regardless of commercial considerations or fear of reprisals. The OFT has a 'margin of appreciation' in deciding whether an undertaking has complied with the obligation of cooperation.[47] Undertakings should also be aware of the possible ramifications in any later private litigation (see paras 5.77–5.80).   **5.51**

It is an offence for a person (including an undertaking) to provide false or misleading information to the OFT in connection with a competition law infringement investigation.[48]   **5.52**

(d) Confidentiality

An undertaking applying for leniency will naturally be concerned that its role is not disclosed to its competitors, suppliers, or the public at large, for fear of commercial repercussions (including in relation to potential damages actions), adverse publicity, and diminished share value. Confidentiality is usually an important consideration for an undertaking, in relation to both the fact that a leniency application has been made and the content of the application.   **5.53**

As a general matter, there are certain confidentiality obligations which apply to   **5.54**

---

[45] ibid, paras 3.1–3.10.

[46] *Umbro Holdings Ltd v OFT* [2005] CAT 22 (where Umbro was refused leniency as it tried to gauge the amount of information given: instead it had to cooperate outside the leniency regime).

[47] ibid, para 327; and *Argos Ltd and Littlewoods Ltd v OFT* [2005] CAT 13, paras 107 and 128.

[48] Competition Act 1998, s 44. See Chapter 7 for further information on the offences connection with OFT investigations (paras 7.73–7.75).

the OFT in the exercise of its functions. In particular, as a public authority, the OFT is bound by the disclosure rules set out in the Enterprise Act 2002, which provides that disclosure of specified information may not be made except in accordance with the specific 'gateways' provided for in the Enterprise Act. The gateways are, in essence: disclosure with the consent of the parties; disclosure in accordance with a Community obligation; disclosure pursuant to a statutory function; and disclosure in connection with criminal proceedings.[49]

5.55 In addition to the general obligations restricting disclosure, the OFT may set its own policies on disclosure, within certain boundaries. Confidentiality in the context of a leniency application is important not only to the undertaking but also to the OFT. The effectiveness of the OFT's leniency programme would be undermined if applicants were unable to rely upon confidentiality being maintained by the OFT. There are also incentives for the OFT to maintain confidentiality at the early stages of a leniency application, as the element of surprise is essential to the effectiveness of any inspection of pre-mises (dawn raid) the OFT plans to conduct.[50] Finally, the information provided by the leniency applicant is often used to assess the veracity and reliability of the submissions made by other parties, and disclosure of such information may jeopardise the OFT's investigation. For these reasons, leniency is an area where the OFT has a real interest in limiting the scope for disclosure of information.

5.56 The OFT's policy on disclosure in the context of a leniency application is set out in its published guidance as follows:

> An undertaking coming forward with evidence of cartel activity may be concerned about the disclosure of its identity as an undertaking which has volunteered infor-mation. The OFT will therefore endeavour, to the extent that it is consistent with its statutory obligations to disclose information, and allowing for the exchange of information as required within the ECN, to keep the identity of such undertakings confidential throughout the course of its investigation until the issue of a statement of objections.[51]

5.57 Statutory obligations on the OFT to disclose information may include, for example, the provision of information pursuant to a Freedom of Information Act application. This will depend on the circumstances of each case: if provision of the information is restricted under Pt 9 of the Enterprise Act 2002, that

---

[49] Information on the Enterprise Act 2002 and these gateways is set out in detail in Chapter 8. The CAT is not bound by these Enterprise Act gateways, but is bound by the restrictions in paras 1(2) and (3) of Sch 4 to the Enterprise Act.

[50] See Chapter 7.

[51] OFT423, *OFT's guidance as to the appropriate amount of a penalty* (December 2004) para 3.18.

restriction takes precedence over the disclosure approach of the Freedom of Information Act 2000.[52]

The possibility of disclosure of documents such as witness statements creates **5.58** additional problems for leniency applicants, as the fact of the leniency application itself could give rise to exposure to damages claims. This is particularly serious in US civil damages cases, where an undertaking is exposed to the possibility of treble damages. This puts undertakings which voluntarily cooperate by revealing cartels in a significantly worse position in respect of civil claims than other cartel members which refuse to cooperate. The European Commission has recently proposed amendments to its leniency programme with the aim of minimising the risk of discovery of corporate leniency applications. These amendments formalise the European Commission's existing arrangements for accepting oral leniency applications. An oral application is effectively a statement recorded on tape but never recorded in documentary form.[53] The OFT also accepts oral applications.

The OFT also has certain obligations in relation to the European Competition **5.59** Network (**ECN**), and there are special rules which apply to restrict the exchange of information provided by leniency applicants in this context. This is discussed in the final section of this chapter. As a matter of policy, the OFT has stated:

> Information supplied by an undertaking as part of an application for Type A or B immunity, corporate immunity or Type B or C leniency will also never be passed to an overseas agency without the consent of the provider save, again, for one exception. Such information may be disclosed to the Commission and/or another EU national competition authority but only in accordance with the provisions and safeguards set out in paragraphs 40 and 41 of the Network Notice. Again, and for the reasons set out above where the OFT was considering such a disclosure to the Commission or to another EU national competition authority, the OFT would always consult the provider.[54]

A leniency applicant's information is not provided solely for the purpose of the **5.60** specific case to which it relates. Subject to the OFT's policy to keep the identity of a leniency applicant confidential throughout the course of the investigation, and any specific promises given to a particular undertaking, the OFT is able to use a leniency applicant's information for other purposes such as Article 82/ Chapter II investigations, market investigations, and sectoral regulation. Such use is also subject to the more general rules applying to the OFT in relation to

---

[52] Decision of the Information Commissioner in relation to the OFT, 25 July 2006, FS50090136, paras 5.5–5.7.
[53] Information on the procedure for oral applications is set out at para 5.73 below.
[54] Interim note, para 5.9.

the treatment of information which is confidential in the sense of business or personal confidentiality.[55]

5.61 Although the OFT will endeavour to keep the fact of the leniency application secret and will not attribute the source of any documents that it has to disclose as part of the access to the file, there is a risk that other parties may become suspicious of the extent to which a particular member of the cartel is cooperating with the OFT.[56] Leniency applicants should therefore ensure that mechanisms are put in place to protect the timing and context of their submissions and that they are seen to participate during the rest of the investigation in the same way as other undertakings under investigation. Leniency applicants can attend private confidential hearings separate from the other parties if necessary.[57]

5.62 The OFT is required to provide a statement of objections to 'each person who the OFT considers is a party to the agreement, or is engaged in conduct, which the OFT considers infringes one or more of the prohibitions'.[58] Where a statement of objections contains matters which will affect a third party, the OFT may provide a redacted version of a statement of objections to a third party.[59] The OFT will redact details of the leniency applicant in the statement of objections, but successful leniency applications will be revealed when the OFT issues a final decision at the end of the investigative process.

5.63 Leniency applicants should also be aware that there is no guarantee that the fact and contents of their application will be kept secret for posterity, even where the application is unsuccessful. In the *Replica Kit* proceedings, in the course of the subsequent appeal, the Competition Appeal Tribunal (**CAT**) held that the CAT is not bound by the gateways in Pt 9 of the Enterprise Act 2002 and that the appellants' rights of defence will prevail over other parties' competing rights to confidentiality.[60] Disclosure of reductions will be necessary for any appeal on the level of the fine (particularly if it raises an allegation of unfair treatment).

---

[55] The OFT's treatment of this type of confidential information is discussed in Chapter 8.

[56] The index of the documents on the OFT's file tends to be chronological so it can be easy to work out if a document is submitted 'out of synch' and at an earlier stage than the responses to the s 26 notices. The provision of witness statements before the statement of objections is another indicator. Applicants should ensure that any correspondence revealing the date and leniency negotiations is kept confidential and is itemised in a neutral manner on the list. For a discussion of confidentiality in the course of an entire investigation, see Chapter 8.

[57] See Chapter 9 for details on procedure.   [58] OFT's Procedural Rules, r 4(2).

[59] This was done, for example, in *MasterCard UK Members Forum Ltd* (OFT decision No CA98/05/05, 6 September 2005, Case CP/0090/00/S), where the OFT provided a redacted version of the statement of objections to Visa, whose arrangements were similar to those condemned by the OFT (see paras 59, 64, and 68).

[60] *Umbro Holdings Ltd v OFT* [2003] CAT 26, paras 43–45 (judgment concerning Umbro's unsuccessful application to protect the fact that it had applied for leniency and prevent the disclosure of its leniency submissions to the other appellants).

Although the CAT will take account of confidentiality claims as part of its assessment under Sch 4 to the Enterprise Act, it restricts confidentiality to business secrets of less than two years old. The majority of information supplied for leniency purposes will fall outside this narrow definition.[61] Leniency applicants should therefore be aware that they may be required to participate in protracted appeals (even if they do not appeal themselves) and, as part of their ongoing cooperation obligation, may be asked to provide even more extensive business information than they had envisaged at the administrative stage.

(i) Withdrawal or rejection of a leniency application

An undertaking may withdraw its application for leniency at any time. Such **5.64** withdrawal will not stop the OFT's investigation, nor will it mean the undertaking is able to take back the information it has provided to the OFT.

In event of the rejection or withdrawal of a leniency application, the OFT will **5.65** retain the information provided by the undertaking. Any use of the information by the OFT could have significant implications for the applicant's rights of defence and freedom from self-incrimination, so it is unlikely that the OFT would seek to make any use of such material. The CAT has commented on this issue in the final judgment on penalty in *Umbro Holdings Ltd v OFT*:

> We also find that the OFT indicated to Umbro that if its application for leniency did not proceed, the OFT would not use the information supplied by Umbro for the purposes of its investigation: see e.g. the OFT's letters of 9 January, 12 and 28 February 2002. Indeed, it would, it seems to us, be highly invidious if an undertaking were to give the OFT information in the hope of obtaining leniency, but then found that the OFT declined to enter into a leniency agreement, but proposed to use the information anyway to the detriment of the undertaking providing it. Any such approach would not encourage undertakings to come forward. Moreover, leniency applications will usually need to be protected, at least initially, by confidentiality. If the leniency application is not proceeded with, it is reasonable for the undertaking concerned to expect that confidentiality would continue to be respected by the OFT, as far as possible, and subject to any overriding requirements that may later arise in proceedings before the Tribunal: see e.g. *Umbro v. OFT (request for confidential treatment)* [2003] CAT 26 at paragraph 34 and *Argos & Littlewoods v. OFT (disclosure)* [2004] CAT 5.[62]

In Umbro's case, the OFT put the leniency materials (including its internal **5.66**

---

[61] This interpretation may well have a negative impact on the OFT's aims with respect to the effectiveness of its leniency programme. This possibility was noted and dismissed by the CAT in *Umbro Holdings Ltd v OFT* [2003] CAT 26, para 43, where the CAT commented: 'We are not persuaded that, in this particular case, there would be any lasting harm to the leniency system. Persons who genuinely seek leniency are still able to come forward and, if successful, will profit thereby. Those who come forward on some failed basis simply have to run the risk that that fact may be identified in due course in the event of appellate proceedings before the Tribunal.'

[62] *Umbro Holdings Ltd v OFT* [2005] CAT 22, para 315.

notes of leniency meetings) to one side and did not use them in the course of the rest of the investigation. The case officers were completely unaware of their existence until they came to light in the subsequent appeal. At that point the OFT raised concerns about the effectiveness of its leniency programme should the CAT order disclosure of the failed leniency application in the appeal proceedings. However, following the CAT's judgment on this issue in *Umbro Holdings Ltd v OFT*, it is clear that both the fact of a rejected leniency application and the material provided by the unsuccessful applicant may be required to be disclosed in subsequent appeals in accordance with the same principles noted above.[63]

(e) Procedure

(i) A place in the queue

5.67 The first contact by a prospective leniency applicant is generally made by a telephone call to the Director or Deputy Director of Cartel Investigations, on 020 7211 8117. This personal point of contact is part of the 'marker' system which allows certainty for undertakings as to their place in the queue from the outset.[64] There are no restrictions on the time frame for prospective applicants to apply for leniency: this telephone call can even be made while a dawn raid is still being carried out by the OFT.[65] This will not stop the dawn raid from taking place.

5.68 If an undertaking simply wishes to ascertain whether it is first in the queue, this call can be made anonymously (usually by a lawyer on behalf of an undisclosed client). The only information needed is the market in question, and the OFT will advise during the call whether or not there is already a queue in place in relation to the particular cartel. The OFT will consider itself bound by the views it gives during this call[66] and it will not use the information supplied during the call provided there is no evidence of bad faith.[67] This type of telephone call does not entitle the undisclosed applicant to a place in the queue, but the OFT will expect that if immunity is still available, the undertaking's legal adviser will have instructions to apply for immunity then and there.[68]

5.69 The telephone call to make a leniency application must be made by a person

---

[63] *Umbro Holdings Ltd v OFT* [2003] CAT 26.

[64] Similarly, each sectoral regulator has an equivalent contact person to receive telephone calls for leniency applications. There is no need to decide which is the 'right' contact point, as the OFT and the Regulators have co-extensive powers.

[65] However, where an application is made during a dawn raid, the OFT has stated that it may have to mark the place in the queue on a provisional basis for a short time (Interim note, para 2.31).

[66] ibid, para 2.2.   [67] ibid, paras 2.23–2.26.   [68] ibid, paras 2.5 and 2.8.

authorised to represent the prospective leniency applicant. The information which will need to be provided during the call in order to secure a place in the queue is the applicant's name, the representative's name, and the market involved. The applicant should be able to identify a concrete basis for its suspicion of having participated in a cartel, and should be prepared to specify the nature of the evidence it has uncovered so far. The OFT will record the date and time of the call, and will advise whether or not the applicant is first in the queue. The applicant's place in the queue will be held from the date and time of this telephone call. The OFT will agree to a short amount of time for the applicant to provide details of its application (perhaps one or two days), although most applicants have already gathered some information which can be provided immediately after the call. The OFT may also make arrangements for the applicant to meet with the OFT for an interview and to bring forward information.

By contrast, the European Commission recommends that the first contact from **5.70** a leniency applicant should be by fax, whereby the time and date of receipt are accurately recorded. The dedicated fax number provided is +32 2 299 45 85.[69] The European Commission previously operated an evidence-based system, but has now introduced a discretionary marker system.[70] In order to be eligible to secure a marker, the applicant must provide key information about the alleged cartel, such as the parties to the alleged cartel and the relevant product and territory.[71] Where a marker is granted, the applicant must then perfect its marker by making a formal (but not hypothetical) application within a time frame set by the Commission.[72] If it becomes apparent that immunity is not available, the European Commission has stated that it will inform the undertaking in writing.[73] In order to make a formal application, the undertaking must provide all evidence available to it or present the evidence in hypothetical terms (by producing a descriptive list of evidence). If requested, the Directorate General for Competition will provide an acknowledgement of receipt confirming the date and time of the application. The European Commission has stated that it will not consider any other application for immunity until it has taken a position in relation to an existing application, irrespective of whether the immunity application is presented formally or by requesting a marker.[74] On verification of the evidence and consideration of the requirements for immunity,

---

[69] See press release, 'DG Competition Reorganisation—Information related to anti trust activity—The fight against cartels and applications for immunity from fines and reduction of fines in cartel cases': <http://www.europa.eu.int/comm/competition/antitrust/legislation/cartel_leniency.pdf>.

[70] Immunity Notice, para 15. The European Commission also offers an alternative process which allows for anonymous applications (ie a hypothetical application).

[71] ibid, para 15.   [72] ibid, para 15.   [73] ibid, para 20.   [74] ibid, para 21.

if the application is successful, the applicant will be provided with immunity
from fines (subject to conditions).

(ii) Providing evidence

5.71 Once the first contact has been made, the leniency process moves to the next
stage: information gathering. This process is extremely 'lawyer intensive' and
subject to tight deadlines.

5.72 The most comprehensive method for gathering the information required is for
the company to conduct its own internal investigation by interviewing its staff
about the extent of their knowledge of the cartel, the key events surrounding the
formation of the cartel and their participation in the cartel. The company (or its
lawyers) will need to gather and review all key contemporaneous documents
(such as minutes, correspondence, emails, diaries) and question executives on
their relevance and contents. The best way of presenting information to the
OFT, if sufficient time is available, is by way of a comprehensive report, written
by external lawyers, with annexed documents and sworn witness statements.

5.73 If an undertaking has a particular concern about providing statement evidence,
perhaps due to the risk of exposure to treble damages in US civil damages
claims, there is the option of providing oral evidence.[75] The OFT will accept
oral leniency applications, but still requires undertakings to make witnesses
available as appropriate to be interviewed and sign statements.[76] The European
Commission's procedure for oral evidence is set out in the European Commission's Immunity Notice,[77] which procedure was created in order to minimise
the risk of discovery of corporate statements in procedures that are not in
application of the European competition rules.[78] The OFT does not have a
similar procedural note on such applications. This issue is evolving as it essentially concerns the application of US discovery rules by US courts to documents
held by foreign tribunals.[79] It is by no means certain that the oral process will
provide the protection from discovery the undertaking might desire in each

---

[75] Note this procedure does not circumvent third parties' rights: the tape still needs to be
accessible for third parties who have a right to access the information, such as complainants.
Under the European Commission's procedures for oral evidence, such third parties may listen to
the tape and make notes, as long as this documentary record is not left with the European
Commission.

[76] Interim note, para 2.17.   [77] Immunity Notice, paras 31–35.

[78] See the draft amendment to the 2002 notice produced by the European Commission, at
<http://europa.eu.int/comm/competition/antitrust/legislation/leniency.html>.

[79] This appears to be based on the argument that the foreign tribunal will not be requested to
produce any documents comprising its own internal records and that a tape recording would fall
within that class of documents. There is also some recognition of the possibility of a discovery
request damaging the foreign tribunal's leniency programme: see *Intel Corp v Advanced Micro
Devices, Inc* 542 US 241, 124 S Ct 2466 (2004).

particular case. Nevertheless, it is clear that the European Commission and the OFT are not only aware of this issue, but are prepared to seek actively to assist undertakings in resolving the issue.

The information provided by the applicant will help to focus the leniency **5.74** meetings and can be supplemented by making senior personnel available for interviews with the OFT. The OFT will then make a decision as to whether to proceed to investigate the case. If the OFT decides to do so, and if the applicant has satisfied the OFT that it qualifies for lenient treatment, then a letter will be provided to the applicant setting out the terms of the agreement with the OFT for lenient treatment. The letter will set out extensive duties of cooperation and, subject to any request to participate in covert surveillance, will require the applicant to terminate the infringement immediately. This letter will be effective immediately although, as a matter of formality, the applicant will be required to sign and return a copy. Provided the undertaking breaches none of the conditions during the course of the investigation, the letter is the undertaking's guarantee of lenient treatment in relation to the imposition of fines. The amount of the actual reduction in fine will not be decided until the fine is decided and set out in the OFT's final decision.

(iii) Rejection of a leniency application

The most likely grounds for the OFT refusing a leniency application will be **5.75** that the applicant has not satisfied the necessary conditions, or has breached any of the conditions set out in the leniency letter. An obvious example is where the application is made out of time.[80] Another ground may be linked to the applicant's conduct during the leniency process. Tipping off other members in the cartel or giving misleading evidence would terminate any offer of leniency. In *Umbro Holdings Ltd v OFT*, the OFT rejected Umbro's application as it was 'holding back' information for fear of commercial repercussions and the OFT did not believe that its witnesses were being fully cooperative. The application was also hampered by the fact, as found by the CAT in the subsequent appeal, that the witness statements submitted as part of the leniency application were incomplete, hastily prepared without the necessary attention to detail, inconsistent, and unreliable in important respects.[81]

There is nothing to stop an unsuccessful applicant re-submitting the leniency **5.76**

---

[80] See, eg, the position of Sports Soccer in *Replica Kit*, who as the whistleblower in the replica football kit cartel, provided extensive information on a voluntary basis to the OFT without making a formal application for leniency until after the OFT had started its investigation. Undertakings must ensure that they complete all the formal requirements as soon as possible.

[81] *Umbro Holdings Ltd v OFT* [2005] CAT 22 (judgment on penalty), paras 323–325 (and see also the paragraphs of the judgment on liability referred to therein).

materials as part of its response to the subsequent Statement of Objections and asking the OFT to take them into account by way of general cooperation as a mitigating factor for the level of the fine. In *Umbro Holdings Ltd v OFT*, Umbro re-submitted much of its earlier leniency material as part of its response to the OFT's Rule 14 Notice (Statement of Objections), and for that cooperation Umbro received a reduction of 40 per cent. On appeal, the CAT commented that this reduction was 'already generous' and declined to make a further reduction despite Umbro's request that its earlier submission of leniency materials should be taken into account as well. In making this decision, the CAT noted that the earlier leniency materials submitted by Umbro were incomplete and were not used in the OFT's investigation.[82]

(f) Effect on private litigation

5.77 The OFT's leniency programme does not protect an applicant from private litigation. The provision of total immunity or a reduction in fines only affects the imposition of fines and does not have any effect on the voidability of agreement, or the undertaking's liability for damages in private actions.

5.78 The lenient treatment provided by the OFT will not absolve the applicant from any finding of its involvement in the infringement, as the lenient treatment only attaches to the imposition of penalties. Thus where an infringement decision is made by the OFT, the applicant undertaking will be the subject of a formal administrative finding that it has breached competition law provisions. Although it is possible in theory, it is difficult to appeal against the OFT's decision in relation to liability where a leniency application has been successful (although there is always the possibility of appealing against the penalty decision).

5.79 Once an administrative finding of infringement is made, it is generally easier for third parties to bring private damages claims, as the competition authority has already established the relevant facts. In the United Kingdom, ss 47A(9) and 58A of the Competition Act 1998 provide that the courts are bound by any findings of infringement by the Commission or the OFT when determining monetary claims.[83] This saves the claimant having to 're-invent the wheel' in establishing liability under Article 81 or the Chapter I prohibition.[84] Although the claimant will not be able to use directly in civil proceedings the materials it has obtained as part of any access to the file arrangements during the investigation,[85] its

---

[82] ibid, paras 329–333.   [83] See Chapter 12 for more information on this topic.
[84] This is an example of the general move towards increasing private litigation in competition law, which remains a priority for the European Commission.
[85] Case C-60/92 *Otto BV v Postbank NV* [1993] ECR I-5683.

prospects for disclosure will have been considerably improved. Accordingly, the authorities' findings may dramatically increase the chances of third parties bringing successful private damages claims in the courts.

This places a leniency applicant in a delicate position, as the duties of complete **5.80** cooperation under the leniency regime are likely to involve the undertaking providing the very evidence that will determine its liability and, perhaps, quantum in subsequent damages proceedings.[86] This is a serious factor to take into account in deciding whether or not to seek leniency.

C. Leniency in the UK Criminal Context

(a) Immunity from criminal prosecution in the United Kingdom

(i) No-action letters

The Enterprise Act 2002 introduced criminal sanctions for individuals dis- **5.81** honestly engaging in 'hardcore' cartel agreements, such as agreements to fix prices, limit supply or production, share markets, or rig bids.[87] The cartel offence applies in relation to Article 81 infringements as well as infringements of the Chapter I prohibition. The cartel offence may be prosecuted by the OFT, the Serious Fraud Office (**SFO**), or in certain circumstances, an individual.

Lenient treatment granted to an *undertaking* as part of an investigation under **5.82** Article 81 or the Chapter I prohibition does not protect the *individuals* involved from the possibility of a cartel offence finding. However, individuals can apply to the OFT for a 'no-action letter', which provides full immunity from prosecution for the cartel offence (whether by the OFT, the SFO, or an individual) in England, Wales and Northern Ireland. In Scotland, a guarantee of immunity cannot be given because the cartel offence is prosecuted by the Lord Advocate who has the final say in whether to bring a prosecution, but an individual who cooperates with the prosecuting authority can nevertheless expect to receive lenient treatment.[88]

Situations of conflict may arise between a company and its employees and **5.83** directors, for example where the best interests of an individual might be served by obtaining a no-action letter but the company being investigated does not wish to apply for leniency (or vice versa). It therefore may be appropriate for individuals facing possible prosecution to be separately represented, and to consider obtaining from the company (if appropriate) an agreement to fund the

---

[86] Where the undertaking has been involved in an investigation by the European Commission, this could potentially have ramifications in any of the European Member States.
[87] See paras 1.126–1.135 above. [88] OFT513 (April 2003) para 3.2.

individual's legal fees, a guarantee against dismissal, and making garden leave arrangements until the matter is resolved.[89]

5.84 Sources of information about the offer of no-action letters are:

- *OFT's guidance as to the appropriate amount of a penalty;*[90]
- *The cartel offence: Guidance on the issue of no-action letters for individuals;*[91]
- *Leniency and no-action—OFT's draft final guidance note on the handling of applications.*[92]

(ii) The effect of a no-action letter

5.85 As noted above, a no-action letter provides full immunity from prosecution for the cartel offence (whether by the OFT, the SFO, or an individual) in England, Wales and Northern Ireland. A no-action letter is effective immediately, and continues to be effective unless its terms are breached.[93]

5.86 The OFT will not seek CDOs against individuals who benefit from a no-action letter.[94]

5.87 It is envisaged from the form of the OFT's sample no-action letter that the immunity will only apply in relation to one single offence, but it is quite possible that the letter could encompass more than one offence (for example, where an undertaking has been participating in more than one cartel arrangement). However, if another case comes to light during the investigation, after the no-action letter has been issued, an individual may need to seek an additional letter in relation to the second cartel agreement.

5.88 The Director of the SFO has confirmed that as a matter of policy the SFO would not attempt to prosecute a recipient of a no-action letter for the 'alternative' offence of conspiracy to defraud.[95]

(b) Conditions

(i) Overview

5.89 To obtain immunity from prosecution by way of a no-action letter, an individual must provide the OFT with all information available to them regarding the existence and activities of the cartel, and must maintain continuous and complete cooperation throughout the investigation and until the conclusion of

---

[89] Such arrangements may well be subject to the individual's compliance with the conditions of a no-action letter and/or assisting with the company's own obligations.

[90] OFT423 (December 2004).   [91] OFT513 (April 2003).

[92] OFT803 (November 2006).   [93] OFT513 (April 2003) Annex, para 9.

[94] OFT510, *Competition disqualification orders: Guidance* (May 2003) para 4.27.

[95] Interim note, para 5.12.

any criminal proceedings arising as a result of the investigation.[96] The individual must not have taken steps to coerce another undertaking to take part in the cartel and must refrain from further participation in the cartel from the time of its disclosure to the OFT (except as may be directed by the investigating authority).[97] The OFT must also consider that it does not have sufficient evidence already for the successful prosecution of the individual(s) concerned. An individual applicant is also likely to be required to admit participation in the criminal offence in certain circumstances.

5.90 These conditions are essentially the same as the conditions for civil leniency noted above, with the additional likely requirement to admit participation in the cartel offence.

(ii) Requirement to admit participation in the offence

5.91 The OFT's published no-action guideline states that all individuals applying for a no-action letter are required to admit their participation in the cartel offence. This published position has been altered slightly as a result of the OFT's Interim Note. Under the Interim Note, the OFT's policy is that in exceptional cases individuals may not be required to admit dishonesty, but the OFT has given no indication of the types of circumstances that might be viewed as exceptional.[98] Where admission is required, it will need to be a full admission, including admission as to dishonesty. As a result of the OFT's policy (as at November 2006), in practice most individuals applying for no-action letters will be required to admit their participation in the cartel offence. It is, however, possible that this policy may alter again with the publication of the final session of the Interim note.

(iii) Cooperation

5.92 The same principles apply for cooperation in the criminal context as for civil leniency. These principles are set out above at paras 5.50–5.52.

5.93 In addition, it is worth noting that where a global immunity is provided for all current and former employees and directors of an undertaking, the obligation to cooperate is a separate obligation for each individual covered by the guarantee. A failure of one individual to cooperate will not affect the immunity of another

---

[96] OFT513 (April 2003) para 3.3.

[97] eg, the individual may be asked to act as a covert human intelligence source.

[98] Interim note, paras 4.2–4.4. Note that in a previous version of the Interim Note, the OFT indicated that it would not require an admission of dishonesty unless the person is 'clearly a principal offender in a dishonest cartel arrangement and whose evidence is likely to be needed to support a prosecution case against other principals'. However, this was not included in the final draft published in November 2006, where the OFT indicated that it would be sufficient in less serious cases for the OFT to issue a comfort letter rather than a no-action letter (see para 4.3).

individual. Thus individuals can provide information under the guarantee that they will get individual immunity provided they cooperate. In this situation, undertakings are expected by the OFT to use their best endeavours to secure the cooperation of individuals.[99]

(iv) Coercion

5.94 The test of coercion in relation to obtaining a no-action letter is the same test as for obtaining civil immunity. This is set out at para 5.49 above in relation to civil leniency, and, in effect, involves a test which is unlikely to be fulfilled in anything other than extreme circumstances.

5.95 The OFT has also clarified the operation of the coercion test in the context of individual coercion, as follows:

> . . . the question is whether another *undertaking* has been coerced, not specifically whether one individual has coerced another or others within the undertaking. Therefore, if the undertaking is not deemed a coercer, no employee or director within it will be refused individual immunity on the coercer ground, save in any exceptional circumstances where somehow an employee enjoyed a position of power independent of their position within the undertaking and used it to coerce another undertaking.
>
> If an undertaking *is* found to be a coercer, individuals within the undertaking who did not themselves play a coercing role will not be denied individual immunity on coercer grounds.[100]

(c) Procedure

5.96 An application for a no-action letter is made by contacting the OFT's Director of Cartel Investigations. This may be done in conjunction with an undertaking's application for leniency from the OFT/Regulator or from the European Commission. When an undertaking submits an immunity application, it can at the same time apply for automatic individual immunity for all of its current and former individual employees and directors.[101] Thus the approach to the OFT may be made by the individual or by the undertaking (on behalf of all current and former employees and directors), or by a legal representative of either.

5.97 As with civil leniency applications, the first approach to the OFT may be made on an anonymous basis if necessary. Where an application is made by an undertaking on behalf of all current and former employees and directors, there is no need to provide a list of names of the individuals. If the civil immunity application is accepted, and the individuals' immunity is guaranteed, the OFT anticipates that the identity of the relevant individuals will become apparent as the

---

[99] ibid, para 4.31.   [100] ibid, paras 4.6 and 4.7 (original emphasis).
[101] ibid, para 2.17.

investigation progresses, and no-action letters will be issued to those individuals who need them (provided they cooperate).[102]

The OFT will make a preliminary decision as to whether it is prepared to issue a **5.98** no-action letter.

(d) Confidentiality and use of information provided

Interviews will be conducted under the protections set out in the no-action **5.99** guideline:

> Any information they provide in such interviews will not be used against them in criminal proceedings except in the following circumstances:
> - where a no-action letter is not issued, if the individual applying for immunity from prosecution has knowingly or recklessly provided information that is false or misleading in a material particular, or
> - where a no-action letter is issued, if it is subsequently revoked . . .[103]

Thus the OFT has provided comfort for individuals that the information **5.100** provided in initial interviews will not be used against the individual concerned (even if a no-action letter is *not* issued) unless the individual has knowingly or recklessly provided false or misleading information, or (where a letter is issued) if the letter is subsequently revoked.

These principles will also be applied by the OFT in respect of information **5.101** provided in documentary form.

In some cases an individual immunity applicant may act as a secret source of **5.102** information about the cartel. In such circumstances, which are likely to be rare, if the individual's safety would be in serious jeopardy if his or her approach to the OFT were to become known, the OFT would not disclose the identity of the individual immunity applicant.[104]

In relation to the provision of information to other authorities, the OFT has **5.103** stated its policy as follows:

> If we want to pass information deriving from an immunity applicant to another UK agency such as the SFO, we will always discuss this with the applicant or his/her legal adviser first.
> Information supplied as part of an application for individual immunity will never

---

[102] ibid, paras 4.11–4.14. Note this policy differs from the official statements as to the OFT's position in OFT513, *The cartel offence: Guidance on the issue of no-action letters for individuals* (April 2003).

[103] OFT513, *The cartel offence: Guidance on the issue of no-action letters for individuals* (April 2003) para 3.7.

[104] Interim note, para 5.4.

be passed to an overseas agency without the consent of the provider save for one exception. The OFT may wish to provide the information to the European Commission to pursue administrative proceedings against two or more undertakings under Article 81 EC Treaty. The European Commission would be required to guarantee to the OFT that the information would not be provided to any other agency. Also, where such a disclosure to the European Commission was considered by the OFT, the OFT would always consult the provider. The OFT recognises that to do otherwise would be seriously detrimental to its leniency policy.[105]

(e) Revocation of a no-action letter

5.104 Revocation of a no-action letter may occur where the recipient of the letter does not satisfy all of the conditions listed in the letter, or the recipient knowingly or recklessly provides false or misleading information. Before any revocation is made, the OFT has stated that the recipient will be notified in writing and will be given an opportunity to make representations.[106] The procedure and timing for a revocation is not clear from the OFT's guideline.

(f) Exposure to criminal offences in other jurisdictions

5.105 Other jurisdictions also operate criminal regimes in respect of an individual's participation in a cartel, some with the power to impose criminal custodial sentences on individuals.[107] Although the ECN members (including the OFT and the Regulators) may exchange information with each other, there are specific restrictions relating to the use of information supplied by a leniency applicant for the purpose of criminal proceedings. Importantly, information obtained from a leniency applicant in one Member State cannot be used to prosecute a criminal offence in another Member State.[108] This is discussed further below in the context of leniency and cross-border cartels.

D. Leniency and Cross-border Cartels

5.106 As leniency programmes are operated by competition authorities as part of their procedural armoury, and do not form part of substantive competition law, there is no requirement for any form of cross-operation of leniency programmes. This applies both within and outside the European Community. There is no mutual

---

[105] ibid, paras 5.7 and 5.8.   [106] OFT513 (April 2003) para 3.13.
[107] Austria, Estonia, France, Germany, Hungary, Ireland, Norway, Slovenia, and the UK.
[108] Council Regulation (EC) 1/2003 of 16 December 2002 on the implementation of the rules on competition laid down in Articles 82 and 82 of the Treaty [2003] OJ L1/1, Art 12.

recognition, harmonisation, or 'one stop shop' across jurisdictions.[109] Globally, there are many countries where the competition enforcement bodies operate leniency programmes with the intended result of assisting the detection and deterrence of cartel activity. These include Austria, Australia, Belgium, Brazil, Canada, Cyprus, Czech Republic, Finland, France, Germany, Hungary, Ireland, Israel, Japan, Korea, Latvia, Lithuania, Luxembourg, the Netherlands, New Zealand, Poland, Portugal, Romania, Slovakia, South Africa, Sweden, the United Kingdom, and the United States.[110] The European Commission and the European Free Trade Association also operate leniency programmes.

In Europe, despite the increased cooperation between the national competi- **5.107**
tion authorities introduced by Regulation 1/2003, there was no attempt to harmonise leniency programmes as part of the modernisation changes. Thus the situation with respect to leniency programmes remains unchanged: there is no mutual recognition of the competition authorities' leniency programmes, no harmonisation between the various programmes which exist and, indeed, no requirement for a competition authority even to have a leniency programme. The European Commission's Leniency Notice does not apply to any other competition authority, even where the other authority is conducting an investigation in the same case and is applying Article 81 in a case. More recently, however, some steps have been taken by the ECN to move towards a unified leniency programme, and to this end the ECN has published a model leniency programme which may be used by national competition authorities in developing national programmes.[111]

(a) Leniency applications in more than one jurisdiction

(i) Making simultaneous applications

There is nothing preventing a leniency applicant from applying for leniency in **5.108**
more than one jurisdiction apart from the significant work involved in making multiple applications. This is often encouraged by authorities, for the very reason that there is no mutual recognition of leniency programmes. It is therefore recommended by many authorities that leniency applicants apply for leniency in as many jurisdictions as they believe the cartel activity covers, in all

---

[109] Harmonisation or even mutual recognition may be on the agenda as a future change in competition law enforcement, particularly within the European Member States. There appears to be growing support for such a change.

[110] International Competition Network, *Anti-Cartel Enforcement Manual* (April 2006) Ch 2, Appendix 2. In addition, a list of the competition authorities within the European Community which operate a leniency programme is published at <http://europa.eu.int/comm/competition/antitrust/legislation/authorities_with_leniency_programme.pdf>.

[111] This is available from the ECN website at <http://ec.europa.eu/comm/competition/ecn/index_en.html>. See also para 5.110 below.

jurisdictions where it is possible to do so. In theory, such applications ought to be made simultaneously, or as close together in time as possible, to avoid a situation where another applicant could become first in the queue. In practice, the amount of work involved in making a leniency application means that an undertaking is more likely to prioritise applications to focus only on those jurisdictions where a leniency application is likely to yield a real benefit.

5.109 Given the work involved in making multiple applications, it will be important to assess which of the leniency programmes should take priority for an applicant. Each competition authority is operating within its own national legal system and as a result there are many differences between the various authorities as to the incentives on offer and the leniency procedure. There are also some differences in the various programmes according to the particular policy priorities of the competition authority concerned. Some of the differences between programmes which may be of particular relevance in making this assessment are:

- whether the authority operates a 'marker' system based on the timing of an application, or a system based on the quality of the evidence provided (where applicants cannot reserve a place in the queue);
- the treatment given to second or subsequent applicants;
- the conditions imposed on leniency applicants for the duration of the investigation in order to ensure lenient treatment is obtained;
- whether the leniency programme covers the type of cartel activity in question.

If a prospective leniency applicant is considering applying for leniency in more than one European jurisdiction, in order to prioritize those applications, it may also assist to make an initial assessment as to which authority is likely to take the case forward. For example, if it is a case that the European Commission would be likely to take forward, this may mean an applicant ought to prioritise an application to the European Commission. See paragraphs 5.111–5.113 below.

5.110 The OFT is also taking some measures to allow an interaction between the respective leniency programmes of the Commission and the OFT. To this end, the OFT has stated that it will allow a 'no-names' Type A immunity marker application to be made in cases where the undertaking's legal adviser confirms that he or she also has instructions to make an application for immunity to the Commission under section A of the Commission's leniency notice. This is designed to provide certainty to undertakings in relation to the risk of exposure to criminal prosecution as a result of a leniency application being made to the Commission (and thus assist the effectiveness of the Commission's leniency programme).[112] The OFT will also accept short form summary applications

---

[112] Interim note, paras 2.18 and 2.19.

where the applicant has already made an appropriate application for immunity to the European Commission, and is in a 'Type A' position in the United Kingdom.[113] This type of short form application is contemplated in the ECN's model leniency programme.

(ii) Determining which European authority is likely to take up the case

Some guidance on which European authority is likely to take up the case is available from the case allocation criteria in the Network Notice.[114] This sets out the criteria applied by national competition authorities and the European Commission in allocating cases between them. The key concept for this purpose is to be able to recognise when it is likely that the European Commission would take a case forward, because where the European Commission initiates proceedings for the adoption of a decision, all other national competition authorities are automatically relieved of their competence to apply Articles 81 and 82 in the same case.[115] According to the Network Notice, the criteria for the European Commission being 'particularly well placed' to take a case is where: **5.111**

(1) 'one or several agreement(s) or practice(s), including networks of similar agreements or practices, have effects on competition in more than three Member States';[116] and/or

(2) the case 'is closely linked to other Community provisions which may be exclusively or more effectively applied by the Commission, if the Community interest requires the adoption of a Commission decision to develop Community competition policy when a new competition issue arises or to ensure effective enforcement'.[117]

Provided the European Commission is not taking a case forward, a national competition authority may take up a case if it is 'well placed' to do so.[118] For a particular authority to be 'well placed', the following cumulative criteria need to be met:[119] **5.112**

(1) the agreement or practice has substantial direct, actual, or foreseeable effects

---

[113] ibid, paras 2.21 and 2.22.

[114] Commission notice on cooperation within the network of competition authorities (2004/C 101/03) [2004] OJ C101/43.

[115] Regulation 1/2003, Art 11(6).   [116] Network Notice, para 14.

[117] ibid, para 15. The types of cases the European Commission is likely to take forward are discussed in further detail in Chapter 6.

[118] *Joint Statement of the Council and the Commission on the functioning of the Network of Competition Authorities*, document 15435/02 ADD1 (**Joint Statement**), para 12, available at <http://register.consilium.eu.int>.

[119] Network Notice, para 8.

on competition within its territory, is implemented within or originates from its territory;[120]

(2) it can gather, possibly with the assistance of other authorities, the evidence required to prove the infringement; and

(3) the authority is able to bring to an end effectively to the entire infringement and restore or maintain competition in the market, ie it can adopt a cease-and-desist order the effect of which will be sufficient to bring an end to the infringement and it can, where appropriate, sanction the infringement adequately.[121]

5.113   However, these statements of principle do not provide any fixed rule for when the European Commission or any other authority will take up a case. Indeed, the European Commission lacks the resources to handle all the cases for which it is 'particularly well placed'. Hence, cases affecting more than three Member States may be taken forward by one or more national authority rather than the European Commission. The national authorities may conduct cases in conjunction with each other, as no jurisdiction takes precedence over any other. Authorities may also transfer cases to each other. This means that as a matter of precaution it is best to apply for leniency in all jurisdictions covered by the cartel activity, wherever it is possible to do so. The case allocation criteria should only be considered in the context of prioritising the timing of multiple applications.

(b) Exchange of leniency applicants' information

(i) General rules on disclosure

5.114   Disclosure of a leniency applicant's information is subject to the same governing laws as other types of disclosure by the OFT and the Regulators. There are only two differences with respect to leniency applicants: first, the OFT operates different policies in respect of leniency applicants (discussed at paras 5.53–5.63 above in relation to confidentiality); and secondly, the ECN has made special provision for the exchange of leniency applicants' information.

5.115   The rules on information disclosure to foreign authorities generally are discussed in Chapter 8. In general, disclosure to any authority outside the European Community is governed by national law provisions. Under national law, there is taken to be an inherent power on the part of the OFT allowing the OFT to disclose information in the course of its functions as a competition authority. The main restrictions on the OFT's use and disclosure of information are those

---

[120] eg, the parties to the agreement or conduct are established in that country and the anti-competitive effects are experienced in that Member State: Joint Statement, para 16.

[121] ibid, para 15.

set out in Pt 9 of the Enterprise Act 2002.[122] There is a general restriction on the disclosure of such information, subject to some exceptions, in relation to all the information obtained or held by the OFT relating to the affairs of an individual or any business of an undertaking. One of the exceptions relates to overseas disclosures, whereby a public authority may disclose information to an overseas public authority for the purpose of facilitating the exercise by the overseas public authority of any function which it has relating to investigations and enforcement of relevant legislation.[123] Thus the OFT's power to disclose individual or business information to an overseas public authority is restricted by the Enterprise Act Pt 9 'gateways'. More information on the operation of these gateways is set out in Chapter 8.

(ii) ECN restrictions

With the decentralisation of enforcement of Article 81 to multiple authorities, **5.116** and the new powers enabling information exchange between competition authorities under Regulation 1/2003, there was a real issue with allowing for information exchange whilst not jeopardising the future of the leniency programmes operated by various authorities. On the one hand it is important for competition authorities applying the same law to be able to provide each other with information as freely as possible. On the other hand, to be 'free' with information provided by leniency applicants where another authority was not obliged to respect the leniency offered would result in much less effective leniency programmes and would ultimately mean that fewer cartels were detected.

Regulation 1/2003, although providing for full power to disclose information **5.117** between the national competition authorities, did not provide for any constraints or changes to the various leniency programmes in operation. In the circumstances, Regulation 1/2003 introduced a serious new risk to the effectiveness of the various leniency programmes in operation by introducing a relatively unlimited power to exchange information.

The solution to these problems lies in the authorities' agreement to cooperate **5.118** on rules surrounding the use of their enforcement and information exchange powers, as set out in the Network Notice. This is an agreement between all competition authorities that they will not use another authority's case information where the case involves a leniency applicant, except in very limited circumstances. This agreement between the authorities is set out in the Network Notice and is intended to create legitimate expectations upon which undertakings may rely.

---

[122] These restrictions also apply to the SFO, and to the Regulators.
[123] Enterprise Act 2002, s 243.

5.119 Paragraphs 37 to 42 of the Network Notice provide for a number of principles, which may be summarised as follows:

(1) an application to an authority is not to be considered as an application for leniency to any other authority;

(2) the basic information about a case which is initiated as a result of a leniency application and is submitted to the network pursuant to Article 11 cannot be used by other competition authorities as the basis for an investigation— subject to the following subparagraphs;

(3) information voluntarily submitted by a leniency applicant will only be disclosed pursuant to Article 12 with the consent of the leniency applicant, except that consent is *not* required where:

- the receiving authority has also received a leniency application from the same applicant and related to the same infringement; or

- the receiving authority provides a written commitment that it will not use such information to impose sanctions on the leniency applicant; or

- the transfer of information pursuant to Article 12 is made in response to a specific request to gather information under Article 22(1) of Regulation 1/2003;[124]

(4) case information submitted pursuant to Article 11(3), where the case has been initiated as a result of a leniency application, will only be made available to those national competition authorities that have committed themselves to respecting the principles set out in the Network Notice.[125]

5.120 Each of these basic principles gives rise to difficulties in understanding the practical effect and the interpretation of these principles. The key areas where difficulties appear to arise are discussed below.

5.121 **Article 11(3) information** Article 11(3) information is information submitted to the ECN at the commencement of a case, which provides basic information about the case. There are two main points to be aware of with respect to information provided to the ECN pursuant to Article 11(3).

5.122 The first point is that where Article 11(3) information is provided pursuant to a case which has been initiated as a result of a leniency application, such information should only be able to be accessed by those competition authorities that have expressly agreed to abide by the principles set out in the Network Notice. The statement of intention to abide by such principles is set out as an annex

---

[124] Network Notice, para 41.   [125] ibid, para 42.

to the Network Notice. The European Commission maintains a list of the competition authorities which have signed this statement.[126]

The second point is that Article 11(3) information may not be used for any purpose other than to trigger a request for the supply of information pursuant to Article 12. Article 12 sets out the provision for the exchange of information between ECN members. Paragraph 39 of the Network Notice makes it clear that this should not be used by other members of the ECN as the basis for starting an investigation on their own behalf 'whether under the competition rules of the Treaty or, in the case of NCAs, under their national competition law or other laws'. There is also a further carve-out noted in relation to the use of Article 11(3) information, which expressly retains the ability of a national authority to open an investigation on the basis of information received from other sources. Thus, if an undertaking were able to establish that a national competition authority initiated an investigation on the basis of Article 11(3) information (which information was not available from some other source at that time), that undertaking would, in theory, be able to claim that the entire investigation against it was based upon a wrongful investigation and seek to have the entire proceeding struck out. In any event, it is quite likely that cases commenced as a result of a leniency application would normally be the types of cases where Article 11(3) information would not be submitted to the ECN until after the first formal investigative measure had been carried out. This is the very type of case where a competition authority would be likely to consider utmost secrecy prior to investigating to outweigh any need to notify the ECN. **5.123**

The protected information   Paragraph 40 of the Network Notice states that the following information may not be disclosed to another member of the ECN pursuant to Article 12: **5.124**

• information voluntarily submitted by a leniency applicant; and

• other information which has been obtained during or following an inspection or by means of or following any other fact-finding measures which, in each case, could not have been carried out except as a result of the leniency application.

However, this protection would not cover information obtained by a national authority as a result of an investigative measure carried out before the leniency applicant came forward. This would clearly provide very little benefit to a leniency applicant who comes forward after the first inspection has been carried out, for example.

---

[126] <http://ec.europa.eu/comm/competition/antitrust/legislation/list_of_authorities_joint_statement.pdf>.

5.125 **Where the consent of the leniency applicant is not required** The general rule is that the consent of the leniency applicant is required before its information may be transmitted. The first exception to this rule covers a situation where the receiving authority has also received a leniency application. This application must relate to the 'same infringement' and be from the 'same applicant'. However, this exception is only an option provided that 'at the time the information is transmitted it is not open to the applicant to withdraw the information which it has submitted to that receiving authority'. This is a reference to a situation where a competition authority's leniency programme allows for the withdrawal of a leniency application, usually relating to a procedure where final leniency is not determined by the authority until later in the case. This is how, for example, the European Commission's leniency programme worked for many years. Many of the Member States' competition authorities have based their leniency programmes on the programme run by the European Commission. The OFT's leniency programme, however, does provide for a guaranteed leniency in the early stages of the case. Thus, in such cases which are being conducted by the OFT, it is not usually open to the applicant to withdraw that information (although it can withdraw the *application* at any time—see para 5.65 above).

5.126 A written commitment not to use an applicant's evidence to impose sanctions on that applicant will cover not only the information transmitted by the relevant competition authority, but also any information which the receiving authority 'may obtain following the date and time of transmission'.[127] This is one of the most important protections for a leniency applicant. It provides a general and easily determined cut-off date beyond which such information obtained by the relevant competition authority may not be used as evidence in order to impose sanctions upon the leniency applicant. Thus, regardless of where or how the later information is obtained, the applicant remains protected as such information cannot be used to impose sanctions on that applicant.

5.127 In addition, a written commitment by the receiving authority not only covers the leniency applicant but also covers 'any other legal or natural person covered by the favourable treatment offered by the transmitting authority as a result of the application made by the applicant under its leniency program' and any employee or former employee of such a person, or of the leniency applicant. In this way, the protection offered by the receiving authority is, in some cases, more extensive than the protection offered by the original leniency programme.

5.128 **Enforceability** On the basis of the statement annexed to the Network Notice, which has been signed by the OFT and the Regulators, along with all other

---

[127] Network Notice, para 41(2).

national competition authorities, an undertaking which believes that it has received treatment contrary to the principles set out in the Network Notice (in particular those relating to the treatment of leniency applications) would be likely to have a cause of action based on legitimate expectations. In addition, where a written commitment has been made, the relevant leniency applicant would have a further basis for a legitimate expectations claim.[128]

However, a claim based on legitimate expectations may not be recognised by all **5.129** national courts as providing a sufficiently binding commitment on the part of the relevant authority. The written commitment provided by the receiving authority is in fact a commitment made to the transmitting authority, and not to the leniency applicant itself. For this reason, it may be preferable for a leniency applicant to consent to a transmission of its information pursuant to Article 12, subject to a specific agreement with each of the transmitting authority and the receiving authority. This type of agreement could impose the requirement that the receiving authority shall not disclose the information any further, it could detail the information to be covered and, if possible, it may note that the written commitment is not to bring proceedings at all (rather than simply agreeing not to use evidence to impose sanctions). It would need to describe the infringement and the facts very carefully and also note the date and time of the transmission of the information. Such an agreement could also detail the parties against whom the proceedings can be brought. In this way, the principles set out in the Network Notice can be tailored to a specific case, and in doing so, would clarify the scope of the powers of the receiving authority in question and would also provide a direct, contractual-type obligation as between the leniency applicant and both authorities in relation to the transmission of the leniency applicant's information.

It is unfortunate that a more simple solution was not available to the ECN **5.130** members: a result of the sheer complexity and variety of the leniency programmes operated by the various Member States. Without a major change such as the introduction of a 'one-stop-shop', it seems unlikely that this 'legal certainty' of creating legitimate expectations by agreeing to abide by a set of principles will ever be clear-cut enough for an undertaking to feel confident in challenging a wrongful disclosure of information under this system. Thus an undertaking's confidence in the ECN restrictions on disclosure must, at least primarily, depend upon trusting the authority to whom a leniency application is made. However, the ECN members are continuing to work towards a 'soft convergence' of leniency programmes, which may well achieve the desired result over time.[129]

---

[128] A copy of the receiving authority's written commitment is to be provided to the leniency applicant: Network Notice, fn 1(2).
[129] See para 5.110 above.

(iii) Other ECN restrictions

5.131 In addition to the above ECN restrictions relevant to leniency applicants, there are other restrictions on the use of information which apply equally to leniency applicants. For example, there are restrictions on the use of ECN information in the application of national criminal laws by national competition authorities. These and other restrictions are discussed in Chapter 8.

6

STARTING AN INVESTIGATION IN THE UNITED KINGDOM

A. Introduction

6.01 This chapter sets out the principles for determining which particular competition authority (or, where appropriate, one or more authorities) will investigate a potential competition law infringement in the United Kingdom and which competition law regime they will seek to enforce. Issues concerning parallel enforcement and choice of investigative authorities arise in relation to the application of both national and EC competition law in three specific instances in the United Kingdom:

(1) in relation to the enforcement of Articles 81 and 82, each member of the European Competition Network (**ECN**) has jurisdiction and power to enforce these provisions in parallel with every other member (except the European Commission, which operates under different provisions);

(2) for the enforcement of the Chapter I and II prohibitions under the Competition Act 1998, the Office of Fair Trading (**OFT**) and the Regulators all have concurrent jurisdiction to take proceedings against undertakings; and

(3) the enforcement of the cartel offence may be done by either (or both) the OFT or the Serious Fraud Office (**SFO**) in the United Kingdom, as both bodies have criminal jurisdiction.

6.02 Each of these situations gives rise to concerns regarding how cases are allocated as between the various authorities having concurrent jurisdiction and overlapping enforcement powers. There are also concerns regarding the ongoing management of cases that are subject to joint investigation, or cases where an investigation is conducted in parallel with a private action. There are many statements of policy and law addressing these matters, and these are discussed in the first part of this chapter. In addition, Chapter 11 also addresses the risk of double jeopardy for undertakings that arises as a result of the possible interaction between the multiple regulatory regimes.

6.03 The second part of this chapter deals with the factual, legal and policy considerations which are relevant to the commencement of an investigation in the United Kingdom. This covers the receipt of information, including a discussion of the various sources of information which may be used to bring a case to the attention of a competition authority. It also covers the various legal requirements necessary for an investigation to commence, including threshold legal requirements under competition law and more general time limits which may be relevant to commencing an investigation. This part also addresses the key policy and resources issues facing the authorities which may enforce competition law in the United Kingdom. Administrative and case priority issues can impact significantly on a competition authority's decision as to whether a case is to be investigated or not, despite all the legal threshold requirements being clearly satisfied.

B. Jurisdiction for the Enforcement of Articles 81 and 82

(a) Effect on trade between Member States (Summary)

From 1 May 2004, the enforcement of Articles 81 and 82 EC has been decentral- **6.04** ised across the European Union. In addition to the European Commission, designated national competition authorities[1] have the power and the responsibility to enforce Articles 81 and 82.[2] The jurisdictional criteria for the application of Articles 81 and 82 turns on whether or not there may be an effect on trade between Member States, regardless of whether it is the European Commission or a national competition authority applying EC competition law. This is a jurisdictional test rather than a test related to anti-competitive effects, and this 'effect on trade' test is therefore the key factor which establishes whether an agreement or conduct falls to be assessed under Article 81 or 82[3] or on the basis of national competition law alone.

In the United Kingdom, since almost all of the substantive competition law **6.05** provisions now mirror the EC competition law provisions, the penalties are the same, and the OFT would be the relevant body conducting the case under either set of laws,[4] in most cases the practical outcome of the 'effect on trade' test will be irrelevant. However, there are, for example, occasionally differing levels of protection such as the application of UK exclusions, as discussed at paras 1.110–1.112 above, and in Chapter 4.[5]

A summary of the key principles and the key factors relevant to the application **6.06** of the test of effect on trade is set out at paras 1.38–1.54 above. Set out below for ease of reference is a quick checklist which focuses on factors indicating that there is *no* effect on trade, since, by falling into one of such categories, the undertaking concerned can avoid the application of Community law so the agreement or conduct undergoes an examination under only UK national competition law.

On the basis of the statements of principle and the case law to date, there are **6.07** particular circumstances which have resulted in setting a limit to the application

---

[1] A list of the designated national competition authorities is set out at Appendix 4.
[2] Council Regulation (EC) 1/2003 of 16 December 2002 on the implementation of the rules on competition laid down in Articles 81 and 82 of the Treaty [2003] OJ L1/1 (**Regulation 1/ 2003**) Art 3 (see Chapter 3 above for a discussion of the application of Art 3).
[3] Case 22/78 *Hugin Kassaregister AB v Commission* [1979] ECR 1869.
[4] See Chapter 3 above for a discussion of the obligation to apply Community competition law.
[5] The distinction may also have an impact on the OFT's exercise of its power to create UK block exemptions in future: it is likely that such block exemptions will be created only if they relate to agreements which are unlikely to have an effect on trade between Member States.

of the effect on trade test (and thereby setting a limit to the jurisdiction of EC competition law). These circumstances are summarised below and may be used as a quick checklist of possible ways of excluding jurisdiction for the application of EC competition law. Thus, it has been established that there is no effect on trade between Member States in the following situations:

(1) There is only a very limited effect on trade (appreciability). This is defined in both case law and by a new statement of the threshold criteria which will be applied by the European Commission (and the OFT).[6] This essentially requires less than 5 per cent market share (combined) and less than 40 million euros annual turnover (combined).

(2) There is no cross-border element at all (geographical or contextual—note that contextual cross-border elements may exist even where there is no geographical cross-border element).

(3) Any possible effect on trade is too vague (even if potential or indirect, the effect on trade is too theoretical).

(4) Any possible effect on trade is too far removed from the European Union (where the agreement or undertaking is entirely outside of the European Union and the agreement or conduct has at most a very limited effect on any EU market).

(b) Allocation of cases between ECN members

(i) Overview

6.08 All of the designated national competition authorities have parallel jurisdiction to enforce Articles 81 and 82 and are obliged to work in 'close cooperation'.[7] A case may be investigated by the European Commission, or by several authorities acting in parallel, or by a single national competition authority, assisted by other authorities.

6.09 As this unstructured decentralisation of jurisdiction for enforcement would have been unworkable without more detail on the circumstances in which several authorities could bring a case in parallel, the European Council and European Commission published a joint statement on the functioning of the network of competition authorities (**Joint Statement**).[8] Subsequently, the European Commission published a Notice on the interaction of the competition network[9] (**Network Notice**). The principles in the Network Notice have been adopted by

---

[6] See paras 1.49–1.54 above. This is sometimes called the 'NAAT Rule'.
[7] Regulation 1/2003, Art 11(1).
[8] <http://ec.europa.eu/comm/competition/antitrust/others/js_en.pdf>.
[9] Commission notice on cooperation within the network of competition authorities (2004/C 101/03) [2004] OJ C101/43.

the designated competition authorities. The basic principle is that case allocation within the network is determined (both for the Commission and the national competition authorities) according to which authority is 'well-placed' to take the case.[10]

(ii) Notifying the ECN when a case commences

Where there may be an effect on trade between Member States, and a competition authority intends to take the case forward,[11] an obligation arises to notify the case to the ECN, which then starts the process known as case allocation.[12] Note that in practice almost every case remains with the notifying authority, ie there is not really a process of case allocation as such: this is explained further below. The 'case allocation' process is described in the Network Notice and the Joint Statement.[13] Essentially, the notification of a case to the ECN by a network member must be made before or without delay after the authority carries out its first investigative measure. The notification must contain information about the authority's proposed investigative measures and may provide other limited information about the case such as the products, territories, and parties concerned, and the basis for the alleged infringement. In order to make the process as efficient as possible, members aim to provide each other regularly with updates to pending cases.[14]

6.10

In 2005, a total of 204 cases were submitted to the ECN: 22 by the European Commission and 182 by the national competition authorities. In the one month period from 1 February to 28 February 2006, there were five new investigations and four envisaged decisions by ECN members.[15]

6.11

From the OFT's perspective, the point at which the ECN will be notified of a case is when the criteria under s 25 of the Competition Act 1998 are met, which are the criteria allowing the OFT to use its formal investigative powers under the Competition Act. The OFT may then notify the ECN either before or 'without delay after' the first investigative measure is taken. It is quite possible that the undertaking(s) subject to the investigation will not be aware of the investigation at this stage. In OFT cases, in order to ensure secrecy (particularly

6.12

---

[10] ibid, para 8.   [11] Regulation 1/2003, Art 11(3); Network notice, para 17.
[12] Regulation 1/2003, Art 11(3). The notification of a case to the ECN by a network member is sometimes called an 'Article 11(3) notice'.
[13] Network Notice, paras 16–17 and Joint Statement, para 10.
[14] Notification to the ECN itself may give rise to some issues of information disclosure, which are discussed in Chapter 8.
[15] See <http://ec.europa.eu/comm/competition/antitrust/cases/ecn_1.pdf>. Note that there was an unusually high number of cases for the European Commission in 2004 (101 cases): this is explained by the fact that the European Commission submitted all of its pending cases in 2004, whereas the national competition authorities submitted only new cases.

surrounding the potential investigation of a cartel), it appears likely that the OFT will notify the ECN of a case after having conducted its first investigative measure, unless there is clearly an effect on another Member State which might require joint investigative efforts at the outset of a case. There is always the option of informal communications between authorities at any stage, as well as the formal ECN notification process. There are often close working relationships between authorities.

(iii) Time period for case allocation

6.13 Upon notification of the case to the ECN, a theoretical allocation time period of two months starts to run.[16] This time period is theoretical because there is nothing in Regulation 1/2003 or the Network Notice to prevent another national competition authority (or the European Commission) from taking up the case at any time.

6.14 However, any conflict should be minimised by the mutual recognition and cooperation provisions in the Joint Statement.[17] The Network Notice also contains statements to the effect that the European Commission will generally not take up a case outside the two month allocation period other than in exceptional circumstances.[18] In practice, national competition authorities tend to have a significant workload and are unlikely to wish to take up cases where it is apparent that another authority is already conducting the case. Also, as a result of the often close working relationships between authorities, it seems likely that national competition authorities will be in a position to avoid any such conflict situation developing.

(iv) Case allocation for the ECN members

6.15 Case allocation is based upon a set of agreed criteria. The agreed criteria are set out in the Network Notice and the Joint Statement, which provide that a national competition authority (or the European Commission) will be allowed to pursue and take up a notified case if it is 'well placed' to do so and there are no objections during the two month case allocation time period.[19] For a particular authority to be 'well placed', the following cumulative criteria need to be met:[20]

(1) the agreement or practice has substantial direct actual or foreseeable effects on competition within its territory, is implemented within or originates from its territory;[21]

---

[16] Joint Statement, para 12.   [17] ibid, para 8.
[18] Network Notice, paras 18, 19, and 54.   [19] Joint Statement, para 12.
[20] Network Notice, para 8.
[21] eg, the parties to the agreement or conduct are established in that country and the anti-competitive effects are experienced in that Member State: Joint Statement, para 16.

(2) it can gather, possibly with the assistance of other authorities, the evidence required to prove the infringement; and

(3) the authority is able effectively to bring to an end the entire infringement and restore or maintain competition in the market, ie it can adopt a cease-and-desist order the effect of which will be sufficient to bring an end to the infringement and it can, where appropriate, sanction the infringement adequately.[22]

The 'well placed' criteria are all widely drafted, and would be likely to allow the European Commission or a national competition authority to claim it is well placed for any type of case which has a loose connection with the relevant Member State. Most national competition authorities have sufficient powers to gather evidence and effectively bring an infringement to an end. In particular, the OFT would certainly have sufficient powers to meet these two criteria in every case. The first criterion, relating to territorial connection, at the very least requires that the relevant agreement or conduct originate from the United Kingdom, even if there are no effects felt in the United Kingdom.   **6.16**

The fact that a national competition authority is well placed to take a case does not oblige it to do so: in fact, there is provision in Regulation 1/2003 for a national competition authority to decline to take a case on the basis that another national competition authority (including one from a different Member State) is already conducting the case.[23]   **6.17**

The OFT also has its own administrative priorities for the use of its resources,[24] which are more likely to limit the cases the OFT will take on than the case allocation criteria as set out in the Network Notice.[25] Other national competition authorities are likely to be in a similar position.   **6.18**

(v) Case allocation for the European Commission

In addition to those criteria applying to all ECN members discussed above, there are further criteria relevant to the European Commission. According to the Network Notice, the criteria for the European Commission being 'well placed' to take a case are where: **6.19**

---

[22] ibid, para 15.

[23] Regulation 1/2003, Art 13. 'Well placed' is not the same as 'best placed' in the sense of *forum non conveniens*.

[24] See OFT's competition prioritisation framework, published on the OFT's website on 12 October 2006.

[25] In the same way as market share thresholds are now dealt with: see OFT446, *Response to points raised during the consultation on the competition law guidelines, guidance and the OFT's Rules* (December 2004) paras 2.12–2.14.

(1) 'one or several agreement(s) or practice(s), including networks of similar agreements or practices, have effects on competition in more than three Member States';[26] and/or

(2) the case 'is closely linked to other Community provisions which may be exclusively or more effectively applied by the Commission, if the Community interest requires the adoption of a Commission decision to develop Community competition policy when a new competition issue arises or to ensure effective enforcement'.[27]

6.20 Where the European Commission initiates proceedings[28] in a case, all other national competition authorities are automatically relieved of their competence to apply Articles 81 and 82 in the same case.[29] A national competition authority that has already started a prior investigation will be consulted by the European Commission before it is relieved of its competence.[30] Note that Article 11(6) has not yet been used, and its equivalent in Regulation 17/62[31] was never used.

(vi) Case allocation where more than one authority is 'well placed'

6.21 The basic 'rule of thumb' for case allocation is that a national competition authority commencing a case will in most cases be the only authority to continue with the case, and the European Commission will normally take a case where it involves more than three Member States. This is also borne out by experience: according to the 2004 Annual Report,[32] re-allocation of notified cases is extremely rare (less than 1 per cent) and cases tend to remain with the authority that has started an investigation. In 2005, the European Commission confirmed that situations where cases change hands are rare in comparison with the overall number of cases dealt with by the ECN members.[33] This experience may be partly explained by the general tendency for most competition cases to involve either only one Member State (in which case that relevant national competition authority would act), or several Member States (ie more than three, in which case the European Commission would be particularly well placed to act). That said, there are examples of cases involving a few national competition authorities where authorities worked jointly or assisted each other in gathering and exchanging information. Further, the European Commission does not always act when there are more than three Member States involved, as its

---

[26] Network Notice, para 14.   [27] ibid, para 15.

[28] 'Initiate proceedings' means a formal act by which the European Commission indicates its intention to adopt a decision: see Network Notice, para 52 and fn 21. Eg, the issue of a Statement of Objections is likely to comprise the initiation of proceedings.

[29] Regulation 1/2003, Art 11(6).   [30] ibid, and Joint Statement, para 21.

[31] First Regulation implementing Articles [81] and [82] of the Treaty [1962] OJ 13/204.

[32] European Commission's Report on competition policy 2004, Vol 1, para 106.

[33] European Commission's Report on competition policy 2005, para 211.

workload may not allow for particular cases to be taken up in some circumstances. It is possible that other reasons why there are few reallocations relate to the close working relations between authorities such that informal discussions are common at a very early stage in the case, and that heavy workloads minimise the desire for authorities to take on further work from each other.

Nevertheless, there is provision for cases to be re-allocated between national **6.22** competition authorities according to the principles in the Joint Statement. As a starting point, the Joint Statement establishes a presumption in favour of cases being dealt with by a single competition authority as often as possible.[34] However, that will not always be the case. If the agreement or practice substantially affects competition in more than one Member State, the ECN members will agree between themselves who is 'best placed' to deal with the case successfully.[35] It may be that the investigation is coordinated between one or more authorities, with one authority acting as the lead institution.[36]

Cases may also move from national competition authorities to the European **6.23** Commission. For example, it is generally unlikely that more than three authorities would act together, since more than three would mean the European Commission was 'particularly well placed' (although not obliged) to conduct the case. There have also been circumstances where a complaint lodged with the European Commission has, following bilateral discussions between the European Commission and the national competition authority concerned, been accepted by a national competition authority instead.

In deciding whether a national competition authority is unable to take up a case **6.24** because another authority is conducting the case and the allocation period has expired, it is important first to work out whether the two cases are the same case for the purposes of the Network Notice. Where an authority is in fact taking up a *different* case, the allocation rules will not apply. Similarly, the prohibition from acting where the European Commission is conducting the case will not apply where the case is not the same case. The definition of the 'same case' in the Network Notice is very narrow: it must be not only the same product but also the same geographic market to be defined as the 'same case'. Therefore, where a national competition authority is taking up a case but only in respect of its own territory, there is no limit on another authority taking up the same case albeit with a different geographic scope.[37] The natural geographic limitation of cases may well mean that two or three authorities conducting the 'same case' will be a very rare occurrence.

---

[34] Joint Statement, para 16.   [35] ibid, para 17.   [36] ibid, para 18.
[37] See the pending investigations into Visa and MasterCard's domestic interchange rates currently being conducted by the UK, Spanish, Polish, and Swedish authorities.

(c) Forum shopping

(i) Forum shopping by an undertaking under investigation

6.25 The forum or location of the investigation can have important ramifications for the conduct of the investigation, for the procedural rights (such as privilege and leniency) of the undertaking(s) concerned, and the penalties that may be imposed. The choice of forum may also have consequences for any subsequent damages claims.[38]

6.26 The ability of an undertaking under investigation to 'forum shop', seeking out the most favourable jurisdiction or authority for its own case, is very limited at best—and may be non-existent. Where a complaint has been made, the accused will not have had any control over the initial location of the investigation. It could lobby other national competition authorities or the European Commission to take the case (or a leading role in the case) during the case allocation procedure (assuming it is aware of the case at that stage). However, it is doubtful whether this would have any effect at all. The only possible opportunity for an undertaking to influence the choice of authority is in its choice when submitting a leniency application before an investigation has been commenced, or when requesting informal advice or a formal opinion/guidance. However, it would be dangerous for an undertaking to assume it was able to influence the choice of authority to take up a case through the making of a leniency application. As there is no 'one-stop-shop', there is no certainty that the European Commission will take up a particular case at all, and even if it does commence an investigation, Article 11(6) may not apply until the Statement of Objections is issued, which would leave the undertaking potentially exposed for a considerable period of time.

(ii) Forum shopping by a complainant

6.27 A complainant, on the other hand, may have some scope to forum shop as it may choose which authority to lodge its complaint with. However, this will depend on the facts of the case, as in many cases it will be clear which Member States the complaint affects. As noted above, many complaints only really affect one Member State. In practical terms, most complainants will not wish to incur the expense and complexities of submitting a complaint to an authority in another jurisdiction with different national competition law, investigation

---

[38] eg, in the UK, ss 47A and 47B of the Competition Act 1998 enable third parties to rely on an infringement decision by the OFT or the European Commission in subsequent damages actions before the CAT. The CAT is bound by the findings of liability in the decision, leaving the claimant to establish quantum and causation. See also s 33(4) of the revised German ARC which is even broader as the binding status attaches to decisions by other national competition authorities: <http://www.bundeskartellamt.de/wEnglisch/download/pdf/06_GWB_7__Novelle_e.pdf>.

procedures, and quite possibly a different language. Since the general rule is that the authority commencing the case will continue to conduct the case, the choice of authority (or court) by a complainant is likely to dictate the forum in which the case is conducted. However, for any authority, the case allocation criteria will still need to be met, and there are also the administrative priorities of each particular authority to consider. There is nothing to prevent a complaint being lodged with more than one authority, including the European Commission.

Factors that should be borne in mind when deciding where to lodge a complaint **6.28** include: the particular authority's statistics for acting on complaints and the comparative efficiency of the investigative procedure; its history of rejecting complaints and the relevant appeal procedures should this occur; its willingness to grant interim relief; the extent of complainants' rights to participate in the procedure; comparative statistics regarding accepting commitments rather than proceeding to a full decision with directions; appeal procedures from a final decision; and the prospects for subsequent damages proceedings.

In relation to the OFT and the Regulators, relevant information may be found **6.29** in the annual reports and published accounting information.[39] In relation to other national competition authorities, information may be available through each of their websites, and see also the ECN website which itself provides links to the national competition authorities' websites.[40]

(d) Double jeopardy

(i) Circumstances giving rise to double jeopardy

With the possibility of concurrent action by national competition authorities, **6.30** and the application of EC law alongside national competition laws, the possibility of double jeopardy (or *ne bis in idem*[41]) arises. There are two ways this might arise: in relation to a duplicated process, or in relation to the imposition of a duplicate penalty. This part deals with double jeopardy in relation to process. The possibility of double jeopardy concerning duplicate or overlapping penalties is discussed in Chapter 11 below.

Before turning to the issue of double jeopardy *within* the EU, it is worth **6.31** briefly mentioning the argument that the *ne bis in idem* principle applies to proceedings commenced in the European Union where proceedings based on the same facts are being conducted by other authorities *outside* the European Union. This argument appears unlikely to succeed. In *Tokai Carbon Co Ltd*

---

[39] See Chapter 2 for information on the OFT and each of the Regulators.
[40] <http://ec.europa.eu/comm/competition/ecn/index_en.html>.
[41] Also known as *non bis in idem*.

v Commission[42] the Court of First Instance held that the principle of *ne bis in idem* did not apply in respect of penalties imposed by Canada and the United States because the aim of the fines imposed by the European Commission was to prevent the distortion of competition in the European Union, whereas the aim of the Canadian and US proceedings was to protect those markets. There does not seem to be any reason why this principle would not also apply in respect of the investigation itself.

6.32 Turning to the position with the EU, the practical implications for an undertaking subject to simultaneous multiple investigations in the new decentralised regime can be significant. Considerable management and legal resources can be expended in answering repeat information requests and responding to duplicate statement of objections. The undertaking will face differing national standards of protection for confidential and legally privileged information and may face criminal sanctions in certain countries. It may have to ensure consistency across multi-lingual proceedings and may have to instruct different lawyers in different legal jurisdictions. These costs are a significant factor, especially when there are no means of recovering legal costs expended at the administrative stage.

6.33 In the modernised competition enforcement regime, there are a number of scenarios in which double jeopardy might become an issue:

(1) two or three national competition authorities are conducting the *same* case in cooperation with one another (although note the comments above in relation to the investigation process);

(2) a number of authorities, which may include the European Commission, are conducting cases which are *related* but are not considered to be the *same* case under the Network Notice;

(3) the European Commission conducts a case subsequent to a national competition authority having taken a decision in the case; and

(4) a national competition authority conducts a case simultaneously under its national competition law as well as under EC law (however, this possibility seems quite remote).

(ii) Legal basis for a double jeopardy claim

6.34 Any claim by an undertaking based on double jeopardy would rely upon the European Convention on Human Rights (**ECHR**)[43] or the same provision as set out in the Charter of Fundamental Rights of the European Union.[44] These are said to enshrine the fundamental *ne bis in idem* principle of EC law.[45] This

---

[42] Case T-236/01) [2004] ECR II-1181.   [43] Protocol No 7, Art 4.   [44] Art 50.
[45] Case C-238/99 P *Limburgse Vinyl Maatschappij NV (LVM) v Commission* [2002] ECR I-8375.

principle is set out in Article 4 of Protocol No 7 ECHR, which provides that '[n]o one shall be liable to be tried or punished again in criminal proceedings under the jurisdiction of the same State for an offence for which he has already been finally acquitted or convicted in accordance with the law and penal procedure of that State'.

There are essentially three key issues which require careful consideration before this provision would apply in the context of competition law enforcement to any of the situations noted above. **6.35**

The first issue is whether the enforcement of competition law amounts to criminal proceedings. The competition authorities generally take the view that competition enforcement proceedings are civil or administrative proceedings only, but courts have tended to take the view that competition enforcement proceedings can be considered to be criminal or quasi-criminal proceedings for certain purposes. In *Napp* and later cases, the Competition Appeal Tribunal (**CAT**) has confirmed that competition enforcement proceedings may be regarded as criminal for the purposes of Article 6 ECHR, but this does not mean that competition law infringements comprise criminal offences in domestic law, nor does it mean that the criminal standard of proof applies.[46] **6.36**

The second issue is whether the concurrent enforcement of competition law in different Member States may be described as proceedings 'under the jurisdiction of the same State'. The fact that the authorities would be enforcing the same provisions would have to be balanced against the probability that each national competition authority would, in most cases, only conduct its proceeding in respect of its own territory. **6.37**

The third issue is to define what amounts to being 'tried [or punished] again' in the context of multiple enforcement of competition law. The reference to being 'tried' again brings in the possibility that duplicate proceedings may amount to a violation of the *ne bis in idem* principle. **6.38**

In relation to the latter two issues, the rules governing the consistent application of competition law across the European Union (and also between EC laws and national laws) are likely to be relevant. On one view, it does not seem right that an undertaking subject to a European Commission investigation which is limited to one Member State can then be subject to any number of other similar investigations conducted by national competition authorities. Nevertheless, it appears as though such situations are not only allowed, but are in fact anticipated by the European Commission in its decisions. This issue has surfaced in **6.39**

---

[46] *Napp Pharmaceutical Holdings Ltd v Director General of Fair Trading* [2002] CAT 1 and *Allsports Ltd v OFT* [2004] CAT 17 (see paras 9.19–9.26 below).

the *Visa/MasterCard* proceedings. The European Commission and various national competition authorities, including the OFT, have all investigated credit card interchange fees following different notifications and complaints. In particular, the OFT disagreed with the European Commission's economic analysis. A compromise was reached with the European Commission framing its exemption in terms of cross-border interchange, leaving the OFT (and several other national competition authorities) clear to investigate the domestic implications of the interchange regime. However this means that Visa and MasterCard have been open to multiple investigations rather than a one-stop-shop.

6.40 Some of these issues have been the subject of interesting and informative debate by other authors, from which it is clear that regardless of whether it constitutes a technical breach of the *ne bis in idem* principle, it undoubtedly creates an additional burden for an undertaking facing multiple proceedings.[47] It appears that a precedent case will be needed before there is clarification of the interaction of the ECHR with the modernised competition enforcement regime.

C. Jurisdiction and Threshold Requirements for an OFT Investigation

6.41 This part addresses the threshold legal and policy requirements which apply to the OFT (and the Regulators) in deciding to commence an investigation. Under the Competition Act 1998, there are jurisdictional and legal threshold conditions which must be fulfilled before the OFT can use its powers of investigation. The two key legal conditions relate to threshold evidence requirements and time limitation periods. The OFT also has policy constraints, since it does not have the resources to investigate fully every matter which is brought to its attention. Thus the OFT may exercise its discretion in deciding which matters it will investigate using its full powers.

6.42 There are also limits on the use to which certain evidence and information received by the OFT may be put: for example, the OFT may not commence an investigation on the basis of information provided to it via the ECN where that information relates to a leniency application in another Member State. These types of issues are reviewed in the section below, on receiving information before commencing an investigation.

---

[47] R Nazzini, *Concurrent Proceedings in Competition Law—procedure, evidence and remedies* (Oxford University Press, 2004) paras 5.27 et seq; see also W Wils, 'The Principle of Ne Bis in Idem in EC Antitrust Enforcement: a Legal and Economic Analysis' (2003) 26 World Competition 131–48.

(a) Obtaining evidence before commencing an investigation

(i) Complaints

In order to trigger an investigation, the OFT must receive information from **6.43** a source. With notifications no longer available, this essentially leaves three methods by which information may be received and acted upon by an authority: complaints, leniency applications, or 'own initiative' (including by the receipt of information in the conduct of its other functions). This latter category may include, for example, gathering information from the ECN, or from the Competition Commission (**CC**) following a market investigation, or information gathered for OFT market studies and through consumer powers.

Complaints are the most common source of information for the OFT.[48] In **6.44** competition enforcement, the OFT reviews more than 1,000 complaints each year, and around 50 of these normally result in further investigation.[49] The OFT has established a Preliminary Investigations Unit which is tasked with reviewing complaints received by the OFT. The OFT's guideline on third parties also incorporates guidance on the submission of complaints[50] which sets out detailed information on the OFT's treatment of complainants and advice on submitting a complaint to the OFT.

The OFT, like the European Commission,[51] generally requires complaints to **6.45** reach a certain minimum standard before the complainant will be accorded the status of 'Formal Complainant', thus allowing the complainant certain rights. A complaint not reaching this standard will be treated merely as the provision of information.[52]

The OFT will grant Formal Complainant status to any person: **6.46**

---

[48] The OFT Annual Report and Resource Accounts 2005–06 reported that 1,350 complaint cases were opened, as compared to 22 conditional leniency agreements having been entered into. No other method of receiving initial information is mentioned in the Report.

[49] The OFT Annual Report and Resource Accounts 2005–06 reported that 1,350 complaint cases were opened, with formal investigations being launched on 23 occasions, and seven decisions were made.

[50] OFT451, *Involving third parties in Competition Act investigations: Incorporating guidance on the submission of complaints* (April 2006) (**Third Parties Guideline**).

[51] The European Commission has published a guideline on the handling of complaints which came into effect on 1 May 2004: Commission notice on the handling of complaints by the Commission under Articles 81 and 82 of the EC Treaty (2004/C 101/05) [2004] OJ C101/65.

[52] This will, in broad terms, result in the complainant having very few rights regarding matters such as access to files and information about the case. The OFT's categorisation of Formal Complainants and its policy statements in the Third Parties Guideline do not affect the general rights of third parties in accordance with case law and legislation. However, it appears that the OFT's Third Parties Guideline is largely intended to reflect the legal requirements concerning third parties.

- who has submitted a written, reasoned complaint to the OFT containing certain specified information;
- who has requested Formal Complainant status; and
- whose interests are, or are likely to be, materially affected by the agreement(s) or conduct which is the subject-matter of the complaint.[53]

The benefits of being treated as a Formal Complainant are set out in the OFT's Third Parties Guideline, and relate to specific rights to be included in the progress of the investigation at certain stages, including receiving information and being provided with an opportunity to respond on certain aspects. The rights of third parties are discussed in detail in Chapter 9 (and see also Chapter 10 in relation to interim measures).

6.47 The OFT's Third Parties Guideline annexes a list of information required to be provided in a written, reasoned complaint, as well as a further list of 'optional' information.[54] In general terms, the required information is: information on the complainant and the complainee; details of the complaint; factual evidence supporting the complaint; and information about any related complaints/investigations or litigation. The optional information comprises: further details about the complainant; the relevant product and geographic markets; the competitive conditions in the relevant markets; the legal basis for the complaint; and information likely to be relevant to particular types of agreement or conduct. Complainants may substantiate their complaint by the provision of relevant documents, by the provision of witness information (in the form of witness statements) and allowing the OFT access to those witnesses, and also (as noted above) by providing legal and/or economic analysis of the factual information. All of these measures will assist the OFT in making an assessment as to whether to take the case forward,[55] and will also assist the complainant to decide whether its complaint is well-founded.

6.48 Information provided by way of a complaint may contain confidential information. The rules governing the OFT's responsibilities for the treatment of confidential information are set out in Pt 9 of the Enterprise Act 2002 and the OFT's Procedural Rules.[56] A detailed assessment of the applicable statutory restrictions contained in s 237 of the Enterprise Act and the gateways in Pt 9 of the Enterprise Act are set out at paras 8.09–8.60 in relation to information disclosure. It is

---

[53] OFT's Third Parties Guideline, para 2.6.   [54] ibid, Annexes B and C.
[55] In general, a decision of the OFT not to investigate a complaint will result from a combination of factors, comprising both legal and policy considerations, which are discussed at paras 6.67–6.78.
[56] Competition Act 1998 (Office of Fair Trading's Rules) Order 2004, SI 2004/2751.

important to note that the Enterprise Act takes precedence over the OFT's Rules, and that the Enterprise Act restrictions in Pt 9 do not apply to the CAT.[57]

6.49 The types of confidential information which a complainant may be concerned about providing could include, for example, such information as the identity of the complainant, information that is sensitive for market or other reasons, and information which is subject to obligations of confidentiality owed to other parties. A complainant should take care not to reveal information in breach of its contractual obligations in these circumstances.

6.50 At the outset, a complainant may choose not to provide certain information to the OFT unless the OFT agrees to treat it as confidential, as the OFT can enter into an agreement with an undertaking regarding the treatment of its information by the OFT.[58] However, this could limit the OFT's ability to take the case forward. Usually, as the OFT's and the complainant's interests are aligned, there will be a way of dealing with the complainant's concerns. For example, the OFT may later issue a Section 26 Notice to compel disclosure of the information, or may obtain the information by some other source, or may agree with the complainant that from a certain point in the investigation it will be able to disclose the information.

6.51 If the complainant decides to provide information to the OFT without first reaching agreement on the treatment of confidential information, but later wishes to have some of the information treated as confidential, the complainant must identify to the OFT that it is confidential information and give specific reasons in support of its legitimate protection. The standard practice for doing this is to denote such information with '[***][C]'), and provide an explanation for the confidentiality in a schedule of reasons.[59] The key reasons for treating information as confidential are likely to be reasons which meet the tests set out in s 244(3) of the Enterprise Act 2002, being either commercial information whose disclosure might significantly harm the legitimate business interests of the undertaking to which it relates, or information relating to the private affairs of an individual whose disclosure might significantly harm the individual's interests. The OFT is not required to treat a request for confidentiality at face value and it may undertake its own independent analysis of the underlying reasons. In practice, it is more likely to do this if it appears that the complainant

---

[57] Enterprise Act 2002, s 237(5).

[58] The OFT cannot prevent the information from being disclosed in all circumstances, eg, pursuant to an order by the CAT.

[59] Where certain documents contain parts that are confidential *and* are not relevant for the OFT's purposes, the standard practice is to redact those parts (and explain the reason for the redaction).

has not properly assessed confidentiality of the information provided. Thus making a blanket request for confidentiality is unlikely to be helpful.

6.52 Even though the OFT has particular responsibilities in its treatment of confidential information, it is possible that information may be ultimately treated by the OFT as not being confidential, or that the information may be required to be revealed by the OFT at a later point in the process, such as on appeal to the CAT.

6.53 Where information is regarded as confidential, the OFT has an obligation to advise of any intended disclosure and allow a reasonable opportunity to make representations about the proposed disclosure.[60] The OFT may also seek further explanations for the need to treat documents as confidential. These obligations and powers apply in respect of a person who has 'supplied information to the OFT'. This may not in all cases be the actual person supplying the information, but may be a person the OFT believes has some connection to the particular document or whose interests are affected by the information.[61] For example, a company may supply documentation, but some of it may relate to an individual who may have concerns about the disclosure of the document. Rule 6(5) of the OFT's Rules provides that 'where, in the OFT's opinion, information supplied to the OFT by any person relates to or originates from another person, that other person may be treated as a person who has supplied information to the OFT'. Thus the OFT may, in theory, satisfy its obligations regarding an intended disclosure by advising a different person of the disclosure other than the person who actually supplied the information.

6.54 Information which has been supplied by a complainant may be retained by the OFT and may be used at a later stage, even if the complaint has been rejected. The most obvious scenario is where one or two complaints about a particular type of behaviour are followed by a much greater number of complaints indicating that the relevant behaviour is more widespread than originally thought. The OFT may then decide to take the case further even though its initial decision was not to do so. Information which has been retained by the OFT or the Regulators may also be disclosed to each other or to other members of the ECN in some circumstances.[62]

6.55 In deciding not to investigate a complaint, the OFT may in some cases be making an appealable decision pursuant to s 46(3) of the Competition Act. Appealable decisions of the OFT are considered in further detail in Chapter 12, below.

---

[60] OFT's Procedural Rules, r 6.   [61] Enterprise Act 2002, Pt 9.
[62] Further details on such disclosures are set out at paras 8.103–8.137.

(ii) Other sources of information

Leniency applications   According to the OFT, almost all of its cartel cases are **6.56** triggered by the supply of information from a whistleblower pursuant to a leniency application. The European Commission reports a similar statistic. This is therefore arguably the most valuable source of information to the OFT and it is certainly a source which the OFT seeks to maintain and protect. Leniency applications are discussed fully in Chapter 5, including the consequences for the information provided by a leniency applicant whose application is unsuccessful.

'Own initiative'   In the course of its functions, the OFT has access to informa- **6.57** tion from many other sources. As the OFT may start an investigation of its own initiative, the OFT may use the information from these sources to commence an investigation, subject to any specific rules on the use of information in certain circumstances. The types of sources from which the OFT may obtain information leading to the commencement of an investigation include court cases, the CC, the ECN, US investigations and cases, and other regulatory bodies such as the Financial Services Authority. The OFT will also obtain information from OFT market studies and consumer investigations. The OFT's 2006–07 Annual Plan states that the OFT intends to increase the extent of own initiative cases.[63]

(iii) Limits on use of information received

There are some legal restrictions on the OFT's use of particular types of infor- **6.58** mation in commencing an investigation. The key legal restrictions result from:

- Enterprise Act 2002, Pt 9;
- the Network Notice;
- restrictions relating to the use of privileged information.

The application of these legal restrictions is set out in detail in Chapters 7 and 8 on information gathering and information disclosure.

(b) Threshold evidence requirement

(i) Section 25 of the Competition Act 1998

The threshold evidence requirement is set out in s 25 of the Competition **6.59** Act 1998. The OFT must ensure that the threshold criteria contained in s 25 are satisfied before it is able to use its powers of investigation under the Act. This applies to all investigations by the OFT or the Regulators, and applies to investigations conducted in relation to the prohibitions under the Competition Act as well as investigations under Article 81 or Article 82.

---

[63] OFT's Annual Plan 2006–07, 13.

6.60   Section 25 of the Competition Act 1998 essentially provides that the OFT 'may' commence an investigation where 'there are reasonable grounds for suspecting' that one of the competition law prohibitions has been (or is being) infringed. The fact that an agreement or conduct has come to an end does not exclude it from being investigated by the OFT.

6.61   This section therefore contains two key elements. First, it sets an objective evidential threshold which must be met before the investigative powers in the subsequent sections can be invoked, and secondly, it provides a discretionary power to commence an investigation once the threshold criteria are met. These two elements have come to have quite different effects in the context of the rejection of complaints by the OFT.

6.62   There has been some judicial consideration given to the type of evidence needed to establish reasonable grounds for suspecting a competition law infringement, in the context of applications for a warrant to enter and search premises. These cases have tended to confirm that some evidence is required, but that the threshold is not high. The key reason for a low threshold is obvious: the use of investigative powers is to obtain evidence to check the existence and scope of a factual and legal situation concerning which the authority already possesses some information. If the evidential threshold for the use of such powers is too high, it would defeat the purpose of the investigative powers.[64]

6.63   The same criteria also apply in the context of the OFT assisting another national competition authority or the European Commission. As the OFT is not the authority making the initial decision to take a case forward, it must rely on information provided to it by the requesting authority to meet the criteria. However, the OFT may refuse to carry out the required investigation if it takes the view that the threshold criteria are not met.[65]

(ii) Consideration of exemptions and exclusions under section 25

6.64   The amendments to the Competition Act in 2004 substantially increased the complexity of s 25, which was previously a relatively short and simple section. The changes were made, however, in an attempt to retain the same effect of s 25 within the modernised regime. The changes were required in order to deal with problems associated with the OFT making a preliminary assessment of an agreement, in circumstances where the notification system had been abolished and any agreement may be exempt under the individual exemption conditions

---

[64] See Case C-94/00 *Roquette Frères SA v Directeur Général de la Concurrence, de la Consommation et de la Répression des Fraudes* [2002] ECR I-9011, paras 54, 61, 70, and 100; and *OFT v X* [2003] EWHC 1042 (Comm), [2003] 2 All ER (Comm) 183, para 3.
[65] Competition Act 1998, s 65D.

without the need for prior notification. Thus it was no longer appropriate for the OFT to make a preliminary assessment of whether an agreement was exempt. The burden of proving exemption falls to the undertaking, not to the OFT.

Section 25 of the Competition Act 1998, as it is now drafted, requires the OFT **6.65** to consider only whether the agreement falls within the provisions of a block exemption (or an exclusion). An undertaking cannot successfully argue that the OFT ought not to have commenced an investigation simply because the conditions for exemption were in fact satisfied, unless there is an individual exemption decision which is still valid,[66] or the agreement falls within one of the block exemptions or exclusions. Under s 25, the OFT is not required to consider whether the individual exemption conditions apply to the particular agreement in question. This issue is one to be raised by the undertaking itself once an investigation has commenced, as the burden of proof falls to the undertaking in such a case.

The extent to which the provisions of s 25 of the Competition Act 1998 **6.66** might prevent the OFT from opening an investigation where the European Commission has made a non-infringement decision is yet to be tested.

(iii) Rejection of complaints under section 25

No reasonable grounds for suspecting a breach   Approximately 80 per cent of **6.67** all complaints received are dismissed by the OFT and the Regulators at or prior to the s 25 stage. Initially, under the Competition Act 1998, these complaints were dismissed on the basis that there were no reasonable grounds for suspecting a breach of the competition law prohibitions. The question of the rights of a complainant in such a case was raised in the CCAT (now the CAT) decision in *Bettercare v Director General of Fair Trading*.[67] In that case, the CAT considered whether the rejection of a complaint under s 25 could amount to an appealable decision under the Competition Act. The Director General of Fair Trading (now the OFT) had stated in a letter to the complainant: 'Our response to your complaint is based on a lack of reasonable grounds to suspect an infringement of the Competition Act 1998.'[68] However, the CAT found that it was clear from previous correspondence between the OFT and the complainant that the reason underlying the rejection of the complaint was, based on the facts in question, that the party complained of was not an undertaking for the purposes of the Competition Act. The CAT noted:

---

[66] This is not specifically provided for in s 25, but it stands to reason that an individual exemption decision made before 1 May 2004 which remains valid ought to be taken into account by the OFT in considering whether the threshold criteria under s 25 are met.

[67] *Bettercare Group Ltd v Director General of Fair Trading (Admissibility of Appeal)* [2002] CAT 6.

[68] ibid, para 32.

It is true that . . . the Director's decision that North & West is not an undertaking also precludes him from launching an investigation under section 25 of the Act since, on the Director's view, it necessarily follows that he has 'no reasonable grounds for suspecting' an infringement. However, in our view, one cannot convert what is in substance an appealable decision into an unappealable decision by the simple device of describing it as the exercise of the Director's administrative discretion not to proceed further on the basis of lack of reasonable grounds for suspecting an infringement. It all depends on the substance. In our view, if, as a matter of substance, the Director's statement that he has no reasonable grounds for suspecting an infringement in fact masks a decision by the Director that the Chapter II prohibition is not infringed, there is still a 'relevant decision' for the purposes of section 47(1). In the present case, in our view, the Director has, in effect, decided that the conduct in question does not infringe the Chapter II prohibition, with the consequence that he cannot proceed under section 25. But that consequence, in our view, is merely the secondary result of the primary decision that there has been no infringement.[69]

6.68 Thus the CAT found in *Bettercare* that there had been a 'relevant decision' (ie a decision that the Chapter II prohibition had not been infringed) despite the Director General of Fair Trading's purported exercise of discretion under s 25 of the Competition Act 1998. Therefore, it is possible that a complaint rejection under s 25 can amount to an appealable decision under the Competition Act, depending on the amount of information the OFT has reviewed in coming to its conclusion and the reasons it provides for rejecting the complaint.[70] This issue is also discussed further in Chapter 12, in relation to appeals and judicial review.

6.69 **Exercise of discretionary power** In *Bettercare*, the CAT expressly acknowledged that s 25 allowed for the exercise of a discretionary power by the Director General of Fair Trading (now the OFT).[71] The OFT's discretion to decide not to proceed with a complaint (even under s 25) can be exercised without the need for a decision that there are no reasonable grounds to suspect a competition law infringement.[72] The CAT noted on this point:

---

[69] ibid, para 87.

[70] See more recently the comments of the CAT in *Brannigan v OFT* [2006] CAT 28, paras 64–72, where the CAT held that a complaint rejected in accordance with the OFT's administrative priorities arguably gave rise to an appealable decision because the OFT had reached a view, either expressly or by necessary implication, that neither the Chapter II nor the Chapter I prohibition had been infringed, on the material before the OFT.

[71] *Bettercare Group Ltd v Director General of Fair Trading (Admissibility of Appeal)* [2002] CAT 6, para 80. The tribunal accepted that (subject to any possibility of judicial review) 'the Director has a discretion under the Act whether to (i) open an investigation under section 25, or (ii) proceed to a decision as to whether or not there has been an infringement'.

[72] However, in *Brannigan v OFT* [2006] CAT 28, the CAT moved toward equating the s 25 threshold with the test for deciding whether or not there was an appealable decision under s 46(3) of the Competition Act 1998, which is arguably too low a threshold for the purposes of s 25.

The Director may decide to 'reject a complaint' for many reasons. For example, he may have other cases that he wishes to pursue in priority (compare Case T-24 and 28/90 Automec v Commission [1992] ECR 11–2223); he may have insufficient information to decide whether there is an infringement or not; he may suspect that there may be an infringement, but the case does not appear sufficiently promising, or the economic activity concerned sufficiently important, to warrant the commitment of further resources. None of these cases necessarily give rise to a decision by the Director as to whether a relevant prohibition is infringed.[73]

The exercise of this discretion is normally based on policy considerations, which are considered in the following section. **6.70**

(iv) Policy requirements for commencing an investigation

Policy considerations   Any decision of a competition authority to take a case **6.71** forward and use its investigative powers will involve not only a legal assessment of the available evidence, but also an assessment of whether the case fits with the authority's current administrative policies. This will include its policies on prosecuting various types of infringements, as well as ensuring in each case that resources to investigate the case are available and will be allocated in accordance with the overall policies.

The OFT's policies leading to the rejection of complaints or the decision not to **6.72** proceed with an investigation may relate to one or more of a number of factors, including the industry involved, the number of complaints received about a particular issue, the market share of the undertaking(s) the subject of the complaint, whether any similar cases have been or are being conducted by the OFT, whether a case is already the subject of investigation by another competition authority,[74] and whether the OFT is already developing a policy to address the particular issues raised by a complaint.

As a government body, the OFT is required to make its decision-making pol- **6.73** icies transparent, so there is generally information available on when the OFT is more likely to choose to take a case forward. For example, the OFT has described its priority areas for 2006/07 as including healthcare, construction and housing, and the interaction between government and markets.[75] It has also set out its criteria for taking on competition enforcement cases as follows: the likely consumer harm from the anti-competitive behaviour; strength of the

---

[73] *Bettercare Group Ltd v Director General of Fair Trading (Admissibility of Appeal)* [2002] CAT 6, para 83.

[74] Note that if a case is already being conducted by another national competition authority within the ECN, the OFT may choose not to take the case forward on the basis of a power set out in Art 13 of Regulation 1/2003. If proceedings have been initiated by the European Commission, the OFT will not have jurisdiction to conduct the case under Art 81 or Art 82.

[75] OFT's Annual Plan, 2006–07, 9.

evidence provided to the OFT; type of case (for example, is it a 'hardcore' cartel?); special features of the particular case; any precedent or policy value—especially if the case is in an OFT priority area; and whether the OFT is best placed to take action.[76]

6.74 Each year the OFT also publishes its Annual Report and Resource Accounts, which contains an analysis of the OFT's performance against its objectives. Each of the Regulators publishes similar reports and/or business plans.[77] In addition, the OFT has published a 'competition prioritisation framework' which briefly lists a number of factors to be considered when deciding whether to prioritise a particular case, on a step-by-step basis.[78]

6.75 Some of these policy factors may relate to both policy and legal considerations. For example, the market share of the undertaking(s) the subject of the complaint may mean that as a matter of law, there can be no infringement of competition law.[79] However, a policy consideration based on the market share of an undertaking may be more generous than the strict legal limitations allow. In superseded guidelines the OFT had advised that, as a matter of policy, it would not generally consider cases where the combined market share of undertakings was less than 25 per cent. The current guidelines have removed this percentage reference, instead referring to the (lower) market share limits set out in the European Commission's notice on appreciable effect on competition.[80] However, the OFT notes that it retains its right to 'consider, on a case by case basis, whether an agreement falls within its administrative priorities so as to merit investigation'.[81] It is probable that the previously published 25 per cent level may be taken as a guide to the OFT's current policy on market share thresholds.

6.76 **Availability and allocation of resources** Part of the rationale behind the changes associated with Regulation 1/2003 related to the European Commission's desire to re-allocate its resources, reducing the time spent on dealing with notifications and increasing the time spent on investigations of cartel

---

[76] ibid 14.

[77] Ofcom publishes an Annual Report and Annual Plan; Ofgem publishes a Corporate Strategy and Plan; Ofregni publishes an Annual Report; Ofwat publishes an Annual Report; and ORR publishes a Business Plan. See Chapter 2 for further information on each of the Regulators.

[78] OFT, *Competition prioritisation framework* (October 2006).

[79] The market share an undertaking holds is relevant to the consideration of legal issues, such as whether there may be an effect on trade between Member Sates, whether there is an appreciable effect on competition, and whether an undertaking is dominant in a particular market.

[80] Commission Notice on agreements of minor importance which do not appreciably restrict competition under Article 81(1) of the Treaty establishing the European Community (*de minimis*) (2001/C 368/07) [2001] OJ C368/13 (which essentially sets the threshold levels at 10% for horizontal and 15% for vertical agreements), and OFT401, *Agreements and concerted practices* (December 2004) paras 2.15–2.21.

[81] OFT401, *Agreements and concerted practices* (December 2004) para 2.28.

infringements. The UK government had a similar objective in making the same change with respect to the OFT's procedures.[82]

The appropriate use of resources is a matter for which the OFT's board has **6.77** responsibility. The OFT's annual budget is approximately £55.5 million. Of this, competition enforcement activities are allocated a budget of £11.4 million and market studies are allocated a budget of £4.8 million. In addition, communications (£3.7 million), corporate services (£9.1 million), and accommodation (£5.9 million) are accounted for separately.[83]

Thus the OFT will consider not only whether the case is one which is able to be **6.78** taken forward on a legal and a general policy basis, but also whether doing so would fit with the proper use of resources. This is listed as a factor in the OFT's published competition prioritisation framework. The OFT has also been implicitly criticised by the CAT for refusing to take on a case citing resource constraints when a substantial proportion of the OFT's sizeable budget was devoted to competition matters.[84]

(c) Time limits for commencing an investigation

(i) Time limits applicable to the OFT and the Regulators

Limitation Act 1980   As the Competition Act 1998 does not set any specific **6.79** time limits for the OFT to commence an investigation, the Limitation Act 1980 applies to the OFT in the conduct of its functions.[85] According to a statement by the Department of Trade and Industry in 2003, '[t]his means that the OFT has six years to impose penalties for infringements of the Competition Act [and the] period within which the OFT may recover penalties imposed under the Competition Act is also six years'.[86]

Time limit for recovery of a penalty imposed   For recovery of penalties **6.80** imposed by the OFT, the Competition Act 1998 provides that the penalty is to be treated as if it were 'a civil debt due to the OFT'.[87] The Limitation Act 1980 provides that a six year time limit applies to actions founded on simple contract,[88] which would be the most common basis for a civil debt recovery (although there are other provisions for special cases in the Limitation Act 1980). The section relating to simple contract actions provides that '[a]n action founded on simple

---

[82] DTI, *UK Competition Law (Modernisation—a consultation on the Government's proposals for amendments to the Competition Act 1998 in light of Regulation 1/2003)* (April 2003).

[83] OFT's Annual Plan 2006–07, 13, 16, 18, and 21.

[84] *Brannigan v OFT* [2006] CAT 28, para 13.   [85] Limitation Act 1980, s 37(1).

[86] DTI's consultation document, *Modernisation—a consultation on the Government's proposals for giving effect to Regulation 1/2003 EC and for re-alignment of the Competition Act 1998* (April 2003) 57.

[87] Competition Act 1998, s 37.   [88] Limitation Act 1980, s 5.

contract shall not be brought after the expiration of six years from the date on which the cause of action accrued'.[89] Thus where the OFT imposes a penalty in respect of a competition law infringement, the six year time period would run from the date it is imposed.

6.81 Where an infringement decision and/or the penalty imposed are the subject of an appeal following the decision of the OFT, this will either freeze the time period from the date the appeal is lodged to the date of the judgment (if the OFT's penalty is upheld on appeal) or start a new time period running in respect of any replacement penalty decision (which will run from either the date of the appellate judgment or the date of the new penalty imposed by the OFT following the appeal decision). This is on the basis that the new penalty gives rise to a new cause of action.

6.82 The related questions of whether the OFT may claim interest on the period, or whether there is a requirement to pay in the meantime, are addressed in Chapter 10 below.

6.83 **Time limit for commencing an investigation** For the commencement of an investigation by the OFT, there is no clear application of the Limitation Act 1980. As noted above, the consultation paper on modernisation issued by the DTI stated that the OFT has six years to impose penalties for infringements of the Competition Act 1998. No further details were provided as to how this conclusion was arrived at, or which provision of the Limitation Act 1980 would apply to this situation. It should also be noted that in relation to competition law offences where the evidence is concealed by the perpetrator (which is usually the situation in cartel cases), any applicable time restrictions will only apply from the date the OFT becomes aware (or ought to have been aware) of the facts revealing the existence of an infringement.[90]

6.84 Assuming the Limitation Act 1980 does limit the OFT's ability to commence an investigation, it is likely to be s 9 (sums recoverable by statute) which bears the most relevance to the commencement of an investigation by the OFT. This section limits commencement of actions to a six year period from the date on which the cause of action accrued. On this assumption, the next issue is the point from which the six year limit applies.

6.85 On one view, the relevant cause of action could come into existence from the date the OFT becomes aware of the potential infringement. If this was the case, it would be open to the OFT to commence a case (and/or impose penalties) within six years from the time it became aware of the potential infringement, provided that the relevant prohibitions applied at the time. The problem with

---

[89] ibid.   [90] Limitation Act 1980, s 32.

this is that any agreement or conduct, no matter how old, would always be within the grasp of the OFT as long as the potential infringement had not yet come to the OFT's attention (however that may be defined).

Another more limited view is that the relevant cause of action comes into existence from the date the infringement ceases. This is the way in which the European Commission's investigations are limited.[91] The problem with this interpretation is that the repercussions of the agreement or conduct could be felt well into the following years, necessitating some action to be taken by an authority. Since there is no legislative guidance to balance properly the need for regulatory involvement with the need for past issues to remain in the past, this would be difficult for a court to apply. This might also lead to cases where a third party might be able to bring an action for damages, but the competition authority is unable to act. **6.86**

Alternatively, the time period could run from the time at which damage is suffered by a third party. This would be an unlikely option because with competition law infringements it is not always easy to identify any particular person as having suffered loss. **6.87**

Given that the Competition Act 1998 itself has only been in force (or enforced) for just over six years, there has been no occasion to test the application of the Limitation Act 1980 to an investigation commenced by the OFT concerning national competition laws. However, with decentralisation of EC competition law, Articles 81 and 82 must now be applied by the OFT. Since these provisions have existed in their current form[92] and have applied in the United Kingdom since 1 January 1973,[93] there is arguably a broader temporal scope to the application of the OFT's investigative powers, although it is doubtful whether this will ever have any relevance in a case. **6.88**

(ii) Time limits applicable to the SFO

As a UK government body, the SFO is subject to the time restrictions set out in the Limitation Act 1980 (although the same interpretation difficulties may apply as noted in relation to the OFT in paras 6.83–6.87 above). However, it should be borne in mind that in relation to competition law offences where the evidence is concealed by the perpetrator (which is usually the situation in cartel cases, where the SFO may be involved), the time restrictions will only apply **6.89**

---

[91] Council Regulation (EEC) 2988/74 concerning limitation periods in proceedings and the enforcement of sanctions under the rules of the European Economic Community relating to transport and competition [1974] OJ L319/1.

[92] Although previously numbered Arts 85 and 86 respectively.

[93] The European Communities Act came into force in 1973 and the UK joined the EU in the same year.

from the date the SFO becomes aware (or ought to have been aware) of the facts revealing the existence of an infringement.[94]

(iii) Time limits applicable to the European Commission

6.90 In contrast to the unclear position with respect to the OFT, the time limits applicable to the European Commission's use of its investigative powers are set out clearly in Council Regulation 2988/74. This Regulation essentially provides for four types of time limits:

- making a decision to impose a fine;
- making a decision to impose an interim fine or periodic penalty;
- enforcing an infringement fine;
- enforcing an interim fine or periodic penalty payment.

6.91 In relation to the first of these categories, Regulation 2988/74 provides that the European Commission may impose fines for competition law infringements within five years from the date the infringement is committed (or the date it ceases, if the infringement is continuing or repeated). This time limit will start running afresh with any action taken by the European Commission to further an investigation. Thus the time limit can be extended, but only to a maximum of ten years in total.

6.92 In relation to interim fines or periodic penalties, the European Commission has only three years from the date the infringement is committed (or the date it ceases, if the infringement is continuing or repeated).

6.93 Once a decision is made, the European Commission has a further five years in which to enforce its decision imposing a fine. For these purposes, time begins to run from the day on which the decision becomes final.

6.94 The limitation period is suspended for as long as the decision of the European Commission is the subject of proceedings pending before the European Court of Justice.[95]

6.95 For the purposes of these provisions, it is reasonable to assume that a decision means a decision actually and directly applicable to a particular undertaking. Accordingly, a decision addressed to a number of undertakings, which is appealed by some undertakings and not by others, is treated as being a number of separate decisions,[96] and each decision will therefore trigger the applicable limitation periods at different times.

---

[94] Limitation Act 1980, s 32.

[95] See Cases T-22/02 and T-23/02 *Sumitomo v Commission*, 6 October 2005 where the time bar applied to the decision as well as the fine.

[96] Case T-227/95 *AssiDomän Kraft Products AB v Commission* [1997] ECR II-1185, para 56.

7

INFORMATION GATHERING

A. Introduction

7.01   The Office of Fair Trading (**OFT**), the Serious Fraud Office (**SFO**), the European Commission and, to some extent, other national competition authorities each have specific information gathering powers relevant to the collection of information from within the United Kingdom. This chapter deals with the powers of these competition authorities to gather information in the United Kingdom and the extent of cooperation that is expected of an undertaking during the exercise of these investigative powers. The next chapter, on information disclosure, deals with the gathering, transmission and use of information by UK authorities where the information is located outside the United Kingdom, as well as the onward transmission and use of information in the United Kingdom.

7.02   The two main types of information gathering powers for any authority are the power to require an undertaking to deliver up documents and information pursuant to a written request, and the power to attend at premises in order to obtain documents. There are also additional ways such as conducting research, gathering publicly available information, and using surveillance methods. Notably, the OFT does not have any powers to gather information for the purpose of market studies, but instead relies upon s 5(1) of the Enterprise Act 2002.[1] According to the OFT's Annual Report 2001, it commenced investigations under the Competition Act 1998 into 63 cases, issued 1,040 Section 26 Notices, and conducted 15 inspections of premises covering 64 different locations. The more recent information provided by the OFT in its annual reports is less detailed, but indicates that the OFT uses its information gathering powers in approximately 18 cases per year.

The powers and sanctions which are applicable to any particular information **7.03** gathering exercise depend on several factors—most significantly, on the type of offence being investigated, the body conducting the investigation, and the undertaking or person which is the recipient of a request or the subject of an inspection. For UK authorities, the powers and procedures relevant to information gathering and transmission methods are set out in UK legislation.[2] For the European Commission, the relevant powers and procedures are contained in Regulation 1/2003,[3] together with, in relation to information in the United Kingdom, the Competition Act 1998. Other national competition authorities do not have any direct power to gather information in the United Kingdom, but they may do so with the assistance of the OFT using specific powers in the Competition Act.

This chapter is divided into sections according to the type of method being used **7.04** to gather information. Where more than one of these methods is available to an authority, it may use more than one method in conjunction with others, simultaneously if necessary. Authorities may also receive information which has been collected by other authorities, both within and outside the United Kingdom. The powers and issues dealing with that are set out in Chapter 8 on information disclosure.

---

[1] Note there are no sanctions in relation to Enterprise Act 2002, s 5(1).
[2] Competition Act 1998, Enterprise Act 2002, Regulation of Investigatory Powers Act 2000, and Police and Criminal Evidence Act 1984.
[3] Council Regulation (EC) 1/2003 of 16 December 2002 on the implementation of the rules on competition laid down in Articles 81 and 82 of the Treaty [2003] OJ L1/1.

B. Key Concepts

(a) Grounds for exclusion from production

7.05 In general, it is advisable for an undertaking subject to an investigation to cooperate with the authorities by providing the documents requested in accordance with the terms of the inspection or written notice (subject to possible discussion and agreement with the authority on relevance and the scope of the request/search). Documents or information falling within one of the categories allowing it to be withheld from production may be excluded from production. The sanctions associated with failing to cooperate or comply with an authority's requests are severe, in some cases including the possibility of imprisonment. There may also be tangible benefits associated with cooperation.[4]

7.06 For all of the UK authorities, for the European Commission and also for other national competition authorities when being assisted by the OFT, the basic grounds upon which documents may be excluded from production are the same. These grounds are:

- the document does not fall within the description of the documents sought by the authority;
- the authority's request for a particular document or class of documents is unreasonable;
- the document is not in the possession, custody, or control of the person or undertaking to whom the notice, warrant, or request is addressed;
- the document or information is subject to legal privilege;
- the document or information is subject to self-incrimination privilege.

7.07 The key concepts underlying the latter two categories are described in detail below, as these are important concepts and are not always easy to apply.

7.08 It is also important to understand that confidentiality is not a ground for excluding a document or information from production. However, confidentiality can give rise to different treatment of such information, and this is also discussed below.

(b) Legal professional privilege

(i) General principles

7.09 Legal professional privilege is an aspect of the English and European laws of evidence, which describes a class of documents protected from production. The principle underlying legal professional privilege is that 'the administration of

---

[4] For further information on the benefits of cooperation, see Chapters 5 and 10.

justice requires that everyone should be able to consult a lawyer, or to prepare his case for litigation, without fear that any information given to the lawyer, or which he collects himself, will later be revealed in Court against his wishes and interests'.[5] Thus, in general terms, authorities such as the OFT and the European Commission may not compel production of, or use as evidence, a document subject to legal professional privilege unless privilege has been waived by the undertaking.[6] The technical definition of legal professional privilege under English law differs from that applicable under European law. In the context of competition investigations in the United Kingdom, there are some occasions where the European definition applies (usually where the investigation is being conducted by the European Commission), but for the majority of circumstances the English definition will apply.

An assertion of privilege over a communication may be made at the point at which disclosure is sought: assertion of privilege over a communication need not wait (and should not wait) until the Statement of Objections or final decision. The most effective way of asserting a claim of privilege over a communication during, for example, a dawn raid, is to place the document into an envelope and mark it confidential and subject to privilege so that the document may not be viewed by the OFT, even if it is removed by the OFT.   **7.10**

(ii) English law

Legal basis for privilege   In the context of competition investigations in the   **7.11**
United Kingdom, the application of legal professional privilege is governed by both statute and common law. Under the Competition Act 1998 and the Enterprise Act 2002, express provision is made in identical terms for the protection of privileged communications:

> (1) A person shall not be required, under any provision of this Part, to produce or disclose a privileged communication.
> (2) 'Privileged communication' means a communication—
>   (a) between a professional legal adviser and a client, or
>   (b) made in connection with, or in contemplation of, legal proceedings and for the purposes of those proceedings,
>   which in proceedings in the High Court would be protected from disclosure on grounds of legal professional privilege.[7]

As a result of the reference to proceedings in the High Court, this provision has   **7.12**

---

[5] See C Passmore, *Privilege* (CLT Professional Publishing, 1998) (*Passmore on Privilege*) 2.
[6] Although privilege attaches to a document, the claim of privilege belongs to the owner of the document, who may also waive such a claim.
[7] Competition Act 1998, s 30(1) and (2).

been interpreted in line with the common law application of legal professional privilege by UK courts.

7.13 There are essentially two types of legal professional privilege which the OFT is required to recognise: legal advice privilege and litigation privilege. Although it is beyond the scope of this work to give a very detailed legal analysis of these two types of privilege, the paragraphs below set out the essential elements in relation to each type of privilege.[8] It is also worth noting that there is an extension of legal professional privilege known as 'joint' or 'common interest' privilege, which operates to protect documents that are disclosed between interested parties so that their disclosure does not amount to a waiver, but the documents must first satisfy the requirements of legal professional privilege for this to apply.[9]

7.14 **Legal advice privilege** For legal advice privilege to apply to a document, it must be (a) a communication, (b) made confidentially, (c) made between a client and his or her lawyer, and (d) made for the dominant purpose of seeking or giving legal advice or assistance. Taking each of these elements in turn:

7.15 *'Communication'* This is a broad term, which includes oral as well as written communications, and can include any form of communication such as a voicemail message, email, or simply a handwritten note of a conversation. It will include accompanying documents prepared by the client for the purpose of obtaining the legal advice, for example, a summary of background events. Notes made of information received from a third party will also be privileged where they are made for the purpose of obtaining legal advice.

7.16 *'Made confidentially'* The communication must have been made in confidential circumstances, and such confidentiality must also have been maintained over the communication in question.[10]

7.17 *'Between a client and lawyer'* The definition of 'client' in this context has narrowed considerably as a result of developments in the English case law: only those representatives of the client which have been charged with seeking legal advice from a lawyer may engage in privileged communications. Communications between a lawyer and any other member of the client will not be subject to legal advice privilege.[11]

---

[8] There are a number of excellent text books available which discuss in some detail the development of English law in relation to legal professional privilege: eg, *Passmore on Privilege*; and B Thaki, *The Law of Privilege* (Oxford University Press, 2006).

[9] See Thaki, ibid, 273 et seq for a discussion of the law applicable to this type of privilege.

[10] The procedures and rights which relate to purely confidential documents and information are an entirely separate consideration from communications over which privilege is claimed.

[11] *Three Rivers DC v Bank of England (Disclosure) (No 5)* [2004] UKHL 48, [2005] 1 AC 610. Note that this part of the decision was made by the Court of Appeal: the House of Lords did not overrule the Court of Appeal on this point, although Lord Scott remarked that 'the Court of

The meaning of 'lawyer' is also important. In-house counsel in the United **7.18**
Kingdom are considered to be independent lawyers for the purpose of claiming
legal professional privilege. Lawyers qualified outside the United Kingdom are
also considered to be independent lawyers for the purpose of claiming legal
professional privilege, including lawyers qualified outside the European Union.
The lawyer must be acting in his or her professional capacity at the time the communication is made, but there is no requirement to hold an English practising
certificate, and solicitor's employees such as paralegals or trainees can also create
privileged communications provided the other elements of the test are met.[12]

This 'client/lawyer' requirement does not exclude documents which are made **7.19**
between a solicitor and another lawyer or counsel in the course of preparation of
legal advice, nor does it exclude the solicitor's own working notes and other
preparatory documents.

'Made for the dominant purpose of seeking or giving legal advice or assistance' This **7.20**
requires the communication to be made as part of 'that necessary exchange of
information of which the object is the giving of legal advice as and when
appropriate'.[13] The purpose test is applied as at the date the document was
created, as the purpose test relates to the reason for which the document was
prepared or created. It has been suggested that in this context the practical
emphasis should be on the retainer, so that if the dominant purpose of
the retainer is the seeking and giving of legal advice, then in all likelihood
documents created pursuant to that retainer will be created for that purpose.[14]
Where a single document has been created for a dual purpose, such as for the
giving of legal advice and for some commercial purpose as well, it is likely, but
not certain, that such documents will be covered by legal advice privilege
provided the legal advice purpose is the dominant purpose.

The meaning of legal advice in this context was raised in the *Three Rivers* case, **7.21**
where the Court of Appeal[15] interpreted this question narrowly (holding that
the documents had to record the legal advice given), but the judgment in this
regard was overturned on appeal by the House of Lords.[16] Thus the position
remains that legal advice is not confined to telling a client the law but also

---

Appeal judgment may have gone too far in treating communications between Freshfields and the
employees of the Bank (other than BIU) . . . as being communications between third parties'.

[12] *IBM Corp v Phoenix International (Computers) Ltd* [1995] 1 All ER 413.

[13] *Balabel v Air India* [1988] 1 Ch 317, 332 (CA), per Taylor LJ.

[14] *Hellenic Mutual Risks Association (Bermuda) Ltd v Harrison (The Sagheera)* [1997] 1 Lloyd's
Rep 160, 168.

[15] *Three Rivers DC v Bank of England (Disclosure) (No 3)* [2003] EWCA Civ 474, [2003]
QB 1556.

[16] *Three Rivers DC v Bank of England (Disclosure) (No 4)* [2004] EWCA Civ 218, [2004]
QB 916.

includes advice on what should be prudently and sensibly done in the relevant legal context, which includes presentational advice in the context of inquiries.

7.22 **Litigation privilege**   Litigation privilege is generally of a broader application, and will apply to (a) a communication, which is made confidentially, (b) made between either a client and a third party, or the lawyer and a third party, (c) for the dominant purpose of use in litigation, and (d) where litigation is either proceeding or in contemplation at the time the communication is made. Taking each of these elements in turn:

7.23 *'Communication' and 'confidentially'*   These terms have the same definition as noted above in relation to legal advice privilege (see paras 7.15–7.16).

7.24 *'Lawyer'/'Client'/'Third party'*   This requirement is much broader than that required for legal advice privilege, for it will cover almost all communications which are made for the purpose of the litigation even where they are made directly between a client and a third party. The meaning of 'lawyer' is the same as for legal advice privilege, as noted at para 7.18 above. The meaning of client, although broader than that as for legal advice privilege, does have some limits: in the *Three Rivers* case, the issue of who is deemed to be the client was interpreted narrowly by the Court of Appeal,[17] and this issue was not raised before the House of Lords.[18] Thus the position remains that not all employees can be regarded as 'the client' for the purposes of asserting privilege over a document. It is only employees with responsibility for obtaining and seeking legal advice. In the context of litigation privilege, this may mean that only employees who are providing instructions or are otherwise directly involved in the litigation are able to be defined as 'the client'.

7.25 *'Dominant purpose of use in litigation'*   A protected communication may be made for a number of purposes, and privilege will be maintained provided that such purposes include a dominant connection with litigation.[19] The purpose may be that of the author or that of the person under whose direction the document is created. The purpose is that established at the time the document is created: thus, privilege may be maintained even though the document is not ultimately used in the litigation.[20]

7.26 *'Litigation'*   Litigation includes contemplated litigation, and means judicial or quasi-judicial proceedings. Although competition investigations are not true adversarial litigation in the traditional sense, an investigation by the OFT or

---

[17] *Three Rivers DC v Bank of England (Disclosure) (No 3)* [2003] EWCA Civ 474, [2003] QB 1556.

[18] *Three Rivers DC v Bank of England (Disclosure) (No 4)* [2004] EWCA Civ 218, [2004] QB 916.

[19] *Grant v Downs* (1976) 135 CLR 674; cited with approval in *Waugh v British Railways Board* [1980] AC 521.

[20] *Southwark Water Co v Quick* (1878) 3 QBD 315.

another competition authority is likely to be regarded as litigation (or 'legal proceedings') for the purpose of claiming litigation privilege over documents.[21] The question of whether such litigation is 'contemplated' at a particular point in time has been described as a test of whether litigation is 'reasonably in anticipation', or is 'very probable', or is 'in real prospect'. This will be a question of fact in each case, and will depend upon such evidence as instructions given to solicitors, or communications with the other party.[22] The guiding principle behind this limb of legal professional privilege links to the rights of defence, and in particular the right to prepare a defence without being required to disclose the preparation of the case to the opponent.

(iii) The European Court of Justice application of legal professional privilege

This application is relevant to information gathering in the United Kingdom **7.27** where the European Commission is gathering information for its own investigations. It does not apply where any other authority is gathering documents or information in the United Kingdom, even if the documents are being used in an investigation of a potential infringement of Article 81 or Article 82. In general terms, the definition of legal professional privilege applied by the European Court of Justice (**ECJ**) is largely the same as the UK definition, as set out above, except that the ECJ only recognises one single category of legal privilege, rather than two. Thus the definition under EC law appears to be a hybrid of the two types of privilege, extending beyond legal advice privilege to the protection of communications connected to the investigation and the undertaking's rights of defence. However, there are some substantive differences which make the European definition of legal professional privilege narrower (in the sense that it applies to fewer documents) than the UK definition.

The European definition of legal professional privilege was set out in *AM & S*,[23] **7.28** where it was confirmed that the ECJ does not accord legal privilege to documents created pursuant to the relationship between a client and an in-house lawyer,[24] or between a client and a lawyer based in a country outside the European

---

[21] Support for this contention is derived from s 30 of the Competition Act 1998, as well as common law principles: see *R (Morgan Grenfell & Co Ltd) v Special Commissioners of Income Tax* [2002] UKHL 21, [2003] 1 AC 563; and further support may be derived from Joined Cases T 125 & 253/03 R *Akzo Nobel Chemicals Ltd v Commission* [2003] ECR II-4771 (which may in theory be incorporated into UK procedure through s 60 of the Competition Act 1998).

[22] Although note it is not necessary for solicitors to have been engaged, nor for any communications to have passed between the parties, in order for litigation privilege to be claimed.

[23] Case 155/79 *AM & S Europe Ltd v Commission* [1982] ECR 1575.

[24] But note that this element was based on principles dating from 1982, and it is possible that it will be altered in the future: see in particular the comments of the CFI in Joined Cases T-125 & 253/03 R *Akzo Nobel Chemicals Ltd v Commission* [2003] ECR II-4771, paras 124–130; and see also para 8.190 below.

Union. In addition, the European definition will not cover documents that are prepared for the predominant purpose of litigation, but are not generated by the lawyer himself (such as experts' reports and witness statements).

7.29 In *AM & S*, the ECJ held:

> In Regulation no 17 itself, in particular in the eleventh recital in its preamble and in the provisions contained in Article 19, care is taken to ensure that the rights of defence may be exercised to the full, and the protection of the confidentiality of written communications between lawyer and client is an essential corollary to those rights. In those circumstances, such protection must, if it is to be effective, be recognised as covering all written communications exchanges after the initiation of the administrative procedure under Regulation No 17 which may lead to a decision on the application of Articles [81] and [82] of the Treaty or to a decision imposing a pecuniary sanction on the undertaking. It must also be possible to extend it to earlier written communications which have a relationship to the subject-matter of that procedure.[25]

These principles were confirmed by the CFI in *Akzo*[26] who reiterated the importance of privilege for the rights of defence in proceedings imposing sanctions. It regarded privilege as an essential corollary to the rights of defence which must be protected even if the Commission proceedings are administrative in nature.

(c) Self-incrimination privilege

(i) Origin and application to competition law proceedings

7.30 The privilege against self-incrimination is closely linked to the right to silence and, in the United Kingdom, provides that in civil proceedings a person may refuse to answer any question if to do so would expose that person to criminal proceedings or proceedings leading to the imposition of a penalty.[27]

7.31 It is clear that the privilege against self-incrimination does apply in the context of a competition investigation in the United Kingdom,[28] and will apply to undertakings as well as individuals who are the subject of an investigation.[29] The

---

[25] ibid, para 23.

[26] Joined Cases T 125 & 253/03 R *Akzo Nobel Chemicals Ltd v Commission* [2003] ECR II-4771, para 95. This case involved a dispute between the Commission and undertakings as to whether certain documents seized by the Commission were privileged. The dispute arose as a result of a dawn raid carried out by the Commission and staff of the OFT.

[27] *Blunt v Park Lane Hotel* [1942] 2 KB 253.

[28] The economic rationale for the application of this privilege in the context of competition law enforcement has been suggested to relate to the need for ensuring the reliability of information obtained under compulsion. Without the privilege, it is possible that staff of the undertaking may give misleading answers in the hope of escaping detection, or alternatively such persons may be induced by pressure to make untruthful inculpatory statements: W Wils, 'Self-incrimination in EC antitrust enforcement: A legal and economic analysis' (2003) 26 World Competition 567.

[29] Note that this privilege does not apply to third parties who are not the subject of the relevant investigation.

rights of defence must be observed not only during the administrative process which may lead to the imposition of penalties, but also during the preliminary phases of an investigation, such as requests for information, as these may be decisive in providing evidence of the unlawful nature of conduct engaged in by undertakings and for which they may be liable.[30] Thus it is clear that the self-incrimination privilege applies to any use of compulsory powers by the European Commission, the OFT, the Regulators, the SFO, and also to the use of any such powers by the OFT on behalf of other national competition authorities in order for them to obtain information in the United Kingdom.

(ii) Legal basis for the self-incrimination privilege

Article 6 of the European Convention on Human Rights In *Saunders*,[31] the **7.32** European Court of Human Rights (**ECtHR**) established that the right not to incriminate oneself is a generally recognised international standard which lies at the heart of the requirement of a fair trial in Article 6(1) of the European Convention on Human Rights (**ECHR**). This line of case law has been developed in further judgments of the ECtHR. Although this legal basis does not apply to the European Commission (see para 7.33 below), it does apply to the national competition authorities and national courts of the Member States.

General rights of defence Under the principles set out in *Mannesmann*,[32] it **7.33** was established that although the ECHR does not bind the European Commission,[33] nevertheless Community law does recognise as fundamental principles both the rights of defence and the right to a fair legal process. In that case the ECJ was required to consider a set of questions which the European Commission had required the applicant to answer pursuant to a written request for information and documents in the context of an administrative competition investigation. The ECJ held that although there was no absolute right to silence in this context, the applicant could not be compelled to answer such questions as would require the applicant to give its own assessment of the nature of the subject matter of the questions. Thus, to the extent that such questions did not concern purely factual information, the applicant was not required to answer such questions, and the asking of such questions infringed the applicant's rights

---

[30] Case 374/87 *Orkem v Commission* [1989] ECR 3283, 3351. Prior to *Orkem*, there were initial suggestions that the privilege did not apply to the investigative process, but would only apply to a later use of such evidence in proceedings. This distinction was drawn on the basis of case law in other areas such as tax investigations, but it has since been made clear that a competition investigation is, in this respect, more akin to adjudicatory process than an administrative process.

[31] *Saunders v UK* Application 19187/91, (1997) 23 EHRR 313.

[32] Case T-112/98 *Mannesmannrohren-Werke v Commission* [2001] ECR II-729.

[33] This appeared to contradict the position previously taken by the CFI in Case 374/87 *Orkem v Commission* [1989] ECR 3283, where the CFI held that Art 6 could be relied upon by an undertaking subject to an investigation related to competition law (para 30).

of defence. The ECJ held that requests of that kind were such 'that they may compel the applicant to admit its participation in an unlawful agreement contrary to the Community rules on competition'.[34]

7.34 **UK statutes** The privilege against self-incrimination in relation to a cartel offence investigation by the OFT or the SFO is enshrined in the Enterprise Act 2002, which provides safeguards in relation to the use of information gained by the OFT using its compulsory powers of investigation.[35] This essentially prevents the powers of investigation of the OFT and the SFO being used in such a way as compulsorily to require the accused to provide information which tends to incriminate himself. Thus, statements made by a person in response to a requirement imposed by the OFT using its powers of investigation under the Enterprise Act, may only be used as evidence in criminal proceedings against that person in two circumstances. The first is where that person has knowingly or recklessly made a false or misleading statement in response to that requirement and is then prosecuted for an offence of knowingly or recklessly making a false or misleading statement. The second is where that person is being prosecuted for some other offence and he makes a statement that is inconsistent with his statement in response to the Enterprise Act requirement and if evidence relating to the Enterprise Act statement is adduced or a question relating to it is asked by him or on his behalf.[36]

7.35 Further, a person's answers to questions required under s 2 of the Criminal Justice Act 1987 may only be used in evidence in criminal proceedings against the person under the same two circumstances,[37] and similar restrictions apply to the use in evidence of answers given to questions required under s 28 of the Criminal Law (Consolidation) (Scotland) Act 1995. Finally, statements made by a person in response to a requirement imposed by the OFT using its compulsory powers of investigation under the Competition Act 1998 may only be used as evidence in a cartel prosecution against the person who made it if, in giving evidence during a prosecution of the cartel offence under the Enterprise Act 2002, he makes a statement inconsistent with the Competition Act 1998 statement and if evidence relating to it is adduced or a question relating to it is asked by him or on his behalf.[38]

(iii) What does the self-incrimination privilege cover?

7.36 **Response to questions (testimony)** It is clear from all the relevant case law that the privilege against self-incrimination applies with respect to a requirement to provide testimony (answer questions), where the answers to such questions

---

[34] Case T-112/98 *Mannesmannrohren-Werke v Commission* [2001] ECR II-729, para 71.
[35] Enterprise Act 2002, s 197. [36] ibid, s 197.
[37] Criminal Justice Act 1987, s 2. [38] Competition Act 1998, s 30A.

'might involve an admission on its part of the existence of an infringement which it is incumbent on the [authority] to prove'.[39] Thus, in *Orkem*, the CFI refused permission for the European Commission to seek answers to a number of questions all of which were essentially seeking an acknowledgement of participation by Orkem in the alleged infringement.

Provision of derived factual information such as explanations of documents or responses to purely factual questions There have been some cases which suggest that the privilege against self-incrimination extends to a requirement that the accused provide explanations of documents and responses to purely factual questions.[40] However, in recent times, the more consistent view has been that such requests do not fall foul of the self-incrimination privilege and rights of defence since they are only concerned with purely factual information and are thus more akin to provision of documents.[41]   **7.37**

In practical terms this means that only where an authority's request for information or an oral explanation of a document goes beyond that which is purely factual, and instead requires the recipient to provide information regarding the nature of the conduct or event or document, may the recipient refuse to answer such questions on the ground that to do so would undermine the rights of defence.   **7.38**

Provision of documents or other direct factual material In almost all cases, the privilege against self-incrimination has been held *not* to apply with respect to a request for the provision of documents or other material which has 'an existence independent of the will of the accused'.[42] However, there are some cases which present an anomaly in the regard: in *Funke*, the ECtHR found that a request for certain documents from a taxpayer infringed that taxpayer's rights under Article 6 ECHR because the requesting authority was not certain that the documents existed. This was viewed by some as a rationale based on preventing 'fishing expeditions',[43] but it has not generally found favour with other courts grappling with similar issues, and the general view, as expressed in *Saunders*, is that where material exists independently of the will of the   **7.39**

---

[39] Case 374/87 *Orkem v Commission* [1989] ECR 3283, paras 34 and 35.
[40] *Funke v France* Series A No 256-A, (1993) 16 EHRR 297; *Saunders v UK* Application 19187/91, (1997) 23 EHRR 313.
[41] Case 374/87 *Orkem v Commission* [1989] ECR 3283; Case T-112/98 *Mannesmannrohren-Werke v Commission* [2001] ECR II-729.
[42] *Saunders v UK* Application 19187/91, (1997) 23 EHRR 313, paras 68 and 69.
[43] For a further discussion on this view, see G Stessens, 'The obligations to produce documents versus the privilege against self-incrimination: human rights protection extended too far?' ELR 22 (1997).

accused, such material cannot be withheld on the basis of the privilege against self-incrimination.[44]

7.40   The self-incrimination privilege need not be exercised, in the sense that there is nothing to prevent an undertaking or natural person from making voluntary statements or voluntarily answering questions of their own free will. For this reason, it is very important that any claim of the self-incrimination privilege is made at the time the question is asked, and that the relevant information is accordingly withheld on this basis.[45]

(d) Confidentiality

7.41   Information sought by a competition authority may include commercially confidential documents or information. Information and documents cannot be excluded from production on the ground of confidentiality. However, where some other ground for excluding information applies to the same information, such as relevance, such information may be excluded from production (or masked) on that ground.

7.42   Where no other ground applies to exclude the information from production, there are nevertheless some steps which may be taken to keep information confidential during the authority's investigative and decision-making process. It is important at the point of production to advise the authority (in writing) that the information provided contains confidential material.[46] As soon as there is sufficient time, the confidential material should be specifically identified and the authority advised accordingly. It will also be helpful (to both the undertaking and the authority) to set out the reasons why such information is confidential. These reasons will inform the OFT's decisions on what material may be disclosed to other undertakings and third parties in the decision-making process.

7.43   Confidentiality can have different meanings depending on the circumstance, but the OFT and other UK authorities (except the Competition Appeal Tribunal (**CAT**)) are always bound by the restrictions on disclosure set out in Pt 9 of the Enterprise Act 2002. Part 9 imposes limits on the disclosure of information

---

[44] See Case C-301/04 P *Commission v SGL Carbon*, judgment of 29 June 2006, which confirms that the company must produce documents even where these could be self-incriminatory (see paras 39 and 48). The ECJ overturned part of the CFI's decision on this and increased the fine.

[45] See, eg, *Archer Daniels Midland Co v European Commission*, Case T-59/02, Judgment of the Court of First Instance, 27 September 2006, at paras 261–270 (also discussed at para 8.150 below).

[46] 'Blanket' statements of confidentiality are not encouraged by authorities and should only be used as a temporary solution where there is not sufficient time to carry out the exercise of properly identifying specific material which is confidential.

that relates to the affairs of any individual or to any business of an undertaking which has been obtained by the OFT as a result of using its powers of investigation.[47] The Enterprise Act requires that such information must not be disclosed during the lifetime of that individual or while the undertaking continues in existence unless consent has been obtained from the person who provided the information (if the information was lawfully obtained by the person and the person's identity is known) and the individual to whose affairs the information relates, or the person carrying on the business to which the information relates.

There are, however, a number of 'gateways' which allow for the disclosure of such information, but even where a gateway applies, s 244 requires that, before disclosing the relevant information, a public authority must undertake a three step evaluation: **7.44**

- The first consideration is the need to exclude from disclosure (so far as practicable) any information whose disclosure the authority thinks is contrary to the public interest.[48]

- The second consideration is the need to exclude from disclosure (so far as practicable) information whose disclosure the authority thinks might significantly harm the legitimate business interests of the undertaking or the interests of the individual to whom it relates (otherwise known as confidential information[49]).[50]

- Thirdly, the public authority must evaluate the extent to which it is necessary to disclose information that would cause significant harm to the interests of the business or individual to which it relates.[51]

Section 244 requires the disclosing authority to balance the potential harm to the interests of an individual or a business (s 244(2)) against the extent to which the disclosure is necessary (s 244(3)). **7.45**

For a discussion on how confidential material is treated during the early investigative process, particularly in relation to disclosure to other authorities, see Chapter 8 on information disclosure. For information on how confidential material is treated during the OFT's decision-making process, including provision of such material to other parties, see Chapter 9 on the decision-making process. The treatment of confidential information by the CAT in the course of an appeal is different again, and this is discussed in Chapter 12. **7.46**

---

[47] See Chapter 8 for a detailed discussion on the operation of Pt 9 of the Enterprise Act. Further information on the disclosure of information can also be found in the OFT guidance 'Controls on overseas disclosure of information'.
[48] Enterprise Act 2002, s 244(2).   [49] OFT's Procedural Rules, r 1.
[50] Enterprise Act 2002, s 244(3).   [51] ibid, s 244(4).

C. Written Requests for Information

(a) Section 26 Notices

(i) Power

7.47 The OFT and the Regulators have powers under the Competition Act 1998 to issue formal written requests for information where they have 'reasonable grounds for suspecting'[52] an infringement of Chapter I or II or Article 81 or 82. This power is set out in s 26(1) of the Competition Act, which states: 'For the purposes of an investigation, the OFT may require any person to produce to it a specified document, or to provide it with specified information, which it considers relates to any matter relevant to the investigation.' A written request made pursuant to this power is referred to as a 'Section 26 Notice'.

7.48 The OFT may issue any number of written requests for information to any person or undertaking,[53] regardless of whether they are actually the subject of the investigation. A request may be withdrawn or amended by the OFT at any time. The OFT may issue additional requests for information from the same undertaking in the course of an investigation.

7.49 The OFT will use this procedure as one of the first steps in any investigation, once the 'reasonable grounds for suspecting' an infringement are satisfied, although this is not a high threshold. However, where it seems likely that the undertaking might destroy the relevant information, a dawn raid will be carried out as the first step. The OFT may issue a Section 26 Notice at any time during the investigation, up until the final decision.

7.50 A Section 26 Notice must specify the document or describe a category of documents or information. In making a request, the OFT will normally state the date by which and place at which the information must be produced. It may also specify the manner and form in which the documents or information are to be produced. A request will normally list categories of documents rather than single documents, and it may also be used to ask questions about particular matters.

(ii) Meaning of 'document' and 'information'

7.51 Documents or information include electronic documents, recordings, and pictures. The OFT cannot request the creation of new documents, but it can request the provision of specific information. Once a document is produced, the OFT may take copies of it and may also require an explanation of the document's contents.

7.52 Where the request includes a request for information or for explanations of

---

[52] Competition Act 1998, s 25   [53] ibid, s 59.

documents, undertakings should be vigilant in ensuring that the questions are not such as to undermine the rights of defence. The OFT is not entitled to use its compulsory powers to seek answers to questions which undermine the rights of defence as provided in Article 6 ECHR. If it does so, the accused may refuse to answer such questions, citing the privilege against self-incrimination. For further detail, see the discussion on the self-incrimination privilege at paras 7.30–7.40.

(iii) On-going obligation to provide documents

There is no on-going obligation on the recipient of a Section 26 Notice to **7.53** continue to provide the OFT with documents if they are created or come into the possession of the undertaking after the date on which the OFT has requested production of the documents. However, such information will have to be provided if it is covered by a subsequent written request. Further, the timely and voluntary provision of documents going beyond the scope of a Section 26 Notice will be taken into account as a mitigating factor for the level of the fine if an infringement is proven. Conversely, the retention of incriminating evidence (even if not strictly covered by the terms of the Section 26 Notice) may, in some circumstances, operate as an aggravating factor.[54]

(iv) Not falling within the description

The requirement is to produce all documents falling within the categories set out **7.54** in the written notice. Documents falling outside the specified categories are not required to be produced. If a category of documents is drafted in an ambiguous way, on the normal principles of construction it should generally be construed in a way which favours the recipient of the notice. Nevertheless, it may be worth advising the authority of the particular construction being taken, so as to avoid any later perception of being misleading in responding to the request. If this is not the intended construction, it may result in a further request being issued.

The authority may issue a written request listing categories which appear to **7.55** encompass documents that are not relevant to the subject matter of the investigation. It is a requirement for the authority to state the subject matter of the investigation—this needs to be done in sufficient detail for the recipient to be able to judge the relevance of the listed classes of documents. If it appears that the classes of documents are not properly relevant to the investigation, or have been drafted so widely as to encompass many irrelevant documents, the recipient may seek judicial review of the authority's use of its power.[55] In practical terms,

---

[54] eg, in *Umbro Holdings Ltd v OFT* [2003] CAT 26, an important piece of evidence was produced for the first time during the appeal, and the CAT was critical of the possible attempt by Allsports to withhold material evidence from the OFT and the CAT, even though the Section 26 Notice did not specifically ask for it.

[55] See Chapter 12 for information on the appeal process.

the best course of action may be to discuss the matter with the authority concerned, as the notice may be able to be amended, or a particular construction
agreed upon. Any agreement on limitations to the notice should be formally
recorded in the response and backed up by attendance notes.

(v) Unreasonable requests

7.56 There is no legislative limit on the amount of documents which may be sought,
or the trouble to which a recipient may be put in order to comply with a request
for information. However, there is an over-riding requirement for the authority
to conduct itself in a reasonable manner in accordance with the principle of due
process. Requests should be proportionate to the size and resources of the
undertaking concerned and the severity of the infringement. The time limit set
by the authority for a reply should also be reasonable. Failure to do so gives rise
to a possible excuse for non-compliance or incomplete compliance with a written request, but will probably not afford a ground for judicial review in all but
the most exceptional cases. As noted in para 7.55 above, a useful course of
action may be to contact the OFT to agree on limitations (such as geographical
restrictions, documents relating to particular companies, exclusion of email
searches, or former employees).

7.57 Proportionality will be relevant where, for example, the request lists categories
which encompass documents of very high volumes, or documents which are
difficult to locate or so costly so as to be unreasonable to produce. Often the
authority will not be in a position to ascertain the practical ramifications of
the production of documents at the time the request is drafted. Thus it would
be desirable, less costly (and quite possibly necessary) first to advise the authority of the particular difficulties the recipient is facing. This will provide the
authority with an opportunity to amend the request: something a review court
would almost certainly provide if judicial review proceedings were brought
without such an opportunity having been given.

7.58 The costs of complying with a written request for information are borne by the
recipient of the request, unless a court orders otherwise (in the context of an
appeal or judicial review).

(vi) Not in possession, custody, or control

7.59 The request extends to documents within the possession or control of the
addressee, but if a document is not produced, the OFT may require a statement
explaining where the document is located.

7.60 A person is not required to produce a document over which he or she does not
have possession, custody, or control. This stems from the common law position
developed in relation to ordinary disclosure procedure in litigation. It is not set

out directly in the Competition Act 1998 or the Enterprise Act 2002, other than through the wording of the sanctions for providing 'false or misleading' information. The usual response in a litigation context is to provide information as to the document's existence and when/if it was last in the possession of the recipient of the notice. For example, documents may have become lost or been discarded simply due to the passage of time. The OFT has a specific power to require a statement as to the location of a document which is not produced, to the best of the knowledge and belief of the recipient of the request.[56]

Deliberately destroying or otherwise getting rid of relevant documents after the **7.61** notice has been received is an offence. It may also be an offence where the destruction of documents takes place before the written request for documents is received.[57]

Where documents are in possession of a subsidiary or related undertaking not **7.62** named in the Section 26 Notice, the strict legal obligation under the terms of the notice will only apply to the extent that such other documents are in the control of the entity named in the notice. However, as the OFT can issue any number of Section 26 Notices, it is likely that such documents will be required to be produced at some stage, and therefore it is generally advisable to cooperate with the OFT and produce the documents regardless of the strict legal terms of the Section 26 Notice. Where the documents are held by an undertaking located outside the United Kingdom, the OFT's powers of investigation do not extend to the compulsion of such documents. However, within the European Union, where the OFT is able to cooperate with the relevant national authority which does have such powers, the OFT is able to obtain such documents through those channels. Thus the same considerations apply, although it is worth noting that the relevant national authority's powers of investigation and the defendant's rights would apply to any such collection of information so, for example, a narrower meaning of legal privilege and different rules regarding confidentiality may apply. This is discussed in greater detail in Chapter 8 on information disclosure, at paras 8.103–8.137.

(vii) Subject to privilege

Where documents are subject to legal privilege there is no obligation to produce **7.63** them to the OFT pursuant to a Section 26 Notice. The UK definition of legal privilege applies to a Section 26 Notice. This is described in detail at paras 7.09–7.26 above.

Where the Section 26 Notice seeks information—in contrast to documents or **7.64**

---

[56] Competition Act 1998, s 26(6)(b) and Enterprise Act 2002, s 193(4).
[57] Competition Act 1998, s 43 and Enterprise Act 2002, s 201.

other direct factual material—which is subject to the privilege against self-incrimination, the undertaking may refuse to answer such questions on this basis. This is described in detail at paras 7.30–7.40 above.

(viii) Excluding documents—practicalities

7.65   Any documents or information which may be rightfully excluded from the documents provided to the OFT in response to a Section 26 Notice, may be withheld so that such documents or information remain in the possession of the recipient of the request. The recipient should, however, provide a list explaining how many and which documents have been retained, noting the reason for the document being excluded from production (or stating the information request is not required to be answered on the basis of the self-incrimination privilege). The excluded documents need to be listed in as much detail as is necessary for the authority to be able to assess whether the ground for excluding the document is properly made out in each case. If the authority believes that documents have been wrongfully withheld, it may use its powers under s 44 for misleading or incomplete replies.[58]

(ix) Resolving disputes

7.66   The first step for resolving any dispute is to consult with the authority, to try to reach an agreed solution. In the event of an unresolved dispute as to the application of a particular ground for exclusion, or about the confidentiality of a document, the recipient of the request may apply to the High Court for judicial review of the authority's decision. Pending review, it is generally sensible for a document which is claimed to be subject to privilege to remain unseen by the authority, given its dual role as both prosecutor and judge in the first instance. It is very difficult for the case officials to 'wipe their memory clean' or be seen to have done so once they have seen the document concerned. However, there are no legislative or other rules governing this procedure. There may also be a method which the parties can agree. It may, for example, be appropriate to arrange for the authority's independent representative to view the document after giving an undertaking as to confidentiality.

7.67   In one case concerning the European Commission, during a dawn raid, case officers viewed documents which were potentially subject to privilege and then, forming the view that some of the documents were not privileged, took copies of those documents. These actions were later the subject of a dispute before the CFI, where the applicants argued that these actions amounted to an infringement of legal professional privilege and also constituted a breach of the fundamental

---

[58] Competition Act 1998, s 44 (offences relating to provision of false or misleading information).

rights forming the foundation of professional privilege. The President of the CFI commented that although an undertaking is entitled to refuse to produce written communications between itself and its lawyer, it must nevertheless provide the Commission with relevant material of such a nature as to demonstrate that the communications fulfil the conditions for being granted legal protection. Where the Commission is not satisfied with those explanations, the Commission is not prima facie entitled to examine the documents, but ought to order production of the documents and if necessary impose fines or periodic penalty payments (and the undertaking can then apply for annulment of the Commission's decision).[59]

(x) Access to and return of documents

The authority is entitled to hold the documents for as long as is reasonably **7.68** necessary in order to conduct its investigation. It is acceptable for the recipient to retain a full set of copies of the documents provided to the authority. Alternatively, the authority may take copies or extracts and return the original.[60] Once the investigation is closed, the documents should be returned to the recipient. At any time, the recipient of the request may seek access to the documents and should be granted access in accordance with the general principles applicable to access to the authority's file (see Chapter 9 for further detail on this topic).

(xi) Use of documents and information in other proceedings

Any documents obtained by the OFT using its powers of investigation under **7.69** the Competition Act 1998 may be admissible in any subsequent criminal prosecution of the cartel offence under the Enterprise Act 2002.[61] The OFT has stated that it intends, when conducting its Competition Act investigations in relation to horizontal cartels, that its procedures in relation to exhibit and property handling, and the storage, management and control of documents should conform to the standards of a criminal investigation.

The OFT may also use any documents obtained to commence new investiga- **7.70** tions into separate proceedings, provided the evidential threshold under s 25 is met.

For more details on the OFT's use of information obtained, see Chapter 8 on **7.71** information disclosure.

---

[59] Joined Cases T 125 & 253/03 R *Akzo Nobel Chemicals Ltd v Commission* [2003] ECR II-4771, paras 132–4.
[60] Competition Act 1998, s 26(6).
[61] OFT515, *Powers for investigating criminal cartels* (January 2004) para 4.9.

(xii) Sanctions for non-compliance

7.72   A person who fails to comply with a Section 26 Notice without a valid defence is liable to a fine of up to £5,000 (on summary conviction) or an unlimited fine (on conviction on indictment).[62]

7.73   A person who takes some deliberate or reckless action to destroy or otherwise tamper with a document is liable to a fine of up to £5,000 (on summary conviction) or to an unlimited fine or imprisonment for up to two years, or both (on conviction on indictment).[63] The same liability applies if false or misleading information is provided (whether intentionally or recklessly).[64]

7.74   These sanctions are criminal in nature, and may only be imposed by a court on the commencement of criminal proceedings by (or on behalf of) the OFT. As these sanctions are criminal sanctions, the relevant standard of proof is the criminal standard of proving the elements of the offence beyond reasonable doubt. The sanctions apply to undertakings as well as to individual persons,[65] although the sanction of imprisonment will not apply to a company.

7.75   To date, the OFT has not exercised its powers to seek the imposition of sanctions for non-compliance with a written request for information, on the ground that it has not yet been necessary to do so—although it is understood to have contemplated using the powers on at least one occasion.[66]

7.76   Apart from the sanctions directly applicable to such offences, there are also other consequences which may follow from tampering with evidence or providing incomplete information. For example, in *Umbro*[67] one of the undertakings had withheld a relevant document (a diary) and when it was produced, the owner had scored out entries with a black marker pen; it was, though, possible to uncover them using forensic examination. This action led to the CAT increasing the ultimate penalty imposed on the undertaking. Another example in the same case concerned the provision of inaccurate sales figures, which again the CAT took into account in its assessment of the final penalty to be imposed. There may also be some impact resulting from falsifying evidence in that it may contribute to the evidence of dishonesty in a subsequent cartel prosecution or competition disqualification order.[68]

---

[62] Competition Act 1998, s 42.   [63] ibid, s 43.   [64] ibid, s 44.
[65] ibid, s 59.   [66] See the OFT's Annual Reports.
[67] *Umbro Holdings Ltd v OFT* [2003] CAT 26.
[68] *R v Ghosh* [1982] QB 1053.

(b) Article 18 written request by the European Commission

(i) Power

The European Commission has a power to make a written request for informa- **7.77**
tion in the United Kingdom, pursuant to Article 18 of Regulation 1/2003. This
provides: 'In order to carry out the duties assigned to it by the Regulation, the
Commission may, by simple request or by decision, require undertakings and
associations of undertakings to provide all necessary information.'

As a provision in a Council Regulation, Article 18 does not need any UK **7.78**
legislation to make it effective, and it is directly applicable in all Member States.
Thus a direct request from the European Commission is enforceable against
individuals within the European Community.[69] There is, however, a requirement
for the European Commission to forward a copy of the request to the Member
State in whose territory the recipient of the request is situated.

(ii) Requirements for a valid request

Article 18 provides for two mechanisms: a simple request and a decision. There **7.79**
are no obligations to comply with a simple request, whereas there are penalties
for not complying with a decision.

Pursuant to Article 18(2), when sending a simple request for information to an **7.80**
undertaking, the European Commission is required to state the legal basis and
the purpose of the request, specify what information is required and fix the time
limit within which the information is to be provided, and the penalties for
supplying incorrect or misleading information.

Under Article 18(3), where the European Commission requires undertakings to **7.81**
supply information by decision, it shall state the legal basis and the purpose of
the request, specify what information is required and fix the time limit within
which it is to be provided. It is also required to indicate the penalties which
apply for non-compliance, and to indicate the right to have the decision
reviewed by the ECJ.

In relation to the previous provision (Article 11 of Regulation 17/62, which was **7.82**
in all relevant respects identical to Article 18), in *Société Générale*, the CFI held
that the European Commission is required to demonstrate:

> that the information requested of the undertakings concerned is justified and also
> to enable those undertakings to assess the scope of their duty to cooperate while at
> the same time safeguarding their rights of defence. It follows that the Commission
> is entitled to require the disclosure only of information which may enable it to

---

[69] Case C-253/00 *Antonio Munoz y Cia SA v Frumar Ltd* [2002] ECR I-7289.

investigate putative infringements which justify the conduct of the enquiry and are set out in the request for information.[70]

7.83 The connection between the document or information requested and the infringement under investigation must be such that the European Commission could reasonably suppose that the document or information would help it to determine whether the alleged infringement had taken place. Further, the obligation of an undertaking to provide information should not represent a burden for the undertaking which is disproportionate to the needs of the investigation.[71]

7.84 The European Commission must ask for documents or information in a manner causing least inconvenience possible to the undertaking.[72]

7.85 The European Commission is required without delay to forward a copy of the simple request or of the decision to the competition authority of the Member State in whose territory the seat of the undertaking is situated and the competition authority of the Member State whose territory is affected. At the request of the European Commission the governments and competition authorities of the Member States are required to provide the European Commission with all necessary information to carry out the duties assigned to it by Regulation 1/2003.[73]

(iii) Grounds for excluding production of documents

7.86 In general, the grounds for excluding documents from production and the method of doing so are the same as for a response to a Section 26 Notice, as detailed in paras 7.51–7.65, above. However, there are some differences in relation to the basis for any claim for legal privilege. In particular, in the context of a written request from the European Commission, the European definition of legal privilege will apply. This is described at paras 7.27–7.29.

(iv) Sanctions for non-compliance

7.87 The relevant sanctions for failure to comply with a request by decision are set out in Article 24 of Regulation 1/2003. This provides for periodic penalty payments which may be imposed directly by the European Commission, by decision.[74] The penalties are envisaged to be calculated daily, at a rate not

---

[70] Case T-34/93 *Société Générale v Commission* [1995] ECR II-545, para 40.
[71] Case C-36/92 P *SEP v Commission* [1994] ECR I-1911.
[72] Case 136/79 *National Panasonic (UK) Ltd v European Commission* [1980] ECR 2033.
[73] Regulation 1/2003, Art 18(5) and (6).
[74] The terms of Art 24 are tougher than the previous sanctions contained in Regulation 17/62. The new sanctions do not apply retrospectively; they apply to any failure to comply with the requirements relevant to a written request, where the request is issued after 1 May 2004.

exceeding 5 per cent of the average daily turnover of the undertaking in the preceding business year. They may be calculated from a retrospective date, but the European Commission may also reduce the total penalty amount payable once compliance has been achieved.

There are no sanctions for failure to comply with a 'simple request' for **7.88** information. However, if a response is provided to a simple request, sanctions will apply in relation to the supply of incorrect or misleading information.

Under Article 18(4) of Regulation 1/2003, the owners of the undertakings or **7.89** legal bodies, or their representatives are required to supply the information requested on behalf of the undertaking concerned. Lawyers duly authorised to act may supply the information on behalf of their clients, but the latter shall remain fully responsible if the information supplied is incomplete, incorrect, or misleading.

(c) Written request by another national competition authority in the United Kingdom

(i) Power

Theoretically, a competition authority outside the United Kingdom could make **7.90** a written request directly to a company or individual in the United Kingdom. However, such measures are not enforceable under UK law, so compliance with such a request would be a matter of discretion for the recipient concerned. In order to satisfy Article 22[75] of Regulation 1/2003, Pt 2A of the Competition Act 1998 was introduced to provide the OFT with specific powers of investigation to assist another national competition authority with an investigation. These powers do not extend to the UK Regulators: they are provided solely to the OFT, although the Regulators may participate in inspections under warrant carried out by the OFT for other national competition authorities where the industry being investigated falls into their area of expertise.

Where a competition authority from another Member State requests the OFT **7.91** to assist it in the gathering of evidence from within the United Kingdom, the OFT may (but is not obliged to) assist, provided that there are 'reasonable grounds for suspecting' an infringement of Article 81 or 82.[76]

---

[75] Art 22(1): 'The competition authority of a Member State may in its own territory carry out any inspection or other fact-finding measure under its national law on behalf and for the account of the competition authority of another Member State in order to establish whether there has been an infringement of Article 81 or Article 82 of the Treaty. Any exchange and use of the information collected shall be carried out in accordance with Article 12.'

[76] Competition Act 1998, s 65D.

(ii) Requirements for a valid information request

7.92 The powers in Pt 2A of the Competition Act 1998 mirror the powers set out in Pt 1 of the Act, including the power to make a written request for information: see paras 7.47–7.50 above.

(iii) Grounds for excluding documents from production

7.93 The grounds for excluding documents or information from production are identical to the grounds for Section 26 Notices: see paras 7.51–7.65 above. Thus it is the UK rules which apply on matters such as legal professional privilege, for example, and not the rules of the national competition authority which is conducting the case.

(iv) Sanctions for non-compliance

7.94 The sanctions are also the same as for a Section 26 Notice, as are the documents which may be excluded from production: see paras 7.72–7.74 above.

(v) Resolving disputes

7.95 Any dispute as to the *collection* of information pursuant to Pt 2A is between the aggrieved party and the OFT: the remedy does not lie with the national competition authority conducting the case.[77] However, any dispute as to the actual *use* of the information in the conduct of a case is between the aggrieved party and the national competition authority conducting the case. The competition authority is thus entitled to assume that any information it receives from the OFT has been lawfully collected, unless the OFT advises that there is a dispute. Thus it is possible that a dispute with the OFT concerning the collection of evidence could hold up an investigation by another national competition authority (at least in part).

(d) Written request under the Enterprise Act

(i) Power

7.96 The OFT can conduct a criminal investigation against an individual under the Enterprise Act 2002 if there are reasonable grounds for suspecting that a cartel offence has been committed,[78] and the OFT has 'good reason' to exercise its investigatory powers.[79] Under the cartel offence, an individual can be prosecuted if he or she 'dishonestly agrees' with a competitor to enter into

---

[77] Network Notice, para 29. Note that a dispute as to collection of information is not an appealable decision to the CAT under the Competition Act 1998. Any appeal would be based on a judicial review relating to the use of the OFT's powers under Pt 2A of the Act, in the same way as a party would seek review of any use of the powers under Pt 1 of the Act.
[78] Enterprise Act 2002, s 192(1).   [79] ibid, s 192(2).

certain categories of horizontal anti-competitive agreements: market sharing; bid rigging; price fixing; and product/selling quotas.

The OFT has indicated that where it starts an investigation of a potential **7.97** cartel offence using its Competition Act powers, it will bear in mind the possibility that a criminal cartel offence may have been committed, and will therefore act in accordance with the Police and Criminal Evidence Act 1984, all the relevant Codes of Practice, and the Criminal Procedure and Investigations Act 1996, or in Scotland, the equivalent Scottish criminal procedure requirements.[80] Any documents obtained by the OFT using its powers of investigation under the Competition Act 1998 may be admissible in any subsequent criminal prosecution of the cartel offence under the Enterprise Act 2002.[81]

The OFT's power to require the production of documents or information in **7.98** relation to the criminal cartel offence is set out in s 193 of the Enterprise Act 2002. This provides for two types of requests: one requiring a person to answer questions with respect to any matter relevant to the investigation or otherwise provide information;[82] and one requiring a person to produce documents.[83] The requests may be sent to any person or undertaking,[84] regardless of whether they are actually the subject of the investigation. A request may be withdrawn or amended at any time.

The OFT has also stated that it may also use its formal criminal powers of **7.99** investigation under the Enterprise Act 2002 to obtain original versions of documents obtained under a Competition Act investigation.[85]

(ii) Requirements for a valid written request

In making a request, the OFT or SFO are required to indicate the subject **7.100** matter and purpose of the investigation, and to state the nature of the offences for failure to comply (see below).[86] The request must also state the date by which and place at which the information or documents must be produced. A request for documents may (and is more likely to) list categories of documents rather than single documents.[87] The OFT or SFO can require immediate compliance with a notice.

---

[80] OFT515, *Powers for investigating criminal cartels* (January 2004) para 4.1.

[81] ibid, para 4.9.

[82] Enterprise Act 2002, s 193(1). Note this is a wider power than the equivalent power under Competition Act 1998, s 26.

[83] Enterprise Act 2002, s 193(2).

[84] Interpretation Act 1978, Schedule 1 (meaning of 'person' includes a body of persons corporate or unincorporate).

[85] OFT515, *Powers for investigating criminal cartels* (January 2004) para 4.9.

[86] Enterprise Act 2002, s 193(5).   [87] ibid, s 193(2).

(iii) Requirement to answer questions

7.101 The power of the OFT or SFO to require a person to answer questions is essentially a compulsory interview power, which has no equivalent under s 26 of the Competition Act 1998, although the latter includes a compulsory power to provide an explanation of a document.

7.102 In using s 193 of the Enterprise Act 2002 to require an individual to answer questions, such questions need not be limited to any document or information which has been requested. The individual is entitled to seek legal advice before answering questions, but will face criminal sanctions if he or she fails to answer all questions put to him or her without proper grounds for such failure, or provides false or misleading answers.

(iv) Grounds for excluding documents or information from production

7.103 'Documents' includes 'information recorded in any form, and, in relation to information recorded otherwise than in a form in which it is visible and legible references to its production include references to producing it in a form in which it is visible and legible or from which it can readily be produced in a visible and legible form'.[88] Accordingly, they cover paper and electronic documents, computer files, emails, and audio or visual recordings such as tapes or voicemail messages. Once documents have been produced pursuant to a written request under s 193(2) of the Enterprise Act 2002, the OFT may take copies or extracts from those documents, and may also require the person producing the documents to provide an explanation of any of them.[89]

7.104 The grounds for excluding documents or information from production are essentially the same as those applicable to a Section 26 Notice (see paras 7.51–7.65 above). In particular, the application of legal privilege is the UK definition,[90] and the self-incrimination privilege applies as well (subject to the various safeguards and limitations under the Enterprise Act, as set out in paras 7.43–7.45 above). In addition, confidential communications between a bank and its client are treated as privileged pursuant to s 196(2) of the Enterprise Act.

7.105 In relation to questions asked of individuals, the OFT/SFO cannot require the individual to answer self-incriminating or leading questions, or questions unconnected to the subject matter of the investigation.[91]

---

[88] ibid, s 202.
[89] ibid, s 193(3) The OFT is likely to need originals rather than copies for any criminal trial.
[90] ibid, s 196(1).   [91] See paras 7.30–7.40 above.

(v) Sanctions for non-compliance

The offences relevant to the use of the OFT's powers under s 193 of the **7.106**
Enterprise Act 2002 are the same as those under the Competition Act 1998.
The offences are, essentially, failure to comply with a requirement imposed on
a person under s 193 without reasonable excuse, and making a statement which
is false or misleading in a material particular (either knowingly or recklessly).[92]
At the time of writing, the OFT has not brought any proceedings for failure to
comply with a request issued under s 193 of the Enterprise Act.[93]

In order to impose sanctions, the OFT or the SFO must commence criminal **7.107**
proceedings.

(e) Written request for information by the SFO [94]

(i) Power

The SFO's standard powers of investigation are provided by s 2 of the Criminal **7.108**
Justice Act 1997, which sets out special powers for information gathering by
the SFO, including interviewing and taking statements. The SFO may also use
these powers in connection with a criminal cartel offence investigation. Under
s 2, the SFO may require a person to answer questions, provide information, or
produce documents for the purposes of an investigation. Normally, written
notice will be given, but in urgent cases the powers can be exercised on the spot
and require immediate compliance.

Section 2 powers may only be used for the purposes of an investigation of a sus- **7.109**
pected offence which appears on reasonable grounds to the Director (of the SFO)
to involve serious or complex fraud and where there is good reason to do so for
the purpose of investigating the affairs, or any aspect of the affairs of any person.

Section 2 Notices can be issued to banks, financial institutions, accountants, **7.110**
and other professionals who may, in the ordinary course of their business,
hold information or documents on behalf of their clients. The Section 2 Notice
will override any conflicting duties of client confidentiality and obliges them
lawfully to provide information and documents, except for confidential communications between a bank and its client which are treated as privileged
similarly to those under the Enterprise Act 2002.[95]

---

[92] Enterprise Act 2002, s 201.   [93] Based on a review of the OFT's annual reports.
[94] In Scotland, the Lord Advocate is responsible for all prosecutions and exercises the same
powers as the SFO, under the Criminal Law (Consolidation) (Scotland) Act 1995, through the
International and Financial Crime Unit in the Crown Office.
[95] Criminal Justice Act 1987, s 2(10)(a) and (b).

(ii) Requirement to answer questions

7.111 The power of the SFO to require a person to answer questions is essentially a compulsory interview power, which has no equivalent under s 26 of the Competition Act 1998.

7.112 In using the notice procedure to require an individual to answer questions, such questions need not be limited to any document or information which has been requested. The individual is entitled to seek legal advice before answering questions, but will face criminal sanctions if he or she fails to answer all questions put to him or her without proper grounds for such failure, or provides false or misleading answers.

(iii) Grounds for excluding documents or information from production

7.113 The grounds for excluding documents or information from production are essentially the same as those applicable to a Section 26 Notice, as set out above at paras 7.51–7.65. In particular, the application of legal privilege uses the UK definition,[96] and the self-incrimination privilege applies.

7.114 The rights of defence in relation to criminal investigations are more extensive, and there are specific restrictions on the use to which certain evidence gathered may be put. For example, a person may refuse to answer questions or provide information or documents if he or she has a reasonable excuse for not doing so. Further, a person's answers to questions required under s 2 of the Criminal Justice Act 1997 may not be used in evidence against them at their trial (unless the trial is in relation to an offence of providing misleading information during the s 2 interview itself).

7.115 In relation to a requirement to answer questions, the SFO cannot require the individual to answer self-incriminating or leading questions, or questions unconnected to the subject matter of the investigation.[97]

(iv) Sanctions for non-compliance

7.116 The sanctions for non-compliance with a warrant obtained under the Criminal Justice Act 1997 are set out in s 2 of that Act. These provide for offences in relation to failure to comply with a requirement imposed under s 2 (such as a warrant for inspection),[98] making a false or misleading statement,[99] and falsifying, concealing, or destroying documents.[100] The sanctions available include both fines and imprisonment, with the applicable maximum length of imprisonment (up to seven years) and maximum amount of any fine dependent upon the

---

[96] Enterprise Act 2002, s 196(1). [97] See paras 7.30–7.40 above.
[98] Criminal Justice Act 1997, s 2(13). [99] ibid, s 2(14) and (15).
[100] ibid, s 2(16) and (17).

type of offence and whether it is brought on indictment or as a summary conviction.

In order to impose sanctions, the SFO must commence criminal proceedings. **7.117** The SFO cannot use the answers given to compulsory questions against that individual in a criminal prosecution unless he has knowingly or recklessly made a false or misleading statement; or he is being prosecuted for some other offence and makes a statement that is inconsistent with it and if evidence relating to it is adduced or a question relating to it is asked by him or on his behalf.

D. Inspections of Premises (Dawn Raids)

(a) Introduction

(i) Dawn raids—practical checklist

The initial procedure for dealing with a dawn raid from an undertaking's **7.118** perspective is largely the same regardless of the power being used. The following is a checklist of the most important matters of practical concern in the event of a dawn raid by a competition authority.

(1) *Authorisation*: Check and keep a copy of the documents which the authority is presenting as proof of its authority to conduct an inspection. Note that the court may have imposed additional conditions in the warrant, so it is important to check the limits on the OFT's powers (for example, there may be controls imposed on removing computers or papers where these are needed to run the business).

(2) *Legal representation*: There is a limited right[101] to have a lawyer present during the inspection.

(3) *Leniency*: Consider whether it would be beneficial to apply leniency, or at least to ascertain whether first place in the queue is still available. This will involve calling the Director or Deputy Director of Cartel Investigations, on 020 7211 8117.[102]

(4) *Dealing with privileged documents*: The undertaking has a right to review its own documents during the inspection in order to set aside documents over which privilege is likely to be claimed. These documents should be enclosed in envelopes and agreement reached with the authority on the time frame for establishing privilege.

---

[101] This is a limited right based on the rights of defence—it is not a statutory right. Generally, the OFT is prepared to wait for up to half an hour, but where an in-house lawyer is present they may not agree to wait.

[102] See paras 5.67–5.69 for further details of this procedure.

(5) *Dealing with confidential material.* Where appropriate, confidential material may need to be masked, or special treatment may be sought for such material (see paras 7.41–7.46 above in relation to confidentiality).

(6) *Interviews and oral explanations.* Interviews can only be conducted under the criminal powers of investigation. Inspections conducted under Article 20 of Regulation 1/2003, however, include a requirement to provide 'explanations on facts . . . relating to the subject-matter and purpose of the inspection' as well as explanations of documents. Persons being interviewed should be aware of the limits on the powers of the OFT to ask questions which would infringe the right against self-incrimination (see paras 7.30–7.40 above) as well as the potential sanctions for providing false or misleading answers.

(7) *Sealing premises.* If the authority intends to use its power to seal premises, the time period must be appropriate for the problem to be addressed. For example, the authority may arrange for offices or cabinets to be sealed overnight to enable the inspection to continue the following day, or for a short period while waiting for the undertaking's legal representative to arrive. In any event, seals should not be left in place for more than 72 hours.[103]

(8) *Access to and return of documents.* Documents may be kept for three months under s 28 or 28A Competition Act inspections, which is the power to enter and search premises with a warrant.[104] Where the investigation relates to the cartel offence, the documents will be kept until any trial under the cartel offence. Access will be granted in accordance with the OFT's Procedural Rules.[105]

(9) *Keeping a record of the process.* It will be important to have a full record of the process should any dispute later arise as to the specific powers and procedures used by the relevant authority. This could prove to be invaluable evidence, particularly where the record of the event is both detailed and contemporaneous.

(ii) Powers to conduct inspections in the United Kingdom

7.119 Inspections[106] of premises in the United Kingdom in the course of an investigation of a competition law infringement may be carried out by the OFT, the SFO, or the European Commission. Inspections of premises may also be carried out

---

[103] OFT404, *Powers of investigation* (December 2004) para 4.5.

[104] There is no power to take original documents under s 27 which is the power to enter a business premises without a warrant.

[105] See Chapter 9 for a discussion of access to documents.

[106] 'Inspection' in this book is a term used to describe the entry into premises, whereas the term 'investigation' is used to describe the overall conduct of a case by an authority, usually after the initial decision is made to proceed with a case (upon satisfaction of the criteria in s 25 of the Competition Act 1998).

in the United Kingdom by the OFT on behalf of other national competition authorities. Inspections will normally be carried out without notice to the undertaking, which is why inspections are often called 'dawn raids' (although civil inspections rarely take place at dawn). In fact, ordinarily, inspections are required to take place within reasonable working hours.

The powers of the authority and the relevant procedural laws applicable in respect of inspections of premises differ depending on the type of inspection being carried out. The types of inspections are: **7.120**

(1) Inspections by the OFT or a Regulator in relation to a potential competition law infringement:
  • Competition Act 1998, s 27 (enter business premises, with at least two working days' notice,[107] no warrant required);
  • Competition Act, s 27 (enter business premises, without notice, no warrant required);
  • Competition Act 1998, s 28 (enter and search business premises, without notice, requires a warrant);
  • Competition Act 1998, s 28A (enter and search domestic premises, without notice, requires a warrant).

(2) Inspections by the OFT or the SFO in relation to a potential cartel offence:
  • Enterprise Act 2002, s 194 (OFT, enter and search any premises, without notice, requires a warrant);
  • Criminal Justice Act 1987, s 2 (SFO, enter and search any premises, without notice, requires a warrant).

(3) Inspections by or for the European Commission with the OFT's[108] assistance:
  • Regulation 1/2003, Article 20 (European Commission with OFT's assistance, enter business premises, without notice, no warrant required);
  • Competition Act 1998, s 62 (European Commission with OFT's assistance, enter and search business premises, without notice, requires a warrant);
  • Competition Act 1998, s 62A (European Commission with OFT's assistance, enter and search non-business premises, without notice, requires a warrant);

---

[107] Notice must be given under s 27 unless the premises are occupied by a party or parties which the OFT is investigating under s 25 or it has not been able to give notice despite taking all reasonably practical steps to do so.

[108] These powers do not extend to the Regulators although they may participate in inspections under warrant carried out by the OFT for the Commission where the industry being investigated falls into their area of expertise.

- Competition Act 1998, s 62B (OFT for the European Commission, enter business premises, without notice, no warrant required);
- Competition Act 1998, s 63 (OFT for the European Commission, enter and search business premises, without notice, requires a warrant).

(4) Inspections by the OFT[109] on behalf of another national competition authority in relation to a potential competition law infringement:

- Competition Act 1998, s 65F (enter business premises, with at least two working days' notice,[110] no warrant required);
- Competition Act 1998, s 65F (enter business premises, without notice, no warrant required);
- Competition Act 1998, s 65G (enter and search business premises, without notice, requires a warrant);
- Competition Act 1998, s 65H (enter and search domestic premises, without notice, requires a warrant).

Each of these types of inspection is discussed in the following sections.

(b) OFT inspections under the Competition Act

(i) Business or domestic premises?

7.121 Where the OFT is investigating a potential infringement of the Chapter I or II prohibitions, or of Article 81 or 82, the OFT's powers to conduct inspections of premises are set out in Pt 1 of the Competition Act 1998. Section 27 provides powers to enter business premises, s 28 provides powers to enter and search business premises, and s 28A provides a power to enter and search domestic premises. Use of one procedure does not preclude the use of another procedure at any time. It is very important for a record of the procedure to be made to ensure that the correct powers are being used at any given time.

7.122 Business premises are defined in s 27(6) as 'premises (or any part of premises) not used as a dwelling'. This definition applies to inspections under both ss 27 and 28.[111]

7.123 Domestic premises are defined as premises or any part of premises that are used as a dwelling and also used in connection with the affairs of an undertaking or

---

[109] These powers do not extend to the Regulators although they may participate in inspections under warrant carried out by the OFT for other national competition authorities where the industry being investigated falls into their area of expertise.

[110] Notice must be given under s 65F unless the premises are occupied by a party or parties which the OFT is investigating because there are reasonable grounds for suspecting an infringement of Arts 81 or 82 or it has not been able to give notice despite taking all reasonably practical steps to do so.

[111] ibid, s 28(8).

where documents relating to the affairs of an undertaking are kept.[112] Thus the power to enter domestic premises is limited to domestic premises having some connection with documents relevant to an investigation.

In most circumstances it will be perfectly clear whether the relevant premises are **7.124** business or domestic. It is the use to which the premises are put which determines their nature as business or domestic premises. Ownership of the premises is entirely irrelevant except insofar as it may help to demonstrate the use to which the premises are put. It is the 'grey area' that may cause some difficulty, where the same premises are used for both business and domestic purposes. For example, a study in a home that is used partly for work related matters, or a business being run from part of a home. Based on a practical interpretation, it is likely that where premises are used for both purposes, the domestic premises procedure will apply unless the business part of the premises can be accessed directly, without passing through the domestic part of the premises. A vehicle is included in the definition of 'premises' and therefore it may be either business or domestic, again depending on the use to which the vehicle is put.[113]

(ii) Section 27 inspection

Under s 27 of the Competition Act 1998, the OFT may enter[114] business **7.125** premises without a warrant, and in most circumstances, without providing notice. Notice is not required where the OFT has a reasonable suspicion that the premises are or have been occupied by a party to an agreement which it is investigating, or by an undertaking the conduct of which it is investigating. Notice is also not required where the investigating officer has attempted to give notice but has been unable to do so. In all other cases, the notice must be in writing and must provide at least two working days' notice of the intended entry, as well as setting out various particulars including the subject matter and purpose of the investigation.[115]

Where the OFT is conducting an inspection without notice under s 27, the **7.126** investigating officer (any officer of the OFT) must produce evidence of his or her authorisation and a document indicating the subject matter and purpose of the investigation and the nature of the offences relevant to the inspection. There are no specific time limits on the inspection itself, or on the number of times which an officer may enter premises under the same authorisation, provided it is still in connection with the relevant investigation described in the authorisation or the accompanying documents.

---

[112] ibid, s 28A(9).   [113] ibid, s 59.   [114] But not by using force.
[115] Competition Act 1998, s 27(2).

7.127   Once on the premises, an investigating officer has a number of powers which may be exercised. These are set out in s 27(5), as follows:

> (a)   take with him such equipment as appears to him to be necessary;
> (b)   require any person on the premises—
>> (i)   to produce any document which he considers relates to any matter relevant to the investigation; and
>> (ii)   if the document is produced, to provide an explanation of it;
> (c)   require any person to state, to the best of his knowledge and belief, where any such document is to be found;
> (d)   take copies of, or extracts from any document which is produced;
> (e)   require any information which is stored in any electronic form and is accessible from the premises and which the investigating officer considers relates to any matter relevant to the investigation, to be produced in a form—
>> (i)   in which it can be taken away; and
>> (ii)   in which it is visible and legible or from which it can readily be produced in a visible and legible form;
> (f)   take any steps which appear to be necessary for the purpose of preserving or preventing interference with any document which he considers relates to any matter relevant to the investigation.

7.128   Notably, the OFT has no power in these circumstances to enter premises by force. Nor has the OFT any power to take possession of the documents produced (unless this is considered to be a necessary step for preventing interference with the documents). The s 27 power is also not a power of search. It allows for peaceable entry to premises and allows an officer to require the production of relevant documents, but does not permit the officer to conduct a search.

7.129   Generally, the power to take steps necessary for preventing interference with documents is a reference to the power to seal offices, cabinets and the like, in order to prevent tampering with evidence once an inspection has started. This would generally be seen as necessary where the investigating officers leave the premises (usually overnight) and later return to continue the inspection. The use of the power to seal is subject to a self-imposed obligation on the OFT to limit the time period for which the seals remain in place to 72 hours.[116] Seals are normally stickers or tape placed across the opening of a cabinet, so that it will be apparent if the cabinet has been opened. Sealing may also be a way of resolving any concerns of the OFT if a delay is requested by the undertaking, such as a delay while waiting for a legal adviser to attend an inspection.

7.130   The grounds upon which an undertaking may refuse to produce documents or information during an inspection are: legal professional privilege; self-incrimination privilege; not relevant; and not in the undertaking's possession,

---

[116]   OFT515, *Powers for investigating criminal cartels* (January 2004).

power, or control. These grounds are discussed above (see paras 7.51–7.65). Where the inspection appears to be an unreasonable use of powers, this may be subject to judicial review, but the threshold would be high and an urgent hearing would be difficult to obtain.

In the context of an investigation, it is not possible to argue successfully that **7.131** a document is not in the undertaking's possession, power, or control where the document is actually located on the undertaking's premises. Any issue concerning relevance should be determined by reference to the authorisation documents produced by the OFT authorising the inspection. However, the OFT has a wide discretion to determine relevance, as set out in its powers above. Self-incrimination privilege may be claimed in the context of a possible offence, so there will generally only be limited situations where this is applicable. This means that in most circumstances, protecting documents and information subject to legal professional privilege is one of the key tasks for an undertaking to focus on during a s 27 inspection.

(iii) Section 28 inspections

A warrant procedure is available to the OFT for inspecting business premises, **7.132** pursuant to s 28 of the Competition Act 1998. In order to obtain the warrant, the OFT must make an application to the High Court[117] and is required to establish to the judge's satisfaction that:

    (a) there are reasonable grounds for suspecting that there are on any business premises documents—
        (i) the production of which has been required under section 26 or 27, and
        (ii) which have not been produced as required;
    (b) there are reasonable grounds for suspecting that—
        (i) there are on any business premises documents which the OFT has power under section 26 to require to be produced; and
        (ii) if the documents were required to be produced, they would not be produced but would be concealed, removed, tampered with or destroyed; or
    (c) an investigating officer has attempted to enter the premises in the exercise of his powers under section 27 but has been unable to do so and that there are reasonable grounds for suspecting that there are on the premises documents the production of which could have been required under that section.

If the judge is satisfied that one of the above criteria is fulfilled, then he or she **7.133** may issue a warrant. The issue of a warrant remains in the judge's discretion, even if the criteria are fulfilled.[118] The threshold of 'reasonable grounds' is not a

---

[117] The applicable procedure is under the Civil Procedure Rules for warrants, but note that a different court and rules apply where the application is made in Scotland.

[118] Compare with s 62A of the Competition Act 1998, where the statute says the judge 'shall' issue a warrant.

particularly high hurdle for the OFT to satisfy, but nevertheless the OFT must provide evidence to support its argument that such reasonable grounds exist. Some guidance as to the type of evidence required may be found in the case of *OFT v X*,[119] involving a potential price fixing infringement, where the OFT applied to the High Court for a warrant under s 28 of the Competition Act 1998. In his judgment, Morison J set out the reasons for finding that the OFT had established that there were reasonable grounds for suspecting that the documents required to be produced would be concealed or destroyed, as follows:

> [T]he evidence shows that a 'warning shot across the defendants' bows' has already been fired by the Director General of Fair Trading. The target companies, if they have been doing what the OFT suspect, are likely to have taken steps to make detection difficult and to be continuing so to act. The stakes are high, since the penalties if guilt is established are likely to be high. The entities being investigated include one of a substantial size, and whose reputation, apart from its financial position, may be damaged if incriminating material is found. There is, therefore, a strong inducement or motive for hiding the truth. The material which the OFT are most interested to see is relatively easy to conceal, given advance notice. For these reasons, I am satisfied that there are reasonable grounds for suspecting that the written material would be concealed or destroyed. It is in the public interest that if there has been wrongdoing it is uncovered and revealed.[120]

7.134 Although most (if not all) warrant applications made by the OFT have been granted, on at least one occasion a warrant was initially refused by a judge of the High Court (Chancery Division) but then granted on certain conditions imposing further limits on the OFT's powers. The warrant was re-drafted to include these conditions.

7.135 Where the OFT is conducting an inspection under s 28, the investigating officer (any officer of the OFT) must produce the warrant or, if no one is present, take reasonable steps to inform the occupier of the intended entry.[121] The warrant must indicate the subject matter and purpose of the investigation and the nature of the offences created by ss 42 to 44 of the Competition Act 1998. The warrant will also name the persons authorised to conduct the inspection. The persons who may be authorised are staff of the OFT and assisting experts, such as IT professionals.[122] There is no statutory limit to the numbers of people who may attend on the part of the OFT. The warrant will continue in force for one month beginning from the day on which it is issued.[123] During this period, there is no limit to the number of times which an authorised officer may enter premises under the same warrant, provided it is still in connection with the relevant investigation described in the warrant.

---

[119] *OFT v X* [2003] EWHC 1042 (Comm), [2003] 2 All ER (Comm) 183.
[120] ibid, para 5.   [121] Competition Act 1998, s 29.   [122] ibid, s 28(3A).
[123] ibid, s 28(6).

Inspections of business premises under a warrant provide the OFT with greater **7.136** powers than those under a s 27 procedure. The powers which the OFT may exercise under a warrant procedure are set out in s 28(2) and are essentially the same as the s 27 powers set out at para 7.127 above, with the additional powers allowing the OFT to enter using such force as is reasonably necessary for the purpose,[124] to search the premises,[125] and to take possession of documents if such action appears necessary for preserving the documents or preventing interference with them or if it is not reasonably practicable to take copies of the documents on the premises.[126] In practical terms, this type of inspection is much more forcible and is generally preferred by the OFT as it provides greater scope for ensuring entry to the premises and the ability to find documents and to take originals if necessary.

(iv) Section 28A inspections

The OFT has a power to enter and search domestic premises pursuant to s 28A **7.137** of the Competition Act 1998, but only under the issue of a warrant.[127] There is no power for the inspection of domestic premises without a warrant.

In order to obtain a warrant under s 28A, the OFT must make an application **7.138** to the High Court[128] and is required to establish to the judge's satisfaction that:

    (a) there are reasonable grounds for suspecting that there are on any domestic premises documents—
        (i) the production of which has been required under section 26, and
        (ii) which have not been produced as required; or
    (b) there are reasonable grounds for suspecting that—
        (i) there are on any domestic premises documents which the OFT has power under section 26 to require to be produced; and
        (ii) if the documents were required to be produced, they would not be produced but would be concealed, removed, tampered with or destroyed.

If the judge is satisfied that one of the above criteria is fulfilled, then he or she **7.139** may issue a warrant. The issue of a warrant remains in the judge's discretion, even if the criteria are fulfilled,[129] but the powers granted under the warrant may not be limited or changed from those set out in the statute.[130]

---

[124] ibid, s 28(2)(a). Where the OFT is using a warrant procedure to search business premises, it may call upon the police to enforce the warrant if necessary but not to conduct the search.

[125] ibid, s 28(2)(b).   [126] ibid, s 28(2)(c).

[127] This power was added to the Competition Act from 1 May 2004, but is in fact a limitation on the previous power as there was no distinction between business and domestic premises prior to 1 May 2004, which meant the OFT could previously inspect all premises using either a warrant or a non-warrant procedure.

[128] The applicable procedure is under the Civil Procedure Rules for warrants, but note that a different court and rules apply where the application is made in Scotland.

[129] Compare with s 62A, where the statute says the judge 'shall' issue a warrant.

[130] This interpretation is based on the use of the word 'shall' in s 28A(2).

7.140   The threshold test of 'reasonable grounds' is subject to the same interpretation as noted above in relation to a s 28 inspection (see para 7.133 above). The court will also need to consider whether the OFT's proposed actions are justified and proportionate in accordance with Article 8 ECHR, which provides for the right to respect for private and family life and limits the interference by a public authority with the exercise of such right. Where domestic premises are concerned, the Article 8 test will be more difficult for the OFT to satisfy.[131]

7.141   Where the OFT is conducting an inspection under s 28A, the authorised OFT officer described in the warrant as the named officer must produce the warrant or, if no one is present, take reasonable steps to inform the occupier of the intended entry.[132] The warrant must indicate the subject matter and purpose of the investigation and the nature of the offences created by ss 42 to 44 of the Competition Act 1998. The subject matter and purpose of the investigation may refer to more than one potential competition law infringement. The warrant will also name all the persons authorised to conduct the inspection. The persons who may be authorised are staff of the OFT and assisting experts, such as IT professionals.[133] There is no statutory limit to the numbers of people who may attend on the part of the OFT. The warrant will continue in force for one month beginning from the day on which it is issued.[134] During this period, there is no limit to the number of times which a named authorised officer may enter premises under the same warrant, provided it is still in connection with the relevant investigation described in the warrant.

7.142   The powers which the OFT may exercise under a warrant procedure for domestic premises are set out in s 28A(2). These powers are identical to the powers which may be exercised under a s 28 warrant for business premises (see para 7.136 above).

(v) Sanctions for non-compliance

7.143   Sections 42 to 44 of the Competition Act 1998 set out the offences in connection with the use of the OFT's powers of investigation, including the powers to conduct inspections under ss 27, 28, and 28A. These offences are directed at individuals rather than at undertakings, but 'person' is defined in s 59 of the Competition Act to include any undertaking.

7.144   The relevant provisions state, in brief, that a person is guilty of an offence if:

---

[131] *OFT v X* [2003] EWHC 1042 (Comm), [2003] 2 All ER (Comm) 183, para 13. See also Case C-94/00 *Roquette Frères SA v Directeur Général de la Concurrence, de la Consommation et de la Répression des Fraudes* [2002] ECR I-9011, para 29.
[132] Competition Act 1998, s 29.   [133] ibid, s 28A(4).   [134] ibid, s 28A(7).

- he fails to comply with a requirement imposed on him under s 27, 28, or 28A;[135]
- he intentionally obstructs an officer acting in the exercise of his powers under s 27;
- he intentionally obstructs an officer in the exercise of his powers under a warrant issued under s 28 or 28A;
- having been required to produce a document under s 27, 28, or 28A he intentionally or recklessly destroys or disposes of it, falsifies it or conceals it, or he causes or permits its destruction, disposal, falsification, or concealment;
- he provides information (either to the OFT or to a person knowing it will be provided to the OFT) which is false or misleading in a material particular, and he knows it is or is reckless as to whether it is.

Where a person is convicted of any of the above offences, if it is a summary conviction (ie in a magistrates' court), the person is liable to a fine of up to the statutory maximum (currently £5,000) for each offence. If the conviction is made on indictment (ie in a superior court), a fine may be imposed for each offence and there is no statutory limit to the amount of the fine. Further, in relation to the final three offences listed above (obstructing an officer in the exercise of powers under a warrant, concealing or destroying documents, and providing false or misleading information), if the conviction is made on indictment, the person is also liable to imprisonment for a term not exceeding two years, in place of or in addition to the unlimited fine. The OFT has the initial discretion to decide in which court the case is to be brought. **7.145**

The OFT has not as yet brought any proceedings for an offence under these provisions of the Competition Act 1998. The OFT has stated that it is the severity of the penalties which has encouraged full compliance with the inspection provisions by the undertakings and persons concerned. **7.146**

(c) Inspections in relation to the cartel offence

(i) *The Enterprise Act*

The trigger for the OFT's use of its investigative powers in relation to the cartel offence is set out in s 192(1) of the Enterprise Act 2002. This provides that the OFT can conduct a formal investigation under the Enterprise Act if there are reasonable grounds for suspecting that a criminal cartel offence has been committed. This is an objective test and will depend upon the information the **7.147**

---

[135] There are a number of defences set out in the Competition Act 1998 in relation to an offence of failing to comply with a requirement imposed under a power of inspection. These essentially provide defences of reasonableness, where it is not reasonable to comply with the particular requirement, or where the person imposing the requirement has failed to act in accordance with the relevant section.

OFT has obtained prior to the use of its formal powers of investigation. In its guideline on the use of such powers, the OFT has stated that:

> Examples of sources of information that may lead to reasonable grounds for suspecting that the criminal offence has been committed include statements provided by employees or ex-employees or former members of a cartel, correspondence evidencing the existence of a secret cartel agreement or information provided in an application made by an undertaking or an individual under the OFT's leniency programmes.[136]

7.148 When conducting an investigation on the basis of a suspected cartel offence, the OFT may use the powers given under s 194 of the Enterprise Act 2002 to enter premises under a warrant. The use of this power is subject to an over-riding consideration that it appears to the OFT that there is good reason to exercise the power for the purpose of investigating the affairs of the person under investigation.[137] There is no guidance as yet on what will constitute 'good reason', but it is clear that this provides a further hurdle for the OFT in applying to the court for a warrant under this section.

7.149 On application by the OFT, the judge[138] may issue a warrant if he or she is satisfied there are reasonable grounds for believing:

(a) that there are on any premises[139] documents which the OFT has power under s 193[140] to require to be produced for the purposes of an investigation; and

(b) that—

  (i) a person has failed to comply with a requirement under that section to produce documents;

  (ii) it is not practicable to serve a notice under that section to that person; or

  (iii) the service of such a notice in relation to that person might seriously prejudice the investigation.

7.150 If the judge is satisfied that one of the above criteria is fulfilled, then he or she may issue a warrant. The issue of a warrant remains in the judge's discretion, even if the criteria are fulfilled.[141] However, once a warrant is issued, the powers granted under the warrant may not be limited or changed from those set out in the statute.[142]

---

[136] OFT515, *Powers for investigating criminal cartels* (January 2004) para 2.2.

[137] Enterprise Act 2002, s 192(2).   [138] Or sheriff in Scotland.

[139] The warrant power in this case does not provide for any distinction between business and domestic premises.

[140] See paras 7.96–7.107 above.

[141] Compare with s 62A of the Competition Act, where the statute says the judge 'shall' issue a warrant.

[142] This interpretation is based on the use of the word 'shall' in s 194(2).

The powers which the OFT may exercise under this warrant procedure are set **7.151** out in s 194(2) of the Enterprise Act 2002 as follows:

(a) to enter the premises specified in the warrant, using such force as is reasonably necessary for the purpose;
(b) to search the premises and
    (i) take possession of any documents appearing to be of a kind, or
    (ii) take, in relation to any documents appearing to be of the relevant kind, any other steps which appear necessary for preserving them or preventing interference with them;
(c) to require any person to provide an explanation of any document appearing to be of the relevant kind or to state, to the best of his knowledge and belief, where it may be found;
(d) to require any information which is stored in any electronic form and is accessible from the premises and which the named officer considers relates to any matter relevant to the investigation, to be produced in a form—
    (i) in which it can be taken away; and
    (ii) in which it is visible and legible or from which it can readily be produced in a visible and legible form.

These powers are essentially the same as the inspection powers set out in the **7.152** Competition Act 1998 for inspections under a warrant (see para 7.136 above), except that they apply to all premises without limitation. Where the OFT is using a warrant procedure to enter and search premises, it may call upon the police to enforce the warrant if necessary but not to conduct the search. The SFO may join the OFT in conducting an inspection under the Enterprise Act 2002, pursuant to s 195 of the Enterprise Act.

The OFT may also use powers to seize and sift material, pursuant to the Criminal **7.153** Justice and Police Act 2001, which allows the OFT to remove material from premises for examination elsewhere.[143] This may be necessary, for example, because there is insufficient time to conduct an effective examination on the premises, or there may be a need to use technical equipment which is not available on site. These powers also allow for the retention of an entire disk or hard drive where that is necessary to prove when specific items were created.[144] There are various limits on these powers: for example, it must be impracticable to separate the material out or to determine whether the material found includes material the subject of the warrant.[145] A person the subject of a warrant where the seize and sift powers are used may apply to a judge for the return of material which has been seized, and restrictions on how such material may be retained and used.[146]

---

[143] Criminal Justice and Police Act 2001, s 50.
[144] Home Office Circular 019/2003, 'Guidance on operating the new powers of seizure in Part LI of the Criminal Justice and Police Act 2001'.
[145] Criminal Justice and Police Act 2001, s 50(1) and (2).   [146] ibid, s 59.

7.154 The Police and Criminal Evidence Act 1984 Code B (**PACE Code B**)[147] also offers detailed guidance on carrying out inspections under warrant, and the OFT's guidance often refers to this code. In relation to the use of seize and sift powers, the OFT has stated that it will comply with relevant provisions of PACE Code B.[148] This refers to issues such as the treatment of seized material, including advising that, when originals are taken, officers must be prepared to facilitate the provision of copies or images for the owner when reasonably practicable. It also comments on the desirability of allowing the person from whom the property was seized, or a person with an interest in the property, an opportunity of being present or represented at the sifting examination.[149]

7.155 Documents collected by the OFT using the Enterprise Act powers may be used in procedures under the Competition Act against undertakings.[150]

(ii) Enterprise Act: Sanctions for non-compliance

7.156 The offences associated with non-compliance with an OFT inspection under the Enterprise Act 2002 provisions are more severe than the equivalent provisions in the Competition Act 1998, in that imprisonment is an option in all cases. The provisions are directed at 'persons' but are also applicable to undertakings where necessary, even though there is no specific definition set out in the Enterprise Act. Although the cartel offence is itself directed only at individuals, the OFT's information gathering powers under the Enterprise Act may need to be directed to undertakings in some circumstances, for example where an undertaking owns the premises being inspected.

7.157 The relevant sanctions are set out in s 201 of the Enterprise Act 2002, providing as follows:

(1) Any person who without reasonable excuse fails to comply with a requirement imposed on him under section 193 or 194 is guilty of an offence and liable on summary conviction to imprisonment for a term not exceeding six months or to a fine not exceeding level 5 on the standard scale or to both.

(2) A person who, in purported compliance with a requirement under section 193 or 194—
   (a) makes a statement which he knows to be false or misleading in a material particular; or
   (b) recklessly makes a statement which is false or misleading in a material particular,
   is guilty of an offence.

(3) A person guilty of an offence under subsection (2) is liable—

---

[147] PACE Code B, 'Searching premises and seizing property' (2004).
[148] OFT515, *Powers for investigating criminal cartels* (January 2004) para 3.14.
[149] PACE Code B, paras 7.7–7.17.
[150] OFT515, *Powers for investigating criminal cartels* (January 2004) para 4.4.

   (a) on conviction on indictment, to imprisonment for a term not exceeding two years or to a fine or to both; and

   (b) on summary conviction, to imprisonment for a term not exceeding six months or to a fine not exceeding the statutory maximum, or to both.

(4) Where any person—

   (a) knows or suspects that an investigation by the Serious Fraud Office or the OFT into an offence under section 188 is being or is likely to be carried out; and

   (b) falsifies, conceals, destroys or otherwise disposes of, or causes or permits the falsification, concealment, destruction or disposal of documents which he knows or suspects are or would be relevant to such an investigation,

he is guilty of an offence unless he proves that he had no intention of concealing the facts disclosed by the documents from the person carrying out such an investigation.

(5) A person guilty of an offence under subsection (4) is liable—

   (a) on conviction on indictment, to imprisonment for a term not exceeding 5 years or to a fine or to both; and

   (b) on summary conviction, to imprisonment for a term not exceeding six months or to a fine not exceeding the statutory maximum, or to both.

(6) A person who intentionally obstructs a person in the exercise of his powers under a warrant issued under section 194 is guilty of an offence and liable—

   (a) on conviction on indictment, to imprisonment for a term not exceeding 2 years or to a fine or to both; and

   (b) on summary conviction, to a fine not exceeding the statutory maximum.

7.158 At the time of writing, these provisions have not yet been used by the OFT. It is possible that as a result of compliance with the inspection provisions it may be some time before the OFT has any need to invoke these sanctions.

(iii) Criminal Justice Act 1987

7.159 The SFO may decide to investigate a potential criminal cartel offence where it appears on reasonable grounds to involve serious or complex fraud. In such cases, the OFT may be involved and even lead the investigation at early stages, but when the SFO determines that it should take up the investigation it will lead the investigation from that point forward. The OFT will still be involved in the investigation, but the SFO will take the lead. According to the Memorandum of Understanding between the OFT and the SFO,[151] the factors taken into account by the SFO in deciding to investigate include:

- Does the value of the alleged fraud exceed £1million? (This is simply an objective and recognisable signpost of seriousness and likely public concern rather than the main indicator of suitability.)

---

[151] OFT547, *Memorandum of Understanding between the Office of Fair Trading and the Director of the Serious Fraud Office* (October 2003).

- Is the case likely to give rise to national publicity and widespread public concern? For example, those involving government departments, public bodies, the governments of other countries, and commercial cases of public interest.
- Does the case require highly specialist knowledge of, for example, Stock Exchange practices or regulated markets?
- Is there a significant international dimension?
- Will legal, accountancy, and investigative skills need to be brought together?
- Is there a need to use the SFO's special powers, such as Criminal Justice Act, s 2 powers?[152]

7.160 Where the SFO is involved in an investigation concerning a potential criminal cartel offence, s 2(4) of the Criminal Justice Act 1987 allows the SFO to apply to a Justice of the Peace for a warrant to enter and search premises for specified documents in connection with an investigation which the SFO is conducting. A warrant obtained under this power will authorise the police to enter premises and take possession of documents. The police will be directed by the SFO in their search. The SFO can also use seize and sift powers, pursuant to the Criminal Justice and Police Act 2001.[153]

(iv) Interviews under the Criminal Justice Act

7.161 The SFO also has powers to require persons to answer questions for the purposes of a criminal investigation pursuant to s 2 of the Criminal Justice Act 1987. This power may be used as part of an inspection process. See paras 7.108–7.117 for further information on the use of this power by the SFO.

(v) Criminal Justice Act—sanctions for non-compliance

7.162 The sanctions for non-compliance with a warrant obtained under the Criminal Justice Act 1987 are set out in s 2 of that Act. These provide for offences in relation to failure to comply with a requirement imposed under s 2 (such as a warrant for inspection),[154] making a false or misleading statement,[155] and falsifying, concealing, or destroying documents.[156] The sanctions available include both fines and imprisonment, with the applicable maximum length of imprisonment (up to seven years) and maximum amount of any fine dependent upon the type of offence and whether it is brought on indictment or as a summary conviction.

(vi) OFT and SFO working together

7.163 The OFT has published a Memorandum of Understanding between the SFO and the OFT which sets out basic principles for the two organisations working

---

[152] ibid, background note, 5. [153] See para 7.153 for an explanation of these powers.
[154] Criminal Justice Act 1987, s 2(13). [155] ibid, s 2(14) and (15).
[156] ibid, s 2(16) and (17).

together in relation to cartel cases.[157] In Scotland, the International and Financial Crime Unit is the equivalent to the SFO, and there is a similar Memorandum of Understanding between the OFT and the International and Financial Crime Unit.[158]

There is a presumption that the SFO and the OFT, when jointly conducting an investigation, will use the SFO's powers under the Criminal Justice Act 1987 to conduct the investigation, rather than using the Enterprise Act powers.[159] If the OFT has already been refused a search warrant by the High Court (under the Enterprise Act powers), the SFO will not seek a search warrant from a Justice of the Peace (under the Criminal Justice Act) in relation to the same premises, unless new evidence has come to light during the course of the investigation that would justify the application for such a warrant.[160] **7.164**

Any documents obtained by the SFO using its powers under the Criminal Justice Act 1987 may be disclosed to the OFT for the purposes of the OFT's administrative procedures under the Competition Act 1998.[161] In the case of *Kent Pharmaceuticals Limited v SFO*,[162] Kent Pharmaceuticals challenged the disclosure of material collected by the SFO to another authority (in that case, the Department of Health). The challenge was brought on the basis that the SFO's decision to disclose was not 'in accordance with law' within the meaning of Article 8(2) ECHR. The court held that, as a result of the restrictions in and surrounding the disclosure power in s 3(5)(a) of the Criminal Justice Act 1987, the SFO's disclosure decision was in accordance with law and did not offend Article 8(2). This aspect of the decision was upheld by the Court of Appeal, where it was noted that any attempt to give further guidance in s 3(5)(a) of the Criminal Justice Act 1987 as to the circumstances in which the discretion to make further disclosure may be exercised would introduce undesirable rigidity. Such discretion must, however, always be exercised reasonably and in good faith.[163] **7.165**

In the *Kent Pharmaceuticals* case, the court also found that the SFO had acted unfairly in failing to give Kent Pharmaceuticals sufficient notice of the intended **7.166**

---

[157] OFT547, *Memorandum of Understanding between the Office of Fair Trading and the Director of the Serious Fraud Office* (October 2003).

[158] OFT546, *Memorandum of Understanding between the Office of Fair Trading and the International and Financial Crime Unit, Crown Office, Scotland* (October 2003).

[159] OFT547, *Memorandum of Understanding between the Office of Fair Trading and the Director of the Serious Fraud Office* (October 2003) para 8.

[160] OFT515, *Powers for investigating criminal cartels* (January 2004) para 3.22.

[161] Criminal Justice Act 1987, s 3(5)(a). See also OFT515, ibid, para 4.5.

[162] *Kent Pharmaceuticals Limited v SFO* [2003] EWHC 3002 (Admin), [2004] ACD 23.

[163] *R (Kent Pharmaceuticals Limited) v SFO* [2004] EWCA Civ 1494, [2005] 1 WLR 1302, para 20, per Kennedy LJ.

disclosure to allow it to make legal representations about the disclosure, and indicated that in most circumstances, principles of fairness required the SFO to inform an interested party of its intention to disclose material to another authority, so as to permit representations to be made by that party if necessary.[164] Furthermore, in the absence of such advance notice, it is incumbent on the SFO to give notice as soon as possible after the disclosure for the same purposes.[165] This decision was also upheld on appeal, where the Court of Appeal held that fairness demands the starting point should always be that the owner of the documents is entitled to be kept informed rather than the reverse:

> . . . unless there is good reason not to do so in the particular case, the person from whom documents have been seized under the powers conferred by the 1987 Act (and, if seized from some person other than the owner, the owner of the documents) ought to be told if and when the Serious Fraud Office determines that it will exercise the power to disclose those documents to others.[166]

(d) Inspections by or for the European Commission

7.167 The European Commission may conduct inspections in the United Kingdom for the purposes of an investigation under Article 81 or 82. Its powers in this regard stem from Regulation 1/2003. However, the European Commission's powers of investigation alone do not allow for situations where the European Commission requires the assistance of a UK warrant to ensure effective entry onto premises and to provide greater powers where necessary. The OFT therefore has additional investigative powers which allow it to assist the European Commission in an inspection.[167] These powers are set out in Regulation 1/2003 and in Pt 2 of the Competition Act 1998. In this section, references to the OFT do not include the Regulators, since the Regulators do not have any powers under Pt 2 of the Competition Act (although they may participate in inspections carried out by the OFT for the Commission where the industry being investigated falls into their area of expertise).

7.168 The OFT's powers to assist the European Commission, as set out in Pt 2 of the Competition Act 1998, are essentially divided into two types. The first type is where the OFT is actually leading the inspection, where there are no European Commission officials required to be present (even though it is conducted as part of a European Commission investigation) (**OFT-led inspections**). The

---

[164] *Kent Pharmaceuticals Limited v SFO* [2003] EWHC 3002 (Admin), [2004] ACD 23, para 32.

[165] ibid, para 36.

[166] *R (Kent Pharmaceuticals Limited) v SFO* [2004] EWCA Civ 1494, [2005] 1 WLR 1302, para 40 per Chadwick LJ and see also para 29, per Kennedy LJ.

[167] These powers are not given to the Regulators, although staff from a Regulator may participate in an inspection with the OFT as specialist personnel.

second type is where the European Commission is leading the inspection and the OFT officials are attending only to assist the European Commission (**Commission-led inspections**). The procedures applicable to each of these types of inspections are different.

OFT-led inspections may be carried out on *business premises* only[168] with or without a warrant. Where an OFT-led inspection is conducted without a warrant, the powers of the OFT stem from s 62B of the Competition Act 1998. With a warrant, the powers stem from s 63 of the Competition Act. The sanctions for non-compliance with these inspections are set out in s 65 of the Competition Act. These sanctions provide that a person who intentionally obstructs a person in the exercise of his or her powers under a warrant is guilty of an offence, and is liable to a fine of up to £5,000, or where the conviction is made on indictment, to imprisonment for a term of up to two years, or a fine, or both. **7.169**

The most relevant procedural aspect of this type of OFT-led inspection is that it is the UK definition of legal professional privilege which applies to information collected under this power, rather than the European definition.[169] This is specifically set out in s 65A of the Competition Act 1998. This may mean that, in future, the European Commission will only rarely request the OFT to undertake this type of inspection. When conducting inspections for the Commission the OFT can require not only documents but also 'explanations on facts . . . relating to the subject-matter and purpose of the inspection' as well as explanations of documents.[170] **7.170**

Commission-led inspections may be conducted with or without a warrant. The European Commission's power to conduct an inspection in the United Kingdom *without* a warrant is derived solely from Article 20 of Regulation 1/2003 and is confined to *business premises*. OFT officials are also given specific powers under Articles 20(5) and 22 of Regulation 1/2003 to assist the European Commission with such inspections. **7.171**

Where the European Commission is leading an inspection of *business premises* which requires a warrant, the powers to do this are provided in s 62 of the Competition Act 1998. OFT officials will almost always attend this type of inspection, since the warrant is sought by the OFT before the High Court. **7.172**

Inspections of *domestic premises* by the European Commission are only possible under warrant by virtue of s 62A of the Competition Act 1998, together with Article 21 of Regulation 1/2003. **7.173**

---

[168] Domestic premises may only be inspected where the separate warrant procedure under s 62A is used, which is not an OFT-led inspection.

[169] See paras 7.09–7.29 for a discussion on legal professional privilege.

[170] Competition Act 1998, s 62B(1) and Regulation 1/2003, Art 20(2).

7.174 The OFT has stated that the European definition of legal professional privilege applies to inspections conducted under ss 62 or 62A, so the documents able to be collected by the European Commission will not be limited by the application of the UK definition. However, the Competition Act is silent on the application of legal professional privilege in relation to these inspections, so the main basis for this position is the OFT's own statement in its guideline.[171]

7.175 The sanctions for non-compliance with an inspection led by the European Commission are set out in Articles 23 and 24 of Regulation 1/2003 (where the failure to comply relates to the non-warrant inspection procedure) and in s 65 of the Competition Act 1998 (where the failure relates to the warrant procedure or to the procedure for inspecting domestic premises). The sanctions under Regulation 1/2003 provide for fines of up to 1 per cent of an undertaking's turnover in the preceding business year where, intentionally or negligently, they refuse to submit to an inspection, or supply incorrect or misleading information, or break any seals affixed during an inspection. Where an undertaking refuses to submit to an inspection, the European Commission may also impose periodic penalty payments of up to 5 per cent of the average daily turnover of the undertaking in the preceding business year per day, in order to compel compliance. The sanctions under s 65 of the Competition Act 1998 provide that a person who intentionally obstructs a person in the exercise of his or her powers under a warrant is guilty of an offence, and is liable to a fine of up to £5,000, or where the conviction is made on indictment, to imprisonment for a term of up to two years or to a fine or to both.

(e) Inspections for other national competition authorities

7.176 National competition authorities from other Member States may seek the assistance of the OFT in order to conduct an inspection in the United Kingdom. Assistance may be given, at the OFT's discretion, in accordance with its powers set out in Pt 2A of the Competition Act 1998. In this section, references to the OFT do not include the Regulators, since the Regulators do not have any powers under Pt 2A of the Competition Act, although they may participate in inspections under warrant carried out by the OFT for other national competition authorities where the industry being investigated falls into their area of expertise. Essentially, the powers under Pt 2A are the same as those set out in Pt 1 of the Act. The only difference is that the inspection is being conducted for a different European competition authority, and this may mean that

---

[171] OFT515, *Powers for investigating criminal cartels* (January 2004). This view also reflects the OFT's practice to date, and the rationale set out in Case 155/79 *AM & S Europe Ltd v Commission* [1982] ECR 1575.

personnel from the other competition authority may be authorised to accompany authorised OFT staff.

As with written requests, there is a separation as to the *collection* of the docu- **7.177**
ments and the *use* of those documents in a case. Even though the case is being
conducted by another national competition authority, the rules applicable to
the *collection* of documents are the same as if the OFT was conducting the
case. Issues or disputes concerning the inspection itself, or the documents over
which legal privilege is claimed are between the subject of the inspection and
the OFT. Disputes as to the relevance of documents to the subject matter of the
investigation are between the subject of the inspection and the OFT, since it
is the extent of the power under Pt 2A of the Competition Act 1998 which is
in question.

Subsequent *use* of the documents is the responsibility of the competition author- **7.178**
ity conducting the case. Thus questions of disclosure of confidential material
and access to the file are ultimately for the competition authority conducting
the case, rather than the OFT. The later use of the material by the authority
conducting the case is governed first by the provisions as to information
disclosure (see Chapter 8 on information disclosure) and also by the national
laws applicable to the authority conducting the case.

The extent to which the OFT (or other authorities) can use the material collected **7.179**
under Pt 2A of the Competition Act 1998 is governed by the rules on use of
information for a different purpose to that for which it was collected. These are
not always clear, and a full discussion is set out in Chapter 8.

E. Other Methods for Gathering Information

(a) Publicly available information

Any authority may use information which is publicly available as general **7.180**
background for its investigation. The usual sources for information gathered
in this way include news articles, journals, company information, trade or
industry reports, market research and statistics, and previous findings by
other authorities such as the Competition Commission and the European
Commission. To the extent that any specific power is required to allow the
OFT to obtain such information, the power may be found in s 5(1) of the
Enterprise Act 2002. The OFT may also prepare and publish reports based
on its findings, pursuant to s 4(4) of the Enterprise Act (and subject to any
copyright restrictions).

(b) Voluntarily provided information

7.181 Authorities may, of course, receive information at any time provided voluntarily by undertakings or members of the public. Where such information is provided in the context of a complaint, a request for an opinion or informal guidance, or a leniency application, there are specific statutory limits or rules which govern the treatment of such information. These specific situations are discussed elsewhere in this text.

7.182 In general, where information (including witness statements) is provided voluntarily, the undertaking providing the information may wish to attach some conditions to the OFT's use of such information. Undertakings may be concerned, for example, about the possible waiver of any privilege, or the onward disclosure of confidential elements of the information. The OFT's general obligations in relation to disclosure of information are discussed at paras 7.41–7.46 (and see also Chapter 8), but regardless of the OFT's obligations it is always possible for the OFT to agree with the relevant undertaking on the treatment of information before it is voluntarily provided to the OFT.

7.183 In the context of an investigation, it may be beneficial for an undertaking that is the subject of the investigation to provide information voluntarily over and above the information sought by the OFT. This type of assistance may be considered by the OFT to go beyond the normal duty of cooperation[172] during an investigation and could be taken into account as a mitigating factor to reduce the level of any eventual fine. Information can be supplied voluntarily at any point during the investigation, but it is likely to be most beneficial if provided at an early stage, when the OFT may not already have gathered such information through exercising its statutory powers. The provision of voluntary information is not explicitly mentioned as a mitigating factor in relation to the calculation of penalties, although it would clearly fit into 'co-operation which enables the enforcement process to be concluded more effectively and/or speedily'.[173]

7.184 In some circumstances, the voluntary supply of information could mean that the person or undertaking providing the information is subject to potential sanctions if the information is false or misleading.[174] This will depend upon whether the supply of such information would be described as the provision of information 'in connection with any function of the OFT under [Pt 1 of the Competition Act 1998]'.[175] There are also possible sanctions associated with the

---

[172] See paras 10.80 and 10.85.
[173] OFT423, *OFT's guidance as to the appropriate amount of a penalty* (December 2004), para 2.16. See also paras 10.80 and 10.85.
[174] Competition Act 1998, s 44. See also Chapter 5, in relation to leniency.
[175] ibid, s 44(1) and (2).

granting of leniency where false or misleading information is provided on a voluntary basis in connection with a leniency application (see Chapter 5 for further information on leniency applications).

(c) Commissioned information

The OFT may engage the services of a consultant in the course of an investiga- **7.185**
tion, such as an expert economist, or a market research organisation. In such circumstances, some of the material obtained by the OFT in relation to the consultant's instructions and work product is likely to be treated as 'internal' material and will be withheld from access pursuant to the OFT's Procedural Rules. This is explained at paras 9.61–9.62. In relation to carrying out market studies and gathering general information in relation to matters concerning the carrying out of its various functions, the OFT has a specific power to commission or support research under s 5(3) of the Enterprise Act 2002.

(d) Surveillance and human intelligence

(i) Surveillance

The OFT may already gather publicly available information (see notes above), **7.186**
and this includes forms of overt surveillance, such as viewing premises to ascertain the size and exact location of premises preparatory to an inspection. In some cases, the OFT may choose to obtain an authorisation to conduct certain forms of overt surveillance, in order to ensure that any evidence obtained will be admissible. This may include, for example, CCTV camera recordings. The form of authorisation is the same as that which may be obtained for covert directed surveillance activities (set out below).

The OFT may also conduct covert surveillance as part of its investigations into a **7.187**
cartel offence under the Enterprise Act 2002 or (to a limited extent) cartel investigations under the Competition Act 1998 or Article 81 EC.[176] The legislation governing this power comprises the Regulation of Investigatory Powers Act 2000[177] and the Police Act 1997. The term 'covert' in this context means that the surveillance is not apparent or not intended to be apparent to the subject of the surveillance.[178] The term 'surveillance' is used to describe monitoring, observing or listening to persons, their movements, their conversations or their other activities or communications; recording any such surveillance; and includes

---

[176] OFT738, *Covert surveillance in cartel investigations: Code of practice* (August 2004) para 1.5.
[177] The OFT has been added as an approved public authority for the use of powers under Pt II of the Regulation of Investigatory Powers Act 2000.
[178] ibid, s 26(9)(a).

surveillance with the assistance of a surveillance device.[179] It also includes the interception of postal and telephone communications where one of the parties consents to the interception.[180]

7.188 The OFT is bound by the Home Office's code of practice on covert surveillance[181] and its own code of practice (**OFT's Covert surveillance code of practice**).[182]

7.189 **Authorisation required** For evidence gathered by covert surveillance to be admissible (able to be used as evidence) it must be lawfully gathered, which requires the OFT to obtain an authorisation before conducting covert surveillance. Covert surveillance is divided into two types for the purposes of authorisation for government authorities. These are directed and intrusive surveillance. In broad terms, directed surveillance describes any surveillance which does not involve being within any residence or private vehicle (such as video recording from the outside of a property).[183] Intrusive surveillance is any type of surveillance which involves surveillance from within a residence or private vehicle (for example, taking photographs or a recording from within a person's home).[184] Covert surveillance activities may also involve entry onto and interference with property (for example, entry into a house to install a recording device). Where this occurs, it requires a separate authorisation procedure in addition to the covert surveillance authorisation procedure.

7.190 The authorisation for directed surveillance may be granted by the Director of Cartel Investigations. The criteria for an authorisation are that it must be considered necessary and proportionate for the required purpose.[185] Directed surveillance may be carried out by the OFT for the purpose of obtaining evidence in relation to criminal cartel investigations under the Enterprise Act 2002, or in relation to some Competition Act 1998 investigations (being investigations of a suspected cartel[186] agreement to fix prices, limit production or supply, share markets, or rig bids).[187] An authorisation will be valid for three months from the date it is issued. It may also be renewed, without any limit to the number of renewals.[188]

---

[179] ibid, s 48(2). There are also some specific carve-outs listed in ibid, s 48(3) where certain types of surveillance are governed by other provisions.
[180] ibid, s 48(2).
[181] Home Office, *Covert surveillance: Code of Practice* (November 2005).
[182] OFT738, *Covert surveillance in cartel investigations: Code of practice* (August 2004).
[183] Regulation of Investigatory Powers Act 2000, s 26(2).
[184] ibid, s 26(3).   [185] ibid, s 28(2).
[186] In respect of Competition Act investigations, this definition of a cartel can embrace some vertical price fixing arrangements as well as purely horizontal ones. See OFT's Covert surveillance code of practice, para 1.5.
[187] ibid, paras 1.5, 4.9 and 4.10.
[188] Regulation of Investigatory Powers Act 2000, s 43.

The authorisation for intrusive surveillance may be granted by the Chairman of **7.191**
the OFT, subject to the approval of the Surveillance Commissioner.[189] The
criteria for an authorisation are that it must be considered necessary and proportionate for the required purpose and there must be no less intrusive means of
obtaining the desired evidence.[190] In the context of an OFT investigation, the
purpose of intrusive surveillance is limited to preventing and detecting a serious
offence under s 188 of the Enterprise Act 2002.[191] An authorisation will be valid
for three months from the date it is issued. It may also be renewed, without any
limit to the number of renewals.[192]

Where the intrusive surveillance would involve entry onto or interference with **7.192**
any property (or with wireless telegraphy) a separate authorisation is required,
which may be combined with the intrusive surveillance authorisation.

Part III of the Police Act 1997 provides for powers to authorise the entry upon **7.193**
and interference with property (or with wireless telegraphy). An authorisation is
necessary to carry out such activities unless the OFT has the consent of a person
able to give permission in respect of the relevant property. The authorisation for
interference with property may be granted by the Chairman of the OFT.[193] This
authorisation will be subject to the approval of the Surveillance Commissioner
where the property in question is a dwelling or a hotel bedroom or constitutes
office premises, or where the action is likely to result in obtaining confidential
information.[194] The criteria for an authorisation are that it must be considered
necessary for the action specified to be taken on the ground that it is likely to be
of substantial value in the prevention or detection of serious crime, and that what
the action seeks to achieve cannot reasonably be achieved by other means.[195]
An authorisation will be valid for three months from the date it is issued. It may
also be renewed, without any limit to the number of renewals.[196] This type of
authorisation may be ceased by order, in which case it may, if its terms allow,
be extended briefly to allow the retrieval of any equipment on the property.[197]
The Police Act 1997 also provides a complaints procedure and allows the
Commissioner power to quash authorisations and order the destruction of
records in certain circumstances.[198]

---

[189] OFT's Covert surveillance code of practice, para 5.16.
[190] Regulation of Investigatory Powers Act 2000, s 32(2), (3) and (4)
[191] OFT's Covert surveillance code of practice, para 5.7.
[192] Regulation of Investigatory Powers Act 2000, s 43.
[193] OFT's Covert surveillance code of practice, para 6.2. Other senior members of the OFT
may also be involved in the authorisation process (see ibid, paras 6.7 and 6.8).
[194] Police Act 1997, s 97; OFT's Covert surveillance code of practice, paras 6.12–6.14.
[195] ibid, s 93(2).   [196] ibid, s 95.
[197] OFT's Covert surveillance code of practice, para 6.26.
[198] Police Act 1997, ss 102 and 103.

7.194   Where any of the above types of authorisation are granted under urgent circumstances, the authorisation will be valid for 72 hours, and this may be renewed without any limit to the number of renewals.[199]

(ii) Covert human intelligence sources

7.195   The OFT is empowered to use covert human intelligence sources in certain circumstances, in order to gather evidence for use in a cartel offence investigation under the Enterprise Act 2002 or in a cartel investigation under the Competition Act 1998 or under Article 81 EC. The OFT's powers are contained in Pt II of the Regulation of Investigatory Powers Act 2000 and their use is governed by both the Home Office's code of practice on covert human intelligence sources,[200] published pursuant to s 71 of that Act, as well as the OFT's own code of practice (**OFT's Human intelligence code of practice**).[201]

7.196   Section 26(8) of the Regulation of Investigatory Powers Act 2000 sets out the definition of a covert human intelligence source as follows:

> For the purposes of this Part a person is a covert human intelligence source if—
> (a) he establishes or maintains a personal or other relationship with a person for the covert purpose of facilitating the doing of anything falling within paragraph (b) or (c);
> (b) he covertly uses such a relationship to obtain information or to provide access to any information to another person; or
> (c) he covertly discloses information obtained by the use of such a relationship, or as a consequence of the existence of such a relationship.

7.197   According to the OFT's Human intelligence code of practice, a source is likely to be an informant or a whistleblower.[202] A source may be tasked by the OFT to engage in conduct or obtain information. Section 29(4) of the Regulation of Investigatory Powers Act 2000 sets out what is included in the meaning of 'conduct of a source'. This encompasses conduct which is described in the relevant authorisation, is carried out by the person named as the source, and which is carried out for the purposes of, or in connection with, the investigation or operation specified.

7.198   **Authorisation required**   An authorisation is required before the OFT may use a covert human intelligence source.[203] The authorisation may only be granted by

---

[199]   Regulation of Investigatory Powers Act 2000, s 43(3)(a); Police Act 1997, s 95(2)(a).

[200]   Home Office, *Covert Human Intelligence Sources: Code of Practice* (September 2005).

[201]   OFT739, *Covert human intelligence sources in cartel investigations: Code of practice* (August 2004).

[202]   ibid, para 4.2.

[203]   Regulation of Investigatory Powers Act 2000, ss 27(1) and 29. Note that the OFT has stated that it believes such authorisation is not strictly necessary under the Act's provisions, but where there is an interference by the OFT with the right to respect for private and family life

the Director of Cartel Investigations, except in urgent circumstances when it may be granted by a principal investigations officer of the OFT. The criteria for an authorisation is that it must be considered necessary and proportionate, and there must be no less intrusive means of obtaining the desired evidence.[204] There must also be arrangements in place to protect the welfare of the source.[205] An authorisation will be valid for 12 months from the date it is issued. It may also be renewed, without any limit to the number of renewals. Where an authorisation is granted under urgent circumstances, it is valid for 72 hours, and this may be renewed without any limit to the number of renewals.[206]

The conduct of the source is subject to a limited protection whereby conduct **7.199** which would otherwise be criminal may be rendered lawful by virtue of ss 26(7) and 27 of the Regulation of Investigatory Powers Act 2000, provided it is under the terms of the authorisation.

If a source wears or carries a surveillance device and is invited into residential **7.200** premises or a private vehicle, there is no need to obtain a separate authorisation for the use of the device or for the intrusion onto property. It is only where the source is not present that an additional type of authorisation will be required for such activities.[207]

(iii) Confidential information

When it appears likely that the proposed surveillance or human intelligence **7.201** activity will result in the obtaining of confidential information, the authorisation required is subject to a 'high level of authorisation', which usually means the Chairman of the OFT.[208] In the context of covert surveillance or human intelligence, the term 'confidential information' means privileged, personal, or journalistic information.

Information subject to legal professional privilege[209] is considered to be con- **7.202** fidential information. The OFT considers that where a lawyer is the subject of an investigation or an operation, it is likely that information will be obtained which is subject to legal professional privilege. In such a case, additional

---

guaranteed under Art 8 ECHR, and where there is no other lawful authority, the consequences of not obtaining an authorisation under the 2000 Act may be that the action is unlawful by virtue of s 6 of the Human Rights Act 1998 (see paras 2.2 and 2.3 of the OFT's Human intelligence code of practice).

[204] Regulation of Investigatory Powers Act 2000, s 29(2) and the OFT's Human intelligence code of practice, paras 2.4–2.6.
[205] ibid, s 29(2)(c) and (5).   [206] ibid, s 43.
[207] OFT's Human intelligence code of practice, paras 4.39 and 4.40.
[208] This requirement has been self-imposed by the OFT: see ibid, paras 3.1 and 3.2.
[209] See paras 7.09–7.29.

consideration will be given to the request for authorisation, and the authorisation will only be granted in 'exceptional and compelling circumstances'.[210]

7.203 Personal information in this context means information 'held in confidence relating to the physical or mental health or spiritual counseling concerning an individual (whether living or dead) who can be identified from it'.[211]

7.204 Journalistic information which would be considered confidential includes material 'acquired or created for the purposes of journalism and held subject to an undertaking to hold it in confidence, as well as communications resulting in information being acquired for the purposes of journalism and held subject to such an undertaking'.[212]

7.205 In the context of surveillance by the OFT, where confidential information is acquired and retained by the OFT, it will be reported to the Surveillance Commissioner (or Inspector).

(iv) Use of surveillance and human intelligence material

7.206 In general terms, the use and disclosure of surveillance and human intelligence material, properly obtained, is subject to the same general limitations as any other material gathered by the OFT.[213]

7.207 In the OFT's code of practice, it is stated that '[m]aterial obtained through covert surveillance may be used as evidence in criminal proceedings in respect of the cartel offence and, in the case of directed surveillance, in administrative procedures instituted by the OFT under the Competition Act'.[214] However, it also states that '[t]here is nothing in the 2000 Act which prevents material obtained from properly authorised surveillance from being used in other investigations'.[215]

7.208 In relation to human intelligence material acquired and retained by the OFT, it is clearly very important for the safety and welfare of a source that the identity of the source is kept confidential before, during and after the relevant conduct has been carried out. For this reason, the OFT has indicated that access to its file would not include any documents 'that might give rise to even the slightest possibility that the identity of a source would be revealed'.[216] This principle extends to the OFT's record-keeping procedures in relation to the authorisation itself and any renewals or reviews of the authorisation.[217]

---

[210] OFT's Human intelligence code of practice, para 3.6.   [211] ibid, para 3.10.
[212] ibid, para 3.12.   [213] See Chapter 8 in relation to information disclosure.
[214] OFT's Covert surveillance code of practice, para 1.8.   [215] ibid, para 2.16.
[216] OFT's Human intelligence code of practice, para 1.8.   [217] ibid, para 2.16.

(v) Access to surveillance and human intelligence material

The code of practice notes that '[t]he undertakings the subject of the proposed **7.209** decision will have an opportunity to inspect the OFT file although the file would not include documents to the extent that they contain confidential information'.[218] The rules on access to documents are described in Chapter 9 on the decision-making process. All authorisations for covert surveillance (and related documentation) are retained by the OFT for three years from the end of the authorisation period. Other material may be retained indefinitely.

(vi) Where a dispute arises over admissibility

An undertaking or individual may dispute the admissibility of evidence in the **7.210** proceedings being conducted by an enforcement authority, or by a court. A dispute as to the admissibility of evidence in a case being conducted by an enforcement authority may be raised as a judicial review point, during the course of the proceedings, or after the final decision has been made (since it may not be apparent that the material is being relied upon by the authority until the final decision is issued). Judicial review in competition law cases is discussed in Chapter 12.

---

[218] ibid, para 1.8. Note that confidential information in this context is a reference to the broader concept of confidential information, as discussed in Chapter 8.

8

INFORMATION DISCLOSURE

A. Introduction

8.01   Regulation 1/2003 requires the Commission and the numerous national competition authorities across 25 Member States to cooperate closely in applying the EC competition rules.[1] It is a prerequisite, for successful cooperation and an effective and consistent application of Articles 81 and 82 EC, that all national competition authorities should be able to disclose relevant information relating to the application of Articles 81 and 82 to one another with confidence.

8.02   Not only is information exchange critical to the successful decentralised application of Articles 81 and 82, but as patterns of trade are increasingly more globalised, the expansion in cross-border anti-competitive activity makes increased

---

[1] Council Regulation (EC) 1/2003 of 16 December 2002 on the implementation of the rules on competition laid down in Articles 81 and 82 of the Treaty [2003] OJ L1/1, Art 11(1).

concertation and disclosure of information between authorities necessary to apprehend behaviour which spans across several states (and sometimes continents).[2]

However, the disclosure of information relating to undertakings and to indi- **8.03** viduals carries a cost: information relating to undertakings and individuals is protected under Article 8 ECHR, as it is a vital aspect of the right to privacy.[3] In many cases, the information is obtained pursuant to compulsory powers, so that subsequent use thereof in another context may erode the privilege against self-incrimination protected under Article 6 ECHR and/or principles of fair administration.

The tension between, on the one hand, allowing disclosure so that competition **8.04** authorities have sufficient enforcement capability, and on the other, protecting the legitimate interests of those to whom the information relates, has given rise to a very complex legal regime on the issue of information exchange. This is further complicated by the fact that one must consider overlapping regimes— domestic law, Community law, the European Convention on Human Rights (**ECHR**), and sometimes international treaties—before reaching a conclusion as to whether any individual piece of information can be disclosed by one authority, and used by another.

This chapter begins at section B by considering domestic law provisions relating **8.05** to disclosure (including ECHR law by means of the Human Rights Act 1998). It then turns in section C to look at the powers provided to disclose information under Community law before examining the restrictions that apply to these powers in section D. In section E, consideration is given to the disclosure relating to leniency applications. Once the various relevant legal contexts have been set out in sections B, C, D, and E, section F examines how the provisions take effect in practice, in the main situations in which information disclosure by competition authorities applying UK and EC competition law arises. The chapter concludes with a brief examination of disclosure to authorities outside the European Community.

---

[2] See OFT507, *The overseas disclosure of information: Consultation paper* (April 2003) para 1.5: 'cross-border trade is becoming an ever more significant part of the modern world. For these reasons, cooperation between enforcement agencies is increasingly necessary: for example to . . . combat cartels which cross international boundaries'.

[3] For several years it has been debatable whether legal entities such as companies had a right to privacy. The position has now been clarified by the ECJ in Case C-94/00 *Roquette Frères SA v Directeur Général de la Concurrence, de la Consommation et de la Répression des Fraudes* [2002] ECR I-9011, and, in the UK, in *OFT v X (also known as OFT v D)* [2003] EWHC 1042, [2003] All ER (Comm) 183.

B. Disclosure under Domestic Law

8.06 Prior to the enactment of the Enterprise Act 2002, in deciding whether or not to disclose information in their possession, competition authorities had to apply different pieces of consumer and competition legislation, each carrying its own disclosure regime.[4] Part 9 of the Enterprise Act was intended to clarify the position and to introduce one information disclosure regime for all UK competition authorities.

8.07 The Enterprise Act 2002 does not provide a one-stop-shop solution to the question as to whether any particular piece of information is disclosable under UK law. Although it introduces a certain coherence to information disclosure by UK public authorities, it does so by providing a single over-arching framework for information disclosure, rather than by exhaustively setting out the various domestic law powers of disclosure or constraints on disclosure.

8.08 In order to determine whether a piece of information may be disclosed, it is nearly always necessary, in addition to the Enterprise Act (which should be the first port of call), to consider additional legislation permitting or restraining disclosure in the particular matter at hand. For example, competition authorities have, in addition to their obligations under the Enterprise Act, to bear in mind their obligations under the Human Rights Act 1998 and the Data Protection Act 1998, not to mention any constraints that may be imposed on them by European law over and above the domestic regime. The purpose of this particular section is to set out the key features of the main applicable UK statutes. We will consider the issues that arise from the interaction between the various UK and European disclosure regimes when we look at the particular context in which disclosure arises in practice (see section F below).

(a) Part 9 of the Enterprise Act 2002

8.09 Although Part 9 of the Enterprise Act 2002 came into force on 20 June 2003, it affects disclosure of all information, including that received before the Act was enacted.[5] The disclosure scheme in Pt 9 is simple: s 237 of the Act imposes a general restriction on disclosure of specified information (**the statutory restriction**), which is followed by a number of exceptions or 'gateways' (ss 239–243) permitting regulators to disclose such information. Finally there is a compulsory 'balancing exercise' under s 244 which regulators must undertake prior to making permitted disclosure of specified information.

---

[4] Inter alia, Fair Trading Act 1973, s 133 and Competition Act 1998, ss 55 and 56.
[5] s 238(2) provides that it is immaterial whether information comes to a public authority before or after the passing of the Enterprise Act 2002.

(i) The statutory restriction

Section 237(2) of the Enterprise Act 2002 prohibits the disclosure by public **8.10** authorities of 'specified information' that relates to the affairs of an individual or to any business of an undertaking. This restriction applies during the lifetime of such individual or the existence of the undertaking, unless the disclosure is permitted elsewhere in Pt 9. A person breaching this restriction commits a criminal offence, carrying a maximum penalty of two years' imprisonment or a fine (or both).[6]

What information is caught?   The restriction applies to all 'specified' informa- **8.11** tion relating to the affairs of an individual or to any business of an undertaking.

'Specified information' is broadly defined to include information coming to a **8.12** public authority in connection with the exercise of any function it has under (amongst other enactments) Enterprise Act 2002 Pt 3 (mergers), Pt 4 (market investigations), Pt 6 (cartel offence), and the Competition Act 1998.[7] Such information may be obtained compulsorily or voluntarily. Information collected by the Office of Fair Trading (**OFT**) in conducting Article 81 and Article 82 investigations under the Competition Act is specified information, as these investigations are conducted by the OFT exercising functions conferred on it by the Competition Act.[8]

It is unclear whether information received by the OFT from the European **8.13** Competition Network (**ECN**) constitutes 'specified information'—on the one hand, the power to receive and provide information within the ECN is not conferred on the OFT by the Competition Act but by Regulation 1/2003 itself. However, one could argue, certainly where the information is transmitted to the OFT with a view to the OFT using it in the context of an investigation into Chapter I, Chapter II, Article 81 or Article 82, that such information comes to it in connection with the functions it has under the Competition Act.

Who is bound?   The restriction affects all 'public authorities' as construed in **8.14** accordance with s 6 of the Human Rights Act 1998,[9] and therefore binds the OFT, the Competition Commission (**CC**), and the Serious Fraud Office (**SFO**) amongst others. Public authorities under the Human Rights Act 1998 include

---

[6] ibid, s 245.   [7] ibid, s 238(1).

[8] The Competition Act 1998 was amended to empower the OFT to conduct investigation of suspected breaches of Arts 81 and 82 by the Competition Act 1998 and Other Enactments (Amendment) Regulations 2004, SI 2004/1261.

[9] Human Rights Act 1998, s 6 does not provide a comprehensive definition of the term public authority. It provides (s 6(3)) that the term includes a court or a tribunal and any person certain of whose functions are functions of a public nature. See *R (Heather) v Leonard Cheshire Foundation* [2002] EWCA Civ 366, [2002] 2 All ER 936; *R (Johnson) v Havering LBC* [2006] EWHC 1714 for judicial consideration of the meaning of 'public authority' and 'public function'.

courts and tribunals, as well as any person exercising functions of a public nature. The Competition Appeal Tribunal (**CAT**) is, however, expressly excluded from the application of Pt 9.[10]

(ii) The scope of the statutory restriction

8.15 The statutory restriction does not prevent disclosure where the information is already in the public domain (providing that the earlier disclosure was lawful).[11]

8.16 The statutory restriction does not affect powers or duties to disclose information that exist 'apart from this Part [Pt 9]'.[12] This wording is broad, and would appear to allow disclosure pursuant to powers and duties to disclose information arising in statute and at common law or pursuant to a court order. Accordingly, where a competition authority is empowered or obliged to disclose information (for example, the OFT is obliged to provide certain information to the CC under s 170 of the Enterprise Act 2002) the statutory restriction will not prevent its disclosure (though Pt 9 will affect the disclosure in other ways).[13]

(iii) Exceptions to the statutory restriction

8.17 The general prohibition on disclosure contained in s 237(2) of the Enterprise Act 2002 is subject to a number of limited exceptions. Disclosure may be possible if it comes within one of the 'gateways' provided in Pt 9, providing also that the disclosure satisfies the balancing test set out in s 244 of the Act.

8.18 Part 9 does not authorise any disclosure that would contravene the Data Protection Act 1998.[14]

8.19 The gateways in the Enterprise Act are discretionary in so far as they provide authorities with the means to effect certain types of disclosure, but they do not oblige such disclosure.[15] However, there is little margin for discretion when it comes to determining whether disclosure is permitted under any of the gateways. Contrary to the s 244 balancing test, which is predicated on the basis of the disclosing authority's (subjective) view, the gateways are framed objectively. For example, disclosure under s 240 is authorised only where the disclosure is 'required for the purpose of a Community obligation'—not where, in the view of the disclosing authority, it is required for the purpose of a Community obligation. This considerably reduces the scope of the exceptions, and, together with the criminal sanctions that apply in the event of breach of the statutory

---

[10] Enterprise Act 2002, s 237(5).   [11] ibid, s 237(3).   [12] ibid, s 237(6).
[13] ibid, the balancing test in s 244 applies to such disclosure, see para 8.34 below.
[14] ibid, s 234(4). See paras 8.96 et seq for a brief description of the data protection regime.
[15] The gateways either provide that the authority 'may' make the permitted disclosure, or that the permitted disclosure is not prohibited by Pt 9.

restriction, explains why the competition authorities construe the gateways narrowly in practice.

If disclosure of specified information does not fall within one of the specified **8.20** gateways below, and there is no prior lawful publication of the specified information, nor a power or duty to disclose it that exists apart from Pt 9, then disclosure is prohibited.

Part 9 provides five gateways: disclosure by consent, disclosure required for the **8.21** purpose of a Community obligation, disclosure for the purpose of facilitating the exercise of statutory functions, disclosure in connection with criminal proceedings or investigation, and finally overseas disclosure. The first four gateways are considered below, whereas overseas disclosure is considered in section G.

Consent (Enterprise Act 2002, s 239) A public authority may disclose **8.22** specified information where it has obtained the necessary consents. It may be necessary to obtain several consents in relation to a single piece of information:

- Where the identity of the provider of the information is known, the authority must satisfy itself that the provider was legally in possession of the information and that the provider consents to further disclosure before the authority can release the information.
- Where the information relates to the affairs of an individual, the consent of the individual is required.
- Where the information relates to the business of an undertaking, the consent of 'the person for the time being carrying on the business' is required. This concept is defined further in s 239(5) as:
  - (a) in the case of a company by a director, secretary or other officer of the company;
  - (b) in the case of a partnership by a partner;
  - (c) in the case of an unincorporated body or association by a person concerned in the management or control of the body or association.

The OFT must have regard to the provisions of s 244 of the Enterprise Act **8.23** before disclosing any information under this gateway (see below at paras 8.34 et seq).

Community obligations (Enterprise Act 2002, s 240) Section 240 provides **8.24** that Pt 9 'does not prohibit' the disclosure of information if it is required for the purpose of a Community obligation. Public authorities may therefore make all disclosures necessary for the purpose of discharging a Community obligation.

The scope of this gateway depends on how broadly one construes the term **8.25** 'Community obligation'. Where a provision of Community law mandates the provision of certain information (for example, Article 11(3) of Regulation

1/2003 requires national competition authorities to provide the Commission with certain information on commencement of a case), this clearly amounts to a Community obligation. What is less clear is whether 'Community obligation', for the purposes of s 240 of the Enterprise Act, extends to include disclosure of information made pursuant to the obligation of sincere cooperation under Article 10 EC. For example, Article 12 of Regulation 1/2003 empowers authorities to disclose information without 'requiring' them to do so in the narrow sense of the term. National competition authorities disclosing information under Article 12 are not strictly speaking required to do so under Community law, but could be viewed to be subject to a twofold Community obligation to exchange information under Article 12 of Regulation 1/2003 to secure the effective application of Articles 81 and 82: first, by virtue of the 'close cooperation' between the Commission and the national competition authorities that is required by Article 11(1) of Regulation 1/2003, and secondly, pursuant to the obligation of sincere cooperation under Article 10 EC.

8.26 Accordingly, it is unclear whether, when UK competition authorities disclose information to the ECN under Regulation 1/2003, the disclosure is made pursuant to s 240 (in discharge of a Community obligation set out in Regulation 1/2003 and the general obligation of loyal cooperation under Article 10 EC) or pursuant to s 237(6) (pursuant to a power to disclose that exists apart from Pt 9). Whether information is disclosed under s 240 or s 237(6) is significant because it potentially affects the application of the balancing test under s 244 of the Enterprise Act. Whereas disclosure under s 237(6) is subject to the application of the balancing test set out in s 244, it is unclear whether public authorities are obliged to have regard to the balancing test set out in s 244 prior to making disclosure under s 240 (this issue is discussed below at paras 8.35–8.37).

8.27 **Statutory functions (Enterprise Act 2002, s 241)**   The statutory functions gateway is one of the broadest and most important gateways in Pt 9 of the Enterprise Act. It consists of two limbs.

8.28 The first limb, s 241(1), allows public authorities holding specified information to disclose the information for the purpose of facilitating the exercise by that authority of any function it has under or by virtue of the Enterprise Act or any other enactment. This clearly permits authorities to disclose specified information in pursuance of many and various functions, provided that these have a statutory basis. Disclosure under s 241(1) entails a judgment as to whether or not disclosure would facilitate the pursuance of its statutory functions. The wording of s 241(1) is objective, and does not entrust the determination to the subjective evaluation of the disclosing authority: the issue is not whether in the OFT's view, the disclosure facilitates the exercise of a statutory function, but whether, viewed objectively, disclosure facilitates such exercise.

The disclosure under s 241(1) may be general—by means of publication (for **8.29** example, information may be disclosed by the OFT in the context of a published decision or a consultation document) or it may be selective (for example, disclosure of certain evidence to third parties and complainants in the context of an investigation under the Competition Act 1998).[16] Part 9 contains safeguards to ensure that where disclosure is selective (as opposed to general publication), recipients of the information will only use it for the purposes for which it was disclosed—see s 241(2). It is an offence under s 245 of the Enterprise Act (punishable by a maximum of two years' imprisonment or a fine or both) for a recipient of information to use the information for a purpose that is not permitted under Pt 9.

The second limb, s 241(3), permits disclosure of specified information to any **8.30** other person for the purpose of facilitating the exercise *by that other person* of a function conferred by the Enterprise Act and a number of other enactments, including the Competition Act 1998.[17] For example, the OFT may use this gateway to disclose information to the CC for use by the CC in a market investigation, or to a Regulator for use in a Competition Act investigation. Information disclosed under s 241(3) must not be used by the person to whom it is disclosed for any purpose other than a purpose relating to a function mentioned in that subsection.[18] It is an offence under s 245 of the Enterprise Act (punishable by a maximum of two years' imprisonment or a fine or both) for a recipient of information to use the information for a purpose which is not permitted under Pt 9.

The disclosing authority must have regard to the provisions of s 244 of the **8.31** Enterprise Act before disclosing any information under this gateway.

Criminal proceedings (Enterprise Act 2002, s 242) A public authority may **8.32** disclose specified information to any person in connection with any criminal investigation or proceedings in the United Kingdom. Therefore, information obtained by the OFT in a Chapter I/Chapter II investigation may be disclosed

---

[16] eg, the OFT explained in *Pernod Ricard*, in its skeleton argument submitted for the hearing of 27 January 2004, that it exercised its discretion in certain limited cases to disclose Rule 14 Notices to third parties and complainants to facilitate its functions under the Competition Act. The CAT held: 'In circumstances such as those, it seems to us, it would generally be proper, as a matter of fairness in administrative law, for the OFT, in exercising its discretion, to disclose a non-confidential version of the Rule 14 notice to a complainant in a position equivalent to that of Pernod. Such a course, in our view, enables the complainant, if he wishes, to put forward his point of view on an informed basis, instead of being largely in the dark. It is also likely to facilitate the OFT's understanding of the case and its implications, and lead to a sounder decision. Such a course is also likely, in our view, to introduce an important element of transparency and balance into the administrative proceedings which are conducted behind closed doors.' *Pernod Ricard SA v OFT* [2004] CAT 10, para 237.
[17] Enterprise Act 2002, s 241(3) and Sch 15.   [18] ibid, s 241(4).

to the SFO for an investigation into the cartel offence. Prior to disclosure, in addition to the balancing test set out in s 244 (see paras 8.34 et seq), the public authority must also apply the proportionality test set out in s 242(3) which is designed to protect the defendant's ECHR rights, in particular Article 8 ECHR (the right to privacy).

8.33 The recipient of the information is bound not to use it for any purpose other than that for which it is disclosed.[19] There are several additional constraints on *the use* to which such information may be put by the receiving authority in other statutes and by virtue of fundamental rights protected under the ECHR such as the privilege against self-incrimination; these are discussed at paras 8.62 et seq below.

(iv) Balancing exercise under Enterprise Act 2002, s 244

8.34 **When does it apply?**   Section 244 provides in terms that it applies to the disclosure of *any* specified information within the meaning of Pt 9. The wording is unequivocal: 'A public authority must have regard to the following considerations before disclosing any specified information (within the meaning of section 238(1)'. There are no caveats or exceptions in s 244 itself. Further, Article 237(6) of the Enterprise Act 2002 expressly extends the application of s 244 to disclosure that is made pursuant to a power or duty that arises apart from Pt 9. Section 244 will therefore apply to disclosure of specified information by a public authority, even if disclosure is made under another statute.

8.35 Yet there is a question mark as to whether the OFT, when disclosing information under s 240 of the Enterprise Act to discharge a Community obligation, is obliged to apply s 244 prior to disclosure. Section 240 provides that Pt 9 (as a whole, including the s 244 test therefore) does not *prohibit* the disclosure of information if it is required for the purpose of a Community obligation. Some commentators read this as meaning that if s 244 cannot prevent disclosure that is mandated by Community law, it does not apply at all.[20] It is true that it is questionable whether it is compatible with primacy of Community law and the duty of loyal cooperation, for an authority to subject disclosure to a pre-condition of satisfying the s 244 test under domestic law.

8.36 On the other hand, the balancing test set out in s 244 could be viewed as sufficiently flexible for this not to be viewed as an interference with the OFT's obligations under Community law. It is difficult to argue that national competition authorities should be transmitting confidential information that it is practicable to exclude under s 244(3) and that is not necessary within the

---

[19] ibid, s 242(2).
[20] R Nazzini, *Concurrent Proceedings in Competition Law* (Oxford University Press, 2004), paras 8.59 and 8.60.

sense of s 244(4). Given that proportionality is a Community law principle (and s 244 can be viewed as an articulation of proportionality), it is consistent for public authorities acting pursuant to Community law powers or Community obligations to take account of proportionality prior to disclosing confidential information.[21]

The OFT will be applying the s 244 test prior to making disclosure pursuant to the Modernisation Regulation, even though some of that disclosure would appear to be required pursuant to a Community obligation within the meaning of s 240.[22] **8.37**

The s 244 balancing exercise Section 244 of the Enterprise Act 2002 requires that, before disclosing the relevant information, a public authority must undertake a three-step evaluation: **8.38**

- The first consideration is the need to exclude from disclosure (so far as practicable) any information whose disclosure the authority thinks is contrary to the public interest.[23]

- The second consideration is the need to exclude from disclosure (so far as practicable) (a) commercial information whose disclosure the authority thinks might significantly harm the legitimate business interests of the undertaking or the interests to whom it relates, or (b) information relating to the private affairs of an individual whose disclosure the authority thinks might significantly harm the individual's interests (collectively known as confidential information[24]).[25]

- Third, the public authority must evaluate the extent to which it is *necessary* to disclose confidential information.[26]

Section 244 requires the disclosing authority to balance the potential harm to the interests of an individual or a business (s 244(2)) against the extent to which the disclosure is necessary (s 244(3)). **8.39**

Each of the three limbs of s 244 is cast in subjective terms revolving around what the disclosing authority thinks. This provides it with a margin of discretion in undertaking the evaluation that the section requires.[27] **8.40**

---

[21] Member States, in applying Community law, must respect the general principles of Community law; see Case 5/88 *Wachauf v Germany* [1989] ECR 2609, para 19.

[22] OFT442, *Modernisation* (December 2004) para 9.7 and OFT404, *Powers of investigation* (December 2004) para 6.13. The OFT takes the view that its disclosure under Regulation 1/2003 is made under s 237(6) of the Enterprise Act, and not s 240. For a contrary view, see R Nazzini, *Concurrent Proceedings in Competition Law* (Oxford University Press, 2004), paras 8.59 and 8.60.

[23] Enterprise Act 2002, s 244(2).   [24] OFT's Rules of Procedure, r 1.

[25] Enterprise Act 2002, s 244(3).   [26] ibid, s 244(4).

[27] *Umbro Holdings Ltd v OFT* [2003] CAT 26.

8.41 **Public interest** The application of s 244(2) only arises where information disclosure has passed several statutory hurdles. First, the information must have qualified as 'specified information'[28] (and so has been identified as information in which there is an interest to protect). Secondly, the proposed disclosure nonetheless qualifies for disclosure under the exceptions to the statutory restriction, because it is already in the public domain (s 237(3)), pursuant to powers and duties that exist apart from Pt 9 (s 237(6)) or under the Enterprise Act gateways. These exceptions and gateways can, in themselves, be viewed as the statutory articulation of public interests that favour disclosure. For example, it is in the public interest to allow disclosure to another authority to facilitate the investigation of crime.[29] Proposed disclosure evaluated under s 244 has therefore already undergone a two-step public interest test of kinds. Accordingly, the subsequent public interest evaluation under s 244 is fairly complex.

8.42 A wide number of additional possible public interest factors arise for consideration by the disclosing authority at this stage. For example, in *Umbro*[30] the applicant sought to oppose disclosure (in the context of an appeal before the CAT) of the fact that it had applied for leniency and cooperated with the OFT. It did so on two public interest grounds (both of which were endorsed by the OFT):

> The first public interest is that persons should be free to seek leniency in confidence and without fear of disclosure, and that the efficiency of the leniency programme should be protected, because that will lead to the discovery, or more effective detection of cartels.

> Secondly, it is submitted that the parties before the Tribunal should not be at the risk of suffering commercial sanctions in the market place as a result of a perception that they had 'shopped' or 'sneaked' on their customers or competitors.[31]

8.43 In *Umbro*, the CAT accepted that the OFT had acted properly in not disclosing the documents related to Umbro's leniency application to the other members of the cartel that was being investigated.[32] However, it took a different view of where the balance of interest lay in the context of disclosure at the appeal stage, finding that 'the needs of fairness and transparency clearly outweigh any other

---

[28] Enterprise Act 2002, s 238(1).

[29] *R v Brady* [2004] EWCA Crim 1763, [2004] 1 WLR 3240, para 27 per Tuckey LJ: 'Once the DTI or the official receiver is satisfied that section 235 material is required by another prosecuting authority for the purpose of investigating crime it should be free to disclose it without an order of the court or notice to the person who provided it. It is self-evidently in the public interest that the appropriate prosecuting authority should have such material to aid its investigation . . .'

[30] *Umbro Holdings Ltd v OFT* [2003] CAT 26.   [31] ibid, paras 27 and 28.

[32] ibid, para 34 : 'We entirely see and accept the public interest considerations which lie behind Umbro's application and which are particularly emphasised by the OFT. It is, in our judgment, desirable that those who seek leniency should be able to do so, at least in the first instance, in confidence and should not be denied that confidence, unless there are important countervailing reasons. It is equally desirable that parties who seek leniency should not be placed unnecessarily at risk of some kind of commercial retaliation in the market place.'

interests there may be in keeping this matter confidential'.[33] This is a good example of the flexibility of the notion of 'public interest' and the margin of discretion that each disclosing authority enjoys—what is in the public interest will differ depending on the relevant circumstances at the time of disclosure and the particular context in which the disclosure is made.

Confidential information   Section 244(3) is aimed at protecting the interests **8.44** of those to whom the information relates. It obliges the disclosing authority, prior to making any disclosure, to assess whether any of the information that it is proposed to disclose may harm the interests of the individual or the legitimate business interests of the undertaking to whom it relates. It gives rise to a presumption that, confidential information, so far as practicable, should be excluded from disclosure. The CAT indicated in *Aberdeen Journals v Director General of Fair Trading*,[34] that 'commercial information' such as market shares, revenues, costs, etc that was over three years old was too old to be capable of causing significant harm to the interests of the undertaking concerned. Accordingly there was no 'legitimate' business interest that still required protecting.

Like s 244(2), s 244(3) is cast in subjective terms revolving around information **8.45** that is in the disclosing authority's view confidential: there is no obligation on the public authority to consult with the person supplying the information prior to making the disclosure.[35] However, in general, where the UK authorities request or require information using their compulsory or voluntary powers, they usually ask that the party supplying the information identify all information which they consider to be confidential, in order to assist the authority in undertaking the s 244 evaluation.[36] In many cases (but not all) the party providing the information will be the party (or one of the parties) to whom the information relates for the purposes of step 2 of the test set out above, so that the risk of error on the part of the disclosing authority is lessened if it has consulted the party producing the information. The CC has indicated that early identification of sensitive material gives it a better chance to consult those concerned prior to disclosure. A 'blanket' assertion of confidentiality over all the information provided will not suffice for these purposes.[37]

Necessary   Once the regulator has identified whether the proposed disclosure **8.46** contains confidential information under s 244(3) and considered the need to

---

[33] ibid, para 43.   [34] [2003] CAT 14.

[35] At para 24 of *Umbro Holdings Ltd v OFT* [2003] CAT 26, the CAT emphasises that a similar, but not identically worded, test set out for the CAT under the Enterprise Act 2002 is subjective.

[36] See, eg, CC7, *Chairman's Guidance on Disclosure of Information in Merger and Market Inquiries* (July 2003) para 4.1 and OFT's Rules of Procedure, r 6.

[37] CC7, ibid, para 41.

exclude disclosure of such information, s 244(4) requires it to have regard, as against the identified need to exclude the disclosure, to what extent it is in its view nonetheless *necessary* to disclose the information. Following the CAT's approach to s 60 of the Competition Act 1998 in *Pernod Ricard*,[38] it might be relevant, in considering necessary disclosure under the Competition Act, to consider what disclosure is made by the European Commission in the context of its own proceedings.

8.47   To determine what disclosure is necessary involves the evaluation of competing interests. Competition proceedings are characterised by the various and conflicting interests of the participants: parties, third parties, complainants and even competitors will often seek access to the information that others have supplied, while simultaneously fighting hard to protect the confidentiality of the information they have themselves supplied. In view of the frequently diametrically opposite interests (for example, a whistleblower will fight hard to protect the confidentiality of its leniency application, whereas the other members of the cartel will argue that they should have access to the application to enable them to conduct their defence), authorities have a difficult task in drawing the line at what disclosure is and is not necessary. The task is particularly onerous in view of the criminal penalties that are attached to disclosures made in breach of Pt 9.

8.48   The OFT takes quite a narrow view of what disclosure is 'necessary'. This is epitomised by the OFT's approach to disclosure in the context of appeals to its decisions before the CAT. It has taken the view, endorsed by the CAT, that the disclosure of confidential information held on the OFT's file is not 'necessary' for the purpose of facilitating the CAT appeal process.[39] Even if the OFT considers disclosure to the parties to the appeal would aid the conduct of the appeal, it does not rely on s 241 (statutory functions) and s 244 to make disclosure. In the past, the OFT has in such a situation sought to proceed under s 239 by seeking the consent of the relevant persons. Alternatively it has sought an order from the CAT mandating the disclosure, so that s 237(6) (obligation to disclose apart from Pt 9) applies to permit the disclosure.[40] This issue is discussed further at paras 8.55 et seq below.

8.49   Where information is deemed confidential, the OFT may, in appropriate cases, seek to accommodate the conflicting interests by not altogether withholding the documents, but instead redacting them to remove the confidential information.[41]

---

[38] *Pernod Ricard SA v OFT* [2004] CAT 10.
[39] *Umbro Holdings Ltd v OFT* [2004] CAT 3, para 5, and *Makers UK Ltd v OFT* [2006] CAT 13.
[40] *Umbro Holdings Ltd v OFT* [2003] CAT 26, and *Makers UK Ltd v OFT* [2006] CAT 13.
[41] OFT404, *Powers of investigation* (December 2004) para 6.11 and OFT507, *The overseas disclosure of information: Consultation paper* (April 2003) para 5.2.

The CC (which frequently relies on the voluntary provision of information) has **8.50**
published a guide which gives a good indication of its approach to the balancing
test in s 244 of the Enterprise Act and by analogy,[42] to the approach of other
authorities in its position. Paragraph 3.1 of the CC's guideline[43] provides:

> When considering whether to disclose particular information and to whom,
> groups should have regard to the following objectives:
>
> - the need to make sufficient information available to main parties so that they
>   have sufficient understanding of the case against them, are able to comment
>   upon the information supplied by other parties when appropriate and are able to
>   draw to the Commission's attention any inaccuracies, incomplete or misleading
>   information;
>
> - the desirability of making sufficient information available to the public so that
>   the public may become aware of the main issues arising in an inquiry and are in a
>   more informed position to provide information to the group; the need to dis-
>   close information supplied to the Commission so that interested parties are able
>   to comment upon the information supplied and can draw to the Commission's
>   attention any inaccuracies, incomplete or misleading information;
>
> - the need to conduct the investigation effectively and efficiently and to make
>   properly reasoned decisions within the prescribed timetable.

For a discussion of access to files and disclosure of information by UK author- **8.51**
ities in the context of various investigations under the Competition Act, see
paragraphs 9.54 and 9.102. For access to files in the context of market investigation references by the OFT, see Chapter 13. See Chapter 14 for access to files in
market investigation inquiries. The position of disclosure by the regulators to
civil litigants for the purpose of civil proceedings for damages for infringements
of competition law is considered below at paras 8.235 et seq.

The considerations discussed above are relevant to disclosure made by a com- **8.52**
petition authority in the context of its own proceedings. When considering
disclosure of information to another authority under the statutory functions
gateway, how does the disclosing authority gauge whether the disclosure is
'necessary'? The CC has indicated that it will determine whether the disclosure
is necessary by asking the requesting authority to demonstrate that the information is or is very likely to become relevant to its investigation or other statutory
function. In addition, it will consider whether the requesting authority would

---

[42] Note however that the context in which disclosure is made is relevant to the balancing
exercise—for example, unlike OFT investigations under the Competition Act 1998, CC procedure does not qualify as 'criminal' for the purposes of Art 6 ECHR, so that considerations may
differ when the OFT considers disclosure.

[43] CC7, *Chairman's Guidance on Disclosure of Information in Merger and Market Inquiries*
(July 2003).

be able to obtain the information from another source.[44] Although the OFT has indicated that it will apply s 244 prior to making disclosure to the ECN under Regulation 1/2003, it is unclear whether it will be making such requests to determine whether the transmission is necessary when asked to disclose specified information to another national competition authority.

(v) Notice of intended disclosure?

8.53 The Enterprise Act 2002 does not provide any obligation on the disclosing authority to consult or give notice to the person to whom the information relates prior to disclosure. However, in practice, both the CC and the OFT tend to give notice to the persons concerned and to allow them to make representations, certainly when it comes to disclosures made in the context of their own proceedings.[45] This is consistent with EC law, and in particular with the obligation of professional secrecy as enunciated in *Akzo Nobel Chemie BV*.[46] Rule 6(1) of the OFT's Rules of Procedure provides that where the OFT proposes to disclose under the Rules, information that has been identified as confidential, the OFT shall take all reasonable steps to inform the supplier of the information of the OFT's proposed action and give that person a reasonable opportunity to make representations to the OFT on the OFT's proposed action. The Rules apply to disclosure made in the context of an OFT investigation or enforcement action in relation to the Chapter I prohibition, the Chapter II prohibition, Article 81(1) and Article 82.[47] They do not cover disclosure to the ECN.[48]

8.54 It should be noted that a right to notice of disclosure may arise out of the common law duty of fairness, or alternatively, to allow the undertakings concerned access to the courts as required under Article 6 ECHR.[49] This issue is discussed in more depth at paras 8.70 et seq below.

---

[44] CC12, *Disclosure of Information by the Competition Commissioner to other public authorities* (April 2006) para 10.

[45] CC7, *Chairman's Guidance on Disclosure of Information in Merger and Market Inquiries* (July 2003) paras 4.5 and 4.6 and CC4, *General Advice and Information* (March 2006) para 6.30.

[46] Case 53/85 *Akzo Nobel Chemie BV v Commission* [1986] ECR 1965, para 29: 'It is undoubtedly for the Commission to assess whether or not a particular document contains business secrets. After giving an undertaking an opportunity to state its views, the Commission is required to adopt a decision in that connection which contains an adequate statement of the reasons on which it is based and which must be notified to the undertaking concerned. Having regard to the extremely serious damage which could result from improper communication of documents to a competitor, the Commission must, before implementing its decision, give the undertaking an opportunity to bring an action before the court with a view to having the assessments made reviewed by it and to preventing disclosure of the documents in question.' See also Case T-353/94 *Postbank NV v Commission* [1996] ECR II-921.

[47] OFT's Rules of Procedure, r 2(1).

[48] OFT404, *Powers of investigation* (December 2004) para 6.13.

[49] *R (Kent Pharmaceuticals Ltd) v Director of the SFO* [2004] EWCA 1494, [2005] 1 WLR 1302. This is discussed at para 8.70 below.

(vi) Enterprise Act prohibition on CAT disclosure

Although s 237 does not apply to the CAT, the Enterprise Act 2002 provides a **8.55**
separate restriction on disclosure for the CAT. Paragraph 1 of Sch 4 to the
Enterprise Act 2002 provides as follows:

> (2) In preparing [the final decision or judgment] the Tribunal shall have regard to
> the need for excluding so far as practicable—
> (a) information the disclosure of which would in its opinion be contrary to
> the public interest;
> (b) commercial information the disclosure of which would or might, in its
> opinion, significantly harm the legitimate business interests of the under-
> taking to which it relates;
> (c) information relating to the private affairs of an individual the disclosure of
> which would, or might, in its opinion, significantly harm his interests.
> (3) But the Tribunal shall also have regard to the extent to which any disclosure
> mentioned in sub-paragraph (2) is necessary for the purpose of explaining the
> reasons for the decision.

Scope of the restriction   In *Umbro Holdings Ltd v OFT*,[50] the CAT held that **8.56**
although the Enterprise Act 2002 deals only with what is to be included in the
Tribunal's judgment, the same principles apply to the protection, during the
appeal proceedings, of information that is likely to be regarded as confidential:

> Although that statutory provision deals only with what is to be included in the
> Tribunal's judgment, the Tribunal takes the view that, for that provision to be
> effective, the Tribunal should protect, during the appeal proceedings, information
> that it would be likely to regard as confidential for the purposes of its judgment
> subject, of course, to the overriding requirement of ensuring the fairness of the
> appeal proceedings.[51]

The test in practice   The test is similar to that undertaken under s 244 of the **8.57**
Enterprise Act 2002, in that it revolves on balancing the interests of those to
whom the confidential information relates on the one hand, as against the need
for the CAT to disclose the information. In practice, the CAT does not only
consider the need for disclosure to enable it to provide reasons for its judgment,
but will also consider whether disclosure is necessary to ensure the fairness of the
appeal proceedings or the interests of justice. If anything, the conflict in the
various interests of the parties involved becomes more acute in the context of an
appeal, as the CAT must additionally have regard to Article 6 ECHR and the
rights of the defence. Confidentiality must be maintained in open court, as all
parties (including competitors) are seated in the same room, and regard must
also be had to ensuring the transcripts do not contain confidential information.
In *Umbro Holdings Ltd v OFT*,[52] the CAT explained the evaluation it undertakes
as follows:

---

[50] [2003] CAT 26.   [51] ibid, para 23.   [52] [2004] CAT 3.

(i)   is the information confidential in the sense that its disclosure would or might harm the legitimate business interests of the undertaking in question?

(ii)   is the information relevant to the appeal?

(iii) is any harm that might be caused to the party disclosing the document *outweighed by the interests of justice?*[53]

8.58 In *MasterCard v OFT*[54] the CAT summarised its approach to disclosure of confidentiality in similar terms:

> In any case, where confidentiality is claimed, there are essentially three questions: first of all, is confidentiality properly claimed having regard to the test which is set out in Schedule 4 of the Enterprise Act? Secondly, if, at first sight, the material is properly confidential, is it nonetheless something that is very likely to be necessary for explaining the reasons for the Tribunal's decision, in which case it is extremely difficult, for obvious reasons, to keep the matter confidential? Thirdly, and in any event, what is the balance of interest between the various parties which requires disclosure? . . .

8.59 The CAT has to weigh competing interests in determining whether or not to grant confidentiality. On balance, it has indicated that it will favour disclosure where the right to a fair trial is at stake:

> The Tribunal takes the view that its proceedings should be conducted on the basis that is as fully open as possible, subject only to the protection of vital business secrets or for some other overriding reason . . . In the event of a conflict between the rights of the defence and other claims to confidentiality there must, in our judgment, be a presumption that the rights of defence prevail.[55]

8.60 Although the CAT's approach to ordering disclosure in practice is cautious, it is more generous than the OFT's primarily because the context of disclosure in an appeal is different. In *Argos Ltd and Littlewoods Ltd v OFT*[56] the CAT identified the factors that meant its approach to disclosure was broader than that of the OFT:

> In our view, the scheme envisaged by the 2002 Act and the earlier, now repealed, provisions of the 1998 Act, is that information which was quite properly protected from disclosure by the OFT during the administrative stage may, depending on the circumstances, become disclosable in the course of appeal proceedings before the Tribunal. That may happen, for example, because information that was once commercially confidential has become less sensitive with the passage of time; because the balancing exercise that the Tribunal is required to perform under paragraph 2(1) of Schedule 4 gives a different result to that which obtained at the OFT stage; or because the overriding interest of fairness in the appeal requires disclosure. In that latter connection, the Tribunal has held that it is the Tribunal's role to ensure that the requirements of Article 6(1) of the ECHR are respected: see

---

[53] ibid, para 34 of the order on confidentiality.   [54] [2006] CAT 2, para 8.
[55] *Umbro Holdings Ltd v OFT* [2003] CAT 26, para 32.   [56] [2004] CAT 5.

Napp Pharmaceuticals Limited v Director General of Fair Trading [2001] CAT 3 and [2002] CAT 1.[57]

The CAT may encourage the parties to agree to disclosure before making an **8.61** order for disclosure.[58] It may also seek to accommodate conflicting interests by means of selective disclosure to a 'confidentiality ring' consisting of the parties' named legal representatives and external advisers (such as economic experts) rather than the parties themselves.[59] Other practices include colour coding documents in court bundles to ensure that certain material is not read out in open court. Further, it will not make an order for disclosure when the issues in the proceedings are not sufficiently defined to allow it to balance the various interests at stake. In *MasterCard*,[60] when an intervener sought disclosure for the purposes of informing its pleading in intervention, the CAT held that disclosure would be better considered by it once the key pleadings in the case (including the intervention) had been lodged so that it could form an idea as to the relevance of the documents before it in determining where the balance of interest lay.

(b) Human Rights Act 1998

Section 6(1) of the Human Rights Act makes it unlawful for a public authority **8.62** to act in a way which is incompatible with a ECHR right. Accordingly, in exercising their powers to disclose information, regulators must act in a matter that is compatible with relevant ECHR rights. The most relevant ECHR provisions in this context are Articles 8 and 6 ECHR. We address each in turn below.

(i) Article 8 ECHR

Article 8 ECHR provides: **8.63**

1. Everyone has the right to respect for his private and family life, his home and his correspondence.
2. There shall be no interference by a public authority with the exercise of this right except such as is in accordance with the law and is necessary in a democratic society in the interests of national security, public safety or the economic well-being of the country, for the prevention of disorder or crime, for the protection of health or morals, or for the protection of the rights and freedoms of others.

Article 8 ECHR applies to undertakings as well as individuals.[61] Its relevance in **8.64**

---

[57] ibid, para 56.   [58] *Umbro Holdings Ltd v OFT* [2004] CAT 3, para 8.
[59] CAT's Guide to Proceedings (October 2005) para 13.10.
[60] *MasterCard UK Members Forum Ltd v OFT* [2006] CAT 2.
[61] In Case C-94/00 *Roquette Frères SA v Directeur Général de la Concurrence, de la Consommation et de la Répression des Fraudes* [2002] ECR I-9011, and, in the UK, in *OFT v X (also known as OFT v D)* [2003] EWHC 1042, [2003] All ER (Comm) 183.

this context is that disclosure of information relating to an undertaking may amount to an interference with the undertaking's right to correspondence.[62]

8.65 In *R (Kent Pharmaceuticals Ltd) v Director of the Serious Fraud Office*,[63] the Court of Appeal considered whether a 'statutory gateway' allowing disclosure by the SFO to other government departments (similar, but not identical, to the statutory functions gateway in the Enterprise Act 2002) was compatible with Article 8 ECHR. The SFO had raided the premises of Kent Pharmaceuticals in the context of its investigation under s 2(4) of the Criminal Justice Act 1987 into price fixing of certain generic drugs. The Department of Health, which wanted to initiate civil proceedings for damages in relation to the price fixing, requested disclosure of the documents for the purpose of these proceedings. The SFO disclosed the documents collected to the Department of Health under s 3(5)(a) of the Criminal Justice Act 1987, which permits, amongst others, disclosure by the SFO of material to any government department discharging functions on behalf of the Crown. The Court of Appeal considered the terms of s 3(5)(a) of the Criminal Justice Act 1987 to determine whether disclosure pursuant to that provision amounted to an excessive inroad into the undertaking's rights under Article 8 ECHR. In particular, Kent Pharmaceuticals submitted that s 3(5)(a) did not meet the requirements of Article 8 ECHR because the authorised disclosure was not sufficiently precise to be 'in accordance with law'. The section was in its view too vague because it did not define:

(1) how or in what circumstances the discretion to disclose may be exercised by the SFO;
(2) for what purpose or purposes the government department may use the information disclosed; and
(3) it imposed no restrictions on the disclosure or use that may be made of the documents.

8.66 The Court of Appeal held that the section was necessarily worded in wide terms and any attempt to give further guidance in the section as to the circumstances in which the discretion to make further disclosure might be exercised would introduce undesirable rigidity. Provided the discretion was exercised reasonably and in good faith the disclosure of documents under s 3(5)(a) of the Criminal Justice Act 1987 was 'in accordance with law' for the purposes of Article 8(2) ECHR.

8.67 In *R v Brady*[64] the Court of Appeal considered the disclosure of information obtained under compulsory powers by one authority (the Official Receiver) to

---

[62] *R (Kent Pharmaceuticals Ltd) v Director of the SFO* [2004] EWCA 1494, [2005] 1 WLR 1302, para 4.
[63] ibid.   [64] [2004] EWCA Crim 1763, [2004] 1 WLR 3240.

another (the Inland Revenue), for the latter to use in a prosecution of the individual providing the information. When winding up a company, the Official Receiver had taken statements from Mr Brady under s 235 of the Insolvency Act 1986. It disclosed the information to the Inland Revenue, who relied on the information obtained for the purposes of obtaining search warrants against Mr Brady, but did not rely on the information in the subsequent criminal prosecution against him (for cheating the Inland Revenue). The Insolvency Act 1986 does not include a general 'gateway provision' allowing the transmission of information by the Official Receiver to other government authorities. Nonetheless, the Court of Appeal held that the transmission was not in breach of any obligation of confidentiality. The Insolvency Act expressly permitted transmission of information by the Official Receiver to the Department of Trade and Industry (DTI) for criminal prosecution, and the court held it would be anomalous if the material might be used by the DTI, but not by any other prosecuting authority. There was no breach of confidentiality, because anyone providing the information should be taken to be aware of the wide uses to which it could be made and the purpose of the Insolvency Act included the identification of potential criminal or other misconduct.

(ii) Article 6 ECHR

Article 6(1) provides: **8.68**

> In the determination of his civil rights and obligations or of any criminal charge against him, everyone is entitled to a fair and public hearing within a reasonable time by an independent and impartial tribunal established by law.

The right to a fair trial (including its adjuncts, the rights of the defence and the   **8.69**
right of access to the courts[65]) is highly relevant in the context of disclosure. The right to a fair trial is versatile and can be relied upon in certain contexts to prevent disclosure and in others to request it.

Right to notice of disclosure   In *Kent Pharmaceuticals*,[66] discussed above at   **8.70**
para 8.65, the Court of Appeal considered whether there is a right to notice of disclosure. Although s 3(5)(a) of the Criminal Justice Act 1987 does not provide for the SFO to give notice to the owner of documents seized when it makes a disclosure, the Court of Appeal considered whether such an obligation arose either by virtue of the common law duty to act fairly or under Article 6(1) ECHR. It acknowledged that there was force in the submissions made by Kent Pharmaceuticals that, in order not to impede its right of access to the court, it

---

[65] *Golder v UK* (1975) 1 EHRR 524; *Tinnelly & Sons Ltd v UK* (1998) 27 EHRR 249.
[66] [2004] EWCA 1494, [2005] 1 WLR 1302.

should have been given prior notice of the SFO's intention to disclose documents that were seized from it:

> [Kent] submits, with some force, that the document owner cannot seek the assistance of the courts to challenge impending or recent disclosure if he knows nothing of it, so keeping him in ignorance curtails his right [of access to the courts].[67]

8.71 The Court of Appeal did not determine whether Article 6 applied, as it evaluated whether Kent had a right to notice under the common law duty to act fairly, which it accepted could give rise to the right to advance or subsequent notice of disclosure, depending on the circumstances of the case. In the Court of Appeal's view the disclosing authority should consider whether to give notice on a case-by-case basis. The starting point for this consideration was always that the owner of the documents was entitled to be kept informed. However, the Court of Appeal acknowledged that in some cases it may not be appropriate or practicable to give notice; for example, where disclosure would hamper investigations.

8.72 In *R v Brady* (discussed at para 8.67 above), the Court of Appeal, in addition to finding that the disclosure of information by the official receiver to the Inland Revenue (acting as an investigating and prosecuting authority) was legitimate for the purposes of Article 8 ECHR, found that there was no need for notice: 'It is self-evidently in the public interest that the appropriate prosecuting authority should have such material to aid its investigation which might well be considerably hampered by any requirement to obtain court approval or to give notice to the person who had approved the material.'[68]

8.73 In the context of the provisions under both Regulation 1/2003 and the Enterprise Act 2002 which provide for the transmission of information between competition authorities without any notice being given to the owner of the document, this question is of some importance.

8.74 **Protection of the rights of the defence**   The right to a fair trial includes the right of the undertaking to defend itself. Access to information is a prerequisite for the exercise of this right. The CAT has acknowledged this right:

> Equally, in a case such as the present, which takes place in a setting in which parties have had penalties imposed upon them, it is, in the Tribunal's judgment, of overriding importance that the parties should be able to exercise their rights of defence without having possibly relevant material held back or inaccessible.[69]

8.75 The right to access to relevant information stems from the principle that a fair

---

[67] ibid, para 30, per Kennedy LJ.
[68] *R v Brady* [2004] EWCA Crim 1763, [2004] 1 WLR 3240, para 27, per Tuckey LJ.
[69] *Umbro Holdings Ltd v OFT* [2003] CAT 26, para 33.

trial under Article 6 ECHR entails 'equality of arms'. An undertaking cannot be said to be in an equal position to defend itself where it does not have access to information that is relevant to its defence. In *Solvay and ICI v Commission*[70] (*Soda-ash*) the Court of First Instance (**CFI**) relied on this principle to annul Commission decisions for failure to grant access to the file to the undertakings concerned: 'the general principle of equality of arms . . . presupposes that in a competition case the knowledge which the undertaking concerned has of the file used in the proceedings is the same as that of the Commission'. Since *Soda-ash*, the Commission has made frequent reference to the obligation to grant access to both the incriminating and potentially exculpatory documents in its file, based on the general principle of equality of arms.[71] Further, the obligation to ensure equality of arms is not confined to the administrative procedure—it extends to the conduct of the appeal before the CFI.[72]

(iii) Privilege against self-incrimination

The precise ambit of the privilege against self-incrimination is not entirely **8.76** clear.[73] At its heart lies the principle that the prosecution must prove its case without resort to evidence obtained through coercion or oppression of the will of the accused. The OFT's approach is that the privilege against self-incrimination prevents it from compelling the provision of answers that might involve the admission of a competition law infringement, but that it might request documents or information relating to facts.[74]

The privilege is highly relevant in the context of disclosure of information, as **8.77** an answer provided under compulsion in one context, may be incriminating, and hence cannot be compelled, in another context. Disclosure of information for another authority to use, possibly in another context, can therefore erode the privilege afforded to individuals and undertakings. In *Saunders v UK*,[75] the privilege prevented the use of statements obtained under compulsory powers of DTI inspectors in a subsequent criminal prosecution. The privilege did not extend to prevent the use of pre-existing documents, which

---

[70] Case T-30/91 *Solvay v Commission* [1995] ECR II-1775, para 83; Case T-36/91 *ICI v Commission* [1995] ECR II-1847, para 93.

[71] *Solvay*, ibid, para 83; *ICI*, ibid, para 93; Case T-305/94 *Limburgse Vinyl Maatschappij NV (LVM) v Commission* [1999] ECR II-931, para 1012; Case T-25/95 *Cimenteries CBR v Commission* [2000] ECR II-491, para 143; Case T-141/94 *Thyssen Stahl v Commission* [1999] ECR II-347, para 97; Case T-175/95 *BASF Lacke + Farben v Commission* [1999] ECR II-1581, para 46.

[72] See Koen Lenaerts, 'De quelques principes généraux du droit de la procédure devant le juge communautaire', in *Mélanges en l'honneur du Professeur Jean-Victor Louis* (Éditions de l'Université de Bruxelles, 2003).

[73] For a broader discussion, see paras 7.30 et seq.

[74] OFT404, *Powers of investigation* (December 2004) paras 6.5–6.7.

[75] (1997) 23 EHRR 313.

had an independent existence and were not created through coercion.[76] Further, the European Court of Human Rights did not preclude reliance on self-incriminating evidence obtained by compulsion to assist in the investigative inquiries relating to the criminal offence.[77] In *R v Brady*, the Court of Appeal held that the Inland Revenue's reliance on statements obtained under compulsion by the Official Receiver under s 235 of the Insolvency Act 1986 to obtain search warrants for a criminal investigation was not a breach of the privilege against self-incrimination under Article 6 ECHR, as the information was not relied upon by the prosecution in the trial itself, and the principle did not extend to preventing the use of information compulsorily obtained for the purpose of investigative extra-judicial inquiries (such as obtaining a search warrant).[78]

(c) Freedom of Information Act 2000

8.78 The Freedom of Information Act 2000 was enacted in order to introduce more transparency into public administration. It entered into force on 1 January 2005. It applies to England, Wales and Northern Ireland. The Freedom of Information (Scotland) Act 2002 applies to Scotland.

(i) Process

8.79 Under the Freedom of Information Act 2000, any person, regardless of their standing in relation to a Competition Act investigation, may request information from public authorities (which includes the OFT and the CC, but not the CAT).[79] Section 1 grants persons making a request for information the following rights:

- the right to be informed whether or not the information requested is held by the authority; and
- if so, the right to have that information communicated to him or her. There is no obligation to give reasons for the request.

8.80 The public authority must tell the applicant (normally within 20 working days) whether it holds the information. If it holds the information the authority must supply it, unless the information is exempt.

---

[76] However, the subsequent *JB v Switzerland* [2001] Crim LR 7481 takes a different approach to pre-existing documents.

[77] *Saunders v UK* (1996) 23 EHRR 313, para 67.

[78] [2004] EWCA Crim 1763, [2004] 1 WLR 3240. The Court of Appeal relied on *Saunders*, ibid.

[79] Freedom of Information Act 2000, Sch 1, Pt VI expressly applies to the CC (which at the time included the Competition Commission Appeal Tribunal) only 'in relation to information held by it otherwise than as a tribunal'.

The public authority need not provide all or part of the information (and **8.81** sometimes need not confirm or deny its existence)[80] if:

- an exemption applies; or
- the request is vexatious or similar to a recent previous request; or
- the cost of the compliance would exceed the 'appropriate limit', currently set at £600.

There are two types of exemption. Exemptions can be absolute[81] (in which **8.82** case information is protected from disclosure) or qualified.[82] If an exemption is qualified, this means that, in addition to establishing that the information falls within the terms of the qualified exemption, the public authority must consider whether the public interest in using the exemption outweighs the public interest in releasing the information before refusing to disclose.

The OFT and the CC deal with freedom of information requests in accordance **8.83** with their Freedom of Information Act 2000 publication schemes[83] which have been approved by the Information Commissioner's office. The publication scheme explains to whom freedom of information requests should be addressed and gives an overview of the classes of information that can be disclosed.

If an authority refuses a freedom of information request a complaint should first **8.84** be made to the authority itself according to its internal complaints procedure.[84] If it does not deal with the complaint properly, the complainant may contact the Information Commissioner's Office.[85] This should be done as soon as possible or in any case within two months following the final response. The Information Commissioner will notify the authority that a complaint has

---

[80] 'The Duty to Confirm or Deny' Freedom of Information Act Awareness Guidance No 21.

[81] Information accessible by other means (s 21); Information supplied by or relating to, bodies dealing with security matters (s 23); Court records (s 32); Public Affairs in so far as relating to information received by the House of Commons or the House of Lords (s 36); Parliamentary privilege (s 34); Personal information (s 40); Information provided in confidence (s 41); Information whose disclosure is prohibited by law (s 44).

[82] The qualified exemptions are as follows: Information intended for future publication (s 22); National security (s 24); Defence (s 26); International relations (s 27); Relations within the UK (s 28); The economy (s 29); Investigations and proceedings (s 30); Law enforcement (s 31); Audit functions (s 33); Formulation of government policy (s 35); Prejudice to effective conduct of public affairs (s 36); Communications with Her Majesty (s 37); Health and safety (s 38); Environmental Information (s 39); Some personal information (s 40); Legal professional privilege (s 42); Commercial interests (s 43).

[83] OFT622, *Freedom of Information Act 2000 publication scheme* (January 2005); Competition Commission Publication Scheme (2005) <http://www.competition-commission.org.uk/rep_pub/freedom_info/request.htm>.

[84] In respect of the OFT, by writing to the Office of Fair Trading, Fleetbank House, 2–6 Salisbury Square, London EC4Y 8JX or by sending an email to foiaenquiries@oft.gov.uk.

[85] FOI/EIR Complaints Resolution, Information Commissioner's Office, Wycliffe House, Water Lane, Wilmslow, Cheshire SK9 5AF.

been received about it. If the complaint cannot be resolved informally, the Information Commissioner will issue a Decision Notice, outlining the Information Commissioner's final assessment as to whether or not the authority has complied with the Freedom of Information Act. There is a further right of appeal to the Information Tribunal.

(ii) What information is disclosed?

8.85 When the Freedom of Information Act 2000 was introduced, there was great excitement amongst competition practitioners, who viewed it as a potential vehicle to extract information from regulators that was not otherwise available. The Act has not given rise to the expected disclosure bonanza, primarily because of two factors. First, the regulators can rely on a number of applicable exemptions to refuse disclosure.[86] The most relevant exemptions in a competition context are considered below. Secondly, the costs threshold of £600 means that, in practice, a request will not yield very much information.

(iii) Absolute exemptions

8.86 **Section 44(1)**   This section of the Act provides an absolute exemption from the freedom of information provisions if disclosure by the public authority holding the information is prohibited (inter alia) by another enactment. The interaction of this exemption with the statutory restriction on disclosure in the Enterprise Act 2002 is somewhat circular.

8.87 Part 9 of the Enterprise Act 2002 contains a general restriction on disclosure of 'specified information' by public authorities (the statutory restriction).[87] If specified information requested under the Freedom of Information Act 2000, an absolute exemption under s 44(1) would appear to apply. However, the restriction in the Enterprise Act is itself not absolute: it is expressed not to affect any power or duty to disclose information which exists outside Pt 9 of the Enterprise Act.[88] If the Freedom of Information Act amounts to a power or duty to disclose, the restriction in Pt 9 does not apply and hence the s 44(1) exemption under the Freedom of Information Act does not apply.

8.88 The OFT, in its Freedom of Information Act 2000 publication scheme,[89] indicates that it will rely on the exemption in s 44(1). It considers that Pt 9 of the Enterprise Act 2002 overrides the Freedom of Information Act, and that there is a presumption of non-disclosure relating to specified information under the

---

[86] In the first quarter of 2006, the OFT received 107 information requests under the Freedom of Information Act, of which 24 requests were granted in full and 10 were partially withheld. In 2005, a total of 298 requests were made to the OFT, of which 27.5% were granted in full. Not all of these requests relate to competition enforcement: some relate to the OFT's other functions.

[87] Enterprise Act 2002, s 237(2). See paras 8.10 et seq above.   [88] ibid, s 237(6).

[89] <http://www.competition-commission.org.uk/rep_pub/freedom_info/request.htm>.

Enterprise Act. The OFT considers that its position is supported by the fact that disclosure in breach of Pt 9 of the Enterprise Act amounts to a criminal offence, whereas there is no equivalent sanction in the Freedom of Information Act.

Two Decision Notices by the Information Commissioner have shed light on **8.89** this issue. The first relates to the OFT's refusal to disclose under the Freedom of Information Act 2000, information relating to consumer complaints made against a named undertaking. The OFT relied (inter alia) on s 44, on the basis that the information requested was specified information subject to the statutory restriction on disclosure under Pt 9 of the Enterprise Act 2002. The Information Commissioner considered the relationship between Pt 9 and the Freedom of Information Act. In the Commissioner's view, s 44 of the Freedom of Information Act 2000 requires the public authority to consider whether disclosure, otherwise than under that Act, is prohibited. When considering the application of the exemption, the Freedom of Information Act itself cannot be considered as an enactment imposing an obligation to disclose. Section 44 was therefore engaged and the information exempt. The OFT was accordingly right to refuse the information by applying s 44.[90] The second Decision Notice only considers the issue in passing. However, the view expressed is clear: s 44 operates as an absolute exemption in respect of specific information under Part 9 of the Enterprise Act 2002.

Section 41: duty of confidentiality An absolute exemption exists from disclos- **8.90** ing information that establishes a duty of confidentiality on the part of the OFT. The exemption will only apply where a person would be able to bring a claim for breach of confidence. This exemption (in its strongest form) would most likely involve information that was given voluntarily and in confidence. There is some authority in support of the proposition that information provided pursuant to mandatory powers also gives rise to a common law duty of confidentiality.[92]

(iv) Qualified exemptions

Public interest test Information that benefits from a qualified exemption is **8.91** subject to a public interest test. The public authority must consider whether there is a greater public interest in confirming or denying the existence of the information requested and providing the information to the applicant or in maintaining the exemption.

There is no definition of the public interest in the Freedom of Information Act **8.92** 2000. The Information Commissioner's Awareness Guidance No 3 on the

---

[90] Decision Notice, 25 July 2006, Case Ref FS50090136, 25/07/2006, para 5.6.
[91] See page 5 of Decision Notice F 550070739, 06/06/2006.
[92] *R v Brady* [2004] EWCA Crim 1763, [2004] 1 WLR 3240.

public interest test explains that when applying the test, the public authority is simply deciding whether in any particular case it serves the interests of the public better to withhold or to disclose information. It would seem therefore that the test is broad and flexible, permitting the consideration of a multiplicity of factors by the disclosing authority, providing that the interests of the public, and not those of the disclosing authority are considered. The Guidance identifies a number of interest factors that would encourage the disclosure of information, including the interests below that are relevant in a competition context:

• Promoting accountability and transparency by public authorities for decisions taken by them. Placing an obligation on authorities and officials to provide reasoned explanations for decisions made will improve the quality of decisions and administration.

• Allowing individuals and companies to understand decisions made by public authorities affecting their lives and, in some cases, assisting individuals in challenging those decisions.

8.93 **Relevant qualified exemptions**   Possible qualified exemptions on which competition authorities could rely include:

• Commercial secrets: a qualified exemption applies to information relating to business secrets, the disclosure of which would, or would be likely to, prejudice the commercial interests of any person (s 43).

• Future publication: where the authority intends to publish the information and it is reasonable to withhold it until it is published (s 22).

• Where disclosure may be prejudicial to the economic interests of the United Kingdom or any part of the United Kingdom or the financial interest of any government body (s 29).

• Where information is held for purposes of a criminal investigation or criminal proceedings (s 30).

• Where information is held for the purpose of an investigation (including non-criminal investigations) or criminal proceedings and relates to the obtaining of information from a confidential source (s 30(2)).

• Law enforcement: an exemption applies if disclosure would be likely to prejudice matters such as the prevention and detection of crime, the administration of justice and the exercise of functions specified in s 31(2) such as: investigations to find out whether any person has failed to comply with the law, ascertaining whether a person is responsible for any conduct which is improper or whether circumstances which justify regulatory action arise (s 31).

(v) Costs limit

Even if the information requested is not covered by one of the exemptions **8.94** mentioned above, there is a further hurdle to disclosure. One of the main obstacles to obtaining information under the Freedom of Information Act 2000 is the costs limit imposed therein. Section 12 provides an exemption from disclosure where the estimated cost of disclosure exceeds the appropriate limit. The Freedom of Information and Data Protection (Appropriate Limit and Fees) Regulations[93] provide that the cost limit is £600. Further, the regulations provide that the cost to a public authority of extracting information is to be estimated at £25 an hour. A request may therefore give rise to a maximum of 24 hours' work, excluding photocopying costs (which, at Law Society's photocopying rates, are not inconsiderable).

The *Pernod Ricard* case is a good example of the effect this restriction has **8.95** in practice. On 6 January 2005 Pernod Ricard made a Freedom of Information Act request to the OFT for access to all internal communications during a two-and-a-half-year investigation by the OFT into possible competition law infringements by Bacardi, one of Pernod's major competitors. The OFT refused the request, primarily in reliance on s 12 of the Act. In addressing Pernod's complaint, the Information Commissioner endorsed the OFT's approach. In the Commissioner's view, even the production of a redacted list of documents held by the OFT would have exceeded the appropriate limit.[94]

(d) Data Protection Act

The Data Protection Act 1998 came into force on 1 March 2000. It is a complex **8.96** statute and what follows is just a brief overview of the provisions that may be relevant in the competition context. Readers are referred to specialist textbooks and guidance published by the Information Commissioner for comprehensive guidance on this issue.[95]

The Data Protection Act 1998 obliges anyone 'processing' personal information **8.97** (data about living individuals (not companies) who can be identified from that information) to comply with eight principles of good information handling. The eight data protection principles are that data relating to individuals must be:

• fairly and lawfully processed;
• processed for limited purposes;
• adequate, relevant, and not excessive;

---

[93] SI 2004/3244.
[94] Decision Notice, 6 June 2006, Case Ref FS50070739, p 4.
[95] <http://www.ico.gov.uk/upload/documents/library/data_protection/detailed_specialist_guides/data_protection_act_legal_guidance.pdf>.

- accurate and up to date;
- not kept longer than necessary;
- processed in accordance with the individual's rights;
- secure;
- not transferred to countries outside the European Economic Area, unless there is adequate protection.

8.98 In addition, ss 7 to 9 of the Data Protection Act 1998 provide extensive rights of access to the subjects of the information. Upon making a request in writing and paying the appropriate fee, an individual is entitled to be told whether a data controller[96] or someone else on his or her behalf is processing that individual's personal data, and if so, to be given a description of the personal data; the purposes for which they are being processed; and those to whom they are or may be disclosed. The individual is also entitled to have communicated to him or her in an intelligible form, all the information which forms any such personal data.

8.99 Some of the above provisions may take effect either to prevent or to compel disclosure of information, depending on the circumstances. The Data Protection Act 1998 takes precedence over the Enterprise Act 2002, in so far as nothing in Pt 9 of the Enterprise Act may authorise a disclosure which contravenes the Data Protection Act 1998.[97]

8.100 In practice, the impact of the Data Protection Act 1998 on disclosure of information by the competition regulators is limited, for two reasons. First, the Data Protection Act imposes obligations only with respect to personal data[98] relating to living individuals. Generally the information in the possession of competition authorities tends to concern undertakings, rather than individuals. Further, even where the competition authorities do hold personal data, there are potentially several relevant exemptions in the Data Protection Act 1998 that apply.

8.101 Section 29 may be relevant in relation to information relating to individuals suspected of the cartel offence. The section provides several exemptions in relation to the processing and disclosure of information for the prevention and detection of crime and the apprehension or prosecution of offenders. The exemptions are not blanket exemptions, but apply only to the extent necessary.

8.102 Section 31 of the Act provides an exemption from the subject information provisions in relation to personal data used for certain defined regulatory purposes. The exemption is only available to the extent that the subject infor-

---

[96] As defined in s 1 Data Protection Act 1998.   [97] Enterprise Act 2002, s 237(4).
[98] Data Protection Act 1998, s 1(1) defines personal data.

mation would be likely to prejudice the proper discharge of those functions. Section 31(2) is particularly relevant to information on individuals relating to director disqualification proceedings. It provides an exemption in the context of the protection of the public against financial loss due to dishonesty, malpractice (etc) of persons in the management of bodies corporate, and dishonesty (etc) of persons authorised to carry on any profession or other activity. Further, s 31(5) provides an exemption from right of access provisions for personal data processed for the purpose of discharging any function which is conferred by or under any enactment on the OFT, and is designed:

- for protecting members of the public against conduct, by persons carrying on a business, which may adversely affect their interests;
- for regulating agreements or conduct which have as their object or effect the prevention, restriction, or distortion of competition in connection with any commercial activity; or
- for regulating conduct on the part of one or more undertakings which amounts to the abuse of a dominant position in a market.

C. Information Disclosure under Community Law

This section begins by setting out the provisions of Regulation 1/2003 that **8.103** variously mandate and facilitate information disclosure within the ECN. Section D considers the limitations that Regulation 1/2003 itself places on the disclosure and usage of such information, before going on to consider additional limitations that apply by virtue of Community case law and principles. It is vital to bear in mind, when reading Section C, that this is only a relatively small piece of the information exchange puzzle: for a fuller picture it is critical to consider both the limitations on information exchange that arise by virtue of Community law under Section D, and any limitations or process requirements that arise by virtue of domestic law under Section B. We attempt such an exercise in section F when we consider information disclosure as it arises in practice in different contexts.

(a) Regulation 1/2003: mandatory information disclosure

Article 11 of Regulation 1/2003 sets out the key elements of the cooperation **8.104** between the European Commission and the national competition authorities. It provides that the Commission and the national competition authorities shall apply the Community competition rules in close cooperation. Two provisions mandate the provision of information by the national competition authorities to the Commission.

(i) Article 11(3) of Regulation 1/2003: notification of commencement of a case

8.105 Article 11(3) requires that national competition authorities shall inform the European Commission of any case they initiate under Article 81 or Article 82. Article 11(3) sets out minimum requirements. It does not prevent any ECN member from disclosing information more widely (to other ECN members as well as the Commission for example), or from exchanging information at an earlier time, pursuant to Article 12 of Regulation 1/2003. In cartel cases, for example, there may be disclosure of information under Article 12 before any notification is made under Article 11(3), in order to agree a coordinated investigation across several jurisdictions.

8.106 **Why?** The purpose of this measure is to inform the Commission of all new Article 81 and Article 82 cases 'in order to detect multiple procedures and to ensure that cases are dealt with by a well placed competition authority'.[99] It is truly in all parties' interest that any case allocation issues should be addressed as early on as possible.

8.107 **Which cases are notified and when?** Article 11(3) is aimed at facilitating case allocation. It does not require national competition authorities to notify the ECN of every complaint received, as not every complaint received becomes a case. For a matter to be notified there are two key conditions in the text of Article 11(3). First (and rather self-evidently), the case must be one involving Article 81 and/or Article 82 (so it must potentially affect trade between Member States). Secondly, the requirement to inform the ECN is triggered by '*the first formal investigation measure*' by the national competition authority. The Network Notice explains[100] that a formal investigation measure is a measure akin to the Commission's powers of investigation under Articles 18 to 21 of Regulation 1/2003 (namely its powers to request or order the provision of information and to undertake inspections). Therefore, an evaluation of the case must have been undertaken and a decision reached to take a 'formal investigation measure' for the obligation to notify to be triggered. Notification can be before or shortly after the formal investigative measure is taken. Applying this test to the OFT process, a case which has passed the threshold for investigation under s 25 of the Competition Act 1998 is likely to be notified to the ECN pursuant to Article 11(3) of Regulation 1/2003.

8.108 Where a case is investigated solely by reference to domestic law, but it is subsequently discovered that Article 81 and/or Article 82 apply (long after the first formal investigative measure), it is the authors' view that the OFT would be

---

[99] Commission notice on cooperation within the network of competition authorities (2004/C 101/03) [2004] OJ C101/43 (**Network Notice**) para 16.
[100] ibid, para 17.

required to notify the ECN pursuant to Article 11(3) of Regulation 1/2003 as soon as it becomes apparent that Article 81 or Article 82 should apply to the case, in order to comply with its obligation of cooperation in Article 11(1) and its more general duty of sincere cooperation under Article 10 EC.

What information? The information provided to the ECN is that which **8.109** would enable the Commission and national competition authorities to form a sufficient impression of the case for the purpose of identifying any similar such cases in other Member States. This would include details of the parties to the agreement or conduct, the relevant territorial extent of the agreement or conduct, and an indication of relevant products or services covered by the agreement or conduct. The Network Notice also states that ECN members will 'provide each other with updates when a relevant change occurs'.[101] Presumably as an investigation progresses, the national competition authority's understanding of the parties and definition of the product and geographic market may alter, so that updates are necessary to ensure the ECN is correctly informed. There must also be a note of the original source for the case, in particular where this was via a leniency application.

Who receives the information? Article 11(3) also notes that, in addition to **8.110** informing the Commission, national competition authorities may transmit the information to the other competition authorities. It is apparent from the Network Notice that the ECN members have agreed that they will inform each other of such cases at the same time as they inform the European Commission.[102] Nothing prevents national competition authorities from using information which is provided to the ECN pursuant to Article 11(3) for the purpose of commencing their own investigation, with the notable exception of cases which involve leniency applicants, which are subject to special restrictions[103]—see further paras 8.191 et seq below and Chapter 5.

Process Article 11(3) requires notification 'in writing'. Notification in all cases **8.111** involves the electronic submission of a set of information to a secure database to which the ECN members have exclusive access.

(ii) Application to cases pre-existing 1 May 2004

From 1 May 2004, the OFT was required to apply Article 81 and/or Article 82 **8.112** to relevant cases with an effect on trade between Member States in which it applied national competition law.[104] This meant that the OFT had to review its

---

[101] ibid.   [102] ibid, para 17.
[103] ibid, para 39 provides that information submitted to the ECN under Art 11 will not be used by other members of the network as the basis for starting an investigation.
[104] Article 3(1) of Regulation 1/2003. For a full discussion of this obligation, see Chapter 3, above.

on-going cases and, where necessary, apply Article 81 and/or Article 82 in addition to Chapter 1 and/or Chapter 2. In normal circumstances, the initiation of a case involving the application of Article 81 or Article 82 would give rise to an obligation pursuant to Article 11(3) of Regulation 1/2003 to notify the ECN. However, given the Article 11(3) notification procedure is primarily designed to allow for case allocation at the outset of a case, it appears that the ECN took the pragmatic view that it would not be sensible to notify cases which had already long passed their first formal investigative measure.

(iii) Article 11(4) of Regulation 1/2003: notification of proposed decision

8.113 Article 11(4) provides:

> No later than 30 days before the adoption of a decision requiring that an infringement be brought to an end, accepting commitments or withdrawing the benefit of a block exemption Regulation, the competition authorities of the Member States shall inform the Commission. To that effect, they shall provide the Commission with a summary of the case, the envisaged decision or, in the absence thereof, any other document indicating the proposed course of action.
>
> This information may also be made available to the competition authorities of the other Member States. At the request of the Commission, the acting Competition Authority shall make available to the Commission other documents it holds which are necessary for the assessment of the case. The information supplied to the Commission may be made available to the Competition Authorities of the other Member States. National Competition Authorities may also exchange between themselves information necessary for the assessment of a case that they are dealing with under Article 81 or Article 82 of the Treaty.

8.114 **Why?** According to the Network Notice,[105] Article 11(4) is intended to create a cooperation mechanism that allows for the consistent application of EC competition rules. Article 11(4) provides the European Commission with a means of seeking to ensure that potential problems relating to the application of Article 81 and/or Article 82 by a national competition authority are dealt with before the final decision is made.

8.115 **Which cases are notified and when?** Article 11(4) requires that, where a national competition authority intends to adopt an infringement decision, a decision accepting commitments or one requiring that an infringement be brought to an end, it should provide the European Commission with details of the intended decision. Article 11(4) does not give rise to an obligation to notify decisions finding that Article 81 and Article 82 do not apply. Under Article 5 of Regulation 1/2003, national competition authorities are not empowered to make non-infringement decisions as such, but rather decisions that 'there are no

---

[105] Network Notice, paras 43–49.

grounds for action on their part'. Such decisions are not intended to have precedent value given that no conclusive finding is made as to the application of Articles 81 and 82 by the national competition authority, and so have not been included under Article 11(4). Although Article 11(4) only relates to prospective types of 'infringement' decision, para 48 of the Network Notice states that national competition authorities can inform the network of any other types of decisions under Article 11(5) of Regulation 1/2003 (such as decisions rejecting complaints or ordering interim measures) in which EC competition law is applied. This is not an obvious use of Article 11(5) which allows national competition authorities to consult the Commission on any case involving the application of Community law.

The national competition authorities must inform the European Commission of **8.116** the intended decision not later than 30 days before the adoption of a relevant decision.

What information?   Article 11(4) is designed to allow the Commission to carry **8.117** out some sort of 'quality control' on proposed decisions by national competition authorities applying Article 81 and/or Article 82. The information provided must therefore be sufficient for the Commission to gain a good insight into the competition authority's reasoning in reaching its conclusions. Article 11(4) therefore requires the provision of 'a summary of the case, the envisaged decision or, in the absence thereof, any other document indicating the proposed cause of action'.

Who receives the information?   The Network Notice provides that although **8.118** the obligation is to inform the Commission, the information may be shared with the other members of the ECN.

Process   Once the intended decision has been notified (in writing), the **8.119** Commission has 30 days in which it can, if necessary, make written observations on the case[106] or initiate proceedings itself (therefore depriving the national competition authority of any competence to take the decision under Article 11(6) of Regulation 1/2003). The European Commission has noted that the use of Article 11(6) is an option of last resort.[107] Given the European Commission's limited resources, it is unlikely that written observations will be made in respect of many cases. It appears, however, there are a number of informal oral exchanges between the Commission and the national competition authorities.[108] There are

---

[106]   Network Notice, para 46.
[107]   According to Kris Dekeyser, Head of Unit of DG Competition, in his paper prepared for the IBC Conference of Advanced European Law, 5 May 2006, this power has not yet been used.
[108]   According to Kris Dekeyser, ibid, 'The possibility to submit (oral or written) comments has proven to be a very useful tool that has triggered creative, informative and productive dialogues,' para 19.

no sanctions if the national competition authority decides not to take account of the observations. It appears that the views expressed by the Commission under Article 11(4) 'only reflect the views of the services in which name they have been submitted and can therefore not be regarded as stating an official policy of the European Commission'.[109] Provided the European Commission has not initiated proceedings pursuant to Article 11(6), once the 30-day deadline has expired, the national competition authority is free to adopt its decision as final. The 30-day time period may also be expedited in special circumstances, pursuant to a request by the relevant national competition authority.

(b) Regulation 1/2003: facilitating transfer of information between national competition authorities

(i) Article 12 of Regulation 1/2003

8.120 Article 12 is the main vehicle for information transfer between the Commission and the national competition authorities. It consists of several limbs:

- Article 12(1) provides the Commission and the national competition authorities with a general power to provide one another with information (including confidential information). In addition to a power to disclose, it also authorises the receiving authority's reliance in evidence on the information received.

- Article 12(2) introduces restrictions on the ability of the receiving authority to rely on the information received in evidence in proceedings.

- Article 12(3) introduces certain further restrictions on the reliance on information provided in evidence in proceedings involving criminal sanctions for individuals.

8.121 In this section, we will confine ourselves to considering the 'enabling' aspect of Article 12 in Article 12(1). Article 12(2) and 12(3) are considered in section D below in the context of the limitations on information disclosure. It is important to bear in mind that in addition to the limitations within Article 12 itself, the general principles of Community law will apply to constrain the exercise of powers under Article 12.[110]

8.122 **Article 12(1)**   Article 12(1) provides:

> For the purpose of applying Article 81 and Article 82 of the Treaty the Commission and the competition authorities of the Member States shall have the power to provide one another with and use in evidence any matter of fact or of law, including confidential information.

8.123 Article 12(1) is an enabling provision—it provides a power, and not an obligation. The Commission and the national competition authorities, including

---

[109] ibid, para 17.   [110] These are considered below at paras 8.138 et seq.

the OFT, may accordingly impose restrictions on their own use of this power, for various policy or other reasons, providing of course that they are acting consistently with their duty of sincere cooperation under Article 10 EC.[111]

Why? For the network to function properly, it is essential that the various 8.124 authorities responsible for the enforcement of Articles 81 and 82 should be able to transmit information to each other freely, in order to ensure consistent and effective application of the competition rules. As the Network Notice remarks, it is a precondition for efficient allocation and handling of cases.[112]

When does it apply? There is no need for a case to have reached a particular 8.125 stage for a national competition authority to disclose information relating to it—indeed, no case need formally have been initiated at all as long as the transmission of information is 'for the purpose of applying Articles 81 and 82'. Article 12 of Regulation 1/2003 is the main basis for information transmission within the ECN: it has been broadly drafted so that it applies at any time provided that the disclosure can be related to the application of Articles 81 and 82 EC.

What information? '*Any* matter of fact or law, including confidential informa- 8.126 tion': provided the purpose of the transmission of the information is to assist in the application of Article 81 and/or Article 82, the power in Article 12 applies to allow the exchange and use of such information. In principle, Article 12(1) provides an extremely broad power, although there are restraints on this power in Article 12(2) and (3) as well as those which arise by virtue of general principles of Community law which we consider separately at paras 8.138 et seq below. Viewed in isolation, Article 12(1) would permit disclosure and use of any materials that may be relevant to application of Articles 81 and 82: past OFT investigation material (relating to Chapter I or Chapter II prohibitions), current OFT investigation material (general information received by the OFT—for example, relating to complaints or market investigation information—information the OFT gathers in relation to the cartel offence, information supplied by a leniency applicant,[113] and any other information the OFT obtains in the conduct of its functions, including that received from other UK

---

[111] The Member States and the Commission have agreed self-imposed restraints on the use of their power in Art 12(1) in the context of leniency (see paras 8.183 et seq), see further S Blake and D Schnichels, 'Leniency following modernisation' [2004] ECLR 765. The OFT has indicated that it will be applying the 'balancing tests' set out in s 244 of the Enterprise Act 2002 before transmitting information—see para 8.37 above.

[112] Network Notice, para 26.

[113] Note that although the power to transmit leniency-related information exists in theory, in practice the ECN members have chosen to adhere to certain self-imposed restrictions with respect to the transmission of information resulting from a leniency application under Art 12 of Regulation1/2003; see paras 8.183 et seq below more generally.

authorities). Any 'matters of fact or law' can be disclosed. This broad formulation allows the authorities a wide scope to transmit many types of information: economists' reports, documentary evidence, legal pleadings,[114] and policy materials all come within the ambit of Article 12(1). Further, Article 12, in conjunction with Article 22(1) of Regulation 1/2003, allows the national competition authorities to undertake new fact-finding measures for the purpose of transmission to another competition authority. Conversely, it would appear to authorise the OFT to rely, by way of evidence, on similar such material that is collected by other national competition authorities.

8.127 **Process** No process is prescribed for the transmission of information by Regulation 1/2003—it may occur orally or in writing and to as many or as few members of the ECN as the disclosing authority wishes. Under domestic law, the disclosure of information under Article 12 is compatible with s 237 of the Enterprise Act 2002 either by virtue of s 237(6) (which the OFT has indicated is the vehicle for information disclosure under Regulation 1/2003)[115] or under s 240 (if one takes a broad approach to the concept of Community obligation).[116]

8.128 Although the power in Article 12 is described in Preamble 16 of Regulation 1/2003 as 'notwithstanding' contrary provisions of national law, the OFT has indicated that the disclosure it makes under Regulation 1/2003 will be subject to the s 244 test.[117] It will therefore undertake an evaluation of the information disclosed under s 244 of the Enterprise Act 2002 prior to disclosure. This may involve consulting those concerned, should the OFT wish to, but there is no obligation on the OFT to consult prior to transmission, either under Regulation 1/2003 or under domestic law.[118] See paras 8.70 et seq above for a discussion as to whether Article 6 ECHR requires undertakings to be given notice of disclosure of information to enable them to have access to the courts.

8.129 **Article 12 enjoys precedence over national law provisions to the contrary** Article 12 is described as overriding any national law to the contrary. Preamble 16 of Regulation 1/2003 provides that:

---

[114] The OFT disclosed its pleadings in the *MasterCard* case to another competition authority without consulting the CAT, thereby provoking certain negative comments from the CAT, see para 8.137 below.

[115] OFT442, *Modernisation* (December 2004) para 9.7 and OFT404, *Powers of investigation* (December 2004) para 6.13.

[116] See paras 8.25 and 8.26 for a discussion of this issue.

[117] For an explanation of this test, and a discussion as to whether the application of s 244 is compatible with Community law, see paras 8.34 et seq.

[118] Note that r 6(1) of the OFT's Rules of Procedure does not apply to disclosure to the ECN. OFT404, *Powers of Investigation* (December 2004), para 6.13.

Notwithstanding any national provision to the contrary, the exchange and the use of information in evidence should be allowed between members of the network even where information is confidential

Paragraph 27 of the Network Notice is to similar effect. This does not alter the intrinsic character of the provision—which remains fundamentally an enabling provision—but it does mean that where the national competition authorities choose to use the power, any national rules that may prevent the disclosure or use of the information do not take effect.

One example of this precedence is the use in evidence of information that was **8.130** lawfully collected in its state of origin, but would not meet the requisite procedural standards in the state in which it is adduced as evidence. Preamble 16 to Regulation 1/2003 provides: 'When the information exchanged is used by the receiving authority to impose sanctions on undertakings, there should be no other limit to the use of the information than the obligation to use it for the purpose for which it was collected.'[119] Similarly, the Network Notice provides that the question as to whether information was lawfully collected is determined by reference to the law applicable to the transmitting authority.[120] The receiving authorities and courts should not therefore subsequently call into question the legality of the use of the information received through the ECN by reference to their own law. A contentious example of this principle in practice relates to legal professional privilege. In the United Kingdom, higher standards of protection apply than in the continent, notably in some Member States no privilege attaches to communications from in-house legal advisers. The OFT's view is that, in accordance with the scheme in Regulation 1/2003, it may rely on material (such as communications from in-house legal advisers) received through the ECN in the context of its proceedings under the Competition Act 1998, although the material would be considered privileged under English law (see paras 8.188 et seq for a discussion of this issue).

Who receives the information?   The disclosing authority may rely on Article 12 **8.131** to disclose information to whichever authorities within the network it chooses— the disclosure can be network wide or can be selective[121] (to a few national competition authorities particularly affected by a cartel, for example). The power in Article 12 is to disclose only to authorities that are designated as national competition authorities under Article 35 of the Regulation. Transmission outside the ECN is forbidden by Article 28 of the Regulation.

---

[119] See para 8.153 et seq below for a discussion of the obligation to use it for the purposes for which it was collected.
[120] Network Notice, para 27.   [121] ibid, para 27.

8.132 **Exchange of information subject to conditions**   Article 12(1) provides national competition authorities with a power which they may exercise at their discretion, subject to the authority's obligation of faithful cooperation under Article 10 EC. It is not excluded therefore, that an authority should, in a particular case, attach conditions to its disclosure of information. The terms of Regulation 1/2003 do not preclude it. In certain cases, the ability to impose conditions on the disclosure of information may be helpful, particularly where the information has been provided to the transmitting authority on a voluntary basis. However, competition authorities are unlikely to do so often, particularly in view of the difficulties of enforcing adherence to the conditions on which the information is disclosed.

(ii) Disclosure under Articles 14, 11(5), and 15 of Regulation 1/2003

8.133 **Disclosure under Article 14 or Article 11(5)**   Regulation 1/2003 establishes an Advisory Committee made up of representatives of the national competition authorities. The Advisory Committee must be consulted by the Commission prior to taking infringement and other significant decisions applying Article 81 or Article 82. National competition authorities may also raise for discussion at the Advisory Committee cases that they wish the Committee to consider. The consultation may take the form of a meeting, but there is also a written procedure. Article 14 implicitly permits the information disclosure that is necessary for the proper functioning of the Advisory Committee procedure. Article 11(5) of Regulation 1/2003 provides another 'sounding board' process for national competition authorities. It provides that authorities may consult the Commission on any case involving the application of Community rules. Paragraph 48 of the Network Notice states that authorities can use this mechanism to inform the network of (and discuss with it) a number of decisions applying Community law that would not otherwise be notified under Article 11(4) of Regulation 1/2003.

8.134 **Disclosure under Article 15**   Article 15 of Regulation 1/2003 provides for cooperation between the Commission (and the national competition authorities) and the national courts. It provides for disclosure from the competition authorities to the courts and vice versa.

8.135 Article 15(1) provides that the courts of the Member States may ask the Commission to transmit to them information in its possession or its opinion concerning the application of Community rules. There is no absolute obligation for the Commission to provide the requested information opinion, beyond the duty of loyal cooperation under Article 10 EC. It is expected that the Commission will meet such requests as far as resources permit. In *Postbank*, the CFI held:

> The principle of sincere cooperation inherent in Article 5 of the Treaty requires the Community institutions, and above all the Commission, which is entrusted with the task of ensuring application of the provisions of the Treaty, to give active assis-

tance to any national judicial authority dealing with an infringement of Community rules. That assistance, which takes various forms, may, where appropriate, consist in disclosing to the national courts documents acquired by the institutions in the discharge of their duties (see the order of the Court of Justice of 13 July 1990 in Case C-2/88 Imm. Zwartveld and others [1990] ECR I-3365, paragraphs 16 to 22).

In proceedings for the application of the Community competition rules, this principle implies in particular, as held by the Court of Justice, that the national court is entitled to seek information from the Commission on the state of any procedure which the Commission may have set in motion and to obtain from that institution such economic and legal information as it may be able to supply to it (Case C-234/89 Delimitis [1991] ECR I-935, paragraph 53, and Joined Cases C-319/93, C-40/94 and C-224/94 Dijkstra and others [1995] ECR I-4471, paragraph 36).[122]

Article 15(3) provides that the national competition authorities and the European Commission may submit written observations to the national courts of the relevant Member State on issues relating to Articles 81 and 82. This is a power as of right and it may be used by a competition authority acting on its own initiative. By contrast, the competition authorities and the Commission may also make oral observations to national courts, but this requires the permission of the court in question.[123] Article 15(3) provides for information exchange to facilitate the preparation of observations: **8.136**

> For the purpose of the preparation of their observations only, the competition authorities of the Member States and the Commission may request the relevant court of the Member State to transmit or ensure the transmission to them of any documents necessary for the assessment of the case.

Although there do not appear to be any limits on the types of documents which may be transmitted to the competition law authority, it is clear that those documents may only be used for the purpose of the preparation of observations to be submitted in the claim in question. There is a question mark as to how disclosure of pleadings and related documents under Article 15 interacts with the power of disclosure under Article 12 of Regulation 1/2003. Where a national competition authority is party to the proceedings, it may transmit pleadings in its possession to other authorities under Article 12, thus by-passing the involvement of the court that is envisaged in Article 15. This happened in *MasterCard*,[124] when the OFT disclosed its defence to another authority within the ECN, without informing the CAT thereof. The requesting authority had **8.137**

---

[122] Case T-353/94 *Postbank NV v Commission* [1996] ECR II-921, paras 64 and 65.

[123] For the procedure for participation in proceedings before courts in England and Wales, see Civil Procedure Rules, *Practice Direction (Competition law—Claims relating to the application of Articles 81 and 82 of the EC Treaty and Chapters 1 and 2 of Part 1 of the Competition Act 1998).*

[124] *MasterCard UK Members Forum Ltd; MasterCard International Incorporated and MasterCard Europe Sprl; and Royal Bank of Scotland Group v OFT*, transcript of hearing of 19 June 2006.

not approached the CAT for the pleadings under Article 15 (presumably because it did not wish to use it for the purpose of making observations).[125] The CAT indicated that in future it wishes to be consulted prior to disclosure in such situations, so that it can discharge its responsibility to ensure that the proceedings remain fair.[126] In response, the OFT emphasised its obligations under Article 12 and indicated that it could not in all situations be expected to consult the CAT prior to making a disclosure under Article 12.

D. Information Received Pursuant to Regulation 1/2003: Limitations on Use and Disclosure of Information

(a) Introduction

8.138 Regulation 1/2003 (in particular Article 12(1) thereof) provides national competition authorities with broad powers to disclose information to each other. The authorities have a formidable weapon to combat anti-competitive activity across the European Union in a coordinated and resource-intensive fashion. Conversely, the exercise of these powers is potentially devastating to the undertakings that are subject to them. As a matter of practice, they increase the likelihood and effectiveness of enforcement proceedings, with the consequent risk of civil proceedings for damages. As a matter of law, the powers affect the undertakings' fundamental rights. In many cases, the information disclosed will have been obtained by the use of compulsory powers that may involve intrusion into the undertakings' premises and interference with their correspondence, as when the OFT obtains information in the course of an on-site inspection under warrant under s 28 of the Competition Act 1998. The exchange and use that is made of such information engages both Article 8 ECHR (in particular, the right to non-interference with premises and correspondence) and Article 6 ECHR (the right to a fair trial, which carries a right of access to the courts, the privilege against self-incrimination, and the rights of the defence).[127]

---

[125] According to the CAT in this case the authority subsequently made 'some sort order requiring the appellants before us to produce all the documents that have been lodged before this court under pain of serious financial penalty within a five day period in a matter that prima facie involved some kind of interference with these proceedings'; ibid.

[126] 'It seems to us that if, as far as pleadings are concerned, (which are obviously not public documents) any party who wishes to disclose its pleadings it is at the very least prudent to inform the Tribunal of what is proposed, first so that a check can be made as to whether there is in fact no issue as to confidentiality, but more particularly as well so that the Tribunal can satisfy itself that there is no prejudice to the case going on before it if such disclosure were to take place. So we would hope that if a similar point arises in future we would at least be informed before anything was done so that those points can be dealt with'; ibid.

[127] See paras 8.68 et seq above.

The Competition Act 1998 requires that undertakings be given notice of the **8.139** subject matter and purpose of the investigation[128] for good reason, namely to enable an undertaking to defend itself and to assert those rights of the defence that depend on knowledge of the charge made against it. To permit the use of information collected in one Member State in one set of proceedings, in other proceedings in another Member State, undermines the rights of the defence by removing the defendant undertaking's opportunity to oppose the disclosure of the information with knowledge of the charge. Further, standards of procedural protection vary throughout the Community, yet it is the law that applies in the collecting authority's state which applies to determine whether the information was collected in a legal manner.[129] Disclosure may accordingly deprive undertakings of higher standards of procedural protection than apply in the recipient authority's state.

In order to address these problems, a number of restrictions apply to the **8.140** use that UK authorities may make of information that they receive under Regulation 1/2003.

(1) National competition authorities are bound to respect general principles of Community law when acting pursuant to Community law powers,[130] including as an integral part thereof, ECHR principles (see paras 8.62 et seq on the human rights aspects of information exchange).

(2) Regulation 1/2003 provides for two types of limitation:
   • It protects the right of the defence by introducing restrictions on the circumstances in which national competition authorities may rely in evidence on information received through the ECN (Article 12(2) and (3)).
   • It prohibits disclosure of information outside the ECN (Article 28). This prohibition on onwards disclosure serves a double function: it minimises the intrusion on the undertakings' ECHR rights (and in particular Article 8 ECHR), but it also serves to encourage national competition authorities to disclose information to each other, in the knowledge that the information will not be leaked outside the ECN.

(3) National competition authorities are bound to respect self-imposed restrictions publicly undertaken. Article 12(1) is an enabling provision, which leaves the authorities a discretion as to how to make use of the power provided therein, subject to their obligations of faithful cooperation under Article 10 EC. Where national competition authorities publicly

---

[128] Competition Act 1998, ss 26(3)(a), 27(2)(b), 29(1)(a)–(2).
[129] Network Notice, para 27 provides that it is the law that applies in the collecting authority's state which applies to determine whether the information was collected in a legal manner.
[130] Case 5/88 *Wachauf v Germany* [1989] ECR 2609, paras 17 and 19.

acknowledge a self-imposed restriction on their handling of information—for example as is the case in relation to leniency cases—this gives rise to a legitimate expectation that they will abide by the restriction.[131]

8.141 In considering the various restrictions that apply to the handling of information by national competition authorities, it is important at the outset to distinguish clearly between the various uses authorities may make of information.

- an authority may rely on information in evidence when taking a decision applying Article 81 or Article 82;
- an authority may disclose information (either selectively or by means of publication);
- an authority may use information as intelligence. This means that it will use the information to direct its searches and investigations. It may even extend to relying on the information to get a search warrant.[132]

8.142 The overwhelming majority (if not all) of restrictions relating to the use of information considered below relate to information disclosure or use in evidence.

8.143 We begin this section by considering the most important general principles of EC law that apply to information disclosure. These are an important starting point, as they will inform our approach to construing the restrictions contained in Regulation 1/2003.

(b) General principles of EC law

8.144 This section highlights the most relevant principles of EC law that are relevant in the context of information disclosure and the use of transmitted information. It does not aspire to cover the topic comprehensively, given its breadth.

(i) Professional secrecy and rights of the defence

8.145 Professional secrecy and the rights of the defence are fundamental principles of EC law that have a direct bearing on information exchange. There are two seminal cases that consider the restrictions that apply by virtue of these two principles when information is collected in one legal context and subsequently used in another. In *Dow Benelux NV v Commission*[133] the Commission formally ordered an investigation of an undertaking's premises on the basis of information that it had obtained in the context of an earlier separate investigation into different undertakings and another cartel. The ECJ considered the use to which

---

[131] Case T-72/99 *Meyer v Commission* [2000] ECR II-2521.
[132] [2004] EWCA Crim 1763, [2004] 1 WLR 3240; Case C-67/91 *Spanish Banks* [1992] ECR I-4785.
[133] Case 85/87 [1989] ECR 3137.

the Commission could put the information it had collected in the earlier investigation, in particular whether it was open to the Commission to rely on the information in evidence in its subsequent infringement decision. In *Dirección General de Defensa de la Competencia v Asociación Española de Banca Privada*[134] (**Spanish Banks**), the Spanish national competition authority relied on information that certain Spanish credit institutions had submitted to the European Commission under the notification provisions of Regulation 17/62[135] in its own proceedings against those credit institutions for breach of EC and Spanish competition law.

In both cases, the ECJ considered the rights of the defence and the obligation of **8.146** professional secrecy by which a competition authority is bound and balanced them against the public interest in the Commission and competition authorities performing their function in enforcing the competition rules. The balance it struck between these competing interests is as follows:

- To protect the rights of the defence, information which is obtained under powers of compulsion must not subsequently be used in evidence outside the legal context in which it was obtained[136] (this right is linked to the right of undertakings to be informed of the legal basis for the investigation and the purposes of the information request).

- The obligation of professional secrecy also forbids authorities to use in evidence information for a reason other than that for which it was collected *in the absence of an express provision allowing them to do so.*

- On the other hand, the Commission and national authorities are not precluded from relying on information obtained in another context to initiate a new investigation[137] (or to use it as intelligence)—they can then go on to request the very same information from the undertakings should they wish to rely on the information in evidence.

The ECJ's judgment in *Dow Benelux NV* explains: **8.147**

> [I]t should be pointed out that it does indeed follow from Article 20(1) and Article 14(3) of Regulation No.17 that information obtained during investigations must not be used for purposes other than those indicated in the order or decision under which the investigation is carried out.

> As has been pointed out above, in addition to professional secrecy, expressly mentioned in the aforesaid Article 20, that requirement is intended to protect the rights

---

134 Case C-67/91 [1992] ECR I-4785.
135 First Regulation implementing Articles [81] and [82] of the Treaty [1962] OJ 13/204.
136 Case C-67/91 *Spanish Banks* [1992] ECR I-4785, paras 36 and 48.
137 Case 85/87 *Dow Benelux v Commission* [1989] ECR 3137, para 19 and Case C-238/99 P *Limburgse Vinyl Maatschappij NV (LVM) v Commission* [2002] ECR I-8375.

of the defence of undertakings guaranteed by Article 14(3). Those rights would be seriously endangered if the Commission could rely on evidence against undertakings which were obtained during an investigation but was not related to the subject-matter or purpose thereof.[138]

8.148 Turning to the possible use of such information as intelligence, the ECJ then stated:

> On the other hand, it cannot be concluded that the Commission is barred from initiating an enquiry in order to verify or supplement information which it happened to obtain during a previous investigation if that information indicates the existence of conduct contrary to the competition rules in the Treaty. Such a bar would go beyond what is necessary to protect professional secrecy and the rights of the defence and would thus constitute an unjustified hindrance to the performance of the Commission of its task of ensuring compliance with the competition rules in the common market and to bring to light infringements of Articles 85 and 86 of the Treaty.[139]

8.149 The ECJ extended the above principle in *Spanish Banks*, holding that Member States authorities were entitled to use as intelligence information that was disclosed by the Commission.[140] Both *Dow Benelux* and *Spanish Banks* were subsequently confirmed in *LVM*.[141] This case also establishes that there is nothing to preclude the Commission, in the subsequent proceedings on the basis of the intelligence, from making a fresh request for the information to enable its use in evidence.[142]

(ii) Privilege against self-incrimination, legal professional privilege

8.150 When determining the use to make of information transmitted through the ECN, authorities must bear in mind certain procedural rights that have been defined as fundamental principles of EC law. The privilege against self-incrimination has the status of a fundamental principle of Community law.[143] In *Archer Daniels Midland v Commission*,[144] the CFI examined the application of the privilege, in the context of the Commission's reliance in evidence on certain materials provided by the FBI, which the latter it had obtained by compulsion in the course of antitrust proceedings. The CFI found that the

---

[138] ibid, paras 17 and 18.   [139] ibid, para 19.

[140] 'The Member States are not required to ignore the information disclosed to them and thereby undergo—to echo the expression used by the Commission and the national court—"acute amnesia". That information provides circumstantial evidence which may, if necessary, be taken into account to justify initiation of a national procedure'; Case C-67/91 *Spanish Banks* [1992] ECR I-4785, para 39.

[141] Case C-238/99 P *Limburgse Vinyl Maatschappij NV (LVM) v Commission* [2002] ECR I-8375.

[142] ibid, paras 301–306.

[143] For a fuller analysis of the principle, see paras 7.30 et seq above.

[144] Case T-59/02, judgment of 27 September 2006.

Commission was not altogether precluded from relying on such evidence, subject to certain safeguards; in particular, the Commission had to give the undertaking concerned notice of its intention to rely on the document, and the opportunity to make its objections known beforehand. In this case, the appellant was given such opportunity and had not disputed that the Commission could rely on the document before the Commission, in fact it had itself relied on the incriminating document. The CFI reasoned as follows:

> [I]t is acknowledged that one of the general principles of Community law, of which fundamental rights are an integral part and in the light of which all Community laws must be interpreted, is the right of undertakings not to be compelled by the Commission, under Article 11 of Regulation No 17, to admit their participation in an infringement (Orkem v Commission, paragraph 238 above, paragraph 35). The protection of that right means that, in the event of a dispute as to the scope of a question, it must be determined whether an answer from the undertaking to which the question is addressed would in fact be equivalent to the admission of an infringement, such as to undermine the rights of the defence (see Joined Cases C-238/99 P, C-244/99 P, C-245/99 P, C-247/99 P, C-250/99 P to C-252/99 P and C-254/99 P LimburgseVinyl Maatschappij and others v Commission [2002] ECR I-8375, paragraph 273, and Case T-112/98 Mannesmannröhren-Werke v Commission [2001] ECR II-729, paragraph 64) . . .

> . . . where, as in the present case, the Commission, when freely assessing the evidence in its possession, relies on a statement made in a context different from that of the procedure initiated before it, and where that statement potentially contains information that the undertaking concerned would have been entitled to refuse to provide to the Commission by reason of the Orkem v Commission case-law, paragraph 238 above, the Commission is required to guarantee to the undertaking concerned procedural rights equivalent to those conferred by that case-law.

> Compliance with those procedural safeguards entails, in a context such as this one, the need for the Commission to carry out an examination automatically if, prima facie, there is serious doubt as to whether the procedural rights of the parties concerned were complied with in the procedure during which they provided such statements. If there is no such serious doubt, the procedural rights of the parties concerned must be deemed to have been adequately safeguarded if, in the statement of objections, the Commission clearly indicates, if necessary by annexing the relevant documents to it, that it intends to rely on the statements in question. In this way, the Commission makes it possible for the parties concerned to comment not only on the content of those statements, but also on any irregularities or special circumstances concerning their composition or submission to the Commission.[145]

The ECJ defined legal professional privilege in *AM & S v Commission*.[146] The **8.151** scope of legal professional privilege as defined in *AM & S* is narrower than that applicable under competition law in several respects:

---

[145] ibid, paras 262–265.　　[146] Case 155/79 [1982] ECR 1575.

- it does not extend to communications from in-house lawyers;
- it does not extend to litigation privilege (which extends to documents produced by non-lawyers such as expert reports);
- it does not extend to communications from lawyers based abroad.

8.152 The standard of protection defined in the ECJ jurisprudence is a minimum standard which must be applied, by virtue of supremacy, when national authorities and the courts are applying Community law.[147]

(iii) Article 12(2): Use in evidence for the application of Articles 81 and 82

8.153 Article 12(2) of Regulation 1/2003 provides:

> Information exchanged shall only be used in evidence for the purpose of applying Article 81 or Article 82 of the Treaty and in respect of the subject-matter for which it was collected by the transmitting authority.

8.154 **Receiving authority only** Article 12(2) provides a clear limit on the use that may made of exchanged information by the receiving authority. There is no obligation on the disclosing authority to have regard to the recipient's intended use of the information. In practice, the OFT is likely to do so, as it applies s 244 of the Enterprise Act 2002 in deciding to make a disclosure to the ECN, which involves gauging whether the disclosure is necessary.

8.155 **Rationale and background** The restriction in Article 12(2) is designed to protect the rights of the defence. The restriction is not new to EC law—in fact Article 12(2) echoes long established EC case law which recognises that fundamental rights arise for undertakings compelled to provide information to the Commission.[148] To understand the ambit of Article 12(2), therefore, one must consider the case law. When undertakings are compelled to provide information in the context of a dawn raid or other compulsory power, they are informed of the legal basis of the request as well as the subject matter of the investigation, so that they may verify that the demand is soundly based in law and object in the event that the authority seeks to collect information that falls outside the scope of the investigation.[149] These rights of the defence are potentially lost when information is collected by one authority towards a specific purpose, and trans-

---

[147] For a fuller analysis of the principle, see paras 7.09 et seq.

[148] Case 85/87 *Dow Benelux v Commission* [1989] ECR 3137; Case C-67/91 *Spanish Banks* [1992] ECR I-4785, see para 8.145 et seq above.

[149] Case 85/87 *Dow Benelux v Commission* [1989] ECR 3137, para 5: 'However, the exercise of the wide powers of investigation conferred on the Commission is subject to conditions serving to ensure respect for the rights of undertakings. In that regard, the Commission's obligation to specify the subject-matter and purpose of the investigation is a fundamental requirement not merely in order to show that the investigation to be carried out on the premises of the undertakings concerned is justified but also to enable those undertakings to assess the scope of their duty to cooperate while at the same time safeguarding the rights of the defence'.

mitted to another authority. Article 12(2) seeks to protect the rights of the defence in such situations, by imposing restrictions on the purpose for which the receiving authority may use information.

Purpose of applying Articles 81 and 82   It should not be a difficult matter for   **8.156**
the recipient authority (on whom the restriction applies) to determine whether it is, in a particular case, relying on information on the evidence to apply Article 81 or Article 82.

A more difficult issue arises, where the information was not collected for the   **8.157**
purposes of applying Articles 81 and 82 by the collecting authority, but the recipient authority proposes to rely on it in evidence in such a case. At first glance, the general principles of EC law defined in *Dow Benelux* and *Spanish Banks* would seem to preclude reliance in evidence on such information for two reasons: first, because use is being made in a 'different legal context' (thus infringing the rights of the defence); and secondly, because the information is being used for another reason than that for which it was collected (thus breaching the obligation of professional secrecy).

However, in respect of the first objection, Regulation 1/2003 arguably defines   **8.158**
the legal context to include such disclosure—undertakings are aware, when they provide information to competition authorities under domestic law, that the power to exchange the information exists. An analogy can be drawn with the Court of Appeal's reasoning in *R v Brady*,[150] and *Kent Pharmaceuticals*,[151] in which it held that the interference with the undertakings' right to correspondence under Article 8 ECHR was not infringed by the transmission of information from one authority to another for the latter's use, because the undertaking was taken to be aware of the broader statutory context allowing transmission and use by the other authority. In respect of the second objection, this can be met by the fact that Article 12(2) now expressly provides for such use, so that there is no breach of the obligation of professional secrecy.

Same subject matter   The limitation that the information transferred be used in   **8.159**
evidence only in respect of the 'subject matter' for which it was collected is a more difficult concept, which may give rise to some disputes. The Network Notice refers to *Dow Benelux* for a definition of 'subject matter'. In that case, the ECJ held that the description of the subject matter of the investigation— essentially the product market, the parties and the alleged infringement—had been sufficiently, if very vaguely, described to the defendants to allow their rights of defence to take effect. The question as to whether the information transmit-

---

[150] [2004] EWCA Crim 1763, [2004] 1 WLR 3240.
[151] *R (Kent Pharmaceuticals Ltd) v Director of the SFO* [2004] EWCA 1494, [2005] 1 WLR 1302.

ted is used for the same subject matter in any one case will revolve around how broadly or narrowly the transmitting authority framed the terms of reference for its original investigation in the documents authorising the collection of evidence (in the formal decision ordering investigation, or the request for informa-tion).[152] If the authority transmits information it collected in the context of a cartel between A, B, and C, can another authority use it against party D, who, it emerges, is also part of the cartel? In the authors' view, it is not necessary that the exact detail of the alleged infringement be identical (including exact parties/ product and geographic market definition), providing the essence is the same. This can be contrasted with the requirements in the second limb of Article 12(2), that where evidence is to be used in support of the application of national competition law, it must concern the 'same case' as that where Article 81 or Article 82 are applied.

8.160 **Use as intelligence** The restrictions in the case law and in Article 12(2) solely restrict the *use* of the information in *evidence*. Actual disclosure of the informa-tion, and its subsequent use by the recipient authority *as intelligence*, are not restricted both under Article 12(2) and in the case law. As regards the terms of Article 12(2), the restriction is formulated only to apply to the use of the information in evidence. There is no restriction on the initial power to disclose in Article 12(1) or on other usage by the recipient authority. As regards the case law, this makes clear that use may be made in intelligence of information that was obtained in a different context. In *Dow Benelux*,[153] the ECJ found that although information obtained in one proceeding cannot be used in evidence in the context of different proceedings, such information could nonetheless be used *in intelligence* for the purpose of initiating different proceedings.[154] Further, in *Spanish Banks*, the ECJ extended this principle: it accepted that the Commission could disclose information that it had received in one context to the Spanish competition authorities so that they could use it as intelligence in the different context of a case commenced under national procedures.[155] As regards the protection of the rights of the defence (but not necessarily Article 8 ECHR) this would appear to be consistent with ECHR case law on the privilege against self-incrimination. In *Saunders v UK*, the privilege against self-incrimination, whilst prohibiting the subsequent *use in evidence* of self-incriminating materials obtained by compulsory powers, was held not to extend to prohibiting their use for the purpose of extra-judicial investigative inquiries.[156] The Court of Appeal

---

[152] In the UK, the Section 26 Notice, Section 27 Notice, or search warrant.
[153] [1989] ECR 3137.   [154] ibid, para 19.
[155] The possibility of using information towards a different purpose as intelligence was con-firmed in Case C-238/99 P *Limburgse Vinyl Maatschappij NV (LVM) v Commission* [2002] ECR I-8375.
[156] *Saunders v UK* (1997) 23 EHRR 313, para 67.

has read this as permitting authorities to rely on evidence compulsorily obtained for one purpose, for the purpose of obtaining a search warrant in aid of different proceedings.[157]

Information collected prior to 1 May 2004 Article 12 of Regulation 1/2003 **8.161** does not provide any restriction on the disclosure of information collected prior to 1 May 2004. However, information collected by many national competition authorities prior to 1 May 2004 cannot have been collected for the purpose of applying Article 81 or Article 82. It is submitted that such information, even if exchanged, may not be used in evidence by the recipient competition authority under Article 12(2). Its subsequent use in evidence would appear to be precluded by *Dow Benelux* and *Spanish Banks* as it would not have been collected in the same legal context (Reg 1/2003 did not apply) and there was no provision at the relevant time expressly providing for its use in Article 81 or Article 82 proceedings. The authors understand that the OFT has taken the view, in practice, that it may disclose to other national competition authorities and the European Commission information which it collected prior to 1 May 2004, pursuant to Article 12(1) of Regulation 1/2003. It may be that this is because Article 12(2) and the general principles of EC law as defined in *Dow Benelux* and *Spanish Banks* prevent the use of such information in evidence, rather than its disclosure.

(iv) Article 12(2): Use in evidence for the application of national law

Article 12(2) goes on to provide that: 'However, where national competition law **8.162** is applied in the same case and in parallel to Community competition law and does not lead to a different outcome, information exchanged under this Article may also be used for the application of national competition law.'

National competition law can only be applied in 'the same case', 'in parallel to **8.163** EC competition law', and where it 'does not lead to a different outcome'. Considering each of these conditions in turn:

- The requirement of the same case: the Joint Statement of the Council and the Commission on the functioning of the network[158] defines same cases as cases that relate to the same market, same parties, same conduct/agreement.[159] The possibility for the application of national competition law is considerably curtailed by this requirement: it suffices that one of the parties should differ, arguably, for the matter no longer to be the same as the Community law case with reference to which the information was collected. There may be room to

---

[157] In *R v Brady* [2004] EWCA Crim 1763, [2004] 1 WLR 3240, the Court of Appeal held that *Saunders* did not apply where the Inland Revenue had relied on information compulsorily obtained for the purpose of obtaining search warrants, but not in the prosecution proceedings.

[158] <http://ec.europa.eu/comm/competition/antitrust/others/js_en.pdf>.

[159] ibid, para 20.

draw on the jurisprudence developed in the context of national courts' and authorities' obligation to avoid inconsistent decisions with Commission decisions on the same matter. In *Inntrepreneur Pub Co (CPC) v Crehan*,[160] the House of Lords considered the ambit of the obligation to avoid decisions that conflict with Commission decisions under Article 16 of Regulation 1/2003. It approved Advocate General Cosmas' Opinion in *Masterfoods*[161] to the effect that the obligation to avoid inconsistent decisions does not arise 'where the legal and factual context of the case being examined by the Commission was not completely identical to that before the national courts'.[162] Parties wishing to argue for a narrow approach to what amounts to the same case may also usefully draw on European case law in relation to *ne bis in idem*, which takes a very narrow approach to what two cases are the same (see generally Chapter 11 below).

• In parallel to EC competition law: this imposes a requirement that the competition authority should use the evidence in a case that is conducted simultaneously with an Article 81/82 case. It appears that the situation which Article 12(2) is aimed at permitting is the case where an authority receives information and uses it to initiate a case against undertakings both under national law and under EC law. Further, the requirement of a parallel Community competition law case in effect precludes the use of information in national law cases where there is no effect on trade.

• The information cannot be relied upon in the context of a case that 'may lead to a different outcome' from that reached in the Article 81 and Article 82 case. This requirement is aimed at avoiding the use of transmitted information in cases where national authorities find an infringement under stricter national laws relating to unilateral conduct.[163] In the author's view 'the same outcome' does not imply that the penalties that are imposed in relation to the infringement must be the same: first, Regulation 1/2003 does not seek to harmonise penalties, provided that national law ensures the effective application of Article 81 or Article 82, and secondly, Community law itself requires that competition authorities take account of fines that are imposed in relation to the same matter by another authority, where necessary reducing any penalty in light of these.[164] Rather, the substantive finding of breach must not differ.

8.164 In view of these stringent conditions, it is unlikely that the OFT will rely on evidence received through the ECN in the application of national

---

[160] [2006] UKHL 38, [2006] 3 WLR 148.
[161] Case C-344/98 *Masterfoods Ltd (t/a Mars Ireland) v HB Ice Cream Ltd* [2000] ECR I-11369.
[162] [2006] UKHL 38, [2006] 3 WLR 148, para 49.
[163] This is permitted by Article 3(2) of Regulation 1/2003; see Chapter 3 above.
[164] Case 14/68 *Wilhelm v Bundeskartellamt* [1969] ECR 1; see para 11.59 below.

law except when it applies Chapter I or Chapter II as well as Article 81 or Article 82.

(c) Information for the application of national competition law: cartel offence and director disqualification

For reasons that are set out in Chapter 3, the cartel offence and director dis-   **8.165**
qualification are not considered by the OFT to be 'national competition law' for the purposes of Regulation 1/2003. Accordingly, in principle, the possibility of using information for the purposes of the 'application of national competition law' provided in Article 12(2) does not arise in this context.

Assuming that the OFT's position on the cartel offence and director   **8.166**
disqualification is incorrect, and that these fall to be considered as national competition law, it is not clear that Article 12(2) would permit the use of network information in such proceedings. This is because, addressing each of the three conditions set out in Article 12(2) in turn:

- It is unlikely that cartel proceedings or director disqualification proceedings amount to the 'same case' as an Article 81/Article 82 case: they relate to different parties (individuals rather than undertakings) and give rise to fundamentally different legal issues.

- The requirement that the case be conducted in parallel with the Article 81/Article 82 case would seem to rule out use of such evidence in cartel proceedings (where the prosecution will normally precede Competition Act proceedings) and in director disqualification proceedings (which in practice will follow Competition Act proceedings).

- 'The same outcome' from Article 81 or Article 82 proceedings does not follow in the context of cartel or director disqualification proceedings. The issues for decision by the court relate primarily to the state of mind and actions of particular individuals—the issue of infringement of competition rules just being a prerequisite element of the factual matrix. It is true that a successful prosecution of an individual for the cartel offence could be viewed as the 'same outcome' as a finding of infringement in the related Article 81 case, in the sense that it would amount to a complementary penalty. However, the difficulty is that given the different issues that a court is asked to determine in a cartel prosecution, a finding of infringement under Article 81 does not necessarily entail a successful cartel prosecution. The prosecuting authority using such information cannot therefore guarantee the 'same outcome'.

For all these reasons, it is unlikely that information that is disclosed to the   **8.167**
UK authorities under Article 12 will be relied upon in evidence in cartel or director disqualification proceedings. It is important to emphasise that Article

12, interpreted in the light of *Dow Benelux* and *Spanish Banks*,[165] would not appear to preclude the use of information received through the ECN as intelligence in respect of the cartel offence or director disqualification (see paras 8.146–8.149, and para 8.160 on the use of information as intelligence).

(d) Article 12(3): restrictions on the use of information for the imposition of sanctions on individuals

8.168 Where the relevant national competition law provides criminal sanctions in relation to competition offences, there are further restrictions (additional to those set out in Article 12(2), that must be met before information exchanged under Article 12 can be relied upon in evidence. Article 12(3) of Regulation 1/2003 provides:

> Information exchanged pursuant to paragraph 1 can only be used in evidence to impose sanctions on natural persons where:
> - the law of the transmitting authority foresees sanctions of a similar kind in relation to an infringement of Article 81 or Article 82 of the Treaty or, in the absence thereof,
> - the information has been collected in a way which respects the same level of protection of the rights of defence of natural persons as provided for under the national rules of the receiving authority. However, in this case, the information exchanged cannot be used by the receiving authority to impose custodial sanctions.

8.169 Article 12(3) of Regulation 1/2003 provides for a further limitation such that information exchanged pursuant to Article 12(1) can only be used in evidence to impose sanctions on natural persons in limited circumstances. The reason for this limitation is explained in Recital 16 of Regulation 1/2003. This recital distinguishes between sanctions on undertakings which are of the same type in all systems, and the position of individuals, who may be subject to substantially different types of sanctions across the various systems. Recital 16 notes that accordingly 'the rights of defence enjoyed by undertakings in the various systems can be considered as sufficiently equivalent'. This is not the case for individuals, given the difference in sanction that can arise between the sanction provided in the state of collection and that in the state in which evidence is relied upon.[166] Further, the rights of the defence accorded to individuals are

---

[165] Case 85/87 *Dow Benelux v Commission* [1989] ECR 3137; Case C-67/91 *Spanish Banks* [1992] ECR I-4785.
[166] Although all Member States are bound by the general principles of Community law including, as an integral part thereof, the ECHR, there are considerable disparities between relevant procedural safeguards in the various Member States. For example, the ambit of legal professional privilege is considerably narrower than in the UK in many continental Member States.

usually more extensive than those enjoyed by undertakings, for example the right to remain silent.[167]

Article 12(3) provides two situations in which evidence may be used to impose **8.170** sanctions on natural persons. The first is where the law of both the transmitting and receiving authorities foresee 'sanctions of a similar kind' in relation to an infringement of Article 81 or 82. Paragraph 28(c) of the Network Notice emphasises that in determining whether sanctions are of a similar kind for the purposes of Article 12(3), the qualification of the sanctions by national law as 'administrative' or 'criminal' is irrelevant. The distinctions that are relevant are issues relating to the severity of the sanction itself, such as fines or custody.

The second situation envisaged in Article 12(3) is where, although the sanctions **8.171** imposed are different, the information has been collected in a way which 'respects the same level of protection of the rights of defence of natural persons as provided for under the national rules of the receiving authority'. However, in such cases, the information exchanged may not be used by the receiving authority to impose custodial sanctions.

The aim of Article 12(3) is to ensure that the procedural safeguards[168] from which **8.172** individuals benefit in criminal proceedings are equivalent wherever the information is collected. It aims to prevent situations where information collected from undertakings is used in a way which would circumvent the higher protection of individuals that applies in the state of enforcement action. The need for such a protection is particularly acute given the fact that the question of whether the information was collected in a lawful manner is governed on the basis of the law applicable to the collecting authority.[169] It should be noted, however, that the first limb of Article 12(3) permits the use of information where similar sanctions are imposed under the laws of the transmitting and receiving authority, when this does not necessarily mean that the procedural safeguards are the same.

(e) Article 28(1): professional secrecy in Commission investigations

Article 28(1) provides that without prejudice to Articles 12 and 15, information **8.173** collected pursuant to Articles 17 to 22 of Regulation 1/2003 shall be used only for the purpose for which it was acquired.

This provision is mainly of relevance to the Commission (Articles 17 to 21 **8.174** provide for the Commission's powers of investigation), but is of some relevance

---

[167] Network Notice, para 28(c).
[168] The exercise of mandatory powers to collect information (in particular where this involves intrusive devices such as surveillance and taping) engages rights under Arts 8 and 6 ECHR. Member States provide different safeguards for the protection of such rights.
[169] Network Notice, para 27.

to national competition authorities in relation to inspections which they carry out at the request of another national authority or the Commission under Article 22 of Regulation 1/2003.

8.175   The principle that 'information should only be used for the purpose for which it was acquired' was first defined in ECJ case law in relation to Regulation 17 in *Dow Benelux* and *Spanish Banks*.[170] These cases defined the ambit of the obligation of professional secrecy under Regulation 17/62. As explained in *Spanish Banks* and *Dow Benelux*, a competition authority may not, by virtue of the principle of professional secrecy, use information in evidence towards another purpose in the absence of an express provision allowing this.

8.176   Regulation 1/2003 expressly provides for other usage: the obligation to make use of information only for the reasons for which it was acquired is expressed to be without prejudice to Articles 12 and 15 of Regulation 1/2003. The Commission may accordingly disclose information under Article 12 or Article 15 without infringing the principles established in *Dow Benelux* and *Spanish Banks*. It may not, however, rely in evidence on information it has itself collected towards another purpose. The same principle precludes a national competition authority collecting information on behalf of another competition authority or the Commission pursuant to Article 22(1) of Regulation 1/2003 from relying on such information towards another purpose.

(f) Article 28(2)

8.177   Article 28(2) of Regulation 1/2003 provides that:

> Without prejudice to the exchange and to the use of information foreseen in Article 11, 12, 14, 15 and 27, the Commission and the competition authorities of the Member States, their officials, servants and other persons working under the supervision of these authorities as well as officials and civil servants of other authorities of the Member States shall not disclose information acquired or exchange by them pursuant to this Regulation and of the kind covered by the obligation of professional secrecy. This obligation also applies to all representative and experts of all Member States attending meetings of the Advisory Committee pursuant Article 14.

8.178   Article 28(2) of Regulation 1/2003 serves a dual function:

- Article 28 of Regulation 1/2003 is a key safeguard for undertakings and individuals.[171] It is intended to protect those providing information by creating 'a common minimum level of protection throughout the Community'.

---

[170] Case 85/87 *Dow Benelux v Commission* [1989] ECR 3137; Case C-67/91 *Spanish Banks* [1992] ECR I-4785. See paras 8.145 et seq above.
[171] Network Notice, para 28(a).

- Article 28 has a second, related purpose, which is not explicitly stated. It is designed to encourage the free exchange of information within the ECN by preventing the disclosure of such information outside it. This means that national competition authorities can exchange information within a closed loop without having to undertake an assessment of the confidentiality of the information and the confidentiality procedures of the receiving authority.

(i) *The prohibition*

Article 28(2) strictly prohibits the disclosure of any information of the kind **8.179** covered by the obligation of professional secrecy outside the ECN. The OFT, Commission and the national competition authorities read this as precluding any such disclosure, even to another government authority. The prohibition applies to 'information acquired or exchanged pursuant to this Regulation' that is covered by professional secrecy. Given that it is Article 5 of Regulation 1/2003 which empowers national competition authorities to apply Articles 81 and 82, it could be argued that all information collected in the context of Article 81 and Article 82 investigations by the OFT is acquired 'pursuant to' Regulation 1/2003 and hence covered by the obligations contained in Article 28(2). This may therefore impact on the OFT's ability to transmit such information to other UK authorities outside of the ECN, such as the CC.[172]

(ii) *What information is covered by professional secrecy?*

The concept of professional secrecy is broad. In practice, it imposes an obliga- **8.180** tion of confidentiality in respect of almost all information that may be received by an authority or a person in the course of conducting their functions relating to competition enforcement, except for information already in the public domain.

Paragraph 28(a) of the Network Notice states that the term professional secrecy **8.181** is a 'Community law concept and includes in particular business secrets and other confidential information'. It is clear that confidential information and 'business secrets' are but a subset of the information that is covered by the obligation. The ECJ defined business secrets as 'information of which not only disclosure to the public but also mere transmission to a person other than the one that provided the information might seriously harm the latter's interests'.[173] In general the ECJ will look to the undertaking's commercial interests in considering whether information is a business secret.[174] 'Other confidential information' has been defined by the Commission as information other than

---

[172] For a discussion of this issue, see paras 8.232 et seq, and Chapter 13.
[173] Case T-353/94 *Postbank v Commission* [1996] ECR II-921, para 87.
[174] Case 53/85 *Akzo Nobel Chemie BV v Commission* [1986] ECR 1965.

business secrets, which may be considered as confidential in so far as its disclosure may have a significant adverse effect upon the supplier of the information.[175] For example, some third parties may wish to protect their anonymity for fear of repercussions. In his Opinion in *Akzo Nobel Chemie BV v Commission*,[176] Advocate General Lenz suggested that the obligation of professional secrecy not only covered business secrets but also internal information of the competition authority.

(iii) *Who is bound by Article 28?*

8.182 It appears that the wording of Article 28 is sufficiently broad to cover any authority or person who might legitimately acquire information pursuant to the various provisions of Regulation 1/2003. The transfer of information under Article 12 is limited to that between designated national competition authorities. But other provisions in Regulation 1/2003, such as Articles 14 and 15, to which express reference is made in Article 28, permit certain disclosure of information to other officials (for example, additional Member States representatives attending Advisory Committee meetings under Article 14). The obligation in Article 28(2) therefore applies to all information: for example, it includes appellate and review courts receiving information under Article 15 of the Regulation, although use for the purposes envisaged in Article 15 itself would not be impeded.

(iv) *Self-imposed restrictions*

8.183 National competition authorities can, in so far as is consistent with their obligations under Article 10 EC and Article 11(1) of Regulation1/2003, impose restrictions on themselves as to the way in which the Article 12 power will be exercised, and if necessary make transmission to the ECN subject to certain conditions.

8.184 The OFT may (and has) placed certain self-imposed restrictions upon its own power to disclose information. There are certain types of information which may be held by the OFT and which, by self-imposed restraints, it will not disclose (or will only disclose subject to certain conditions) pursuant to Article 12 of Regulation 1/2003. These self-imposed restraints fall into three categories: information received from a leniency applicant; information received from another Member State national competition authority pursuant to Article 12; and information which the OFT holds only subject to conditions or other obligations.

---

[175] Eighteenth Report on Competition Policy (1988) para 43.
[176] [1986] ECR 1965, paras 5.2 and 5.3.

Leniency information The European Commission and the competition **8.185** authorities share a concern to ensure that the broad information exchange provisions in Regulation 1/2003 do not deter leniency applications. Accordingly, the Network Notice provides for a number of self-imposed restraints relating to the exchange of leniency related information. Information relating to leniency applications is subject to strict and detailed rules concerning any potential disclosure which may take place pursuant to Article 12. These are considered in section E below.

Information subject to obligations Where information is provided to the **8.186** OFT on a voluntary basis, but subject to conditions or obligations that have been agreed with the provider of the information, for example relating to confidentiality, the OFT will be bound by its agreement to adhere to those conditions in relation to any potential disclosure under Article 12 (the restriction on disclosure does not stem from a national provision to the contrary, and so is not overridden by Article 12). Those conditions may in some cases prevent such disclosure altogether. However, the more likely scenario is an agreement between the OFT and a particular undertaking that documents will not be disclosed unless the same confidentiality obligations are also imposed upon the recipient of such information. Parties considering voluntarily disclosing information to the OFT should consider carefully whether the terms upon which that disclosure is made will cover the OFT's use of its Article 12 power.

Information not to be passed on again within the ECN Although there is no **8.187** legal prohibition on any exchange of information within the ECN (subject to the leniency issues, which are discussed at paras 8.191 et seq) there is a general understanding among ECN members that information received from one competition authority will not be passed on to another competition authority pursuant to Article 12 of Regulation 1/2003. The requesting competition authority should direct its request to the party from whom the information originated. This understanding is revealed by para 27 of the Network Notice which assumes that the transmitting authority is the same authority as the gathering authority (which is obviously not the case where there is onward transmission).[177] This is the only way in which competition authorities may be certain as to the legality of the collection of the information (which is determined by reference to the law applicable to the authority that gathered the information). Further, it protects transmitting authorities by ensuring that any conditions they impose upon the information transmitted by them will remain effective. However, as it is not a legal or binding requirement upon any competition authority, an undertaking

---

[177] Network Notice, para 27.

voluntarily disclosing information to the OFT may wish to consider seeking an additional condition to address this issue.

8.188 **Information protected by legal professional privilege** One of the more contentious areas of difference between the various legal regimes of the Member States is the concept of legal professional privilege. The definition of legal professional privilege applied under s 30 of the Competition Act 1998 is quite broad, and includes litigation privilege (which extends to documents prepared by non-lawyers for the purpose of legal proceedings), as well as communications between lawyers (including in-house lawyers and lawyers qualified outside the European Union) with their client.[178] The definition of legal professional privilege under Community law as established in *AM & S v Commission*[179] is much narrower. Regulation 1/2003 would appear to permit the OFT to use information that would be considered privileged under the Competition Act, if it were received from another competition authority that had lawfully collected it in a Member State with a narrower concept of privilege.[180] This is the case even though that information could not have been collected by the OFT itself under the Competition Act in the United Kingdom.

8.189 In its guideline on powers of investigation,[181] the OFT states:

> Whilst UK privilege rules will apply to cases being investigated in the UK by the OFT on its own behalf, the OFT could be sent the communications of in-house lawyers, or lawyers qualified outside the EU, by an NCA from another member state where the communication of such lawyers are not privileged. Under those circumstances, the OFT may use the documentation received from the other NCA in its investigation.

8.190 In the OFT's response to the original consultation on the competition law guidelines, it notes that 'some concern was expressed in relation to the OFT's proposal that it would use in evidence documents which might have benefited from legal professional privilege if they had been collected by the OFT in the UK but which do not benefit from legal professional privilege in the Member State where the documents were actually collected'. The OFT's response relies on the 'supremacy of Article 12' argument.[182] It relies on Recital 16 of Regulation 1/2003 and para 27 of the Network Notice to argue that Article 12 prevails over any conflicting provision of national law obstructing disclosure and/or use

---

[178] See Chapter 7 above for a discussion on the UK and EU definitions of legal professional privilege.

[179] Case 155/79 [1982] ECR 1575.   [180] See para 8.130 above.

[181] OFT404, *Powers of investigation* (December 2004) para 6.3.

[182] OFT446, *Response to points raised during the consultation on the competition law guidelines, guidance and the OFT's Rules* (December 2004) paras 2.23–2.27.

of disclosed information in evidence.[183] However, Article 12 is an enabling provision that does not give rise to any duty on the recipient authority to use information transmitted to it. Accordingly, this analysis ignores the question of whether or not the OFT's policy should be to restrict its own use of such information. The disparity in relation to the rules on legal professional privilege across the European Community may be remedied if the issue were raised again before the European courts. In considering an interim remedies application in *Akzo Nobel Chemie BV v Commission*, the CFI showed a willingness to reconsider the rules on privilege:

> . . . the solution in AM & S v Commission . . . is based, inter alia, on an interpretation of the principles common to the Member States dating from 1962. It is therefore necessary to determine whether, in the present case, the applicants and the interveners have adduced serious evidence of such a kind as to demonstrate that, taking into account developments in Community law and in the legal orders of the Member States since the judgment in AM & S v Commission . . . it cannot be precluded that the protection of professional privilege should now also extend to written communications with a lawyer employed by an undertaking on a permanent basis.[184]

E. Leniency and Information Disclosure within the ECN

At the outset, it is important to note that the OFT's leniency programme lies at the core of its competition enforcement functions. The leniency programme operates to generate information about cartels where the OFT would otherwise be very unlikely to obtain such information. Further, it generates the production of the best information quickly and voluntarily, where the OFT would otherwise have to use extensive resources and powers to obtain the information. The European Commission, like the OFT, is very committed to its leniency programme. It considers that it is in the Community interest to grant favourable treatment to undertakings which cooperate with it in the investigation of cartel infringements.[185] The Commission and the national competition authorities (most of which have a leniency programme) therefore have a shared concern to protect the viability of leniency in the context of the broad powers of information disclosure provided by Regulation 1/2003.

8.191

---

[183] Recital 16 provides that: 'Notwithstanding any national provision to the contrary, the exchange of information and use of such information in evidence should be allowed . . .'. Network Notice, para 27 provides that Art 12 takes precedence over any contrary law of a Member State. Further it states that the question as to whether the information was gathered in a legal manner by the transmitting authority is governed on the basis of the law applicable to this authority.

[184] Case T-125/03 R [2003] ECR II-4771, para 122. Note that the ECJ partially overturned the interim measures granted by the CFI in this case on appeal, Case C-7/04P [2004] ECR I-8739.

[185] Network Notice, para 37.

8.192 It is for this reason that the OFT and the other members of the ECN went to great lengths to ensure that the information provided by leniency applicants is protected (at least in the short term). The commitment of the ECN members to protect leniency is manifested in the Network Notice, which provides for self-imposed restrictions on the exchange of leniency related information that may be made within the ECN. All Member States have indicated that they shall abide by the principles set out in the Network Notice.

(a) ECN and leniency

(i) *Regulation 1/2003 and leniency*

8.193 Regulation 1/2003 does not make any attempt to create a one-stop-shop leniency procedure, nor to ensure that all Member States have a leniency programme, nor to harmonise the leniency programmes which currently exist across Europe. As at December 2006, 19 Member States have a national leniency programme and two more will soon come into force.[186] The current list is available online.[187] In addition, the European Commission operates a leniency programme.

8.194 However, Regulation 1/2003 gave rise to a serious new risk to the effectiveness of existing leniency programmes by introducing a relatively unlimited power for national competition authorities to exchange information, including leniency information. This gave rise to a possibility that leniency applicants applying for leniency in one jurisdiction would face enforcement action in other jurisdictions on the basis of the information supplied to the first jurisdiction—a significant deterrent for any undertaking considering whistleblowing.

(ii) *Agreement between national competition authorities*

8.195 The risk to leniency programmes was addressed in the Network Notice. Paragraphs 37 to 42 of the Network Notice set out the principles that were agreed between the competition authorities and the European Commission relating to the disclosure and use of information relating to leniency applications. These paragraphs set out a number of principles, which may be summarised as follows:

- a leniency application to one competition authority is not to be considered as an application for leniency to any other competition authority;

- the basic information about a case which is submitted to the ECN at the outset of a leniency case pursuant to Article 11(3) of Regulation 1/2003 cannot be used by another competition authority to start an investigation;

- case information submitted pursuant to Article 11(3), where the case has been

---

[186] <http://ec.europa.eu/comm/competition/ecn/index_en.html>.
[187] <http://ec.europa.eu/comm/competition/antitrust/legislation/authorities_with_leniency_programme.pdf>.

initiated as a result of a leniency application, will only be made available to those competition authorities that have committed themselves to respecting the principles set out in the Network Notice;[188]

- information relating to a leniency application will only be disclosed to another member of the ECN pursuant to Article 12 with the consent of the leniency applicant, except:
  - where the receiving authority has also received a leniency application from the same applicant and related to the same infringement; or
  - where the receiving authority provides a written commitment that it will not use such information to impose sanctions on the leniency applicant; or
  - the transfer of information pursuant to Article 12 is made following a specific request by the authority to whom the leniency application was made to gather information under Article 22(1) of Regulation 1/2003.[189]

The practical effect and interpretation of these principles is not immediately **8.196** apparent. The key areas where difficulties arise are discussed below.

Article 11(3) information Paragraph 39 of the Network Notice makes it clear **8.197** that where a case has been initiated as a result of a leniency application, information provided to the ECN pursuant to Article 11(3) may not be used by other members of the network as the basis for starting an investigation on their own behalf whether under the competition rules of the Treaty or, in the case of national authorities, under their national competition law or other laws. However, the restriction in Article 11(3) does not prevent a national authority from opening an investigation on the basis of information received from other sources.

The protected information There are also limitations on the exchange of **8.198** other information relating to a leniency application. Such information may only be exchanged under Article 12 of Regulation1/2003 with the consent of the leniency applicant, or under the specific conditions provided at para 41 of the Network Notice. According to para 40, protected information relating to a leniency application includes:

- information voluntarily submitted by a leniency applicant; and
- other information which has been obtained during or following an inspection or by means of or following any other fact finding measures which, in each case, could not have been carried out except as a result of the leniency application.

---

[188] Network Notice, para 42. This safeguard is no longer relevant, as all Member States, including Greece and Spain, have now indicated that they will abide by the principles set out in the Network Notice.
[189] Network Notice, para 41.

8.199 This would, therefore, exclude information obtained by a national authority as a result of an investigative measure carried out before the leniency applicant came forward. This would clearly provide very little benefit to a leniency applicant who comes forward after the first inspection has been carried out, for example. It is also going to be unhelpful to a leniency applicant who provides very little additional or new information to a case. Thus a leniency applicant who is second or third in line is unlikely to benefit from these provisions unless it can deliver to the competition authority information which the authority had not yet obtained and was vital or very important to establishing a case.

8.200 **Where the consent of the leniency applicant is not required**   The first exception to the general rule that the consent of the leniency applicant is required before protected information may be transmitted relates to a situation where the receiving authority has also received a leniency application. This application must relate to the 'same infringement' and be from the 'same applicant'. However, this is only an option provided that 'at the time the information is transmitted it is not open to the applicant to withdraw the information which it has submitted to that receiving authority'.

8.201 In a circumstance where information is transmitted pursuant to a written commitment not to use such evidence to impose sanctions, the relevant evidence includes not only the information transmitted by the relevant competition authority, but also any information which the receiving authority 'may obtain following the date and time of transmission'.[190] Note that the commitment is not to impose sanctions, rather than not to bring proceedings or make a bare finding of infringement (the latter is significant as such a finding can give rise to exposure to civil claims for damages).

8.202 In respect of the few national competition authorities that do not yet have a leniency programme, this is one of the most important protections for a leniency applicant. It provides a general and easily determined cut-off date beyond which such information obtained by the relevant competition authority may not be used as evidence in order to impose sanctions upon the leniency applicant. This does not require any test as to whether or not such information may or may not have been able to be obtained without the leniency applicant's information. Where competition authorities do have leniency programmes, applications would normally be made to the relevant national authority and/or to the European Commission.

8.203 A written commitment by the receiving authority not only covers the leniency applicant but also covers 'any other legal or natural person covered by the

---

[190] ibid, para 41(2).

favourable treatment offered by the transmitting authority as a result of the application made by the applicant under its leniency program' and any employee or former employee of such a person, or of the leniency applicant. In this way, the protection offered by the receiving authority is, in some cases, more extensive than the protection offered by the original leniency programme.

Enforceability   On the basis of the statement annexed to the Network Notice,   **8.204** which has been signed by the OFT, along with other national competition authorities, an undertaking which believes that it has received treatment contrary to the principles set out in the Network Notice (in particular those relating to the treatment of leniency applications) would be likely to have a cause of action based on legitimate expectations. In addition, a leniency applicant in respect of whose information a written commitment had been provided by the receiving authority, would have a further basis for a claim based on legitimate expectation.[191]

The written commitment provided by the receiving authority is in fact a com-   **8.205** mitment made to the transmitting authority, and not to the leniency applicant itself. For these reasons, it may well be the preferred course for a leniency applicant to consent to a transmission of its information pursuant to Article 12, subject to a specific agreement with each of the transmitting authority and the receiving authority. This agreement would cover the requirement that the receiving authority not disclose the information any further, it would detail the information to be covered, and, if possible, it may note that the written commitment is not to bring proceedings at all (not simply to agree not to use evidence to impose sanctions). It would need to describe the infringement and the facts very carefully and also note the date and time of the transmission of the information. Such an agreement could also detail the parties against whom the proceedings can be brought. In this way, the principles set out in the Network Notice can be tailored to a specific case, and in doing so, would make most of the powers of the receiving authority in question and would also provide a direct, contractual-type obligation as between the leniency applicant and both authorities in relation to the transmission of the leniency applicant's information. For further discussion of leniency under Regulation 1/2003, see Chapter 5.

(b) Information disclosure to the United States and other countries where leniency applicant involved

OFT guidelines provide that where an individual has voluntarily provided   **8.206** information as part of a leniency application, the OFT will not disclose the information to an overseas authority for the purpose of a criminal cartel

---

[191] A copy of the receiving authority's written commitment is to be provided to the leniency applicant: Network Notice, footer 1(2).

prosecution unless the individual were granted immunity from prosecution.[192] Further, where a company has provided information as part of a leniency application, the OFT will not disclose this information to the overseas authority for the purposes of cartel enforcement against that company, unless the company benefits from a similar leniency arrangement with the overseas authority. The OFT might however disclose the information for the purpose of enforcement against a company or individual other than the provider of the information.

F. Disclosure and Use of Information in Practice within the United Kingdom

8.207 The interests and functions of the various UK regulators overlap to varying degrees. Consequently, regulatory authorities will frequently need (or wish) to disclose information to one another to facilitate a coordinated and effective approach to competition enforcement. There are two main types of constraint to such 'pooling of information' by the competition authorities.

8.208 First, there are constraints on disclosure that arise by virtue of domestic law. In making disclosure, an authority will have to consider the Enterprise Act 2002, the Human Rights Act 1998, the Data Protection Act 1998, and administrative law principles of fairness of procedure. See section B above for a discussion of these constraints.

8.209 Secondly, separate limitations under European law restrict the use to which certain of the information received may be put by the receiving authority (see section D above).

8.210 In the sections below, we consider the various situations in which UK competition authorities may need or may be tempted to disclose information to another UK competition authority, and whether and to what extent sharing the information is possible by reference to the various applicable provisions of European and domestic law.

(a) Disclosure between the OFT and the Regulators

(i) OFT and the Regulators

8.211 The OFT and the Regulators[193] interact with each other in two separate guises.

8.212 First and foremost, they work together in applying the Competition Act 1998.

---

[192] OFT507, *The overseas disclosure of information: Consultation paper* (April 2003) paras 5.7–5.9.

[193] Defined at paras 2.14–2.18 above.

Sectoral regulators have powers to apply the Competition Act concurrently with the OFT in relation to the regulated sectors.[194] As the Regulators have all the powers of the OFT to apply and enforce the Competition Act in their designated sector, there is a need for close coordination between the Regulators and the OFT to avoid inefficient and possible over-enforcement of the Competition Act. To this end, the OFT and the Regulators meet regularly in a group known as the 'Concurrency Working Party'.

Secondly, the OFT and the Regulators are designated as UK competition **8.213** authorities empowered to apply Articles 81 and 82 for the purposes of Regulation 1/2003 in the United Kingdom (within their respective sectors). They are accordingly all members of the ECN and liaise with each other with powers for disclosure of information that are provided in Regulation 1/2003 (these powers are considered at section C above).

(ii) What regime applies to govern information disclosure?

When the OFT and the Regulators obtain information in the context of an **8.214** Article 81 or Article 82 investigation which they have conducted under Pt I of the Competition Act 1998, do they exchange this under domestic law facilitating such exchanges or under the scheme for exchange of information between national competition authorities set up in Regulation 1/2003? The OFT and the Regulators have indicated that the exchange of all information obtained by them in the exercise of Pt I powers, be it for a suspected Chapter I, Chapter II, Article 81 or Article 82 infringement, shall be governed by Pt 9 of the Enterprise Act 2002 rather than Regulation 1/2003 (for reasons that are not elaborated).[195]

There is a question mark over whether these exchanges of information should **8.215** not also be conducted in a way that complies with Regulation 1/2003 and the general principles of Community law. Information collected in relation to possible Article 81/Article 82 infringements is collected under powers provided to national competition authorities in Article 5 of Regulation 1/2003, and arguably collected 'pursuant' to Regulation 1/2003. Article 28 of Regulation is expressed to apply to information acquired pursuant to Regulation 1/2003. Further, by virtue of the primacy of Community law, Member States must apply general principles of EC law when they apply Community law.[196]

Whatever the merits of this argument, the practice is that the OFT and **8.216** Regulators apply Pt 9 of the Enterprise Act 2002 to information exchange.

---

[194] Competition Act 1998, s 54.
[195] OFT405, *Concurrent application to regulated industries* (December 2004) para 5.4.
[196] Case 5/88 *Wachauf v Germany* [1989] ECR 2609, paras 17 and 19.

8.217 **Concurrency Regulations**   The Competition Act 1998 (Concurrency) Regulations 2004[197] enable certain exchanges information between the OFT and the Regulators, in the context of deciding whether a case ought to be conducted by the OFT or one of the Regulators, and to enable the transfer of a case both before and after any investigation has taken place. Such disclosure is compatible with Pt 9 by virtue of s 237(6) of the Act, as it amounts to a power to disclose which exists separately from Pt 9. Section 3 of the Concurrency Regulations allows a 'competent person' (defined as the OFT or a Regulator) to send to any other competent person any details of any information received relating to an infringement of the Chapter I prohibition, the Chapter II prohibition, or the prohibition in Article 81(1) or Article 82.

8.218 Further, reg 7 of the Concurrency Regulations provides for the ability to transfer a case between the OFT and/or any of the Regulators upon reaching agreement for such transfer to take place. In the event of such a transfer, there are provisions in the Concurrency Regulations for the undertaking the subject of the investigation to be notified of the transfer.[198] Further, s 241(2) of the Enterprise Act 2002 enables the OFT to disclose to the Regulators any information that facilitates the exercise by that authority of a function under, inter alia, the Competition Act 1998 and any enactment specified under Sch 15 to the Enterprise Act.[199] Disclosure under s 241(2) is subject to the balancing test set out in s 244 of the Enterprise Act. In all cases, prior to effecting disclosure, the disclosing authorities will have to consider whether the Human Rights Act 1998 and the duty to act fairly give rise to a right to give the undertaking notice of the disclosure.[200]

8.219 **Regulation 1/2003**   As the OFT and each of the Regulators are also members of the ECN, the provisions of Regulation 1/2003 which relate to the disclosure of information between ECN members also apply to any disclosure of information between the OFT and the Regulators in their role as fellow ECN members. However, as indicated above, exchange in this context will only relate to those cases which have been notified to the ECN and will not apply to domestic exchanges of information relating to cases that are being investigated by the OFT and the Regulators under Articles 81 and 82 EC.

---

[197] Competition Act 1998 (Concurrency) Regulations 2004, SI 2004/1077.
[198] ibid, reg 7(2)–(4).
[199] Sch 15 specifies relevant sectoral legislation such as the Gas Act 1986, the Water Act 1989, the Electricity Act 1989, etc.
[200] See paras 8.70–8.73 above.

(b) Disclosure and use of information collected in a regulatory context for the prosecution of the cartel offence

(i) Disclosure and use

As we saw above at paras 8.32 and 8.33, s 242 of the Enterprise Act 2002 **8.220** authorises the disclosure of specified information by public authorities to any person in connection with a possible or on-going criminal investigation in the United Kingdom, or for criminal proceedings. Therefore, the OFT and the CC may disclose information collected in the context of their investigations under the Competition Act and Enterprise Act to the SFO for the purposes of an actual or potential prosecution of the cartel offence under s 188 of the Enterprise Act. Alternatively the OFT may itself disclose the information in the context of such a prosecution, by virtue of s 241(1) of the Enterprise Act (which permits disclosure by the collecting authority for any of its stat-utory functions). There are, however, several restrictions on the power to disclose or use information collected in a regulatory context towards a criminal prosecution.

(ii) Restrictions

Enterprise Act 2002, ss 244 and 242(3)   In addition to the balancing test set **8.221** out in s 244 (see paras 8.34 et seq above for a discussion of this test), s 242(3) requires that the disclosing authority satisfy itself, prior to disclosure under the s 242 gateway, that the making of disclosure is proportionate to what is sought to be achieved by it.

Human Rights Act 1998/administrative fairness   Further, it will have to con- **8.222** sider whether there is any requirement, either by virtue of the common law duty to exercise statutory powers fairly, or under Article 6 ECHR, to give notice to the person concerned either prior to or after the disclosure is made.[201]

Competition Act 1998, s 30A and the privilege against self- **8.223** **incrimination**   The SFO and the OFT are precluded from relying on certain information in prosecution in order to protect the privilege against self-incrimination. Sections 30A, 65B, and 65K of the Competition Act 1998 pro-vide that statements made to the OFT pursuant to the OFT's compulsory powers under Pts I, II, and IIA of the Competition Act respectively may not be relied upon in evidence against that person in a prosecution under s 188 of the Enterprise Act 2002 unless, in giving evidence, the person makes a statement that is inconsistent with it or the person adduces evidence relating to it. Similar

---

[201] See paras 8.70 et seq above.

restrictions apply to information collected by the SFO using its compulsory powers under the Criminal Justice Act 1987.[202]

8.224 **Criminal standards of evidence collection**   Further, where the SFO/OFT are unable to prove to criminal standard the origin of the documents, they may not adduce them as evidence in criminal proceedings. The OFT has indicated that it intends that, when conducting investigations under the Competition Act 1998 in relation to horizontal cartels, its procedures in relation to exhibit and property handling, and the storage, management, and control of documents conform to the standards of a criminal investigation. The OFT may also use its formal criminal powers of investigation under the Enterprise Act 2002 to obtain original versions of documents obtained under a Competition Act investigation.[203]

8.225 **Articles 12 and 28(2) of Regulation 1/2003**   Article 28(2) of Regulation 1/2003 precludes disclosure of information covered by the obligation of professional secrecy from a national competition authority outside the ECN. Information received from the ECN cannot therefore be disclosed by the OFT to the SFO. Further, Article 12(2) would appear to preclude the use of network information by the OFT itself towards prosecuting the cartel offence, because the cartel offence is not 'national competition law'.[204] The OFT may, however, use network information as intelligence to initiate an investigation into the cartel offence.[205]

(c) Disclosure of information collected in the context of the cartel offence for the application of the competition prohibitions or market investigations

(i) Disclosure and use

8.226 This section addresses the use by the OFT of information collected pursuant to its powers to investigate criminal cartels under the Enterprise Act 2002. Information collected by the OFT pursuant to Pt 6 of the Act is specified information to which Pt 9 applies. Where the OFT finds, in the course of an investigation under Pt 6, information that would assist OFT itself or another authority in the performance of any statutory function, it may disclose that information for the purpose of its own statutory functions or disclose the information to the other authority under s 241 of the Act—the statutory functions gateway. The SFO, for its part, is empowered to provide documents obtained under its own powers to the OFT or the CC under s 3(5)(a) of the Criminal Justice Act 1987.

---

[202] See Chapter 7 more generally for a discussion of the privilege against self-incrimination.
[203] OFT515, *Powers for investigating criminal cartels* (January 2004) para 4.9.
[204] See paras 8.165–8.167 above.   [205] See para 8.167 above.

(ii) Restrictions

Human Rights Act 1998/privilege against self-incrimination   The OFT has   **8.227**
indicated that it will not rely in evidence on compulsory statements taken from
individuals in the context of a cartel investigation under the Enterprise Act
against the undertakings employing the individual in an investigation under
the Competition Act.[206] As with any disclosure, the disclosing authority (be it
the OFT or the SFO) should also consider whether it should provide the
undertaking concerned with notice of intended disclosure.[207]

(d) OFT and the CC

(i) Disclosure

The OFT has a statutory obligation, under s 170 of the Enterprise Act 2002,   **8.228**
to pass to the CC such information that it has in its possession that the
Commission may reasonably require to carry out the market investigation
reference or that would in the OFT's opinion be appropriate to give to the
Commission for the purpose of assisting it in carrying out its functions.
The OFT can therefore avail of two gateways to make the disclosure under the
Enterprise Act. First, s 241(3) permits disclosure for the purpose of facilitating
any of the disclosing authority's statutory obligations. Alternatively, s 241(3)
permits disclosure to another person to facilitate the exercise by that person of
any function conferred by the Enterprise Act 2002, the Competition Act 1998,
and a number of other enactments.[208]

Conversely, should the CC need to transmit information to the OFT—for   **8.229**
example where it 'remits' potential Article 81 agreements to the OFT—it is able
to transmit the information related thereto under s 241(3) to facilitate the
OFT's exercise of its statutory functions.

(ii) Restrictions

Regulation 1/2003   The OFT cannot, under Article 28(2) of Regulation   **8.230**
1/2003 (which takes precedence over any conflicting provision of national law)
transmit any information it has received from the ECN to the CC, as the
Commission has not been designated as a UK competition authority, and is thus
not a member of the ECN.[209]

Human Rights Act 1998/administrative fairness   The OFT and CC will have   **8.231**
to consider whether there is any requirement, either by virtue of the common

---

[206] OFT515, *Powers for investigating criminal cartels* (January 2004) para 4.3.
[207] See para 8.70 above.
[208] See Enterprise Act 2002, Sch 15 for a list of these enactments.
[209] See paras 8.177 et seq above for the restraints on disclosure of information on national
competition authorities under Article 28(2) of Regulation 1/2003.

law duty to exercise statutory powers fairly, or under Article 6 ECHR, to give notice to the person or undertaking concerned either prior to or after the disclosure is made.[210]

8.232 **Information collected under the Competition Act** OFT guidance indicates that it is able to use information collected under the Competition Act 1998 towards making a market investigation reference.[211] There are arguably some impediments to this usage under Community law. Domestic law is subject to any overriding provisions of Community law.[212] Community law potentially threatens the OFT's ability to use information it has collected under the Competition Act towards another purpose in two ways.

8.233 First, it is arguable that Regulation 1/2003 takes effect to prevent the OFT from transmitting information it received in investigating Article 81 and Article 82 cases under the Competition Act to the CC (or any other party), or to disclose that information in a market investigation reference. Article 28(2) of Regulation 1/2003 imposes a requirement of professional secrecy in relation to all information acquired pursuant to Regulation 1/2003. This obligation precludes disclosure by the OFT of such information outside the ECN, even if the disclosure is to another UK statutory body.[213] Arguably, OFT investigations of suspected breaches of Article 81 and/or Article 82 are carried out *pursuant to* Articles 5 and 35 of Regulation 1/2003, which (respectively) empower national competition authorities to apply Articles 81 and 82 EC and impose an obligation on the Member States to designate the authorities responsible for applying Articles 81 and 82. On this view, Article 28(2) bites on information collected by the OFT in the course of such investigations, even if the investigatory powers used by the OFT are provided by national law. The restriction on disclosure contained in Article 28(2) may therefore operate effectively to prevent the OFT from disclosing information to make a reference. It would not appear to be able to pass the information on to the CC (which is not a member of the ECN) nor could it rely on it in the context of market investigation references, which it is obliged to publish. There is some scope for the OFT to use information acquired pursuant to Regulation 1/2003 as intelligence, which is explored in greater detail at paras 8.146–8.149.[214]

8.234 Secondly, one could seek to rely on the general principle that information

---

[210] See para 8.70 above.

[211] OFT511, *Market investigation references: Guidance about the making of references under Part 4 of the Enterprise Act* (March 2006) para 3.4.

[212] See Chapter 3, generally, for a discussion of the supremacy of European law.

[213] On Art 28(2), see paras 8.177 et seq above.

[214] See paras 8.146–8.149 relating to the OFT's ability to use information collected or received under Regulation 1/2003 as intelligence, despite Art 28.

cannot subsequently be used in a different legal context,[215] to preclude such usage. This argument is difficult though, where the legal context includes statutory provisions authorising the disclosure[216] and express guidance that such disclosure is envisaged by the collecting authority.

(e) Disclosure to courts in the United Kingdom

(i) National courts in the United Kingdom

Enterprise Act 2002   Part 9 does not provide public authorities with a gateway **8.235** to disclose specified information to business and individuals for the purpose of civil proceedings enforcing the competition prohibitions (or any other proceedings). The general prohibition in s 237 of the Act therefore applies to prohibit such disclosure. Litigants wishing to have access to information held by the OFT to assist their case must seek a court order for non-party disclosure under s 34 of the Supreme Court Act 1981 (as amended) and CPR r 31.17. If ordered to make disclosure, the OFT and other regulators can disclose information without breaching the prohibition in the Enterprise Act.[217]

The Companies Act 2006 added a new section 241A to Part 9 of the Enterprise **8.236** Act to allow disclosure for civil proceedings. At time of writing the DTI is conducting a consultation exercise on secondary legislation allowing such disclosure.[218]

Article 15 of Regulation 1/2003   Pursuant to Regulation 1/2003, the Com- **8.237** petition Law Practice Direction[219] provides a right for the OFT to make written observations to national courts. The OFT may also apply for permission to make oral representations at the hearing of the claim.[220] In this way, the OFT may provide information to a national court, as information disclosed pursuant to its power to make representations is compatible with the Enterprise Act 2002 (disclosed pursuant to a statutory function) and with Regulation 1/2003 (Article 28 is expressed to be without prejudice to Article 15). Similar rights also apply to the European Commission in respect of national courts in the United Kingdom.

(ii) The CAT and appeals

Enterprise Act 2002   The OFT has no power to disclose specified information **8.238** under Pt 9 for the purpose of civil proceedings. Further, it takes the view that it

---

[215] Case 85/87 *Dow Benelux v Commission* [1989] ECR 3137 and Competition Act 1998, s 60.

[216] Enterprise Act 2002, Pt 9.

[217] ibid, s 237(6) provides that Pt 9 will not affect a duty to disclose that exists apart from the Act.

[218] <http://www.dti.gov.uk/consultations/page35922.html>.

[219] Civil Procedure Rules, *Practice Direction (Competition law—Claims relating to the application of Articles 81 and 82 of the EC Treaty and Chapters 1 and 2 of Part 1 of the Competition Act 1998).*

[220] ibid, para 4.

cannot disclose, pursuant to s 244, any confidential information held on its files to parties to an appeal before the CAT under an Enterprise Act gateway unless the CAT orders the disclosure.[221] Parties to an appeal who wish to have sight of confidential material held by the OFT to inform their submissions on appeal must therefore apply to the CAT for disclosure. The CAT's approach to disclosure is discussed at paras 8.55 et seq.

8.239 Regulation 1/2003 Under Regulation 1/2003, disclosure of information from an ECN member to an appellate body or court is not treated as a disclosure of information contrary to Article 28 of Regulation 1/2003. This is because the disclosure to the appellate body is treated as use of the information for the purpose of applying Article 81 or Article 82 EC, permitted therefore under Article 12 of the Regulation. However, this assumption has not been tested. In the United Kingdom, the competition authorities which have been designated for the purposes of Regulation 1/2003 have not included appellate bodies. Therefore, the CAT, for example, has not been designated as a competition authority pursuant to Regulation 1/2003. This is different to those Member States which operate systems involving judicial authorities at the initial decision making stage.[222]

(iii) Other UK persons/bodies

8.240 Arbitrators There is no legislative or policy basis allowing for the disclosure of information to or from arbitrators and the OFT, or the European Commission. Any such disclosure would therefore have to be made with the agreement of the relevant parties.

8.241 Interested parties Main and third parties to proceedings being conducted by the OFT, the SFO, or the CC, may have certain rights of access to the relevant files. Those rights are discussed in detail in Chapters 9, 13, and 14. Apart from those rights, there is no general right for an interested party to receive information from any UK authority.

(f) Disclosure by UK authorities to the ECN

(i) OFT disclosure to the ECN

8.242 Enterprise Act 2002 The OFT's competition law guidelines take the view that the information disclosed to the ECN is disclosed pursuant to a *power*

---

[221] In which case disclosure is made pursuant to a duty that exists outside Pt 9.

[222] Recital 35 of Regulation 1/2003 draws a distinction between a situation where a prosecuting authority brings a case before a separate judicial authority and cases where courts are acting as review courts.

that exists apart from Pt 9, so that the s 244 balancing test applies to any disclosure.[223]

The OFT guidelines confirm that the OFT will be applying the s 244 test prior **8.243** to making disclosure pursuant to the Modernisation Regulation.[224] This provides a useful lever for those undertakings who wish to resist onward disclosure by the OFT of confidential information affecting their interests.

(ii) CC disclosure to the ECN

As the CC is not designated as a national competition authority for the purposes **8.244** of Regulation 1/2003, it is not empowered to disclose information to the ECN under Article 12 of Regulation 1/2003. If it is required to make a disclosure of specified information under the Enterprise Act 2002 to the ECN pursuant to its obligation of faithful cooperation under Article 10 EC, it could possibly seek to make the disclosure under s 240.

(g) Decisions to transmit information to and from UK authorities: challenge?

(i) Commission decision to transmit to UK authorities

Regulation 1/2003 does not provide a right of appeal regarding any transmis- **8.245** sion of information to the network. In fact there is no obligation even to inform any of the parties or third parties of the transmissions of information, there is only mention of informing parties and complainants as soon as possible if a case is reallocated.[225]

Those wishing to challenge transmission of information by the Commission to **8.246** UK authorities under Regulation 1/2003 will have to rely on Article 230 EC which provides for judicial review of Community acts. An undertaking wishing to challenge transmission of information under Article 230 EC has two hurdles to overcome.

First, it has to establish that there is a challengeable act within the meaning of **8.247** Article 230. Whether an undertaking can challenge the transmission will depend on whether it can characterise the decision to transmit the information to the network or the transmission itself as a challengeable 'decision' or 'act' within the jurisprudence of the ECJ. Any measure which produces binding legal effects such as to affect the interests of an undertaking by bringing about a

---

[223] Enterprise Act 2002, s 237(6). However, there is some uncertainty on the appropriate gateway, see paras 8.25 and 8.26 above.
[224] OFT442, *Modernisation* (December 2004) para 9.7 and OFT404, *Powers of investigation* (December 2004) para 6.13. For a contrary view, see R Nazzini, *Concurrent Proceedings in Competition Law* (Oxford University Press, 2004) paras 8.59 and 8.60.
[225] Network Notice, para 34.

distinct change in its legal position is an act or decision that may be subject of an action under Article 230 EC.[226] The difficulty is that the decision to transmit, like many other investigatory steps, may simply be viewed as a preparatory measure leading to a decision. In *Nefarma v Commission*[227] a letter by the Commissioner for competition expressing the Commission's views on an agreement and factual suggestions for amendment of the agreement did not qualify as a challengeable act, even though the letter affected the course taken by the Dutch authorities in relation to the agreement.

8.248 Secondly, the undertaking has to establish standing—that it is directly and individually concerned by the decision or act it wishes to challenge.[228] Although this is generally a very difficult hurdle to overcome, in competition matters it is more readily satisfied.[239] Readers are referred to dedicated textbooks on procedure before the European courts for a fuller explanation as to standing and what amounts to a challengeable act and under Article 230 EC.[230]

(ii) UK law

8.249 A disclosure and breach of the Enterprise Act 2002 may be subject to offences, as set out in s 245. The individual or undertaking to which the information relates would (presumably) also have a right of civil redress for breach of a statutory duty.

8.250 A decision by the OFT to disclose information to the ECN most probably does not amount to a decision as to whether or not there has been an infringement under s 46 of the Competition Act 1998, and so does not give rise to an appeal to the CAT.[231] However, there is always the possibility of proceeding by way of judicial review before the High Court.[232] An undertaking wishing to challenge a decision making disclosure of information by UK competition authorities must proceed by the usual judicial review channels.[233] The difficulty in bringing such a challenge is that there is usually no notice of such decisions to the undertaking concerned.[234]

---

[226] Case T-125/97 *Coca-Cola Co v Commission* [2000] ECR II-1733.

[227] Case T-113/89 [1990] ECR II-797.

[228] Case 25/62 *Plaumann & Co v Commission* [1963] ECR 95.

[239] See Case 26/76 *Metro-SB-Grossmarkte GmBH v Commission* [1977] ECR 1875.

[230] H Schermers and D Waelbroeck, *Judicial Protection in the European Union* (Kluwer Law International, 2002); A Arnull, *The European Court of Justice* (2nd edn, Oxford University Press, 2006); Lasok, Millet and Howard, *Judicial Control in the EU* (OUP, USA, 2004).

[231] See Chapter 12 for a discussion of what amounts to an appealable decision under the Competition Act.

[232] See Chapter 12 on judicial review before the High Court.

[233] *R (Kent Pharmaceuticals Ltd) v Director of the SFO* [2004] EWCA 1494, [2005] 1 WLR 1302.

[234] See paras 8.53 and 8.70.

Alternatively, if a judicial review claim is not brought against the relevant **8.251** decision making the disclosure, it may subsequently be possible to challenge the disclosure when an authority places reliance in evidence on information wrongfully received from another authority.[235]

In relation to a transmission of information in breach of a particular obligation, **8.252** the undertaking may be able to challenge the transmission on the basis that the OFT was in breach of its undertaking not to disclose such information. Where a specific obligation has not been provided to the undertaking in question, but the OFT has stated its position (as for example, in relation to the transmission of information received from a leniency applicant), the review of transmission could be based upon breach of a legitimate expectation.

G. Overseas Disclosures

Section 243(1) of the Enterprise Act 2002 provides that a public authority may **8.253** disclose information to an overseas public authority for the purposes set out in s 243(2), namely:

> facilitating the exercise by the overseas public authority of any function which it has relating to—
>
> (a) carrying out investigations in connection with the enforcement of any relevant legislation by means of civil proceedings;
> (b) bringing civil proceedings for the enforcement of such legislation or the conduct of such proceedings;
> (c) the investigation of crime;
> (d) bringing criminal proceedings or the conduct of such proceedings;
> (e) deciding whether to start or bring to an end such investigations or proceedings.

Overseas public authority is broadly defined in s 243(11) as 'a person or body in **8.254** any country or territory outside the United Kingdom which appears to the discloser to exercise functions of a public nature in relation to any of the matters mentioned in paragraph (a) to (e) of sub-section (2)'. This definition allows disclosure to other competition authorities within the ECN. However, the OFT has indicated[236] that it will not disclose information pursuant to s 243 where other relevant Enterprise Act gateways are available, including where:

- disclosure is made for the purpose of a Community obligation (s 240);
- disclosure is made under powers or duties which exist apart from Pt 9 (Regulation 1/2003 is one such source of powers/duties).[237]

---

[235] *R v Brady* [2004] EWCA Crim 1763, [2004] 1 WLR 3240.
[236] OFT507, *The overseas disclosure of information: Consultation paper* (April 2003).
[237] ibid, para 3.7.

8.255 Section 243(3) of the Enterprise Act 2002 provides for certain exceptions to the power to disclose specified information to an overseas public authority. The power does not apply with respect to particular types of information identified in s 243(3). Information that comes to a public authority in connection with an investigation in relation to mergers or market investigations, for example, is one of the categories of information excluded from disclosure.[238] In addition, there is also a general power for the Secretary of State to direct that a particular disclosure must not be made if the Secretary of State thinks that the relevant investigation or proceedings are better carried out or conducted in the United Kingdom or in some other country.[239]

8.256 The OFT must have regard to the provisions of s 244 of the Enterprise Act 2002 before disclosing any information to an overseas public authority. These requirements are set out in more detail in para 8.38 above.

8.257 Additionally, s 243(6) of the Enterprise Act lists a number of considerations to which the OFT must have regard in deciding whether to disclose information to an overseas authority. These include consideration as to the seriousness of the matter, whether the law of the relevant country provides appropriate protection against self-incrimination in criminal proceedings or in relation to the storage and disclosure of personal data. A further consideration is whether there are arrangements in place for the provision of mutual assistance as between the United Kingdom and the relevant country.

8.258 This latter consideration is considered somewhat differently. Where the OFT considers that the first three criteria in s 246(3) are met, the absence of a mutual assistance agreement will not prevent disclosure. If, however, there is doubt as to whether one of the first three criteria is met, the OFT will take particular account of mutual assistance arrangements.[240] It will generally assume that, in the absence of evidence to the contrary, where the United Kingdom has entered into bilateral or multilateral mutual assistance arrangements this will indicate that the first three criteria in s 246(3)(a) to (c) are met. Relevant mutual assistance arrangements include:[241]

- European Convention on Mutual Legal Assistance in Criminal Matters (1959), and Additional Protocol;

- Treaty on Mutual Assistance in Criminal Matters (UK/Canada, 1988);

---

[238] Enterprise Act 2002, s 243(3)(d).   [239] ibid, s 243(4).

[240] OFT507, *The overseas disclosure of information: Consultation paper* (April 2003) para 4.20.

[241] Note that the OECD has encouraged cooperation in law enforcement against cartels in two Recommendations: C(95)130/Final and C(98)35/Final.

- Treaty Between the Government of the United Kingdom of Great Britain and Northern Ireland and the Government of the United States of America on Mutual Legal Assistance in Criminal Matters (1994);

- Agreement between the Government of the United Kingdom of Great Britain and Northern Ireland and the Government of the Hong Kong Special Administrative Region of the People's Republic of China concerning Mutual Legal Assistance in Criminal Matters (1998).

The OFT takes the view that the disclosure of information for the purpose of **8.259** bringing civil and criminal proceedings on matters relating to competition law will generally be sufficiently serious for the purposes of s 243(6).[242] Further, as regards self-incrimination, the OFT has indicated that the laws of any signatory of the ECHR are considered to meet the requirements of adequate protection.[243] Regarding protection of personal data, EEA Member States who have implemented the Data Protection Directive meet these requirements.

The United States is considered by the OFT to meet the requirements of **8.260** s 243(6)(b) by virtue of protection afforded in relation to self-incrimination by the Fifth Amendment to its Constitution. Further, in the OFT's view, it has in place sufficient statutory safeguards to prevent the onward disclosure of information for the purposes of s 243(6)(c).[244]

The OFT may, pursuant to s 243(10), disclose information subject to the **8.261** condition that it must not be further disclosed without the agreement of the OFT. This sub-section also provides that information disclosed to an overseas authority must not otherwise be used by the overseas public authority for any purpose other than that for which it is first disclosed.[245] An overseas authority is obviously not bound by Article 243(10). But the OFT may, where relevant, consider an overseas authority's record relating to the use it made of information that has been provided to it by the OFT or other authorities in the past.[246] Alternatively, the mutual assistance arrangement relating to the disclosure may provide relevant safeguards. Section 243(10) is consistent with the non-binding OECD Best Practices for the formal exchange of information between competition authorities in Hard Core Cartel Investigation (October 2005), which provides that the requesting jurisdiction should use the information provided solely for the cartel in respect of which the request was made.

---

[242] OFT507, *The overseas disclosure of information: Consultation paper* (April 2003) para 4.3.
[243] ibid, para 4.8.   [244] ibid, paras 4.18 and 4.19.
[245] Enterprise Act 2002, s 243(10)(b).
[246] OFT507, *The overseas disclosure of information: Consultation paper* (April 2003) paras 5.12 and 5.13.

9

THE OFT'S DECISION-MAKING PROCESS

A. Introduction

9.01 This chapter deals with the competition enforcement decision-making procedures under the Competition Act 1998, including the Office of Fair Trading's (**OFT**) enforcement of Articles 81 and 82 EC. These procedures apply to both the OFT and the Regulators, and form part of the administrative procedure for competition enforcement. Essentially, the decision-making process commences with the issue of a Statement of Objections (previously known as a Rule 14 Notice) and concludes with the issue of a final decision or other means of disposal of the case.

9.02 The Competition Appeal Tribunal (**CAT**) has taken the opportunity from time to time to comment on the role of the OFT and, in particular, the dividing line between the appellate procedure before the CAT and the administrative procedure carried out by the OFT. In *Argos and Littlewoods*, the CAT commented:

> In the system as set up under the 1998 Act, the OFT in the administrative stage acts as investigator, prosecutor and, ultimately, decision maker. Broadly speaking, the OFT moves from the mode of investigation to the mode of prosecution when it is decided to issue a [Statement of Objections]. At that stage, however, the safeguards provided under [Rule 4] apply.[1]

9.03 The Statement of Objections is effectively a draft decision and sets out the evidence relied on and the factual and legal conclusions of the OFT. The Statement of Objections represents the culmination of what can be years of work on the part of the OFT. Once the Statement of Objections has been provided, the recipient undertaking is provided with an opportunity to respond to the Statement of Objections, both orally and in writing.

9.04 During this process, a number of important procedural issues arise, primarily concerning access to the OFT's file, protection of confidentiality, and third party involvement. In examining these procedural issues, it is apparent that many of the difficulties which arise during the decision-making process stem from the OFT's responsibility to act as both prosecutor and judge simultaneously. The OFT does not have a Hearing Officer (unlike the European Commission where the Hearing Officer reports directly to the Competition Commissioner) and, apart from the possibility of judicial review, there is no independent party to make decisions on these important issues until any appeal process against the final decision.[2]

---

[1] *Argos Ltd and Littlewoods Ltd v OFT* [2003] CAT 16, para 63.
[2] Note that there is no interim right of appeal: see Case C-51/92 P *Hercules Chemicals NV v Commission* [1999] ECR I-4235; Case T-7/89 *Hercules NV v Commission* [1991] ECR II-1711; Case C-238/99 P *Limburgse Vinyl Maatschappij NV (LVM) v Commission* [2002] ECR I-8375.

The decision-making process can take up to 18 months or more as there are no **9.05** specified legislative time limits. The longest case to date is the September 2005 *MasterCard* decision by OFT which took five and a half years.[3] The OFT has anticipated providing average time frame information, but this has not yet been published.[4] There may be any number of iterations of the Statement of Objections (called Supplementary Statements of Objections), thus further elongating the process.

B. Statement of Objections

(a) Basic requirements for a Statement of Objections

Before making an infringement decision, the OFT is required to provide a **9.06** Statement of Objections[5] to each person whom the OFT considers is a party to the alleged agreement, or is engaged in conduct which the OFT considers infringes one or more of the relevant competition law prohibitions.[6] In providing the Statement of Objections, the OFT must comply with the Competition Act 1998—and Articles 81 and/or 82 where appropriate—and the OFT's Procedural Rules, which specify the form and content of the Statement of Objections. In general, the OFT has an interest in delivering the broadest possible Statement of Objections, as it cannot raise new issues in the decision without having first given an undertaking the opportunity of addressing those issues in the Statement of Objections. Any attempt to do so could lead to the decision being, at least partly, annulled in any appeal.[7]

The Statement of Objections is required to state the facts on which the OFT **9.07**

---

[3] In a case management conference in *Floe Telecom Ltd (in administration) v Office of Communications*, case nos 1024/2/3/04 and 1027/2/3/04, 1 December 2004, Ofcom made a submission to the effect that it generally expects an investigation to be completed within 6 months in the case of a decision that there are no grounds for action, and within 12 months in the case of an infringement decision: transcript, p 7, Mr Hoskins.

[4] OFT's Annual Plan 2006–07.

[5] The Statement of Objections was previously known as a 'Rule 14 Notice' (as a reference to the relevant rule in the OFT's Rules), but following changes to the OFT's Rules, the OFT decided to adopt the language used by the European Commission to describe the notice as a Statement of Objections rather than by reference to a particular rule.

[6] The requirement to provide a Statement of Objections is set out in r 4 of the OFT's Procedural Rules.

[7] See *Allsports Ltd v OFT* [2004] CAT 1 (judgment on Allsports' application for summary judgment, 29 January 2004). The OFT is able to expand its case on appeal if the issue was raised and addressed during the administrative process, as this has no impact on the rights of defence. Note also that the Court of First Instance partly annulled the European Commission's decision against Archer Daniels Midland in Citric Acid Cartel for having introduced new elements not in its Statement of Objections: Case T-224/00 *Archer Daniels Midland Co v Commission* [2003] ECR II-2597.

relies, the objections raised by the OFT, the action the OFT proposes, and its reasons for the proposed action.[8] The substance of the Statement of Objections is discussed further below. Although the Statement of Objections does not need to provide any calculation of the proposed penalties, or state the amount of any proposed penalty, it does need to refer to the intention of the OFT to impose a financial penalty on the undertaking. In practice, the OFT will often set out in the Statement of Objections any other remedies which the OFT intends to impose, such as directions ordering cessation of the relevant conduct.

9.08 In the Statement of Objections, the OFT is also required to state the period in which the recipient may make written representations to the OFT identifying the information contained in the Statement of Objections which the recipient considers should be treated as confidential information.[9] The OFT's Procedural Rules do not specify a particular time period, and leave this to the OFT's discretion.

9.09 The Statement of Objections is also required to state the period within which the undertaking may make written representations to the OFT on the matters referred to in the Statement of Objections.[10] There is no specified time period and the time frame is left to the OFT's discretion. Eight weeks is likely to be the minimum period. During this period the undertaking has access to the OFT's file on the case. If written representations are not received by the OFT within the specified time period, the OFT may proceed with the case in the absence of such representations.[11]

(b) Publicity and confidentiality

(i) Is the Statement of Objections itself confidential?

9.10 The starting point is that the Statement of Objections in each case is a confidential document. There is no obligation on the OFT to publish a Statement of Objections, and it is very unlikely that the OFT would ever do so, as it is a criminal offence for the OFT to disclose confidential information.[12]

9.11 However, the OFT may publicise the fact that a Statement of Objections has been issued to the relevant parties and may include a certain amount of basic information in its press release. This is particularly likely where the fact of the investigation is already public knowledge or may become so, for example, where the case involves many parties, all of whom will receive a Statement of Objections. An OFT press statement can allow interested third parties to be

---

[8] OFT's Procedural Rules, r 5(2)(a).   [9] ibid, r 5(2)(b).   [10] ibid, r 5(2)(c).
[11] ibid, r 5(5).   [12] Enterprise Act 2002, Pt 9.

aware of the existence of the Statement of Objections and to participate in the decision-making process.[13]

Publicly listed undertakings will also need to consider whether they are under an **9.12** obligation pursuant to the Stock Exchange Rules to notify the market by way of a press release, once they have received a Statement of Objections. Such obligations may apply even though the Statement of Objections is a confidential document.

The confidentiality of the Statement of Objections may be limited in time. In **9.13** the case of an eventual appeal, it is likely that the Statement of Objections will itself become a relevant document and, in the same way as leniency applications, may be treated as a non-confidential document (with appropriate excisions) by the CAT in the course of the appeal.

(ii) Who receives a copy of the Statement of Objections?

The OFT is required to provide a Statement of Objections to 'each person **9.14** who the OFT considers is a party to the agreement, or is engaged in conduct, which the OFT considers infringes one or more of the prohibitions'.[14] A Statement of Objections is necessarily tailored to the undertaking which is the subject of the Statement of Objections. Where the OFT is alleging infringements on the part of more than one undertaking based on the same set of facts, the OFT will provide different versions of the Statement of Objections depending on the party receiving the Statement of Objections. Where a Statement of Objections contains matters which will affect a third party, the OFT will generally provide a redacted version (ie a non-confidential version) of the Statement of Objections to a third party.[15]

The OFT may also send a version of the Statement of Objections to the **9.15** European Commission (and possibly to other members of the European Competition Network (**ECN**)).[16] Where an OFT decision involves the application of Community competition law, the OFT is required to provide a copy of its draft decision to the European Commission.[17] The Statement of Objections would constitute a draft decision for this purpose. This requirement is intended to allow the European Commission an opportunity to review the proposed decision and, if necessary to ensure consistency in the application of European competition law, to intervene in the process by initiating proceedings pursuant

---

[13] Further information on third party involvement is set out at paras 9.84–9.107.

[14] OFT's Procedural Rules, r 4(2).

[15] OFT451, *Involving third parties in Competition Act investigations* (April 2006) para 3.15. In some cases the right to receive a non-confidential version is automatic: see discussion on third party involvement at paras 9.84–9.107, below.

[16] Pursuant to Enterprise Act 2002, s 240 (relating to Community obligations).

[17] Council Regulation (EC) 1/2003 of 16 December 2002 on the implementation of the rules on competition laid down in Articles 82 and 82 of the Treaty [2003] OJ L1/1, Art 11(4).

to Article 11(6) of Regulation 1/2003 (thereby taking over the case). Such interventions will, however, be exceedingly rare in practice. The provisions of Article 28 of Regulation 1/2003 are intended to keep such documents confidential within the ECN.[18] There is no specific restriction on whether the version sent should be the non-confidential version, but the OFT is likely to provide a non-confidential version for this purpose as that would be sufficient to fulfil the requirements of Regulation 1/2003.

9.16 In certain circumstances where parallel proceedings are being conducted by a national court, the OFT may provide a version of the Statement of Objections to the court.[19] The court should already be aware of the OFT's investigation, as (in the United Kingdom) there is a duty on the parties to inform the court if the OFT initiates an investigation.

(c) Burden and standard of proof

(i) Burden of proof

9.17 The legal burden of proof rests on the OFT to prove the infringement in question. This burden only applies in relation to the prohibition itself, and not to the question of whether the exemption conditions are satisfied in a particular case. For the latter question, the burden of proof rests on the undertaking claiming the benefit of the exemption conditions. Where this is raised by an undertaking the OFT must also decide whether the standard of proof has been satisfied by the evidence put forward by the undertaking.[20]

9.18 In some cases the evidential burden may switch by the operation of a legal presumption. For example, in relation to predatory pricing alleged under Article 82, certain evidence can give rise to a presumption that predatory pricing has occurred. If this evidence is sufficiently strong, the OFT may consider that the burden of proof switches to the undertaking whereby it would be required to establish that it has not engaged in infringing conduct.[21]

(ii) Standard of proof

9.19 Given the seriousness of the penalties which may apply in respect of breaches of competition law and the objective of setting a penalty with deterrence in mind,

---

[18] For a discussion on disclosure to the ECN and Art 28, see paras 8.138–8.190, above.

[19] By virtue of the gateways in Pt 9 of the Enterprise Act 2002.

[20] Competition Act 1998, s 9(2); Regulation 1/2003, Art 2.

[21] Note that the issue of whether legal burden of proof—as opposed to evidentiary burden—can switch, given Art 2 of Regulation 1/2003, was raised by a number of those commenting on the European Commission's *DG Competition discussion paper on the application of Article 82 of the Treaty to exclusionary abuses* (for links to the discussion paper and comments, see <http://ec.europa.eu/comm/competition/antitrust/others/article_82_review.html>).

there was a real question as to whether the appropriate standard of proof should be the criminal standard of 'beyond reasonable doubt', rather than the civil standard of the 'balance of probabilities'. This issue was raised before the CAT in *Napp v Director General of Fair Trading*,[22] where the CAT accepted the Director's concession that competition infringement proceedings under the Competition Act 1998 are 'criminal' for the purposes of Article 6 of the European Convention on Human Rights (**ECHR**). However, the CAT went on to find that the fact that Article 6 applies does not of itself lead to the conclusion that such proceedings must be subject to the rules and procedures that apply to the investigation and trial of offences classified as criminal offences under domestic law.[23] The CAT concluded:

> In those circumstances the conclusion we reach is that, formally speaking, the standard of proof in proceedings under the Act involving penalties is the civil standard of proof but that standard is to be applied bearing in mind that infringements of the Act are serious matters attracting severe financial penalty. It is for the Director to satisfy us in each case, on the basis of strong and compelling evidence, taking account of the seriousness of what is alleged, that the infringement is duly proved, the undertaking being entitled to the presumption of innocence, and to any reasonable doubt there may be.[24]

This wording created some confusion in relation to the applicable standard, and the standard of proof debate was raised again in the *Allsports* case before the CAT. The CAT took the opportunity to examine a number of wide ranging cases discussing the application of the standard of proof in quasi-criminal cases under domestic law, and to further clarify its judgment in *Napp*.[25] The CAT expressed concern that *Napp* 'might be interpreted by the OFT or other regulators in an unduly cautious way, inhibiting the enforcement of the Act'[26] and that it 'should not be interpreted as introducing the criminal standard through the back door'.[27]

9.20

The CAT accordingly noted that:

9.21

> It also follows that the reference by the Tribunal to 'strong and compelling' evidence

---

[22] *Napp Pharmaceutical Holdings Ltd v Director General of Fair Trading* [2002] CAT 1.

[23] ibid, para 101. Note that competition infringement proceedings are not 'criminal' for the purposes of national criminal law.

[24] ibid, para 109.

[25] *JJB Sports Plc and Allsports Ltd v OFT* [2004] CAT 17, paras 164–208. The judgment referred to cases including: *Re H (Minors) (Sexual abuse: Standard of proof)* [1996] AC 563; *B v Chief Constable of Avon and Somerset* [2001] 1 WLR 640; *Secretary of State for the Home Department v Rehman* [2001] UKHL 47, [2003] 1 AC 153; *R (McCann) v Crown Court of Manchester* [2002] UKHL 39, [2003] AC 787; *Gough v Chief Constable of Derbyshire* [2002] EWCA Civ 351, [2002] QB 1213; *Re T (Children) (Sexual abuse: Standard of proof)* [2004] EWCA Civ 558, [2004] 2 FLR 838; and *Re U (A child)* [2004] EWCA Civ 567, [2005] Fam 134; *Woolmington v DPP* [1935] AC 462.

[26] *JJB Sports Plc and Allsports Ltd v OFT* [2004] CAT 17, para 205.

[27] ibid, para 203.

at [109] of Napp should not be interpreted as meaning that something akin to the criminal standard is applicable to these proceedings. The standard remains the civil standard. The evidence must however be sufficient to convince the Tribunal in the circumstances of the particular case, and to overcome the presumption of innocence to which the undertaking concerned is entitled.

What evidence is likely to be sufficiently convincing to prove the infringement will depend on the circumstances and the facts . . .[28]

9.22 There is a subtle but significant distinction between the applicable standard of proof test on the one hand, and the nature, quality, and weight of the evidence required to satisfy the test on the other hand.[29] It is the latter measure which varies according to the individual circumstances of each case, and some assistance can be gleaned from the cases thus far to demonstrate the types of factors which are relevant. For example, it is clear that the gravity of the infringement, including whether it attracts a penalty, is a significant factor. In *Allsports*, the CAT held:

198. First, we accept that in the present case an allegation of an infringement of the Chapter I prohibition is a serious matter involving penalties.

199. Secondly, in our judgment it is important to distinguish between two different things: what the test is, on the one hand, and what is the nature of the evidence necessary to satisfy the test, on the other. As regards the test, the civil standard is the balance of probabilities. As regards the nature of the evidence, the authorities cited above show that where serious matters are in issue, for example conduct akin to dishonesty, the quality and weight of the evidence needs to be stronger than it would need to be if the allegations were less serious. As we understand *Re H*, the law in effect presumes that conduct akin to dishonesty, or capable of attracting penalties, is less likely than honest conduct. In addition, in a case such as the present, the presumption of innocence applies.

200. In these circumstances, in applying the balance of probabilities in a case involving penalties, the Tribunal must be satisfied that the quality and weight of the evidence is sufficiently strong to overcome the presumption that the party in question has not engaged in unlawful conduct. For example, if in a borderline case the decision is finely balanced and the Tribunal finds itself to-ing and fro-ing, the correct analysis is that the evidence is not sufficiently strong to satisfy the Tribunal on the balance of probabilities that the infringement occurred.

201. In other words, the Tribunal will not apply what Lord Bingham described in *B v Chief Constable* at [31] as a 'bare balance of probabilities' but will direct itself in accordance with the speech of Lord Nicholls in *Re H* at p. 586, that '. . . even in civil proceedings a court should be more sure before finding serious allegations proved than when deciding less serious or trivial matters'. We take the reference to 'more sure' in the speech of Lord Nicholls to be a reference to the quality and weight of the evidence to which the test is to be applied: the more serious the allegation, the more cogent should be the evidence before the court concludes that

---

[28] ibid, paras 204 and 205.
[29] ibid, para 199; *R (DJ) v Mental Health Review Tribunal* [2005] EWHC 587 (Admin), para 41, per Munby J.

the allegation is established on the preponderance of probabilities. Among many examples in the civil courts, we note in particular that this approach applies in cases involving the disqualification of directors, which is now one of the possible consequences of a finding of infringement under the Act, as mentioned above: see notably the judgment of Neuburger J as he then was in *Re Verby Print* [1998] 2 BCLC 23 [1998] BCC 652 under the heading 'The burden and standard of proof.'[30]

Where the matter involves a small or medium sized enterprise, this may have **9.23** some bearing on the nature and weight of evidence which will satisfy the standard of proof. In *Burgess*, the fact that the undertaking concerned was a smaller enterprise and benefited from immunity from penalties was considered to be relevant by the CAT. However, it was not clear from the decision precisely how this would affect the nature and weight of evidence required to satisfy the civil standard of proof.[31]

Where a case concerns a cartel and thus evidence may be expected to be difficult **9.24** to find, it may be that very little evidence will be required to satisfy the relevant civil standard of proof. In *Allsports*, the CAT commented (relying on the European Court of Justice (**ECJ**) ruling in *Aalborg Portland A/S v Commission*[32]):

> As regards price fixing cases . . . cartels are by their nature hidden and secret; little or nothing may be committed to writing. In our view, even a single item of evidence, or wholly circumstantial evidence, depending on the particular context in the particular circumstances, may be sufficient to meet the required standard.[33]

Thus the OFT must take great care in assessing the quality and weight of the **9.25** evidence it proposes to use in establishing that an infringement has occurred on the balance of probabilities.

Although the standard of proof for an undertaking proving the exemption **9.26** conditions are satisfied has not yet been considered by the CAT,[34] it seems clear that the appropriate standard of proof will also be the civil standard of proof, being proof on the balance of probabilities.

(d) Substance of the Statement of Objections

(i) Legal elements of the alleged infringement

In order to comply with the requirements of r 5(2)(a) of the OFT's Procedural **9.27** Rules, the Statement of Objections needs to address the legal elements of the

---

[30] *JJB Sports Plc and Allsports Ltd v OFT* [2004] CAT 17, paras 198–201.
[31] *Burgess (t/a JJ Burgess & Sons) v OFT* [2005] CAT 25, paras 115–120.
[32] Case C-204/00 P [2004] ECR I-123.
[33] *JJB Sports Plc and Allsports Ltd v OFT* [2004] CAT 17, para 206.
[34] Although this was discussed briefly in passing during the course of a case management conference on 31 March 2006 in *MasterCard UK Members Forum Ltd v OFT*, Case nos 1054, 1055 and 1056/1/1/05.

alleged infringement. New issues or evidence cannot be covered by any sub-sequent decision unless they are addressed in the Statement of Objections. It is important for a number of reasons for the legal case to be clearly set out in the Statement of Objections: first, it determines the parameters of the case against the undertaking; second, it is relevant to the undertaking's rights of defence and determining issues regarding access to file; third, it allows changes to the case to be readily identified so it is clear whether a supplementary Statement of Objections needs to be issued; and fourth, it determines the scope of any appeal, since new issues cannot be raised by the OFT on appeal unless it has addressed these at the administrative stage.[35]

9.28 **Legal elements of alleged infringement** The basic legal elements of the relevant competition law infringements are set out in Chapter 1, above. In essence, Article 81 and the Chapter I prohibition prohibit agreements between undertakings which have as their object or effect the prevention, restriction, or distortion of competition, within the common market (in the case of Article 81) or within the United Kingdom (in the case of the Chapter I prohibition), and which do not satisfy the exemption conditions. Article 82 and the Chapter II prohibition prohibit any abuse by one or more undertakings of a dominant position, within the common market or a substantial part of it (in the case of Article 82) or within the United Kingdom or any part of it (in the case of the Chapter II prohibition). In addition to these requirements, there are further obligations on the OFT resulting from the modernisation changes, concerning the effect on trade test, and the application of the legal exception regime.

9.29 **Effect on trade between Member States** As a result of the obligation on the OFT to apply Articles 81 and/or 82 wherever it applies domestic competition law,[36] the OFT will need to address the question of whether or not there is an effect on trade between Member States, even if the conclusion is that there is no such effect.[37] If there is an effect on trade between Member States, then the Statement of Objections needs to address the application of Articles 81 and/or 82 as well as the application of the Competition Act 1998. The OFT will normally apply both the Competition Act and Articles 81 and/or 82 where an effect on trade is possible.

9.30 **Individual exemption conditions** Where the possibility of the exemption conditions applying has been raised by the undertaking in the process leading up to the Statement of Objections, including exemption by way of block

---

[35] See *Allsports Ltd v OFT* [2004] CAT 1 (judgment on Allsports' application for summary judgment, 29 January 2004).
[36] Pursuant to Regulation 1/2003, Art 3.
[37] The issue of effect on trade between Member States is discussed in detail at paras 1.38–1.54.

exemption or parallel exemption, the OFT's Statement of Objections will need to address whether the undertaking has discharged the burden of proving that an exemption applies. As a matter of procedure, if the undertaking in question has not as yet raised the possibility of exemption, but this is raised by the undertaking in response to the Statement of Objections, then the OFT would need to review the matters raised and, if the OFT did not accept the submission, it would need to provide an explanation of its reasons, usually in the form of a Supplementary Statement of Objections.

(ii) Evidence and findings of fact

In the Statement of Objections the OFT sets out in detail 'the facts it has found **9.31** and the inferences it has drawn on the basis of the material it has, and identifies the items of evidence relied on for that finding or inference'.[38]

The OFT is likely to refer to background information, leniency information, **9.32** documents or information (including interviews) it has gathered during the information gathering process,[39] and the evidence of witnesses. It may also refer to the evidence of experts, market studies or publicly available statistical information.

Documentary evidence Some documentary evidence has more weight (ie it is **9.33** of a higher value) than other evidence. A document created at the time of a relevant event (contemporaneous material) has greater evidential value than a document created some time after the event. In the *Allsports* case, the CAT commented:

> As regards the contemporaneous documents, it seems to us that a document prepared at the time, which the author never anticipated would see the light of day, is likely to be more credible than explanations given later. We have therefore given weight to contemporary documents, unless there is a good reason not to do so.[40]

Where evidence is contradictory it will often be the relative weight of the **9.34** evidence that determines which version is accepted by the OFT or a court. Circumstantial (indirect) evidence can also help add weight to one version of events, and documents may lend support to one witness's version of events over another. For example, documents containing statements of anti-competitive intent may be used to assist in the interpretation of other contemporaneous documents, as well as comprising evidence of knowledge of the unlawful nature of the activities in question. For example, in *Argos and Littlewoods*, an email

---

[38] *Argos Ltd and Littlewoods Ltd v OFT* [2003] CAT 16, para 64.
[39] As to which, see Chapters 7 and 8.
[40] *JJB Sports Plc and Allsports Ltd v OFT* [2004] CAT 17, para 287.

was uncovered which described one witness's view of the anti-competitive arrangement which had been put in place:

> Ian . . . This is a great initiative that you and Neil have instigated!!!!!!!!! However, a word to the wise, never ever put anything in writing, its highly illegal and it could bite you right in the arse!!!! suggest you phone Lesley and tell her to trash? Talk to Dave. Mike.[41]

9.35   Upon reviewing this documentary evidence, the CAT noted that on the basis of the email, this witness was clearly in no doubt that the relevant activities were unlawful.

9.36   **Assertion**   In a judgment delivered by the CAT in *British Horse Racing Board v OFT*,[42] the CAT was critical of the OFT's case, noting that the case was essentially founded on an assertion. That case concerned an agreement relating to the sale of media rights in aid of bookmaking activities across a number of racecourses owned by various entities, which agreement the OFT held infringed the Chapter I prohibition. It was fundamental to the OFT's case that, in practical terms, the sale could have been conducted in a particular way which was different and more competitive than the way the sale was actually conducted. However, this premise was 'founded on the assertion that ATR [Attheraces Plc, one of the parties to the agreement] could have gone about the purchasing exercise in a fundamentally different way from that which ATR originally acknowledged was the only practical way; and that, had it done so, it could have picked up the requisite rights at an appreciably lower price'.[43] The CAT noted that, regarding the OFT's assertion, it was 'a perhaps possible interpretation of the events, but it is not the only one; and in our judgment the evidence before the OFT did not entitle them to be confident as to the correctness of their interpretation of such events'.[44] This criticism of the OFT highlights a clear dividing line between evidence and assertion. Pure assertion or conjecture does not amount to evidence of itself, and assertion which is unsupported by satisfactory evidence will not discharge the applicable burden of proof.

9.37   **Witness evidence**   The OFT may rely on witness evidence produced during the course of its investigation. This evidence may be in the form of interview notes and supporting documents rather than complete witness statements. In the *Argos and Littlewoods* case[45] the OFT was criticised for failing to put its witness evidence in full to the parties in the Statement of Objections, and in the early stages of the appeal the case was remitted back to the OFT so that the

---

[41] *Argos Ltd and Littlewoods Ltd v OFT* [2003] CAT 16, para 558 and see also para 604.
[42] *British Horseracing Board v OFT* [2005] CAT 29.   [43] ibid, para 200.
[44] ibid, para 201.
[45] *Argos Ltd and Littlewoods Ltd v OFT* [2003] CAT 16.

Statement of Objections and response procedure could be properly carried out. In the meantime, the appeal was stayed. This clearly wasted time and resources for all concerned, and as a result the OFT is likely to attempt to provide full and complete witness evidence at the Statement of Objections stage.

The relative quality of witness evidence is very important. The evidence of a **9.38** witness with a better memory of the events in question, or where the documents or other witnesses support their version of events, is likely to be treated as better evidence than a witness with a poor recollection or where their recollection is uncorroborated. It must also be recognised that witnesses are rarely completely independent of the case. Even where witness statements are provided in support of a leniency application and are likely to be reliable in the sense that they are given in full and complete cooperation with the OFT, there may be sub-conscious or hidden agendas for the undertaking to secure immunity or gain an advantage over its competitors. The CAT commented at length on the quality of witness evidence in the *Allsports* case:

> 288. As far as witnesses are concerned, in this case we have no 'independent' witness in the sense of an impartial third party who is free of the suggestion that he may have an axe to grind. On the contrary, all the witnesses in this case are open to the contention that their evidence is coloured, at least sub-consciously, by various factors . . .
>
> 292. Moreover, the hearing before the Tribunal took place four years after the events in question. However conscientious a witness may be, we remind ourselves that memory is apt to play tricks, and recollections may be mistaken or incomplete. It is extremely difficult to remember details regarding dates, times, and the sequence of events even a short time after a particular happening, let alone four years ago. When businessmen are frequently engaged in meetings and conducting business on the telephone, it is difficult to identify precisely what was said at an individual meeting or during a particular phone call.
>
> 293. In addition, witnesses may find themselves in an unfamiliar situation when asked to prepare written statements. They understandably rely on lawyers to turn their raw material into drafts which they then approve. In the course of that process, nuances may be lost, or the draft may not capture, in the witness's words, what the witness is trying to say. Indeed the quality of a witness statement may to some extent depend on whether the lawyer who took the proof did his job properly or not. Similarly the witness may be shown a document, of which he has no particular recollection, and then give an explanation in good faith which turns out to be mistaken. Later events, such as the service of subsequent witness statements by others, may lead a witness genuinely to correct his earlier evidence, or prompt the recollection of matters previously forgotten. In this process inconsistency or late recollection does not necessarily mean that a witness is dishonest: but it does mean that the Tribunal must ask itself whether the witness's evidence is reliable.
>
> 294. In all these circumstances, our general approach to the witness evidence, whether given on behalf of the OFT, or on behalf of the appellants, is to be

cautious, and to look for corroboration, whether from context, documents, or other witnesses, wherever possible.[46]

9.39 While an undertaking may respond to a Statement of Objections by providing its own witness statements, neither the OFT nor the undertaking will have any opportunity to cross-examine each others' witnesses until the appeal stage, after the OFT has made a final decision. This is because the administrative procedure which the OFT follows before taking a decision does not provide for the possibility of questioning witnesses under oath, or cross-examining witnesses in a manner equivalent to the procedures of a courtroom.[47] Where the OFT rejects the evidence of a witness, it should give reasons why it has not believed the witness, or has preferred the evidence of another witness, or an inference drawn from a document.

9.40 **Expert evidence** The OFT may use expert evidence in support of its Statement of Objections and its final decision. There is no prescribed form for such evidence, although it would usually comprise a report and/or a witness statement together with relevant material referred to therein (including market surveys or other empirical evidence to support a theory).

9.41 In a case management conference in *MasterCard*,[48] the CAT commented on the use of expert evidence by the OFT, noting that it comprised not only the economic analysis expected of an expert, but also partly comprised actual factual evidence of systems used in other countries. The CAT remarked that this sort of factual evidence, in order to be relied upon by the OFT, 'would in the ordinary course of events need to be substantiated in some way, need to be proved, or agreed or something, and would or might need some sort of factual investigation. In the normal way one would not allow pure factual evidence in via the route of an expert economic economist's report, because it is a very indirect way of bringing primary facts to the Tribunal's attention.'[49]

9.42 Expert evidence must be provided by an appropriately qualified person. It is quite likely that during the course of an appeal, experts whose evidence has been relied upon by the OFT will be cross-examined as to their background and qualifications, as well as the substance of their expert advice.

---

[46] *JJB Sports Plc and Allsports Ltd v OFT* [2004] CAT 17, paras 288 and 292–294.

[47] *Argos Ltd and Littlewoods Ltd v OFT* [2003] CAT 16, para 16. See also Case C-238/99 P *Limburgse Vinyl Maatschappij NV (LVM) v Commission* [2002] ECR I-8375 and Case C-204/00 P *Aalborg Portland A/S v Commission* [2004] ECR I-123, para 200, where the ECJ held that there was no requirement for the Commission to provide an opportunity for cross-examination and found that this was not a breach of the ECHR.

[48] *MasterCard UK Members Forum Ltd v OFT*, Case nos 1054, 1055 and 1056/1/1/05, case management conference on 31 March 2006.

[49] ibid, 48.

It has been suggested by the Court of Appeal that the OFT's failure to obtain **9.43** manifestly necessary expert advice, or the OFT's reliance on advice or evidence from an unqualified person, may be appropriate grounds for the CAT to remit a case back to the OFT for further investigation, together with an order requiring the OFT to obtain the necessary expert advice.[50]

Use of confidential and privileged material The OFT may use confidential **9.44** material in reaching its decision, such as commercially sensitive information. There are, however, obligations on the OFT in relation to the disclosure of such information (see para 9.83, below). The OFT may not use documents which are subject to legal privilege, where such privilege has not been waived. A detailed discussion of the use of privileged material in competition enforcement is set out at paras 7.09–7.29, above. In addition, the OFT will not use documents which are subject to public interest immunity. Nor will the OFT use material submitted by leniency applicants where the leniency application has been withdrawn or rejected.[51]

(e) Supplementary Statements of Objections

Once the OFT has provided a Statement of Objections, the OFT may also **9.45** supply later supplementary Statement of Objections which may revise the allegations made by the OFT or any of the original matters set out in the first Statement of Objections. It is particularly important for the OFT to issue a supplementary Statement of Objections where it wishes to raise new allegations or where there is a material change in the OFT's case. Provision of a supplementary Statement of Objections allows the undertaking an opportunity to address the new matters raised.

In theory, the OFT may provide an unlimited number of supplementary State- **9.46** ments of Objections. However, should the OFT's use of this process become unreasonable in all the circumstances, an undertaking could seek judicial review on the basis that it is an unjustified use of the OFT's power to require an undertaking continually to answer new and revised allegations without having its case finally determined and thereby being able to be reviewed on full appeal.

(f) Further information gathering

The OFT can also make further requests for information up until the time of **9.47** the final decision, as there is nothing to prevent the OFT from continuing to

---

[50] *Floe Telecom Ltd (in administration) v Ofcom* [2006] EWCA Civ 768, para 55, per Sedley LJ (obiter).
[51] *Umbro Holdings Ltd v OFT* [2005] CAT 22, para 315, and see also Enterprise Act 2002, Sch 4, para 1(2)(a) in relation to the CAT.

use its powers of investigation during the decision-making process. If the OFT intends to rely upon any new information gathered, it will need to issue a supplementary Statement of Objections, or a 'letter of facts' (sometimes known as a 'TACA letter') informing the accused undertaking of additional information to be taken into account in the final decision. This applies even if the OFT does not intend to change its case or introduce new allegations, as it relates to the proposed reliance upon new evidence, where the undertaking ought to be given an opportunity to comment on the new evidence and make submissions as to its meaning and probative value.[52]

(g) Time frame for decision-making process

9.48 Apart from Article 6 ECHR and any time limits set by the CAT during the course of a continuing appeal,[53] there is nothing governing the required time frame for the OFT's decision-making process. Time frames are thus largely within the OFT's discretion, and are subject only to the possibility of judicial review for unreasonable delay. This discretion applies regardless of whether the OFT is making its decision for the first time or is conducting a second process following an order by the CAT that the matter be remitted back to the OFT when the appeal has ended. In the latter circumstance, the CAT has no jurisdiction to order a specified time frame for completion of the OFT's decision-making process.

9.49 This question was considered by the Court of Appeal in an unusual case where all parties consented to the matter being heard by the Court of Appeal despite the fact that none of the parties actually required any order to be made by the Court of Appeal. It was, however, clearly an important question for the future conduct of investigations and clarification of the CAT's jurisdiction. The issue of unreasonable delay was discussed in the context of the application of Article 6 ECHR, where Lloyd LJ stated:

> . . . the CAT has no role in relation to the time taken by a regulator over an initial investigation even if, as in the present case (however exceptional it may be), article 6 applies at that stage. If the complainant considered that Ofcom was guilty of unreasonable delay in pursuing the initial investigation, its remedy would be to

---

[52] Based on the 'TACA' cases: Joined Cases T-191/98, T-212/98 to T-214/98 *Atlantic Container Line* [2003] ECR II-3275. This related to the European Commission's process, but the principles are likely to be equally applicable to the OFT.

[53] Competition Appeal Tribunal Rules 2003, SI 2003/1372. Where the CAT exercises the power in r 19(2)(j) to refer certain points in an appeal back to the OFT or Regulator for consideration, but without determining the appeal itself, the appeal remains live and the CAT is able to give a direction as to the time within which the matters referred have to be dealt with (r 19(2)(h)).

apply for judicial review in the Administrative Court. In my judgment that would also be the correct remedy if the complainant considered that the regulator was guilty of unreasonable delay in proceeding with the investigation after remittal by the CAT.[54]

In that case, there was also some consideration given to the appropriate time for an aggrieved applicant to apply for judicial review on the basis of unreasonable delay, noting that '[i]t would be appropriate for the Administrative Court to consider such a question after the event, if an application for judicial review is made to it, whereas it does not seem to me an appropriate exercise for the CAT to undertake in advance'.[55]   **9.50**

The Court of Appeal also made some comments as to how such a judicial review application ought to be determined in the context of the OFT's investigations: **9.51**

> It does not follow from Lloyd LJ's conclusions that, once remission has been ordered, parties are at the mercy of the OFT in respect of time. Any undue delay falls within the supervisory jurisdiction of the High Court and can be met with a mandatory order. If such an order is sought it may well be relevant that the Tribunal has expressed a view, whether in its judgment or in its order, as to the time within which the remitted matter needs or ought to be dealt with. But this will not be the only factor. The OFT has other demands on its resources and is entitled, within reason, to set its own priorities. The High Court is unlikely to compel it to readjust these to accommodate a particular case unless the interests of justice and good administration plainly require it.[56]

It also seems clear that the threshold of providing a breach of a reasonable time requirement is a high one, and is not easily crossed. If the period which has elapsed is one which on its face gives ground for real concern, it seems that two consequences follow. First, the court must look into the detailed facts of the case, and secondly, the OFT would have an opportunity to explain and justify any lapse of time which appears to be excessive.[57] The delay may not be unreasonable if it is largely due to matters outside of the OFT's control.[58]   **9.52**

---

[54] *Floe Telecom Ltd (in administration) v Ofcom* [2006] ECWA Civ 768, para 45, per Lloyd LJ.
[55] ibid, para 46, per Lloyd LJ.   [56] ibid, para 53, per Sedley LJ.
[57] Lloyd LJ also referred to the case of *Dyer v Watson* [2002] UKPC D1, [2004] 1 AC 379, para 52, per Lord Bingham.
[58] eg, in Case C-238/99 P *Limburgse Vinyl Maatschappij NV (LVM) v Commission* [2002] ECR I-8375 the case process took 12 years, but this was not an unreasonable delay as it was due to appeals brought by the undertakings, which did not adversely affect the ability of the undertakings to defend themselves.

C. Response to Statement of Objections

(a) Overview

9.53 Responding to the Statement of Objections is clearly an important stage for the undertaking concerned. There is an opportunity for providing both written and oral submissions to the OFT and it is important at this stage to consider the party's intention to appeal and what matters (if any) may be left to be raised on appeal rather than put forward in the response to the Statement of Objections. At this stage, parties may also consider the option of commitments (as to which, see Chapter 10). Although once a Statement of Objections has been provided the OFT has invested considerable work in the case, the OFT may nevertheless be receptive in an appropriate case to an alternative means of resolution other than devoting resources to a full decision and any subsequent appeal.

(b) Access to evidence

(i) Access to file

9.54 Under the OFT's Procedural Rules, the OFT is required to provide an undertaking which is the subject of a Statement of Objections with a reasonable opportunity to inspect the documents in the OFT's file that relate to the Statement of Objections.[59] Note that the OFT cannot 'select' which documents it considers to be relevant to the case. The undertaking is entitled to see almost all documents on file, including those documents on which the OFT has not specifically relied in support of its provisional findings. This is important as some documents may undermine the OFT's case or cause a different interpretation to be taken. In providing this inspection opportunity, the OFT may withhold any document to the extent that it contains information which is confidential, or to the extent that it is internal.[60] The undertaking may take copies of the documents it reviews, and in practice it is common for the OFT to provide electronic copies of the file excluding confidential and internal documents.

9.55 **Confidential information** Confidential information is given a broad definition in the OFT's Procedural Rules, and is also based on a subjective test of the OFT's opinion. Confidential information is defined as:

(i) commercial information whose disclosure the OFT thinks might significantly harm the legitimate business interests of the undertaking to which it relates; or

---

[59] OFT's Procedural Rules, rr 4 and 5(1)(c).   [60] ibid, r 5(2).

(ii) information relating to the private affairs of an individual whose disclosure the OFT thinks might significantly harm the individual's interests; or

(iii) information that is, in the OFT's opinion, otherwise confidential.[61]

9.56 The meaning of 'otherwise confidential' is set out in r 1(1)(k) as including information received from other authorities on a confidential basis, documents relating to the OFT's application for a warrant, and information the disclosure of which might prejudice national security.

9.57 In deciding whether material is confidential, the OFT will have regard to submissions as to confidentiality made by the undertaking to which the information relates, and there is a process for the OFT to seek further representations as to confidentiality.[62] The index to the file will show where documents have been excluded as confidential and will also normally state where documents have been partially redacted. Hence, where confidentiality seems to have been improperly asserted over a document, an undertaking wishing to access that document may reasonably seek an explanation from the OFT as to why the document should be treated as such.

9.58 This process is a difficult balancing exercise for the OFT, as it has multiple and often conflicting obligations regarding disclosure of information. On the one hand it is required to conduct a fair process for both third parties and for the undertakings the subject of its Statement of Objections, and on the other hand it must protect its own interests in furtherance of its policies (such as its leniency programme) as well as protecting the confidentiality of documents relating to individuals and undertakings gathered during its investigative process. However, the OFT cannot rely on documents which it is unable to disclose because of confidentiality[63] or because they are internal documents or protected by privilege.

9.59 The OFT is also subject to the requirements of Pt 9 of the Enterprise Act 2002 in relation to the disclosure of information. This essentially restricts the disclosure of information relating to the affairs of an individual or any business of an undertaking by a public authority to specified disclosure gateways, and even if one of the gateways applies, it then requires consideration of whether the disclosure ought to take place having regard to the type of information in question and the purpose of the intended disclosure.[64]

9.60 **Internal documents** The OFT is also entitled to withhold internal documents. Under the OFT's Procedural Rules, a document is 'internal' if it is:

---

[61] ibid, r 1(1)(d).   [62] ibid, r 6.
[63] Unless it can be partly disclosed to the accused, see para 9.82 below.
[64] For further information on Pt 9 of the Enterprise Act 2002, see paras 8.09–8.60, above.

(i) a document, not intended for disclosure, which has been produced by or exchanged between any of the OFT, another competition authority, a regulator or any other authority; or

(ii) a document, not intended for disclosure, which has been produced by any person from time to time retained under a contract for services by any of the OFT, another competition authority, a regulator or any other public authority.[65]

9.61 The phrase 'not intended for disclosure' is separately defined as meaning 'a document concerning a case which, by its nature, could not be relied on by the OFT as evidence'.[66] Essentially, this means the OFT can withhold from access all of its internal working papers and the working papers, correspondence, and drafts produced by its experts or by other authorities, and in some circumstances meeting attendance notes. Sometimes the OFT may decide to disclose internal documents at the later appeal stage to reveal its thinking at the time of investigation.

9.62 **Privileged material**   An assertion of privilege over a communication may be made at the point at which disclosure is sought: assertion of privilege over a communication need not wait (and should not wait) until the Statement of Objections is issued. Unlike confidential material, the OFT may not compel production of such material.[67]

9.63 **Further access on appeal**   If a party considers that it has not been granted adequate access to documents (for example it may consider that another party's assertion of privilege or confidentiality is unfounded) and the OFT is therefore withholding documents that are vital to the defence, the first step is to raise the issue with the OFT, setting out the reasons why access ought to be granted. If the OFT still refuses access, and the party still considers such refusal is unfounded, it may either raise the issue on appeal before the CAT (which will involve waiting until the OFT has made a final decision in the case), or it may bring an action for judicial review in the High Court.

9.64 An action seeking judicial review can be taken immediately, as there is no need to wait until the OFT has made a final decision in the case, provided that the OFT has made a decision in relation to access to the relevant documents. However, seeking judicial review of an OFT decision to withhold documents is not to be done lightly, and there will be many legal and commercial considerations relevant to a company's decision to take such action. For example, taking

---

[65] OFT's Procedural Rules, r 1(1).

[66] ibid, r 1(1). This rule also sets out some inclusive examples of the type of documents meeting these criteria.

[67] Competition Act 1998, s 30; and see also paras 7.09–7.29, above.

this step may well hold up the process of the OFT's final decision in the case and thereby delay any appeal. It is also likely to add considerable cost to the defence of the case. In most cases, the preferable course will be to raise the issue and seek access to the relevant documents on appeal before the CAT.

On appeal, when the question of whether a document is confidential or internal **9.65** is raised again before the CAT, the tests for confidentiality are different and may lead to orders that the OFT disclose information which it had previously with-held. The CAT is not bound by Pt 9 of the Enterprise Act 2002.[68] Schedule 4 to the Enterprise Act sets out factors to which the CAT is required to have regard in preparing its decision.[69] Those factors relate to the need to exclude informa-tion the disclosure of which would be contrary to the public interest, or which might significantly harm the legitimate business interests of an undertaking or the interests of an individual. The CAT is also required to have regard to the extent to which any such disclosure is necessary for the purpose of explaining the reasons for the decision.[70] Since these requirements leave some scope for interpretation, and only relate to the CAT's preparation of its decision, the CAT has devised its own general principles relating to confidentiality. The CAT set out its considerations in the case of *Allsports Ltd v OFT*, where some of the parties sought access to documents which had previously been withheld by the OFT on the basis that they were confidential to Allsports. Allsports objected to the disclosure and the issue was initially heard 'in camera', that is to say, it was heard in a private sitting with limited persons in attendance. Ruling in favour of disclosure, the CAT stated:

> . . . the Tribunal takes the view that its proceedings should be conducted on the basis that is as fully open as possible, subject only to the protection of vital business secrets or for some other overriding reason. It must be remembered that the Tribunal's judgment is a public document that has to be published. The Tribunal's hearings are in public, the transcripts of its hearings are published and so on.
>
> Equally, in a case such as the present, which takes place in a setting in which parties have had penalties imposed upon them, it is, in the Tribunal's judgment, of overriding importance that the parties should be able to exercise their rights of defence without having possibly relevant material held back or inaccessible. In the event of a conflict between the rights of the defence and other claims to confidentiality there must, in our judgment, be a presumption that the rights of defence prevail.[71]

Thus it is clear that in CAT proceedings, disclosure will be the preferred option **9.66** if it is required for the rights of defence. Further, although the CAT will take

---

[68] Enterprise Act 2002, s 237(5).   [69] ibid, Sch 4, para 1(2).
[70] ibid, Sch 4, para 1(3).
[71] *Umbro Holdings Ltd v OFT* [2003] CAT 26, paras 32 and 33.

account of confidentiality claims as part of its assessment under Sch 4 to the Enterprise Act 2002, it restricts confidentiality to business secrets of less than two years old. This will rule out many documents which parties might otherwise claim as confidential. As in *Allsports*, confidentiality disputes can be resolved by the CAT in private hearings if necessary, which may require attendance and submissions by third parties who are not parties to the appeal.

(ii) Freedom of Information Act

9.67 The Freedom of Information Act 2000 entered into force on 1 January 2005 and gives any person a general right of access to information held by public authorities, including the OFT. This means that any 'specified information' (as defined in the Freedom of Information Act) which the OFT holds is prima facie disclosable to any person requesting such disclosure. The OFT can only refuse disclosure of the information requested if it is able to rely on one or more exemptions under the Act, most of which are 'qualified' by being subject to a public interest test.[72] This means that the OFT must consider whether the public interest in maintaining the exemption outweighs the public interest in disclosure.

9.68 The OFT deals with Freedom of Information Act requests in accordance with its 'Freedom of Information Act 2000 publication scheme'[73] which has been approved by the Information Commissioner's office. The publication scheme explains that Freedom of Information Act requests to the OFT should be addressed to its Freedom of Information Act coordinator,[74] and gives an overview of the classes of information that can be disclosed. When considering a request for information under the Freedom of Information Act, the OFT will confirm whether or not it holds the relevant information and also whether this information can be disclosed or if it is subject to exemptions under the Act that prevent its disclosure.

9.69 Under the Freedom of Information Act, any person, regardless of their standing in relation to a Competition Act investigation, may request information from the OFT. On receiving such a request, the OFT must consider whether it can disclose the requested information or whether it can refuse disclosure if one of the exemptions in the Freedom of Information Act applies.

9.70 If the OFT refuses a Freedom of Information Act information request, a complaint should first be made to the OFT itself according to its internal

---

[72] For further information on the exemptions and on the Freedom of Information Act generally, see paras 8.78–8.95.

[73] OFT622, *Freedom of Information Act 2000 publication scheme* (January 2005).

[74] The Freedom of Information Act Coordinator, Communications Division, Room 5C/9, Fleetbank House, 2–6 Salisbury Square, London EC4Y 8JX, Fax: 020 7211 8400, Email: foiaenquiries@oft.gov.uk.

complaints procedure.[75] If the OFT does not deal with the complaint properly, the complainant may contact the Information Commissioner's Office.[76] This should be done as soon as possible or in any case within two months following the final response of the OFT. The Information Commissioner will also notify the OFT that a complaint has been received about it. If the complaint cannot be resolved informally, the Information Commissioner will issue a Decision Notice to both the complainant and the OFT, outlining the Information Commissioner's final assessment as to whether or not the OFT has complied with the Freedom of Information Act. If the Information Commissioner decides the OFT has not given information the complainant is entitled to, it will be instructed to do so. There is a further right of appeal to the Information Tribunal.

9.71 For further information on the application of the Freedom of Information Act in the context of an OFT investigation, see paras 8.78–8.95, above.

(c) Response to the Statement of Objections

(i) Written submissions and supporting evidence

9.72 Undertakings must be given a time frame within which to submit any written representations in response to the Statement of Objections. There is no obligation on the undertaking to make any submissions, and if none are made, the OFT may proceed with the case on the basis of the documents in its possession.[77] An undertaking may seek an extension of time in which to provide submissions, which the OFT, in its discretion, may grant.

9.73 Written submissions will normally comprise a detailed statement of the undertaking's defence, together with supporting evidence in the form of documents, witness statements, and/or expert evidence. This can be a costly and time consuming exercise. It will normally be lawyer-intensive and may involve experts such as economists or industry experts. It may also involve significant management time in providing detailed witness statements from key individuals. Witness statements provided to the OFT should generally be submitted along with a statement of truth, and should comply with the requirements for witness evidence as set out in the Civil Procedure Rules governing civil litigation procedure in the High Court and County Court.

---

[75] By writing to the Director of Resources and Services, 7C/01 Office of Fair Trading, Fleetbank House, 2–6 Salisbury Square, London EC4Y 8JX or by sending an email to foiaenquiries@oft.gov.uk.

[76] FOI/EIR Complaints Resolution, Information Commissioner's Office, Wycliffe House, Water Lane, Wilmslow, Cheshire SK9 5AF.

[77] OFT's Procedural Rules, rr 4 and 5(3). Although technically possible, a strategic decision not to make any submissions may be criticised on appeal.

9.74 In general terms, a response to the Statement of Objections should include: identification of the central allegations made by the OFT; a rebuttal in systematic order going through all of the required elements of the alleged infringement; challenges to the OFT's case (both evidence and assumptions); and putting forward the company's positive case for non-infringement. The accused may also select the most important allegations to deal with and simply reserve all their rights in relation to the remaining allegations.

9.75 A decision not to submit a written response will not prevent the undertaking from appealing any subsequent decision, but it could leave open the prospect that the OFT will submit more extensive evidence in the appeal than it would otherwise be entitled to do, and it may also have costs consequences.

9.76 In the *Allsports* case, Allsports provided written submissions but did not submit any witness statements to the OFT during the administrative procedure. The CAT commented on this in the context of Allsports' appeal, where Allsports challenged the OFT's attempt to submit further evidence during the appeal process, stating that:

> . . . it seems to us that where an appellant produces no witness evidence at the Rule 14 [Statement of Objections] stage, and then serves extensive further evidence at the appeal stage, the OFT cannot reasonably be denied the opportunity to respond. Subject to the requirements of procedural fairness, such response may involve the OFT being permitted by the Tribunal to elaborate its case, so that a proper balance is achieved between the interests of the appellant and the public interest which the OFT represents.[78]

9.77 In that case, Allsports was also penalised on costs, as a result of the extra work incurred at the appeal stage that could have been carried out earlier, had the matters been raised by Allsports in the administrative process before the OFT.

(ii) Oral submissions

9.78 The OFT must provide undertakings with a reasonable opportunity to make oral representations in response to the Statement of Objections, in addition to the written submissions.[79] Oral representations are normally made after the written submissions have been provided, and are conducted before a panel of OFT staff. Although there is no independent hearing officer, the OFT will arrange for a senior staff member who has not been directly involved in the conduct of the case to preside over the oral procedure. Undertakings may be represented by solicitors and counsel at oral hearings. Senior executives or other

---

[78] *Allsports Ltd v OFT* [2004] CAT 1, para 90.
[79] OFT's Procedural Rules, rr 4 and 5(4).

representatives may want to make a short presentation to show the business perspective.

Hearings are not open to the public. They may, however, be held jointly with **9.79** other parties, although the company can ask for a private hearing if there is a need to deal with sensitive issues such as leniency. In some circumstances, complainants and interested parties may also be permitted to attend the main hearing. Oral hearings are opened and chaired by the OFT, and are conducted according to a general format which allows for each party to make submissions (usually about 45 minutes) and provides an opportunity for replying to the submissions made by the other parties. Hearings conclude with a session involving questions from the OFT and an opportunity for undertakings to answer the questions. There is no cross-examination of other parties, or of any witnesses during the oral hearing.

There is no obligation on parties to present oral submissions to the OFT. The **9.80** OFT's Procedural Rules state that if, having given an undertaking a reasonable opportunity to make oral representations, none are made, the OFT may proceed with the case on the basis of the documents in its possession, including any written representations that have been submitted.[80]

(iii) Protecting confidentiality

The OFT may provide other parties with a non-confidential version of the **9.81** written representations submitted by an undertaking and afford them an opportunity to comment. For example, in *Argos and Littlewoods*, the OFT disclosed the representations made by each of Hasbro, Argos, and Littlewoods respectively (other than Hasbro's representations in relation to leniency) to each of the other parties, subject to the excision of confidential business information. Argos and Littlewoods each made further written representations on those redacted representations.[81]

Usually, confidentiality over information obtained by the OFT during the inves- **9.82** tigative procedure will have been dealt with prior to the issue of the Statement of Objections. To the extent that it has not been dealt with, an undertaking should take the opportunity to seek that confidential information be protected from disclosure to third parties or other undertakings. Information that is confidential may still be used by the OFT in order to make its decision as long as it can be sufficiently disclosed to the subject of the decision. Some of the confidential information will, of course, have come from the subject of the decision itself. However, wider disclosure of the information will be subject to restrictions.

---

[80] ibid, r 5(4).
[81] *Argos Ltd and Littlewoods Ltd v OFT* [2004] CAT 24, para 36.

9.83 At this stage, the OFT may also seek to disclose information which has previously been identified as confidential, either to protect the rights of the defence, or perhaps pursuant to a specific request from another party to reveal the information. Where the OFT is considering such disclosure, it must abide by the requirements set out in r 6 of the OFT's Procedural Rules. This requires the OFT to notify the undertaking of its intention to disclose the information and allow a reasonable opportunity to make representations on the proposed disclosure. Ultimately, though, under the OFT's Procedural Rules the decision to disclose rests with the OFT, and the OFT's Procedural Rules simply specify the required process prior to any such disclosure. The OFT remains subject to the obligations in Pt 9 of the Enterprise Act 2002 in making any such disclosure, which would be likely to fall within the gateway relating to facilitating the exercise of a statutory function.[82] In addition, Article 28 of Regulation 1/2003 continues to apply, such that the OFT cannot disclose information which it has obtained from another national competition authority or the European Commission where that information is covered by the obligation of professional secrecy.[83]

D. Third Party Involvement

(a) General rights of third parties

(i) Legal basis for third party involvement

9.84 Third parties have certain rights of appeal under s 47 of the Competition Act 1998, but there is nothing in the Competition Act or the OFT's Procedural Rules expressly providing rights to third parties to be involved in the OFT's decision-making process. Conversely, there is also nothing in the Competition Act or the OFT's Procedural Rules which *prevents* the involvement of third parties.

9.85 Under EC law, the European Commission is required to allow some procedural rights to third parties. In the ECJ decision of *T-Mobile Austria GmbH*[84] it was held that third parties' rights related to the principle of sound administration but this did not go so far as to provide any rights of defence for third parties. Third parties have limited rights under EC law relating to access to the file and to be heard. In the OFT's decision in the *Pernod Ricard* case, on appeal, the CAT considered how the principles of administrative fairness relating to third

---

[82] For more information on Pt 9 of the Enterprise Act 2002, see paras 8.09–8.61, above.

[83] For more information on Art 28 of Regulation 1/2003, see paras 8.173–8.182, above

[84] Case C-141/02 P *European Commission v T-Mobile Austria GmbH (formerly Max.Mobil Telekommunikation Service GmbH)* [2005] ECR I-1283.

party complainants should be viewed in the context of the Competition Act 1998, concluding that s 60 of the Act required the EC procedural principles to be applied in the domestic context:

229. . . . it seems to us that the question at issue does arise 'in relation to competition' within the meaning of section 60(1), at least indirectly, since it concerns the procedural principles to be applied in the application and enforcement of the competition rules. We add that complaints to the OFT and the EC Commission play a central role in both the Community and domestic systems of competition law, and may in many cases be the only means of detecting the abuse of monopoly power or illegal agreements. The procedures by which such complaints are handled have, in our view, a key bearing on how effectively the competition rules set up by Treaty, and adopted in the 1998 Act, are applied and enforced in practice. If that approach is correct, it would follow that we should, so far as possible, decide this case consistently with the corresponding provisions of Community law.

230. As to any relevant differences between the provisions concerned, to which the Tribunal must have regard, there is nothing in the Act or the Director's Rules which *prevents* the participation of the complainant in the ways indicated above. It is not therefore a case of a positive provision of the Act or of subordinate legislation precluding an approach which is in conformity with Community law. It is simply that the existing procedural framework does not *expressly* provide for complainants' rights in the same way as Community law does.

231. Turning to sub-section (2) of section 60, that sub-section does not repeat the words 'in relation to competition' found in sub-section (1), although it is true that sub-section (1) refers to the 'purpose of this section', which phrase may include sub-section (2). However, the OFT has referred us to a passage in the debates on the Competition Bill (see paragraph 110 above) which indicate that 'the principles' referred to in sub-section (2) were intended to include not just the principles of competition law strictly so called, but other principles of Community law relevant to the enforcement of competition law. Thus, it was said on behalf of the Government that section 60 was intended to import 'high level principles, such as proportionality, legal certainty and administrative fairness' into domestic law (Hansard 25 November 1997, column 961). Having been invited to do so by the OFT, in order to resolve any perceived ambiguity in section 60, we take note of that statement having regard to *Pepper (Inspector of Taxes) v Hart* [1993] A.C. 593.

232. In relation to 'administrative fairness' we have already indicated above that in Community law, the principle that the complainant has a 'right to be heard' has stood for forty years, since the Community system was set up in 1962. The implementation of that principle takes the form of two further principles, namely

(i) that the complainant is entitled to be heard when a statement of objections is issued: see variously Article 19(2) of Regulation 17, Article 5 of Regulation 99, Articles 7 and 8 of Regulation 2482/98, Article 27 of Regulation 1/2003 and Article 6 of Regulation 774/2004 [*sic*: should probably be 773/2004] and

(ii) that a complainant is entitled to be heard before the Commission decides not to examine its complaint any further: see Article 6 of Regulation 99, Article 6 of Regulation 2482/98 and Article 7 of Regulation 774/2004 [*sic*: should probably be 773/2004].

233. The consistent development of the case law since 1962 (see e.g. paragraphs 204 and 205 above) reinforces our view that the procedural opportunities afforded to complainants form a basic element of administrative fairness in the system of Community competition law as a whole. The principle of administrative fairness as regards complainants finds its expression in the legislative provisions we have already referred to above.

234. In all these circumstances, we are of the view that, by virtue of section 60 of the Act, we should resolve the questions before us in the same way as they would be resolved under Community law in an equivalent situation. Indeed, it seems to us that section 60(2) of the Act gives us little or no choice in the matter. Nor can we see any good reason for not following Community law in situations such as that arising in the present case as regards complaints by competitors. The system as it has evolved under Community law appears to have worked satisfactorily, and has been an important element in ensuring fairness, transparency and rigour in decision making. We would have thought it undesirable if, at this stage of the development of Community law, the United Kingdom should go the other way on an issue such as this.

235. Turning to domestic administrative law, and looking at it from the point of view as to how the OFT should exercise its discretion under the 1998 Act, we take the general principle to be that where Parliament has conferred an administrative power, that power is to be exercised in a manner which is fair in all the circumstances. What is fair in all the circumstances depends notably, on the context of the particular decision in question and on the 'shape of the legal and administrative system in which the decision is taken', having regard to the particular statute in question: see Lord Mustill in *R v Secretary of State for the Home Department ex parte Doody* [1994] 1 AC 531, at 560, as cited by Lord Woolf in *R v Home Secretary ex p. Fayed* [1998] 1 WLR 763, at 766.[85]

9.86 This extension of s 60 of the Competition Act 1998 to matters of procedure rather than just interpretation of the law is perhaps questionable, but the decision was not appealed, and the full extent of any impact on the OFT's practice and procedure remains to be seen.[86] After the CAT's decision in *Pernod Ricard*, the OFT published a draft guideline for consultation on 'Involving third parties in Competition Act investigations'[87] (**Third Parties Guideline**). This guideline was finalised in August 2006, and sets out the OFT's current policy in relation to complaints and provides a process for the involvement of third parties in the decision-making process. In contrast to the normal position with Competition Act guidelines, the Third Parties Guideline only applies to the OFT and not to the Regulators, although the Regulators were consulted on the draft guideline in accordance with s 52(7) of the Competition Act 1998.

---

[85] *Pernod Ricard SA v OFT* [2004] CAT 10, paras 229–235.

[86] OFT issued a press release on 1 July 2004 stating that it would not appeal the judgment but, among other matters, it did not agree with the CAT's application of s 60 of the Competition Act 1998 to procedural matters.

[87] OFT451, *Involving third parties in Competition Act investigations* (April 2006).

(ii) Which third parties may be involved in the process?

In the *Pernod Ricard* case, the CAT stressed that its comments concerning third **9.87** party rights only applied in the context of the case at hand and did not generally apply to 'the apparently numerous "complaints" received by the OFT which have little or nothing to do with the 1998 Act, or which are too vague or unsubstantiated to form a basis for further investigation'.[88] Nor would it apply to the case of a complainant as a member of the public whose position is no different from other members of the public.[89]

Under the OFT's Third Parties Guideline, at the complaints stage, special status **9.88** is accorded to complainants meeting the criteria for Formal Complainants.[90] A Formal Complainant is essentially any third party who has submitted a written, reasoned complaint to the OFT, has requested Formal Complainant status, and whose interests are, or are likely to be, materially affected by the agreement(s) or conduct which are the subject matter of the complaint.[91] In the decision-making process, the OFT will normally consult any third party who has the status of Formal Complainant at the stage where the OFT issues a Statement of Objections (or a Supplementary Statement of Objections).[92]

The OFT has also stated that it may consult certain other third parties who, **9.89** although not being a Formal Complainant, meet the following criteria:

- they are, or are likely to be, materially affected by the alleged infringement;
- they request to be consulted; and
- they are likely materially to assist the OFT in its investigation.[93]

The OFT has provided examples of third parties which it would be likely to **9.90** regard as being 'materially affected', as follows:

1   actual or potential competitors denied access to a market by another party or parties
2   a competitor who is unable to compete effectively because of the predatory behaviour of a dominant undertaking
3   a customer who has had its choice of supplier restricted by an upstream market sharing agreement
4   a retailer who is refused supply because it has priced below a recommended price, and

---

[88] *Pernod Ricard SA v OFT* [2004] CAT 10, para 245.   [89] ibid, para 245.
[90] This is discussed in Chapter 6.   [91] Third Parties Guideline, para 2.6.
[92] ibid, paras 3.5 and 3.13. The OFT is, of course, likely to have contacted the Formal Complainant prior to the decision-making process, in order to seek further information and informal opinions on the undertaking's responses to the OFT investigative measures.
[93] ibid, paras 3.3–3.8.

5   a trade association whose members are materially affected by the subject-matter of the complaint.[94]

9.91   In assessing whether a third party is likely materially to assist the OFT with its investigation, the OFT will take into account the extent to which a third party has been involved in the investigation prior to the issue of the Statement of Objections,[95] including the nature of the information it has provided, noting that '[i]n general, third parties who have been extensively involved in the investigation and have provided significant information to the OFT prior to the issue of the Statement of Objections are more likely to satisfy this condition'.[96] Otherwise, third parties will be required to submit representations to the OFT explaining why they consider this requirement is satisfied.[97]

9.92   By way of illustration, some guidance may be derived from the CAT's comments in the *Pernod Ricard* case, although it was decided prior to the introduction of the OFT's Third Parties Guideline. The CAT noted that, in that case, Pernod-Ricard was in a special position, setting out the relevant context as follows:

— Bacardi has a 90% market share in the supply of white rum.
— Pernod is a new market entrant challenging that high market share through Havana Club.
— Pernod complained to the OFT about a number of practices having the effect of excluding or eliminating Havana Club from the market.
— The OFT conducted a detailed investigation lasting 2½ years, including resort to external consultants.
— The OFT sought a great deal of information from Pernod, some at least of which was apparently used in the Rule 14 notice.
— Pernod's interests were directly and closely affected by the outcome of the OFT's investigation.
— Pernod provided submissions to the OFT, and regularly sought information about the progress of its complaint and meetings with the OFT, largely unsuccessfully, throughout the 2½ years that the matter was being investigated.[98]

9.93   It is likely that, were this case to have commenced under the new framework and Third Parties Guideline, Pernod would have been accorded the status of a

---

[94] ibid, para 2.10.
[95] eg, a third party may have responded to a Section 26 Notice for information, and may have provided the OFT with witness statements, or attended interviews or meetings with the OFT to provide further information.
[96] Third Parties Guideline, para 3.7.   [97] ibid, para 3.8.
[98] *Pernod Ricard SA v OFT* [2004] CAT 10, para 236.

Formal Complainant, and, on the basis of these factors, would certainly have been regarded as a third party likely materially to assist the OFT.

(b) Third party access to documents and information

(i) *The Statement of Objections*

According to the Third Parties Guideline, when a case reaches the stage where **9.94** a Statement of Objections is issued, the OFT will (except in certain cartel cases[99]) publish a notice on its website giving a brief summary of the case noting that a Statement of Objections has been issued and inviting third parties wishing to comment on the OFT's findings to submit a written request for a non-confidential copy of the Statement of Objections.[100]

A non-confidential version of the Statement of Objections will be automatically **9.95** provided to Formal Complainants and other third parties meeting the criteria noted above.[101] Formal Complainants do not need to request specifically a copy of the Statement of Objections, as it will normally be provided to them in any event.[102]

This was also the approach advocated by the CAT in the *Pernod Ricard* case, **9.96** where the CAT noted that:

> . . . it would generally be proper, as a matter of fairness in administrative law, for the OFT, in exercising its discretion, to disclose a non-confidential version of the [Statement of Objections] to a complainant in a position equivalent to that of Pernod. Such a course, in our view, enables the complainant, if he wishes, to put forward his point of view on an informed basis, instead of being largely in the dark. It is also likely to facilitate the OFT's understanding of the case and its implications, and lead to a sounder decision. Such a course is also likely, in our view, to introduce an important element of transparency and balance into the administrative proceedings which are conducted behind closed doors. It is particularly at the stage of the [Statement of Objections] that defendant companies, often powerful and well resourced concerns, will understandably enough deploy all available substantive or tactical arguments to persuade the OFT to abandon or modify its position.
>
> 238. Moreover, whatever the strict interpretation of section 60, in deciding what would be a fair and reasonable exercise of the OFT's discretion, we think we are entitled to take into account how the EC Commission would proceed in similar circumstances. It is also desirable, in our view, that the OFT's discretion should be exercised on a consistent and predictable basis. For those reasons, absent exceptional circumstances, we think the OFT's discretion should normally be

---

[99] The OFT notes that it may not consult such Formal Complainants or other third parties in cartel cases where consultation could give rise to a risk of prejudice to a related criminal investigation in respect of the cartel offence: Third Parties Guideline, para 3.10.

[100] ibid, para 3.14. Publication may not be made in cartel cases.   [101] ibid, para 3.15.

[102] ibid, para 3.13.

exercised in favour of disclosure of a non-confidential version of the [Statement of Objections] in circumstances comparable to those of the present case.[103]

9.97 Other third parties should apply for a non-confidential copy of the Statement of Objections and seek the right to submit a response. Due to the time lapse between the issue of the Statement of Objections and the provision of a non-confidential version of the Statement of Objections, third parties' responses tend to be submitted after the response of the subject undertaking(s).

9.98 Under the OFT's Third Parties Guideline, when the Statement of Objections is provided to a third party (including a Formal Complainant), comments and/or additional information will be sought within a stated period (generally within four to six weeks).[104] Third parties may only wish to respond on limited issues that concern them. The third party submission may annex evidence including documents and witness statements; however, it would generally be more appropriate to submit substantive material and provide access to witnesses at an earlier stage in the OFT's investigation. Where confidential information is provided as part of a third party's response, a non-confidential version of the response must be submitted within the same time period.[105]

9.99 The OFT will meet with a third party if it is considered appropriate to do so in the circumstances of the case, but will not generally invite third parties to attend the oral hearing in the case.[106]

(ii) Supplementary Statements of Objections

9.100 A Supplementary Statement of Objections may be a completely revised version of the original Statement of Objections, or it may simply address a limited number of additional issues. It is therefore possible that a supplementary Statement of Objections may not touch on any issue concerning a third party.

9.101 The OFT has stated that, although it will generally adopt the same consultation process for a supplementary Statement of Objections, there may be occasions where consultation of third parties and Formal Complainants is 'unlikely materially to assist the OFT in its assessment' and thus the OFT may decide to consult to a more limited extent, or not all, on a supplementary Statement of Objections.[107]

(iii) Access to the file and oral hearings

9.102 Third parties will not generally be given access to documents or information in addition to the Statement of Objections, nor will they be invited to attend any

---

[103] *Pernod Ricard SA v OFT* [2004] CAT 10, paras 237 and 238.
[104] Third Parties Guideline, para 3.16.   [105] ibid, para 3.17.
[106] ibid, para 3.21.   [107] ibid, paras 3.11 and 3.12.

hearing of oral representations in the case (although there are examples where third parties have attended oral hearings).[108] In exceptional circumstances where the OFT considers it necessary to disclose additional information or documents to a Formal Complainant or other third party, such disclosure must be permitted under Pt 9 of the Enterprise Act 2002.[109]

(iv) Further disclosure

The OFT will provide the non-confidential version of any third party submissions to the undertaking the subject of the Statement of Objections, and such undertaking will be given an opportunity to comment (in writing or at the oral hearing).[110] Third parties and Formal Complainants will not normally be given a copy of, or a further opportunity to comment on, the response of the undertaking in question.[111] However, on occasion, the OFT may want assistance from a third party in rebutting the undertaking's defence and to this end may disclose to the third party extracts from the undertaking's response.   **9.103**

(v) Third party involvement in decision to accept commitments

The OFT's power to accept binding commitments is set out in ss 31A to 31E of the Competition Act 1998. The OFT has published guidance on its use of this power.[112] Once binding commitments have been agreed, before they can be finally accepted by the OFT, the OFT must consult third parties. The procedure for this consultation and information on a third party' rights of appeal are set out in Chapter 10.[113] The matters set out below in relation to the *Pernod-Ricard* case concern an OFT decision to accept informal assurances. This took place before the OFT had power to accept binding commitments, but nevertheless has clear relevance to the exercise of the power.   **9.104**

(c) General approach to third party participation

In the *Pernod-Ricard* case, the OFT commenced its investigation on the basis of complaints from a competitor of Bacardi, and following investigation it issued a Statement of Objections against Bacardi. The OFT did not involve the complainant, Pernod-Ricard, in the process that ensued, which ultimately resulted in the OFT accepting informal assurances from Bacardi. On appeal, the CAT considered the question of whether Pernod-Ricard had a right to be heard on the matters set out in the Statement of Objections, and whether it had a right to   **9.105**

---

[108] This is in line with the European position as set out in Case C-141/02 P *European Commission v T-Mobile Austria GmbH (formerly Max.Mobil Telekommunikation Service GmbH)* [2005] ECR I-1283.
[109] Third Parties Guideline, paras 3.19–3.20.   [110] ibid, para 3.17.
[111] ibid, para 3.18.   [112] OFT407, *Enforcement* (December 2004) Pt 4 and Annexe A.
[113] See paras 10.33 and 10.35–10.37, below

have the opportunity to comment before the OFT decided not to take its complaint any further.[114] The CAT noted that, in the context of that case, and having regard to the provisions of Community law on which the UK system is modelled, the OFT should have provided a copy of the non-confidential version of the Statement of Objections, and also should have given Pernod an opportunity to submit observations before deciding to close its file on Pernod's complaint.[115] The CAT commented on the right of appeal of third parties, noting:

> 241. Our conclusions on both the issues considered above are reinforced by the fact that, under section 47 of the Act, Parliament has expressly conferred rights of appeal to the Tribunal on persons demonstrating a sufficient interest, which Pernod has shown in this case. Having regard to the general system of the Act, it seems to us desirable that complainants should be afforded a structured opportunity to be heard by the OFT before decisions are taken, rather than having to raise matters for the first time before the Tribunal in circumstances where the complainant has been kept by the OFT largely at arms-length during the administrative process. If complainants are 'closely associated with the proceedings' as Article 27(1) of Regulation 1/2003 now requires, that in our view is likely to lead to fewer and less costly appeals, and better decision making.

> 242. We emphasise that, in reaching the above conclusions, we accept the OFT's submission that the Act does not envisage an adversarial system in which the function of the OFT is to arbitrate on complaints. Community law is not an adversarial system either (see Cases 142 and 156/84 *BAT and R J Reynolds v Commission* [1987] ECR 4487 at paragraph 19). However, that does not preclude the need to afford the complainant an opportunity to defend its interests during the administrative proceedings (ibid, paragraph 20).[116]

9.106 In a later case, a third party (Burgess) appealed to the CAT following a decision of the OFT that a competitor of Burgess had not abused a dominant position in refusing Burgess access to its crematorium facility. In seeking an order that the OFT's decision be set aside, one of the grounds raised in support was that Burgess had not been given any opportunity to comment on the OFT's decision before it was adopted by the OFT. In dealing with this issue, the CAT referred to its finding in *Pernod-Ricard* regarding third party involvement, and noted that the OFT's decision in *Burgess* 'gave no opportunity for Burgess to comment before its adoption, notwithstanding what was apparently an informal promise to do so made during [a prior meeting with the OFT]'.[117] Although the CAT had already found on other grounds that it was necessary to set aside the OFT's decision, the CAT reaffirmed its view on this issue, stating: 'Had it been necessary, we would have been minded to decide that it was, in any event, necessary to set aside the Decision because of that procedural failure.'[118]

---

[114] *Pernod Ricard SA v OFT* [2004] CAT 10, para 229.   [115] ibid, paras 239–246.
[116] ibid, paras 241 and 242.
[117] *Burgess (t/a JJ Burgess & Sons) v OFT* [2005] CAT 25, para 388.   [118] ibid, para 389.

The CAT has not yet considered in further detail what steps would comprise a **9.107** sufficient opportunity for a third party complainant to defend its interests. Thus the question of whether the OFT's proposed involvement of third parties as set out in its guideline accords with the principles laid down by the CAT in the *Pernod Ricard* case remains to be answered.

E. Final OFT Decision

(a) Required form of final decision

The OFT's final decision in a case will usually take largely the same form as the **9.108** Statement of Objections preceding it, with the main difference being the inclusion of a section dealing with calculation of any penalty or directions applicable. The OFT is required to inform the relevant undertaking in writing of the facts on which it bases the penalty and its reasons for requiring that undertaking to pay the penalty, following the steps set out in its Penalties Guidance,[119] and a rebuttal of the undertaking's final arguments.[120] Where the OFT gives a direction under s 32 or s 33 of the Competition Act 1998, it is required at the same time to inform the recipient in writing of the facts on which it bases the direction and its reasons for giving the direction.[121]

The OFT is likely to set out its decision in as full and complete a way as **9.109** possible, given that the introduction of new facts by the OFT during the appeal process could give rise to an order by the CAT remitting the case back to the OFT. The types of enforcement measures the OFT may take are described in Chapter 10 on enforcement decisions.

(b) Process for final decision

(i) General process

The OFT's Procedural Rules set out the required process for issuing a final **9.110** decision. This provides for different requirements depending on whether the OFT makes a finding of infringement or a finding that there are no grounds for further action.

Where the case involves Article 81 or Article 82, the OFT must also inform the **9.111** European Commission prior to adopting a final decision. The OFT is required, pursuant to Article 11(4) of Regulation 1/2003, to inform the European Commission no later than 30 days before it adopts a decision requiring an infringement to be brought to an end, accepting commitments, or withdrawing

---

[119] OFT423, *OFT's guidance as to the appropriate amount of a penalty* (December 2004).
[120] OFT's Procedural Rules, r 8(2).   [121] ibid, r 8(1).

the benefits of a block exemption Regulation. In that time period, the European Commission may submit written observations on the proposed decision.[122] In extreme circumstances, the European Commission could take up the case itself pursuant to Article 11(6), which would relieve the OFT of any jurisdiction to make a decision.[123]

(ii) Infringement decisions

9.112 Where the OFT makes a finding of infringement, r 7(1) of the OFT's Procedural Rules requires the OFT to, without delay, give notice of the decision to each person the OFT considers is or was a party to the agreement or conduct, stating in the decision the facts on which it bases the decision and its reasons for making the decision. Rule 7(1) also states that the OFT shall, without delay, publish the decision. The OFT is also required to publish any directions given under s 32 or s 33 of the Competition Act 1998.[124]

9.113 The OFT will normally publish a press release on the same day of the infringement decision, setting out information on the parties and the amounts of any fines imposed. The OFT will usually note in its press release that the text of the final decision will be published once commercially sensitive information has been removed. Publication of any decision by the OFT is subject to the requirements of r 6 of the Procedural Rules in relation to confidentiality (duty to consult prior to disclosure).[125] The Enterprise Act obligations regarding disclosure by a public authority also continue to apply to the OFT in relation to any such publication. Decisions are published in non-confidential form on the Competition Act Public Register and are available to download from the OFT's website. Normally the OFT will ask parties in the final weeks before the adoption of the decision to confirm which information is confidential. After the decision is adopted, the parties can make confidentiality requests. This process normally takes around six weeks, which can create problems for parties seeking to intervene in appeals, as interveners may not have a copy of the decision at the time they make their request.

(iii) 'No grounds for action' decisions

9.114 Different requirements apply where the OFT decides that there are no grounds for action. Rule 7(2) provides:

---

[122] There are no powers in Art 11(4) for the European Commission to comment on a draft decision. Hence, any observations submitted by the European Commission only reflect the views of the services in whose name they have been submitted and can therefore not be regarded as stating an official position of the European Commission.

[123] See also Commission notice on cooperation within the network of competition authorities (2004/C 101/03) [2004] OJ C101/43, para 46.

[124] OFT's Procedural Rules, r 8(3).   [125] See para 9.84 for further detail.

If the OFT has made a decision that there are no grounds for action:

(a) in respect of an agreement either because the conditions of the Chapter I prohibition are not met or because the agreement is excluded from the Chapter I prohibition or satisfies the conditions in section 9(1); or

(b) in respect of an agreement either because the conditions of the prohibition in Article 81(1) are not met or because the agreement satisfies the conditions of Article 81(3); or

(c) in respect of conduct because the conditions of the Chapter II prohibition or of the prohibition in Article 82 are not met;

then it shall, without delay, give notice of the decision . . . to any complainant and to any person in respect of whom the OFT or an officer of the OFT has exercised any of the powers of investigation in the Act, stating in the decision the facts on which it bases the decision and its reasons for making the decision, and it may publish the decision.

Thus, although the OFT's decision must be provided to a wider group of **9.115** recipients, the OFT is not required to publish the decision. In practice, some at least of these decisions by the OFT and the Regulators are published.

Once a final decision has been adopted by the OFT, it will retain all documents **9.116** on its file, as these may be required during the course of an appeal. The appeal process may involve the required disclosure of information which had previously been protected as confidential during the administrative process before the OFT.[126]

(iv) Commitment decisions

Article 5 of Regulation 1/2003 permits the OFT to accept binding commit- **9.117** ments in relation to cases under Articles 81 and 82. The power of the OFT to do so, in relation to Article 81, Article 82, and investigations under the Competition Act 1998, is set out in ss 31A to 31E of the Competition Act. In addition, the OFT has published guidance as to the circumstances in which it may be appropriate to accept commitments.[127] Essentially, the OFT may only accept commitments in a case where the OFT has begun an investigation, but has not yet made an infringement decision.[128] Importantly, the OFT has indicated that it is unlikely to accept binding commitments where they are offered at a very late stage in the investigative process where there is some merit in proceeding to full infringement decision. The process followed by the OFT in relation to commitment decisions is set out in Chapter 10.

---

[126] See paras 12.38–12.41, below, for a discussion of this issue.
[127] OFT407, *Enforcement* (December 2004) Annexe A.
[128] Competition Act 1998, s 31A(1).

(c) Time frame for making a final decision

(i) General time frames for procedure

9.118 There is no specified time frame in the Competition Act 1998 or in the OFT's Procedural Rules for the OFT to make a final decision in a case. Usually the OFT's process will take, at least, between six and twelve months from the date of first issuing the Statement of Objections until the date of the final decision. The timing will often depend on the numbers of parties involved (including third parties), as well as the complexity of the case and the OFT's available resources and current priorities. The CAT has indicated that where a case involves small or medium sized businesses operating in local markets, the OFT should ensure that such cases can be dealt with within an acceptable time frame.[129] The CAT cannot, however, seek to impose a deadline on the OFT for reaching a final decision (unless, exceptionally, this is part of an on-going appeal).[130] Where the delay in issuing a final decision is unreasonable, it may give rise to judicial review of the exercise of the OFT's powers, as discussed above in relation to the time frame for the decision-making process at paras 9.48–9.52.

(ii) Whether undue delay can amount to an implied decision

9.119 There appears to be a possibility that a failure by the OFT to make a final decision within a reasonable time frame might in itself amount to an implied decision and therefore be capable of forming the basis for an appeal to the CAT. This question was raised before the CAT by Albion Water Ltd in an appeal brought against Ofwat. In that case, the first draft decision (equivalent to a Statement of Objections) was issued by Ofwat on 6 June 2003 with an indication that a final decision or a revised draft would be available by November 2003. On 2 April 2004, having received no further draft from Ofwat, Albion Water brought an appeal before the CAT claiming that Ofwat's failure to make a decision within a reasonable time itself constituted an implied decision and was, on that basis, an appealable decision. In the course of the hearing, Ofwat indicated that a final draft decision would be issued by July 2004, some 11 months after the first issue of a draft decision. In its ruling, the CAT commented that this was a 'very long delay' and noted that '[t]he Tribunal's experience is that other regulators, certainly at this stage of the proceedings, are capable, in appropriate cases, of dealing with matters expeditiously'.

9.120 The CAT then explored the options available to it, including the option of deciding whether it had jurisdiction to hear the case:

---

[129] *Burgess (t/a JJ Burgess & Sons) v OFT* [2005] CAT 25, para 390.
[130] *Floe Telecom Ltd (in administration) v Ofcom* [2006] EWCA Civ 768, para 55, per Sedley LJ (obiter).

The first option was that the Tribunal should decide in the present appeal whether in fact it has jurisdiction to hear the case. That would involve addressing the question as to whether there had in fact been an appealable decision. One issue that may well arise, as the Tribunal has already indicated in discussion, is whether in circumstances such as those that I have outlined, there has been an implied decision by the Director in this case to the effect that no infringement of the Chapter II prohibition is shown. That would be an important issue from the point of view of the structure of the Act and would affect other regulators. It is also important in view of the situation that arises under the jurisprudence of the European Community, in which the concept of an implied decision is fairly well established. We bear in mind in that context that, as from 1st May 2004, under Regulation 1 of 2003, the United Kingdom authorities have jurisdiction to apply the competition rules of the Treaty. In general terms, the United Kingdom domestic system is required to operate, at least arguably, in a way that is as coherent as possible with the EC system. Section 60 of the Act may also be relevant here.[131]

In the end, the CAT did not need to consider this issue further, as shortly **9.121** afterwards Albion Water applied for and was refused interim relief by Ofwat, providing a clear route for appeal under the Competition Act 1998 (as amended), namely an appeal against a refusal to provide interim relief.[132]

---

[131] *Albion Water Ltd v Director General of Water Services* [2004] CAT 9, 6.

[132] The CAT stayed the original proceedings pending the outcome of the second set of proceedings: see Case no 1031/2/4/04, Order of 21 September 2004.

10

ENFORCEMENT MEASURES

A. Introduction

10.01 The 'teeth' of any enforcement authority relate to its powers to impose hefty fines and make orders backed up by serious sanctions, which are ultimately able to be enforced by an effective court and police system. The Office of Fair Trading (**OFT**) (and the Regulators) each have such powers, given to them by the legislature under a structure which places some boundaries on the use of those powers. The OFT has powers to:

- make interim orders;
- accept binding commitments;
- impose penalties;
- make directions; and
- impose competition disqualification orders (**CDOs**) on individuals.

10.02 The penalties imposed may be significant, as the main constraint on such penalties is the maximum cap of 10 per cent of the undertaking's worldwide turnover in the year prior to the infringement decision. The highest penalty imposed by the OFT to date is £17.28 million. The OFT may also make an infringement decision without imposing any penalty.

10.03 In addition to the enforcement powers of the authorities, competition law infringements can also be the subject of private enforcement in the form of damages claims, or a claim for a declaration that an agreement is void. The penalties which may be imposed by an authority are completely separate to any liability to pay damages, so this is an additional financial consequence of a competition law infringement.

B. Interim Measures

(a) Interim measures directions

(i) Power

10.04 The OFT's power to make interim measures directions in competition enforcement cases is set out in s 35 of the Competition Act 1998, and is similar to the power of the High Court to grant an injunction. The OFT's power relates to cases concerning the Chapter I and Chapter II prohibitions, as well as Articles 81 and 82 EC.[1] This power also applies equally to the Regulators. Pursuant to this power, the OFT may impose interim measures directions where:

(a) the OFT has begun an investigation under s 25 and has not completed it (for as long as the OFT has such power under s 25 to conduct that investigation); and

(b) the OFT considers that it is necessary to act as a matter of urgency for the purpose of preventing serious, irreparable damage to a particular person (or category of person), or of protecting the public interest;[2] and

(c) in cases concerning the Chapter I prohibition or Article 81, where an agreement may benefit from the individual exemption criteria, the OFT must consider that possibility where it is raised by the undertaking the subject of the interim measures decision.

10.05 The OFT need not wait until an application is made by a complainant in order to issue an interim measures direction: it may act on its own initiative in an appropriate case, where the OFT considers that interim measures may be necessary in the public interest as a matter of urgency.[3]

(ii) Section 25 threshold

10.06 This threshold requires the OFT to have reached a preliminary level of certainty about a case. This is not a high threshold, but it does require a reasonable suspicion to be formed. This threshold is discussed in Chapter 6.

(iii) Evidential requirements and application of injunction test

10.07 The first occasion upon which the OFT used its power under s 35 of the Competition Act 1998 was in a case concerning the London Metal Exchange

---

[1] Council Regulation (EC) 1/2003 of 16 December 2002 on the implementation of the rules on competition laid down in Articles 81 and 82 of the Treaty [2003] OJ L1/1, Art 5 permits the OFT to make such interim measures directions in relation to Arts 81 and 82, but does not provide the necessary power to do so: the OFT's power in this regard is provided by s 35 of the Competition Act 1998.

[2] Competition Act 1998, s 35(2).

[3] *London Metal Exchange v OFT* [2006] CAT 19, para 159, and OFT407, *Enforcement* (December 2004) para 3.8.

(**LME**). Spectron, a competitor of LME, applied to the OFT for an interim measures direction to prevent LME from extending its opening hours for a certain part of its trading business, on the basis that in doing so, LME would effectively take all business from Spectron and Spectron would thereafter be unable to re-enter the market.

10.08 The interim measures direction was granted by the OFT, and LME appealed to the Competition Appeal Tribunal (**CAT**). Shortly thereafter, the OFT lifted its interim measures direction and LME consequently withdrew its appeal. An argument ensued concerning costs of the aborted appeal, whereupon the CAT found itself in a position to consider 'whether the process which the OFT adopted in giving the IMD [interim measures direction], including as to the assessment of the quality of the evidence upon which it would rely, was one which an authority acting with due appreciation of its responsibilities under section 35 of the Act would have decided to adopt'.[4]

10.09 The CAT noted that the OFT's use of the power under s 35 was akin to an injunction power, and indicated that it was appropriate to take guidance from the High Court's exercise of the injunction power in relation to the quality of evidence to be relied upon by the OFT in making an interim measures direction. The CAT said:

> We accept that since the OFT is acting as a matter of urgency, the process it adopts before issuing an IMD must necessarily be flexible and must be proportionate to the particular circumstances of the case. However, before the OFT considers it necessary to act, it must be satisfied that the information it is relying upon is of such a quality that it is appropriate to rely upon it in all the circumstances of the particular case.[5]

10.10 In that case, the CAT found that the OFT had relied on evidence of insufficient quality in the circumstances. This was due to the evidence being out of date, having been provided in circumstances where there were no particular safeguards to ensure the accuracy of the evidence, and having been provided solely by the complainant and without any inquiries having been made of any third parties. The CAT found that there had been sufficient time for the OFT to redress each of these matters prior to making the interim measures direction, and in the circumstances the quality of the evidence relied upon by the OFT 'fell below the standard which should normally be required by an authority such as the OFT when carrying out its functions under section 35 of the Act'.[6]

---

[4] *LME*, ibid, para 129.   [5] ibid, para 137.   [6] ibid, para 149.

(iv) Urgency and serious irreparable harm

The OFT has given no guidance on what it will consider to be 'a matter of **10.11** urgency'. In the *LME* case, the CAT considered that there was no real urgency, as the OFT had learned of the complaint and of the possibility of a request for interim measures approximately two months prior to the actual application being made. By not taking any steps until the making of the application, the CAT found that the urgency with which the OFT was confronted at the time of the interim measures application was entirely of its own making.[7]

In relation to the purpose of 'preventing serious, irreparable damage', the OFT **10.12** has stated that this is a question of fact and will depend upon the circumstances of each case. The OFT has given guidance that damage may be considered to be serious where a person may suffer 'considerable competitive disadvantage likely to have a lasting effect on their position'.[8] Further, serious damage is likely to include 'significant financial loss to a person', which is to be assessed with reference to that person's size or financial resources as well as the proportion of the loss as compared to the person's total revenue.[9] The OFT has also stated that irreparable does not mean 'that a person must be threatened with insolvency, though this will generally suffice'. Serious damage may be irreparable insofar as it 'cannot be remedied by later intervention'.[10]

The CAT has considered similar criteria in relation to the exercise of its own **10.13** power to suspend, on an interim basis, the effect of directions made by the OFT. In doing so, the CAT has concluded that:

> the principles normally applied in applications for interim injunctions or similar relief in the civil courts in such well known cases as American Cyanamid v Ethicon [1975] AC 396, while providing many useful and relevant analogies, are not in themselves necessarily determinative of the issues likely to arise under Rule 32(4) [concerning the CAT's power to grant interim relief].[11]

The CAT considered that these principles would not be determinative because **10.14** of the differences in process, such as the fact that CAT proceedings are not party and party litigation, the OFT is not obliged to offer any cross-undertaking as to damages, and the matters arose within a specific statutory framework. Rather, the CAT found that:

> the nearest analogous situation to hand is that of an application to the Court of First Instance of the European Communities for interim relief, pending an appeal

---

[7] ibid, para 160.   [8] OFT407, *Enforcement* (December 2004) para 3.5.
[9] ibid.   [10] ibid, para 3.6.
[11] *Napp Pharmaceutical Holdings Ltd v Director General of Fair Trading*, Case No 1000/1/1/01, judgment of 22 May 2001 (judgment on request for interim relief), para 39.

to that court against a decision taken by the European Commission under Articles 81 and 82 of the EC Treaty.[12]

10.15 The CAT also had regard to s 60 of the Competition Act 1998, which provides that:

> so far as is possible (having regard to any relevant differences between the provisions concerned), questions arising under this Part in relation to competition within the United Kingdom are dealt with in a manner which is consistent with the treatment of corresponding questions arising in Community law in relation to competition within the Community.[13]

On the basis that the same reasons would apply in relation to the OFT's administrative procedures, it is reasonable to assume that the CAT's comments would apply equally to the exercise of the OFT's powers to grant interim relief.

10.16 Most interim measures decisions relate to relief sought by undertakings whose commercial survival is at stake (as was claimed by Spectron in its application for an interim measures direction against LME). However, occasionally, other situations give rise to requests for the interim measures powers to be used. For example, in the case of *AKZO Chemicals Ltd*[14] an application for an interim measures decision was made in order to force the European Commission to return certain documents which the applicants asserted were protected by legal professional privilege. The European Court of Justice (**ECJ**) held that the risk that the documents could be read was not sufficient to establish irreparable harm, given the fact that third parties could not access the information contained therein before judgment was given in the main action.

(v) Exemption conditions

10.17 In the case of a potential infringement under the Chapter I prohibition and/or Article 81, in the context of interim measures, the undertaking accused (ie not the complainant) must produce evidence to the OFT that 'satisfies it on the balance of probabilities that, in the event of it reaching the basic infringement conclusion, it would also reach the conclusion that the suspected agreement is exempt' from the Chapter I prohibition or the prohibition in Article 81(1), as the case may be. Thus the burden of establishing a case for exemption falls to the undertaking the subject of the investigation. In general terms, the standard of proof for Article 81(3) is normally set at a high level, as the OFT demands cogent evidence. Further, it appears that the OFT power is subjective rather

---

[12] ibid, para 40.
[13] For another example where the CAT extends the application of s 60 to procedural matters see *Pernod Ricard* discussed at paras 9.85–9.86, above.
[14] Case C-7/04 P *AKZO Chemicals Ltd v Commission* [2004] ECR I-8739.

than objective in this regard.[15] For these reasons, it may be difficult for any undertaking to satisfy the OFT that the exemption criteria will apply on the balance of probabilities.

(vi) Procedure

The procedure the OFT must follow before making an interim measures deci- **10.18**
sion is set out in the Competition Act 1998 and in the OFT's Procedural Rules.[16] The OFT is required to give written notice to any person to whom it proposes to give the interim measures direction and it must also give that person an opportunity to make representations. The notice given by the OFT must indicate the nature of the direction the OFT is proposing to give and its reasons for wishing to give it. The recipient of such written notice may inspect the OFT's file in relation to the case. The OFT is required to provide a reasonable opportunity to inspect the documents in its file relating to the proposed direction, although the OFT may withhold documents which contain confidential information.

Complainants' rights in such a circumstance are addressed in the OFT's Third **10.19**
Parties Guideline.[17] This provides that when the OFT proposes to adopt an interim measures decision (provisionally or finally), it will consult applicants for interim measures who are 'formal complainants'.[18] Similarly, when the OFT decides to reject an interim measures application made by a complainant, and at the same time proposes to close the investigation file, it will consult applicants for interim measures who are formal complainants before doing so.[19] It is also apparent from the OFT's decision in *LME* that the complainant in that case, Spectron, was closely involved in the procedure as it made the initial request for an interim measures direction and provided the OFT with evidence in support of its application. It is clear from the CAT's judgment in the *LME* case that evidence provided by a complainant will be regarded as significantly more reliable if it is produced in response to the use of a formal investigatory power (such as a Section 26 Notice) rather than being provided voluntarily and without the risk of sanctions for providing misleading or incomplete information. Thus complainants providing information on a voluntary basis should consider whether such information can be provided in a more formal way, such as under cover of a declaration as to the accuracy and completeness of the evidence.[20]

---

[15] Competition Act 1998, s 35(8) and (9).
[16] ibid, s 35(3) and (4); OFT's Procedural Rules, r 9.
[17] OFT451, *Involving third parties in Competition Act investigations* (April 2006) pt 4.
[18] ibid, paras 4.2 and 4.12. In relation to the status of formal complainants, see paras 6.45 and 6.46, above.
[19] ibid, para 4.6.   [20] See also paras 6.45 and 6.46, above.

10.20 There is no power for the OFT to obtain a cross-undertaking as to damages from a third party standing to benefit from the interim relief granted, as confirmed by the CAT in relation to the exercise of its own power to grant interim relief:

> In adopting what I regard as a minimalist approach I have been conscious of the fact that neither the Director nor the Tribunal has, in my view, any power to order a cross undertaking from HH [the third party]. It is true that in one old case NCB/National Smokeless Fuels/NCC OJ 1976 L36/6, [1976] 1 CMLR D82 the European Commission did grant interim relief on the basis of a cross undertaking, but that approach has not been followed since, either by the Commission, the Court of First Instance or the Court of Justice. The 1998 Act does not seem to me to confer any statutory power to obtain a cross undertaking in these proceedings.[21]

(vii) Publication

10.21 Interim measures directions are published on a register maintained by the OFT, which is available to the public on the OFT's website. The OFT has also noted that it may publish the interim measures direction in an appropriate trade journal.[22]

(b) Informal assurances

10.22 While the OFT is considering imposing an interim measures direction, it may accept informal (non-statutory) assurances 'where it is satisfied that these will prevent any harm which might otherwise form the basis for imposition of an interim measures direction'.[23] One possible incentive for undertakings to offer informal assurances in place of an interim measures direction is that an interim measures directions would be published, whereas informal assurances are not required to be published.

(c) Appeals from interim measures decisions

10.23 An interim measures direction made by the OFT may be appealed to the CAT by the undertaking the subject of the direction, as in the *LME* case.[24] An interim measures direction may also be appealed by a third party if the CAT 'considers that he has a sufficient interest in the decision . . . or that he represents persons who have such interest'.[25] Similarly, a decision by the OFT *not* to grant interim measures may be appealed by a third party with sufficient interest, as occurred in the case of *Albion Water*.[26] In another case where this right of appeal was exercised, a third party, Burgess, appealed a decision of the OFT not to grant

---

[21] *Genzyme Ltd v OFT* [2003] CAT 8, para 129.
[22] OFT407, *Enforcement* (December 2004) para 3.14.   [23] ibid, para 3.17.
[24] Competition Act 1998, s 46(1) and (3).   [25] ibid, s 47(1)(d) and (2).
[26] ibid, s 47(1)(e) and (2); *Albion Water v Water Services Regulation Authority* [2005] CAT 19.

interim measures providing Burgess with access to a crematorium operated by a competitor, Harwood Park Crematorium Limited. Harwood Park joined the action as an intervener, and in the early stages of the appeal Burgess and Harwood Park reached an interim arrangement pending determination of the main appeal on the substantive issues. This arrangement was recorded in a formal order by the CAT.[27]

An interim measures direction may also be appealed where there has been a **10.24** change in circumstance such that the factors giving rise to the interim measures direction are no longer present.[28]

The making of an appeal does not suspend the effect of the interim measures **10.25** direction.[29] The procedure for appealing an interim measures decision essentially provides for a time limit of two months from the date of the OFT's decision in which to lodge a notice of appeal with the CAT.[30] The notice of appeal must comply with the requirements of Sch 8, para 2(2) of the Competition Act 1998 in setting out the grounds of appeal. For a discussion on general matters relevant to appeals to the CAT, see Chapter 12, and for an example of a notice of appeal against an OFT interim measures decision, see the *LME* notice of appeal as published on the CAT's website.[31]

The CAT also has power to impose interim measures. This power is found in **10.26** the CAT's Rules, r 19. Thus the CAT may, on any appeal from an interim measures decisions (or a decision not to grant interim measures), impose its own decision in place of the OFT's decision.[32]

(d) Failure to comply with an interim measures direction

An interim measures direction made by the OFT may be enforced by the OFT **10.27** by way of an application to the court for an order requiring compliance with the direction within a specified time limit. The OFT will apply for such an order 'if a person fails to comply with it without reasonable excuse'.[33] This effectively makes the OFT's interim measures direction have the same force and effect as a court order.

---

[27] *Burgess (t/a JJ Burgess & Sons) v OFT* [2005] CAT 25, paras 78–81.
[28] eg, in *IMS Health* [2003] OJ L268/69, the European Commission withdrew an interim measures decision it had previously made, on the basis that changed circumstances no longer justified the maintenance of the interim measures. The change was brought about by a decision of a national court in Germany which meant there was no longer any need for Commission's interim measures.
[29] Competition Act 1998, ss 46(4) and 47(3).   [30] CAT's Rules of Procedure, r 8(1).
[31] <http://www.catribunal.org.uk/documents/Sum1062Metal050506.pdf>.
[32] *Genzyme Ltd v OFT* [2003] CAT 8.
[33] OFT407, *Enforcement* (December 2004) paras 2.9 and 3.16.

C. Commitments

(a) Overview

10.28   Article 5 of Regulation 1/2003 permits the OFT and the Regulators to accept binding commitments in relation to cases under Articles 81 and 82. The power of the OFT to do so, in relation to Article 81, Article 82, and investigations under the Competition Act 1998, is set out in ss 31A to 31E of the Competition Act. In addition, the OFT has published guidance as to the circumstances in which it may be appropriate to accept commitments.[34] The OFT's guidance in relation to commitments is published subject to the approval of the Secretary of State, and the OFT must have regard to the guidance for the time being in force when considering whether to accept any commitments offered to it.[35] Further, the OFT's enforcement guideline contains a section with further detail on how the OFT intends to exercise its power to accept commitments under the Competition Act.[36]

(b) Making binding commitments

(i) Appropriate cases

10.29   The OFT's power to accept binding commitments only applies in relation to particular cases. The case must be one in which the OFT has begun an investigation, but has not yet made an infringement decision.[37] Where the decision whether to accept binding commitments in any particular case is at the discretion of the OFT, the OFT has stated that it is likely to consider it appropriate to accept binding commitments only in cases where the OFT's 'competition concerns' are readily identifiable, are fully addressed by the commitment offered, and where the proposed commitment is capable of being implemented effectively and quickly.[38] The OFT has also set out what it regards as *not* being appropriate circumstances in which to accept binding commitments. Other than in very exceptional circumstances, the OFT will not accept binding commitments in cases involving secret cartels between competitors relating to hardcore cartel offences such as price fixing, market sharing, and bid rigging.[39] It is not clear whether 'cartel' is confined to agreements between competitors or looser forms of arrangements and concerted practices. The OFT has stated that it will also not accept binding commitments in cases involving serious abuse of a

---

[34]   ibid, Annexe A.

[35]   OFT407, *Enforcement* (December 2004) para A.6, incorporating the OFT's guidance as to the circumstances in which it may be appropriate to accept commitments.

[36]   OFT407, *Enforcement* (December 2004) Pt 4.   [37]   Competition Act 1998, s 31A(1).

[38]   OFT407, *Enforcement* (December 2004) para A.14, incorporating the OFT's guidance as to the circumstances in which it may be appropriate to accept commitments.

[39]   ibid, para A.15.

dominant position.[40] In relation to a 'serious' abuse of dominance, the OFT has stated that the assessment will be made on a case by case basis, but has noted that, as a general rule, it will regard predatory pricing as a serious abuse.[41] The OFT has also noted that it will not accept binding commitments where compliance with and the effectiveness of the commitments would be difficult to discern. This is, perhaps, a reference to the difficulty of monitoring commitments which are made.[42] The OFT will also not accept binding commitments where it considers that doing so would 'undermine deterrence'. This factor is quite different, as it is relatively subjective and therefore, wholly outside of the control of the undertaking. It relates more to the OFT's policy agenda, as to which, see Chapter 6.[43] Further, the OFT has indicated that it is unlikely to accept binding commitments where they are offered at a very late stage in the investigative process where there is some merit in proceeding to a full infringement decision. This may involve an assessment of the resources that have been committed to the case.[44]

(ii) Status of informal assurances

Prior to 1 May 2004, the OFT regarded itself as having power to accept **10.30** informal assurances in order to close an investigation. In general terms, many undertakings the subject of investigations would prefer informal assurances to binding commitments, as informal assurances are able to be both private and very quick. It may be arguable that, to the extent that the OFT now has a statutory-based power to accept commitments, it no longer has any non-statutory, implied power. On this basis, only accepting informal assurances *outside* the power to accept commitments would still be valid. This would include, for example, assurances accepted before a case had reached the s 25 investigation stage. However, it is not clear that this would be the correct interpretation, and in the OFT's guideline on enforcement, it is noted that informal assurances may be accepted where an interim measures decision is being contemplated, which indicates that the OFT does not regard its power to accept informal assurances as having been limited in this way.

The CAT made some observations on this issue in an appeal by Pernod-Ricard **10.31**

---

[40] ibid, para 8.15 and fn 6.   [41] ibid, para 8.15 and fn 6.

[42] It is possible that compliance may be monitored by obliging the undertaking to submit compliance reports. See also the provisions of the Enterprise Act 2002 relating to the Competition Commission's powers to accept undertakings in lieu of making a market investigation reference to the Competition Commission. These provisions include a requirement that the OFT keep under review the carrying out of any enforcement undertaking (s 162).

[43] OFT407, *Enforcement* (December 2004) para A.16, incorporating the OFT's guidance as to the circumstances in which it may be appropriate to accept commitments.

[44] ibid, para 4.16.

against a decision of the OFT to accept voluntary assurances from Bacardi-Martini, a competitor of Pernod-Ricard. In that case, the assurances were accepted by the OFT prior to the amendment to the Competition Act 1998 providing for binding commitments, and the CAT noted:

> The issues that then have been canvassed in this Case Management Conference are effectively four in number. First, whether the assurances are acceptable to all parties, and we are assured that they are, so this is a matter that can effectively proceed by agreement. Secondly, we have had during the course of argument some discussion about the effect of the new powers of the Office of Fair Trading under sections 31A and following of the Competition Act 1998 (as amended) to accept binding commitments. The assurances that we have been discussing in this case so far are voluntary assurances, not binding commitments of the kind envisaged under those new statutory provisions.
>
> Since the voluntary assurances given in this case originally pre-date the amendment to the Act I have just mentioned, whether these newly amended assurances offered by Bacardi could (or should) be converted to binding commitments is a somewhat complicated question given the particular background to these proceedings. We think it best in the circumstances not to enter into any further discussion of that point, particularly since Pernod has not pressed for these new assurances to be converted into binding commitments. We would simply say, as neutrally as possible, as far as the future is concerned that from the point of view of the effectiveness of the United Kingdom competition regime, binding commitments have advantages from the point of view of enforcement over voluntary assurances, and may well prove to be a weapon in the OFT's armoury that needs further development. We have not, of course, addressed the problem of whether there remains scope for accepting voluntary commitments after the introduction of section 31A—that is also a matter that we leave open.[45]

(iii) Partial commitments

10.32 The OFT appears to be able to accept binding commitments in relation to part of a case, while continuing to investigate other matters within the same case. The OFT has stated that it is not prevented from taking action in relation to competition concerns which are not addressed by the commitments it has accepted.[46] The OFT has given examples where this may arise, including where an agreement or conduct raises a number of competition concerns, although different aspects of an agreement or conduct raise different competition concerns.[47] This power clearly highlights a need to ensure that any binding commitments are clearly specified to be in relation to a particular matter or part of a matter. Otherwise, the protection which applies in respect of the binding commitments may be weakened or subject to re-interpretation at a later stage.

---

[45] *Pernod-Ricard SA v OFT* [2005] CAT 9, paras 6 and 7.
[46] OFT407, *Enforcement* (December 2004) para A.21, incorporating the OFT's guidance as to the circumstances in which it may be appropriate to accept commitments.
[47] ibid, para 4.10.

(iv) Procedure

The OFT guideline clearly contemplates that the process of accepting binding **10.33** commitments will begin with an offer made by the relevant undertaking. There is no clear guidance on the form of such an offer, but provided the undertaking makes it clear that it is making an offer of binding commitments, the form is probably irrelevant. For example, an offer could be made by way of a letter to the relevant case officer. The OFT will not use the offer of commitments as evidence in any such subsequent decision in relation to the agreement or conduct.[48] Where the commitments offer is made before a Statement of Objections has been issued by the OFT, and provided the OFT considers the case is one in which commitments may be appropriate, the OFT will issue a 'summary of its competition concerns' to the undertaking. This will set out the OFT's concerns and a summary of the main facts on which those concerns are based.[49] Effectively, this statement of competition concerns is made on a 'without prejudice' basis. The OFT has stated that the fact that it has issued such a summary of its competition concerns does not preclude the OFT from making a decision in relation to the agreement or conduct. This, of course, assumes the binding commitments are not accepted by the OFT.[50] Following the statement of competition concerns, the OFT may enter into negotiations with the undertaking in order to reach agreement as to the form and content of acceptable binding commitments. The process therefore involves several phases of negotiation and on average is likely to take a number of weeks before any final position is reached.

Consultation prior to final acceptance   Once binding commitments have **10.34** been agreed, before they can be finally accepted by the OFT, the OFT must consult the third parties and must also consult the European Commission (where the case involves Article 81 or Article 82). The OFT is required pursuant to Article 11(4) of Regulation 1/2003 to submit any proposed decision to accept commitments to the European Commission 30 days before it adopts a final decision. In that time period, the European Commission may comment on the proposed decision, or it may choose to make no comment, or alternatively, in extreme circumstances, it may take up the case itself pursuant to Article 11(6), which would relieve the OFT of any jurisdiction to make such a decision.[51]

---

[48] ibid, para 4.20.   [49] ibid, para 4.17.   [50] ibid, para 4.19.

[51] See also Commission notice on cooperation within the network of competition authorities (2004/C 101/03) [2004] OJ C101/43, part 3. There is no requirement for the OFT to consult with the other ECN members, although they may be informed of the intention to accept binding commitments and may also be provided with a copy of the draft decision.

10.35 **Publication** Once the OFT has made a decision to accept binding commitments, the OFT will publish that decision.[52] The publication will be made on
the OFT's website, and the OFT will have regard for the need to exclude from
publication confidential information, in accordance with Pt 9 of the Enterprise
Act 2002.[53]

(c) Rights of third parties

10.36 If the OFT decides to accept commitments, the OFT will 'give notice' to
affected third parties. The OFT will provide a summary of the case and set out
the proposed commitments, stating the purpose of the commitments and the
way in which they meet the OFT's competition concerns. Interested third
parties may then make representations to the OFT within a certain time limit,
not less than eleven working days.[54] A further consultation period will be
allowed if the OFT then proposes to make any material modifications to the
proposed commitments. The time frame for such consultation is not less than
six working days.[55] Third parties also have certain rights of appeal in relation to
the decision to accept binding commitments: as to which see paras 10.46–10.50
below.

10.37 In the *Pernod Ricard* case, the CAT considered what procedural measures would
be appropriate and fair to an interested third party in circumstances where the
OFT had entered into negotiations with an undertaking and proposed to accept
assurances rather than continue with the investigation:

> We also point out that the Community system, amongst other things, provides for
> the possibility of the EC Commission entering into confidential negotiations in
> order to allow the companies concerned to bring their agreements or practices into
> conformity with the rules laid down by the Treaty: *BAT and Reynolds*, paragraphs
> 23 and 24. The OFT can, therefore, in principle, conduct negotiations about the
> possibility of accepting undertakings in confidence, subject to the possible applica-
> tion of the principles set out in Schedule 4, paragraph 2 of the 2002 Act if the
> matter were subsequently to reach the Tribunal. That is no doubt a valuable tool in
> the OFT's armoury, enabling appropriate cases to be settled. On the other hand, it
> is in our view essential, from the point of view of fairness and transparency, that
> the complainant be informed of the outcome of the negotiations, and given an
> opportunity to be heard *before* the OFT closes its file on the complaint: *BAT and
> Reynolds*, at paragraph 24. That, in effect, means that the OFT cannot definitively
> commit itself to accepting the undertakings without giving the complainant the
> chance to comment.
>
> Such a system, as a system, seems to us to be not dissimilar from the system now

---

[52] OFT407, *Enforcement* (December 2004) para 4.23.
[53] ibid, para 4.24. See also the discussion of Pt 9 of the Enterprise Act 2002 in Chapter 9.
[54] ibid, para 4.21.   [55] ibid, para 4.22.

envisaged when the OFT is minded to accept binding commitments under what is now sections 31A to 31G of the 1998 Act as amended. That system is also similar in principle to that which ordinarily applies where the OFT is minded to accept undertakings in lieu of a merger reference under the Enterprise Act 2002 pursuant to Section 73 and Schedule 10 of that Act, or in lieu of a market investigation under sections 154 and 155 of that Act.[56]

Another issue raised by Pernod Ricard in that case concerned access to the **10.38** 'without prejudice' communications between the OFT and the undertaking giving commitments (Bacardi-Martini). This issue was discussed in the *Pernod Ricard* case during an interlocutory hearing before the CAT. Although the issue remained unresolved, the Chairman made some comments in passing regarding the OFT's obligations, querying whether, making all allowances for seeking to protect the without prejudice nature of the exchange, it may be that if there was a plain admission of a serious infringement of one of the prohibitions, that might not be covered by the 'without prejudice' privilege.[57]

(d) Effect of binding commitments

Once binding commitments are made, the OFT may not continue with its **10.39** investigation in relation to that part of the investigation covered by the binding commitments (unless there is a breach).[58] Further, the OFT may not make an infringement decision or give an interim measures direction where it has accepted binding commitments.[59] These effects do not apply where the OFT has released the commitments (as to which, see below). The fact that binding commitments have been accepted by the OFT does not preclude a third party from bringing an action before a court and obtaining a decision from the court that the relevant undertaking has infringed Article 81, Article 82, the Chapter I prohibition and/or the Chapter II prohibition.

Presumably, the extent of recovery will be limited until the date of acceptance **10.40** of commitments. After that date, there is a presumption that the OFT's competition concerns have been resolved.

(i) Re-opening a case after commitments accepted

After accepting commitments, the OFT may only re-open its case where: **10.41**

- it has reasonable grounds for believing there has been a material change of circumstances;
- it has reasonable grounds for suspecting that the undertaking has failed to adhere to the commitments given; or

---

[56] *Pernod Ricard SA v OFT* [2004] CAT 10, paras 243 and 244.
[57] *Pernod-Ricard*, transcript of interlocutory hearing, 16 January 2004, pp 22 and 23.
[58] Competition Act 1998, s 31B. [59] ibid.

- it has reasonable grounds for suspecting that information which led it to accept the commitments was incomplete, false, or misleading in a material particular.[60]

10.42 Where the OFT re-opens an investigation and goes on to give a direction or make an infringement decision, the commitments are treated as released from the date of that decision or release.[61] There is no statutory requirement for the OFT to advise affected parties or the relevant undertaking where it believes one of these criteria is fulfilled and proposes to continue its investigation as a result. However, the OFT would be required to follow the usual process for making an infringement decision, including issuing a Statement of Objections, as discussed in Chapter 9.

(ii) Variation or substitution of commitments

10.43 The OFT has the power to accept a variation of commitments in force, or to accept substituted commitments.[62] In order to accept a variation or substitution of commitments, the OFT must be satisfied that the varied or new commitments will address its current competition concerns. Before accepting a variation of commitments, the OFT must give notice and consult with any persons likely to be affected by the commitments, in accordance with the same procedure noted above at para 10.36.[63] Although there is no specific written requirement for the OFT to do so, it is almost certain that this consultation procedure would also apply to a substitution of commitments. The need for a variation of the commitments can be raised by the OFT, or by the undertaking the subject of the commitments itself. The OFT may only be able to raise the need for a variation in circumstances where it is able to re-open a case.

(iii) Release of commitments

10.44 The OFT may release an undertaking from binding commitments at the request of the undertaking giving the commitments, or where the OFT has reasonable grounds for believing that the competition concerns which the commitments were intended to address no longer arise.[64] Before releasing the commitments, the OFT is required to give notice to any person likely to be affected by the release of the commitments, setting out the fact that a release is proposed, the reasons for it, and the period within which representations may be made in relation to the proposed release. The period for representations to be made must last at least 11 working days.[65]

---

[60] ibid, s 31B(4).
[61] ibid, s 31B(5) and OFT407, *Enforcement* (December 2004) para 4.9.
[62] ibid, s 31A(3).   [63] OFT407, *Enforcement* (December 2004) para 4.23.
[64] Competition Act 1998, s 31A(4), and OFT407, *Enforcement* (December 2004) para 4.13.
[65] ibid, Sch 6A, paras 10–14.

(e) Enforcement and appeals

(i) Enforcement by court order

The OFT may apply to the court for orders in the same terms as the binding **10.45** commitments. A breach of those orders will then amount to contempt of court.[66]

(ii) Appeals

Appeals in relation to commitments decisions made by the OFT are made **10.46** to the CAT. The CAT is required to determine the appeal, not by determination as a full appeal, but by 'applying the same principles as would be applied by a Court on an application for judicial review'.[67] For a full discussion of the principles applicable to an application for judicial review, see Chapter 12.

Third parties having sufficient interest in the commitments decision may appeal **10.47** against a decision of the OFT to accept or release commitments, or to accept a variation of such commitments other than a variation which is not material in any respect.[68] An appeal by a third party does not suspend the effect of the decision to which the appeal relates.[69]

An undertaking the subject of a commitments decision has a right of appeal **10.48** against a decision of the OFT not to release commitments pursuant to a request made by the undertaking, or a decision to release commitments.[70] The making of an appeal does not suspend the effect of the decision made by the OFT not to release, or to release, commitments.[71]

When the OFT decides not to accept commitments which have been offered to **10.49** it by an undertaking, although this is a decision of the OFT, it is not listed as one which is appealable pursuant to s 46 of the Competition Act 1998. The OFT has clearly taken the view that a decision not to accept commitments is not an appealable decision.[72] It would be very difficult to establish that such a refusal ought to constitute an appealable decision, because of the wide discretion of the OFT in accepting or refusing to accept commitments and, in particular, the possibility of the OFT deciding not to accept commitments due to the need for deterrence. It remains to be seen whether a refusal to accept commitments could be raised as an issue in a later, substantive, appeal—particularly if the need to deter was not part of the reasoning in relation to the commitments issue or part of the reasoning for the main fining decision.

---

[66] ibid, s 31E.   [67] ibid, Sch 8, Pt 1, para 3A(2).   [68] ibid, s 47(1)(c) and (2).
[69] ibid, s 47(3).   [70] ibid, s 46(3)(g) and (h).   [71] ibid, s 46(4).
[72] OFT407, *Enforcement* (December 2004) para 4.25.

10.50 It may also be possible for undertakings to use binding commitments (or informal assurances) as a 'plea bargaining' tool, whereby commitments are offered as a way of accepting liability and cooperating, in exchange for a reduction in the fine.

D. Penalties

(a) Power

10.51 The OFT has the power to require an undertaking to pay a penalty in respect of an infringement of the Chapter I prohibition, the Chapter II prohibition, Article 81(1), or Article 82.[73] The OFT may only impose a penalty where the OFT is satisfied that the infringement has been committed intentionally or negligently by the undertaking.[74] Any penalty imposed by the OFT may not exceed 10 per cent of the undertaking's worldwide turnover.[75] The OFT is also required to publish guidance on how it determines the appropriate amount of any penalty imposed.[76] That guidance must be approved by the Secretary of State and, when setting the amount of the penalty, the OFT must have regard to the guidance for the time being in force.[77] The Regulators have the same power as the OFT, and are also required to follow the guidance published by the OFT. The Regulators are not required to publish any separate guidance. The following sections apply equally to the Regulators as well as the OFT.

10.52 The OFT also has power to make a finding of infringement even where no penalty is imposed. This may occur, eg, where there is no clear evidence of intention or negligence (see paras 10.53 and 10.54 below). A finding of infringement may assist private claims for damages even if no penalty is imposed (see para 10.134 below). In order to make such a finding the OFT needs to show a legitimate interest in making an infringement decision without imposing penalties, such as a need to clarify the legal position or facilitating private enforcement.[78] There also seems to be a generally accepted possibility of 'plea-bargaining', whereby the undertaking admits liability and the admission is accepted by the authority as the basis for a reduction in penalty on grounds of

---

[73] Competition Act 1998, s 36(1) and (2).   [74] ibid, s 36(3).
[75] ibid, s 36(8) and see also the Competition Act 1998 (Determination of Turnover for Penalties) Order 2000, SI 2000/309, as amended by the Competition Act 1998 (Determination for Turnover of Penalties) (Amendment) Order 2004, SI 2004/1259.
[76] ibid, s 38(1).   [77] ibid, s 38(8).
[78] See, eg, *Sumitomo Chemical Co Ltd and another v European Commission*, Joined Cases T-22/02 and T-23/02, Court of First Instance judgment of 6 October 2005.

cooperation (along with any other mitigating factors such as the restitution of any wrongful profits to consumers).[79]

(b) Applicable conditions

(i) Intention or negligence

The OFT's power to impose a penalty on an undertaking only exists 'if the **10.53** OFT is satisfied that the infringement has been committed intentionally or negligently by the undertaking'.[80]

The OFT does not need to decide whether the infringement was committed **10.54** intentionally *or* negligently, so long as it is satisfied that the infringement is *either* intentional or negligent. The question of whether the infringement was intentional *or* negligent goes, at most, to mitigation.[81]

As to the meaning of 'intentionally or negligently', this was considered in **10.55** *Napp*, where the CAT held:

> 456. As to the meaning of 'intentionally' in section 36(3), in our judgment an infringement is committed intentionally for the purposes of the Act if the undertaking must have been aware that its conduct was of such a nature as to encourage a restriction or distortion of competition: see *Musique Diffusion Français*, and *Parker Pen*, cited 206 above. It is sufficient that the undertaking could not have been unaware that its conduct had the object or would have the effect of restricting competition, without it being necessary to show that the undertaking also knew that it was infringing the Chapter I or Chapter II prohibition: see *BPB Industries and British Gypsum*, cited above, at paragraph 165 of the judgment, and Case T-29/92 *SPO and others v Commission* [1995] ECR II-289, at paragraph 356. While in some cases the undertaking's intention will be confirmed by internal documents, in our judgment, and in the absence of any evidence to the contrary, the fact that certain consequences are plainly foreseeable is an element from which the requisite intention may be inferred. If, therefore, a dominant undertaking pursues a certain policy which in fact has, or would foreseeably have, an anti-competitive effect, it may be legitimate to infer that it is acting 'intentionally' for the purposes of section 36(3).

> 457. As to 'negligently', there appears to be little discussion of this concept in the case law of the European Community. In our judgment an infringement is

---

[79] See for example the finding of liability by ORR against EWS noted in the ORR press release of 17 November 2006, at <http://www.rail-reg.gov.uk/server/show/ConWebDoc.8409> and see also para 5.17 above in relation to a settlement reached by the OFT in the independent schools investigation.

[80] ibid, s 36(3). Note OFT407, *Enforcement* (December 2004) paras 5.9–5.12.

[81] *Napp Pharmaceutical Holdings Ltd v Director General of Fair Trading*, Case No 1001/1/1/0115, January 2002, paras 453–5, referring also to Case C-137/95 P *SPO v Commission* [1996] ECR I-1611, Case 100/80 *Musique Diffusion Française v Commission* [1983] ECR 1825, Case T-77/92 *Parker Pen v Commission* [1994] ECR II-549, Case T-65/89 *BPB Industries and British Gypsum v Commission* [1993] ECR II-389.

committed negligently for the purposes of section 36(3) if the undertaking ought to have known that its conduct would result in a restriction or distortion of competition: see *United Brands v Commission*, cited above, at paragraphs 298 to 301 of the judgment. For the purposes of the present case, however, we do not need to decide precisely where the concept of 'negligently' shades into the concept of 'intentionally' for the purposes of section 36(3), nor attempt an exhaustive judicial interpretation of either term.[82]

(ii) One infringement or two?

10.56 Technically, the OFT may impose a separate sanction in respect of each individual infringement. However, in circumstances where the period of time is unbroken between separate infringements, there is some authority to suggest that this should be treated as a single infringement for the purposes of calculating a penalty. However, where the time period is broken, a separate infringement for each period may be sanctioned as such.[83]

(c) Relevant factors in assessing a penalty

10.57 The OFT is required to publish and have regard to guidance explaining the steps which the OFT takes in calculating a penalty.[84] The current OFT guidance was published and came into effect in November 2004 (**Penalties Guidance**).[85] The OFT's Penalties Guidance sets out a five step approach taking into account the seriousness of the infringement, the relevant turnover of the undertaking, any aggravated factors, any mitigating factors, and, lastly, any prospect of double jeopardy (a duplicate fine imposed on the undertaking) and also a reduction in the event that the final amount exceeds the statutory maximum of 10 per cent of the worldwide turnover of the undertaking.

10.58 The requirement to 'have regard' to the Penalties Guidance was considered by the CAT in the *Allsports* case, where the CAT noted:

---

[82] ibid, paras 456 and 457. The CAT also applied these observations in later cases including *Aberdeen Journals (No 2)* [2003] CAT 11, paras 484–6 and *Genzyme Ltd v OFT* [2003] CAT 8, paras 689–91.

[83] *Umbro Holdings Ltd v OFT* [2005] CAT 22 (judgment on penalty), para 204. Note that if treated as separate infringements and fines, the OFT can in each case impose multipliers for repeated infringements as well. The OFT tends not to do this if it is treated as one fine; rather, it will just apply an uplift for deterrence.

[84] OFT423, *OFT's guidance as to the appropriate amount of a penalty* (December 2004).

[85] The European Commission also publishes equivalent guidance, 'Guidelines on the method of setting fines imposed pursuant to Article 23(2)(a) of Regulation no 1/2003', 28 June 2006, copy available on the Commission's website, <http://ec.europa.eu/comm/competition/antitrust/legislation/fines_en.pdf>. Fines are based on a percentage of the yearly sales in the relevant sector (up to 30%), multiplied for each year the infringement has continued. The guidance also incorporates an 'entry fee' (by which the Commission will, in cartel cases, add to the penalty amount a sum equal to 15–20% of the yearly relevant sales—and may add this in other cases); and also an increased fine for repeat offenders, including where the previous infringement decision was made by a national competition authority.

101. We accept, in principle, that when imposing a penalty on an undertaking, the OFT must 'have regard' to the *Guidance:* section 38(8) of the Act. In our judgment, in the statutory context 'have regard' imports a stronger obligation than merely 'take into account'. If the OFT were able to deviate significantly from the *Guidance* that would largely nullify the OFT's obligation not to alter the guidance without consultation (section 38(6) and (7) and render superfluous the need to obtain the approval of the Secretary of State (section 38(4)).

102. On the other hand, in our judgment it is implicit in the fact that the *Guidance* is just that—i.e. guidance, rather than precise statutory rules—that the OFT retains a margin of appreciation, both as to the interpretation of the *Guidance*, and as to its application in any particular case.[86]

The CAT has also made it clear that, although each step of the Penalties **10.59** Guidance is formally distinct, the Penalties Guidance cannot be treated as if the OFT is making a series of mechanical calculations according to a pre-determined mathematical formula. The Penalties Guidance contains a number of subjective and interrelated areas of judgment which necessarily play a part in the OFT setting the final penalty.[87]

(d) Step 1—seriousness and turnover

(i) Seriousness

The seriousness of the infringement is taken into account in determining the **10.60** starting point for a financial penalty imposed by the OFT. Seriousness will be determined by reference to the nature of the infringement, any damage caused to consumers, and other general factors relating to the infringement, such as the nature of the product, the undertaking's market share, and the effect on competitors and third parties.[88] The OFT's assessment of seriousness will determine the percentage of relevant turnover to be used as the starting point. The starting point will not exceed 10 per cent of the relevant turnover of the undertaking.[89]

In *Genzyme*, a case concerning abusive margins squeezing under the Chapter II **10.61** prohibition, a major factor in the CAT's reasoning behind the significant reduc-tion in penalty (from £6,809,598 to £3 million) appeared to relate to the fact that the evidence supported a less serious effect on the upstream market than the OFT's decision had suggested, and that it was difficult to show any gain on the part of Genzyme or any significant financial loss on the part of the affected parties.[90]

---

[86] *Umbro Holdings Ltd v OFT* [2005] CAT 22 (judgment on penalty), paras 101 and 102.
[87] ibid, para 105
[88] OFT423, *OFT's guidance as to the appropriate amount of a penalty* (December 2004) paras 2.3–2.5.
[89] ibid, para 2.8.   [90] *Genzyme v OFT* [2004] CAT 4, para 704.

10.62 Although seriousness is stated to relate to factors including the effect on competitors and other aspects of the infringement, the CAT has made it clear that the profit or 'gain' of the infringing party is not a relevant factor in fixing the penalty.[91] In the *Argos* case, a case concerning price fixing of toys, the CAT held that it was not relevant that the penalty set by the OFT was several times greater than the profit margin earned on the relevant products.[92]

10.63 The types of infringements which justify a starting point at or near the highest point, 10 per cent, are price fixing[93] and predatory pricing.[94] In price fixing cases, the fact that the relevant arrangement is found to be a concerted practice rather than a formal agreement does not make it a less serious infringement.[95] Predatory pricing, even of short duration, is generally considered to be a serious infringement of the Chapter II prohibition, and in the *Aberdeen Journals* case it was considered particularly serious because it was practised by an incumbent monopolist against its sole competitor.[96]

(ii) Relevant turnover

10.64 The OFT has stated that the relevant turnover calculated for the purposes of determining a penalty is 'the turnover of the undertaking in the relevant product market and relevant geographic market affected by the infringement in the undertaking's last business year'.[97] This is, by its very nature, a hypothetical test and resultant turnover may have no connection with the infringement in question.[98] The 'undertaking' in this context may include subsidiary entities as well.[99] Relevant turnover is calculated after deducting sales rebates, VAT, and other taxes directly related to turnover. It is possible for the relevant turnover of an undertaking to be zero. In that case, the starting point for a penalty would also be zero, however this may be adjusted upwards in the subsequent

---

[91] *Napp Pharmaceutical Holdings Ltd v Director General of Fair Trading*, Case No 1001/1/1/0115, January 2002, paras 507–9; *Genzyme v OFT* [2004] CAT 4, para 706.

[92] *Argos Ltd and Littlewoods Ltd v OFT* [2005] CAT 13 (judgment on penalty), para 228.

[93] ibid, para 216. Note that this starting point still has some flexibility: in the OFT's original decision appealed to the CAT in *Umbro Holdings Ltd v OFT* [2005] CAT 22 (judgment on penalty), the OFT applied a reduced starting point of 9% to reflect the fact that the price fixing agreement (for replica football shirts) did not extend to all of the products in the relevant market (such as shorts and socks); paras 78 and 148.

[94] *Aberdeen Journals Ltd v Director General of Fair Trading (No 2)* [2003] CAT 11, para 491, and *Napp Pharmaceutical Holdings Ltd v Director General of Fair Trading*, Case No 1001/1/1/0115, January 2002, paras 518–9.

[95] *Argos Ltd and Littlewoods Ltd v OFT* [2005] CAT 13 (judgment on penalty), para 217.

[96] *Aberdeen Journals Ltd v Director General of Fair Trading (No 2)* [2003] CAT 11, para 491.

[97] OFT423, *OFT's guidance as to the appropriate amount of a penalty* (December 2004) para 2.7.

[98] *Umbro Holdings Ltd v OFT* [2005] CAT 22 (judgment on penalty), paras 113–115.

[99] On the basis that the meaning of 'undertaking' in competition law can extend to subsidiary entities as well: see Chapter 1.

calculation steps. This occurred in the *Richard Price Roofing* case, where the OFT's methodology in this respect (albeit not the final amount) was upheld by the CAT on appeal.[100]

In *Argos*, the CAT observed that in a price fixing case there was no requirement **10.65** for the OFT to assess market power, and noted:

> In our judgment, it follows that in Chapter I cases involving price-fixing it would be inappropriate for the OFT to be required to establish the relevant market with the same rigour as would be expected in a case involving the Chapter II prohibition. In a case such as the present, definition of the relevant product market is not intrinsic to the determination of liability, as it is in a Chapter II case. In our judgment, it would be disproportionate to require the OFT to devote resources to a detailed market analysis, where the only issue is the penalty.[101]

This was later confirmed in the *Allsports* case, where the CAT held it was **10.66** 'sufficient for the OFT to show that it had a reasonable basis for identifying a certain product market for the purposes of Step 1 of its calculation'.[102] This issue was also confirmed by the Court of Appeal in its judgment dealing with the respective appeals of Argos, Littlewoods and JJB Sports:

> We agree that neither at the stage of the OFT investigation, nor on appeal to the Tribunal, is a formal analysis of the relevant product market necessary in order that regard can properly be had to step 1 of the Guidance in determining the appropriate penalty. The process of applying a SSNIP test (small but significant non-transitory increase in price) to determine what product or service is substitutable for any relevant item does not have to be undertaken in this context, nor does any other formal process of analysis need to be applied.

> On the other hand, the OFT and in turn the Tribunal do have to be satisfied, on a reasonable and properly reasoned basis, of what is the relevant product market affected by the infringement.[103]

The OFT may determine the turnover for the starting point taking into account **10.67** not only the turnover for the relevant product directly affected by the infringement but also the turnover in neighbouring or related products which may reasonably be considered to have been 'affected' by the infringement.[104] In a case

---

[100] *Richard W Price (Roofing Contractors) Ltd v OFT* [2005] CAT 5, para 59.

[101] *Argos Ltd and Littlewoods Ltd v OFT* [2005] CAT 13 (judgment on penalty), para 178; and see also *Umbro Holdings Ltd v OFT* [2005] CAT 22 (judgment on penalty), para 111.

[102] *Umbro*, ibid, para 112.

[103] *Argos and Littlewoods v OFT; and JJB Sports v OFT* [2006] EWCA 1318, paras 169 and 170.

[104] *Umbro*, ibid, para 116. In this case, the OFT included turnover in socks and shorts although the infringement only concerned shirts, on the basis that shirt prices had a 'spill over effect' on related products and they were sold together as a kit in the majority of cases. However, this is not subject to a 'cross-substitution' test as would be required for formal market definition. (Note this point was confirmed by the Court of Appeal in *Argos Limited and Ors v OFT* [2006] EWCA Civ 1318 but is on appeal to the House of Lords at the time of writing.)

involving many parties with multiple infringements of various kinds it is also reasonable for the OFT to use the same relevant product market across the board for calculating the penalty on all the parties to the infringement unless there are strong reasons for not doing so, even though there may be some differences of detail between the scope of the agreements in relation to the various related products at different periods of time.[105]

(e) Step 2—Duration

10.68 The starting point penalty may be adjusted (up or down) to take into account the duration of the infringement. This would normally be a straightforward multiplication based on the exact duration of the infringement. However, part years may be treated as full years for the purpose of this calculation.[106] In cases concerning the Chapter I prohibition or Article 81, duration for these purposes commences from the date of the agreement rather than the date the agreement comes into effect.[107] The duration ends on the date on which the undertaking concerned ceases to be involved in the infringement.[108]

10.69 Where the duration is particularly short, this may result in a reduction of the penalty imposed. In *Aberdeen Journals*, the fact that the infringement lasted only one month was taken into account by the CAT where it made an adjustment to reduce the fine by 25 per cent largely as a consequence of the short duration of the infringement.[109] This was raised again in the *Allsports* case (an infringement lasting three months), where the CAT confirmed that a short duration could be taken into account as a mitigating factor, but did not accept that there was any automatic rule built into step 2 that agreements of less than one year should attract a multiplier of less than one, stating:

> We accept that, at some point in the assessment of a penalty, the fact that an infringement was of a relatively short duration may, depending on the circumstances, be taken into account: see *Aberdeen Journals (No. 2)*, cited above, at paragraph 498 of the judgment. Thus, we do not accept that a short duration can never be taken into account, for example as a mitigating factor.
>
> We do not, however, accept that there should, in effect, be built into Step 2 of the *Guidance* an automatic rule that agreements of less than a year should attract a multiplier of less than one. Apart from the unduly mechanistic nature of such a

---

[105] *Umbro*, ibid, para 120. This is necessary for equal treatment to apply.

[106] OFT423, *OFT's guidance as to the appropriate amount of a penalty* (December 2004) para 2.10, and see also *Umbro Holdings Ltd v OFT* [2005] CAT 22 (judgment on penalty), para 182.

[107] *Umbro*, ibid, para 184.

[108] An undertaking may need to provide evidence of the conclusion of its involvement in the infringement, such as a price rise, a circular to clients, or discounts offered.

[109] *Aberdeen Journals Ltd v Director General of Fair Trading (No 2)* [2003] CAT 11, paras 489 and 499.

rule, there are at least two objections. First, as the OFT points out, an important element of the infringement committed is the fact that the agreement was made in the first place, rather than how long it lasted. Secondly, depending on the circumstances, an agreement of short duration of a serious nature may be a more serious infringement than one which lasts longer but has less serious effects.[110]

Delay in the OFT's proceedings cannot generally be regarded as a factor operat- **10.70** ing to reduce a penalty, unless it is excessive.[111] However, where the delay of the OFT causes the infringement to continue for a longer period of time than it would have otherwise done, this may be sufficient to justify a reduction in penalty.[112]

(f) Step 3—Adjustment for other factors

The third step in the OFT's calculation of a financial penalty is to increase or **10.71** decrease the penalty based on deterrence, aggravating factors, and mitigating factors. The list of factors which the OFT may take into account is not exhaustive and it is open to the OFT to take into account other factors which have not been previously considered, or are not listed in the OFT's guidance as to the appropriate amount of a penalty.

Generally, instead of calculating an additional amount to be added (or possibly **10.72** subtracted) from the figure reached after steps 1 and 2, the OFT will apply a multiplier to reach its adjusted amount. There is also a link between steps 1 and 3. The OFT has some flexibility in taking its starting point at step 1 and then, at step 3, if the penalty at that point does not seem high enough 'in the round', applying an appropriate multiplier. On this basis, the CAT dismissed arguments made by Argos and Littlewoods that the OFT set their penalties too high at step 1. The CAT held that in circumstances where the OFT did not impose any multiplier at step 3, had the OFT taken the lower alternative starting point, it would have been justified in taking a multiplier of 2–3 at step 3, thus bringing the penalties up to the same level in any event.[113]

In calculating the adjustment, if any, required for ensuring a deterrent effect, the **10.73** OFT will take into account factors which will be relevant to deterring the

---

[110] *Umbro Holdings Ltd v OFT* [2005] CAT 22 (judgment on penalty), paras 181 and 182. Eg, an infringement which covers a short but high impact selling period such as Christmas may have more serious effects than a longer period over a different time of year.

[111] *Argos Ltd and Littlewoods Ltd v OFT* [2005] CAT 13 (judgment on penalty), paras 230 and 231. It was suggested that an eight year delay might qualify as excessive but a nine month delay in that case did not so qualify.

[112] Case 6/73 *Commercial Solvents Corp v Commission* [1974] ECR 223 and see *Argos*, ibid, para 231. Eg, it may be argued that the undertaking could have stopped its practice as soon as it received a Statement of Objections.

[113] *Argos*, ibid, paras 207–211.

undertaking(s) subject to the decision (private deterrence), as well as factors relevant to deterring other undertakings which might be considering similar activity (public interest deterrence). Thus, as part of private deterrence, relevant factors will include any economic advantage which was made or intended to be made by the infringing undertaking as a result of the infringement.[114] In the CAT decision in *Allsports*, relevant factors included the size, strength, and high profile nature of the company;[115] whether there was a deliberate disregard for the law;[116] and whether there was any other disregard for requirements imposed by the OFT, such as a violation of previous voluntary assurances given to the OFT.[117] Factors relevant to public interest deterrence include extent of similar practices in the industry.

10.74   The issue of fairness to all parties to the same infringement has been raised on occasion by appellants who, upon seeing the details of the OFT's decision-making process as to penalty in relation to other undertakings subject to the same infringement, appeal on the ground that their own penalty is unfair, relative to that imposed on the others. However, the fact that one party to an infringing agreement has escaped penalty as a result of cooperation or leniency does not provide any basis for reduction of the penalties imposed on the other parties to the infringing agreement.[118]

10.75   In the *Price Roofing* case, the OFT conceded 'that it is appropriate for the Tribunal to take into account whether there is proportionality as between the penalties imposed on the various undertakings found to have been party to the concerted practices at issue'.[119] On appeal, the CAT noted:

> The principle of equal treatment in setting penalties is well established in both Community law (see e.g. Joined Cases T-236/01 etc *Tokai Carbon v Commission*, judgment of 29 April 2004, not yet reported, at paragraphs 228 and 244) and English law. On the figures submitted to us we are satisfied that this principle has not been applied when setting the penalty imposed on Price. We take into account the penalties imposed on the other undertakings, the relationship between the turnover of those undertakings and the penalties imposed on them, that Price had no relevant turnover, that Price only committed one infringement but that there was involvement on the part of a director and also that the OFT's calculation of

---

[114] OFT423, *OFT's guidance as to the appropriate amount of a penalty* (December 2004) para 2.11.

[115] *Umbro Holdings Ltd v OFT* [2005] CAT 22 (judgment on penalty), paras 170 and 173.

[116] ibid, paras 171 and 172.   [117] ibid, para 173.

[118] *Argos Ltd and Littlewoods Ltd v OFT* [2005] CAT 13 (judgment on penalty), para 139. See also *Umbro Holdings Ltd v OFT* [2005] CAT 22 (judgment on penalty), where a leniency applicant was given a privileged position versus the other parties to the infringement (para 280).

[119] *Richard W Price (Roofing Contractors) Ltd v OFT* [2005] CAT 5, para 60. See also Joined Cases T 191 & 212–214/98 *Atlantic Container Line* [2003] ECR II-3275, which set out the principle of equal treatment in fining.

Price's penalty for deterrent effect was necessarily based on an arbitrary assessment since Price had no relevant turnover. Having regard to all the above features we consider that the penalty should be reduced to £9,000. We are satisfied that in the circumstances of this case such a level of penalty provides an effective deterrent.[120]

In *Allsports*, the CAT commented on the resultant fine on Umbro being much **10.76** higher than the fine on the other appellants, noting that it was the calculation of turnover which gave some cause for concern:

174. As to the submission that it is unfair to the other appellants that the OFT imposed only a multiplier of 2 on Umbro at Step 3, the Tribunal is concerned by Umbro's penalty in this case, but for a reason opposite to that advanced by the appellants. The situation in the present case is that Umbro's business is to a large extent concerned with replica kit, with the consequence that the infringements related to a far larger proportion of Umbro's total turnover than was the case with the other appellants. In those circumstances the calculation based on relevant turnover envisaged by the *Guidance* is likely to result in a penalty on Umbro which is much higher, when expressed as a proportion of total turnover, or as a proportion of the statutory maximum, than the penalty imposed on other parties such as JJB, Allsports or MU.

175. Thus, for illustrative purposes, the situation can be seen in the following Table, on the basis of the penalties imposed in the Decision:

	Penalty	Penalty as % of UK turnover	Penalty as % of statutory maximum
Umbro	£6.641	7.9	44.6
JJB	£8.373	1.3	8.7
Allsports	£1.350	1.0	9.7
MU	£1.652	1.5	14.5

176. In our view, a penalty which represents 8 per cent of a company's United Kingdom turnover is significantly more severe than a penalty which represents only around 1 per cent of a company's United Kingdom turnover. A company whose penalty is over 40 per cent of the statutory maximum has a heavier penalty to bear than a company whose penalty is only 8 to 14 per cent of the statutory maximum. In our view the solely turnover-based approach of the *Guidance* gives rise to a risk that a company which is no more culpable than another company may find itself facing a penalty which in practice [is] more severe, simply because of differences in the 'mix' of turnover between the two companies. In our view this potentially gives rise to a risk of unfairness, which the OFT should guard against.

177. At this stage of the judgment it suffices to say that in our view the OFT was entirely correct to decide to apply a lower multiplier to Umbro for deterrence, on the ground that the resulting penalty, expressed as a proportion of Umbro's turnover, was sufficiently high to have a deterrent effect. As it is, Umbro's penalty

---

[120] *Price Roofing*, ibid, para 63. Note that the case referred to, *Tokai Carbon*, is now reported and the full citation is [2004] ECR II-1181.

as a proportion of turnover and as a proportion of the statutory maximum is significantly more severe than the penalty imposed on the other appellants, which is a matter to which we revert later in this judgment.[121]

(g) Step 4—Aggravating or mitigating factors

10.77 At this step, the OFT may adjust the financial penalty upwards or downwards depending on relevant factors in the particular case. There are no set aggravating or mitigating factors. However, the OFT has set out in its guidance an inclusive list of aggravating factors and an inclusive list of mitigating factors.

10.78 The OFT has noted that aggravating factors include:

(1) role of the undertaking as a leader in, or an instigator of, the infringement;[122]

(2) involvement of directors or senior management (notwithstanding the prosecution or conviction of individuals under s 188 of the Enterprise Act 2002 in connection with an infringement);[123]

(3) retaliatory or other coercive measures taken against other undertakings aimed at ensuring the continuation of the infringement;

(4) continuing the infringement after the start of the OFT's investigation;

(5) repeated infringements by the same undertaking or other undertakings in the same group;[124]

(6) infringements which are committed intentionally rather than negligently;[125] and

(7) retaliatory measures taken or commercial reprisals sought by the undertaking against a leniency applicant.[126]

10.79 Other aggravating factors which have been referred to in the OFT's decisions include ignoring legal advice, concealing evidence, and breach of assurances given to the OFT.

10.80 The OFT has listed mitigating factors as including:

---

[121] *Umbro Holdings Ltd v OFT* [2005] CAT 22 (judgment on penalty), paras 174–177.

[122] ibid, paras 39 and 203

[123] *Richard W Price (Roofing Contractors) Ltd v OFT* [2005] CAT 5, para 30, which sets out the relevant para of the OFT's decision of 16 March 2004, para 458; *Umbro Holdings Ltd v OFT* [2005] CAT 22 (judgment on penalty), para 203; and *Argos Ltd and Littlewoods Ltd v OFT* [2005] CAT 13 (judgment on penalty), para 47.

[124] *Umbro Holdings Ltd v OFT* [2005] CAT 22 (judgment on penalty), paras 63 and 204 (JJB's involvement in an infringement was counted as a separate and repeated infringement and thus an aggravating factor).

[125] Although the question of intentional or negligent does not need to be decided for the purposes of the preliminary condition for imposing a penalty, the question of whether the infringement was intentional or negligent may go to mitigation: *Aberdeen Journals Ltd v Director General of Fair Trading (No 2)* [2003] CAT 11, para 484.

[126] OFT423, *OFT's guidance as to the appropriate amount of a penalty* (December 2004) para 2.15.

(1) role of the undertaking, for example, where the undertaking is acting under severe duress or pressure;[127]

(2) genuine uncertainty on the part of the undertaking as to whether the agreement or conduct constituted an infringement;[128]

(3) adequate steps having been taken with a view to ensuring compliance with Articles 81 and 82 and the Chapter I and Chapter II prohibitions;[129]

(4) termination of the infringement as soon as the OFT intervenes;[130] and

(5) cooperation which enables the enforcement process to be concluded more effectively and/or speedily.[131]

Other mitigating factors appear to include: an admission of liability;[132] the **10.81** 'failing firm' defence;[133] and a public apology or some other action taken to compensate consumers.[134] The fact that the finding on liability was on the basis of a concerted practice rather than an agreement will not amount to a mitigating factor.[135]

Often the total of aggravating and mitigating factors may cancel each other **10.82** out. In *Price Roofing*, the penalty was increased by 10 per cent to reflect the involvement of a director of Price in the infringement; it was then mitigated by 20 per cent to reflect Price's cooperation and acceptance of the infringements.[136]

In relation to compliance as a mitigating factor, in *Allsports* the CAT did not **10.83** think any mitigation was warranted for introduction of a compliance programme where that took place after the penalty decision and after the appeal had been commenced,[137] although in relation to another party in the same case, some credit was given for evidence of a compliance programme being strengthened after the infringement took place.[138] The CAT noted:

---

[127] *Umbro Holdings Ltd v OFT* [2005] CAT 22 (judgment on penalty), para 346.

[128] *Aberdeen Journals Ltd v Director General of Fair Trading (No 2)* [2003] CAT 11, para 484.

[129] *Umbro Holdings Ltd v OFT* [2005] CAT 22 (judgment on penalty), para 263 (see also the discussion at paras 10.83 and 10.84 below).

[130] It is worth noting that the mitigating factor of prompt termination of the infringing conduct or agreement once the OFT intervenes was not previously considered to be a mitigating factor: in *Argos* an argument to this effect put forward by Littlewoods was rejected by the CAT, observing: 'It seems to us that termination of an infringement when the OFT intervenes should happen as a matter of course and not be a factor justifying a reduction in the penalty' (*Argos Ltd and Littlewoods Ltd v OFT* [2005] CAT 13 (judgment on penalty), para 233). However, this is now quite clearly an option.

[131] OFT423, *OFT's guidance as to the appropriate amount of a penalty* (December 2004) para 2.16.

[132] *Umbro Holdings Ltd v OFT* [2005] CAT 22 (judgment on penalty), paras 201 and 265.

[133] This is not certain—see discussion at para 10.88, below.

[134] *Umbro Holdings Ltd v OFT* [2005] CAT 22 (judgment on penalty), paras 265 and 266.

[135] ibid, para 205.

[136] *Richard W Price (Roofing Contractors) Ltd v OFT* [2005] CAT 5.

[137] *Umbro Holdings Ltd v OFT* [2005] CAT 22 (judgment on penalty), para 194.

[138] ibid, para 263.

While, of course, the introduction of compliance programmes is desirable, to continue to be party to an infringement while simultaneously introducing a compliance programme is in our view capable of being an aggravating factor. It is capable of being an aggravating factor because the circumstances may show that the executives of the company continued to infringe the Act notwithstanding that their attention had been specifically drawn to its provisions.[139]

10.84 It appears that compliance programmes must therefore be adequate, in that they ought to prevent the directors from breaching the competition laws. Some guidance may be derived from the High Court guidance given in the previous regulatory context,[140] which referred to a number of requirements in relation to compliance programmes, including: programmes are to be in writing and to involve lectures and tuition; all levels of staff in the business are to be subject to the programme; principles are to be incorporated into contracts of employments along with sanctions for breach; and staff are to sign acknowledgements of their understanding of the programme and its aims.

10.85 Mitigation for cooperation is an important consideration. In general, cooperation will require the undertaking to stop its involvement in the infringement, provide complete cooperation with the OFT (ie provide all relevant documents and information), and provide continuous cooperation (ie throughout the investigative period and any appeal). There is also a clear distinction between mitigation in the penalty calculation on the basis of cooperation, and a reduction in penalty pursuant to a successful leniency application. In *Allsports*, Umbro attempted to use its failed leniency application in order to gain an additional reduction in penalty for cooperation on top of the 40 per cent it had already received. The CAT found that the leniency application was quite separate from general cooperation as mitigating factor and that the OFT was right not to take it into account. The CAT held that the discount of 40 per cent was already generous, and declined to reduce the penalty further on this basis, noting that any further reduction would have undermined the leniency regime, where a discount of up to 50 per cent may have been obtained in the circumstances.[141]

10.86 The conduct of the appeal before the CAT can also give rise to a reduction in penalty.[142] In *Allsports* this issue was raised by Umbro, and the CAT observed that examples of such mitigation could include a frank acceptance of responsibility, an offer to make amends, or fresh evidence of extenuating circumstances.[143] However, in that case Umbro was not successful in obtaining any further reduction because matters such as provision of witnesses for cross examination and

---

[139] ibid, para 254.   [140] Concerning the Restrictive Trade Practices Act.
[141] *Umbro Holdings Ltd v OFT* [2005] CAT 22 (judgment on penalty), para 333.
[142] *Aberdeen Journals v Director General of Fair Trading (No 2)* [2003] CAT 11, para 496.
[143] *Umbro Holdings Ltd v OFT* [2005] CAT 22 (judgment on penalty), para 336.

responding to document requests were held to be simply 'incidents of litigation' and did not amount to cooperation over and above what might reasonably be expected of a company in that position.[144]

Accepting responsibility and apologising are relevant factors for mitigation, as observed by the CAT in *Allsports*: **10.87**

> At the final penalty hearing MU did, however, accept its responsibility for infringing the Act, and apologised. We would have given much greater credit had that been done earlier in the proceedings, and had it been accompanied by a preparedness to recompense consumers, either directly or by contributing to causes likely to benefit relevant consumer interests, particularly disadvantaged consumers. However, we do give some credit for MU's acceptance of responsibility, however belated.[145]

Financial hardship will also be relevant where it applies: In *Price Roofing* the **10.88** OFT conceded that, had financial hardship been advanced by a party at the time that the penalty was assessed, it would have been considered and not dismissed as entirely irrelevant.[146] This issue was raised before the CAT in *Achilles*, where the CAT noted that it ought as far as possible to act consistently with the principles applicable to comparable situations under Community law. Those principles were referred to as being, in effect, that entities could not pray in aid their economic difficulties and those of the market in seeking a reduction in the penalty. However, the CAT noted that in this respect the OFT's guidance differs from that applicable to the European Commission, and the CAT took the view that 'where the OFT does in fact consider an undertaking's submission concerning financial hardship under Step 3, it must ensure that it bases that consideration on the appropriate and accurate figures'.[147] The CAT also agreed with the OFT's submission that 'the fact that a fine may result in a company going into liquidation and exiting the market is something that the OFT should take into account but is not necessarily a reason for reducing the fine'[148] and also held that the OFT was not required to take into account the legal and professional fees incurred by the undertaking in relation to the investigation when setting the level of the fine.[149] Achilles raised a further argument that its exit from the relevant market might leave one market player with very significant power: this argument did not find favour with the CAT, which noted that limiting fines on this basis would be unworkable, and that consideration of how to balance deterrence as against possible adverse effects on the market structure was a 'consideration within the OFT's margin of appreciation'.[150]

---

[144] ibid, paras 337–9. [145] ibid, para 265.

[146] *Richard W Price (Roofing Contractors) Ltd v OFT* [2005] CAT 5, para 60.

[147] *Achilles Paper Group Ltd v OFT* [2006] CAT 24, paras 21–3, 42 and 43, and see also the case referred to therein: Case T-236/01 *Tokai Carbon Co v Commission* [2004] ECR II-1181.

[148] ibid, paras 55 and 56. [149] ibid, para 57. [150] ibid, paras 58 and 59.

(h) Step 5—Penalties cap and double jeopardy

10.89 The final step in the OFT's assessment of a penalty is to reduce the penalty to the extent that it exceeds the maximum allowable penalty, and to take into account any fines which have already been imposed in relation to that particular infringement.

10.90 The OFT may not impose a penalty which exceeds 10 per cent of the worldwide turnover of the undertaking in its last business year.[151] This statutory maximum applies in respect of decisions in relation to Articles 81 and 82, as well as decisions in relation to the Chapter I prohibition and the Chapter II prohibition. The application of the statutory maximum is applied by the OFT at the end of its fining assessment; thus if, at the end of the fining assessment, the final amount exceeds the statutory maximum, it will be reduced accordingly.

10.91 The assessment of turnover of an undertaking for the purposes of determining the statutory limit is 'the applicable turnover for the business year preceding the date on which the decision of the OFT is taken or, if figures are not available for that business year, the one immediately preceding it'.[152] This test refers to total turnover, not just the turnover in respect of the products affected by the infringement, or in respect of the geographic area of the infringement. The CAT clarified this in *Napp*, stating:

> It is clear from that Order that Parliament intended that it is the overall turnover of the undertaking concerned, rather than its turnover in the products affected by the infringement, which is the final determinant for the amount of the penalty . . .[153]

10.92 In applying the maximum penalty cap in relation to an infringement of an association of undertakings, the calculation depends upon whether the financial penalties are being imposed on the association itself or its members. Where the penalty is being imposed on the association itself, the application of the penalty cap will relate to the turnover of the association. However, where the infringement relates to the activities of the association's members, the relevant cap is set at 10 per cent of the sum of the worldwide turnover of each member active on the market affected by the infringement.[154]

---

[151] Competition Act 1998 (Determination of Turnover for Penalties) Order 2000, SI 2000/309, as amended by the Competition Act 1998 (Determination of Turnover for Penalties) (Amendment) Order 2004, SI 2004/1259. The OFT has noted that the business year on the basis of which turnover is determined is the one preceding the date on which the OFT's decision is taken (see OFT423, *OFT's guidance as to the appropriate amount of a penalty* (December 2004) para 2.17).

[152] SI 2000/309 (as amended by SI 2000/2952, SI 2002/765 and SI 2004/1259) Art 3.

[153] *Napp Pharmaceutical Holdings Ltd v Director General of Fair Trading*, Case No 1001/1/1/0115, January 2002, para 501.

[154] OFT423, *OFT's guidance as to the appropriate amount of a penalty* (December 2004) para 2.19 and see also OFT408, *Trade associations, professions and self-regulating bodies* (December 2004) paras 8.2–8.4.

Prior to 1 May 2004, the relevant penalty cap (which only applied in respect of **10.93**
Chapter I and Chapter II) was set at 10 per cent of the *UK* turnover of the
undertaking. The increase in the maximum cap was made in order to bring the
OFT's maximum penalty applicable into line with that applicable in respect of
decisions taken by the European Commission.[155] In practice, even when the
lower maximum cap was applicable, the OFT has never had to adjust any
penalty as a result of exceeding the maximum.

It is at step 5 that the OFT will also take into account any other penalties which **10.94**
have been imposed on the undertakings. Section 38(9) of the Competition Act
1998 states:

> If a penalty or a fine has been imposed by the Commission, or by a Court or
> another body in another Member State, in respect of an agreement or contract, the
> OFT, an appeal tribunal or the appropriate Court must take that penalty or fine
> into account when setting the amount of the penalty under this Part in relation to
> that agreement or conduct.

The OFT has noted that this is to ensure that an undertaking is not penalised **10.95**
twice for the same anti-competitive effects.[156] In relation to fines imposed in the
United States, such fines have been held to be irrelevant (in the context of fines
imposed by the European Commission) by the Court of First Instance in the
British Airways case.[157] This would similarly apply to fines imposed by the OFT.

It is also worth noting that this step also includes fines which have previously **10.96**
been imposed by the OFT, and in particular this addresses the theoretical problem of a duplicate fine in relation to Article 81 and Chapter I, or Article 82 and
Chapter II. However, it is possible that the fines in such cases may differ, and
the example provided by the OFT is where an infringement commenced
before 1 March 2000, when the Competition Act 1998 entered into force. An
infringement pre-dating that date may still be subject to a penalty in respect of
an infringement of Article 81 or Article 82, even if Chapter I or Chapter II does
not apply.[158]

(i) Immunity from fines

Regardless of the OFT's power to impose penalties and the above steps to be **10.97**
taken in calculating a penalty, there are three ways in which an undertaking may

---

[155] There are certain transitional matters in respect of infringements which pre-dated the
increase in the statutory maximum. These issues are discussed at paras 10.111 et seq, below.
[156] OFT423, *OFT's guidance as to the appropriate amount of a penalty* (December 2004)
para 2.20. See also Chapter 11 on double jeopardy.
[157] Case T-219/99 *British Airways plc v Commission* [2003] ECR II-5197.
[158] OFT423, *OFT's guidance as to the appropriate amount of a penalty* (December 2004)
paras 1.15 and 1.16.

be immune from the application of any penalty. Immunity from the fines relates to certain protections in place for small businesses, protections in relation to agreements which fall within exemptions or exclusions, and undertakings who qualify for lenient treatment pursuant to the OFT's leniency programme.

(i) Protection for small businesses

10.98 In the United Kingdom, small businesses are protected from penalties in respect of most competition law infringements under the Chapter I or Chapter II prohibitions. The protection is set out in the Competition Act 1998, ss 36(4) and (5), 39 and 40, and the Competition Act 1998 (Small Agreements and Conduct of Minor Significance) Regulations 2000.[159] Where an agreement (which would otherwise infringe the Chapter I prohibition) is made between undertakings whose combined annual turnover is less than £20 million, those undertakings may qualify for immunity from fines. In respect of the conduct of an undertaking which infringes the Chapter II prohibition, where the undertaking's turnover is less than £50 million, that undertaking may qualify for immunity from fines. In addition to the turnover requirement, the OFT must also be satisfied that the undertaking or undertakings acted on the reasonable assumption that on the facts they qualified for the limited immunity.[160]

10.99 This protection for small businesses does not cover price fixing agreements, nor does it cover any infringement of Article 81 or Article 82. Further, the OFT has the power to withdraw the immunity in particular cases, although this has not been done to date.

(ii) Exemptions and exclusions

10.100 The effect of block exemptions, exclusions and individual exemptions is discussed in Chapter 4 above. Exemptions and exclusions do not provide any protection in respect of penalties relating to infringements of Article 82 or Chapter II. In summary, where an agreement falls within the scope of a block exemption, the undertakings party to that agreement will be immune from penalties (in relation to both Article 81 and Chapter I) until that block exemption is withdrawn. If however an agreement contains a hardcore restriction, the agreement will not benefit from a block exemption and parties will be exposed to fines. Likewise, an individual exemption under Article 81(3) will protect undertakings from penalties while it remains valid in respect of the relevant competition law infringement to which it is stated to apply. The same applies in relation to an exclusion, except that exclusions are only relevant to UK domestic competition law and therefore do not provide any protection from Article 81 infringements.

---

[159] SI 2000/262.   [160] Competition Act 1998, s 36(4) and (5).

The OFT has powers to withdraw block exemptions, exclusions, and individual **10.101** exemptions which it has issued. However, to date, the OFT has not exercised this power.[161] Once an exemption or exclusion is withdrawn, any penalty may only be applied from that date forward. Where an agreement does not fall within the scope of a block exemption or an exclusion, but the undertakings in question reasonably believed that the agreement did fall within the scope of the exemption or exclusion, this may be taken into account as a mitigating factor at step 4 in the penalties process noted above, but does not provide any certain immunity or benefit.

(iii) Leniency

Where an undertaking qualifies for lenient treatment by the OFT, this will **10.102** result in a reduction of up to 100 per cent of any penalty which might otherwise have been imposed by the OFT. The OFT's leniency programme is discussed in full in Chapter 5 above. The OFT's leniency programme does not apply in relation to infringements of Article 82 or the Chapter II prohibitions. Any reduction in relation to a leniency application is applied after the final step in the OFT's assessment of penalties as noted above.

(j) Procedure for a penalty order

When the OFT issues a Statement of Objections,[162] it must indicate whether it **10.103** intends to impose a penalty, but will not, at that stage, provide reasons or any penalty amount.[163] When a final decision is made, including a penalty decision, the OFT is required to inform the undertaking in writing of the facts upon which it bases the penalty and its reasons for requiring the undertaking to pay the penalty.[164] The OFT will not disclose its reasoning in respect of any other undertakings where to do so would expose confidential information relating to re-turnover. The OFT is also required to publish the penalties it imposes in relation to competition law infringements although the details of its calculation will be redacted for confidentiality reasons.[165]

(k) Payment and enforcement

When the OFT makes a final decision including a penalty decision, the OFT **10.104** is required to serve a written notice on the undertaking required to pay the

---

[161] Note that specific investigative powers apply in relation to the withdrawal of a block exemption or an exclusion by the OFT.

[162] OFT's Procedural Rules, r 4.

[163] The requirement for the OFT to state its intention to impose penalties is derived from Community law.

[164] OFT's Procedural Rules, r 8(2).   [165] ibid, r 8(4).

penalty. That written notice must specify the date by which the penalty is required to be paid. This is normally three months from the date of that notice.[166] The date specified for payment must not be earlier than the end of the period within which an appeal against the notice may be brought under s 46 of the Competition Act 1998.[167]

10.105 Where the time for payment of the penalty has expired (and no appeal has been made) the OFT may recover the amount outstanding as a civil debt due to the OFT.[168] The Limitation Act 1980 applies to the OFT in relation to any action it may take in order to recover a penalty imposed. The Limitation Act 1980 applies to prevent the OFT from bringing any action to recover any sum recoverable after the expiration of six years from the date on which the cause of action accrued.[169]

10.106 The OFT may also recover interest in respect of any amount outstanding, by virtue of the rules of civil procedure for recovery of a debt in the United Kingdom.[170] In relation to the tax position on penalties, para 5.15 of the Enforcement Guideline[171] states:

> It is the view of the Inland Revenue that financial penalties imposed under the Act will not be deductible in computing trading profits for tax purposes. This is because civil or criminal penalties imposed by or under the authority of an act of parliament are not deductible: they are 'losses not connected with or arising out of the trade' and so not deductible by virtue of section 74(1)(e) of the Income and Corporation Company Taxes Act 1988.

(i) Effect of appeal

10.107 The rights of appeal and procedure for appeals of parties and third parties are set out in Chapter 12 below. The only type of appeal which will automatically suspend the effect of a penalty imposed by the OFT is an appeal by the under-taking the subject of the decision against the imposition, or the amount, of a penalty.[172] In those cases, although the requirement to pay the penalty will be suspended until the appeal is determined, the CAT may order that interest is payable from a date as early as the date on which the appeal was made.[173]

---

[166] OFT407, *Enforcement* (December 2004) para 5.38.

[167] Competition Act 1998, s 36(7).   [168] ibid, s 37(1).

[169] Limitation Act 1980, s 9. Also note that the Limitation Act 1980 does not extend to Scotland.

[170] Civil Procedure Rules, available at <http://www.dca.gov.uk/civil/procrules_fin/menus/rules.htm>.

[171] OFT407, *Enforcement* (December 2004). See also *Commissioners of Inland Revenue v Alexander von Glehn and Co Ltd* 12 TC 232 (allowing fines to be deducted as a business expense would encourage undertakings to believe wrongly that they can disregard the fines merely as a business expense item).

[172] Competition Act 1998, s 46(4).

[173] *Napp Pharmaceutical Holdings Ltd v Director General of Fair Trading*, Case No 1001/1/1/0115, January 2002, paras 542 and 543.

Note that in considering the penalty on appeal, the CAT is not bound by the **10.108**
Penalties Guidance and is not even required to have regard to such guidance,[174]
but the CAT stated in *Napp* that 'it does not seem to us appropriate to disregard
the Director's Guidance, or the Director's own approach in the Decision
under challenge, when reaching our own conclusion as to what the penalty
should be'.[175]

On appeal, the CAT can increase the penalty,[176] as it held in *Allsports*, dismissing **10.109**
arguments that the CAT was limited to the remedies sought in the notice of
appeal[177] and could not rely on new matters which had not been the subject of
the Statement of Objections.[178] However, the CAT held that it would only
exercise its powers in exceptional circumstances.[179] In the case of *Allsports*, the
CAT did in fact increase the penalty by revoking a 5 per cent reduction for
cooperation on the ground that Allsports' 'admission' of liability could not
reasonably be regarded as cooperation when the evidence subsequently revealed
during the appeal showed that it was incomplete and misleading.[180]

(ii) Destination of penalty funds

Any sums received by the OFT in relation to penalties imposed are paid into the **10.110**
Consolidated Fund.[181] This applies to penalties paid in respect of the Chapter I
and Chapter II prohibitions and also penalties paid to the OFT in respect of
infringements of Article 81 and Article 82.

(l) Transitional matters

(i) Change in maximum penalty cap

From the commencement of the Competition Act 1998 on 1 March 2000 up to **10.111**
1 May 2004, the applicable cap on penalties was set at 10 per cent of an
undertaking's UK turnover, which could be multiplied by up to three years of
turnover depending upon the time frame of the infringement. This previous
penalty cap continues to apply in respect of infringements of Chapter I or

---

[174] ibid, para 497. This was confirmed by the Court of Appeal in *Argos Limited and Ors v OFT* [2006] EWCA Civ, para 165.
[175] ibid, para 500.
[176] *Umbro Holdings Ltd v OFT* [2005] CAT 22 (judgment on penalty), para 214; Competition Act 1998, Sch 8, para 3.
[177] *Umbro Holdings Ltd v OFT* [2005] CAT 22 (judgment on penalty), para 216.
[178] ibid, para 217.
[179] ibid, paras 218 and 219. This was based on Case T-236/01 *Tokai Carbon Co Ltd v Commission* [2004] ECR II-1181—increase by the ECJ.
[180] ibid, paras 220–235.
[181] Competition Act 1998, s 36(9).

Chapter II where the infringement finished before 1 May 2004.[182] In relation to Article 81 or Article 82 infringements, the OFT has stated that it intends to apply the new penalty cap regardless of whether the infringement spans or was concluded before 1 May 2004. As no cap existed for those infringements as applies by the OFT before 1 May 2004, it could be argued that no fines ought to apply in respect of such infringement. However, the OFT would argue that the infringement always existed (on the basis that Articles 81 and 82 have had direct effect since 1973) and only the enforcement body is different. Further, the OFT would, in most cases, not apply any penalty in respect of the Article 81 or 82 infringement on the basis that to do so would be a duplication of penalties where a penalty had already been imposed in respect of Chapter I or Chapter II infringements.[183]

E. Directions

(a) Powers of the OFT

10.112 Where the OFT has made an infringement decision, it also has the power to make such directions as it considers appropriate to bring the infringement to an end.[184] This power, and the section below, apply equally to the Regulators. The Competition Act 1998 provides that a direction made in this regard may include provisions requiring the parties to an agreement to modify that agreement, terminate the infringing agreement, or, in the case of the Chapter II prohibition, requiring the person concerned to modify the conduct in question or cease that conduct. In this regard, there is an important distinction between 'behavioural' type directions and 'structural' type directions. Although the Competition Act 1998 does not prohibit particular types of directions being made by the OFT, the examples which are given in ss 32(3) and 33(3) are essentially behavioural directions and not structural directions. To date, the OFT has not made any structural directions in relation to competition law infringements and there is an argument available that, were such a direction to be made, it would be ultra vires under the Competition Act. However, the OFT has provided guidance indicating that in some circumstances the directions it may make may be directions requiring an undertaking to make structural changes to its business.[185] There is also a need to interpret the Competition Act

---

[182] OFT423, *OFT's guidance as to the appropriate amount of a penalty* (December 2004) para 2.18.
[183] It is not clear whether it would be different where the Chapter I or Chapter II fine is based on UK turnover—it is possible that the Art 81/82 fine may extend further geographically.
[184] Competition Act 1998, s 32 (in relation to agreements) and s 33 (in relation to conduct).
[185] OFT407, *Enforcement* (December 2004) para 2.3.

consistently with EC law, and provide remedies to ensure the effectiveness of the EC competition rules. Thus the OFT may need to impose structural remedies for infringements of Article 81 or Article 82.[186]

(b) Procedure

Directions made by the OFT must be given in writing.[187] The directions may be **10.113** made against 'such person or persons as [the OFT] considers appropriate'.[188] However, the OFT must allow the person the subject of the direction an opportunity to make written representations, and to request oral representation in relation to the directions.[189]

Generally, the OFT will make any direction at the same time as it makes the **10.114** infringement decision. The OFT has, on occasion, given directions by separate letter issued some time after the infringement decision.[190]

(c) Appeal

Directions made by the OFT may be the subject of appeal to the CAT. **10.115** However, the effect of directions is not automatically suspended by the issue of an appeal against the directions.[191] A party wishing to suspend the effect of a direction to which an appeal relates will therefore need to apply for interim relief to the CAT. Interim relief can be granted before the main appeal is lodged.[192] In making a decision as to whether or not to grant interim relief, the CAT has indicated that it will take various factors into account, and will most likely seek undertakings that the party seeking the interim relief will lodge an appeal expeditiously. Ultimately, the CAT also has the power to reinstate the directions or other commitments for the duration of the appeal. See Chapter 12 below for further information in relation to appeals and the CAT's powers.

---

[186] European Commission powers in this regard stem from Regulation 1/2003, Art 7(1).

[187] Competition Act 1998, ss 32(4) and 33(4).

[188] ibid, ss 32(1) and 33(1). In ORR's decision in EWS, ORR gave directions addressed not only to EWS but also to its power generator customers requiring them to re-negotiate the terms of their contracts so as to bring then into conformity with Article 81. See press release at <http://rail-reg.gov.uk/server/show/ConWebDoc.8409>.

[189] OFT's Procedural Rules, r 5.

[190] See, eg, *Napp Pharmaceutical Holdings Ltd v Director General of Fair Trading*, Case No 1000/1/1/01, judgment of 22 May 2001 (judgment on request for interim relief) where the OFT's letter giving directions was sent five weeks after the infringement decision. The CAT noted that in such a situation complications may arise in calculating the time for appeal, and commented that it therefore seemed desirable that directions given under the Competition Act 1998 should be made in the same document, or at least at the same time, as the substantive decision of infringement upon which the directions are based (para 34).

[191] Competition Act 1998, s 46(4). See also *Napp*, ibid, para 36.

[192] *Napp*, ibid, para 32.

(d) Sanctions for non-compliance

10.116   The enforcement of directions by the OFT is by way of a court order, which effectively converts the OFT's directions into a court order, punishable as contempt of court for further non-compliance. However, in effect, before applying to the court, the OFT must make some form of inquiry into an alleged breach of its directions, as it needs to establish that there has been a failure to comply with a direction, and that the failure occurred without reasonable excuse.

F. Sanctions Against Individuals

10.117   The sanctions set out above in this chapter may also apply to individuals where the individual falls within the definition of an 'undertaking' for the purposes of the competition law (ie a sole trader or partnership). Further, sanctions which may be imposed on individuals in relation to obstruction of the OFT's information gathering powers are dealt with in Chapter 7, above, as these are not enforcement measures as such. However, in addition to the sanctions set out above, there are certain sanctions which may be applied in respect of individuals in the enforcement of competition law. These are competition disqualification orders (**CDOs**), imprisonment, and fines for individuals. Each of these sanctions is addressed below.

(a) Imprisonment and fines

10.118   A person convicted of the cartel offence (introduced by s 188 of the Enterprise Act 2002) may be penalised with a maximum sentence of five years' imprisonment and an unlimited fine. The cartel offence arises when an individual dishonestly agrees with one or more persons that two or more undertakings will engage in certain prohibited cartel arrangements, such as bid-rigging or price-fixing (see Chapter 1 for a discussion of the cartel offence).

10.119   The length of time for imprisonment and the level of any fine depends on the type of conviction. Where the conviction is on indictment, a person guilty of the cartel offence is liable to imprisonment for a term not exceeding five years or to an unlimited fine, or both.[193] Where the conviction is summary, a person found guilty of the cartel offence is liable to imprisonment for a term not exceeding six months or to a fine not exceeding the statutory maximum (currently £5,000), or to both.[194] These sanctions are criminal in nature, and may

---

[193] Enterprise Act 2002, s 190(1)(a).   [194] ibid, s 190(1)(b)

only be imposed by a court on the commencement of criminal proceedings by the Director of the Serious Fraud Office (**SFO**), or by (or with the consent of) the OFT. As these sanctions are criminal sanctions, the relevant standard of proof is the criminal standard of proving the elements of the offence beyond reasonable doubt.

For the first few years of the Enterprise Act 2002 coming into force, there were **10.120** no cartel investigations launched by the OFT, but in November 2006, the OFT launched both a civil and criminal investigation into an alleged price-fixing arrangement between British Airways and Virgin Atlantic in relation to fuel surcharges for long-haul passenger flights to and from the United Kingdom. At the time of writing, it is too early for any knowledge to have developed as a result of this case, but it is likely to be the first case where the procedures to be followed by the OFT (or the SFO) in conducting a cartel offence investigation are explored. The statutory powers applicable to investigation of a cartel offence are set out in Chapter 7.

(b) Competition disqualification orders

A CDO is a particular type of director's disqualification order which may **10.121** be made pursuant to the Company Director's Disqualification Act 1986.[195] Essentially, a court's power to impose a CDO arises in one of two ways: on an individual's conviction of a cartel offence; or pursuant to a specific application made by the OFT or a Regulator under the Company Director's Disqualification Act 1986.

(i) Cartel offence conviction

In relation to the first of these methods, the conviction of a cartel offence is one **10.122** of a number of other offences listed in the Company Director's Disqualification Act 1986 which may be committed in connection with the management of a company. In such a case the court's powers derive from s 2(1) and (2)(b) of the Company Director's Disqualification Act 1986. A CDO may, in these circumstances, be made by any court which convicts an individual of an indictable offence.[196] Where the OFT (or SFO) has provided an individual with a no-action letter,[197] the OFT will not apply for a CDO against that individual.[198] Where the OFT is able to use this method to obtain a CDO, it is unlikely to use its powers under s 9A of the Company Director's Disqualification Act 1986.

---

[195] ss 2 and 9A.
[196] The cartel offence is an indictable offence, pursuant to s 190 of the Enterprise Act 2002.
[197] See paras 5.81–5.105 above.
[198] OFT510, *Competition disqualification orders: Guidance* (May 2003) para 4.27.

(ii) Section 9A method

10.123 Even where an individual has not been convicted of a cartel offence, the OFT (and the Regulators) have a separate power to apply to the court[199] seeking a CDO. The court must impose a CDO where the two required elements are satisfied. These elements are:

- the person is a director of a company that has committed a breach of competition law; and
- the court considers the person's conduct was such as to make him unfit to be concerned in the management or control of a company.[200]

10.124 The first element, set out in s 9A(2) of the Company Director's Disqualification Act 1986, requires the individual to be a director of a company which commits a breach of competition law. The relevant competition law provisions are the Chapter I and Chapter II prohibitions and Articles 81 and 82. The court or authority making the infringement decision does not appear to be relevant.[201] The OFT considers that a director of an infringing company will also include a de facto director of such a company and thus may include directors or officers of a subsidiary's parent company.[202] There is no specific requirement that the individual concerned was a director at the time of the infringement. However, this is addressed by the application of the second element, set out below. Further, although it is not clear from s 9A(2) that the individual need not be a director of the relevant company at the time of the application for a CDO, it is difficult to conceive of any other sensible way of interpreting the legislation.

10.125 In relation to the second element, there are a number of requirements which a court must have regard to in determining whether the conduct of the director makes him unfit to be concerned in the management of a company.[203] Those matters are:

---

[199] The High Court in England and Wales, or the Court of Session in Scotland. There is a specific practice direction in the Civil Procedure Rules relating to Directors Disqualification Proceedings, available at <http://www.dca.gov.uk/civil/procrules_fin/contents/practice_directions/disqualification_proceedings.htm>.

[200] Company Director's Disqualification Act 1986, s 9A(1)–(3), as inserted by Enterprise Act 2002, s 204.

[201] The Company Director's Disqualification Act 1986 does not include any limitation on the entity making the relevant infringement decision. Further, in OFT510, *Competition disqualification orders: Guidance* (May 2003) para 4.6, it is noted that the OFT only intends to apply for CDOs in respect of competition law infringements proven in decisions or judgments of the OFT or a Regulator, the European Commission, the CAT, or the European Court.

[202] This view and the reasons for it are set out in OFT510, *Competition disqualification orders: Guidance* (May 2003), para 2.3.

[203] Company Directors Disqualification Act 1986, s 9A(5)(a).

- the person's conduct as a director contributed to the breach of competition law. It is immaterial whether the director knew that the conduct of the undertaking constituted a breach; or
- the person's conduct as a director did not contribute to the breach, but he or she had reasonable grounds to suspect that the conduct of the undertaking constituted a breach and took no steps to prevent it; or
- as a director of the company, the person did not know but ought to have known that the conduct of the undertaking constituted the breach.

Further, the court may have regard to the person's conduct as a director of a company in connection with any other breach(es) of competition law; but it must not have regard to the matters mentioned in Sch 1 to the Company Directors Disqualification Act 1986.[204] **10.126**

(iii) Penalty for breach

The maximum period for a CDO disqualification is 15 years.[205] A person subject to a CDO may not be a director of a company, act as a receiver of a company's property, be concerned or take part in any way, whether directly or indirectly, in the promotion, formation or management of the company, or act as an insolvency practitioner.[206] Breach of a CDO is a criminal offence.[207] **10.127**

(iv) Immunity from CDOs

In its guidance, the OFT has stated that it will not make an application for a CDO in the following circumstances: **10.128**

- where the breach to which the decision or judgment of a competition law infringement relates does or did not have an actual or potential effect on trade in the United Kingdom;[208]
- in respect of breaches of competition law which ended before the commencement of ss 9A to 9E of the Company Directors Disqualification Act 1986 (20 June 2003);[209]
- where a decision or judgment relating to the breach remains subject to appeal;[210]
- in cases where no financial penalty has been imposed (and, in the event of an appeal, upheld);[211]

---

[204] Sch 1 sets out a number of matters to be considered when determining unfitness of directors in non-CDO cases.

[205] Company Directors Disqualification Act 1986, s 9A(9).   [206] ibid, s 1(1).

[207] ibid, s 13. Also note that it is possible to obtain leave of the court during the period in which the person is subject to a CDO to be a director of a company, act as a receiver of company property or take part in the promotion, formation or management of a company (ibid, s 1(1)(a)).

[208] OFT510, *Competition disqualification orders: Guidance* (May 2003) para 4.7.

[209] ibid, para 4.8.   [210] ibid, para 4.9.   [211] ibid, para 4.10.

- where the individual in question is a current director of a company whose company benefited from leniency in respect of the activities to which the grant of leniency relates;[212]
- the individual concerned is the beneficiary of a no-action letter in respect of the cartel activities specified in that letter;[213] and
- where the OFT has accepted a Competition Disqualification Undertaking (**CDU**) from a person.[214]

(v) Competition disqualification undertakings

10.129 A CDU may be accepted from an individual by the OFT in place of the OFT applying for (or continuing an application for) a CDO. All of the terms of a CDU would be the same as may be expected in a CDO. The legal effect of a CDU is also identical to the legal effect for CDOs. The OFT will publish such undertakings in the same way as it would publish an order. The practical advantages of giving undertakings rather than continuing through to an order relate to the individual's ability to avoid full proceedings and to have some input into the terms of the undertaking.

(vi) Notice requirement

10.130 Before the OFT makes an application for a CDO, it must give notice to the person the subject of that application and provide them with an opportunity to make representations to the OFT.[215] Prior to making an application for a CDO, the OFT may also choose to exercise its powers of investigation under ss 26 to 28 of the Competition Act 1998 in order to gather information to decide whether or not to apply for a CDO.[216]

G. Private Enforcement

(a) Advantages and disadvantages of private enforcement

10.131 Private enforcement of the competition law rules is a very important aspect of competition law as it allows for the effective protection of individual's rights

---

[212] ibid, para 4.12.   [213] ibid, para 4.27.

[214] See discussion at paras 10.129–10.130, below.

[215] Company Directors Disqualification Act 1986, s 9C(4). For a discussion of what the notice will include, see OFT510, *Competition disqualification orders: Guidance* (May 2003) para 5.2.

[216] By way of guidance as to the type of evidence the OFT will be seeking, the OFT has stated that it is likely to apply for a CDO where there is evidence of direct involvement in the breach, such as the person having actively taken steps to carry out the infringement, planning or devising the activity causing the breach, pressuring others to participate in the breach, attending meetings in which the activity constituting the breach occurred or was discussed, and encouraging retaliation against those who were reluctant to participate (see OFT510, *Competition disqualification orders: Guidance* (May 2003), para 4.17).

under Articles 81 and 82 (and under the Competition Act 1998).[217] From 1 May 2004, the competition law infringements in their entirety are determined by national courts as part of the private enforcement of competition law.

The key advantage for a claimant seeking private enforcement of competition law matters is the ability to seek damages to compensate for loss suffered as a result of the infringement, as the OFT fines imposed do not address the claimant's position. Further, the competition law infringements may be used to attempt to have a contract declared void under Article 81(2) (which would ordinarily be used as a defence). Further, in relation to interim or injunctive relief, the procedure before the national courts may well be faster than the procedure which the OFT is required to follow. **10.132**

The key disadvantage in relation to private enforcement of competition law is essentially the cost to the claimant in seeking relief, in terms of both legal and experts' fees, as well as the time cost involved in bringing a case before the courts. A claimant may also be required to give a cross-undertaking as to damages or provide security for costs in certain circumstances. **10.133**

The cost is, however, alleviated somewhat by an unusual procedural advantage for claimants seeking private enforcement of competition law infringements. This advantage allows claimants to use a decision made by the OFT (or the Regulators, the European Commission, or a judgment on appeal by the CAT or the Community courts) as a 'springboard' effectively to form the basis of the claim before a national court. In this way the court is bound by the previous findings of fact and liability, so effectively the litigation relates only to quantum.[218] **10.134**

In 2005, the European Commission published a Green Paper[219] and a Working Paper[220] in relation to private enforcement of competition law, in order to identify the main obstacles to a more efficient system of damages claims. This work related to the national systems across Europe, as private enforcement of the EC competition rules relies on actions before the national courts. **10.135**

Essentially, the main issues identified by the European Commission in the Green Paper relate to access to evidence, the 'fault requirement' imposed in some systems, the scope of damages, the operation of the 'passing on' defence, **10.136**

---

[217] Case C-453/99 *Courage Ltd v Crehan* [2001] ECR I-6297.
[218] Competition Act 1998, ss 47A and 47B. See also para 10.52 above: the OFT may make a decision on liability only, which would be of assistance to a private litigant.
[219] <http://ec.europa.eu/comm/competition/antitrust/actionsdamages/documents.html#greenpaper>.
[220] <http://ec.europa.eu/comm/competition/antitrust/actionsdamages/documents.html#staffpaper>.

the problems associated with small consumer claims, the cost of proceedings, coordination between public and private enforcement, jurisdiction and applicable law issues, and complexities arising from such matters as experts, limitation periods, and the causation requirement.

10.137   Some, but not all, of these problems are apparent in the UK systems for private enforcement.

(b) Civil proceedings before a court

(i) Venue

10.138   A claimant may bring a private competition law claim before the High Court or before the CAT.

10.139   Where a civil claim for damages is brought before the CAT, such claims are able to be commenced under s 47A of the Competition Act 1998[221] and must be commenced within two years of the expiry of the time period for appealing the OFT's (or European Commission's) decision relied upon, pursuant to the CAT's Rules, r 31.

10.140   In relation to a claim brought before the High Court, the UK civil procedure rules now incorporate a practice direction relating to competition law claims, being 'claims relating to the application of Articles 81 and 82 of the EC Treaty and Chapters 1 and 2 of Part 1 of the Competition Act 1998'. This effectively provides that any claim relating to the application of competition law provisions must be commenced in the High Court at the Royal Courts of Justice. In general, such claims will be assigned to the Chancery Division and, where proceedings are commenced elsewhere, they will normally be transferred to the Chancery Division of the High Court.

10.141   The time limit for bringing a claim in the High Court is six years from the date the wrongful act caused the damage in question.[222]

10.142   According to the practice direction, any party whose statement of case raises or deals with an issue relating to the application of competition law must serve a copy of the statement of case on the OFT. This then allows the OFT to comply with its obligation to provide a copy of the statement of case to the European Commission, and for both the OFT and European Commission to consider whether or not to make any written submission to the court and whether or not to apply to the court to make an oral submission, pursuant to Article 15(3) of

---

[221] See, eg, the private damages claim brought before the CAT in *Healthcare at Home v Genzyme Limited*, Case number 1060/5/7/06.
[222] Limitation Act 1980, s 2.

Regulation 1/2003. Given the OFT's focus of its resources on uncovering competition infringements, it is unlikely that the OFT will exercise its powers of intervention in UK civil cases very often.[223] Further, given the potential difficulties associated with cross examination of experts and the use of expert evidence, it seems similarly unlikely that the European Commission will use its powers to intervene in a UK private law case.[224]

References to the ECJ on questions of law relating to the EC Treaty may only be **10.143** made by the House of Lords, as this is the final appellate court in the United Kingdom. This applies to both the CAT and the High Court.[225]

(ii) Who may bring a claim?

Any person or legal entity in a position to allege actionable damage as a result of **10.144** infringement of the competition law provisions under the Competition Act 1998, Article 81 or Article 82 can bring a claim. This includes parties to a relevant agreement as well as third parties in general who may allege loss suffered as a result of an infringing agreement or conduct.[226]

However, where a party to an infringing agreement brings a claim against **10.145** another party to the agreement, the claimant will have an additional hurdle to overcome. Although such a claimant can, in principle, bring a claim, the claimant will also need to establish that he or she does not bear 'significant responsibility' for the infringement.[227]

(iii) Cause of action

The relevant cause of action in a competition law claim is founded on a breach **10.146** of statutory duty, as a claim in tort.[228] The elements of a claim for breach of statutory duty are: that the breach of a statutory standard gives rise to an action; the damage alleged to be suffered falls within the ambit of the statute; the statutory duty was breached; the breach caused the loss in question; and there are no applicable defences.

However, to the extent that the use of the process and tests associated with a **10.147** breach of statutory duty claim under English law would be contrary to the principle of effectiveness in Community law, the procedure and tests must be

---

[223] The OFT has intervened once at the time of writing before the House of Lords, in the case of *Inntrepreneur Pub Company and others v Crehan* [2006] UKHL 38.

[224] In *Mastercard UK Members Forum Limited and others v OFT* [2006] CAT 14, the European Commission declined to submit observations in the case despite the fact that it was concurrently dealing with a related case.

[225] Arts 234 and 68 EC.

[226] Case C-453/99 *Courage Ltd v Crehan* [2001] ECR I-6297.   [227] ibid.

[228] See, eg, *Roche Products Limited and others v Provimi Limited* [2003] EWHC 961 (Comm).

modified.[229] In the case of a competition law infringement, it is clear that the statute gives rise to a civil cause of action and that any loss suffered will be within the scope of the statute.

10.148   In establishing the necessary competition law infringement, a claimant, where appropriate, can rely upon the findings of the OFT, a regulator, or the European Commission.[230]

10.149   A competition law cause of action may also be set out in civil proceedings as a counterclaim and/or set-off. However, in order to do this, the counter-claimant will need to establish that there is a sufficiently close link between the claim and the counterclaim to support an equitable right of set-off.[231]

(iv) Remedies

10.150   In principle, the remedies available to a claimant in competition law will be as extensive as the remedies which the relevant court has power to grant. The most commonly sought remedies in the context of competition law would be injunctive relief, a declaration that the agreement or relevant parts of the agreement are void and/or illegal, a declaration that the conduct in question is illegal, and/or a claim for damages. It is beyond the scope of this text to set out a complete analysis of the assessment of damages for a civil claim under competition law.[232]

10.151   Where such a claim forms the basis for a counterclaim, it must be noted that it is unlikely that any English court would find that a defendant was entitled to retain any goods or services received without paying for them and, on the whole, this type of 'Euro defence' has generally not found favour with the English courts.

10.152   Damages in tort are assessed, in general terms, so as to put the claimant in the position he would have been in had the relevant harm not been suffered. Note that the Limitation Act 1980 will generally operate to exclude any claim for damage suffered more than six years prior to the issue of the claim.[233] Where the claim is brought in the CAT, this limitation on damages arguably may not apply, as a result of s 47A(3) of the Competition Act 1998.[234]

---

[229] *Crehan v Inntrepreneur Pub Co (CPC)* [2004] EWCA Civ 637, para 167.

[230] Competition Act 1998, ss 58 and 58A.

[231] *Esso Petroleum v Milton* [1997] 1 WLR 938. See also A Howard, 'Competition law defences in commercial litigation: Intel v Via' [2003] Competition LJ 36.

[232] For further information, see Richard Whish, *Competition Law* (5th edn, Oxford University Press, 2003) This text explores causation, remoteness, quantum, punitive damages, and the applicable substantive law.

[233] Limitation Act 1980, s 2.

[234] Monetary claims may be brought before the CAT where that claim would be able to be brought in civil proceedings in any part of the UK. Competition Act 1998, s 47A(3) provides that, for the purposes of identifying claims which may be made in civil proceedings, any limitation rules that would apply in such proceedings are to be disregarded. While this provision does

(c) Arbitration proceedings

(i) Powers of arbitral tribunals

Although Regulation 1/2003 does not provide specific powers to arbitral tri- **10.153**
bunals in relation to the application of Article 81(3), in the modernised regime of
'self assessment' it seems that the most practical approach would be to regard the
arbitral tribunal's powers as being set by the parties in each case, and unless those
powers specifically exclude Article 81(3) from competition law as a whole, then
examination of such issues is likely to fall within the power of the arbitral tribunal.

Under the Arbitration Act 1996 in the United Kingdom, parties are able to seek **10.154**
a court's view on the arbitral tribunal's powers under the arbitration agreement
in question.[235] In *Ecoswiss China Time Limited v Benetton International NV*[236]
the ECJ held that the potential breach of EC competition law should be treated
as a matter of public policy so that where, as in that case, under the national law
an arbitration award can be challenged on grounds of public policy, a breach of
competition law would provide such a ground.

(ii) Obligations of the arbitral tribunal

There is no obligation on an arbitral tribunal, other than one agreed by the **10.155**
parties to the arbitration, proactively to seek and determine any breaches of
the competition laws, nor is there any obligation to report an infringement of
the competition laws as this would conflict with the arbitral tribunal's obligations
of confidentiality and the general requirement for the consent of both parties.

It also appears that an arbitral tribunal cannot refer an issue of competition law **10.156**
to the ECJ, as it is not a 'Court or Tribunal' for the purposes of Article 234.[237]
Further, there is no right or obligation for the OFT, a Regulator, or the
European Commission to become involved in an arbitral tribunal proceeding.
In this way, the arbitral tribunal's proceedings are kept confidential and are
not dealt with in the same way as civil enforcement proceedings before a
court.

---

leave it open to argue that this also applies in respect of any limitation on damages, it is
equally arguable that s 47A(3) only operates in respect of the commencement of a claim, and
allows r 31 of the CAT's Rules to operate effectively (it allows a claim for damages to be brought
in the CAT within two years from the later of the time the relevant infringement decision is final
or the date on which the cause of action accrued). See also the comments of the CAT in *Healthcare
at Home Limited v Genzyme Limited* [2006] CAT 29, para 59.

[235] For further discussion, see P Lomas, 'Arbitration: Jurisdiction over EC competition law
issues', Practical Law Company, 27 April 2004.

[236] Case C-126/87 [1999] ECR I-3055.

[237] However, if an arbitral ruling is appealed, the national court would be obliged to comply
with EC competition law and may need to consider whether to make a preliminary reference.

11

MULTIPLE ENFORCEMENT: THE EUROPEAN COMMISSION, UK COMPETITION AUTHORITIES, AND THE EUROPEAN COMPETITION NETWORK

A. Introduction

11.01   On the same day that the European Union grew to 25 Member States, Regulation 1/2003 decentralised the enforcement of Article 81 and Article 82 EC, so multiplying the amount of national competition authorities and national courts applying Articles 81 and 82. Regulation 1/2003 requires national competition authorities and the Commission to apply the rules on competition in close cooperation.[1] It does not, however, provide a developed mechanism to coordinate the action of the national competition authorities, giving rise therefore to possibility of inconsistent and multiple decisions relating to the same behaviour.[2]

11.02   It is the aim of this chapter to examine to what extent, and in what circumstances, undertakings facing multiple prosecution by a number of competition authorities, can rely on the principle of *ne bis in idem* (otherwise known as the rule against double jeopardy) in order to defeat or restrain regulatory action that is initiated against them in the context of the decentralised regime of competition enforcement introduced by Regulation 1/2003.

11.03   The chapter will begin with a brief overview of the principle of *ne bis in idem* as formulated in the context of fundamental rights and in national law before examining how the principle is applied in a competition context. Finally, it briefly examines the associated issue of the precedent value that can be attached to the various decisions made by national competition authorities in respect of anti-competitive behaviour in the United Kingdom.

(a) Multiple prosecution: the risk

11.04   In the past 15 years many Member States have enacted domestic competition legislation that replicates Article 81 and Article 82 on a national scale. In addition to this increase in substantive competition rules, Regulation 1/2003 complicates the procedural landscape by entrusting a large role in the enforcement of Articles 81 and 82 to the numerous national competition authorities across the Member States.

---

[1] Council Regulation (EC) 1/2003 of 16 December 2002 on the implementation of the rules on competition laid down in Articles 81 and 82 of the Treaty [2003] OJ L1/1, Art 11(1).
[2] The European Competition Network (**ECN**) was created (outside the context of Regulation 1/2003) in order to address some of these issues. See Chapter 1 on the ECN more generally.

Three features of Regulation 1/2003, in particular, give rise to a risk of multiple **11.05** prosecution:

(1) Under Regulation 1/2003, as long as trade between Member States may be affected, the ability of the national competition authorities to apply Article 81 and Article 82 is not confined by any jurisdictional criteria. There is no concept of *forum non conveniens* or of 'court first seised' in Regulation 1/2003. The basic presumption is one of parallel competence: each competition authority is empowered to apply Articles 81 and 82 irrespective of where the infringement has occurred.[3] Under Regulation 1/2003, anti-competitive behaviour stretching across national boundaries can therefore give rise to several national competition authorities taking enforcement action under Article 81 and/or Article 82. An informal process of case allocation has been developed by the Commission and the national competition authorities in the context of the European Competition Network (**ECN**), but (with the exception of when the Commission takes on a case)[4] this process is not binding. It can be expected that in the vast majority of cases, the informal allocation process developed in the ECN will prevent multiple prosecution—there is little incentive for regulators to waste resources on a matter that is dealt with by another competition authorities. Nonetheless, under Regulation 1/2003, an undertaking active in the European markets remains at potential risk of multiple prosecution in relation to the application of Articles 81 and 82. By way of example, although the Network Notice[5] indicates that the Commission is particularly well placed to take on cases having effects in four or more Member States and that network members will endeavour to allocate cases to a single well placed competition authority,[6] Visa and MasterCard currently face formal and informal investigations regarding domestic interchange rates in ten Member States (including the United Kingdom).

(2) Regulation 1/2003 does not rule out the parallel application of national competition law and European competition law—quite the contrary, the application of European competition law is mandated when national competition law is applied: under Article 3(1) of Regulation 1/2003, the obligation on national competition authorities and national courts to apply

---

[3] Regulation 1/2003, Art 5. An informal, non-binding process of case allocation has been developed in the context of the ECN, as set out in the Commission notice on cooperation within the network of competition authorities (2004/C 101/03) [2004] OJ C101/43.

[4] Regulation 1/2003, Art 11(6) provides that where the Commission initiates proceedings, this automatically relieves the national competition authorities of their competence in relation to the same matter.

[5] Commission notice on cooperation within the network of competition authorities (2004/C 101/03) [2004] OJ C101/43.

[6] ibid, paras 6–15.

Articles 81 and 82 crystallises upon the application of national competition law in a given case.[7] The Commission has indicated that the practice to date is for national competition authorities to apply both Community and national competition law to cases, even though these could opt just to apply Community law.

(3) Regulation 1/2003 does not provide for a system of precedent at the level of the national competition authorities and courts applying Articles 81 and 82.[8] An undertaking can defend itself successfully before one competition authorities, and yet find that the 'no grounds of action' decision by the first authority does not protect it from a finding of breach by another authority or a court in respect of the same behaviour. Conversely, where one national competition authority has made a finding of breach, there is no obligation for another authority looking at the same issue to reach the same conclusion.[9]

11.06 Taken together, these features (numerous competition authorities empowered to act, no jurisdictional rules, and no system of precedent at the level of national competition authorities) give rise to a risk of over-prosecution and inconsistent outcomes.

(b) Multiple prosecution: the risk in context

11.07 In assessing the risks of multiple prosecution that arise under Regulation 1/2003 it is important to set these in their proper context. Regulation 1/2003 has brought with it raised expectations of coherence and consistency in the application of both Community and national rules on competition. The point of comparison is slightly skewed: the current system for the enforcement of competition rules under Regulation 1/2003, which to some extent embraces both the application of national and Community law, is usually compared only with the European Commission's application of Articles 81 and 82 under Regulation 17/62[10] (although the Commission was not the sole authority applying Community rules on competition under Regulation 17/62). This is not a fair comparison.

11.08 Although Regulation 1/2003 has increased the amount of authorities applying Articles 81 and 82, it should not be forgotten that national courts of the

---

[7] See Chapter 3 generally for a discussion of Art 3(1).

[8] Kris Dekeyser, Head of Unit, DG COMP, indicated that: 'The challenge is to ensure that the rules are applied in a coherent manner, irrespective of which authority happens to act on a case'. See 'Almost 2 Years of cooperation within the ECN', paper prepared for the IBC Conference, Advanced EC Competition Law, May 2005.

[9] The Commission is able, where it anticipates that a decision by a national competition authority is inconsistent with that of another national authority, to initiate proceedings and so relieve the national authorities of competence under Art 11(6) of Regulation 1/2003; see Network Notice, para 54.

[10] First Regulation implementing Articles [81] and [82] of the Treaty [1962] OJ 13/204.

Member States and several national competition authorities applied Article 81(1) and Article 82 prior to 1 May 2004, with none of the safeguards that exist under Regulation 1/2003. It is telling that all three factors itemised above (numerous competition authorities empowered to act, no jurisdictional rules, and no system of precedent at the level of national competition authorities) are flaws relating to the enforcement of Community rules on competition that existed prior to Regulation 1/2003.

Further, many of the risks of multiple prosecution under Regulation 1/2003 **11.09** arise from the application of both national competition law and the Community rules on competition. This feature was also present prior to Regulation 1/2003. It is true that Article 3(1) of Regulation 1/2003 increases this risk by mandating, in certain situations, the application of Community rules on competition wherever national domestic law is applied to relevant conduct. However, Article 3(1) will in some ways improve the position of undertakings. It brings in its wake greater convergence between domestic competition law and Community law, and indirectly brings the various domestic rules on competition of the Member States closer together. For example, the Commission has indicated that all but five Member States have now abolished their notification system in order to bring their domestic system closer into line with Regulation 1/2003. Further, the Commission notes considerable alignment between national investigative powers.[11]

Regulation 1/2003 should also bring greater consistency in decision-making **11.10** across the European Community. Under Article 3(1) of Regulation 1/2003 national competition authorities are less able to apply domestic legislation that is inconsistent with the EU competition rules. Further, Article 3(2) of Regulation 1/2003 expands the requirement for consistency when national competition law is applied to agreements falling within Article 81.[12] Accordingly, although the chapter below by definition focuses on the potential for multiple prosecution under Regulation 1/2003, it is important to bear in mind that Regulation 1/2003 has not necessarily worsened the position overall.

B. Definitions

There is no single agreed definition of the principle of *ne bis in idem* ('not twice **11.11** in the same'). It is a principle of criminal law that protects a defendant from a second prosecution (and punishment) where the defendant has already been

---

[11] Dekeyser (n 8 above).
[12] See Chapter 3 for a discussion of the effects of Art 3(2).

acquitted or convicted for the same offence. It features (in different permuta-
tions) in various multilateral charters of rights. It is recognised by the European
Court of Justice (**ECJ**) as a general principle of Community law.[13]

11.12   Although the principle is well-established, many critical aspects relating to its
application continue to provoke debate. During its presidency, Greece launched
an initiative for a draft Council Framework Decision concerning the application
of the '*ne bis in idem* principle' under the Third Pillar of the Treaty on European
Union (police and judicial cooperation in criminal matters), but Member States
were unable to reach agreement on the proposal. In the criminal justice field, the
European Commission published a Green Paper on the issue in December
2005[14] and promised a new legislative proposal for 2006, which has since been
delayed.[15] Absent an agreed formulation of the principle, it is necessary to
consider the various definitions in multilateral charters that influence both the
European courts and the UK national courts.

11.13   In examining the various definitions of the principle, the discussion below
will consider in particular four aspects of the principle that are critical to its
application in a competition context:

- Its **effect**: is this a legal binding principle or an aspirational text?
- What is its **territorial scope**—does *ne bis in idem* apply solely where both
  offences occur in one and the same Member State or also in transnational
  situations (so that an offence in one Member State precludes prosecution in
  a second Member State)?
- What is the '**same offence**'—must the second prosecution be the same in
  law and in fact or does it suffice if it relates to the same facts?
- How broad is the **prohibition**—is it double prosecution or just double
  punishment that is forbidden?

(a) European Convention of Human Rights

11.14   Article 4 of Protocol 7 to the European Convention on Human Rights (**ECHR**)
provides:

> No one shall be liable to be tried or punished again in criminal proceedings under

---

[13] Case C-238/99 P *Limburgse Vinyl Maatschappij NV (LVM) v Commission* [2002] ECR
I-8375, para 59.

[14] Green Paper on Conflicts of Jurisdiction and the Principle of *ne bis in idem* in Criminal
Proceedings (SEC(2005) 1767), consultation closed in March 2006. One of the questions
posed by the Commission in the Green Paper was: 'Is it feasible and necessary to define the
concept of idem, or should this be left to the case law of the ECJ?'

[15] See also the Communication from the Commission to the Council and the European
Parliament on the mutual recognition of judicial decisions in criminal matters and the
strengthening of mutual trust between Member States (COM(2005) 195 final).

the jurisdiction of the same State for an offence for which he has already been finally acquitted or convicted in accordance with the law and penal procedure of that State.

Effect   The ECJ has endorsed Article 4 as a formulation of the fundamental   **11.15** principle of *ne bis in idem* recognised in Community law.[16] It is therefore of relevance both in respect of Community law, and in domestic law through the medium of Community law[17] even though the United Kingdom has not ratified Protocol 7.[18]

Territorial scope   Article 4 applies to prevent a second prosecution in one and   **11.16** the same state only.[19]

Same offence   The European Court of Human Rights (**ECtHR**) has taken a   **11.17** broad approach to what can be considered as 'the same offence'. In *Fischer v Austria*,[20] in order to determine whether two offences which were nominally different were nonetheless *in idem*, the test adopted by ECtHR was whether the essential elements of the two offences at issue overlapped: 'What is decisive in the present case is that, on the basis of one act, the applicant was tried and punished twice, since [the two offences], as interpreted by the courts, do not differ in their essential elements.'

Prohibition   Article 4 is not confined to the right not to be punished twice,   **11.18** it includes the right not to be tried twice. Accordingly, where there is a second trial, a reduction or withholding of the second penalty in order to 'take account' of the previous penalty will not suffice—the right is not to be tried a second time.[21]

(b) Charter of Fundamental Rights of the European Union

Article 50 of the EU Charter provides: **11.19**

> No one shall be liable to be tried or punished again in criminal proceedings for an offence for which he or she has already been finally acquitted or convicted within the Union in accordance with the law.

---

[16] Case C-238/99 P *Limburgse Vinyl Maatschappij NV (LVM) v Commission* [2002] ECR I-8375, para 59; Case C-289/04 P *Showa Denko KK v Commission*, judgment of 29 June 2006, para 60.
[17] Joined Cases C 20 & 64/00 *Booker Aquaculture Ltd (t/a Marine Harvest McConnell) and Hydro Seafood GSP Ltd v Scottish Ministers* [1993] ECR I-7411, para 65; Case C-94/00 *Roquette Frères SA v Directeur Général de la Concurrence, de la Consommation et de la Répression des fraudes* [2002] ECR I-9011, para 25.
[18] The government has indicated its intention to ratify Protocol 7 once certain changes to domestic family law have been enacted.
[19] *SR v Sweden* Application 62806/00, decision of 23 April 2002; *Graf v Austria* Application 72594/01, decision of 3 June 2003.
[20] Application 37950 [2001] ECHR 352.   [21] ibid, para 129.

11.20 **Effect**   Although the EU Charter is not legally binding, it is nonetheless influential as a source of reference for the CFI and ECJ.[22]

11.21 **Territorial scope**   Article 50 applies *ne bis in idem* within the European Union on a transnational basis, so that a previous prosecution in one Member State prevents a second prosecution for the same offence in another Member State. However, the prohibition under Article 50 hinges on the first prosecution occurring within the Union.[23]

11.22 **Same offence**   Article 50 refers to prosecution for the 'same offence'. It is unclear whether a purposive approach will be adopted to the definition of same offence (as the ECtHR did in *Fischer v Austria*) in order to capture double prosecution for the same acts.

11.23 **Prohibition**   Article 50 is not confined to the right not to be punished twice: it includes the right not to be tried twice.

(c) Convention Implementing the Schengen Agreement[24]

11.24 Article 54 of the Convention Implementing the Schengen Agreement (**CISA**) provides:

> A person whose trial has been finally disposed of in one Contracting Party may not be prosecuted in another Contracting Party for the same acts provided that, if a penalty has been imposed, it has been enforced, is actually in the process of being enforced or can no longer be enforced under the laws of the sentencing Contracting Party.[25]

11.25 **Effect**   The CISA applies to the 13 Member States that have implemented the 1985 Schengen Agreement,[26] the ten EU acceding States[27] and the United

---

[22] Case C-131/03 P *RJ Reynolds Tobacco Holdings Inc v Commission*, judgment of 12 September 2006; Case C-540/03 *Parliament v Council*, judgment of 27 June 2006; Case T-223/00 *Kyowa Hakko Kogyo Co v Commission* [2003] ECR II-2553, para 104.

[23] *Kyowa Hakko Kogyo Co*, ibid, para 104: 'However, independently of the question whether that provision has binding legal force, it is clearly intended to apply only within the territory of the Union and the scope of the right laid down in the provision is expressly limited to cases where the first acquittal or conviction is handed down within the Union.'

[24] Convention implementing the Schengen Agreement of 14 June 1985 between the Governments of the States of the Benelux Economic Union, the Federal Republic of Germany and the French Republic on the gradual abolition of checks at their common borders [2000] OJ L239/19, signed on 19 June 1990 at Schengen, Art 54.

[25] The legal basis for Art 54 CISA is Arts 34 and 31 TEU, in Title VI (Police and Judicial Cooperation in criminal matters).

[26] Belgium, France, Germany, Luxembourg, Netherlands, Portugal, Spain, Italy, Austria, Greece, Denmark, Finland, and Sweden. Iceland and Norway have also implemented the Schengen agreement even though they are not Member States.

[27] Cyprus, Czech Republic, Estonia, Hungary, Latvia, Lithuania, Malta, Poland, Slovakia, and Slovenia.

Kingdom[28] and Ireland.[29] An undertaking that finds it is subject to enforcement action by two CISA Member States could seek to rely on the CISA either directly (by submitting that undertakings qualify as a legal 'person' protected by Article 54 CISA), or by arguing by analogy. The ECJ is likely to be tempted to aim for consistency with the CISA if it is to avoid a two-tier system of *ne bis in idem* protection across the Union.

Territorial scope   Article 54 applies *ne bis in idem* on a transnational basis. The **11.26** application of Article 54 is conditional on the first prosecution occurring in a Schengen State.

Same offence   Article 54 identifies '*idem*' as the same underlying facts, so that **11.27** it is irrelevant if the two offences are formulated in different fashion, so long as the same facts lead to a second prosecution.[30]

Prohibition   The CISA forbids double prosecution as well as double **11.28** punishment.

(d) UK law

In English national law the principle of *ne bis in idem* takes the form of the **11.29** *autrefois acquit* or *convict* rule (in Scotland 'tholed assize'), by virtue of which a person who has previously been acquitted or convicted of an offence may not be prosecuted for the same offence again. The House of Lords restated the principles in *Connelly v Director of Public Prosecutions*.[31] The principle applies only where the same offence, both in fact and in law, is alleged in the second indictment.[32]

Beyond the *autrefois* plea, the principle of abuse of process can apply to protect **11.30** a person prosecuted for an offence arising out of the same or substantially the same facts as a previous prosecution. The House of Lords' decision in *Connelly v DPP* established that although the strict *autrefois* rule does not apply to prevent subsequent prosecution on the same facts, the principle of abuse of process provides protection to a defendant on trial a second time in relation to the same facts. The defendant in such a case is instead protected by a

---

[28] Council Regulation (EC) 2000/365 of 29 May 2000 concerning the request of the UK to take part in some provisions of the Schengen Acquis together with Council Decisions 2004/926/EC [2004] OJ L385/1.

[29] Council Decision (EC) 2002/192 of 28 February 2002 [2002] OJ L64/20.

[30] Case C-436/04 *Van Esbroeck* [2006] 3 CMLR 6; Case C-150/05 *Van Straaten v Netherlands and Italy*, judgment of 28 September 2006.

[31] [1964] AC 1254.

[32] 'The word "offence" embraces both the facts which constitute the crime and the legal characteristics which make it an offence. For the doctrine to apply it must be the same offence both in fact and in law.' Per Devlin LJ in *Connelly*, ibid, 1339–40.

presumption that the proceedings should be stayed in the absence of special circumstances to justify them.[33] Unlike the doctrine of *autrefois*, which gives the defendant a right to relief, abuse of process gives the judge a discretion to stay the proceedings.[34]

(i) Simultaneous administrative and civil proceedings

11.31 The court has a general discretion to stay proceedings[35] having regard to other parallel regulatory proceedings, if the justice of the case required it[36] or where there is abuse of process.[37]

11.32 The burden rests with the party seeking the stay to demonstrate that there were sound reasons for a stay in all the circumstances. The court will also have to consider the other party's right to have issues determined by a court within a reasonable time under Article 6 ECHR. A good example of a case suitable for a stay is where the parallel administrative proceedings are going to be determinative of the issues in the litigation (or at least a significant proportion of them) or otherwise to render a trial unnecessary (or significantly less expensive).[38] The overriding objective of the Civil Procedure Rules[39] and the need to avoid duplication of costs and effort are also relevant in this context.

11.33 In this regard, it is relevant that under ss 58 and 58A of the Competition Act 1998, findings of fact and findings of infringement by the Office of Fair Trading (**OFT**) (and the Competition Appeal Tribunal (**CAT**)) have binding effect in certain circumstances. The High Court considered simultaneous civil proceedings before the court and regulatory proceedings before the CAT in *Synstar Computing*.[40] It identified the factors that would lead to a stay in such a situation:

> The same 'competition' issue may arise in court proceedings and in proceedings

---

[33] *R v Beedie* [1997] 2 Cr App R 167.

[34] For more information on protection against double jeopardy under domestic law see Law Commission Report, *Double jeopardy and prosecution appeals* (Law Com No 267, 2001).

[35] The power to stay is one of the general case management powers of the court; Civil Procedure Rules, r 3(2)(f).

[36] *Wakefield v Channel Four Television Corp* [2005] EWHC 2410; *R v Panel on Takeovers and Mergers, ex p Fayed* [1992] BCLC 938, 947: 'It is clear that the court has power to intervene to prevent injustice where the continuation of one set of proceedings may prejudice the fairness of the trial of other proceedings . . . But it is a power which has to be exercised with great care and only where there is a real risk of serious prejudice which may lead to injustice' per Neil LJ.

[37] *Abraham v Thompson* [1997] 4 All ER 362: '[I]f the court is satisfied that the action is not properly constituted or pleaded, or is not brought bona fide in the sense of being vexatious oppressive or otherwise an abuse of process then the court may dismiss the action or impose a stay whether under the specific provisions of the Rules of Court or the inherent jurisdiction of the court'. Per Potter LJ at 374.

[38] *Wakefield*, ibid, para 13.　　　[39] CPR r 1.

[40] *Synstar Computer Services (UK) Ltd v ICL (Sorbus) Ltd* [2001] CP Rep 98.

before the specialist body. Where it does, the question will arise whether the court in its discretion should stay the proceedings before the court pending the determination by the Director or the Tribunal. In the ordinary case, such a stay may be expected for a number of reasons which include: (1) the need to avoid the risk that inconsistent decisions are reached by the court and the Director or Tribunal; (2) the specialist expertise of the Director and Tribunal; and (3) the indication to this effect implicit in section 58 of the Act that decisions of fact arrived at after investigations by the Director, if not appealed or if confirmed on appeal, shall (unless the court otherwise directs) be binding on the parties as there provided.[41]

Special considerations apply where the parallel administrative investigation is **11.34** conducted by the European Commission under Article 81 or Article 82 EC, and there is a risk of conflicting or inconsistent decisions. In such cases, there is an obligation on the court under Article 16(1) of Regulation 1/2003 to stay proceedings pending a Commission decision on the issue.[42] The Commission Notice on the cooperation between the Commission and the courts of the EU Member States in the application of Articles 81 and 82 EC (**Cooperation Notice**)[43] provides guidance on this issue. National courts in this situation retain a certain amount of procedural autonomy. In *MTV Europe v BMG Record (UK) Ltd*,[44] the Court of Appeal upheld a decision refusing to stay civil proceedings *entirely* pending the outcome of a European Commission investigation. It held that the general undesirability of involving a party in parallel proceedings was not a reason for requiring a *general stay* as a matter of Community law. It was for the national court to ensure that litigants before it were treated fairly: in this case the judge had decided that the potential injustice of prolonged delay before the plaintiff could recover damages, outweighed the potential prejudice to the defendants. The judge's decision to grant a partial stay, permitting certain preparations for trial to proceed (whilst accepting that the case should not be set down for trial before the Commission's decision) was accordingly upheld.[45]

---

[41] Since this decision, s 58A of the Competition Act 1998 now additionally provides for findings of infringement by the OFT and the CAT to have binding effect in actions for damages.

[42] See also Case C-344/98 *Masterfoods Ltd (t/a Mars Ireland) v HB Ice Creams Ltd* [2000] ECR I-11369: 'When the outcome of the dispute before the national court depends on the validity of the Commission decision, it follows from the obligation of sincere cooperation that the national court should, in order to avoid reaching a decision that runs counter to that of the Commission, stay its proceedings pending final judgment in the action for annulment by the Community Courts, unless it considers that, in the circumstances of the case, a reference to the Court of Justice for a preliminary ruling on the validity of the Commission decision is warranted.'

[43] 2004/C 101/04 [2004] OJ C101/54.　　　[44] [1997] 1 CMLR 867.

[45] For a full discussion of the practice of the courts with respect to stays in the context of parallel proceedings, see R Nazzini, *Concurrent Proceedings in Competition Law* (Oxford University Press, 2004) Ch 6.

(ii) Civil and criminal proceedings

11.35   Civil courts have the discretion to stay the proceedings if it appears that the balance of justice between the parties so requires, having regard to concurrent criminal proceedings faced by the defendant. The burden is on the defendant to establish why the plaintiff in the civil action should be precluded from pursuing his action.[46] An application for a stay of the civil proceedings by an undertaking potentially facing Serious Fraud Office (**SFO**) investigations into alleged price fixing as well as civil proceedings for damages for breach of Article 81 was rejected by the High Court in *Secretary of State for Health v Norton Healthcare.*[47] Whilst the court acknowledged there was a discretion to stay civil proceedings where case management of the civil proceedings would not effectively protect a defendant (also facing criminal proceedings) from prejudice in the criminal proceedings caused by participating in the civil action, it held that the defendant undertaking should not be protected from civil proceedings because of the adverse affect of the SFO investigation—the fact that certain witnesses were not available in the civil action for fear of the subsequent criminal prosecution was not a sufficient reason to grant a stay of the civil proceedings. Conversely, in *Re Abermeadow Ltd (No 1)*,[48] the court upheld a stay of director disqualification proceedings on the ground that the applicant, who also faced a criminal trial, had shown that there was a real risk of prejudice to his defence.

(iii) Multiple civil proceedings

11.36   For reasons that are explained below (at para 11.48), civil proceedings for damages for breaches of competition law do not qualify as criminal proceedings so the principle of *ne bis in idem* does not apply to prevent multiple proceedings of this nature. In the United Kingdom a defendant facing several claims across different Member States would rely on the ordinary rules of private international law relating to the allocation of jurisdiction in civil and commercial proceedings. These matters are outside the scope of this book, and the reader is referred to textbooks on private international law for a discussion as to how these rules apply to competition proceedings.[49]

(iv) Calculation of penalties under the Competition Act

11.37   Finally, on a subsidiary note, in the context of the calculation of penalties under the Competition Act 1998, s 38(9) of the Act requires the OFT to take account

---

[46] *Jefferson Ltd v Bhetiha* [1979] 1 WLR 898.
[47] *Secretary of State for Health v Norton Healthcare Ltd* [2003] EWHC 1905 (Ch), [2004] Eu LR 12.
[48] [1998] CLY 681.
[49] See *Cheshire & North's Private International law* (13th edn, Butterworths, 1999).

of any penalty or fine that has been imposed in relation to an agreement or conduct by the Commission or by a court or other body in another Member State. This rule is not, as such, an application of *ne bis in idem*. It does not preclude double prosecution, nor, in fact, does it prevent double punishment. It merely requires that account should be taken of earlier penalties in calculating the penalties under the Competition Act.

C. *Ne bis in idem* in Competition Proceedings: The Pre-conditions

Several questions must be answered before an undertaking can invoke the pro- **11.38** tection of *ne bis in idem* in a competition context. First, are the competition proceedings at issue 'criminal'? Secondly, is the second investigation the 'same' as an earlier one? Thirdly, is there a valid prior decision (or judgment) that can be relied upon to preclude the second investigation?

In searching for an answer to these questions, the discussion below focuses on **11.39** EC and ECtHR case law. EC case law is critical for two reasons. First, where Article 81 and Article 82 proceedings are at issue, it is the ECJ and Court of First Instance (**CFI**) that ultimately determine compatibility of all Article 81 and Article 82 procedure with Community law (including the human rights aspects of these proceedings), even when the rules by which Articles 81 and 82 take effect are national rules of procedure.[50] Secondly, even where Articles 81 and 82 are not at issue, the UK courts and regulators are obliged, in applying Chapters I and II of the Competition Act 1998, to follow relevant ECJ precedent on the scope of fundamental rights (one of which is *ne bis in idem)* whenever applying the Competition Act.[51]

ECHR case law is also highly relevant, for two reasons. First, the European **11.40** courts have endorsed the ECHR generally, and have identified *ne bis in idem,* as enshrined in Article 4 of Protocol 7 ECHR, as a general principle of Community law.[52] Accordingly, the ECJ and CFI, as well as UK courts and national competition authorities, take account of ECtHR precedents in relation to human rights matters that fall within the scope of Community

---

[50] Case C-94/00 *Roquette Frères SA v Directeur Général de la Concurrence, de la Consommation et de la Répression des Fraudes* [2002] ECR I-9011: '[T]he Court has consistently held that, where national rules fall within the scope of Community law and reference is made for a preliminary hearing, it must provide all the criteria of interpretation needed by the national court to determine whether those rules are compatible with the fundamental rights the observance of which the Court ensures and which derive in particular from the ECHR' (para 25).

[51] Competition Act 1998, s 60; see Chapter 3 above.   [52] See para 11.15 above.

law.[53] Secondly, the OFT and the Competition Commission (**CC**) are bound, as public authorities, by the Human Rights Act 1998 so that when the United Kingdom ratifies Article 4 of Protocol 7 ECHR (and the government has indicated its intention to do so), they will be obliged to adhere to Article 4: it will become a Convention right enforceable in the courts of England and Wales. Even without ratification, Article 4 influences UK courts: it is cited and relied upon in judgments, even without the medium of European law.[54]

(a) Are the relevant competition proceedings 'criminal'?

11.41 One feature that is consistent in all the key definitions of *ne bis in idem* provided above, is that the principle only applies to proceedings that can be characterised as having a 'criminal' nature.

11.42 The ECtHR has developed an autonomous concept of what amounts to definition of a 'criminal' charge for the purposes of ECHR rights, including *ne bis in idem*.[55] It will have regard to how the relevant legal system itself classifies the charge, but this is not determinative. It will also consider the nature of the offence and/or the severity of the penalty in order to determine whether a charge is criminal.[56] The latter two criteria are alternative,[57] so that it suffices for one to be satisfied for the proceedings to become 'criminal'.

11.43 The ECJ,[58] CFI, and UK courts such as the CAT[59] apply the ECtHR's approach to the concept of 'criminal' in order to determine whether proceedings are 'criminal'.

11.44 Each of the potential competition proceedings that may arise in the United Kingdom must accordingly be considered in the light of those criteria in order to determine whether or not they can be considered as 'criminal' for the purposes of relying on the principle of *ne bis in idem*.

---

[53] Case C-94/00 *Roquette Frères SA v Directeur général de la concurrence, de la consommation et de la répression des fraudes* [2002] ECR I-9011.

[54] One of many examples is *R v Young (Kerry Rena)* [2005] EWCA Crim 2963.

[55] *Engel v Netherlands (No 1)* (1976) EHRR 647. The criteria are summarised in *Garyfallou AEBE v Greece* (1999) 28 EHRR 344: 'The Court recalls that in order to determine whether an offence qualifies as "criminal" for the purposes of the Convention, the first matter to be ascertained is whether or not the text defining the offence belongs, in the legal system of the respondent State, to the criminal law; next, the nature of the offence and, finally, the nature and degree of severity of the penalty that the person concerned risked incurring must be examined, having regard to the object and purpose of Article 6, to the ordinary meaning of the terms of that Article and to the laws of the Contracting States' (para 32).

[56] *Ozturk v Germany* (1984) 6 EHRR 409.

[57] *Garyfallou AEBE v Greece* (1997) 28 EHRR 344.

[58] See Case C-235/92 P *Montecatini SpA v Commission* [1999] ECR I-4539.

[59] *Napp Pharmaceutical Holdings Ltd v Director General of Fair Trading* [2002] CAT 1.

(i) Article 81 and Article 82

Article 23(5) of Regulation 1/2003 provides that decisions by the European **11.45**
Commission imposing a fine on undertakings for breaches of competition
law 'shall not be of a criminal law nature'. An equivalent provision existed in
Regulation 17/62.

That statement, however, does not dispose of the matter. Applying the approach **11.46**
of the ECtHR, Articles 81 and 82 EC are measures of general application that
carry significant penalties which have both a punitive and deterrent effect. These
would certainly qualify as 'criminal' proceedings for the purposes of the ECHR,
whether brought by the European Commission or by any of the national competition authorities.[60] The ECJ has acknowledged the criminal nature of the
competition prohibitions.[61] The ECJ accordingly reviews Commission decisions
applying Articles 81 and 82 against the standards applicable for criminal proceedings under Articles 6 and 7 ECHR,[62] and it accepts *ne bis in idem* could
arise in relation to competition decisions applying these provisions taken by
the Commission and/or by the Member States' authorities.[63]

(ii) Chapter I and Chapter II

Although UK law does not characterise Chapter I and Chapter II as criminal **11.47**
charges, applying the ECHR case law, the same reasoning as that outlined
above at paras 11.45 and 11.46 applies. The first case before the CAT (*Napp*[64])
established that Chapter I and Chapter II decisions are to be considered 'criminal' for the purposes of Article 6 ECHR,[65] and accordingly for the purposes of
applying *ne bis in idem.*

---

[60] On this issue see W Wils, 'La compatibilité des procedures communautaires en matière de
concurrence avec la Convention européenne des droits de l'homme' (1996) 32 Cahiers de droit
européen 329.

[61] See Case C-235/92 P *Montecatini SpA v Commission* [1999] ECR I-4539, para 176: 'It
must also be accepted that, given the nature of the infringements in question and the nature and
degree of severity of the ensuing penalties, the principle of the presumption of innocence applies
to the procedures relating to infringements of the competition rules applicable to undertakings
that may result in the imposition of fines or periodic penalty payments (see, to that effect, in
particular the judgments of the European Court of Human Rights of 21 February 1984, *Oztürk*)'.

[62] Most recently, in Joined Cases C 189, 202, 205–208 & 213/02 P *Dansk Rørindustri v
Commission* [2005] ECR I-5425, para 202: 'the principle of non-retroactivity of criminal laws,
enshrined in Article 7 of the ECHR as a fundamental right, constitutes a general principle
of Community law which must be observed when fines are imposed for infringement of the
competition rules'.

[63] Case C-238/99 P *Limburgse Vinyl Maatschappij NV (LVM) v Commission* [2002] ECR
I-8375. Case 14/68 *Wilhelm v Bundeskartellamt* [1969] ECR 1.

[64] [2002] CAT 1, para 98: 'As we have already stated in our interim judgment of 8 August
2001, we agree that the Director's concession that these proceedings are "criminal", for the
purposes of Article 6 of the ECHR, is properly made . . . That is particularly so since penalties
under the Act are intended to be severe and to have a deterrent effect.'

[65] See also *OFT v X, also known as OFT v D* [2003] EWHC 1042, [2003] 2 All ER (Comm) 183.

(iii) Private action for damages for breach of the competition prohibitions

11.48 Where Articles 81 and 82, and Chapters I and II are applied in the context of civil proceedings, however, they lose their criminal nature. This is because although private actions for damages for breaches of competition law may lead to significant awards of damages, the payment of damages in the context of litigation between private parties lacks the punitive and deterrent effect that is necessary to lend the proceedings a criminal flavour. The ECJ distinguished between public prosecutions and actions for compensation by victims of crime in *Gözütok and Brügge*: 'The ne bis in idem principle does not preclude the victim or any other person harmed by the accused's conduct from bringing civil action to seek compensation for the damage suffered.'[66] Accordingly, the principle of *ne bis in idem* does not bite to prevent one or more civil proceedings against an undertaking that is subject to investigation. Under domestic procedural law, broader notions of abuse of process and the obligation to ensure a fair trial may assist a defendant facing multiple civil proceedings,[67] as may the rules on jurisdiction relating to civil and commercial matters (in particular Regulation (EC) 44/2001[68]), and, more substantively, a defence of unjust enrichment (the ECJ recognised the concept of unjust enrichment in *Courage v Crehan*[69]).

(iv) Market investigations

11.49 Applying the criteria enunciated by the ECtHR in *Engel*[70] and in *Ozturk*,[71] it appears that the market investigations are not 'criminal'. None of the three criteria appear to be satisfied:

- Market investigations are not designated as 'criminal' under domestic competition law.

- Neither can they be considered, by their nature, to be penal. Whereas the competition prohibitions are measures of general application that prescribe (and prohibit) certain conduct, the same cannot be said for the market investigation provisions. Although of general application, the provisions do not prescribe any conduct either to a class or to the generality of the population. The provisions are entirely devoid of prohibitive or deterrent effect and are forward-looking. They are aimed at enabling the CC to identify problems on a given market with a view to remedying these for the future.

---

[66] Cases C 187 & 385/01 *Gözütok and Brügge* [2003] ECR I-1345, para 47.

[67] *Secretary of State for Health v Norton Healthcare Ltd* [2003] EWHC 1905 (Ch), [2004] Eu LR 12. See further paras 11.31–11.34.

[68] Regulation (EC) 44/2001 of 22 December 2000 on jurisdiction and the recognition and enforcement of judgments in civil and commercial matters [2001] OJ L12/1.

[69] Case C-453/99 *Courage Ltd v Crehan* [2001] ECR I-6297.

[70] *Engel v Netherlands* Series A No 22, (1976) EHRR 647.

[71] *Ozturk v Germany* Series A No 73, (1984) 6 EHRR 409.

- The remedies available to the CC at the conclusion of its investigation, although far-reaching, are not punitive (there is no power to fine, for example).[72] They have no deterrent purpose. Although these remedies may invoke other ECHR rights,[73] on balance the remedies lack the punitive flavour necessary to characterise the proceedings as criminal.

For this reason, although the remedies that are available to the CC can poten- **11.50**
tially impose major costs on businesses, it is unlikely that an undertaking wishing to preclude further regulatory action in relation to the same facts could rely on the principle of *ne bis in idem*. Under domestic law, broader notions of abuse of process and the obligation to ensure a fair trial (without unreasonable delay) may assist a defendant in this position.[74]

(v) The cartel offence

The cartel offence is classified as a criminal offence in the United Kingdom and **11.51**
undoubtedly qualifies as such for ECHR purposes.[75]

(vi) Director disqualification

Director disqualification proceedings have been considered by the ECtHR **11.52**
and held to be proceedings that determine civil rights and obligations for the purposes of Article 6(1) ECHR.[76]

(b) What is the 'same offence'?

Assuming that an undertaking is facing a repetition of proceedings that qualify **11.53**
as 'criminal', it will have to establish that earlier proceedings preclude the initiation of second proceedings. Not all previous proceedings suffice. The earlier proceedings must relate to the same offence as the proceedings the undertaking now faces. Much turns on the issue of what two offences are considered the same: if the two offences must be the same in law (ie in terms of legal classification), it will suffice for one offence to differ from another in a nominal sense to defeat the application of *ne bis in idem*. This is a particular risk in competition cases as cartels and abuse of dominance occur across national boundaries and

---

[72] As the ECtHR pointed out in *Ozturk*, ibid, para 54, the gravity (or, in that case, lack of gravity) of the penalty is not necessarily determinative.

[73] Art 1, Protocol 1 (the right to property) and Art 8 (right to privacy and home).

[74] See further paras 11.31–11.34. On delay in regulatory decision-making, see *Floe Telecom Ltd (in administration) v Ofcom* [2005] CAT 14, paras 119 et seq, and *Association of Convenience Stores v OFT* [2005] CAT 36, para 12.

[75] Enterprise Act 2002, ss 188 and 189.

[76] *Davies v UK* (2002) 35 EHRR CD92, para 25: 'As regards the applicability of Article 6 § 1, it was not disputed between the parties that the proceedings under the CDDA determined "civil rights and obligations" and the Court is of the same opinion.' See also *Eastaway v UK* (2005) 40 EHRR 17.

various authorities apply similar, but not identical, legislation. Very often the same facts can lead to different findings of infringement by various authorities applying legal provisions that differ in their formulation (depending on whether the viewpoint adopted is legal or economic, domestic or international) but that are, in substance, the same. If one does not have regard to the underlying facts (or at least consider whether the key elements of the two offences are substantially the same) for the purposes of applying *ne bis in idem*, there is a risk that undertakings will pay twice (or more) for what is essentially the same offence.

(i) ECHR case law

11.54   As mentioned above, ECHR case law defining what constitutes the 'same offence' takes a broad, purposive approach. In *Fischer v Austria*,[77] the ECtHR emphasised that to determine whether two offences are the same, one needs to look beyond the way an offence is formulated legally, in favour of considering the essential elements of the two offences. In order to determine whether two offences that are formulated differently are nonetheless *in idem*, the ECtHR explained that it was necessary to consider whether the essential elements of the two offences at issue overlapped. In particular, it stated that 'there are cases where . . . only one offence should be prosecuted because it encompasses all the wrongs contained in the others . . . An obvious example would be an act which constitutes two offences, one of which contains precisely the same elements as the other plus an additional one.'[78]

11.55   Applying this approach in the case of the United Kingdom and many other Member States which have enacted domestic competition law which is nearly identical to Articles 81 and 82 (the only different element being the issue of effect in trade), it is hard to resist the conclusion, on an analysis that is consistent with *Fischer*, that a breach of Article 81 and Article 82 encompasses a breach of the equivalent domestic legislation, so, for example, in essence Chapter I and Article 81 amount to the same offence.[79]

(ii) European case law

11.56   The European case law on *ne bis in idem* has to date not been entirely consistent. Three main strands can be distinguished in the jurisprudence.

11.57   *Wilhelm*   The first competition case in which the issue of *ne bis in idem* arose was *Wilhelm*.[80] A preliminary reference from a German court raised the question

---

[77] Application 37950, [2001] ECHR 352.
[78] ibid, para 25.
[79] See W Wils, 'The Principle of Ne Bis in Idem in EC Antitrust Enforcement: a Legal and Economic Analysis' (2003) 26 World Competition 131–48.
[80] Case 14/68 *Wilhelm v Bundeskartellamt* [1969] ECR 1.

as to whether it was compatible with the principle of *ne bis in idem* for the Bundeskartellamt to apply German cartel law to the same set of agreements in relation to which the European Commission had initiated Article 81 proceedings. The ECJ found that *ne bis in idem* did not arise, for two reasons. First, German cartel law and Article 81 could not be considered the same offence. In order to differentiate the German prohibition on cartels from Article 81, the ECJ dwelt on the difference *in object* of European and domestic competition law:

> Community and national law on cartels consider cartels from different points of view. Whereas Articles 85 regards them in the light of obstacles which may result for trade between Member States, each body of national legislation proceeds on the basis of the considerations peculiar to it and considers cartels only in that context.[81]

Secondly, it found that because of the special shared competence between the Community and the Member States it was possible to have concurrent proceedings: **11.58**

> The possibility of concurrent sanctions need not mean that the possibility of two parallel proceedings pursuing different ends is unacceptable . . . the acceptability of a dual procedure of this kind follows in fact from the special system of the sharing of jurisdiction between the Community and the Member States with regard to cartels.[82]

Although the ECJ found that offences under competition law and national competition law were not the same as they pursued different aims, it found that a principle of natural justice (which is to be distinguished from *ne bis in idem*) meant that the two authorities acting in such circumstances were obliged to have regard to any previous fines imposed in relation to the same behaviour: **11.59**

> If, however, the possibility of two procedures being conducted separately were to lead to the imposition of consecutive sanctions, a general requirement of natural justice . . . demands that any previous punitive decision must be taken into account in determining any sanction which is to be imposed.[83]

The approach adopted in *Wilhelm* has been followed and developed in the case law. In *Sotralentz*,[84] the Commission fined several undertakings, including the applicant, for agreements or concerted practices fixing prices and sharing markets in the welded steel mesh market. The French competition authority had already imposed fines on a number of French companies, including the applicant, for taking action and engaging in practices whose object or effect was to restrict competition and hamper the normal functioning of the welded steel mesh market in France. The applicant sought to distinguish this case from *Wilhelm* by emphasising that the particular subject matter of the proceedings **11.60**

---

[81] ibid, para 3.   [82] ibid, para 11.   [83] ibid, para 11.
[84] Case T-149/89 *Sotralentz v Commission* [1995] ECR II-1127.

brought by French authorities and by the Commission was exactly the same, namely an international agreement fixing, on the same national market, quotas for imports and the prices charged by all the traders concerned, including importers. The argument failed: the CFI relied on *Wilhelm* to justify that one and the same agreement could be the subject of parallel proceedings, domestic and European. Further, subject to each authority 'taking account' of the sanction imposed by the other, it was acceptable for each authority to apply a sanction.[85]

11.61   The net effect of this approach is that, even if the facts and the essential elements of two offences that are prosecuted are the same, unless the legislation applied in both cases shares the same objective (viewed extremely narrowly), two proceedings will not be considered the same.

11.62   The approach taken in these cases as to whether two offences are the same is markedly stricter than that adopted by the ECtHR (see para 11.17 above). Applying the approach taken by the ECtHR in *Fischer* to this case,[86] as Article 81 encompasses all the essential elements in the domestic prohibition on agreements that distort competition, the two offences would be considered the same under Article 4 of Protocol 7 ECHR (although Article 4 itself would not apply in this situation because it requires double prosecution under the laws of the same state).

11.63   **After *Wilhelm***   The test in *Wilhelm*—namely to consider not only whether the case relates to the same facts but also whether the legislation at issue in the two offences pursues the same aim—has been developed and refined. Recent cases define the pre-conditions for *ne bis in idem* to apply in a manner that is reminiscent of the principle of *res judicata*. Advocate General Ruiz-Jaramo Colomer in his Opinion in *Gözütok and Brügge*[87] set out the criteria as follows:

> The classic formulation of the ne bis in idem principle requires that three identical circumstances should be present: the same facts, the same offender and the same legal principle—the same value—to be protected.[88]

---

[85] ibid, paras 26 and 29. See, to similar effect, Case T-141/89 *Trefileurope Sales SARL v Commission* [1995] ECR II-791.

[86] Application 37950, [2001] ECHR 352: 'there are cases where . . . only one offence should be prosecuted because it encompasses all the wrongs contained in the others . . . An obvious example would be an act which constitutes two offences, one of which contains precisely the same elements as the other plus an additional one.'

[87] See also his Opinions in Case C-217/00 P *Buzzi Unicem SpA v Commission*, Case C-213/00 *Italcementi SpA v Commission* and Case C-219/00 *Cimentir v Commission*, collectively known as *Aalborg Portland A/S v Commission* [2004] ECR I-123.

[88] Cases C 187 & 385/01 *Gözütok and Brügge* [2003] ECR I-1345, Opinion of AG Ruiz-Jaramo Colomer, para 56.

This test has been adopted by the CFI, for example in *Graphite Electrodes*:[89] **11.64**

> The application of the principle ne bis in idem is subject not only to the infringe-ments and the persons sanctioned being the same, but also to the unity of the legal right being protected (Opinion of Advocate General Ruiz-Jaramo in Case C-213/00 P Italcementi v Commission [2004] ECR I-0000, point 89).[90]

In *Aalborg Portland A/S*,[91] the ECJ endorsed the three identities formulation **11.65**
that had been suggested by Advocate General Ruiz-Jaramo Colomer in his Opinions:

> [T]he application of that principle is subject to the threefold condition of identity of the facts, unity of offender and unity of the legal interest protected. Under that principle, therefore, the same person cannot be sanctioned more than once for a single unlawful course of conduct designed to protect the same legal asset.[92]

It is unclear what constitutes the 'same' legal asset. The requirement that not **11.66**
only should the previous decision relate to the same facts and the same person, but also that *the same legal right* should be at issue could be interpreted as the ECJ approached the 'same objective' in *Wilhelm*, in a manner that is tantamount to a requirement that the two offences should actually be iden-tical. Thus, one could argue that in protecting trade between Member States, European competition law is protecting a different legal asset to that protected by national competition law.

Advocate General Ruiz-Jaramo Colomer took a broad view of what should be **11.67**
considered the same legal right or asset. In his Opinions in *Buzzi Unicem SpA*,[93]
Italcementi SpA[94] and *Cimentir*[95] he forcefully argued that Community com-petition law and national competition law cannot be distinguished from one another as they constitute the same legal asset:

> The unity of the legal right to be protected is beyond doubt. The rules which guarantee free competition within the European Union do not allow a distinction to be drawn between separate areas, the Community area and the national areas, as though they were watertight compartments. Both sectors are concerned with the supervision of free and open competition in the common market, one

---

[89] Case T-236/01 *Tokai Carbon Co v Commission (Graphite Electrodes)* [2004] ECR II-1181. See also Case T-329/01 *Archer Daniels Midland Co v Commission*, judgment of 27 September 2006.

[90] *Graphite Electrodes*, ibid, para 134.

[91] Joined Cases C 204, 213, 217 & 219/00 P *Aalborg Portland A/S v Commission* [2004] ECR I-123.

[92] ibid, para 338.

[93] Case C-217/00 P *Buzzi Unicem SpA v Commission* [2004] ECR I-123.

[94] Case C-213/00 *Italcementi SpA v Commission* [2004] ECR I-123.

[95] Case C-219/00 *Cimentir v Commission* [2004] ECR I-123.

contemplating it in its entirety and the other from its separate components, but the essence is the same.[96]

11.68 To date, the question of what constitutes the same legal asset has not been expressly considered by the ECJ. In *Graphite Electrodes*, the CFI, distinguishing between the aim of Canadian and US antitrust law on the one hand, and that of European competition law on the other, found that the same legal right was not at issue as the procedures pursued different ends:

> . . . the principle ne bis in idem cannot . . . apply in the present case because *the procedures* conducted and penalties imposed by the Commission on the one hand and the United States and Canadian authorities on the other *clearly did not pursue the same ends. The aim of the first was to preserve undistorted competition within the European Union or the EEA, whereas the aim of the second was to protect the United States or the Canadian market . . .*[97]

11.69 In *Archer Daniels Midland Co*, Advocate General Tizzano opined 'when the Commission imposes penalties for an offence, which may derive from a single "international strategy", it seeks to protect a specific "legal asset" namely free competition in the common market and thus distinct from that protected by the authorities of third countries'.[98] The ECJ did not consider the issue, as it considered that the plea raised by the appellant was not a plea of *ne bis in idem* proper.

11.70 On appeal from the CFI's judgment in *Graphite Electrodes*, in *Showa Denko KK*,[99] the ECJ gave an indication that it considers that Community law on competition and Member State law on competition pursue the same ends.[100]

---

[96] Case C-217/00 P *Buzzi Unicem SpA v Commission* [2004] ECR I-123, para 173; see also Case C-213/00 *Italcementi SpA v Commission* [2004] ECR I-123, para 91. In those cases, the AG suggested that there was no identity in the facts (*Buzzi Unicem*, para 180 and *Italcementi*, para 98). (Note that the English version of the Opinion refers to there not being identity in the objectives of the procedure, but that both the Italian and French versions of this Opinion refer to lack of identity on the facts.) The ECJ agreed—Joined Cases C 204, 213, 217 & 219/00 P *Aalborg Portland A/S v Commission* [2004] ECR I-123.

[97] Case T-236/01 *Tokai Carbon Co v Commission (Graphite Electrodes)* [2004] ECR II-1181, para 134. Similar reasoning can be found in Case T-223/00 *Kyowa Hakko Kogyo Co v Commission* [2003] ECR II-2553.

[98] Case C-397/03 P *Archer Daniels Midland Co v Commission*, Opinion of 7 June 2005, para 103.

[99] Case C-289/04 P *Showa Denko KK v Commission*, judgment of 29 June 2006.

[100] Note, to contrary effect, the CFI's judgments in *Graphite Electrodes*. It appears to find that for two cases to be the same they should both be brought by the Commission: 'In the field of Community competition law, the principle precludes an undertaking from being sanctioned by the Commission or made the defendant to proceedings brought by the Commission a second time in respect of anti-competitive conduct for which it has already been penalised or of which it has been exonerated by a previous decision of the Commission that is not amenable challenge.' Case T-236/01 *Tokai Carbon Co v Commission (Graphite Electrodes)* [2004] ECR II-1181, para 131. See to similar effect Case T-223/00 *Kyowa Hakko Kogyo Co v Commission* [2003] ECR II-2553, para 97.

After indicating why competition law in non-Member States meets requirements that are specific to those States (which are not those of the Community), it stated '[o]n the other hand, the legal situation is completely different where an undertaking is caught exclusively—in competition matters—by the application of Community law and the law of one or more Member States'.[101]

***Ne bis in idem* in the European jurisprudence more generally**   The ECJ and **11.71** CFI's approach to *ne bis in idem* in the context of competition is in marked contrast to its approach to the concept under Article 54 CISA.[102] In particular, under the CISA the only prerequisite for the plea to arise is that the prosecution should relate to the same acts—there is no need for their legal classification be the same.[103] In *Van Straaten* the ECJ held that 'the only relevant criterion for the application of Article 54 of the CISA is identity of the material acts, understood as the existence of a set of concrete circumstances which are inextricably linked together'.[104] In her Opinion in *Gasparini*,[105] Advocate General Sharpston suggested that the specific application of *ne bis in idem* in particular areas (be these CISA or competition law) should form part of the core understanding of what the fundamental principle means within the Community legal order.

(iii) Same legislation: one offence or several?

The issue of what two offences are the same need not always arise in the context **11.72** of decisions by two different national competition authorities. Sometimes it arises in the context of decisions taken by one and the same authority applying the same legislation. The difficulty of evidencing factually complex arrangements such as cartels has occasionally led the European Commission to adopt the concept of a single, overall cartel agreement in making a decision.[106] However, as the ECJ remarked in *Aalborg Portland*,[107] one or several elements of an 'overall agreement' can also, taken in isolation, be viewed as separate infringements, and lead to several fines.

Sometimes therefore, the issue of *ne bis in idem* arises in circumstances where **11.73** the same authority prosecutes and punishes agreements concerning closely related products between the same players, and imposes several sanctions, one in

---

[101] Case C-289/04 P *Showa Denko KK v Commission*, judgment of 29 June 2006, para 54.
[102] AG Sharpston comments upon in Case C-467/04 *Gasparini*, Opinion of 15 June 2006, para 63.
[103] Case C-436/04 *Van Esbroeck* [2006] 3 CMLR 6, para 41.
[104] Case C-150/05, judgment of 28 September 2006, para 48.
[105] Case C-467/04, Opinion of 15 June 2006, para 80.
[106] Joined Cases C 204, 213, 217 & 219/00 P *Aalborg Portland A/S v Commission* [2004] ECR I-123, paras 258–62.
[107] ibid, para 258.

relation to each infringement. Arguments of *ne bis in idem* in such situations are difficult: there is nearly always some variance between the factual matrix of the two infringements that a regulator can rely upon as a valid ground of distinction so that there is no identity in the facts underlying the two infringements. Further, the approach of the CFI and ECJ has been unsympathetic to such arguments. Faced with such arguments in *JJB Sports plc v OFT*,[108] the CAT and the Court of Appeal[109] upheld the OFT's finding that the price fixing relating to the MU Centenary Shirts Agreement should be treated as a separate infringement.

11.74   In *Tokai Carbon Co*,[110] one of the parties argued that by imposing on it a fine in respect of graphite electrodes as well as a fine in respect of the neighbouring product of specialty graphites, the European Commission penalised it for the same facts twice. It claimed that the agreements constituted a single continuous infringement based on an overall plan in which the existing cartel for graphite electrodes was extended to specialty graphite. The CFI dismissed the *ne bis in idem* argument on the basis that the participants in the two cartels were not the same, that the product markets for the two products were distinct, and that the anti-competitive practices adopted by the two cartels were not the same.[111] The CFI found that the product markets were distinct partially on the basis of replies provided by the parties to questionnaires. This could lead to a tension for a respondent to questionnaires where several products have been the subject of anti-competitive agreements: on the one hand, defining the product markets narrowly leads to a possibility that several fines will be imposed. On the other, defining the markets more broadly can lead to a larger starting point for the fine.[112]

(c) Is there a valid prior decision?

11.75   In *Limburgse Vinyl Maatschappij NV (LVM) v Commission*,[113] the ECJ decreed that a previous unappealable decision is a prerequisite for *ne bis in idem* to apply in a competition context:

> [It] precludes, in competition matters, an undertaking from being found guilty or

---

[108] *JJB Sports plc v OFT* [2005] CAT 22.
[109] *Argos, Littlewoods and JJB v OFT* [2006] EWCA Civ 1318.
[110] Case T-71/03 *Tokai Carbon Co v Commission* [2005] 5 CMLR 13.
[111] ibid, paras 119 et seq.
[112] The starting point for the calculation of the fine imposed by the UK authorities for breaches of Chapter I, Chapter II, Art 81 and Art 82 is partially based on the relevant turnover in the relevant product market affected by the infringement (OFT423, *OFT's guidance as to the appropriate amount of a penalty* (December 2004) para 2.7).
[113] Case C-238/99 P *Limburgse Vinyl Maatschappij NV (LVM) v Commission* [2002] ECR I-8375, para 59.

proceedings from being brought against it a second time on the grounds of anti-competitive conduct in respect of which it has been penalised or declared not liable *by a previous unappealable decision.*[114]

The ECJ emphasised in that case that it is critical that the earlier decision maker **11.76** has undertaken an evaluation of the legality of the behaviour at issue:

> The application of that principle . . . presupposes that a ruling has been given on the question whether an offence has in fact been committed or that the legality of the assessment thereof has been reviewed.[115]

Assuming the requirement that there be a previous unappealable decision is **11.77** maintained, this has consequences for the application of *ne bis in idem* to the following regulatory decisions that do not, on current authority, involve an evaluation of the merits. In particular, commitment decisions by the European Commission and by national competition authorities, regulatory decisions that are annulled for procedural reasons, and decisions by national competition authorities that they have no grounds for action do not provide an evaluation of the legality of the behaviour at issue and, on this basis, could not give rise to a plea of *ne bis in idem*. Each is considered in turn below.

(i) Commitment decisions

Commitment decisions taken by the European Commission and by the OFT **11.78** do not undertake an evaluation of the legality of the conduct to which they relate.[116] There is some debate as to whether one can rely on a commitment decision to preclude further regulatory action.[117] The ECJ judgment in *LVM* implies that such a decision would be insufficient to prevent a second investigation by another competition authority on the basis of *ne bis in idem* because it does not undertake an assessment of legality of the behaviour. On this argument, one cannot therefore seek to rely on a commitment decision by the European Commission to preclude further investigation by the national competition authorities seeking to apply Article 81 and/or Article 82, or indeed any decision by the courts applying Article 81 and/or Article 82.

---

[114] ibid, para 59 (emphasis added).   [115] ibid, para 60.

[116] As regards European Commission commitments decisions, see Recital 13 to Regulation 1/2003: 'Commitment decisions should find that there are no longer grounds for action by the Commission without concluding whether or not there has been or still is an infringement.' For commitment decisions taken under the Competition Act 1998, see OFT407, *Enforcement* (December 2004) para 4.7: 'A decision by the OFT accepting binding commitments will state that the commitments offered by the undertaking meet the OFT's competition concerns, but will not include any statement as to the legality or otherwise of the agreement or conduct either prior to the acceptance of the commitments or once the commitments are in place.'

[117] See R Nazzini, 'Some Reflections on the Dynamics of the Due Process Discourse in EC Competition Law' (2005) 2 Competition L Rev 5; M Sousa Ferro, 'Committing to Commitment Decisions—unanswered questions on Article 9 decisions' [2005] ECLR 451–9.

11.79   This approach is consistent with Recitals 13 and 22 of Regulation 1/2003 which respectively provide: 'Commitment decisions are without prejudice to the powers of competition authorities and courts of the Member States to make such a finding and decide upon the case' and 'Commitment decisions adopted by the Commission do not affect the power of the courts and the competition authorities of the Member States to apply Articles 81 and 82 of the Treaty.' It is also consistent with Article 4 of Protocol 7 ECHR and Article 50 of the European Charter, which both depend on a final decision to preclude a second prosecution.

11.80   Despite this, some commentators have suggested that a national competition authority is not free, after the Commission has accepted commitments, to investigate and make a decision relating to the same matter under Article 81 and/or Article 82 (inter alia because this would be in breach of its obligations under Article 16 of Regulation 1/2003, or a breach of its duty of loyal cooperation under Article 10 EC).[118] In support of this view, an interesting parallel can be drawn with a recent decision by the ECJ concerning the application of Article 54 CISA to settlements of criminal cases. In *Gözütok and Brügge*,[119] the ECJ found that Article 54 CISA applied to prevent a second prosecution after an earlier out of court settlement involving the prosecuting authority.[120] The ECJ found that the out of court settlement procedure penalised the unlawful conduct because it was dependent on the accused undertaking performing certain obligations prescribed by the public prosecutor. Further, as following such a procedure further prosecution was definitely barred, in the ECJ's view the case must be regarded as 'finally disposed of' for the purposes of Article 54 CISA. The ECJ took a purposive approach to the questions raised:

> Article 54 of the CISA . . . cannot play a useful role . . . unless it also applies to decisions definitively discontinuing prosecutions in a Member State, even where such decisions are adopted without the involvement of a court and do not take the form of a judicial decision.

11.81   In *Miraglia*,[121] the ECJ decided that *ne bis in idem* did not apply where the first decision was a decision by a public prosecutor to close a case for entirely technical reasons with no consideration whatsoever of the merits of the case. It is not clear which way the ECJ will go should it be invited either to apply or to reason by analogy with Article 54 CISA to commitment decisions. The ECJ's judgments in *Gözütok and Brügge* and even in *Miraglia* indicate that the ECJ is prepared to take a broader approach to *ne bis in idem*—it will be difficult for the ECJ to justify standards of protection that are different when it is applied

---

[118] M Sousa Ferro, ibid.
[119] Cases C 187 & 385/01 *Gözütok and Brügge* [2003] ECR I-1345.
[120] ibid, para 38.   [121] Case C-469/03 [2005] ECR I-2009.

in the competition context.[122] A decision accepting commitments falls somewhere in between the decisions taken by the public prosecutor in *Miraglia* and *Gözütok and Brügge.* On the one hand, the acceptance of commitments clearly goes beyond closing a case for technical reasons as in *Miraglia.* On the other, the acceptance of commitments does not definitively preclude further prosecution (both under EC law and the Competition Act 1998 the possibility of re-opening proceedings after commitments are accepted is expressly preserved).[123]

On balance, in view of the wording of the recitals to Regulation 1/2003, the **11.82** need for a decision that finally disposes of the matter under the CISA, the European Charter, and the ECHR, and the ECJ's emphasis on the need for an evaluation of the legality of the behaviour in *PVC II*, an undertaking would be best advised to assume that a commitment decision by the Commission or by a national competition authority will not take effect to preclude a second decision by another authority on the same offence.[124] The policy argument in support of allowing further action by other authorities (after a commitment decision has been accepted by one authority) is that decisions relating to commitments are heavily influenced by an authority's use of resources and do not necessarily imply any favourable judgment of the merits of the competition problem—they merely establish that there are no longer grounds for action on that particular regulator's part. This argument is particularly strong with regard to commitment decisions taken by national competition authorities. When negotiating commitments, an authority will usually require commitments that relate to conduct and agreements that take effect in its own territory—it will not generally have the ability to police or enforce commitments relating to conduct elsewhere. This should not preclude another national competition authority, or the Commission, from taking action, either with a view to obtaining commitments in relation to its own territory or with a view to pronouncing upon the legality of the behaviour (if necessary, imposing a sanction).

(ii) Procedural annulments

Where an earlier decision is annulled or withdrawn for procedural reasons only, **11.83** there is no substantive pronouncement on the charges against an undertaking. In *LVM*,[125] the ECJ held that *ne bis in idem* did not preclude the Commission reopening an investigation into the same anti-competitive conduct where its

---

[122] Undertakings may seek to rely on Art 54 in a competition context.

[123] See Chapter 10 for a discussion of commitments.

[124] The authority accepting commitments is itself precluded from re-opening the matter unless certain conditions are met: Competition Act 1998, s 31B(2) and Regulation 1/2003, Art 9(2).

[125] Case C-238/99 P *Limburgse Vinyl Maatschappij NV (LVM) v Commission* [2002] ECR I-8375.

first decision was annulled for procedural reasons. The ECJ considered that 'the annulment decision cannot in such circumstances be regarded as an acquittal within the meaning given to that expression in penal matters. In such a case, the penalties imposed by the new decision are not added to those imposed by the annulled decision but replace them.'[126] This is in marked contrast to the approach taken by the ECJ in such cases under Article 54 CISA, where it has held that prior acquittals by reason of a time-bar[127] or lack of evidence[128] preclude a second prosecution.

(iii) National competition authority decisions that there are no grounds for action

11.84 Regulation 1/2003 has deliberately moved away from a scheme by which one could obtain a 'clearance' or 'finding of non-infringement' from one authority that would take effect across the European Union.[129]

11.85 Article 5 of Regulation 1/2003 provides national competition authorities with the power to apply Article 81 and Article 82. It lists (apparently non-exhaustively) the types of decision that authorities may take in applying Articles 81 and 82. Article 5 deliberately provides no power for authorities to make non-infringement decisions: where authorities consider that the conditions for prohibition are not met, they are merely empowered to 'decide that there are no grounds for decision on their part'. This language is aimed at retaining the scope for national competition authorities to investigate and decide upon a matter that another authority has decided not to act upon, as there is no finding of non-infringement as such by the first authority.[130] Whether the use of such device should succeed in avoiding the rule in *ne bis in idem* is discussed below at paras 11.96 et seq.

D. Multiple Prosecution in Practice

11.86 Let us now examine how the principle of *ne bis in idem* could apply in practice under Regulation 1/2003.

---

[126] ibid, para 62. [127] Case C-467/04 *Gasparini*, judgment of 28 September 2006.
[128] Case C-150/05 *Van Straaten v Netherlands and Italy*, judgment of 28 September 2006.
[129] Under Regulation 1/2003, the European Commission is the only competition authority that may, exceptionally, make an express finding of 'inapplicability' (under Art 10 of Regulation 1/2003) which takes effect to bind national competition authorities and courts.
[130] Regulation 1/203, Art 9, which empowers the Commission to make commitment decisions, similarly uses 'no grounds of action' language to preserve the ability of national competition authorities to initiate cases in relation to which the Commission has accepted commitments: see Regulation 1/2003, Recital 13.

(a) Prosecution under EC law and under domestic competition law

(i) Domestic proceedings that are not criminal in nature

Where an undertaking is facing proceedings under EC law (be they brought **11.87** by national competition authorities or the Commission) together with domestic proceedings that are not 'criminal' in nature (such as civil proceedings for damages under Articles 81 and 82 or a market investigation reference), *ne bis in idem* will not apply to protect the undertaking from parallel proceedings, given that both proceedings must be of a criminal nature for the plea to arise.

However, where the domestic court or decision-maker is seized with a dispute **11.88** concerning agreements or conduct that is before the European Commission, arguments can be made on grounds of loyal cooperation and primacy,[131] and in some cases under Article 16 of Regulation 1/2003, that the case should be stayed pending the Commission's decision, to avoid the risk of inconsistent decisions.[132] In such cases, national courts retain, despite their obligations under Article 16(1) of Regulation 1/2003, a certain amount of procedural autonomy.[133] A court may for example, as in *MTV Europe*,[134] decide to permit preparation of the proceedings to proceed short of actually holding the trial.

Where the parallel proceedings are between civil proceedings before the UK **11.89** national courts under domestic law, on the one hand, and the OFT or the CAT applying Article 81 or Article 82 EC, on the other, the court has a general discretion to stay the proceedings, inter alia to avoid inconsistent decisions, see paras 11.31 et seq above.

Where the parallel proceedings are conducted by various UK authorities (such **11.90** as the CC and the OFT), it is possible to rely on the protection of the rights of the defence and Article 6 ECHR and principles of fair administration to seek to defer simultaneous investigations that prejudice the rights of the defence.[135] For example, the OFT has indicated that: '[a]s a general rule the OFT will avoid actually investigating a suspected infringement of Articles 81 or 82 simultaneously with a CC investigation of the same agreement, decision, concerted

---

[131] All competition authorities, even those that are not designated under Regulation 1/2003, are bound by the principle of primacy—it is not clear, however, whether an authority such as the CC, which is not designated, would be bound by Art 16(2).

[132] See Cooperation Notice and Case C-344/98 *Masterfoods Ltd (t/a Mars Ireland) v HB Ice Creams Ltd* [2000] ECR I-11369.

[133] See also *Synstar Computer Services (UK) Ltd v ICL (Sorbus) Ltd* [2001] CP Rep 98, discussed at paras 11.33 et seq above.

[134] *MTV Europe v BMG Record (UK) Ltd* [1997] 1 CMLR 867.

[135] *R v Panel of Take Overs and Mergers, ex p Fayed* [1992] BCC 524; *R v ICAEW, ex p Brindle* [1994] BCC 297; *R v Institute of Actuaries* [2004] EWHC 3087.

practice or conduct, both to reduce undue burdens on business and as a matter of administrative good practice'.[136]

(ii) Domestic proceedings that are criminal in nature

11.91 Where an undertaking faces an investigation under European law and the Competition Act 1998, the approach of the ECJ and CFI to such issues prior to Regulation 1/2003 was that *ne bis in idem* does not apply to prevent the same wrongful acts giving rise to prosecution and punishment under both European and national competition law. *Wilhelm* (see paras 11.57 et seq above for a full discussion of this case) established that parallel prosecution of the same conduct or agreements by domestic authorities on the one hand and the Commission on the other is permissible as national competition law and European competition law pursue different aims, and accordingly do not amount to the same offence.[137] In view of the special shared jurisdiction of the European and national competition authorities, the ECJ held it was possible for each to apply a sanction, provided that the authorities take account of the sanctions that have already been imposed in relation to the same behaviour.[138]

11.92 Since the *Wilhelm* judgment in 1969, several changes have taken place that call into question whether the ECJ would take the same approach to the application of *ne bis in idem* if the issue of application of both European and domestic law to the same facts arose for decision in a case before it today in the context of Regulation 1/2003. Should an undertaking facing prosecution under both domestic and European competition law wish to contest the double prosecution, several arguments are available in its defence:

• The premise on which *Wilhelm* is founded, namely that national law and European domestic law pursue different aims, is difficult to sustain now that a majority of Member States have adopted domestic law prohibitions that clone Article 81 and Article 82. In many Member States, the only difference between national and European competition law is that EC law applies only where trade between Member States is affected. In the same vein, as noted by

---

[136] OFT511, *Market investigation references: Guidance about the making of references under Part 4 of the Enterprise Act* (March 2006) para 2.16.

[137] Case 14/68 *Wilhelm v Bundeskartellamt* [1969] ECR 1.

[138] Case T-223/00 *Kyowa Hakko Kogyo Co v Commission* [2003] ECR II-2553, para 98: 'However, a general requirement of natural justice demands that, in determining the amount of a fine, the Commission must take account of any penalties that have already been borne by the undertaking in question in respect of the same conduct where these were imposed for infringement of the law relating to cartels of a Member State and where, consequently, the infringement was committed within the Community (Wilhelm and others, cited above, paragraph 11, Boehringer v Commission, cited above, paragraph 3, Case T-141/89 Tréfileurope v Commission [1995] ECR II-791, paragraph 191, and Sotralentz v Commission, cited above, paragraph 29).'

Advocate General Tizzano in his Opinion in *Archer Daniels Midland Co*,[139] '[s]ince the Court delivered its judgment in *Walt Wilhelm* (more than 30 years ago) the degree of interdependence and integration of Community and national systems for safeguarding competition on which that judgment was based has significantly increased, in particular with the decentralisation of the application of Community antitrust law introduced by Regulation 1/2003'. Advocate General Ruiz-Jaramo Colomer, in his Opinions in *Buzzi Unicem SpA*[140] and in *Italcementi SpA*,[141] recognised that national and European competition law can no longer be considered as different offences. The ECJ, in its judgment in *Showa Denko*,[142] (the appeal from the CFI's judgment in *Graphite Electrodes*) seems also to provide a strong hint in this direction.

- Secondly, since *Wilhelm* the ECtHR's judgment in *Fischer v Austria*[143] provides a powerful precedent which undermines the ECJ's reasoning in *Wilhelm*. If the ECJ were to follow *Fischer* to determine whether *ne bis in idem* applied to prevent double prosecution under national and European competition law, this would almost certainly lead it to reach a different conclusion. It will be recalled that it suffices for the purposes of the ECHR for the essential elements of two offences to overlap for the two offences to be considered the same. Applying the approach taken by the ECtHR in *Fisher* to this case,[144] Articles 81 and 82 would appear to encompass all the essential elements of domestic law replicas such as Chapter I and Chapter II.[145] The ECJ has also recently taken a generous approach to what amounts to the same offence for the purposes of Article 54 CISA.[146]

- There was an important incentive, in *Wilhelm*, for the ECJ to find that *ne bis in idem* did not apply in order to protect the Commission's scope for action. At the time, applying *ne bis in idem* in the context of national and European competition law would in effect have meant that where national competition authorities had acted, the Commission would be precluded from taking further action. This incentive is no longer there: under Regulation 1/2003, if the

---

[139] Case C-397/03 P *Archer Daniels Midland Co v Commission*, Opinion of 7 June 2005.

[140] Case C-217/00 P *Buzzi Unicem SpA v Commission* [2004] ECR I-123, para 173.

[141] Case C-213/00 *Italcementi SpA v Commission* [2004] ECR I-123, paras 91–3.

[142] Case C-289/04 P *Showa Denko KK v Commission*, judgment of 29 June 2006, para 54.

[143] Application 37950, [2001] ECHR 352. See para 11.17 above for a description of the test set out in *Fischer v Austria*.

[144] '[T]here are cases where . . . only one offence should be prosecuted because it encompasses all the wrongs contained in the others . . . An obvious example would be an act which constitutes two offences, one of which contains precisely the same elements as the other plus an additional one.' ibid, para 25.

[145] See Wouter Wils, 'The Principle of Ne Bis in Idem in EC Antitrust Enforcement: a Legal and Economic Analysis' (2003) 26 World Competition 131–48, 143.

[146] Case C-436/04 *Van Esbroeck* [2006] 3 CMLR 6, see also paras 11.27 and 11.71. Case C-150/05 *Van Straaten v Netherlands and Italy*, judgment of 28 September 2006.

ECJ were to find that *ne bis in idem* precluded the application of European and national law competition law to one and the same infringement, it is likely that the fatality would be national competition law.

- Lastly, it can be understood why the ECJ took a conservative stance to the scope of *ne bis in idem* in 1969—it was taking a revolutionary step just in acknowledging that the principle could apply in a transnational context. Since the introduction of Article 50 of the Charter and Article 54 CISA, the application of *ne bis in idem* outside the context of one state's legal system (but within the scope of the European Union only) is not so unusual. The ECJ, in applying Article 54 CISA, has taken a more purposive approach.[147]

11.93 An undertaking should not face prosecution both by the Commission under European law and by a national competition authority under domestic law. Under Article 11(6) of Regulation 1/2003, a national competition authority only loses its competence to apply European law where the Commission initiates a case in relation to the same matter: it does expressly not lose its competence to apply domestic law to the matter. It could, however, be argued that further action under domestic law is precluded by virtue of primacy.[148] In practice, it is unlikely that a national competition authority would choose to waste its resources either to initiate or continue with an investigation to apply domestic law where the Commission takes (or has already taken) action under European law, particularly in light of the views expressed by Commission officials on competence. In the highly unlikely event that a national competition authority would take on such a case under national law, it would be difficult (if not impossible) for an authority to do anything consistent with its duty of cooperation under Article 10 EC other than stay its domestic proceedings and await the outcome of the Commission proceedings to ensure that any decision it makes under domestic law is compatible with European law.[149]

11.94 The application of both European and domestic law to the same facts is much more likely to arise where an undertaking is investigated by one national competition authority under both domestic and European law, or (less frequently) if an undertaking faces investigations by different authorities applying domestic and European law, where there has been no agreement on case allocation in the

---

[147] Cases C 187 & 385/01 *Gözütok and Brügge* [2003] ECR I-1345.

[148] Although some Commission officials argue that the initiation of proceedings by the Commission relieves the national competition authority of all competence to act in relation to the same matter, as the authority is not able to satisfy its obligations under Art 3(1) of Regulation 1/2003. W Wils, *Principles of European Antitrust Enforcement* (Hart Publishing, 2005).

[149] Case C-344/98 *Masterfoods Ltd (t/a Mars Ireland) v HB Ice Creams Ltd* [2000] ECR I-11369. See Chapter 3 for a discussion of the obligations on national courts and national authorities to apply domestic competition law in a manner that is compatible with European law.

ECN or several authorities have agreed to act together in the context of the ECN.[150]

The burdens of double prosecution will be less where the double prosecution **11.95** is at the hands of a UK competition authority, as the relevant Competition Act prohibition and its European equivalent will be investigated by means of one and the same investigation (the OFT may change the charge as the investigation proceeds).[151] Further, although an undertaking will theoretically be penalised twice under European and domestic competition law, in that there will be a finding of breach of both the domestic prohibition and the European prohibition, the OFT has said that an undertaking will not be penalised twice 'for the same anti-competitive effects'.[152] The authors take this to mean that when calculating the starting point for each of the fines, the same turnover cannot be used to fine under both European and domestic law (elsewhere the guidance equates 'effects' with relevant turnover).[153] This means in practical terms that where the OFT applies European and national competition law, an undertaking is not prosecuted twice nor is it fined twice over.

(b) Prosecutions by several authorities applying European law

Under Regulation 1/2003, an undertaking is not intended to face proceedings **11.96** both by the Commission and a national competition authority under European law. The initiation of Article 81 and Article 82 proceedings by the Commission has the effect of relieving national competition authorities of their competence to apply these articles in relation to the same matter.[154] Competence would seem to return to the national authorities after the Commission has reached a decision, since Article 16(2) envisages a national authority applying Articles 81 and 82 to a matter that has already been the subject of a Commission decision, but it is unlikely that an authority will expend resources on investigating a matter that has been investigated and decided upon by the Commission, given that it may not take a decision that runs counter to that of the Commission.[155] It should be noted that Article 16 will not prevent national authorities from investigating matters that are closely related, but not identical, to the matter

---

[150] Art 3(1) exacerbates the risk of simultaneous application of domestic and European law by requiring that European law be applied where national law is applied to agreements that may affect trade or conduct that is prohibited by Art 82.

[151] OFT's Procedural Rules, r 10, provides that the OFT may, at any time prior to making an infringement decision, elect to apply one or more of the Chapter I prohibition, Chapter II prohibition, Art 81 and Art 82.

[152] OFT423, *OFT's guidance as to the appropriate amount of a penalty* (December 2004) para 1.15.

[153] ibid, para 2.6: 'The OFT will take into account effects in another Member State through its assessment of relevant turnover.'

[154] Regulation 1/2003, Art 11(6).   [155] ibid, Art 16(2).

investigated by the Commission[156]—but neither will the principle of *ne bis in idem* as there is not the requisite identity in the facts.

11.97 This issue is likely therefore mostly to arise in the context where several national competition authorities are acting under Article 81 or Article 82. Some of these cases would be those agreed through the ECN where authorities investigate cases jointly—such as multi-jurisdictional cartels—with each focusing on effects in its jurisdiction.

11.98 The case for contesting the application of European law by several national authorities rests on the same arguments as set out above in respect of the parallel application of European and domestic competition law. In addition, several other arguments can be made:

- Such a situation clearly satisfies the test for *ne bis in idem* as most recently formulated by the ECJ[157]—there is the requisite identity in the facts, in the defendant, and in the legal asset to be protected. *Wilhelm* cannot apply where each national authority is applying identical provisions towards the same aim: no valid distinction can be drawn between the various prosecutions, they clearly relate to the same offence.

- The principle of natural justice recognised in *Wilhelm*, whereby authorities 'take account' of each others' decisions, is not sufficient: the right is not to be prosecuted twice, as well as not to be punished twice. This was noted by Advocate General Ruiz-Jaramo Colomer: '[t]he solution whereby the second authority involved reduces the penalty owing to the amount of the fine imposed by the first authority, which was adopted by the Court of Justice in *Wilhelm*, does not satisfy the principle of ne bis in idem'.[158] The need to be protected from double prosecution is particularly acute in a situation where prosecutions in several Member States are likely—these are particularly costly since they demand the retention of different lawyers as well as translators to deal with the linguistic issues. It is clearly far more onerous and punitive a process for an undertaking to defend itself before multiple authorities in different jurisdictions, each proceeding at a different pace and each taking a different view as to the relevant factual and legal issues. The fact that the fine that each national authority imposes only accounts for the effects of anti-competitive behaviour in the particular jurisdiction is no answer to these difficulties.

---

[156] The simultaneous investigations of MasterCard's cross-border interchange fees (by the European Commission) and of its domestic interchange fees (it is investigated, on a formal or informal basis, by up to ten national competition authorities) is a good example of this.

[157] Joined Cases C 204, 213, 217 & 219/00 P *Aalborg Portland A/S v Commission* [2004] ECR I-123; see paras 11.63–11.70 above.

[158] Case C-213/00 *Italcementi SpA v Commission* [2004] ECR I-123, Opinion of AG Ruiz-Jaramo Colomer, para 96.

- It is difficult to see, after Regulation 1/2003, a justification for multiple prosecution based on the 'special shared jurisdiction' between the national competition authorities—if anything the ever closer cooperation between authorities and the Commission in enforcing competition law should mean that there is less risk of multiple prosecution, not more. Regulation 1/2003 provides national authorities with formidable tools to work together to combat anti-competitive activity, for example they may share information with one another and conduct inspections and other fact-finding measures on each other's behalf. Against the background of these shared powers, it is difficult to see how the shared jurisdiction justifies subjecting undertakings to different decision-making processes in different jurisdictions.

(c) Multiple prosecution by EU and non-EU competition authorities

11.99 The ECJ and the CFI have considered and rejected any application of the principle of *ne bis in idem* proper (ie a rule precluding even double prosecution) in the context of the action by the Community and a third state.

11.100 In *Graphite Electrodes*[159] the Commission fined undertakings that had already been fined by the US and Canadian competition authorities in relation to the same cartel. The CFI upheld the Commission decision and rejected an argument of *ne bis in idem* on a classic *Wilhelm* approach, namely on the basis that the procedures did not have the same aim. It emphasised that, given that *Wilhelm* had approved the possibility of parallel European and domestic proceedings on the basis that these pursued different ends:

> In those circumstances, the principle ne bis in idem cannot, a fortiori, apply in the present case because the procedures conducted and penalties imposed by the Commission on the one hand and the United States and Canadian authorities on the other clearly did not pursue the same ends. The aim of the first was to preserve undistorted competition within the European Union or the EEA, whereas the aim of the second was to protect the United States or the Canadian market . . .[160]

11.101 In *Tokai Carbon Co*,[161] despite fairly full argument on the subject (the applicants relied on *Fischer v Austria*[162]), the CFI refused to recognise any application of the principle on the basis that:

> In the present case, under the principle of territoriality, there are no conflicts in the

---

[159] Case T-236/01 *Tokai Carbon Co v Commission (Graphite Electrodes)* [2004] ECR II-1181.

[160] ibid, para 134. Similar reasoning can be found in Case T-223/00 *Kyowa Hakko Kogyo Co v Commission* [2003] ECR II-2553 and Case T-224/00 *Archer Daniels Midland Co v Commission* [2003] ECR II-2597 (the latter is on appeal to the ECJ, see Opinion of AG Tizzano, 7 June 2005).

[161] Case T-71/03 *Tokai Carbon Co v Commission* [2005] 5 CMLR 13.

[162] See para 11.17 above.

exercise by the Commission and by the US authorities of their power to impose fines on undertakings which infringe the competition rules of the EEA and of the United States.[163]

11.102 In *Showa Denko KK*,[164] the ECJ expressly addressed the issue. It found that on account of the specific nature of the interests protected at Community level (taking account of the fact that free competition within the common market constitutes a fundamental objective of the Community under Article 3(1)(g) EC), the Commission's assessments of a competition problem may diverge considerably from those by authorities of non-Member States. Accordingly, it agreed with the CFI that *non bis in idem* does not arise in situations in which the legal systems and competition authorities of non-Member States intervene within their own jurisdiction.[165]

11.103 Theoretically, the case for *ne bis in idem* to apply in the context of a Community and third state prosecution is weaker: most of the arguments for disregarding *Wilhelm* that were made at para 11.92 above in the context of multiple prosecution under EU and domestic law would not apply in the context of multiple prosecution by a Community authority and that of a third state.

(d) Multiple fines by EU and non-EU competition authorities

11.104 Where one of the prosecuting competition authorities is not based in the European Union the principle of *ne bis in idem* does not apply because there is no identity between the legal interests that are being protected by the prosecuting authorities.[166] Further, there is little prospect of defendants relying on *ne bis in idem*'s poor relative, the principle of natural justice, to require authorities to take account of fines previously imposed by other authorities in relation to the same matter.

11.105 In *Boehringer Mannheim GmbH*,[167] the ECJ was invited to apply the principle of natural justice identified in *Wilhelm*, namely that the Commission was obliged to take account of fines imposed by other authorities, in a transatlantic context. The ECJ's finding was ambiguous. It held that:

> It is only necessary to decide the question whether the Commission may also be under a duty to set a penalty imposed by the authorities of a third state against another penalty if in the case in question the actions of the applicant complained of by the Commission, on the one hand, and by the American authorities, on the other, are identical.

---

[163] *Tokai Carbon*, para 113.
[164] Case C-289/04 P *Showa Denko KK v Commission*, judgment of 29 June 2006. This case is an appeal from the CFI judgment in *Graphite Electrodes*.
[165] ibid, para 56.   [166] See para 11.65 above.
[167] Case 7/72 *Boehringer Mannheim GmbH v Commission* [1972] ECR 1281.

In this case, although the fines related to the same cartel, the ECJ found that **11.106** 'although the actions on which the two convictions in question are based arise out of the same set of agreements they nevertheless differ essentially as regards both their object and their geographical emphasis'. It did not therefore specifically rule on whether the principle of natural justice that obliges authorities to take account of other penalties applies in the context of a prior fine by an authority based in a third state.

The CFI has, more recently, rejected any argument that there is any obligation **11.107** to 'take account' of the fines applied under the broader 'principle of natural justice' that was recognised in *Wilhelm*. In its judgments (delivered on the same day) in *Kyowa Hakko Kogyo Co Ltd*[168] and in *Archer Daniels Midland Co*,[169] the CFI found that there was no sufficient interdependence between the competition authorities of the European Union and those of third countries to warrant applying the principle of natural justice recognised in *Wilhelm*:[170]

> [I]t was in view of the particular situation which arises from the close interdependence between the national markets of the Member States and the common market and from the special system for the sharing of jurisdiction between the Community and the Member States with regard to cartels on the same territory, namely the common market, that the Court, having acknowledged the possibility of dual sets of proceedings and having regard to the possibility of double sanctions flowing from them, held it to be necessary, in accordance with a requirement of natural justice, for account to be taken of the first decision imposing a penalty (Wilhelm and others, cited above, paragraph 11, and the Opinion of Advocate General Mayras in Case 7/72 Boehringer v Commission, cited above, ECR 1293, 1301 to 1303).[171]

On appeal before the ECJ, Advocate General Tizzano supported the CFI's **11.108** reasoning on this issue.[172] The ECJ was less clear. Referring to the CFI's reasoning cited above, it stated that:

> Even if that reasoning were erroneous and the sanction imposed by the authorities of a non-member country was a factor to be taken into account in assessing the facts of the present case in setting the amount of the fine, the plea alleging that the Commission failed to take account of the fines already imposed in non-member countries can only succeed if the actions of ADM complained of by the Commission on the one hand and by the authorities of the United States and Canada on the other were identical.

---

[168] Case T-223/00 *Kyowa Hakko Kogyo Co Ltd v Commission* [2003] ECR II-2553.

[169] Case T-224/00 *Archer Daniels Midland Co v Commission* [2003] ECR II-2597.

[170] See also, to similar effect, Case T-236/01 *Tokai Carbon Co v Commission (Graphite Electrodes)* [2004] ECR II-1181, paras 139–45.

[171] Case T-223/00 *Kyowa Hakko Kogyo Co Ltd v Commission* [2003] ECR II-2553, para 110. See also Case T-224/00 *Archer Daniels Midland Co v Commission* [2003] ECR II-2597, para 99.

[172] See para 106 of his Opinion of 7 June 2005.

11.109   The ECJ went on to dismiss the appeal on the basis that as there was no identity in the facts:

> It should be noted in this regard that, where the sanction imposed in a non-member country covers only the applications or effects of the cartel on the market of that State and the Community sanction covers only the applications or effects of the cartel on the Community market, the facts are not identical.[173]

11.110   In *Tokai Carbon Co*,[174] the CFI held that the principle of natural justice or fairness does not give rise to any obstacle even where the fine takes account of the worldwide turnover and market share of the undertakings, since these are only used by the Commission to distinguish the relative impact of the undertakings implicated in the cartel and do not imply that the scope of the offence has been broadened to cover effects outside the European Union.

11.111   Finally, in *Showa Denko KK*,[175] the appeal from *Graphite Electrodes*, the ECJ considered the issue again. It agreed with the CFI judgment in *Graphite Electrodes*[176] that there was no other principle of law that obliged the Commission to take account of proceedings and penalties to which the appellant had been subject in non-Member States. Further, it held that in so far as the appellants had relied on proportionality and equity to argue for consideration of the fines, any consideration concerning fines imposed by non-Member States can be taken into account only at the Commission's discretion—although it cannot be ruled out that the Commission would take account of these, it cannot be required to do so.[177]

E. Precedent Value of Decisions Within the ECN

11.112   One of the most difficult issues arising for decision-makers under Regulation 1/2003 is how to ensure consistency in decision-making throughout the Community.[178] Numerous national competition authorities and courts are empowered to apply Articles 81 and 82 EC. Although there is an established body of case law relating to the application of Articles 81 and 82, this is not sufficient to ensure consistency in view of the complexity of the legal and economic issues that arise for determination by the national authorities. This

---

[173] Case T-224/00 *Archer Daniels Midland Co v Commission* [2003] ECR II-2597, para 69.
[174] Case T-71/03 *Tokai Carbon Co v Commission* [2005] 5 CMLR 13, para 115.
[175] Case C-289/04 P *Showa Denko KK v Commission*, judgment of 29 June 2006.
[176] Case T-236/01 *Tokai Carbon Co v Commission (Graphite Electrodes)* [2004] ECR II-1181.
[177] Case C-289/04 P *Showa Denko KK v Commission*, paras 57–60. The ECJ did not explicitly endorse the passages in the CFI's judgment that addressed Case 7/72 *Boehringer v Commission* [1972] ECR 1281.
[178] Dekeyser (n 8 above).

difficulty has been exacerbated with enlargement, given that many of the authorities in the acceding states would have no significant prior knowledge of Articles 81 and 82. The issue of consistency of decision-making within the ECN as a whole is outwith the scope of this book. However, it is of direct relevance to UK competition authorities and courts to consider the precedent value of decisions made by other authorities applying Articles 81 and 82. This section will focus in particular on the obligations that UK competition authorities have in this regard, given that the focus of this book is on competition enforcement procedure as opposed to civil litigation.[179]

(a) Precedent value of decisions by the European Commission

A Commission decision is in essence a legislative measure, that is usually **11.113** aimed at specific addressees. Under Article 249 EC, decisions are expressed to be binding only on those to whom they are addressed. However, the supremacy of EC law generally, and the obligation of loyal cooperation which binds national courts and competition authorities mean that, in effect, Commission decisions applying the competition rules preclude contrary decisions by the national courts or competition authorities. Article 16 of Regulation 1/2003 codifies existing case law on the effect of decisions by the European Commission.

Article 16(1) provides that when national courts rule on agreements, decisions **11.114** or practices that are already the subject of a Commission decision, they cannot take a decision that runs counter to the Commission decision. Further, they must also avoid giving decisions which would conflict with a decision contemplated by the Commission, if necessary staying the proceedings pending the Commission's decision. This is consistent with earlier European case law on this issue, which draws heavily on the national courts' obligations of faithful cooperation under Article 10 EC.[180] The Cooperation Notice[181] provides further guidance on this issue.

Article 16(2) of Regulation 1/2003 provides that when national competition **11.115** authorities rule on agreements, decisions or practices under Article 81 and Article 82 EC which are already the subject of a Commission decision, they may

---

[179] For a discussion of the obligation of civil courts to avoid decisions that are inconsistent with Commission decisions, see R Nazzini, *Concurrent Proceedings in Competition Law* (Oxford University Press, 2004) Ch 6.

[180] Case C-344/98 *Masterfoods Ltd (t/a Mars Ireland) v HB Ice Creams Ltd* [2000] ECR I-11369; Case C-234/89 *Delimitis v Henninger Brau AG* [1991] ECR I-935.

[181] para 8: 'Furthermore, the application of Articles 81 and 82 EC by the Commission in a specific case binds the national courts when they apply EC competition rules in the same case in parallel with or subsequent to the Commission.'

not take a decision that would run counter to the decision adopted by the Commission. No provision is made under Regulation 1/2003 for national authorities to avoid conflicts with decisions contemplated by the Commission, as under Article 11(6) the initiation of proceedings by the Commission precludes national authorities from applying Articles 81 and 82 in that case). In effect, the Commission's initiation of a case may also deprive the national competition authority of competence to apply domestic law. Article 3(1) obliges national authorities also to apply Community law to agreements within the meaning of Article 81 and abuses of dominance that have an effect on trade. The initiation of proceedings by the Commission means that the national authority is not able, as required by Article 3(1), to apply Community law and national law in such cases.[182]

11.116 In *Inntrepreneur Pub Co (CPC) v Crehan*[183] the House of Lords considered the ambit of the national courts' obligation to avoid conflicting decisions under Article 16(1) of Regulation 1/2003. It found that under the terms of Article 16, 'a relevant conflict exists only when the "agreements, decisions or practices" ruled on by the national court have been or are about to be the subject of a Commission decision. It does not apply to other agreements, decisions or practices in the same market.' In that case, because the Commission decision did not relate to the same parties, the House of Lords held that the national court was free to decide the competition issue itself, and was not obliged to follow the Commission decision. Given that both Article 16(1) and (2) use similar wording on the obligation not to take decisions running counter to the decision adopted by the Commission, the House of Lords' judgment should provide a useful indication of what is a relevant conflict under Article 16 for the purposes of both the courts and the national competition authorities.

11.117 In the United Kingdom, s 47A of the Competition Act 1998 provides that Commission decisions finding infringement of Article 81 or Article 82 are binding on the CAT in the context of monetary claims.

(b) Precedent value of decisions by non-UK competition authorities

11.118 Although the Commission and national competition authorities work in cooperation with each other under Regulation 1/2003,[184] there is no system of precedent at national level, and the national authorities are not expressly requested to take heed of each other's decisions.

---

[182] W Wils, *Principles of European Antitrust Enforcement* (Hart Publishing, 2005).
[183] [2006] UKHL 38, [2006] 3 WLR 148.
[184] Regulation 1/2003, Art 11(1) provides: 'The Commission and the competition authorities of the Member States shall apply the competition rules in close cooperation.'

The Cooperation Notice addresses the issue of consistency in the application of **11.119** EC competition rules across the ECN. The Commission, as guardian of the Treaty, has the ultimate (but not sole) responsibility for safeguarding consistency.

One way that the Commission may seek to ensure consistency is by using its **11.120** powers under Article 11 of Regulation 1/2003, where decisions that conflict with one another are notified to it by the national competition authorities.[185] It may comment on proposed infringement decisions and commitment decisions that are notified to it by the authorities under Article 11(4) EC. However, the Commission does not have the resources to scrutinise all decisions and ensure there are no conflicts. Further, there is no express obligation for the authorities to take account of the Commission's views, nor are there any sanctions for failure to do so (although it is questionable whether this would be compatible with their obligation under Article 10 EC). National authorities, for their part, are requested to respect the rule of convergence in Article 3(2) of Regulation 1/2003[186] and to ensure that no decisions run counter to Commission decisions (Article 16(2) of Regulation 1/2003).[187] They are encouraged to use the Advisory Committee System set up under Article 14 of Regulation 1/2003 to discuss important cases[188] or to consult the Commission under Article 11(5).

Although there is no formal requirement for national competition authorities to **11.121** follow each other's decisions, it can be expected that a decision by certain authorities (such as the Bundeskartellamt) may have persuasive effect.

In Germany, s 33(4) of the Act against Restraints of Competition provides **11.122** that Article 81 and 82 infringement decisions by the Bundeskartellamt, the European Commission, and other national competition authorities are binding on the civil courts in damages actions.

(c) Precedent value of UK competition authority decisions

Section 58 of the Competition Act 1998 provides that findings of fact made **11.123** by the OFT in the course of an investigation are binding on the parties in civil proceedings for infringement of the prohibitions in the Competition Act, Article 81 EC, or Article 82 EC. Further, ss 47A and 58A of the Competition Act enable 'piggy back' claims for damages on infringement decisions by the OFT and the CAT. These sections provide that OFT findings of infringement of the prohibitions in the Competition Act, Article 81 EC, or Article 82 EC

---

[185] Cooperation Notice, para 43. [186] See generally Chapter 3 for a discussion of this.
[187] Cooperation Notice, para 43. [188] ibid, para 61.

are binding on courts and the CAT in the United Kingdom in proceedings in which damages or any sum of money are claimed for infringement of the prohibitions, providing that the decision is no longer capable of being overturned on appeal. Presumably, decisions that there are no grounds for action will also have some persuasive value.

12

APPEALS

A. Introduction

12.01 The Competition Appeal Tribunal (**CAT**) as we know it today was established under the Enterprise Act 2002,[1] but it first made its appearance as the Competition Commission Appeal Tribunal (**CCAT**) under the Competition Act 1998.[2] Prior to the Competition Act, there was no specialist competition tribunal before which appeals from the regulators' decisions could be brought. The only route of challenge was by public administrative law. Administrative courts hearing applications for judicial review under the Fair Trading Act 1973 generally demonstrated deference to the regulators' economic expertise.[3] With the introduction of substantive new competition powers under the Competition Act 1998 and the Enterprise Act 2002, a corresponding need arose for a fast, expert tribunal to determine appeals from regulators' decisions applying the new competition provisions.[4] An effective appeals regime is a fundamental constituent of a successful competition regime.

12.02 Despite its relative youth, the CAT has been entrusted with a wide range of decision-making powers under the Competition Act 1998, the Enterprise Act 2002, and the Communications Act 2003. To name but a few of the tasks devolved upon the CAT, it has jurisdiction, variously: to hear appeals against competition decisions on the merits; to hear applications for review of decisions on the basis of the same principles as would be applied by a court on judicial review in the merger and market investigations fields; to hear appeals on the merits against the majority of decisions taken by Ofcom in the field of electronic communications under the Communications Act 2003 and to adjudicate in civil law 'follow on' claims for damages (or other claims such as restitution) arising from breach of UK or European competition law that has already been established by a decision of the OFT or the European Commission. Its

---

[1] Enterprise Act 2002, s 12 and Sch 2.
[2] Competition Act 1998, s 45(7) and Sch 7, Pt III.
[3] *R v Monopolies and Mergers Commission, ex p South Yorkshire Transport* [1993] 1 WLR 23.
[4] 'The CAT offers a faster and less expensive route to justice than would be possible through the courts via a body expert in competition law and practice', Douglas Alexander, Minister for E-commerce and Competitiveness, *Hansard*, HC Standing Committee B, col 415 (1 May 2002).

workload is therefore varied and complex, and the CAT must demonstrate great versatility as well as expertise in different substantive and procedural fields to accomplish the daunting list of tasks entrusted to it.

This chapter will briefly examine the scope of the CAT's jurisdiction and **12.03** general powers, before turning to look in more depth at the matters central to the subject of this book, namely the various appeal mechanisms from competition decisions taken by UK based competition regulators in relation to Chapter I, Chapter II, Article 81 and/or Article 82 under the Competition Act 1998, and from the market investigation provisions of the Enterprise Act 2002.[5]

B. The CAT: An Overview

(a) Statutory nature of the CAT's jurisdiction

As a statutory tribunal, the CAT only has the jurisdiction to hear appeals where **12.04** statute has expressly conferred it the power to do so. The CAT cannot infer powers going beyond those necessary or incidental to its statutory powers in the absence of explicit statutory provision.[6] In the absence of a statutory provision providing that a particular decision may be appealed to the CAT, the means of redress available is by the usual public law channel of judicial review before the administrative courts.[7]

(b) The CAT's decision-making powers

The CAT's functions can be divided into three categories based on the statutes **12.05** conferring it with the relevant powers.

First, the Competition Act 1998 empowers the CAT to: **12.06**

- hear appeals on the merits against decisions of the OFT and the sectoral

---

[5] The chapter is not intended to address in detail the mechanics of litigation procedure for competition appeals and actions for damages, which exceed the scope of this book. Litigation procedure is addressed in T Ward and K Smith, *Competition Litigation in the United Kingdom* (Sweet & Maxwell, 2005).

[6] See *Floe Telecom Ltd (in administration) v Ofcom* [2006] EWCA Civ 768, para 34 per Lloyd LJ: 'If the regulator fails to discharge its duties, then it may be amenable to an application for judicial review in the Administrative Court but, unless and until it has given a decision which is subject to a statutory right of appeal, the CAT will have no jurisdiction in the matter.'

[7] *Bettercare Group Ltd v Director General of Fair Trading* [2002] CAT 6, para 90; *Floe Telecom*, ibid.

regulators as to whether Chapter I, Chapter II, Article 81, or Article 82 are infringed;[8]

- hear actions for damages and other monetary claims following from decisions finding infringements of Chapter I, Chapter II, Article 81, or Article 82;
- hear applications for judicial review of commitment decisions by the OFT and the sectoral regulators.

12.07 Secondly, under the Enterprise Act 2002, the CAT is empowered to:

- hear applications for judicial review of decisions made by the Secretary of State, Office of Fair Trading (**OFT**), and the Competition Commission (**CC**) relating to merger and market investigation references;
- hear appeals on the merits from penalty decisions taken by the CC under ss 114 and 176(1)(f) of the Enterprise Act 2002 in the context of market and merger investigations.

12.08 Lastly, under the Communications Act 2003, the CAT may hear appeals on the merits against certain decisions made by Ofcom and, in some instances, the Secretary of State relating to:

- electronic communications;
- data services;
- spectrum licensing; and
- the competition aspects of broadcasting.

12.09 In addition to the above three categories which make up the vast majority of the CAT's jurisdiction, the CAT can also hear appeals in respect of decisions made by the OFT applying Article 81 and Article 82 EC in the maritime sectors under the EC Competition Law (Articles 84 and 85) Enforcement Regulations 2001.[9] However, these Regulations are now largely redundant, following Council Regulation (EC) 411/2004 and Council Regulation 14/9/2006 of 25 September 2006.[10] These regulations have removed the remaining exclusions from Regulation 1/2003[11] from which the maritime sector benefited, so that any competition issues arising in this sector now fall to be enforced under Regulation 1/2003 and the Competition Act 1998, as for all other sectors of the economy.[12]

---

[8] These include decisions such as to make, or not to make, interim measures orders in relation to suspected infringements under s 35 of the Competition Act 1998. See paras 12.60 et seq below for a discussion of what amounts to an appealable decision under the Competition Act.

[9] SI 2001/2916.   [10] [2004] OJ L68/1.

[11] Council Regulation (EC) 1/2003 of 16 December 2002 on the implementation of the rules on competition laid down in Articles 81 and 82 of the Treaty [2003] OJ L1/1.

[12] See para 1.14 above.

This chapter will not consider any functions of the CAT under the Communi- **12.10**
cations Act 2003 nor any applications for review of merger decisions, as the
procedure relating to these areas is outside the scope of this book.

(c) Judicial review and full merits review

The Competition Act 1998 and the Enterprise Act 2002 each provide for two **12.11**
different types of appellate jurisdiction—under both statutes, certain appeals are
determined by means of judicial review, others by means of a full merits review.
This distinction may have a material impact on the appellant's prospects of
overturning a decision on appeal, as the appellate scrutiny under the full merits
jurisdiction is far more exhaustive than challenge by way of judicial review.

It was the government's avowed intention that the CAT's merits jurisdiction **12.12**
should be primarily concerned with the correctness or otherwise of the conclusions contained in the appealed decision and not with how the decision was
reached or the reasoning expressed in it.[13] A full merits review entails the CAT
inquiring into the regulator's assessment of the facts, with a view to deciding
whether the correct decision was reached on all the evidence, including new
evidence that may be laid before the CAT on appeal. In challenges by way of
judicial review, the question is whether the regulator erred—it is not an appeal
from the decision, but a review of the soundness of the underlying decision-
making process, which does not normally require a consideration of fresh
evidence. As stated by Lord Bingham in *McDonald*:

> It is important to remember always that this is judicial review of, and not an appeal
> against, the judge's decision. We can only intervene if persuaded that his decision
> was perverse or that there was some failure to have regard to material consider-
> ations or that account was taken of some immaterial considerations or that there
> was some material misdirection. We cannot consider fresh evidence unless perhaps
> it establishes that the judge was misled by the prosecution.[14]

The difference between the CAT's full merits and judicial review jurisdiction **12.13**
permeates the entire procedure for determination of such claims from the very
outset. To begin with, whereas in full merits appeals against an infringement
decision the burden of proof lies on the regulator to establish that the infringement decision was properly founded, in judicial review challenges the burden of
proof is on the applicant to establish that the regulator erred in its decision.[15]

---

[13] See the Statement in the House of Commons by Nigel Griffiths, Minister for Competition
and Consumer Affairs, during the passage of the Competition Bill: *Hansard*, HL Standing
Committee G, col 496 (18 June 1998).

[14] *R v Manchester Crown Court, ex p McDonald* [1999] 1 WLR 841, 855A–B.

[15] Contrast *JJB Sports Plc v OFT* [2004] CAT 17 and *IBA Health Ltd v OFT* [2004] EWCA
Civ 142, [2004] 4 All ER 1103.

Further, although the CAT enjoys essentially the same procedural powers in the context of both procedures (the majority of the CAT's Rules of Procedure apply both to appeals and challenges by way of judicial review),[16] a full merits review influences the CAT's approach to its procedure. In a full merits appeal, it adopts a more generous approach, for example, to the admission of new evidence on appeal and the hearing of witnesses and experts.[17] As the CAT stated in *Napp Pharmaceutical Holdings Ltd v Director General of Fair Trading*:

> There is . . . no inhibition on the applicant attacking the Decision on any ground he chooses, including new evidence, whether or not that ground or evidence was put before the Director. The Tribunal, for its part, is not limited to the traditional rôle of judicial review but is required by paragraph 3(1) of Schedule 8 of the Act to decide the case 'on the merits' and may, if necessary and appropriate, 'make any other decision which the Director could have made': paragraph 3(2)(e) . . . Unlike the normal practice in judicial review proceedings, the Act and the Tribunal Rules envisage that the Tribunal may order the production of documents, hear witnesses and appoint experts (see Schedule 8, paragraph 9 of the Act, and Rule 17 of the Tribunal's Rules) and may do so even if the evidence was not available to the Director when he took the decision: see Rule 20(2) of the Tribunal's.[18]

12.14 Finally, the CAT has much broader remedial powers in the context of appeals on the merits. Not only can it set the regulator's decision aside, but it can substitute its own decision for that of the regulator and even impose or increase penalties.[19]

12.15 The government viewed the full merits review of the CAT as an essential part of ensuring the fairness and transparency of the new competition regime established under the Competition Act 1998.[20] Access to appeal is a highly significant procedural safeguard for the rights of undertakings subject to investigation. The OFT and the CC have extensive decision-making powers that have far-reaching implications for the undertakings subject to investigation. Regulatory decision-making under the Competition Act and the market investigations provisions of the Enterprise Act 2002, as a minimum, affect civil rights and obligations for the purposes of Article 6 ECHR. This is because the decisions applying these provisions affect an undertaking's business activities[21] and rights to property

---

[16] CAT's Rules of Procedure, r 25.

[17] The CAT demonstrated great caution with respect to the additional evidence that the OFT was permitted to adduce in *IBA Health Ltd v OFT* [2003] CAT 27. However, the Court of Appeal took a more generous approach to this issue on appeal—*IBA Health Ltd v OFT* [2004] EWCA Civ 142, [2004] 4 All ER 1103.

[18] [2002] CAT 1, para 117. See also *Freeserve.com Plc v Director General of Telecommunications* [2005] CAT 5, para 116.

[19] Competition Act 1998, Sch 8, para 3(2)(e).

[20] See the Statement in the House of Commons by Nigel Griffiths, Minister for Competition and Consumer Affairs, during the passage of the Competition Bill: *Hansard*, HL Standing Committee G, col 496 (18 June 1998).

[21] *Pudas v Sweden* (1988) 10 EHRR 380.

protected under Article 1 of Protocol 1 ECHR. Moreover, both the CAT and the courts have indicated that, given the considerable sanctions that may be imposed at its conclusion, the administrative procedure under the Competition Act may be deemed 'criminal' for the purposes of Article 6 ECHR.[22] Article 6, which guarantees the right to a fair trial, accordingly entitles undertakings investigated by the OFT or the CC to have (inter alia) access to an independent and impartial tribunal for the determination of their rights.

The OFT and the CC act as investigator, prosecutor, and decision-maker under **12.16** (respectively) the Competition Act 1998 and the market investigation provisions of the Enterprise Act 2002 and, as such, the regulatory decision-makers cannot qualify as an independent tribunal. For the regulatory decision-making process to be ECHR compliant, the Article 6 defects must be cured by giving the undertakings access to an independent and impartial tribunal on appeal.[23] This partly explains why the CAT enjoys a full merits review in respect of certain decisions taken under the Competition Act, as was recognised by the CAT in *Napp Pharmaceuticals*:

> We add that the fact that the administrative procedure before the Director may not itself comply with the requirements of Article 6(1) of the ECHR, does not constitute a breach of the Convention, provided that the Director is subject to subsequent control by a judicial body that has full jurisdiction and does comply with Article 6(1): Albert and Le Compte v Belgium 5 EHRR 533, and the decision of the House of Lords of 9 May 2001 in Alconbury Developments Ltd and others [2001] UKHL 23. As we see it, the Act looks to the judicial stage of the process before this Tribunal to satisfy the requirements of Article 6 of the ECHR.[24]

For those decisions, such as commitments decisions and appeals from merger **12.17** and market investigation decisions, in relation to which appeal lies on judicial review grounds only, it has not yet been determined whether the narrow judicial review appellate jurisdiction is sufficient to render the decision-making process as a whole compliant with Article 6 ECHR. In *Begum*,[25] the House of Lords

---

[22] *Napp Pharmaceutical Holdings Ltd v Director General of Fair Trading* [2002] CAT 1. In *Napp*, the CAT stated: 'As we have just indicated, we accept that both Article 6(1) and (2) of the ECHR apply to proceedings potentially involving a penalty imposed for a breach of the Chapter I and Chapter II prohibitions. We also accept that there is force in the argument that the administrative procedure before the Director does not in itself comply with Article 6(1), notably because the Director himself combines the roles of investigator, prosecutor and decision maker.' See also the High Court's decision in *OFT v X (also known as OFT v D)* [2003] EWHC 1042, [2003] All ER (Comm) 183. See paras 11.45–11.47 for a discussion of the 'criminal' nature of Art 81, Art 82, Chapter I, and Chapter II proceedings.

[23] *Le Compte, Van Leuven and De Meyere v Belgium* (1981) 4 EHRR 1; *Albert and Le Compte v Belgium* (1983) 5 EHRR 533.

[24] [2002] CAT 1, para 74.

[25] *Begum (Runa) v Tower Hamlets LBC* [2003] UKHL 5, [2003] 2 AC 230.

considered the sufficiency of judicial review for ECHR purposes in the context of an administrative decision taken under the Housing Act 1996. It found that, in the circumstances at issue, the appeal mechanism to the county court on normal judicial review principles provided by s 104 of the Housing Act 1996 was sufficient to render the administrative decision-making procedure ECHR compliant.[26] In the course of his judgment, Lord Hoffmann provided an indication that judicial review of 'regulatory decisions' may be suitable for the purposes of Article 6 ECHR:

> The key phrases in the judgments of the Strasbourg court which describe the cases in which a limited review of the facts is sufficient are 'specialised areas of the law' (Bryan's case, at p 361, para 47) and 'classic exercise of administrative discretion' (Kingsley's case, at p 302, para 53). What kind of decisions are these phrases referring to? I think that one has to take them together . . . It seems to me that what the court had in mind was those areas of the law such as *regulatory* and welfare schemes in which decision-making is customarily entrusted to administrators.[27]

12.18   In view of these fundamental differences, the question of which is the applicable appellate jurisdiction has generated much case law on the issue of admissibility. For obvious reasons, prospective appellants seek to engage the full merits based review jurisdiction of the CAT, whereas regulators prefer to frame their decisions to avoid such a review, see paras 12.60 et seq, below.

(d) Constitution

12.19   The CAT's judicial panels are composed of three elements : a President, a panel of chairmen, and a panel of ordinary members.[28] The members of the panel of chairmen are judges of the Chancery Division of the High Court and other senior lawyers. The so-called ordinary members have expertise in various competition related fields such as economics, business, and accountancy, and thus give the CAT cross-disciplinary expertise.

12.20   All cases are heard before a panel consisting of three members: either the President or a member of the panel of chairmen and two ordinary members.[29] There is no need for unanimity for the panel to make a decision—if a panel is unable to agree on any decision, the decision is taken by majority vote.[30] To date all the CAT's decisions have been unanimous.

---

[26] See also *R (Hammond) v Secretary of State for the Home Department* [2005] UKHL 69, [2006] 1 AC 603.

[27] *Begum (Runa) v Tower Hamlets LBC* [2003] UKHL 5, [2003] 2 AC 230, para 56. Emphasis added.

[28] Enterprise Act 2002, s 12(2).   [29] ibid, s 14.   [30] ibid, s 14(4).

(e) Rules

All cases commenced after 20 June 2003 are governed by the Competition **12.21**
Appeal Tribunal Rules 2003[31] (**the Rules**) as amended by the Competition
Appeal Tribunal (Amendment and Communications Act Appeals) Rules 2004.[32]
The CAT has also published a Guide to Proceedings, which expounds its rules
and practice. The Rules are partially inspired by the Civil Procedural Rules
(**CPR**) and by the Rules of Procedure of the Court of First Instance of the
European Communities (**CFI**). The CAT's Guide to Proceedings emphasises
'[t]he Rules are based on the same philosophy as the CPR and pursue the same
overriding objective of enabling the Tribunal to deal with cases justly, in particular by ensuring that parties are on an equal footing, that expense is saved, and that
appeals are dealt with expeditiously and fairly'.[33] Both the CFI's Rules of
Procedure and the CPR are therefore useful to consider, where guidance is sought
on a matter that may not be addressed fully in the Rules. For example, in *Napp
Pharmaceuticals*,[34] the CAT, in considering its own powers to grant interim relief,
drew extensively on the CFI's approach to interim relief in determining its own
approach to interim measures.[35] However, care should be taken in drawing general analogies between the Rules and the CPR or the CFI's Rules of Procedure.
In *BCL Old Co Ltd v Aventis SA*[36] the CAT firmly refused to draw on the CPR:

> We consider that the analogy the Defendants seek to draw with rule 19.5 of the
> CPR is misconceived. First, the Tribunal's Rules are intended, in our view, to be a
> coherent self-standing set of procedural rules governing the conduct of proceedings
> before the Tribunal. The Tribunal's Rules, it seems to us, are both intentionally
> more simply drafted than the CPR and are drafted in a more general and flexible
> manner than the procedural rules in the CPR. In particular, the Tribunal's Rules
> were not drafted, in our view, in such a way that parties to proceedings before the
> Tribunal must constantly have recourse to the CPR (or, bearing in mind that the
> Tribunal has United Kingdom jurisdiction, any other set of procedural rules gov-
> erning litigation before other courts and tribunals in the United Kingdom) in
> order that the true meaning of the Tribunal's Rules can be discerned. That applies,
> in particular, to alleged 'unwritten exclusions' from the procedures contained in
> the Tribunal's Rules which are not apparent on the face of the Rules.

The Rules posit five main principles: **12.22**

(1) early disclosure in writing;
(2) active case management;

---

[31] SI 2003/1372.   [32] SI 2004/2068.   [33] CAT's Guide to Proceedings, para 3.1.
[34] *Napp Pharmaceutical Holdings Ltd v Director General of Fair Trading*, Case No 1000/1/1/01,
judgment of 22 May 2001 (judgment on request for interim relief), para 40.
[35] In considering what amounts to a ground of appeal in *Floe Telecom Ltd (in administration) v
Ofcom* [2004] CAT 7, the CAT looked at European procedure and that of civil continental
jurisdictions, see para 32.
[36] [2005] CAT 1.

(3) strict timetables (in general the CAT will aim to complete straightforward cases in nine months);

(4) effective fact-finding procedures;

(5) short and structured oral hearings.

12.23 In a Competition Act appeal, the first case management conference is normally scheduled four to six weeks after the case has been initiated, before the defence is lodged, and is generally the most important hearing which sets the parameters for the appeal procedure. At the first case management conference, issues such as jurisdiction and forum, interventions, disclosure and confidentiality, expert evidence, and a timetable for the proceedings are considered.

(f) The influence of European law and the Competition Act 1998, s 60

12.24 The CAT is subject to a double obligation to follow relevant European jurisprudence. First, Article 10 EC binds it, as a national court, when applying measures of Community law, to do so in a spirit of loyal cooperation, taking account of relevant European precedent.[37] Secondly, by virtue of s 60, it must ensure that its decisions on questions arising under Pt I of the Competition Act 1998 are consistent with the principles laid down in the Treaty and relevant European jurisprudence. Since its inception, the CAT has drawn heavily on European jurisprudence to determine all substantive questions relating to the Chapter I and Chapter II prohibitions, ranging from its definition of what is an 'undertaking' or 'an agreement' to construing whether certain conduct amounts to an abuse. By way of example, we need look no further than the first decision taken by the CAT, in *Napp Pharmaceuticals*,[38] in which the CAT drew heavily on the concept of abuse under relevant European jurisprudence to determine whether there was an abuse of dominance by Napp under Chapter II of the Competition Act.

12.25 However, European law has an influence that goes beyond substantive questions of competition law. It was initially assumed by the regulators[39] that the obligation in s 60 was confined to ensuring consistency in relation to the meaning and application of the Chapter I and Chapter II prohibitions, but that the CAT's approach to procedural issues arising under the Competition Act could differ from European precedent. This is consistent with the general thrust of Community law: whilst defining substantive rights for individuals, Community law generally leaves the procedure for enforcement and remedies for breaches of

---

[37] Case C-94/00 *Roquette Frères* [2002] ECR 9011, 31.

[38] *Napp Pharmaceutical Holdings Ltd v Director General of Fair Trading* [2002] CAT 1.

[39] J Bridgeman, 'The Competition Act 1998 and EC jurisprudence! Some questions answered', The Denning Lecture 1999.

Community derived rights to national law, subject to two important caveats, namely that the national procedure should provide equivalent protection for EC rights and national rights and that it should not render the exercise of EC rights impossible in practice.[40] Regulation 1/2003 does not harmonise the procedure for enforcement of Article 81 and Article 82, leaving this to the laws of the Member States. However, as is discussed in more depth in Chapter 3, the CAT's decision in *Pernod Ricard*[41] indicates that it will, pursuant to s 60, take account of, and even follow, relevant European jurisprudence in relation to procedural questions arising under the Competition Act. This is so even though the procedure under the Competition Act and the OFT's Rules of Procedure is in some respects very different from the Commission's enforcement procedure.

If the obligation of consistency under s 60 were generally held to apply to **12.26** procedural issues, this would not only affect the CAT's definition of procedural rights arising in relation to undertakings that are subject to investigation under the Competition Act, but it would also have profound implications for the conduct of appeals itself. As it is, European law is already of some influence in respect of the standard review applied by the CAT.

In *Unichem v OFT*,[42] when defining the nature and intensity of the CAT's **12.27** review of challenges to decisions relating to mergers under s 120 of the Enterprise Act 2002, the CAT cited[43] the European Court of Justice (**ECJ**) judgment considering the scope of review of the CFI in *Tetra Laval*.[44] In the *GSM Gateways* case[45] Vodafone unsuccessfully sought to rely on the ECJ's judgment in *Upjohn Limited*[46] to argue that the CAT's usual full merits review should not apply in view of the specialist technical nature of the questions raised by the appeal. This was so despite the fact that the appeals provisions in the Competition Act 1998 were expressly mentioned as a 'relevant difference' for the purpose of s 60 in the debates in Parliament when the Competition Bill was passed.[47]

The above cases reveal the significance of European case law to appeals conducted **12.28** before the CAT. European case law is highly relevant to questions relating to the substance of the competition prohibitions, to the procedure for the enforcement

---

[40] Case 33/76 *Rewe-Zentralfinanz eG and Rewe-Zentral Ag v Landwirtschaftskammer fur das Saarland* [1976] ECR 1989. Joined Cases C 295–298/04 *Manfredi v Lloyd Adriatico Assicurazioni SpA*, judgment of 13 July 2006. For a discussion of the principles of equivalence and practical possibility, see P Craig and G de Burca, *EU Law: Texts, Cases and Materials* (3rd edn, Oxford University Press, 2002) Ch 6.

[41] *Pernod Ricard SA v OFT* [2004] CAT 10.   [42] [2005] CAT 8.

[43] ibid, paras 168 and 169.

[44] Case C-12/03 P *Commission v Tetra Laval BV* [2005] ECR I-987.

[45] [2006] CAT 17.

[46] Case C-120/97 *Upjohn Ltd v Licensing Authority* [1999] ECR I-223.

[47] *Hansard*, HL col 961 (25 November 1997).

of the prohibitions, and to the CAT's approach to its own review function and procedure.

(g) Jurisdiction and forum

12.29 The CAT's jurisdiction extends to the whole of the United Kingdom.

12.30 Rule 18(3) of the CAT's Rules of Procedure provides that in deciding whether the case is to be treated as proceedings in England and Wales, Scotland, or Northern Ireland the CAT may take account all relevant matters, in particular the location of the parties, the place where the events took place, and the location of the documents. The CAT's judgment in *Claymore* provides useful guidance as to its approach to such issues in practice.[48]

12.31 In a Competition Act appeal the forum ought not to affect the substantive determination of the appeal, but it should be noted that:

- in judicial review cases the principles and procedures relevant to judicial review are not identical in England and Wales, Scotland, and Northern Ireland;
- the forum will also affect to which court an appeal lies from the CAT (see s 49 of the Competition Act 1998 by virtue of which appeals of CAT proceedings in England and Wales are appealed to the Court of Appeal, proceedings in Northern Ireland are appealed to the Court of Appeal in Northern Ireland, and proceedings in Scotland to the Court of Session);
- the forum may have an effect on the rules of civil procedure (for example, note the CAT's comments on the rules applicable to recovery and inspection in *Claymore*[49]);
- rules on enforcement of CAT decisions are different in Great Britain and in Northern Ireland (see Sch 4 to the Enterprise Act 2002).

(h) Intervention

12.32 Rules governing intervention are the same for both judicial review challenges and full merits appeals. Rule 16(6) provides that where the CAT is satisfied (having taken account of the parties' submissions) that the intervening party has 'sufficient interest', it may permit intervention on such terms and conditions as it thinks fit. This should be read in the context of r 16(1) that allows any person who considers he has 'sufficient interest in the outcome of the proceedings' to

---

[48] *Claymore Dairies Ltd and Arla Foods UK Plc v OFT* [2003] CAT 3, paras 192–200; see also *Aberdeen Journals Ltd v Director General of Fair Trading* [2001] CAT 5; *Bettercare Group Ltd v Director General of Fair Trading* [2002] CAT 6.

[49] *Claymore Dairies Ltd and Arla Foods UK Plc v OFT* [2004] CAT 16, paras 107–8.

request the CAT for permission to intervene. Rule 16 does not apply to damages actions under s 47A of the Competition Act 1998 and appeals against penalties under ss 114 and 176(1)(f) of the Enterprise Act 2002, presumably because third parties are deemed to have less interest in such matters.

Sufficiency of interest is a matter that is to be determined at the time an appeal **12.33** has been made. It will often be the case that persons with a sufficient interest to intervene in proceedings before the Tribunal will have participated (or will have sought to participate) in the proceedings before the Director at the administrative stage. However, participation in the administrative proceedings is not a necessary pre-condition to having a sufficient interest to intervene before the Tribunal.[50]

In *Floe Telecom Ltd (in administration) v Ofcom*[51] the CAT allowed the interven- **12.34** tion of Vodafone in Floe's appeal from Ofcom's rejection of its complaint regarding Vodafone's alleged breach of the Chapter 2 prohibition. In determining sufficiency, it emphasised that the proceedings would touch on Vodafone's conduct and that the interpretation of certain provisions of legislation at issue (Wireless Telegraphy Act) would also affect it.

In *MasterCard UK Members Forum Ltd*,[52] MasterCard appealed from the OFT's **12.35** decision relating to the settling of multilateral interchange fees. Both Visa (who had participated in the administrative proceedings before the OFT to a limited extent) and the British Retail Consortium (who had also participated in the administrative proceedings) were permitted to intervene. It was acknowledged that Visa had a very real interest in the outcome of the proceedings as it would be bound by the OFT's decision concerning multilateral interchange fees.

When considering an application to intervene, the CAT will consider whether **12.36** the interests of the intervening party are already adequately protected by a main party to the proceedings.[53] In *Umbro Holdings Ltd v OFT*,[54] the CAT, mainly on pragmatic grounds relating to the conduct of the appeal, refused an application to intervene by Sports World Ltd. Sports World Ltd had acted as a whistleblower in relation to the cartel that was the subject of the OFT's infringement decision appealed before the CAT. It submitted that as the whistleblower, and also as it was likely to come in for extensive personal criticism by the appellants, it should be permitted to intervene in the proceedings. The CAT refused the application made at the outset of the proceedings, without altogether ruling out

---

[50] *Albion Water Ltd v Water Services Regulation Authority* [2004] CAT 19, para 67.
[51] [2004] CAT 2.
[52] *MasterCard UK Members Forum Ltd v OFT*, transcript of case management conference, 9 December 2005.
[53] CAT's Guide to Proceedings, para 10.5.   [54] [2003] CAT 25.

intervention at some later stage (either formally or informally). An important part of its reasoning was that the interests of Sports World Ltd were protected by the OFT, and that by this means, it could where necessary ensure its interests were put before the Tribunal.

> As far as we can see there is no objection to Sports World, if so advised and if it so wishes, collaborating with the Office of Fair Trading in supplying information to the Office of Fair Trading and assisting with the presentation of the Office of Fair Trading's case. I stress the Office of Fair Trading's case and not Sports World's case. If circumstances were to arise in which fairness required that we heard directly from Sports World then we, the Tribunal, would be open to a second application, either for a formal intervention or for Sports World to be heard, as it were, informally.[55]

12.37　Rule 16(6) leaves the CAT considerable latitude with respect to the shape an intervention will take. In practice, the level of participation in intervention will reflect the degree of interest the intervener has in the proceedings. For example, the intervener may not get full rights to submit written representations or make oral submissions.[56] The CAT's Guide to Proceedings emphasises that the intervener's role is normally ancillary and that a full exchange of pleadings between the interveners and the main parties may duplicate arguments and delay the final determination of the appeal—so it will not always be appropriate.[57] Lastly, the CAT must have regard to the confidentiality provisions set out in para 1(2) of Sch 4 to the Enterprise Act 2002 in granting permission to intervene.[58] This may restrict the access that interveners have to confidential information relating to the parties.

(i) Confidentiality

12.38　Disclosure is often a contentious issue in competition proceedings. There is a tension between protecting sensitive commercial information belonging to one party, and allowing other parties sufficient information to place them on an equal footing to prepare their case. Applications for disclosure often take up a significant amount of the CAT's pre-hearing case management. There are sensitivities about releasing commercial information that may amount to business secrets from the OFT's file to parties that might be direct competitors. Further, as CAT hearings are heard in public, there is a risk of disclosure of sensitive commercial material to the public if matters are read out in open court. On the other hand, third parties and even the undertakings subject to investigation do

---

[55] ibid, para 10. Note that Sports World provided evidence and was subsequently granted permission to intervene in order to be awarded costs.
[56] *Albion Water Ltd v Water Services Regulation Authority* [2004] CAT 19, para 52.
[57] CAT's Guide to Proceedings, para 10.11.　　[58] CAT's Rules of Procedure, r 16(8).

not get full access to the file at the administrative stage, given the restrictions that regulators must consider in relation to the disclosure of confidential information under Pt 9 of the Enterprise Act 2002.[59] Appeals are therefore the first opportunity for appellants and third parties to obtain wider disclosure of centrally important documents and submit new evidence to the CAT.[60]

12.39 Although the CAT is expressly excluded from the application of Pt 9 of the Enterprise Act 2002,[61] it is subject to statutory confidentiality requirements, under paras 1(2) and (3) of Sch 4 to the Enterprise Act. The CAT determines any applications for confidentiality by reference to these provisions, which are considered in detail at paras 8.55 et seq above. The reader is referred to that section for a discussion of how the CAT applies these provisions and the mechanisms it uses to balance one party's interest in preserving the confidentiality of its business secrets as against another party's rights of the defence.

12.40 As a matter of practice, confidentiality must be claimed in writing within 14 days of filing the document.[62]

12.41 In appropriate circumstances, the CAT has tried to resolve conflicts relating to disclosure by means of a 'confidentiality ring'. Information is not provided to the parties themselves, but to their external legal advisers preparing the case—normally the parties' named legal representatives and possibly (but less likely) external advisers or experts such as accountants and economists.[63] In general, the CAT will only protect business secrets or other confidential information that is less than two to three years old.[64] Guidance on confidentiality is provided in the CAT's Guide to Proceedings.[65]

(j) Effect of appeals and interim relief

12.42 The initiation of an appeal before the CAT generally does not take effect to suspend the regulator's decision, except in the case of appeals on penalties under the Competition Act 1998.[66] The CAT's powers to grant interim relief are therefore highly relevant, particularly in the context of appeals from infringement decisions under the Competition Act, in which the regulator frequently gives directions to undertakings to cease infringing behaviour.

---

[59] See paras 9.54 and 9.102 above.

[60] *Napp Pharmaceutical Holdings Ltd v Director General of Fair Trading* [2002] CAT 1. Whereas appellants and third parties are allowed to submit new evidence as part of an appeal on the merits, the OFT is on the other hand save in exceptional circumstances expected to defend its decision on the evidence available at the time.

[61] Enterprise Act 2002, s 137(5).   [62] CAT's Rules of Procedure, r 53.

[63] *Claymore Dairies Ltd v OFT* [2003] CAT 12; *Genzyme v OFT*, transcript of 27 May 2004.

[64] *Umbro Holdings Ltd v OFT* [2003] CAT 29.

[65] CAT's Guide to Proceedings, 47–51.   [66] Competition Act 1998, s 46(4).

12.43 Under r 61 of its Rules of Procedure, the CAT has broad powers to make interim orders. These powers include the following measures:

- the partial or entire suspension of the regulator's decision;
- granting any remedy which the Tribunal may grant in its final decision;
- giving directions that it considers are necessary as a matter of urgency for the purpose of preventing serious and irreparable harm to a person or persons, or protecting the public interest.[67]

12.44 The CAT's Guide to Proceedings indicates[68] that the principal purpose of interim relief is to preserve the integrity of the appeal and, in particular, to ensure that so far as possible, taking into account the other interest involved, the applicant does not suffer serious and irreparable damage pending the hearing of an appeal which may yet succeed. However, financial loss which cannot be compensated in the event of a successful appeal does not constitute serious and irreparable damage, unless the survival of the undertaking is in question.

12.45 In *Napp Pharmaceuticals*,[69] the CAT indicated that the principles normally applied in applications for interim injunctions or similar relief in the civil courts in cases such as *American Cyanamid v Ethicon*,[70] while providing many useful and relevant analogies, are not in themselves necessarily determinative of the issues likely to arise. It came to the view that applications for interim relief to suspend directions should be dealt with by analogy with the principles applied by the CFI when dealing with applications for interim relief against decisions of the European Commission.[71]

12.46 In *Genzyme*, the CAT indicated that its approach to application for interim relief involves asking five questions:

(i) Are the arguments raised by the applicant as to the merits of its substantive appeal, at least prima facie, not entirely ungrounded, in the sense that the applicant's arguments cannot be dismissed at the interim stage of the procedure without a more detailed examination? . . .

(ii) Is urgency established?

(iii) Is the applicant likely to suffer serious and irreparable damage if interim relief is not granted? . . .

---

[67] Note that the CAT can also hear appeals from interim measures decisions taken by the OFT.

[68] CAT's Guide to Proceedings, para 20.7.

[69] *Napp Pharmaceutical Holdings Ltd v Director General of Fair Trading*, Case No 1000/1/1/01, judgment of 22 May 2001 (judgment on request for interim relief).

[70] [1975] AC 396.

[71] *Napp Pharmaceutical Holdings Ltd v Director General of Fair Trading*, Case No 1000/1/1/01, judgment of 22 May 2001 (judgment on request for interim relief), paras 37–44.

(iv) What is the likely effect on competition, or relevant third party interests, of the grant or refusal of interim relief?

(v) What is 'the balance of interests' under heads (iii) and (iv)?[72]

Applications for interim relief may be made before a notice of appeal is lodged.[73]   **12.47**

(k) Reference to the ECJ

The CAT may make a preliminary reference to the ECJ under Article 234 EC, **12.48** either of its own initiative or on application by a party.[74] Given that European law is of critical importance to the issues that are determined by the CAT, this power is appropriate. To date, the CAT has not made a preliminary reference to the ECJ, although it has had to consider issues of considerable difficulty.[75]

C. The CAT's Merits Jurisdiction

(a) Standing to bring an appeal

(i) Competition Act Appeals

The Competition Act 1998 distinguishes between rights of appeal for 'parties' **12.49** and rights of appeal for 'third parties'. Sections 46 and 47 of the Competition Act identify, respectively, which decisions are appealable to the CAT by parties and which by third parties. Let us first consider what is a party and a third party for these purposes

Parties   Section 46 defines 'parties' as: a party to an agreement in respect of **12.50** which the OFT has made a decision,[76] and any person in respect of whose conduct the OFT has made a decision.[77]

Third parties   Section 47 provides for third party appeals. Section 47(2) gives **12.51** standing to appeal to those persons whom the CAT considers (a) to have 'sufficient interest' in the decision the subject of the appeal, or (b) that represent persons having such an interest. The express provision of standing for those

---

[72] *Genzyme Ltd v OFT* [2003] CAT 8, para 70.

[73] CAT's Rules of Procedure, r 61(6)(e) and (7).

[74] ibid, r 60. Article 234 EC gives the ECJ jurisdiction to give preliminary rulings on questions of law that are raised by national courts, that relate, inter alia, to the interpretation of the EC Treaty.

[75] Contrast the CAT's approach to the definition of an 'undertaking' in *Bettercare Group Ltd v Director General of Fair Trading* [2002] CAT 7, and the subsequent decision of the ECJ in Case C-205/03 P *Federación Española de Empresas de Tecnología Sanitaria (FENIN) v Commission* [2006] 5 CMLR 7. AG Maduro cited the CAT's judgment at para 24 of his Opinion as 'particularly noteworthy'.

[76] Competition Act 1998, s 46(1).   [77] ibid, s 46(2).

representing others having sufficient interest implies that the test for standing under s 47 is fairly broad, intending to capture consumer associations or trade associations.

12.52 'Sufficient interest' is the threshold for standing for judicial review to the administrative court. The leading authority on this concept in the context of administrative law is the House of Lords' decision in *R v Inland Revenue Commissioners, ex p National Federation of Self-Employed and Small Businesses*,[78] which has led to a generous approach to standing by the administrative court.

12.53 It is unclear whether the CAT will follow the lead of the administrative court in considering sufficient interest under s 47 of the Competition Act. Given the breadth of its full merits appeal jurisdiction, it may not be in the public interest (in view of the resources that regulators expend in defending full merits appeals) to allow such a wide category of applicants standing to initiate such an extensive appeal.

12.54 In *Pernod Ricard*, the CAT indicated that it had no doubt that most complainants who are competitors have 'a sufficient interest' for the purposes of s 47.[79] This leaves open that certain other categories of complainant—for example complainants that are consumers—may not have 'sufficient interest'. The CAT has not yet, however, had to consider appeals brought by parties other than complainants that are competitors or downstream users that are affected by the anti-competitive conduct. The OFT has taken no arguments on standing, so consequently no appeal has been rejected on the ground that there is no standing, and the test of 'sufficient interest' has not been fully articulated.

12.55 There has been considerable CAT case law on the meaning of 'sufficient interest', in the context of applications for intervention under r 16 of the CAT's Rules of Procedure, which provide that sufficient interest in the outcome of the appeal proceedings is the test with respect to allowing intervention. In the CAT's view, where a third party has actively participated in the administrative procedure before the regulator, this will nearly inevitably mean that it has 'sufficient interest' in the decision for the purposes of bringing an appeal.

12.56 Although the case law on sufficiency of interest in the context of interventions (considered above at paras 12.33 et seq) provides a useful indication of the circumstances which the CAT considers as relevant in determining whether there is a sufficient interest, it should be borne in mind that the factual context in determining sufficient interest in relation to an intervention is not the same. It is not clear that a sufficient interest in an on-going appeal equates to sufficient

---

[78] [1982] AC 617.   [79] *Pernod Ricard SA v OFT* [2004] CAT 10, para 196.

interest to trigger an appeal. In applications for intervention, for example, the CAT will consider whether the interests of the would-be intervener are already adequately protected by one or other of the principal parties to the proceedings—this is obviously not a relevant factor in the context of sufficient interest for the purpose of appeals.

(ii) Enterprise Act appeals from CC penalty decisions

For reasons which are self-evident, only persons on whom a penalty has been imposed by the CC may appeal the imposition of a penalty.[80] **12.57**

(b) Which decisions can be appealed to CAT on the merits?

(i) Competition Act merits appeals

Schedule 8 to the Competition Act 1998 identifies what type of appeal lies— **12.58**
whether it is on the merits or by judicial review. The vast majority of appeals that lie to the CAT under the Competition Act are appeals on the merits. At the time of writing,[81] ss 46 and 47 of the Competition Act, read together with Sch 8 provide for the following 'appealable decisions' applying Chapter I, Chapter II, Article 81, and/or Article 82 to be appealed to the CAT on the merits:

- Both parties and third parties[82] may appeal decisions by the OFT (or, where relevant, the sectoral regulators):
  - as to whether Chapter I, Chapter II, Article 81, and/or Article 82 have been infringed;
  - cancelling a block or parallel exemption;
  - withdrawing the benefit of a Commission block exemption regulation; and
  - making or abstaining from making interim measures under s 35 of the Competition Act.[83]
- Parties (but not third parties) may appeal to the CAT on the merits in relation to the imposition of any penalty under s 36 or in relation to any remedies imposed by the regulator under s 32 or s 33 of the Competition Act.[84] Such remedies might include structural remedies, such as divestiture, but will usually consist of behavioural remedies, such as directions to undertakings to cease certain behaviour.[85]

---

[80] Enterprise Act 2002, ss 114(1) and 176(1).

[81] The Secretary of State may prescribe further appealable decisions under ss 46(3) and 47(1) of the Competition Act 1998.

[82] For a definition of parties and third parties see paras 12.50 and 12.51.

[83] Competition Act 1998, Sch 8, para 3.   [84] ibid.

[85] Alternatively, where an appeal is already afoot, third parties may choose to challenge remedies by participating in the appeal at the remedies stage, eg in *Genzyme Ltd v OFT* [2005] CAT 32, Healthcare at Home intervened at the remedies stage.

(ii) Enterprise Act merits appeals

12.59 The Enterprise Act 2002, unlike the Competition Act 1998, provides for very few appeals on the merits to the CAT. The only appeals determined on the merits by the CAT are appeals from penalty decisions taken by the CC under ss 114 and 176(1)(f) of the Enterprise Act 2002. These are penalties imposed by the CC where it considers that a person has failed to comply with its mandatory powers to require information in the context of a merger or a market investigation inquiry. To date, the CC has not (to the authors' knowledge) imposed any such penalties, although it has come close to doing so on several occasions.

(c) What is an appealable decision in practice?

12.60 The overwhelming majority of decisions that are identified as 'appealable' to the CAT under the Competition Act 1998 are appealable to the CAT on the merits. However, the Competition Act adopts a selective approach to exactly what decisions are appealable. It individually identifies specific types of decision that are susceptible to appeal to the CAT, rather than providing for a broad category of decisions that may be appealed.[86] It seems fairly straightforward, in principle, for statute to identify which decisions are appealable to the CAT, and what standard of review applies. In practice, however, the dividing line between decisions that are appealable on the merits and those that are not is, in certain cases, unclear. This has led to prolonged disputes before the CAT on the issue of admissibility.

12.61 Decisions taken under the Competition Act 1998 which fall outside the list in ss 46 and 47 of the Act are not appealable to the CAT, so the only means of recourse against such decisions is by way of judicial review before the High Court. There is a clear incentive for regulators to seek to avoid the CAT's full merits jurisdiction by characterising non-infringement decisions (which are appealable to the CAT) as a rejection of a complaint (which is not an 'appealable' decision). Conversely, there is a similar incentive for appellants to characterise case administration decisions made by the regulators in the context of an on-going or possible investigation into Chapter I, Chapter II, Article 81, and/or Article 82 matters as decisions susceptible to appeal under s 46 or s 47 of the Competition Act to engage the full merits jurisdiction of the CAT. As the CAT put it:

> If there is a relevant decision . . . then a disappointed complainant has an appeal to this tribunal. If, on a true analysis, there is no relevant decision, but only an exercise of discretion not involving a decision whether the Chapter I or II prohibition has

---

[86] This is to be contrasted with the far broader Enterprise Act 2002 appeal provisions which predominantly provide for appeal by means of judicial review.

been infringed, then a disappointed complainant may have a remedy, if at all, by way of judicial review at common law. Which route applies depends solely on whether there is a 'relevant decision' or not.[87]

A significant body of case law as to what amounts to an appealable decision **12.62** under the Competition Act 1998 has therefore come into existence. The issue has arisen exclusively in the context of the CAT's merits jurisdiction, and turns in particular on the exact ambit of s 46(3) of the Competition Act, which provides for an appeal on the merits from decisions by the OFT 'as to whether' the Competition Act prohibitions, Article 81, or Article 82 have been infringed.

Litigants have (successfully) sought to include within the concept of a decision **12.63** 'as to whether' there is an infringement, a number of decisions that are not expressly identified in ss 46 and 47 of the Competition Act. The CAT's purposive interpretation of s 46(3) has opened up broader avenues of redress for third party complainants, and has also expanded the CAT's merits jurisdiction.

The question as to what constitutes an appealable decision under s 46(3) arises **12.64** in determining what is a 'non-infringement decision'. Rejections of complaints by regulators are not expressly identified in ss 46 and 47 of the Competition Act as appealable decisions. Where a regulator decides to reject a complaint (sometimes, but not always, after having investigated the matter for quite some time) this can be construed as an implicit negative finding as to whether Chapter I, Chapter II, Article 81, and/or Article 82 (as relevant) has been infringed (and so is reviewable by the CAT on the merits). Alternatively, the rejection of the complaint can be viewed as an exercise by the regulator of its discretion relating to its administrative priorities, which does not involve a finding as to whether there has been an infringement and (as appropriate for the exercise of an administrative discretion) should be reviewed only by the High Court on judicial review.

European case law clearly recognises that when regulators 'filter out' those **12.65** complaints that they do not wish to proceed with, this does not amount to a non-infringement decision, but is in essence an exercise of administrative discretion. In *Automec Srl*[88] the CFI held:

> [T]he rights conferred upon complaints . . . do not include a right to obtain decision . . . as to the existence or otherwise of the alleged infringement . . . [I]t should be observed that, for an institution performing a public-service task, the power to take all the organizational measures necessary for the fulfilment of that task, including settling priorities in the framework laid down by law . . . is an inherent part of public administration.'

---

[87] *Bettercare Group Ltd v Director General of Fair Trading* [2002] CAT 6, para 90.
[88] Case T-24/90 *Automec Srl v Commission* [1992] ECR-II 2223.

(i) The case law to date

12.66 *Bettercare Group Ltd v Director General of Fair Trading*[89]   The issue first
arose in *Bettercare*, in which the Director General rejected a complaint on
the basis that he had no reasonable grounds to suspect an infringement. On
appeal, the CAT held that in determining whether a rejection of a complaint
amounted to a decision for the purposes of s 46 of the Competition Act 1998,
the form a decision takes is not relevant.[90] Looking at the relevant facts (such
as the correspondence between the complainant and the Director General of
Fair Trading) the CAT found that the Director General had given careful
consideration to the matter and formed a concluded view rejecting the complaint. This amounted to a decision. In considering whether the decision
amounted to a decision as to whether Chapter II had been infringed and hence
an 'appealable decision', the CAT again looked to substance. It found that in
finding that North & West did not amount to an undertaking, the Director
General had determined that an essential element of the Chapter II prohibition
had not been infringed. He had accordingly decided that the Chapter II
prohibition was not infringed. It followed that the Director General had taken a
decision as to whether or not the Chapter II prohibition had been infringed
within the meaning of s 46(3)(b) of the Act. The CAT's interpretation of
s 46(3), reading the text as meaning 'whether or not' there has been an
infringement, clarifies that the CAT's jurisdiction extends to both infringement
and non-infringement decisions.[91]

12.67 *Freeserve.com Plc v Director General of Telecommunications*[92]   Next, in
Freeserve, the Director General of Telecommunications rejected a complaint
that BT was abusing its dominant position in relation to the provision of
broadband internet services. The complaint was rejected, after a first stage
preliminary investigation (which took just over a month), on the basis that the
information supplied by the complainant did not provide evidence of anti-
competitive conduct, so that the issues raised did not warrant further
investigation. Unlike *Bettercare*, where the Director General of Fair Trading had
made a legal assessment (as to whether North & West was an undertaking) prior
to rejecting a decision, in this case the Director General of Telecommunications'
decision not to proceed with an investigation was based on an assessment of

---

[89] [2002] CAT 6.

[90] 'Whether such a decision has been taken for the purposes of the Act is, in our view, a
question of substance, not form, to be determined objectively. If there is, in substance, a decision,
it is immaterial whether it is formally entitled "a decision".' Ibid, para 62.

[91] Although the 'paradigm' Competition Act 1998 appeal was predicated on the basis of
appeals from infringement decisions, in fact enforcement activity by the OFT has in practice led
to far more case closure decisions than it has to infringement decisions.

[92] [2002] CAT 6.

the evidence placed before him. The CAT developed the *Bettercare* test as follows:

> [I]f, when rejecting, or closing the file on a complaint, the substance of the matter, judged objectively, is that the Director has decided, either expressly or by necessary implication, that on the material before him there is no infringement of the Chapter II prohibition, then he has taken a decision 'as to whether the Chapter II prohibition has been infringed'.[93]

Looking at the matter in the round and considering the reasoning put forward **12.68** by the Director General of Telecommunications in rejecting the complaint (which was fairly full and addressed each of Freeserve's complaints in turn), the CAT found that '[it] amounts, in our view, in substance to a finding that the evidence does not establish "an abuse" '. Accordingly, the decision by the Director General amounted to a decision that the Chapter II prohibition had not been infringed within the meaning of s 46(3)(b). This was so despite the fact that the Director General had never initiated a full investigation into the matter.

Claymore Dairies Ltd v OFT[94]   In this case, the Director General's letter **12.69** communicating the decision to reject the complaint made express reference to the resource implications of taking the complaint further, and echoed the language the CAT had used in *Bettercare* to describe decisions that were not appealable:

> We are taking the administrative decision to close our files on the Chapter II case on the basis that it is not sufficiently promising in terms of a likely decision of infringement to warrant the commitment of further resources. . .[95]

The CAT looked beyond the wording of the letter to the surrounding circumstances to determine whether the decision was appealable. It noted the amount of time and resources the OFT had invested in investigating the matter and the tone of previous exchanges it had with the complainant. In reaching its conclusion as to whether there was an appealable decision, the CAT stated that a useful approach is to pose two questions:[96]

- Did the Director ask himself whether the Chapter II prohibition has been infringed?
- What answer did the Director give to that question when making his decision?'

---

[93] ibid, para 96.   [94] [2003] CAT 3.
[95] ibid, para 56, and contrast *Bettercare Group Ltd v Director General of Fair Trading* [2002] CAT 6, para 83.
[96] *Claymore*, ibid, para 148.

12.70   In this case the OFT had made an extensive investigation into the complaints and invested considerable resources in so doing. It had collected information under Section 26 Notices and had carried out an on-site inspection. It had clearly asked itself, and carried out an investigation, as to whether the Chapter II prohibition had been infringed. In the CAT's judgment, in closing the investigation, the DGFT had assessed the evidence before him and come to a conclusion that no infringement could be established on that evidence. This amounted to a non-infringement decision.

12.71   The CAT summarised the main principles for determining whether there was an appealable decision as follows (and these remain the key principles to date):[97]

> (i)   The question whether the Director has 'made a decision as to whether the Chapter II prohibition is infringed' is primarily a question of fact to be decided in accordance with the particular circumstances of each case (Bettercare, [24]).
>
> (ii)   Whether such a decision has been taken is a question of substance, not form, to be determined objectively, taking into account all the circumstances (Bettercare, [62], [84] to [87], and [93]). The issue is: has the Director made a decision as to whether the Chapter II prohibition has been infringed, either expressly or by necessary implication, on the material before him? (Freeserve, [96]).
>
> (iii)   There is a distinction between a situation where the Director has merely exercised an administrative discretion without proceeding to a decision on the question of infringement (for example, where the Director decides not to investigate a complaint pending the conclusion of a parallel investigation by the European Commission), and a situation where the Director has, in fact, reached a decision on the question of infringement, (Bettercare, [80], [87], [88], [93]; Freeserve, [101] to [105]). The test, as formulated by the Tribunal in Freeserve, is whether the Director has genuinely abstained from expressing a view, one way or the other, even by implication, on the question whether there has been an infringement of the Chapter II prohibition (Freeserve, [101] and [102]).

12.72   *Aquavitae (UK) Ltd v Water Services Regulation Authority*[98]   Following *Claymore*, the test to determine whether or not the regulator has made an appealable decision turns, in essence, on whether it genuinely abstained from expressing a view in rejecting the complaint. In *Aquavitae*, the CAT narrowed the scope of those situations in which the regulator 'abstains from expressing a view'. It held, obiter, that where regulators close a file after indicating that they will be considering the complaint on the merits, the Tribunal will normally infer

---

[97] ibid [2003] CAT 3, para 122. These paragraphs have been approved subsequently in *Pernod Ricard SA v OFT* [2004] CAT 10, para 141 and *Aquavitae (UK) Ltd v Water Services Regulation Authority* [2003] CAT 17, para 174.
[98] [2003] CAT 17.

from this that the file closure is because there is insufficient evidence of infringement and in most cases the result will be an appealable decision.[99] Further, the inference that the case has been closed because the relevant regulator has concluded that an infringement is not established will normally be irresistible if, at an earlier stage, the regulator has already expressed a view to the effect that he sees little merit in the case.[100] If this approach is followed, regulators can expect little scope to close their files by means of their administrative discretion: once they have considered a complaint on the merits (however briefly) the usual inference will be that the decision to close the file gives rise to a 'non-infringement decision'.

Pernod Ricard SA v OFT[101] This case raised the issue as to whether the **12.73** acceptance of voluntary undertakings amounts to a non-infringement decision. After conducting a substantial investigation into Bacardi's conduct under Chapter II (which went as far as issuing a Rule 14 Notice), the OFT decided to accept voluntary assurances provided by Bacardi as to its behaviour and closed its file.[102] The OFT stated in its letter notifying the decision to close the file to the complainant (Pernod), that Bacardi's assurances 'removed the competition problem'. Its press release indicated that the decision to close its investigation into the agreements was taken in the light of Bacardi's change in behaviour and the OFT's other casework priorities. The CAT held that when the Director General of Fair Trading found that Bacardi's assurances 'removed the competition problem', he also decided, by necessary implication, that on the information then available to him, from date of the receipt of the assurances, there was no abuse of dominance and that there would not be an abuse of any dominant position so long as the assurances were observed.

Brannigan v OFT[103] In this case, the OFT had indicated to Mr Brannigan that **12.74** it had insufficient resources to make further inquiries into his complaint and that it was taking the administrative decision not to proceed with the matter any further, unless further resources became available. On appeal to the CAT, at a private hearing before the CAT, the OFT undertook, in view of Mr Brannigan's personal circumstances (Mr Brannigan was bankrupt and did not have the means to take private enforcement action before the courts) to consider whether there were reasonable grounds to suspect an infringement (ie, to determine whether the case met the threshold for an investigation to be commenced under s 25 of the Competition Act 1998). Subsequently, the OFT sent Mr Brannigan a letter, which rejected the complaint on the basis of administrative priorities. The letter attached a further document in which the OFT assessed whether there were reasonable grounds to suspect an infringement, on the basis of

---

[99] ibid, para 206.   [100] ibid.   [101] [2004] CAT 10.
[102] See paras 10.30 et seq for a discussion of voluntary assurances.   [103] [2006] CAT 28.

information that Mr Brannigan had supplied. The question arose as to whether the OFT had made a 'decision'. The OFT contended that its assessment of the complaint had been made without prejudice to its administrative priorities decision, and that it had undertaken the assessment with a view to assisting Mr Brannigan. The CAT's judgment (obiter) demonstrates an interest in evaluating the OFT's assessment of its administrative priorities.[104] On the issue as to whether there was an appealable decision, the CAT held that, in assessing on the basis of the material before it whether there were reasonable grounds for initiating an investigation under s 25 of the Competition Act, the OFT had in effect made a non-infringement decision:

> If, as the OFT found, that material did not give rise to reasonable grounds to suspect an infringement, it follows in our view that the OFT implicitly reached the view that the Chapter II and Chapter I prohibitions had not been infringed on the basis of that material.[105]

12.75 *Casting Book Ltd v OFT*[106]   In this case, the OFT had commenced a formal investigation and issued several Section 26 Notices to various parties. However, a little over a year after receiving the complaint, against a backdrop of the reorganisation of the entire Competition Enforcement division, the OFT decided to close the file on the basis of administrative priorities. It sent a letter to the appellant explaining why the case did not satisfy the factors the OFT used for the selection and prioritisation of casework. The OFT put considerable evidence before the CAT explaining its administrative priorities. The CAT, considering the evidence, distinguished *Casting Book* from *Claymore* on the basis that there had not been a detailed investigation prior to the case closure decision. It was satisfied, on the basis of the decision letter, the witness evidence, and the contemporaneous documentary evidence that none of the reasons for closing the case related to the merits of the case. Accordingly, there was no decision as to whether the prohibitions had been infringed, and no appealable decision.

(ii) Analysis

12.76 The cases above establish that the CAT will not be deterred from reviewing decisions merely because they are tagged by the OFT's as administrative decisions relating to the organisation of its resources. The CAT considers all the relevant facts closely to determine whether, expressly or by implication, the OFT has formed a view on the substance of the complaint, either on the law (as in *Bettercare*) or on the evidence before it (as in *Freeserve* or *Pernod Ricard*). It

---

[104] 'We are not concerned in this judgment to comment on the question of the OFT's administrative priorities, although we can see that in other contexts major issues could arise in that regard', ibid, para 42.
[105] ibid, para 69.   [106] [2006] CAT 35.

must be correct that the OFT should not be able to preclude appeal by formulating its decisions in a particular way. However, there is a danger that certain of the inferences that the CAT has been prepared to draw (*Aquavitae, Brannigan*) in determining whether there is an appealable decision, stretch the wording of the Competition Act and do not strike the appropriate balance between ensuring that regulators are properly accountable for their decisions, and allowing regulators sufficient leeway to determine their administrative priorities and commit their resources as they see fit.

There is a certain logic to the argument advanced by the CAT in *Brannigan* that **12.77** if the regulator does not have reasonable grounds for suspecting an infringement for the purposes of triggering an investigation under s 25 of the Competition Act 1998, then a fortiori this implies that in its view there is no infringement. However, there are procedural and conceptual difficulties with this approach. First, the decisions that regulators make with respect to their resources are intimately linked to their assessment of the prima facie strength of the complaints they receive. It is difficult to expect regulators to organise their priorities otherwise, and it is not always accurate to construe the prima facie evaluation that regulators undertake prior to rejecting complaints as a full-blown non-infringement decision. Secondly, paradoxically, the CAT's approach, with its readiness to infer that an appealable decision has been taken whenever the regulator acknowledges it is considering a complaint (*Aquavitae*), will actually deter the regulator from communicating with complainants or evaluating the complaints in any great depth, for fear of the CAT finding that they have, by implication, reached a conclusion on the complaint. Thirdly, the CAT's gradual erosion of the situations in which it finds that a regulator has genuinely abstained from expressing a view on the infringement severely curtails the regulators in exercising their discretion as to which complaints to take forward. The CAT had recognised in *Bettercare* that there was considerable scope for regulators to reject complaints by the exercise of administrative discretion.[107] It is questionable whether in the light of subsequent decisions such as *Freeserve* and *Aquavitae*, it is now open to the OFT to dismiss a complaint in the situations envisaged in *Bettercare*.

The CAT's current approach is clearly right to focus on substance, not form. It **12.78** has on many an occasion forced the regulator to reconsider its decision

---

[107] 'For example, he may have other cases that he wishes to pursue in priority (compare Case T-24 and 28/90 Automec v Commission [1992] ECR II-2223); he may have insufficient information to decide whether there is an infringement or not; he may suspect that there may be an infringement, but the case does not appear sufficiently promising, or the economic activity concerned sufficiently important, to warrant the commitment of further resources. None of these cases necessarily give rise to a decision by the Director as to whether a relevant prohibition is infringed', *Bettercare Group Ltd v Director General of Fair Trading* [2002] CAT 6, paras 83 and 84.

entirely.[108] However, its approach is time-consuming and issues of admissibility are contributing to delays in decision-making. Further, admissibility is still relatively uncertain (see para 12.80 below). The uncertainty means that cautious applicants may (in view of the tight time limits within which an appeal must be lodged) be compelled to apply to both the CAT (on the merits) and the High Court on judicial review if they are not to risk their challenge falling between two stools, as in *Casting Book*. Lastly, there are significant costs implications: the CAT, regulators and parties commit considerable resources for the purposes of a preliminary decision on admissibility.

12.79   The Court of Appeal, in *Floe Telecom Ltd (in administration) v Ofcom*,[109] made certain general comments on the nature of the CAT's jurisdiction (albeit in a different context) which may be relevant to this issue in future. First, it noted that the CAT does not have the general statutory function of supervising the regulators. Secondly, it emphasised that the CAT is in no position to judge the competing demands on the resources of a regulator at any given time. Thirdly, the judgment highlights the role the administrative courts have to play in relation to certain aspects of regulators' decision-making: the correct avenue for a complaint of undue delay, for example, is by means of judicial review.[110]

(iii) Drawing the line in practice

12.80   In addition to decisions that are expressly listed in ss 46 and 47 of the Competition Act 1998 as appealable on the merits (see para 12.58 above), CAT jurisprudence establishes that the following decisions amount to decisions 'as to whether' there has been an infringement under s 46(3), and are accordingly appealable on the merits:

- **Non-infringement decisions.** Ever since *Bettercare*[111] (and confirmed in *Claymore* and *Pernod Ricard*[112]) the CAT's interpretation of s 46(3) 'as to whether' there has been an infringement is that this includes non-infringement decisions.

- **Decisions rejecting complaints and closing the file after a case has crossed the s 25 threshold.** In *Claymore* and *Pernod Ricard* the OFT decided to reject complaints after having initiated a formal investigation into the complaint (both cases had passed the threshold of s 25 of the Competition Act 1998[113]) and having undertaken detailed investigations in which it exercised

---

[108] eg, after *Freeserve*, Ofcom re-investigated and subsequently issued BT with a Statement of Objections.

[109] [2006] EWCA 768.   [110] ibid, para 46, per Lloyd LJ.

[111] *Bettercare Group Ltd v Director General of Fair Trading* [2002] CAT 6, para 86.

[112] *Claymore Dairies Ltd v OFT* [2003] CAT 3; *Pernod Ricard SA v OFT* [2004] CAT 10.

[113] See paras 6.59 et seq for a discussion of the s 25 threshold.

information-collecting powers. Following *Claymore* and *Aquavitae*, in such cases the CAT will usually infer that there has been a decision of non-infringement. The length of the OFT investigation which precedes the rejection of a complaint is obviously a factor which would indicate that the OFT has asked itself, as per the *Claymore* test, whether there is an infringement and given a reply to that answer. Where however, a case has passed the s 25 threshold, but the investigation is not detailed or developed, there is a possibility, depending on the facts of the case, that a case closure may not amount to an appealable decision where the OFT clearly did not have the merits of the case in mind when closing the file (*Casting Book*).

It remains unclear whether the following decisions by regulators could be **12.81** construed as non-infringement decisions:

- **Decisions closing the file for administrative priorities prior to the s 25 threshold being met.** The situation remains unclear. In both *Bettercare*[114] and *Freeserve*[115] the CAT remarked that there is no reason why the OFT should not take a 'non-infringement decision' at a preliminary stage of the investigation. In *Freeserve*, the CAT found that a case closure letter sent at the closure of the preliminary stage (and thus prior to the s 25 threshold being crossed) amounted to a 'non-infringement' decision. Further, in *Brannigan*, the CAT found that the 'reasonable grounds' assessment made by the OFT at the s 25 stage necessarily implied a 'non-infringement decision'. There are nonetheless several reasons why it may not, in future, find there has been an appealable decision where the regulator takes a decision to close the file prior to the s 25 threshold:
  - In reaching its decision in *Freeserve*, the CAT relied heavily on the fact that the closure letter addressed four aspects of one overall complaint and Ofcom had reached one overall conclusion on the complaint. Yet Ofcom conceded that the case closure letter had made a non-infringement decision on one aspect of *Freeserve*'s complaint. It was hard to believe therefore that no decision had been reached on the other aspects of the same complaint.[116]
  - In *Freeserve*, the language of the case closure letter was ambiguous. Substantive consideration was given by the regulator to the various arguments advanced by the complainant and it was not clear that the decision was made on grounds of administrative priorities. Similarly, in *Brannigan*, the

---

[114] *Bettercare Group Ltd v Director General of Fair Trading* [2002] CAT 6, para 89.

[115] *Freeserve.com Plc v Director General of Telecommunications* [2005] CAT 5, para 98.

[116] 'In our view it would be highly surprising if, in one and the same document, a conclusion to the effect that the material before the Director "does not provide evidence of anti-competitive behaviour" signifies, in one part of the document, that the Director has taken an appealable decision, but means something different in another part of the document. That result respectfully seems to us to be contrary to common sense.' Ibid, para 88.

OFT undertook a fairly thorough analysis of the issues in assessing why the case did not meet the s 25 threshold.

- The Court of Appeal in *Floe Telecom* (albeit in a different context) took a narrow view of the nature of the CAT's appeal jurisdiction and emphasised its statutory nature. Further, it expressly approved the CFI's judgment in *Automec*[117] on regulators' ability to reject cases on grounds of administrative priorities. It stated: 'The [CAT] cannot know what are the competing demands on the resources of the particular regulator at the given time. It may well be that it cannot properly be told of this by the regulator because of issues of confidentiality as to current investigations. It cannot, therefore, form any proper view as to the relative priority of one case as compared with others.'[118] These, and other similar comments made by the Court of Appeal in that case, may assist the regulators in submitting that they maintain a wide discretion not to proceed with certain complaints, which is only susceptible to challenge on judicial review grounds.

- The OFT has recently established a Preliminary Investigation Unit that will be specifically charged with determining which cases to proceed with. This will draw a clearer line between the decision-making process by which the OFT selects the cases with which it proceeds and organises its administrative priorities on the one hand, and its substantive decision-making on the other.

- **Decisions accepting voluntary assurances:** Although the CAT held in *Pernod Ricard* that a decision to accept voluntary assurances amounted to a non-infringement decision, the continued relevance of that decision is doubtful. Regulation 1/2003 and the amended Competition Act provide a different regime with respect to voluntary assurances.[119] These changes affect the continued relevance of *Pernod Ricard* as follows:

  - *Pernod Ricard* concerned the acceptance of assurances at an advanced stage in the investigation, after a Rule 14 Notice had been issued by the regulator. With the introduction of the express statutory power for the OFT to accept commitments,[120] there is arguably no longer any informal power to accept voluntary assurances after a case has passed the s 25 threshold. The power to accept commitments under the Competition Act arises after the s 25 threshold has been passed: arguably this express power (and the procedural safeguards that come with it) oust any informal power to accept commitments or assurances thereafter.[121] If the facts of

---

[117] Case T-24/90 *Automec Srl v Commission* [1992] ECR-II 2223.
[118] *Floe Telecom Ltd (in administration) v Ofcom* [2006] EWCA Civ 768, para 37.
[119] See paras 10.30 et seq above.
[120] Competition Act 1998, s 31A(2); see paras 10.28 et seq for a discussion of this power.
[121] The extra-statutory power to accept voluntary assurances is ousted by the provision of the power to accept commitments: see paras 10.30 et seq above.

Pernod arose again, the decision adopted by the OFT at such an advanced stage of the investigation would most probably be a commitments decision. Commitments decisions are expressly reviewable by the CAT on judicial review standards.[122] Given the highly discretionary nature of a commitments decision (which involves resource implications), this is appropriate.

- However, the OFT would appear to retain the power to accept voluntary assurances in lieu of an interim measures direction and before a case has reached the s 25 threshold. Under Regulation 1/2003, the acceptance of commitments does not in any way amount to an infringement or a non-infringement decision. Preamble 13 provides that a commitment decision by the Commission finds that there are no longer grounds for action by the Commission without concluding whether there has been or is still an infringement. OFT guidelines[123] also provide 'a decision accepting binding commitments . . . will not include any statement as to the legality or otherwise of the agreement or conduct either prior to the acceptance of the commitments or once the commitments are in place'.[124] If there is no decision as to whether there is an infringement decision in commitment decisions, which under the Competition Act are accepted when a case is advanced beyond the s 25 threshold, then a fortiori, this must also be the case in relation to the acceptance of voluntary assurances, which process is not as developed in terms of procedure and decision-making.

- **Failure to act.** A failure by the OFT to take action at all is not expressly listed in s 46 as an appealable decision. Several factors would seem to indicate failure to act is not appealable to the CAT. First, the legislator is quite clear elsewhere in the Competition Act 1998 where it wishes failure to take a decision to be appealable: see s 47(1)(e) in relation to decisions not to make an interim measures direction. Secondly, the Court of Appeal indicated in *Floe Telecom Ltd (in administration) v Ofcom*[125] that the correct avenue for claims of undue delay (of which failure to act is an extreme species) is to proceed by judicial review before the Administrative Court. However, the CAT has made a few comments that indicate its interest. In *Aquavitae*, it questioned (obiter) the regulator's discretion to reject complaints without investigating them.[126] In this respect, it may be drawing an analogy with the action for failure to act under Article 232 EC, although there is no equivalent provision under the Competition Act.

---

[122] See paras 12.104 et seq.   [123] OFT407, *Enforcement* (December 2004).
[124] ibid, para 4.5.   [125] [2006] EWCA 768.
[126] *Aquavitae (UK) Ltd v Water Services Regulation Authority* [2003] CAT 17, para 205.

(iv) Is a non-infringement decision in reality a decision that there are no grounds for action?

12.82 An analogy can be drawn between the CAT's approach to what amounts to a 'non-infringement decision' under the Competition Act 1998 and a 'decision that there are no grounds for action' under Regulation 1/2003. Regulation 1/2003 does not empower national competition authorities to make any findings of non-infringement as such, but merely decisions that there are 'no grounds for action' on their part.[127] This is consistent with a system in which there are no individual exemptions from Article 81—only the Commission is empowered to make a decision of 'inapplicability' or non-infringement.[128] Were the Competition Act amended so that the OFT no longer takes 'non-infringement decisions' as such, but instead takes decisions that 'there are no grounds for action on its part' (appealable to the CAT), this would have several advantages. First, it would accord more closely with national powers with respect to the application of Articles 81 and 82 under Article 5 of Regulation 1/2003, as national competition authorities are not empowered to make declaratory findings that Article 81 or Article 82 are not infringed. Secondly, it would also accord more closely with the CAT's notion of what the OFT is doing when it makes what is currently termed a non-infringement decision. In *Claymore Dairies*, the Director General of Fair Trading argued that he was genuinely undecided about a case, and hence could not adopt a positive decision finding there was no infringement. The CAT's response was clear:

> The Director seems to be saying that he cannot reach a decision of 'non-infringement' unless he is satisfied on a 'positive assessment' to some absolute level of certainty that there is, in fact, no infringement, i.e. that the Director cannot take a 'decision of non-infringement' unless he is in a position to prove the negative. Hence his argument that if an astronomer says he cannot, with the means available to him, find life on other planets, that does not mean that there is no life on other planets (see paragraph 103 above).
>
> The Director is not, however, an astronomer seeking life on other planets: he is performing a statutory function. In discharging that function, the criteria by which he makes up his mind is not some absolute level of certainty but the much more prosaic civil standard of proof, . . . Applying the appropriate standard of proof to the evidence that he has, the Director then makes a decision as to whether the evidence meets that standard. If it does, an infringement has been established to the requisite standard of proof; if it does not, no infringement has been established to the requisite standard of proof on the evidence available. If the Director then takes as a decision to the latter effect, he makes, it seems to us, a decision, 'as to

---

[127] Regulation 1/2003, Art 5.   [128] See para 4.26 above.

whether the Chapter II prohibition has been infringed' within the meaning of section 46(3)(b) of the Act.[129]

(d) Standard of review in appeals on the merits

(i) Full merits review

Paragraph 3(1) to Sch 8 to the Competition Act 1998 provides that '[t]he **12.83** Tribunal must determine the appeal on the merits by reference to the grounds of appeal set out in the notice of appeal'. The full merits review means that the CAT has a full jurisdiction to find facts, make its own appraisals of economic issues, apply the law to those facts and appraisals, and determine the amount of any penalty.[130] The CAT may, where necessary, take on a role as a primary decision-maker.[131] In *Napp Pharmaceuticals*,[132] for example, the CAT made its own decision of infringement on the basis of the evidence not put before the DGFT.[133] In some cases, the CAT can make extensive findings of fact, as for example in *JJB Sports Plc v OFT*.[134] Any decision that is taken by the CAT has the same effect, and may be enforced in the same manner, as a decision of the OFT.[135]

The breadth of the merits review is reflected throughout the procedure before **12.84** the CAT. In many cases, the CAT will hear a considerable amount of evidence (some of which may be fresh evidence), may cross-examine witnesses, hear economic experts and will generally explore the facts of the case before it in considerable detail. As the CAT remarked in *JJB Sports Plc v OFT*:[136]

> The Tribunal has now heard a great deal of evidence, much of which is not referred to in the decision. Such a situation is a common occurrence in appeals to the Tribunal which are appeals 'on the merits' and effectively take the form of a new hearing: see Schedule 8, paragraph 3(1) of the Act. Indeed, as the Tribunal observed in Napp, cited above, at [134], it is virtually inevitable that, at the appeal stage, matters will be gone into in considerably more detail than was the case at the administrative stage. New witness statements may be filed; new documents may come to light; a witness may say something in the witness box that has never been said before.

---

[129] *Claymore Dairies Ltd v OFT* [2003] CAT 3, paras 154 and 155.
[130] *Freeserve.com Plc v Director General of Telecommunications* [2003] CAT 5, para 107.
[131] Competition Act 1998, Sch 8, para 3(2)(d) and (e).
[132] *Napp Pharmaceutical Holdings Ltd v Director General of Fair Trading* [2002] CAT 1.
[133] ibid, para 263: 'To the extent that we rely on other facts or matters, or express our finding in terms which differ from the Director, we take so far as necessary our own decision that Napp has infringed the Chapter II prohibition, pursuant to our powers in Schedule 8, paragraph 3(2) of the Act.'
[134] [2004] CAT 17.   [135] Competition Act 1998, Sch 8, para 3(3).
[136] [2004] CAT 17, para 284.

The wealth of evidential and economic material considered by the CAT is reflected in the length of its judgments.[137] The exercise of a merits review affects the entire procedure, from the standard of proof, to the remedies available. For a more general discussion of the difference between the CAT's merits review and judicial review, see paras 12.11–12.14 above.

(ii) Rejection of complaints—a lower standard of review?

12.85 The CAT has indicated that there is no difference in principle between an appeal against an infringement decision and an appeal from a non-infringement decision. Take the following dicta as an example:

> In Freeserve v Director General of Telecommunications [2003] CAT 5, since confirmed in JJ Burgess & Sons v OFT [2005] CAT 25, the Tribunal said there was in principle no difference between an appeal against an infringement decision and an appeal against a non-infringement decision.[138]

12.86 However, the CAT has emphasised that the way it exercises its jurisdiction will differ depending on the circumstances.[139] It appears to consider that when it is reviewing appeals from rejections of complaints, the nature of the decision appealed may call for a looser standard of review than a full merits review. The approach it takes is closer to that of judicial review, namely to consider whether the regulator erred, rather than considering whether the regulator's decision was correct.

12.87 In *Claymore*[140] the CAT differentiated between ordinary merits appeals and appeals from non-infringement decisions as follows:

> [T]he primary purpose of this case is to identify whether the OFT has made any material error of law, whether it has carried out a proper investigation, whether its reasons are adequate and whether there are material errors in its appreciation. . . . The Tribunal's function is different, in the present case, from appeals brought by the subject of an infringement decision. Such appeals are full appeals on the merits, in which the Tribunal usually has to come to a view, on the evidence before it, as to whether an infringement has indeed been made out. A detailed examination of the information used by the OFT in reaching its infringement decision will often be necessary. That is not the case here. The Tribunal is not being asked to take a decision as to whether Wiseman did in fact abuse a dominant position; it must simply decide whether the OFT's approach was in error. We should add, however, that this reflects our current view, based on the facts of the present case: we do not rule out further developments in other cases presenting different circumstances.

---

[137] The Court of Appeal invited the CAT to be more concise in *Argos v OFT* [2006] EWCA Civ 1318.

[138] *Albion Water Ltd v Water Services Regulation Authority* [2004] CAT 19, para 243.

[139] *Freeserve.com Plc v Director General of Telecommunications* [2005] CAT 5, para 111.

[140] [2004] CAT 16, paras 109 and 111.

It repeated this view later on in the proceedings and accordingly confined its **12.88** review:

> In our view we should not find, in a case such as the present, that an OFT investigation leading to an appealable decision as to whether the Chapter II prohibition has not been infringed was legally flawed unless we are satisfied that the OFT has made a material error.[141]

In *Claymore*, the CAT expressly indicated that it did not consider all grounds of **12.89** appeal listed in the Notice of Appeal. Its quasi-judicial review approach in appeals relating to rejections of complaints also affects the procedure relating to such appeals, and in particular, the ability of the complainant to adduce evidence that was not before the CAT. In *Bettercare*, the CAT indicated that when considering an appeal from a decision to reject a complaint, it was usually not appropriate to allow the complainant to submit new evidence before the CAT:

> In complainants' appeals . . . it seems to us that the primary task of the Tribunal will usually be to decide whether, on the material put before him by the complainant, the Director was correct in arriving at the conclusion that he did.[142]

Subsequently, in *Freeserve*[143] the CAT, whilst not endorsing a rule that com- **12.90** plainants could not submit new evidence, accepted that, in principle, the original complaint sets the framework within which the correctness of the regulator's decision is to be judged, taking account of the material that he had or ought reasonably to have obtained. It emphasised that an appeal is not an occasion to launch what is in effect a new complaint.

(e) Burden of proof

Contrary to challenges by way of judicial review, in full merits appeals against an **12.91** infringement decision the burden of proof lies on the decision-maker to establish the infringement.[144] This does not preclude the reliance by the regulator on certain inferences:

> It is common ground that the legal burden of proof rests throughout on the Director to prove the infringements alleged (see Napp, cited above, at [100]), albeit that the Director may properly rely on inferences or presumptions that would, in the absence of any countervailing indications, normally flow from a given set of facts: Napp, at [110] to [111].[145]

---

[141] [2005] CAT 30.

[142] *Bettercare Group Ltd v Director General of Fair Trading* [2002] CAT 6, para 96.

[143] *Freeserve.com Plc v Director General of Telecommunications* [2003] CAT 5, para 116.

[144] In *Napp Pharmaceutical Holdings Ltd v Director General of Fair Trading* [2002] CAT 1, para 100, the CAT indicated that: 'In our view it follows from Article 6(2) that the burden of proof rests throughout on the Director to prove the infringements alleged.'

[145] *Aberdeen Journals Ltd v Director General of Fair Trading* [2003] CAT 11, para 123.

Further, under Regulation 1/2003 and the Competition Act 1998, the legal burden is on the undertaking seeking to benefit from Article 81(3) and s 9 of the Competition Act to establish that the agreement at issue satisfies the conditions provided therein.[146]

(f) Standard of proof

12.92 The standard of proof in proceedings before the CAT is the civil standard of proof, ie on the balance of probabilities. However, the evidence required will vary depending on the gravity of what is sought to establish on the balance of probabilities. The CAT first defined the relevant standard of proof in *Napp*:

> . . . the conclusion we reach is that, formally speaking, the standard of proof in proceedings under the Act involving penalties is the civil standard of proof, but that standard is to be applied bearing in mind that infringements of the Act are serious matters attracting severe financial penalties. It is for the Director to satisfy us in each case, on the basis of strong and compelling evidence, taking account of the seriousness of what is alleged, that the infringement is duly proved, the undertaking being entitled to the presumption of innocence, and to any reasonable doubt there may be.[147]

12.93 The CAT has not departed from the above definition.[148] It has however made certain clarifications to prevent the *Napp* definition from being misconstrued, in particular to avoid the possibility of regulators becoming overly cautious. In *JJB Sports Plc v OFT*[149] it stated:

> 204. It also follows that the reference by the Tribunal to 'strong and compelling' evidence at [109] of Napp should not be interpreted as meaning that something akin to the criminal standard is applicable to these proceedings. The standard remains the civil standard. The evidence must however be sufficient to convince the Tribunal in the circumstances of the particular case, and to overcome the presumption of innocence to which the undertaking concerned is entitled.
>
> 205. What evidence is likely to be sufficiently convincing to prove the infringement will depend on the circumstances and the facts. In Claymore Dairies v. OFT [2003] CAT 18 the Tribunal was concerned that Napp might be interpreted by the OFT or other regulators in an unduly cautious way, inhibiting the enforcement of the Act. A similar issue arises in certain Chapter II cases currently pending before the Tribunal.
>
> 206. As regards price fixing cases under the Chapter I prohibition, the Tribunal pointed out in Claymore Dairies that cartels are by their nature hidden and secret; little or nothing may be committed to writing. In our view even a single item of

---

[146] Regulation 1/2003, Art 2; Competition Act 1998, s 9(2).
[147] *Napp Pharmaceutical Holdings Ltd v Director General of Fair Trading* [2002] CAT 1, para 109.
[148] *JJB Sports Plc v OFT* [2004] CAT 17; *Argos Ltd v OFT* [2004] CAT 24.
[149] [2004] CAT 17.

evidence, or wholly circumstantial evidence, depending on the particular context and the particular circumstances, may be sufficient to meet the required standard: see Claymore Dairies at [3] to [10].

(g) CAT remedies in full merits appeals under the Competition Act

Under para 3(2) of Sch 8 to the Competition Act 1998 the CAT has been given **12.94** a broad remedial power. It is empowered to:

- confirm or set aside the decision (or any part of it) on appeal;
- remit the matter to the OFT;
- impose or revoke or vary the amount of any penalty;
- give such directions, or take such other steps, as the OFT itself could have given or taken;
- make any decision which the OFT itself could have made.

The Court of Appeal recently described some of the options available to the CAT: **12.95**

> If the appellant challenges a decision by a regulator, and establishes, on grounds taken in the notice of appeal, that the decision was wrong, whether as a matter of procedure or because of some misdirection of law or because the CAT takes a different view of the facts on the evidence before it, the Tribunal has a choice of a number of courses open to it. It may set aside the decision and remit the case to the regulator. It may feel able to decide itself what the correct result should have been, so that no remission or reference back is necessary. It may wish to retain for itself the task of deciding the eventual outcome but require further findings from the regulator, in which case it will not remit but may refer all or part of the decision back under rule 19(2)(j), with a view to deciding the appeal with the benefit of the result of that referral.[150]

(i) Varying the penalty

In *JJB Sports Plc v OFT*,[151] the CAT confirmed that para 3(2)(b) of Sch 8, **12.96** which provides that the CAT may 'vary a penalty', confers the CAT with the jurisdiction to increase the penalty.[152]

(ii) Give such directions, or take such steps, as the OFT itself could have given or taken

The extent of the CAT's power in para 3(2) of Sch 8 to give any directions **12.97** that the OFT could itself have given came under scrutiny in *Floe Telecom Ltd (in administration) v Ofcom*.[153] The CAT has, in certain cases, remitted cases to

---

[150] *Floe Telecom Ltd (in administration) v Ofcom* [2006] EWCA Civ 768, para 25.
[151] [2005] CAT 22, para 214.
[152] The Court of Appeal took the CAT's right to increase the penalty as read on appeal, see *Argos v OFT* [2006] EWCA Civ 1318, para 257, per Lloyd LJ.
[153] [2006] EWCA Civ 768.

the regulator, together with directions as to the timetable in which the regulator is to reconsider the matter. Where the appeal is still subsisting (for example where the CAT remits an aspect of the matter for a particular factual determination but keeps the appeal subsisting),[154] then the CAT may rely upon its broad case management powers with respect to appeals to give the regulator directions as to a timetable in the context of the subsisting appeal.[155] However, in *Floe Telecom*,[156] the CAT set aside the decision taken by the Director General of Telecommunications and remitted the matter as a whole to Ofcom. The question arose as to whether it had the power to specify the timetable by which Ofcom had to reinvestigate the matter. The CAT considered that it had the power to impose a timetable on Ofcom for its reinvestigation of the matter, primarily on the basis that (despite having remitted the case as a whole back to Ofcom) it treated the appeal as still subsisting so that its broad case management powers with respect to on-going appeals still applied. It also relied on para 3(2) of Sch 8 which enables it to give any directions that the OFT could itself have given.

12.98 On appeal, the Court of Appeal disagreed. Its judgment[157] notes that in previous cases the CAT made certain directions as to timetable, but none was exactly on point. In *Freeserve.com Plc v Director General of Telecommunications*,[158] the CAT gave directions with respect to the timing by which the Director General should provide a fuller statement of his reasons—but the Director General had volunteered to provide this in order to avoid the case being remitted to him. In *Aberdeen Journals*[159] and in *Argos*,[160] the appeals were still subsisting.

12.99 The Court of Appeal judgment clarifies that the appeal can no longer be treated as subsisting if the CAT has set aside the decision and remitted the matter back as a whole to the regulator (note, however, that it did not question that the CAT's case management powers extended to giving such directions where the appeal subsisted). Further, the CAT's powers to give directions that the regulator might have given under para 3(2)(d) of Sch 8 do not extend to 'directions' which the regulator could have given to itself by way of the internal

---

[154] eg, in *Argos Ltd and Littlewoods Ltd v OFT*, cases 1014 & 1015/1/11/03, the CAT stayed both cases on 30 July 2003 and remitted to the OFT the decision on which the appeals were founded to permit certain witness evidence to be the subject of an administrative procedure.

[155] CAT's Rules of Procedure, r 19(1) and (2) provides, inter alia, the following case management powers to the CAT: '(1) The Tribunal may at any time, on the request of a party or of its own initiative, at a case management conference, pre-hearing review or otherwise, give such directions as are provided for in paragraph (2) below or such other directions as it thinks fit to secure the just, expeditious and economical conduct of the proceedings.'

[156] [2005] CAT 14.

[157] *Floe Telecom Ltd (in administration) v Ofcom* [2006] EWCA Civ 768.

[158] [2003] CAT 6.

[159] *Aberdeen Journals Ltd v Director General of Fair Trading* [2002] CAT 4.

[160] *Argos Ltd v OFT* [2003] CAT 16.

management of an investigation. In emphatic wording, the Court of Appeal reminded the CAT of the statutory nature and the extent of its jurisdiction—it is worth quoting the judgment extensively to obtain its full flavour:

> The Tribunal, as a statutory body, has the task of deciding such appeals as are brought to it in accordance with the provisions of the 1998 Act and the rules, but it does not have a more general statutory function, of supervising regulators. On that basis it seems to me that the CAT's reasoning is based on a misconception of the relationship between the Tribunal and the regulators. When a decision is set aside and remitted to the relevant regulator, that particular matter is then to be dealt with by that regulator in accordance with its own statutory duties and functions . . . Of course the CAT can properly express its own view as to how urgently the case should be dealt with after remission, just as it may express opinions on other aspects of the consequent re-investigation. But it does not seem to me to be a proper or necessary incident of the power to remit that the CAT should be able to give directions. . .
>
> [T]he CAT has no role in relation to the time taken by a regulator over an initial investigation even if, as in the present case (however exceptional it may be), article 6 applies at that stage. If the complainant considered that Ofcom was guilty of unreasonable delay in pursuing the initial investigation, its remedy would be to apply for judicial review in the Administrative Court. In my judgment that would also be the correct remedy if the complainant considered that the regulator was guilty of unreasonable delay in proceeding with the investigation after remittal by the CAT.[161]

(iii) Make any decision which the OFT could have made

The CAT's broad remedial powers are the natural compliment to its extensive merits review jurisdiction. The logic is readily perceivable: if the CAT is to fully review the regulators' decision, where necessary considering new evidence in this context, it would be wasteful of resources not to provide it with the power, where it finds fault with the regulators' decision, to take a decision itself on the matters before it. This avoids remitting the matter back to the regulator for a second decision, with all the attendants costs associated therewith. The government's intention was that 'wherever possible, we want the tribunal to decide a case on the facts before it, even where there has been a procedural error, and to avoid remitting the case'.[162]   **12.100**

The CAT exercises caution in deciding whether to decide a case itself or remit it to the regulator for further investigation and a fresh decision. It is relatively common for the CAT to substitute its decision for that of the regulator in the   **12.101**

---

[161] *Floe Telecom Ltd (in administration) v Ofcom* [2006] EWCA Civ 768, paras 34 and 45 (Lloyd LJ).
[162] See the Statement in the House of Commons by Nigel Griffiths, Minister for Competition and Consumer Affairs, during the passage of the Competition Bill: *Hansard*, HL Standing Committee G, col 496 (18 June 1998).

context of appeals against penalties.[163] Further, it may, in upholding the regulator's decision, make its own decision on liability which is not necessarily based on the same material that was before the regulator.[164] However, it is more seldom that the CAT will reach a different view to the regulator's on liability, and substitute its own view for the regulators. In *Institute of Independent Insurance Brokers v Director General of Fair Trading*[165] the CAT found (contrary to the OFT) that certain aspects of the General Insurance Standards Council Rules infringed Chapter I, and remitted other aspects of the Rules to the OFT for further investigation. In *JJ Burgess & Sons v OFT*,[166] the CAT, contrary to the OFT, found that Harwood Park and Austins had infringed the Chapter II prohibition. In neither case did it impose a penalty.

12.102 The CAT considered the underlying rationale for its ability to substitute its decision for that of the regulator at some length in *Burgess*. Although it was mindful of the fact that it should not turn itself into a primary decision-maker without good reason, it noted that its merits jurisdiction was wider than judicial review. It noted also the government's intention that, wherever possible, it should decide a case before it. The CAT indicated that its decision whether to make its own decision or remit to the regulator primarily turned on what was necessary to meet the justice of the case, bearing in mind the overriding need for fairness and the need for expedition and saving costs. Three factors that would favour the CAT taking its own decision:

(i)   it has or can obtain all the necessary material;

(ii) the requirements of procedural fairness are respected; and

(iii) the course the Tribunal proposes to take is desirable from the point of view of the need for expedition and saving costs.[167]

12.103 There are clear advantages for the CAT, where it sets aside a regulator's decision, to substitute its own decision on the merits for that of the regulator. Providing it has sufficient materials to hand, and that the rights of the defence are respected (by giving the concerned undertaking a full opportunity to be heard), it is a more efficient way of dealing with appeals. Particularly in view of the small size of the undertakings involved, incurring further costs where these are not necessary would be pointless. However, there are some drawbacks for undertakings: an undertaking which only has the status of an intervener in the context of an appeal may find itself subject to an infringement decision by the CAT. Clearly (as the CAT is aware) there are important Article 6 ECHR issues to bear in mind. In *VIP Communications Ltd v Ofcom*,[168] the intervener, T-Mobile,

---

[163] In *Allsports Ltd v OFT* [2005] CAT 22, the CAT varied the fines imposed on Umbro, JJB, Allsports and Manchester United.

[164] *Napp Pharmaceutical Holdings Ltd v Director General of Fair Trading* [2002] CAT 1.

[165] [2001] CAT 4.   [166] [2005] CAT 25.   [167] ibid, para 132.   [168] [2007] CAT 3.

submitted the CAT had no jurisdiction to substitute, for the regulator's finding of non-infringement, its own finding of infringement. It argued, inter alia, that this would undermine the procedural protection provided by an effective administrative procedure and deprive T-Mobile of a two-tier structure of competition decisions. The CAT firmly rejected this submission. It emphasised that the appeal on the merits jurisdiction gives the intervener at least equivalent rights of defence to those it would have in respect of a Statement of Objection.[169] Further, it will be interesting to consider, as the case law develops, whether the CAT is able, in the context of an appeal, to meet the rigorous standards in decision-making that it has set the regulators. For example, it is not entirely clear whether the CAT met the *Aberdeen Journals* standard for market definition in *Burgess*.

(h) CAT remedies to full merits appeals under the Enterprise Act 2002

Given that the CAT's merits review under the Enterprise Act 2002 is limited to reviewing decisions by the CC imposing penalties on undertakings who have failed to comply with its requests for information, the CAT has been amply provided with remedial powers. Sections 114(5) and 176 of the Enterprise Act 2002 empower the CAT to: **12.104**

- quash the penalty imposed by the CC;
- substitute a penalty of a different nature or of such lesser amount or amounts as it considers appropriate; and
- in certain cases, substitute the date which the CC fixed for the penalty to be paid.

D. Judicial Review before the CAT

In essence, three 'types' of decision may be challenged before the CAT by way of judicial review: commitment decisions under the Competition Act 1998, merger decisions under the Enterprise Act 2002, and market investigation decisions under the Enterprise Act. Although it is not proposed to address appeals from merger decisions (given that mergers fall outside the scope of this book), this section may make reference to certain judgments resulting from challenges to merger decisions. This is for two reasons: first, there are relatively few decisions to date in which the CAT has exercised its 'judicial review' powers; secondly, the approach that the CAT will take in reviewing merger and market investigation challenges is likely to be the same, given that the provisions **12.105**

---

[169] ibid, para 45.

that enable it to hear such challenges from merger and market investigations decisions are near identical.[170]

(a) Which decisions can be appealed to the CAT on judicial review?

(i) Commitment decisions under the Competition Act

12.106 Unlike other decisions that are 'appealable' under the Competition Act 1998, decisions relating to commitments are not subject to the CAT's full merits review jurisdiction on appeal. Instead, the Competition Act provides for the CAT to review certain commitment decisions (but not all) by way of judicial review. The legislator's choice of judicial review reflects the highly discretionary nature of commitment decisions, which involve the regulator making finely balanced evaluations (with resource implications) relating to the benefits of continuing an investigation as opposed to accepting a commitment that meets its competition concerns. Under s 46 of the Competition Act, parties (ie those the subject of the decision) may apply for judicial review of:

- decisions refusing to release commitments pursuant to a request for release;[171] and
- decisions taken by the OFT releasing commitments where it has reasonable grounds for believing that there are no longer competition concerns.

12.107 No appeal lies for parties from a decision to accept commitments. Such an appeal would amount to an abuse of process, as a commitment decision is a two-way process: the decision to accept commitments only arises where the party/ies have voluntarily offered commitments to the regulator. No appeal lies from a refusal to accept commitments, presumably because it is the OFT's prerogative to pursue an investigation to its conclusion—there is no right for an undertaking to avoid a finding of infringement by way of offering a commitment.[172] The legislator's wish to ensure that infringements are investigated, where necessary, to their conclusion is also apparent from the fact that the OFT is not empowered to accept commitments in relation to the most extreme infringements.[173]

12.108 Third parties may appeal from a decision to accept, release, or vary commitments, and a decision refusing to release commitments pursuant to a request made from the person giving the commitments. All of these decisions may potentially, depending on the circumstances, affect third parties. For example, a

---

[170] Enterprise Act 2002, ss 120(1) and 179(1).
[171] Competition Act 1998, s 31A(4)(b)(i).
[172] OFT407, *Enforcement* (December 2004) para 4.25.
[173] See paras 10.29 et seq.

pricing commitment undertaken by a dominant undertaking may, if not released, affect a downstream user of that product.

(ii) Market investigations under the Enterprise Act

Section 179(1) of the Enterprise Act 2002 provides that 'a decision of the OFT, **12.109** the appropriate Minister the Secretary of State or the [Competition] Commission in connection with a reference or possible reference under this Part' may be challenged to the CAT by way of judicial review. This generous wording enables a wide range of decisions relating to market investigations to be challenged before the CAT on judicial review, provided they are connected with a market investigation reference. Clearly, the range of reviewable decisions is broader than just the final decision by the OFT making a reference or the CC making a finding in relation to the market referred. There is scope to review decisions taken in the context of an on-going investigation. In *Stericycle International LLC v CC*,[174] the applicant undertakings challenged an interim measures order and subsequent directions made by the CC with a view to precluding further integration of the merged entities pending the outcome of the Commission's investigation of the merger.

A 'decision' that may be challenged includes a failure to take a decision.[175] The **12.110** CAT has intimated that there may be circumstances in which it would be appropriate to consider whether undue delay on the part of the decision-maker amounts to a de facto failure to take a decision, so that undue delay may be challenged by this route.[176]

(b) Standing

(i) Enterprise Act

Section 179(1) of the Enterprise Act 2002 provides that 'any person aggrieved' **12.111** by a decision of the OFT, CC, or Secretary of State in connection with a market investigation reference or a possible reference may apply to the CAT for a review of that decision.

The origin of the 'person aggrieved' threshold for standing can be traced to **12.112** certain public law remedies. It is currently given a broad interpretation by the administrative courts:

> In several cases the courts had already favoured a generous interpretation of 'person aggrieved' and it is now less likely that these words will be made an obstacle to any person who may reasonably consider himself aggrieved. Judicial statements suggest that they are likely to cover any person who has a genuine grievance of whatever

---

[174] [2006] CAT 21.   [175] Enterprise Act 2002, s 179(2)(b).
[176] *Association of Convenience Stores v OFT* [2005] CAT 36.

kind—and that is tantamount to any person who reasonably wishes to bring proceedings.[177]

12.113 It is unclear to what extent, if at all, this test differs from that of 'sufficient interest'. Administrative law commentators do not seem to consider there is material difference between a 'person aggrieved' and a person with 'sufficient interest', though the matter is yet to be determined by a court.[178]

12.114 The OFT has never, to date, challenged standing of judicial review applicants. Accordingly, the scope of the person aggrieved threshold has not been tested judicially. It appears clear from the CAT's limited case law to date that, a person aggrieved includes third parties such as competitors, downstream users, and associations representing end-use consumers that may be affected by the agreements or conduct.

12.115 In *Association of Convenience Stores v OFT*[179] the Association (supported by Friends of the Earth) sought to review the OFT's decision not to refer the UK market for groceries to the CC. There was no argument on admissibility: the sufficiency of interest of the association, which represented smaller grocery stores that compete with supermarkets, was not contested. In *Federation of Wholesale Distributors v OFT*,[180] the Federation was allowed to review the OFT's approval of an acquisition of 45 convenience stores by Tesco. In *IBA Health Ltd v OFT*,[181] the standing of IBA, the third party appellant, was not contested. IBA was a competitor of the merging parties, and was also party to a distribution agreement with one of the merging parties, and so had a financial interest in the agreement.

(ii) Competition Act

12.116 Under s 47 of the Competition Act 1998, the test for standing is that of 'sufficient interest'. The concept is considered above at paras 12.52 et seq.

(c) Standard of review

(i) The statutory provisions

12.117 Section 179(4) of the Enterprise Act 2002 provides:

> In determining such an application the Competition Appeal Tribunal shall apply *the same principles as would be applied by a court on an application for judicial review.* [emphasis added]

12.118 Schedule 3A(2) to the Competition Act 1998 provides:

---

[177] W Wade and C Forsyth, *Administrative Law* (9th edn, Oxford University Press, 2004) 739.
[178] See also T Ward and K Smith, *Competition Litigation in the UK* (Sweet & Maxwell, 2005) para 4.074.
[179] [2005] CAT 36.   [180] [2004] CAT 11.   [181] [2003] CAT 27.

The Tribunal must, by reference to the grounds of appeal set out in the notice of appeal, determine the appeal by applying *the same principles as would be applied by a court on an application for judicial review.* [emphasis added]

(ii) Application of the principles of judicial review by the CAT

It is not entirely clear what the 'same principles as would be applied by a court on judicial review' entails in real terms, when applied by a specialist competition tribunal such as the CAT. When the Enterprise Bill was debated in Parliament, one area of criticism of this aspect of the Bill was that it was unrealistic to expect a panel of competition experts to withhold examination of the merits of the case before it, and to apply instead the administrative standards of review: **12.119**

> If the Government want a tribunal that is expert in administrative law, they should set one up . . . However, the Government are setting up a Tribunal that is intended to be expert in competition law. At the same time, they are saying that experts in competition law, who understand the economic rationale of decisions by the Competition Commission, will not be able to examine the economic rationale of decisions by the Competition Commission, will not be able to examine the economic merits of the decisions. They must examine them in terms of administrative law . . . It is good if the Government want to have a review of ten remedies, but that should be conducted in line with competition law on its merits rather than as an aspect of trying to mirror judicial review through the courts as part of administrative law.[182]

To some extent this criticism has been borne out in the subsequent case law, which has seen the CAT adopting a high intensity standard of review in the determination of challenges brought to it by way of judicial review. **12.120**

In *IBA Health Ltd v OFT*[183] the CAT first exercised its judicial review jurisdiction. It did so in the context of reviewing the OFT's decision not to refer a merger. As with market investigation challenges, the CAT is required in merger cases to apply the same principles as would be applied by a court in an application for judicial review. The CAT took a broad view of its review powers. It placed emphasis on its specialised nature, which distinguished it from the 'normal situation where a non-specialised court is called upon to review the decision of a specialised decision-maker'.[184] Further, instead of applying the administrative law test of *Wednesbury* unreasonableness, it chose instead to adopt a more generous approach to its review powers: 'the broad question we ask ourselves is whether we are satisfied that the OFT's decision was not erroneous in law, and one which it was reasonably open to the OFT to take, giving the word "reasonably" its ordinary and natural meaning'.[185] **12.121**

---

[182] *Hansard*, HL col 418 (1 May 2002).   [183] [2003] CAT 27.
[184] ibid, para 220.   [185] ibid, para 225.

12.122 The CAT's decision was appealed by the OFT to the Court of Appeal inter alia on the ground that the CAT had not applied the normal principles that would be applied by a court on an application for judicial review. Although the Court of Appeal dismissed the appeal (essentially because it agreed that the CAT's decision to quash the OFT's decision was correct), it discussed the appropriate principles of judicial review at some length.[186] It held that, irrespective of the CAT's special expertise, s 120(4) required the CAT to apply ordinary principles of judicial review. Further, if the CAT had applied the ordinary meaning to the word reasonably, it was wrong to do so.[187]

12.123 Carnwath LJ's judgment goes into detail on the scope and flexibility of the principles of judicial review, emphasising the versatility of the concept of reasonableness and the varying intensity of the review undertaken depending on the issues before the Tribunal. At one end of the spectrum, he identified those cases calling for low intensity review (such as where the issues before the court essentially depended on political judgment), and at the other end decisions infringing human rights where a higher intensity review prevails. Another relevant factor to the intensity of review he emphasised was whether the issue was within the province of the court. The present case (ie the merger reference by the OFT) was not concerned with policy or discretion (which courts are less well equipped to judge)—the test for a merger referral, although cast in subjective terms, essentially called for a factual judgment by the OFT. Accordingly, there was no doubt in Carnwath LJ's view that the CAT was entitled to inquire whether there was adequate material to support the OFT's decision.[188] In Carnwath LJ's view 'the Tribunal did not need to rely on some special dispensation from the ordinary principles of judicial review. Those principles, whether applied by a court or by a specialised Tribunal, are flexible enough to be adapted to the particular statutory context'.[189]

12.124 In *Unichem Ltd v OFT*,[190] the CAT applied the Court of Appeal's guidance. The CAT took its cue from the high-intensity review examples cited in Carnwath LJ's judgment and emphasised that the intensity of review varies according to the statutory context and will depend upon the particular circumstances. It rejected the OFT's submission that it had a wide discretion as to the evaluation of

---

[186] *IBA Health Ltd v OFT* [2004] EWCA Civ 142, [2004] 4 All ER 1103.
[187] ibid, para 61.
[188] Carnwath LJ drew on *Education Secretary v Tameside BC* [1977] AC 1014, 1047 per Lord Wilberforce: 'If a judgment requires, before it can be made, the existence of some facts, then although the evaluation of those facts is for the Secretary of State alone, the court must inquire whether those facts exist, and have been taken into account, whether the judgment has been made upon a proper self-direction as to those facts, whether the judgment has not been made upon other facts which ought not to have been taken into account'. Ibid, para 85.
[189] ibid, para 100.   [190] [2005] CAT 8.

the facts in making a merger reference. In particular, it noted that s 33(1) of the Enterprise Act 2002 placed a duty on the OFT to make a merger reference, and that it was not concerned with policy or political issues, but with an assessment of facts. Accordingly, the test set out by Lord Wilberforce in *Education Secretary v Tameside BC* applied.[191] The first question was whether the OFT had correctly evaluated the primary facts, and the second question was whether it was entitled to draw the conclusion that there was an insufficient likelihood of substantial lessening of competition. The case at issue turned on the first question. The CAT adopted as a starting point for its review: 'Could the decision maker acting reasonably have reached this decision?' In approaching this question in the context at issue the CAT indicated that it had jurisdiction 'to determine whether the OFT's conclusions are adequately supported by evidence, that the facts have been properly found, that all material factual considerations have been taken into account and that material facts have not been omitted'.[192] In reaching its conclusions, the CAT also drew on the ECJ's judgment in *Tetra Laval*[193] which deals with the scope of review that the CFI applies to European Commission merger decisions.[194]

In *Somerfield Plc v CC*[195] and in *Stericycle International LLC v CC*[196] the CAT **12.125** was invited to review decisions by the CC in the context of merger inquiries. In *Somerfield,* the applicant challenged the CC's choice of remedy, whereas in *Stericycle* the challenge was to interim measures adopted by the CC. The CAT refused to embark on an elaborate exercise to determine whether the standard of review should differ in view of the CC's statutory role. In both cases, it adopted as its starting point essentially the same approach it had defined in *Unichem.*[197] In conducting its review, the CAT recognised that the CC enjoyed a clear margin of appreciation in relation to the choice or remedies open to it.[198] Further, in *Somerfield,* it clearly indicated its reluctance to allow the parties to adduce new evidence or to raise points that had not been made in the initial inquiry.[199]

(d) Burden and standard of proof

In the context of challenges by way of judicial review, the burden rests on the **12.126**

---

[191] [1977] AC 1014, 1047.
[192] [2005] CAT 8, para 174.
[193] Case C-12/03 P *Commission v Tetra Laval BV* [2005] ECR I-987
[194] [2005] CAT 8, para 168.   [195] [2006] CAT 4.   [196] [2006] CAT 21.
[197] [2005] CAT 8, paras 174 and 175.   [198] *Somerfield Plc v CC* [2006] CAT 4, para 88.
[199] eg, Somerfield had not objected to the disposal of three stores before the CC. The CAT held (ibid, para 71) that only in exceptional circumstances should Somerfield be permitted to challenge before the CAT a remedy to which it had not objected before the CC. Accordingly, the CAT did not consider those aspects of Somerfield's challenge.

applicant throughout.[200] The burden is the civil burden, ie on the balance of probabilities.

(e) Grounds of review

12.127 The grounds of judicial review are outside of the scope of this book. Essentially, three main grounds of review are relevant in a competition context. First, the decision-maker must act upon the correct interpretation of the law (illegality). Secondly, the decision must fall within the bounds of reasonable judgment (irrationality). Thirdly, the decision must be reached by procedurally fair means (procedural impropriety). These grounds are not exhaustive. For an examination of the grounds of review, readers are referred to textbooks on judicial review.[201]

(f) CAT remedies in judicial review

(i) The statutory provisions

12.128 The Competition Act 1998 and the Enterprise Act 2002 provide for the remedies available to the CAT on judicial review in near-identical terms.

12.129 Paragraph 3A of Sch 8 to the Competition Act empowers the CAT to:

(a) dismiss the appeal or quash the whole or part of the decision to which it relates; and

(b) where it quashes the whole or part of that decision, remit the matter back to the OFT with a direction to reconsider and make a new decision in accordance with the ruling of the Tribunal.

12.130 Section 179(5) of the Enterprise Act 2002 provides that the CAT may:

(a) dismiss the application or quash the whole or part of the decision to which it relates; and

(b) where it quashes the whole or part of that decision refer the matter back to the original decision maker with a direction to reconsider and make a new decision in accordance with the ruling of the Competition Appeal Tribunal.

12.131 The CAT's remedial powers in the context of judicial review are accordingly much narrower than those available when exercising its full merits jurisdiction. They are also narrower than the traditional remedies available in judicial review.

12.132 In *Association of Convenience Stores v OFT*,[202] the CAT briefly considered, obiter,

---

[200] 'It is common ground that the legal onus or burden of proof on an application for judicial review rests on the applicant throughout', *IBA Health Ltd v OFT* [2004] EWCA Civ 142, [2004] 4 All ER 1103, para 54, per Sir Andrew Morritt V-C.

[201] For an analysis of these principles as applied to competition cases, see N Parr, R Finbow and M Hughes, *UK Merger Control, Law and Practice* (2nd edn, Sweet & Maxwell, 2004) Ch 10.

[202] [2005] CAT 36.

whether, in exercising its power to remit a decision, the words 'make a new decision in accordance with the ruling of the Competition Tribunal' empowered the CAT to set a timetable within which the OFT should re-take the decision when the matter was remitted to it. It seemed to consider the wording was sufficiently broad: '[o]ur present view is that in an appropriate case the Tribunal would have power under that provision to set—or at least indicate—a timetable in which the new Decision in question was to be taken in order to ensure justice between the parties'. It is not clear to what extent the CAT would maintain this view since the Court of Appeal gave its judgment in *Floe Telecom*.[203] In *Floe Telecom*, the Court of Appeal placed great emphasis on the statutory nature of the CAT's powers, and took a narrow approach to construing what these powers are. It held that the CAT was not able to set the timetable if it quashed a regulator's decision and decided to remit a case to the regulators exercising the remedial powers available to it under its full merits jurisdiction under the Competition Act (see discussion at paras 12.95–12.97 above). However, there may be another way for frustrated appellants to tackle undue delay in re-taking a decision. The CAT hinted in *Association of Convenience Stores* that a challenge for failure to take a decision could provide a remedy for undue delay.[204]

(g) Fall-back judicial review applications to High Court

As mentioned in *Bettercare*,[205] where there is no statutory provision for appeal to the CAT, appellants may appeal by way of the normal judicial review channel before the administrative division of the High Court. Where an appellant chooses to apply to the administrative court in preference to an existing statutory mechanism of appeal, it is unlikely that the administrative court would entertain the application for judicial review where there is a statutory mechanism for appeal that has not been pursued. In *R (Davies) v Financial Services Authority*,[206] Mummery LJ held: 'the legislative purpose evident from the detailed statutory scheme was that those aggrieved by the decisions and actions of the Authority should have recourse to the special procedures and the specialists tribunal rather than to the general jurisdiction of the Administrative Court'. Given that there is still considerable uncertainty as to whether some decisions rejecting complaints are appealable to the CAT under ss 46 and 47 of the Competition Act 1998, it is difficult for appellants wishing to appeal from those borderline decisions to choose the appropriate route of appeal, particularly in view of the tight time limits that apply before both the CAT and the administrative court.

12.133

---

[203] *Floe Telecom Ltd (in administration) v Ofcom* [2006] EWCA 768.
[204] Enterprise Act 2002, s 179 defines a 'decision' that may be challenged as including a 'failure to take a decision'.
[205] *Bettercare Group Ltd v Director General of Fair Trading* [2002[CAT 6.
[206] [2003] EWCA Civ 1128, [2004] 1 WLR 185.

12.134 With the introduction of Regulation 1/2003, the OFT has acquired an entire range of new decision-making powers. Many decisions, such as decisions to transmit information to the European Competition Network (**ECN**) under Article 12 of Regulation 1/2003,[207] or decisions relating to case allocation taken in the context of the ECN, are not communicated to those affected by the decision. Those that are affected by these decisions do not have an obvious means of recourse against such decisions—there is certainly no statutory mechanism for appeal. It may be that would-be appellants in such a situation will proceed by means of judicial review through the administrative courts. There is precedent to the effect that the right to a fair trial under Article 6 ECHR implies the right to notice of certain decisions, to enable the subjects of the decision access to the courts.[208] Given the importance that European Community case law attributes to the duty to give reasons[209] and the rights of those whose legal position is affected by an administrative act or decision to appeal therefrom,[210] those wishing to raise an appeal have some material to draw upon, to argue that certain of the newer decisions by the UK regulators in the context of the ECN are appealable by way of judicial review.

E. Other Appeals

(a) Director disqualification appeals

12.135 Applications for director disqualification under s 9A of the Company Directors Disqualification Act 1986 in England and Wales are made at the High Court, before the companies court registrar in the Royal Courts of Justice. The CPR Directors Disqualification Practice Direction provides that rr 7.47 and 7.49 of the Insolvency Rules[211] apply to an appeal from a decision made by the court in the course of disqualification proceedings under s 9A of the 1986 Act. Under rr 7.47 and 7.49 appeal lies from the registrar to a single judge of the High Court, and from there, with the leave of that judge or the Court of Appeal, to the Court of Appeal.

12.136 In *Secretary of State for Trade and Industry v Paulin*,[212] Sir Andrew Morritt VC held that first appeals from disqualification orders under the Company Directors Disqualification Act 1986 are 'insolvency proceedings' and, as such, do not require the permission of the lower or appeal court. Accordingly, directors

---

[207] See generally, Chapter 8.
[208] See paras 8.70 et seq above.
[209] Case 222/84 *Johnston v Chief Constable of the RUC* [1986] ECR 1651.
[210] Joined Cases 8–11/66 *Noordwijks Cement Accoord* [1967] ECR 75; Case 17/74 *Transocean Marine Paint Association v Commission* [1974] ECR 1063.
[211] SI 1986/1925, as amended.   [212] [2005] EWHC 888 (Ch), [2005] BCC 927.

who are subject to a director's disqualification order have a right of appeal to a single judge in the High Court in any event.

(b) Cartel appeals

The appeal process will vary depending on the jurisdiction of prosecution and **12.137** whether the cartel offence is tried summarily or by indictment.[213] The appeal process is determined by rules of criminal procedure relating to appeals that lie outside the scope of this book.

(c) Appeal from the CAT's decision

Essentially the same provision is made for appeals from CAT decisions under **12.138** the Competition Act 1998 and under the Enterprise Act 2002.[214] An appeal lies from the CAT's decision on a point of law or, in cases involving penalties under the Competition Act, as to the amount of the penalty (on unlimited grounds). The appeal lies to the Court of Appeal in England and Wales, in Scotland to the Court of Session, or in the case of proceedings in Northern Ireland to the Court of Appeal of Northern Ireland. It is necessary in all cases to obtain either the consent of the CAT or that of the court to which appeal is made.

The CAT's Guide to Proceedings provides that a request to the Tribunal for **12.139** permission to appeal from a decision of the Tribunal may be made orally at any hearing at which the decision is delivered by the Tribunal or in writing to the Registrar within one month of notification of that decision.

---

[213] Enterprise Act 2002, s 190(1).
[214] Competition Act 1998, s 49 and Enterprise Act 2002, ss 120(6)–(8) and 179(6)–(8). Section 49 of the Competition Act provides that an appeal may be made by a party to the proceedings before the CAT or by a person who has sufficient interest in the matter.

13

MARKET INVESTIGATION REFERENCES: MAKING THE REFERENCE

A. Introduction

13.01   The government proposed and adopted the market investigation regime contained in Pt 4 of the Enterprise Act 2002[1] (replacing and modernising the provisions on complex and scale monopolies contained in the Fair Trading Act 1973) on the basis that 'the ability to investigate markets as a whole is an important feature of our competition regime' and that the provisions of the Enterprise Act 'allow broad investigations into markets to see how they are working, what the problems might be, and how to solve them, without necessarily attaching any blame to the participants'.[2]

13.02   The ability of UK competition authorities to investigate markets viewed in their entirety with a view to resolving any problems for the future by imposing prospective remedies complements the more traditional '*ex post*' sanction and deterrent-based competition prohibitions contained in the Competition Act 1998 and in Articles 81 and 82 EC. It provides a flexible tool to address a range of competition problems arising on markets that cannot easily be analysed in a prohibitionist framework. By way of example, a market investigation may resolve the problem of parallel oligopolistic behaviour falling short of actual cooperation, a phenomenon which can still escape the competition prohibitions aimed at concerted anti-competitive behaviour and unilateral abuse of dominance.[3] Further examples of competition problems arising in markets that are better addressed in the context of market investigation references include information asymmetries (where there is inequality in the information held by

---

[1] See Chapter 1 above for a brief overview of the substantive features of the market investigation reference regime. Useful guidance is provided by the CC pursuant to s 171(3) of the Enterprise Act 2002, see *Market Investigation References: Competition Commission Guidelines*, June 2003, see also OFT511, *Market investigation references: Guidance about the making of references under Part 4 of the Enterprise Act* (March 2006).

[2] DTI White Paper, *Productivity and Enterprise: A world class competition regime*, Cm 5233 (2001).

[3] See, eg OFT796, *Personal current account banking services in Northern Ireland: The OFT's reasons for making a reference to the Competition Commission* (May 2005).

the participants at different levels of the market) and regulatory, legal, or other structural barriers to entry.

The market investigation regime has an awkward hybrid nature, cooperative **13.03** and yet also semi-penal in nature. The ethos of the market investigation reference regime is that no single undertaking or individual is 'in the dock', as the focus of the investigation is on the competitive process in the relevant market *as a whole.* However, in practice and in substance the consequences for an undertaking whose conduct is under scrutiny in the context of an investigation into a market can be as serious as if the investigation were carried out under the Competition Act. The Competition Commission (**CC**) is empowered to impose extremely far-reaching behavioural and structural remedies (such as divestiture) on undertakings active in a market at the conclusion of its investigations.[4] Further, now that Article 3(1) of Regulation 1/2003[5] obliges Member State authorities, wherever they apply national competition law provisions to an agreement within Article 81 or to conduct prohibited by Article 82, also to apply Article 81 and/or Article 82 EC (as relevant), an undertaking active in a market that is referred could find that a market reference investigation triggers the application of Article 81 and/or Article 82 to its conduct. The consequences of the procedure should therefore not be underestimated.

The hybrid nature of the market investigation regime can also be seen in its **13.04** procedure. On the one hand, heavy reliance is placed, both in theory and in practice, on voluntary collaboration and communication between the competition authorities and the undertakings active in the markets subject to investigation. On the other hand, should the softly-softly cooperative approach fail to yield results, the Enterprise Act 2002 provides the regulators with mandatory powers to collect information that are reinforced by severe sanctions for undertakings that do not comply.

The market investigation regime consists of two distinct stages. First, the **13.05** Office of Fair Trading (**OFT**) (or the relevant sectoral regulator) undertakes a preliminary investigation. If it considers that the test for reference is met, it makes a reference to the CC. The referral process is dealt with in this chapter. Secondly, on receipt of the reference, the CC investigates the issues referred and reports upon them. Chapter 14 addresses the market investigation process.

---

[4] See further paras 14.63 et seq, below. The Explanatory Notes to the Enterprise Act 2002 provide, at para 133, that the remedies that the CC may impose 'may engage rights under Article 1 of Protocol 1 to the Convention'.

[5] Council Regulation (EC) 1/2003 of 16 December 2002 on the implementation of the rules on competition laid down in Articles 81 and 82 of the Treaty [2003] OJ L1/1.

B. Market Investigation References

13.06 The CC is a specialist second stage investigatory authority. It has no powers to begin investigations of its own initiative and relies on references from other primary investigators in order to undertake its work. It is not able to select and prioritise the investigations it undertakes: it cannot reject references and is under a statutory obligation to investigate and report thereupon within a defined timetable. It is therefore critical, in the absence of the ability to regulate its own work, that those bodies making references to the CC make their selection carefully, on an informed basis, and after applying appropriate selection criteria. Since March 2004, when the OFT made the first market investigation reference to the CC, it has made a further five such references, so that to date the CC has received an average of two references a year from the OFT.[6] No market investigation references have been made as yet by the sectoral regulators.[7]

13.07 Section 131(1) of the Enterprise Act 2002 provides the following power for the OFT to make a reference:

> The OFT may . . . make a reference to the Commission if the OFT has reasonable grounds for suspecting that any feature, or combination of features, of a market in the United Kingdom for goods or services prevents, restricts or distorts competition in connection with the supply or acquisition of any goods or services in the United Kingdom or a part of the United Kingdom.

(a) Who may refer

13.08 The power to refer contained in s 131 is provided to the OFT. However, sectoral regulators are provided with concurrent powers within their regulated sectors by virtue of amendments to the relevant legislation for each sectoral regulator effected by Sch 9, Pt 2 to the Enterprise Act 2002. At time of writing, the following sectoral regulators have concurrent powers: the Office of Communications,[8] the Gas and Electricity Markets Authority,[9] the Civil Aviation Authority,[10]

---

[6] An up-to-date list of market investigation references to date is kept by the CC at <http://www.competition-commission.org.uk/inquiries/reference_type/market.htm>.

[7] Peter Freeman, Chairman of the CC, considered why the sectoral regulators are not making full use of their powers to make references in 'Regulation and Competition: Chalk and Cheese? The role of the Competition Commission', CRI Frontiers of Regulation Conference, Keynote Speech, University of Bath, 7 September 2006.

[8] Communications Act 2003, s 370.

[9] Electricity Act 1989, s 43, as amended by Enterprise Act 2002, Sch 9, para 18, and Gas Act 1986, s 36A, as amended by Enterprise Act 2002, Sch 9, para 17.

[10] Transport Act 2000, s 86, as amended by Enterprise Act 2002, Sch 9, para 23.

the Water Services Regulatory Authority,[11] the Northern Ireland Authority for Energy Regulation,[12] and the Office of Rail Regulation.[13]

Despite the government's intention (on reforming the complex and scale mon- **13.09** opolies provisions contained in the Fair Trading Act 1973) to remove political intervention from the market investigation process,[14] s 132 of the Enterprise Act 2002 contains a reserve power for the Secretary of State (acting singly or jointly with other ministers) to make a reference to the CC. This power is discussed at paras 13.135–13.136 below.

(b) Reasonable grounds for suspecting

The government's intention was to create a flexible reference test which would **13.10** allow the OFT scope for action, and it appears that this has been achieved. OFT guidelines[15] provide that the OFT is not required to reach firm conclusions before making references and it would be inappropriate for it to engage in extensive research. Provided it has reasonable grounds for suspecting that there are market features that adversely affect competition, the reference test has been met. Although the legal and evidential threshold which the OFT has to meet in order to have 'reasonable grounds for suspecting' prior to making a reference has as yet not fully been considered in the case law, the preliminary judicial indications are that the threshold for market investigation references is easily met.[16] In *Association of Convenience Stores v OFT*,[17] the Association challenged an OFT decision not to refer the market for grocery retailing by way of judicial review to the Competition Appeal Tribunal (**CAT**) under s 179 of the Enterprise Act 2002. It requested guidance as to the correct legal interpretation of s 131. Although the appeal was not heard (the decision was quashed by order of the

---

[11] Water Act 2003, s 36 and Water Industry Act 1991, s 31, as amended by Enterprise Act 2002, Sch 9, para 19.

[12] Electricity (Northern Ireland) Order 1992 (SI 1992/231 (NI1)) and Gas (Northern Ireland) Order 1996 (SI 1996/275 (NI 2)) as amended by Enterprise Act 2002, Sch 9, paras 20 and 22.

[13] Railways Act 1993, s 67, as amended by Enterprise Act 2002, Sch 9, para 21.

[14] 'It is one of the Government's principles that competition decisions should be taken by strong, pro-active and independent competition authorities. Under the monopoly provisions, decisions are still taken by Ministers. The Government intends to reform the monopoly provisions—replacing them with a new power to investigate markets—where the overwhelming majority of decisions will be taken by independent competition authorities.' DTI White Paper, *Productivity and Enterprise: A world class competition regime*, Cm 5233 (2001) paras 6.4 and 6.5.

[15] OFT511, *Market investigation references: Guidance about the making of references under Part 4 of the Enterprise Act* (March 2006) para 4.7.

[16] The 'reasonable grounds for suspecting' test is also used in s 25 of the Competition Act 1998. For a discussion of this concept in the context of the Competition Act, see para 6.60, above.

[17] [2005] CAT 36.

CAT at the request of the OFT, which voluntarily undertook to reinvestigate), the initial indication from the CAT, was the threshold for the test is low:

> There is, if we may say so, some risk that one may mistake the height of the hurdle which s.131(1) presents. It is a 'reasonable ground to suspect' test. The scheme of the Act is that a full investigation is carried out at the stage of the CC not at the stage of the OFT, although admittedly the OFT has to address the matter sufficiently to decide whether there are reasonable grounds 'to suspect', and sufficiently in order to consider the question of undertakings under s.154 of the Act in lieu of making a reference.[18]

13.11 In *IBA Health Ltd v OFT*,[19] the Court of Appeal, in considering the test for merger references under the Enterprise Act 2002, made a number of comments that are relevant to construing the 'reasonable grounds for suspecting' test under s 131(1) of the Enterprise Act. The Vice-Chancellor highlighted that both the merger and the market investigation provisions of the Act distinguish between a belief on one hand and a suspicion on the other. In the Vice-Chancellor's judgment (which was the leading judgment) there is a clear hierarchy between these two thresholds: 'Thus [for a belief] some form of mental assent is required as opposed to the less positive frame of mind connoted by a suspicion. As pointed out in the Shorter Oxford Dictionary 3rd Edition a suspicion is but a "slight belief".'[20] Accordingly, providing it has reasonable grounds for its view, it would appear that the OFT need only have a 'slight belief' in order to make a reference.

13.12 After the CAT quashed its first decision dated 3 August 2005 in *Association of Convenience Stores v OFT*,[21] the OFT made a second decision on 9 May 2006, in which it took the view, contrary to its earlier decision, that it should refer the grocery retail market to the CC (*Groceries*).[22] Whilst it is clear that the OFT's change of heart was influenced by additional evidence that it had obtained, it may also have been influenced by the Court of Appeal's and the CAT's above remarks on the reasonable grounds to suspect test. The text of the OFT's reasons for making a reference in *Groceries* is littered with references to the preliminary nature of its analysis. From the very outset the OFT makes its position clear by emphasising that it has not sought to carry out a detailed analysis of competition in the market, nor to reach firm conclusions as to whether competition is being harmed.[23] This is consistent with the OFT's preliminary role as a referral authority.

---

[18] ibid, para 7.   [19] [2004] EWCA Civ 142, [2004] 4 All ER 1103.
[20] ibid, para 44.   [21] [2005] CAT 36.
[22] See OFT845, *The grocery market: The OFT's reasons for making a reference to the Competition Commission* (May 2006). For analysis of this decision, see David Bailey, 'The parable of the supermarkets', Competition Law Insight, 4 July 2006, 13–15 and 1 August 2006, pp 10–11.
[23] OFT845, ibid, para 1.2.

(c) Feature or combination of features of a market in the United Kingdom for goods or services prevents, restricts, or distorts competition

Section 131(1) of the Enterprise Act 2002 requires the OFT to consider **13.13** whether it has reasonable grounds for suspecting that any feature (or combination of features) of the market referred prevents, restricts, or distorts competition in relation to the supply of any goods or services in the United Kingdom or any part of it. This is also known as the adverse effect on competition test (**AEC**).[24] The competition analysis undertaken under the AEC test is considerably more wide-ranging than that required by the behaviour-centric Competition Act prohibitions, Article 81, or Article 82 EC.[25] This is primarily because of the breadth of the concept of a 'feature of the market'.

A feature of the market covers both behavioural and structural issues, and **13.14** includes a diverse range of matters, such as government regulations and information asymmetries. Section 131(2) defines a feature of the market as any of:

(a) the structure of the market concerned or any aspect of that structure;[26]

(b) any conduct (whether or not in the market concerned) of one or more than one person who supplies or acquires goods or services in the market concerned;[27] or

(c) any conduct relating to the market concerned of customers of any person who supplies or acquires goods or services.

The inclusion of non-behavioural elements in the definition of 'feature of the **13.15** market' gives expression to the government's intention that, in addition to direct observable conduct of particular undertakings, indirect indicators of lack of competition (such as high barriers to entry, the cost or difficulty of switching from one supplier to another[28]) should also provide grounds for reference. The Explanatory Notes to the Enterprise Act 2002 provide:

---

[24] Enterprise Act 2002, s 134(4).

[25] See the comments to this effect by Peter Freeman, Chairman of the CC, in 'Regulation and Competition: Chalk and Cheese? The role of the Competition Commission', CRI Frontiers of Regulation Conference, Keynote Speech, University of Bath, 7 September 2006.

[26] eg, in OFT845, *The grocery market: The OFT's reasons for making a reference to the Competition Commission* (May 2006), one of the features of the market giving rise to the reference was the planning system, which was suspected of restricting competition by raising the cost of, and limiting the scope for, new local market entry.

[27] eg, in OFT845, ibid, one of the features of the market giving rise to the reference was the large supermarkets' pricing behaviour. In OFT796, *Personal current account banking services in Northern Ireland: The OFT's reasons for making a reference to the Competition Commission* (May 2005), one of the features of the market was customer inertia.

[28] The difficulty of switching was one of the features that led to a reference in OFT769, *Home Credit: The OFT's reasons for making a reference to the Competition Commission* (January 2005).

In considering whether it has reasonable grounds to suspect that features of a market are preventing, restricting or distorting competition, the OFT will have to evaluate the evidence available to it in each case. In some cases, it will be possible for a reference decision to be justified wholly or partly on the basis of indirect evidence, such as the prevailing levels of prices charged for goods or services in a market, or the prevailing levels of profitability or productivity of firms operating in that market (particularly when observed over time, or when compared to another market, in the UK or elsewhere, for similar or related products).

13.16 The three categories of features identified in s 131(2) are loose and not mutually exclusive—certain features may be considered both 'structural' and 'conduct'.[29] There is no need for the OFT to identify whether the feature falls exclusively under any of (a), (b), or (c), as the Explanatory Notes to the Enterprise Act 2002 explain:

In some cases, it will be open to debate whether a given feature of a market is structural or an aspect of conduct (for example, information asymmetries and barriers to entry arising from the behaviour of incumbents could equally well belong in either category). However in indicating the range of features of a market which the competition authorities may take into account, the separate references to structure and conduct in section 131 do not require either the OFT under section 131 or the CC under section 134 to identify particular features of markets that are the subject of a reference as falling entirely within the terms of one of subsections (a), (b) or (c) to the exclusion of the others.[30]

13.17 The breadth of s 131(1) would appear to allow the OFT to consider the effects of the various features in the round. The features that are identified may give rise to a reference by reason of their interaction: for example in *Groceries*, the OFT indicated that the potential concerns with respect to each of the features identified were interlinked.[31]

13.18 Turning to 'prevents, restricts or distorts competition', this language echoes that of Chapter I of the Competition Act 1998 and Article 81 EC and also that of the Fair Trading Act 1973. The substantive concept is well defined in both national and European competition law.[32] The OFT market investigation reference guidance states '[t]he past practice of the CC and EC case law both

---

[29] See OFT511, *Market investigation references: Guidance about the making of references under Part 4 of the Enterprise Act* (March 2006) para 1.9, which provides a further example of a feature that may be viewed as both structural and conduct related: a firm's supply contracts or distribution arrangements (a matter of conduct) may add to entry barriers in a market (a structural feature).

[30] Explanatory Notes to the Enterprise Act 2002, para 302.

[31] OFT845, *The grocery market: The OFT's reasons for making a reference to the Competition Commission* (May 2006), para 8.4.

[32] For a brief discussion of the concept see Chapter 1 above. For more detailed analysis see R Whish, *Competition Law* (5th edn, Butterworths, 2003) Ch 11; *Bellamy & Child: European Community Law of Competition* (5th edn, Sweet & Maxwell, 2001) paras 2.056 et seq.

indicate that the phrase should be interpreted broadly to encompass any reduction or dampening of actual or potential competition'.[33]

(d) In connection with the supply or acquisition of any goods or services in the United Kingdom or a part of the United Kingdom

In making a market investigation reference, the OFT must identify the goods or **13.19** services at issue. OFT guidance indicates that this will require some consideration of the definition of the relevant market.[34] The geographic market can be broader than the United Kingdom, as long as it includes the United Kingdom or a part of it.[35] OFT guidance on market investigation references explains[36] that, conceptually, its approach to market definition in this context will be the same as in other competition cases (see paras 1.77–1.81 for a discussion of the OFT's approach to market definition). However, the OFT does not need to have defined the exact geographic and product market, provided it has formed an initial view of the market.[37]

C. Investigation Powers

Within the OFT, market investigation references are dealt with not by the **13.20** Competition Enforcement Division, but by the Markets and Policy Initiatives Division (**MPI**). This is consistent with the non-punitive nature of market investigation references.

Prior to making a reference, the OFT will carry out a preliminary investigation **13.21** in order to determine whether the criteria for reference are satisfied. This preliminary investigation usually takes the shape of a short market study carried out under s 5 of the Enterprise Act 2002.[38] However, market investigations references can also be made following a super-complaint made to the OFT

---

[33] OFT511, *Market investigation references: Guidance about the making of references under Part 4 of the Enterprise Act* (March 2006) para 4.2.

[34] ibid, para 4.8.

[35] Enterprise Act 2002, s 131(6).

[36] OFT511, *Market investigation references: Guidance about the making of references under Part 4 of the Enterprise Act* (March 2006) para 4.9.

[37] OFT706, *Store Cards: Report of the OFT's inquiry* (March 2004) at para 4.41: 'In the case of action under Chapter II of the Competition Act, a firm conclusion on the definition of the relevant market must clearly be reached. In the case of a reference to the CC, however, the OFT need come only to a preliminary view as to the definition of the market: it is then for the Commission to reach a firm conclusion.' See also OFT845, *The grocery market: The OFT's reasons for making a reference to the Competition Commission* (May 2006) para 2.1.

[38] Enterprise Act 2002, s 5 applies to the OFT only, although concurrent regulators have powers under sectoral legislations that enable similar pro-active research to be undertaken.

under s 11 of the Enterprise Act, following an initial investigation commenced by the OFT under the Competition Act 1998 or following the exercise of the OFT's powers of investigation for market investigation references under s 174 of the Enterprise Act. Each of these possible routes to making a reference is discussed in turn below.

(a) Market studies

13.22 Market studies are general exploratory studies undertaken by the OFT (usually under s 5 of the Enterprise Act 2002) into markets that do not appear to be working well but in respect of which it is not immediately apparent what action is appropriate.[39] Although sectoral regulators do not have concurrent powers under s 5, in effect they have similar powers in the sectors they regulate as part of their general regulatory powers.[40]

13.23 The OFT conducts general market studies in order to identify whether perceived problems in the markets concerned should be addressed through any of its functions. One of the many possible outcomes[41] of a market study is that the OFT will make a market investigation reference to the CC, for example *Store Cards*.[42]

13.24 There are two types of market study, both of which may, depending on the circumstances, lead to a reference—a short study lasting three to six months (for example, the Public Sector Procurement study[43]) and a full study (approximately one year) (for example, Private Dentistry[44]).

13.25 The OFT aims, where practicable, to avoid waiting until the end of a full study before deciding on a market investigation reference to the CC, as it is conscious

---

[39] See Chapter 1 for an outline of the procedure relating to market studies.

[40] eg, s 69 of the Railways Act 1993 provides that ORR must, so far as it appears practicable from time to time, keep under review the provision of railway services. For guidance on its approach, see ORR publication, *ORR's approach to reviewing markets* (April 2006). See generally Department of Trade and Industry and HM Treasury, *Concurrent competition powers in sectoral regulation* (May 2006).

[41] OFT519, *Market studies: Guidance on the OFT approach* (November 2004) lists the following possible outcomes of a study: giving the market a clean bill of health; publishing information to help consumers; encouraging firms to take voluntary action; encouraging a consumer code of practice; making recommendations to the government or sector regulators; investigation and enforcement action against companies suspected of breaching consumer law or competition law.

[42] OFT706, *Store Cards: Report of the OFT's inquiry* (March 2004).

[43] OFT press release 16/04, 'OFT to review public sector procurement', 5 February 2004.

[44] OFT630, *The private dentistry market in the UK* (March 2003). This super-complaint was made before s 11of the Enterprise Act 2002 came into operation but was treated by the OFT as if s 11 had taken effect. The market study was carried out under the now-repealed s 2 of the Fair Trading Act 1973, which empowered the then Director General of Fair Trading to keep markets under review and collate information thereto.

that such an investigation is lengthy and has consequences in terms of resources and continuing uncertainties for those concerned.[45] The CAT's approach to delay in *Association of Convenience Stores v OFT* should reinforce this intention. In that case, the OFT indicated it wished to take eighth months to reconsider a market investigation reference decision quashed by the CAT. The CAT demonstrated it was prepared to take a firm line as regards undue delay:

> If we may say so the competition authorities must equip themselves in a way that enables them to address the kinds of issues that arise in a case like this within a reasonable timescale. Our present view is that the indicative timescale [8 months] we have been told of this afternoon is not a reasonable timescale in which to reach the preliminary decision envisaged by s.131.[46]

The OFT has no express investigatory powers to carry out market studies. **13.26** There is no obligation on those consulted to provide the information requested. There are no sanctions for failure to comply or for providing misleading information. It relies on its informal fact-finding powers such as consulting consumers, competitors and undertakings operating in the market concerned. For example, as part of the *Store Cards* market study, the OFT commissioned a mystery shopping exercise which comprised 763 mystery shopping visits across Great Britain covering all the main retailers who operate a store card scheme. It also commissioned a consumer survey of a representative sample of 550 consumers. Great importance was attached to the result of both these exercises.[47] In *Private Dentistry*, the OFT consulted widely with dental professionals and key organisations including the General Dental Council, trade and professional organisations, and consumer groups. It also carried out surveys of 2,000 consumers and 2,200 dental practices, undertook a 'mystery shop' of 750 dental practices, commissioned a report on the evaluation of the role of clinical decision-making in the need and demand for dentistry, and undertook an international study looking at how markets for dental services operate in some other countries.[48] These market studies reveal that considerable amounts of information are available to the OFT without any need for it to exercise formal fact-finding powers.[49]

---

[45] OFT519, *Market studies: Guidance on the OFT approach* (November 2004) para 3.18.
[46] *Association of Convenience Stores v OFT* [2005] CAT 36, para 8.
[47] OFT706, *Store Cards: Report of the OFT's inquiry* (March 2004) paras 4.13, 4.15, 4.17, 4.18, 4.19, and 5.3.
[48] OFT630, *The private dentistry market in the UK* (March 2003) paras 1.3 and 2.4.
[49] OFT706, *Store Cards: Report of the OFT's inquiry* (March 2004).

(b) Super-complaints

13.27 Super-complaints under s 11 of the Enterprise Act 2002 are made by designated consumer bodies to the OFT or sectoral regulators[50] where a feature or features of a market allegedly result in 'significant harm to consumers'.[51] Within 90 days, the OFT is required to publish a considered response to a super-complaint, setting out what action, if any, it proposes to take under its competition or consumer powers.[52]

13.28 After the 90 day period available to the OFT to consider a super-complaint, it may decide that a market study is an appropriate response.[53]

13.29 Alternatively, the OFT may, if it considers that the test for reference is met without the need to obtain additional information, make a market investigation reference at the end of the 90 day period in which it has considered the super-complaint, without launching a market study beforehand.[54] For example, in both its Response to the super-complaint on personal current account banking[55] and in its Response to the super-complaint on home credit,[56] the OFT found, after consultation with interested parties during the 90 day period available to it, that the test for a market investigation reference to the CC under s 131 of the Enterprise Act 2002 was satisfied and that (bearing in mind the CC's broader remedial powers) a market study by the OFT would not be a sufficient response to the complaint. Accordingly, the OFT response to these super-complaints consisted of launching a consultation paper about its proposed market investigation reference under s 169 of the Enterprise Act.

13.30 No formal investigatory powers are provided to the OFT to collect information in the 90 day period available to it before responding to a super-complaint. As with market studies, the OFT relies on informal powers to gather information.

(c) Competition cases started under the Competition Act

13.31 Some market investigation references will arise out of investigatory work initially carried out by the Competition Enforcement Division of the OFT

---

[50] In 2003, the ability to receive super-complaints was extended to the concurrent regulators (see Enterprise Act 2002, s 205 and Enterprise Act (Super-complaints to Regulators) Order 2003 (SI 2003/1368)).

[51] See Chapter 1 for a brief overview of super-complaints.

[52] Enterprise Act 2002, s 11(2).

[53] eg, OFT825, *Response to the super-complaint on payment protection insurance made by Citizens Advice* (December 2005).

[54] OFT514, *Super-complaints: guidance for designated consumer bodies* (July 2003) para 25.

[55] OFT771a, *Response to the super-complaint on personal current account banking in Northern Ireland made by Which? and the General Consumer Council for Northern Ireland* (February 2005).

[56] OFT747a, *Response to the super-complaint on home credit made by the National Consumer Council* (September 2004).

under the Competition Act 1998. After an initial review of a case, if the Enforcement Division decides that no Chapter I, Chapter II, Article 81, or Article 82 issue arises, but some competition concerns remain, it may pass the case to MPI for further consideration. For example, in one case the OFT concluded that there were no grounds for action under the Chapter II prohibition of the Competition Act regarding pricing policies in the online property search sector and rejected a complaint alleging abuse of a dominant position made by one of three online providers of property conveyance services about a competitor.[57] However, despite rejecting the complaint under the Competition Act, the OFT indicated that as a whole the market required further in-depth study, and a market study into the property search market was launched on 8 December 2004.[58]

The background work carried out under the Competition Act in relation to **13.32** such cases may mean that it is not necessary for MPI to undertake a separate market study before deciding to make a market investigation reference. The OFT states in its guidance on market investigation references[59] that it is able to use information obtained under the Competition Act towards making a market investigation reference.

Of course, the use of the investigatory powers under the Competition Act in **13.33** the first instance must have been legitimate—both bona fide and with the requisite level of suspicion relating to possible infringements of the Competition Act required under s 25 of the Act.[60] It is therefore not open to the OFT to use powers of investigation provided to it under the Competition Act for the sole or predominant purpose of obtaining information for a market investigation reference. This is acknowledged by the OFT in guidance, which states 'the OFT will use its powers of investigation in good faith and will not use powers available under one piece of legislation if it has already decided to proceed under another'.[61] The possible constraints on the OFT's ability to use information collected under the Competition Act towards another purpose (such as making a market investigation reference) are discussed below at para 13.39.

---

[57] OFT press release 130/04, 'Online property search companies not anti-competitive', 19 August 2004.

[58] OFT press release 201/04, 'New study into property search market', 8 December 2004.

[59] OFT511, *Market investigation references: Guidance about the making of references under Part 4 of the Enterprise Act* (March 2006) para 3.4.

[60] On investigative powers under the Competition Act 1998, see further Chapter 7; on s 25 of the Competition Act, see paras 6.59 et seq.

[61] OFT511, *Market investigation references: Guidance about the making of references under Part 4 of the Enterprise Act* (March 2006) para 3.5.

(d) Section 174 of the Enterprise Act

13.34 Section 174 of the Enterprise Act 2002 provides the OFT with formal investigative powers relating to market investigation references. Provided the OFT already believes that it has power to make a market investigation reference (or to accept an undertaking in lieu thereof), it may exercise the investigative powers provided in s 174 for the purpose of assisting it in coming to a decision. Under s 174, the OFT may give notice to any person requiring that person:

- to attend at a time and place specified in order to give evidence;
- to produce specified documents;
- to supply to the OFT such estimates, forecasts, returns, or other information as may be specified.

13.35 It may seem surprising that the threshold for the use of these investigative powers is the same as that for making a reference. However, the threshold for making a reference under s 131(1) of the Enterprise Act 2002 is itself more akin to a threshold for the use of investigatory powers: it suffices that the OFT should have 'reasonable grounds for suspecting' (see paras 13.10–13.12 above). A similar threshold of 'reasonable grounds for suspecting' is also contained in s 25 of the Competition Act 1998 for the OFT to use investigative powers in relation to suspected breaches of Chapter I, Chapter II, Article 81, and/or Article 82.

13.36 The OFT has not frequently exercised its powers under s 174 before making a market investigation reference, relying instead on the informal powers described above. It has even indicated[62] that it is unlikely to summon parties to give evidence.

13.37 Although these powers may be used infrequently, they carry a certain weight: non-compliance with a request made under s 174 gives rise to criminal penalties. Under s 175 of the Enterprise Act, a person commits an offence where he or she intentionally fails to comply with a notice or he or she intentionally alters, suppresses or destroys documents that he or she has been required to produce. The punishment for either of these offences may be a fine up to the statutory maximum and/or imprisonment of up to two years. Section 175 also provides that it is an offence for a person intentionally to obstruct or delay the OFT or any person in carrying out their investigative functions under s 174, although this offence is punishable by fine only.

---

[62] ibid, para 3.3.

(e) Use and onward disclosure of information provided to the OFT

(i) Information provided on a voluntary basis

Undertakings that are consulted by the OFT and receive a request to provide **13.38** information on a voluntary basis will want to bear in mind the open ended nature of market studies and super-complaints. At the conclusion of either, it is open to the OFT to exercise a number of statutory powers, including commencing formal Chapter I, Chapter II, Article 81, or Article 82 investigations under the Competition Act or making a market reference. There is a priori nothing to prevent information voluntarily provided to the OFT for a market study from subsequently being relied upon in evidence against the undertaking providing the information, both by the OFT and the CC in the context of such subsequent proceedings. Indeed, the OFT may even transmit the information to other authorities.[63] Undertakings providing information to the OFT are taken to be aware of the range of subsequent uses to which its information may be put. It is therefore essential that undertakings providing the information consider carefully the implications of the release of such information to the regulator and that, where necessary, confidentiality and other restrictions on the use the OFT may make of such information are put in place. Confidentiality and other such restrictions have their limitations: even where an undertaking imposes certain restrictions on the usage that may be made of the information it has provided, the OFT need only make a second request for the same information using its compulsory powers under s 174 of the Enterprise Act 2002 or under the Competition Act 1998 to re-obtain the information and make such use of it as it wishes.[64]

(ii) Information provided to the OFT pursuant to compulsion under the Competition Act

As regards information that has been provided to the OFT pursuant to its **13.39** compulsory powers under the Competition Act 1998, the OFT is confident that it is able to use information collected under the Act towards making a market investigation reference. Its guidance on market investigation references provides that:

> Where the OFT is considering a reference to the CC following a CA98 investigation in which it used its powers under that Act, the information it has obtained

---

[63] Enterprise Act 2002, s 241(3) permits certain onwards disclosure to other domestic authorities to facilitate those authorities' exercise of certain statutory functions, and s 237(6) together with Art 12 of Regulation 1/2003 permit onward disclosure of such information to the European Commission and the national competition authorities that are part of the European Competition Network. See Chapter 8 for a general discussion of these provisions.

[64] Case C-238/99 P *Limburgse Vinyl Maatschappij v Commission* [2002] ECR I-8375, paras 301–6.

from the earlier investigation may be used as a basis for making a reference. Conversely, when the OFT has used its investigatory powers under the Act but subsequently decides to proceed by means of a CA98 investigation rather than by a reference to the CC, the information it has obtained under Enterprise Act powers can be used for the purposes of the CA98 investigation.[65]

13.40 There is no statutory restriction preventing the OFT from making further use of information lawfully obtained for one purpose, such as an investigation conducted under the Competition Act, in the context of another investigation (for example, a market investigation reference). In the absence of any provision expressly authorising multiple use of the information, it is arguable that to permit the use of information collected in one set of proceedings towards other proceedings could be said to undermine the rights of the defence by removing the defendant undertaking's opportunity to oppose the disclosure of the information with knowledge of the charge made against it.[66] It could also amount to a breach of the undertaking's rights under Article 8 ECHR, one of which is to non-interference with correspondence, except in accordance with law. In *R v Brady*,[67] the Court of Appeal acknowledged that the public interest required that information obtained under compulsion should only be used for the purposes for which it was obtained.

13.41 However, such arguments are difficult in view of the relevant statutory context. The Enterprise Act 2002 expressly authorises public authorities to *disclose* information received or collected in one context to facilitate the exercise of **any** statutory function (not necessarily in the same context, therefore). It is implicit from s 241(1) of the Act, which permits *disclosure* of specified information for the purpose of exercising any other statutory function, that the authorities have the ability to make lesser use (falling short of disclosure) of the information in their possession and that the lack of statutory restriction thereon is deliberate. In practice, reliance by the OFT on evidence or information obtained under the Competition Act 1998 in a (published) market investigation reference amounts to disclosure of specified information to facilitate the exercise of the OFT's market investigation reference functions, as expressly authorised by s 241(1).[68]

13.42 This statutory context, and the fact that the OFT has clearly signalled its intention to use information provided to it in this manner, would seem to suggest that it is difficult to mount an argument based on the rights of the defence and

---

[65] OFT511, *Market investigation references: Guidance about the making of references under Part 4 of the Enterprise Act* (March 2006) para 3.4.

[66] The argument could draw on EC case law on fundamental rights of the defence, see Case 85/87 *Dow Benelux NV v Commission* [1989] ECR 3137; Case C-67/91 *Dirección General de Defensa de la Competencia v Asociación Española de Banca Privada* [1992] ECR I-4785.

[67] [2004] EWCA Crim 1763, [2004] 1 WLR 3240.

[68] The power to disclose is not entirely unfettered, see Enterprise Act 2002, s 244.

non-interference with correspondence arising under Article 8 ECHR. In *R v Brady*[69] the Court of Appeal readily inferred, as against the interest that information should only be used for the purposes for which it was obtained, that those providing information to authorities should be taken to be aware of the wide uses to which it may be put. Similar arguments can be made, drawing on the relevant statutory context, to justify the interference with correspondence as one that is 'in accordance with law' for the purposes of Article 8 ECHR.[70] The balance of opinion therefore clearly favours the OFT's view, namely that the OFT can use information collected under the Competition Act towards a market investigation reference.[71]

However, domestic law does not entirely determine the issue: it is subject to any **13.43** overriding provisions of Community law.[72] Even in those cases where a matter is investigated entirely under Chapter I and Chapter II, the general principles of Community law will take effect by virtue of s 60 of the Competition Act 1998.[73]

Certain arguments could be made on the basis of Community law to restrict the **13.44** OFT's ability to use information under the Competition Act investigation towards another purpose. These are discussed at paras 8.227–8.229.

(iii) Information obtained by the OFT through the ECN

Article 12(2) of Regulation 1/2003 provides that information exchanged shall **13.45** only be used in evidence for the purpose of applying Article 81 or Article 82 by the receiving authority (and in respect of the subject matter for which it was collected by the transmitting authority[74]). The OFT is therefore not able to use network information as evidence towards making a reference under national competition law, although it is not excluded that network information may be used as intelligence to prompt the OFT to collect information in respect of a particular market.[75]

Although Article 12(2) exceptionally permits the reliance upon European **13.46** Competition Network (**ECN**) information by national competition authorities in applying their national competition law, none of the pre-conditions for usage

---

[69] [2004] EWCA Crim 1763, [2004] 1 WLR 3240, discussed at paras 8.67 and 8.72 above.

[70] *R (Kent Pharmaceuticals) v Director of Serious Fraud Office* [2004] EWCA Civ 1494, [2005] 1 WLR 1302, discussed at paras 8.65 and 8.70–8.71 above.

[71] See, for further discussion, para 8.228 above. See also R Nazzini, *Concurrent Proceedings in Competition Law* (Oxford University Press, 2004) 222.

[72] See paras 3.03 et seq above for a discussion of the supremacy of European law.

[73] On s 60 of the Competition Act 1998, see paras 3.94 et seq above.

[74] For a discussion of what amounts to the same subject matter for the purposes of Art 12, see Chapter 8.

[75] On the use of information received through the network as intelligence in the context of domestic law investigations more generally, see Chapter 8.

of such information (namely that national competition law should be applied at the same time and for the same case and should not lead to a different outcome as the Article 81/Article 82 case[76]) are satisfied in the context of a market investigation reference by the OFT.

(iv) Disclosure of information between the OFT and the CC

13.47   As the market investigation regime involves several authorities, it is clear that there has to be a certain amount of information exchange between the authorities for the system to work effectively. Chapter 8 considers issues relating to information exchange in some depth. What follows below is a brief examination of some the issues as they arise in the context of market investigations.

13.48   **OFT disclosure to CC**   The OFT is obliged under s 170 of the Enterprise Act 2002 to pass to the CC such information that it has in its possession that the CC may reasonably require to carry out the market investigation reference or that would in the OFT's opinion be appropriate to give to the CC for the purpose of assisting it in carrying out its functions.

13.49   Section 241(3) of the Enterprise Act 2002 expressly permits disclosure of information collected by the OFT to the CC to facilitate the exercise by the CC of any function it has under the Enterprise Act, the Competition Act 1998, and a number of other enactments.[77]

13.50   However, the OFT will not, under Article 28(2) of Regulation 1/2003 (which takes precedence over any conflicting provision of national law), be able to transmit to the CC any information it has received from the ECN, as the CC is not a member of the ECN.[78] Further, as mentioned above in respect of the OFT's ability to use information collected under the Competition Act in relation to market investigation references, certain arguments can be made on the basis of Community law to restrict the OFT's ability to transmit to the CC information it has itself collected in the course of an investigation conducted under the Competition Act, for the CC to use towards another purpose.[79]

13.51   **CC disclosure to OFT**   Section 241(1) of the Enterprise Act 2002 empowers public authorities (such as the CC) which hold specified information[80] to disclose that information for the purpose of facilitating the exercise by the

---

[76] For further discussion as to the circumstances in which a national competition authority is able to use network information in the application of national competition law, see Chapter 8 paras 8.162 et seq.

[77] See Enterprise Act 2002, Sch 15.   [78] See paras 13.69 below.

[79] See paras 8.227–8.229 above.

[80] Specified information includes, inter alia, information obtained under Enterprise Act 2002, Pt 4, see s 238 of the Act.

disclosing authority of any function it has under or by virtue of the Enterprise Act 2002 (or any other enactment) and even[81] to facilitate the exercise by the recipient authority of any function it has under the Enterprise Act 2002, the Competition Act 1998, and a number of other enactments.[82] Accordingly, should the CC need to transmit information to the OFT—for example where it 'remits' potential Article 81 agreements to the OFT—it is able to transmit the information related thereto to facilitate the OFT in exercising its functions.

D. Interaction of the Market Investigation Regime with Articles 81 and 82

Article 81 and 82 EC are relevant to market investigations in two ways. First, **13.52** since 1 May 2004, Article 3(1) of Regulation 1/2003 obliges national competition authorities, wherever they apply national competition law to agreements within the meaning of Article 81(1) or to abuses prohibited by Article 82, also to apply Articles 81 and 82 (as relevant).[83] Whenever a market investigation is initiated, the question therefore arises whether Article 81 and/or Article 82 should also be applied. Secondly, general principles of EC law oblige national courts and competition authorities to apply domestic competition law in a manner that is consistent with European competition law.[84] Article 3(2) of Regulation 1/2003 has extended this obligation of consistency by precluding the application of stricter national competition law to agreements that do not breach Article 81 EC. This section begins by examining how Article 81 and Article 82 issues arise in the context of a market investigation reference. It then considers when the obligation to apply Articles 81 and 82 is triggered, before looking at how the obligation to apply Article 81 or 82 will be accommodated in theory and in practice.

(a) The extent of the overlap

The OFT's guidance[85] indicates that market investigation references giving **13.53** rise to Article 81 issues should be rare: this is because one of the key factors to which the OFT has regard before exercising its discretion to make a market investigation reference to the CC, is whether it would not be more appropriate

---

[81] ibid, s 241(3).   [82] See ibid, Sch 15 for a list of enactments.
[83] See paras 3.49 et seq for a discussion of the obligation under Art 3(1) generally.
[84] Case 14/68 *Wilhelm v Bundeskartellamt* [1969] ECR 1.
[85] OFT511, *Market investigation references: Guidance about the making of references under Part 4 of the Enterprise Act* (March 2006) para 2.14.

to act under the Competition Act 1998. The intention is that those cases giving rise to Article 81 and Article 82 issues (and indeed to Chapter I/Chapter II issues) will be filtered out so that they can be addressed by the OFT under the Competition Act.

13.54   The implication arising from OFT and CC guidance on this issue is that, because the OFT will not refer cases best dealt with under the Competition Act, market investigations will not frequently give rise to an obligation to apply Article 81 or Article 82. This view is based on the assumption that '[m]arket investigations are concerned with something different from particular anticompetitive agreements or abuses of dominance. Their purpose is to determined whether the process of competition is working effectively in markets as a whole.'[86] However, in practice the Competition Act and market investigation regimes do not operate in mutually exclusive spheres. Anticompetitive conduct or agreements can form part of the reasons leading to a market investigation reference, given that 'features' that may prevent competition for the purposes of s 131 include behavioural issues (see para 13.14 above). The ORR's guidance clearly illustrates this point, in providing that 'if the anti-competitive conduct of a single firm or a number of firms is associated with structural features, it may still be appropriate to make a reference to the CC'.[87]

13.55   Where the OFT refers a market to the CC, the markets referred may therefore also contain agreements falling within the meaning of Article 81 or conduct prohibited by Article 82. As the (then) Deputy Chairman of the CC, Peter Freeman stated: 'A market . . . under investigation by the Competition Commission may well be characterized by agreements and abuses of a dominant position that are subject to EC competition law.'[88] This is particularly the case given the generous approach adopted by the jurisprudence of the European Court of Justice (**ECJ**) on the jurisdictional criterion of effect on interstate trade.[89] The broad definition of interstate trade may give rise to difficulties for the OFT in maintaining its stated policy of filtering out all cases that give rise to Article 81 and Article 82 issues as unsuitable for reference.[90] To date, despite the relative novelty of the market investigation regime and of Regulation 1/2003, several references to the CC have already included potential Article 81 and Article 82 concerns. For example:

---

[86] ibid, para 2.2.   [87] *ORR's approach to reviewing markets* (April 2006) para 2.7.

[88] P Freeman, Lord Fletcher Lecture, 15 March 2005, p 12, available from the CC website.

[89] Effect on trade between Member States is the jurisdictional criterion which determines whether or not Art 81 or Art 82 is applicable: see paras 1.38 et seq above.

[90] Michael Rowe, *Store Cards: due credit to modernisation?* Practical Law Company (PLC) Competition, 6 April 2004.

- The *Store Cards*[91] reference raised inter alia the competition issues that were associated with a network of vertical agreements between credit providers and retailers. These were 'agreements' within the meaning of Article 81 which were likely to satisfy the effect on trade test.[92] Both the OFT reference and the CC's Final Report[93] refer to the obligation not to reach a result that would be incompatible with Article 3(2) of Regulation 1/2003, but no mention is made of the obligation to *apply* Article 81 wherever national competition law is applied to agreements within the meaning of Article 81(1).

- In *Classified directory advertising services*,[94] the OFT made a reference relating to the market in directory advertising services, in which the largest supplier (Yell), held a position of strength on the market (an extremely high market share[95] on a market with significant barriers to entry) that would most likely amount to dominance for the purpose of Article 82 EC. Further, the OFT's concerns centred primarily on the pricing policies and profitability of the leading suppliers.

- In *Personal current account banking services in Northern Ireland*,[96] the OFT identified, amongst other factors, clear evidence of parallel pricing among four undertakings (with one identified price leader) and lack of price competition between them as features leading to the reference.

Notwithstanding the OFT's best endeavours, references will in some cases **13.56** necessarily include agreements and/or conduct that may affect trade between Member States. The question as to what, if any, obligation there is under Article 3(1) of Regulation 1/2003 to apply Article 81 and Article 82 in these circumstances is therefore of some importance.

(b) Is the obligation triggered?

In order to determine whether a market investigation triggers the obligation to **13.57** apply Article 81 and Article 82 under Regulation 1/2003, several preliminary questions must be answered. First, can the market investigation provisions be considered as the application of national competition law for the purposes of

---

[91] OFT706, *Store Cards: Report of the OFT's inquiry* (March 2004).
[92] In this respect, a parallel can be drawn with other network agreement cases under Art 81 EC, such as Case C-234/89 *Delimitis v Henninger Brau AG* [1991] ECR I-935.
[93] *Store cards market investigation*, 7 March 2006, para 10.9.
[94] OFT787, *Classified directory advertising services: The OFT's reasons for making a reference to the Competition Commission* (April 2005).
[95] The OFT indicates that the market shares are much the same as those reported by the Monopolies and Mergers Commission in 1996, in which it found that Yell's predecessor had an 84% market share, and Thomson had 14%.
[96] OFT796, *Personal current account banking services in Northern Ireland: The OFT's reasons for making a reference to the Competition Commission* (May 2005).

Article 3(1)? If yes, at what stage of the lengthy market investigation process is national competition law 'applied'?

(i) National competition law

13.58 This question is uncontroversial: both the OFT and the CC acknowledge that market investigation references are national competition law[97] (for discussion of this issue, refer to paras 3.17–3.20 above). Accordingly, wherever market investigation provisions are 'applied' to an agreement within the meaning of Article 81(1), or to an abuse of dominance prohibited by Article 82, Article 3(1) of Regulation 1/2003 gives rise to an obligation to apply Articles 81 and 82.

(ii) Applied to an agreement within the meaning of Article 81(1) or to an abuse prohibited by Article 82

13.59 **Applied**   It is unclear when national competition law is applied for the purposes of Article 3(1).[98] On one view, national competition law is applied at the very outset of every investigation, whenever the regulator first exercises its statutory powers to initiate the investigation. On another view, national competition law is only applied when the national competition authority makes a final finding relating to relevant agreements/abuses.

13.60 The policy position adopted by both the OFT and the CC on this issue is that national competition law is only 'applied', for the purposes of Article 3(1), at the conclusion of a market investigation reference, when remedies are imposed by the CC following a reference and it is accordingly only at this stage that the obligation to apply Articles 81 and 82 is triggered.[99] Articles 81 and 82 are thus applied *after* the CC has completed its investigation. The advantage of this approach is that it leaves the CC free to follow its own Enterprise Act procedure to its completion before there is a need to embark upon the application of Articles 81 and 82. Given the tight statutory timetable that the CC is obliged to follow in conducting market investigation references, this is administratively convenient (not to mention that the CC is currently not empowered to apply Articles 81 and 82).

13.61 The policy of the CC and the OFT is clearly articulated in the guidance:

---

[97] OFT511, *Market investigation references: Guidance about the making of references under Part 4 of the Enterprise Act* (March 2006) paras 2.12 and 2.13. See also CC3, *Market Investigation References: Competition Commission Guidelines* (June 2003) para 1.13; P Freeman, Lord Fletcher Lecture, 15 March 2005, p 12, available from the CC website.
[98] On this issue more generally, see paras 3.71 et seq above.
[99] OFT511, *Market investigation references: Guidance about the making of references under Part 4 of the Enterprise Act* (March 2006) para 2.12 and CC3, *Market Investigation References: Competition Commission Guidelines* (June 2003) para 1.13.

In the context of a market investigation by the CC, the obligation to apply Articles 81 or 82 in parallel with national competition law will arise only at the stage where remedies are imposed by the CC following a reference.[100]

In the authors' view, this statement cannot be taken to mean that the obligation **13.62** to apply Article 81 and/or Article 82 only arises where the CC chooses to impose remedies (this would mean that the CC could circumvent any obligation to apply Articles 81 and 82 by choosing not to impose a remedy in any particular case). Rather, 'the application of competition law' under Article 3(1) does not comprise investigatory steps taken by the authority (which are of a procedural nature) but refers to the application of *substantive* competition law at the end of an investigation.

The interpretation of Article 3(1) is consistent with Regulation 1/2003, which **13.63** does not harmonise the procedure for the enforcement of Articles 81 and 82 (procedures for enforcement are essentially left to be governed by national law). It also accords with the purpose of Article 3, which is to ensure the effective enforcement of Community competition rules:[101] this purpose would not be served by imposing a requirement on competition authorities to apply European competition law at the investigatory stage, when the nature and ambit of the competition problem is as yet unclear.

Consistent with the analysis undertaken above, the OFT takes the view that **13.64** procedural matters such as the exercise of investigatory powers by the OFT and the CC do not trigger the obligation to apply Article 81 or Article 82. The OFT's guidance provides:

> The obligation [to apply Articles 81 or 82] does not affect any investigation carried out by the OFT to determine whether to make a reference, the making of a reference to the CC or the investigation by the CC.[102]

The OFT and CC's policy can readily be understood in so far as it implies that **13.65** the obligation in Article 3(1) does not arise until the investigatory stages have been completed and a substantive competition finding has been made. What is less clear is the emphasis on *the application of remedies* as a trigger for the obligation to apply European law to arise. This approach leaves the door open for national authorities to clear anti-competitive agreements under national competition law without applying European law to them and so defeating the purpose of Article 3(1).

---

[100] OFT511, *Market investigation references: Guidance about the making of references under Part 4 of the Enterprise Act* (March 2006) para 2.12. See also CC3, *Market Investigation References: Competition Commission Guidelines* (June 2003) para 1.13.

[101] See Recital 8 to Regulation 1/2003.

[102] OFT511, *Market investigation references: Guidance about the making of references under Part 4 of the Enterprise Act* (March 2006) para 2.12.

13.66   Arguably, an 'application' of national competition law occurs when a national competition authority publishes its final findings of law on a particular competition issue, irrespective of whether it imposes any remedies. It is clear from the wording of Article 3(1) that the obligation to apply Articles 81 and 82 is not made dependent upon an adverse finding under national competition law—it is triggered by *any* finding that amounts to an application of national competition law. It should therefore be triggered by any CC finding on agreements within the meaning of Article 81(1) and abuse within the meaning of Article 82. Accordingly, in the authors' view, it is at the stage when there is an application of substantive national competition law provisions (either with or without the imposition of remedies) that the obligation to apply Articles 81 and 82 arises under Article 3(1).

13.67   It is arguable that an OFT market investigation reference under s 131(1) of the Enterprise Act 2002 should not be viewed as a mere procedural investigative step. Such a market investigation reference does after all amount to a published decision by a competition authority containing a *substantive* (albeit preliminary) analysis of the restriction, prevention, or distortion of competition on a particular market. The analysis comprises sophisticated (if not definitive) market definition as well as an identification of the competition problems on that particular market, and one could make a purposive argument that the Article 3(1) obligation should accordingly bite at this stage if the effective application of Articles 81 and 82 is not to be undermined. On balance, given that market investigation references do not provide final findings regarding the competition issues arising on a particular market, and in view of the extremely low threshold that the OFT has to meet in making such references under s 131(1) of the Enterprise Act 2002,[103] the authors favour the view that a reference by the OFT to the CC does not amount to an application of national competition law for the purposes of Article 3(1).

13.68   **To an agreement within the meaning of Article 81(1) or to an abuse prohibited by Article 82**   For an explanation of 'agreement within the meaning of Article 81(1)' and 'abuse prohibited by Article 82' see Chapter 3. Assuming it is agreed that competition law is only applied when the CC reports on a market, the question arises as to when one can say that competition law is applied to a particular agreement or conduct, when it is the market within which such conduct or agreement features that is usually the subject of the reference. The mere *presence* of an agreement within the sense of Article 81(1) in a market referred should not mean that the CC is applying national law to such an

---

[103] Under Enterprise Act 2002, s 131 it need only have 'reasonable grounds for suspecting' the restriction, prevention, or distortion of competition.

agreement—most markets referred must indeed include such agreements. However, wherever the CC undertakes an evaluation of the competitive effects of agreements or of conduct in the market—be it either adverse or neutral—then it must be applying national competition law in such a way as to trigger the obligation to apply Articles 81 and 82 as relevant.

(c) The corresponding obligation to apply Articles 81 and 82

(i) *Which authority will apply Articles 81 and 82?*

The Competition Act 1998 and Other Enactments (Amendment) Regulations **13.69** 2004[104] designate national competition authorities responsible for the application of Articles 81 and 82 in the United Kingdom. These regulations designate the OFT and the concurrent regulators, but they do not designate the CC. This means that, as matters stand, the CC is not empowered to apply Articles 81 and 82. For the United Kingdom to avoid breaching Regulation 1/2003, the OFT (as the main authority responsible for applying Articles 81 and 82) must apply Articles 81 and 82 as relevant should the obligation arise in the context of a market investigation reference.[105] The Department of Trade and Industry is currently reviewing whether the CC should be designated to apply Articles 81 and Article 82.[106]

(ii) *When will it do so?*

As was explained at paras 3.71–3.77, Article 3(1) does not expressly mandate **13.70** the *simultaneous* application of Article 81 and/or Article 82 by national competition authorities, merely providing that *where* (and not *when*) national competition law is applied in particular circumstances, Article 81 and/or Article 82 should also be applied. The United Kingdom negotiated this wording (previous wordings referred to Articles 81 and 82 being applied in parallel with national competition law) with a view to the market investigation regime.

---

[104] SI 2004/1261.

[105] OFT511, *Market investigation references: Guidance about the making of references under Part 4 of the Enterprise Act* (March 2006) paras 2.14 and 2.15. Peter Freeman (then Deputy Chairman of the CC) provides useful guidance on this issue in the Lord Fletcher Lecture, 15 March 2005, available from the CC website.

[106] 'The "Modernisation Regulation" (EC Regulation 1/2003), which decentralised the application of EC competition law to member states, came into effect in May 2004, and we are in discussions with the DTI as to how this will affect our market investigations', CC's Annual Review and Accounts 2004/2005, 8. See also CC's Annual Review and Accounts 2005/2006, 6: 'We have been discussing with the Department for Trade and Industry (DTI) and the OFT how the market investigation regime can be made to work most effectively within the framework for enforcement of EU competition rules. One option under consideration is for the CC to be designated to apply Articles 81 and 82 where relevant in the course of a market investigation.'

13.71 It can be appreciated why, given the very recent introduction of the market investigation regime at the relevant time, the United Kingdom sought to negotiate wording of Regulation 1/2003 that would not cut across the market investigation reference regime by compelling the immediate and simultaneous application of Articles 81 and 82. The United Kingdom is unusual in having two distinct systems of competition regulation—on the one hand, essentially behavioural prohibitions aimed at deterring undertakings under the Competition Act 1998, and on the other, more comprehensive scrutiny of the competition process in markets with a view to resolving problems for the future under the Enterprise Act 2002. The change to the wording of Article 3(1) was intended to preserve the CC's ability to act under the Enterprise Act. Arguably, in the absence of an obligation to apply Articles 81 and 82 immediately, the CC retains its ability to conclude investigations and to remedy all issues (including Article 81 and Article 82 issues) arising on a market referred, without having to interrupt a market investigation to apply Articles 81 and 82 whenever these issues arise in a market referred.[107]

13.72 It is unclear whether the view that Article 3(1) permits a subsequent application of Articles 81 and 82 by national competition authorities will prevail when this provision is considered by the ECJ. This interpretation places a lot of weight on the ambiguous use of the word *where* in Article 3(1). Further, this construction of Article 3(1) is also arguably at odds with one of the objectives of Regulation 1/2003 as stated in Recital 2, namely to simplify administration to the greatest possible extent. When one considers the application of Regulation 1/2003 in the other Member States, none of which possess a system similar to the UK market investigation regime, it is hard to envisage the ECJ endorsing a construction of Article 3(1) that would permit national competition authorities to apply their national competition law first, and only subsequently to apply Articles 81 and 82.

(d) How will Article 81 and/or Article 82 be applied in practice?

13.73 Should the CC, in the course of a market investigation, identify a competition issue to which Article 81 or Article 82 applies (despite the OFT's endeavours not to refer issues better addressed under the Competition Act 1998), OFT and CC guidance indicates that Article 81 and/or Article 82 will usually not be applied until after the CC has reported on the market concerned and that the OFT will avoid simultaneously investigating with the CC to avoid undue burdens on business.[108] As a matter of practice, it is difficult to evaluate whether it is

---

[107] OFT511, *Market investigation references: Guidance about the making of references under Part 4 of the Enterprise Act* (March 2006) para 2.15.
[108] ibid, paras 2.15 and 2.16.

more burdensome to business to be subject to simultaneous investigations (and therefore to have to battle on several fronts at the same time) or potentially lengthy sequential investigations (a market study, leading to a two-year market investigation, followed by a two- to three-year OFT investigation). As a matter of principle, as market investigation references are not 'criminal' for the purposes of Article 6 ECHR,[109] it is unlikely that an undertaking in this unhappy situation could seek to rely on *ne bis in idem* (otherwise known as the rule against double jeopardy) to prevent simultaneous or subsequent investigations relating to the same matter—the rule only takes effect to prevent double prosecution of criminal offences.[110] However, there are other arguments (such as undue delay) that can be made relating to the burdens that are imposed on undertakings subjected to simultaneous or overly lengthy investigations. The CAT has recently given very clear signals that it will not tolerate undue delay in the context of market investigations.[111]

However, it is possible, in respect of both Article 81 and Article 82, to envisage, **13.74** despite the OFT and CC guidance described above, that there will be certain situations where there will be a simultaneous Enterprise Act and Article 81/ Article 82 investigations. The OFT, as the body responsible for applying Article 81 or Article 82, will not always be able to await the outcome of a market investigation to begin its own investigation under Article 81 or Article 82.

It is best to consider how Articles 81 and 82 will be applied in practice separately **13.75** as each gives rise to different considerations.

(i) Article 81

With regard to Article 81, OFT guidance envisages that the CC, upon discover- **13.76** ing an agreement within the meaning of Article 81 in the market referred, can nonetheless choose to continue with its investigation and make a report, or alternatively, it can remit the agreement back to the OFT for its consideration under Article 81.[112] There are various difficulties with this proposition.

Remitting the agreements to the OFT   It is open to question whether the CC **13.77** has the power to 'remit' a matter that has been referred to it given that:

---

[109] See para 11.49 above for an analysis of why the market investigation provisions are unlikely to be qualified as criminal.

[110] See Chapter 11 for a full discussion of the conditions that must be satisfied for *ne bis in idem* to apply.

[111] See *Association of Convenience Stores v OFT* [2005] CAT 36, paras 8 et seq.

[112] OFT511, *Market investigation references: Guidance about the making of references under Part 4 of the Enterprise Act* (March 2006) para 2.14: 'If an agreement within the meaning of Article 81(1) is uncovered during the course of the CC's investigation the CC would consider whether to remit the agreement back to the OFT for consideration under Article 81.'

- it has a statutory obligation under the Enterprise Act 2002 to report on matters referred to it within a defined timetable;
- s 138 of the Enterprise Act imposes a duty on the CC to remedy the adverse effects on competition that it has identified;
- the Enterprise Act does not empower the CC to suspend or refuse to undertake a market investigation.

13.78 There are two indirect ways that a matter could be remitted:

- First, the CC could request that the OFT vary its terms of reference under s 135 of the Enterprise Act 2002 so as expressly to carve out the agreements at issue from the reference (this is suitable only where the Article 81 agreements are not covert and there is no need to preserve an element of surprise). The OFT would have to consult industry before varying its reference[113] as it did in varying the references (for other reasons) in *Store cards*[114] and in *Domestic LPG*.[115]

- Alternatively, should the suspected agreements be of a covert nature, so that (by reason of the publicity) a variation of the reference is inappropriate, the CC could draw the OFT's attention to the agreements and pass on any relevant information to the OFT as soon as it suspects their existence.[116] The OFT could then investigate and retain the benefit of a surprise element to any inspection. Section 241(3)(b) of the Enterprise Act 2002 permits the transmission of the relevant information from the CC to the OFT in these circumstances as in transmitting it the CC would be facilitating the exercise of the OFT's functions under the Competition Act.[117]

13.79 **Which agreements are remitted?**   In determining whether to deal with the Article 81 agreement itself or to 'remit' it back to the OFT, much will depend on the type of agreement at issue.

13.80 Where the agreements falling under Article 81 are of a covert nature, for example where the CC uncovers evidence of a cartel or other covert agreements in a market referred, it is likely that the CC would immediately draw the suspected cartel to the OFT's attention. An immediate investigation by the OFT will be necessary in order not to lose vital time and evidence. As the CC is not equipped with sufficiently far-reaching investigatory powers to investigate cartels, the most effective way of addressing this issue is to inform the OFT. This situation may arise in respect of markets (such as that for *Personal current*

---

[113] Enterprise Act 2002, s 169.   [114] Reference varied on 3 March 2005.
[115] Reference varied on 20 October 2004.
[116] Enterprise Act 2002, s 141(3) empowers the CC to disclose specified information for the purpose of facilitating the exercise by the authority of its functions.
[117] The Competition Act 1998 is one of the Acts specified in Enterprise Act 2002, Sch 15.

account banking services in Northern Ireland) are referred to the OFT in light of what appears to be uncoordinated parallel behaviour, but where the conduct of the undertakings may, on further scrutiny by the CC, turn out to be more coordinated than anticipated.

After informing the OFT of the suspicious agreements and transmitting any **13.81** other relevant information pertaining thereto, the CC remains subject to its statutory obligation to report on the reference. It will therefore be obliged to proceed with the market investigation and make a report. It may be that there are other aspects of the market which the CC will wish to remedy, but it is presumed that as regards the covert Article 81 agreements, the CC would merely comment on the possible existence of such agreements and/or recommend further action by the OFT or other regulator in its final report.

Where the agreements at issue are not covert, there may be good reason for the **13.82** CC to proceed with its investigation of the market including considering the relevant Article 81 agreements—for example where the Article 81 agreements are incidental to a larger bundle of issues present in the market such as in *Store Cards*. In such cases, if the CC goes on to make a report which includes an analysis of the competitive effects of agreements falling within Article 81, this application of national competition law (whether the analysis is favourable or not) triggers the obligation to apply Article 81 under Article 3(1) of Regulation 1/2003. As the CC is not empowered to apply Article 81, the OFT should, at the conclusion of the CC's investigation and taking account of the CC's findings, itself apply Article 81 to the agreements—which entails initiating a separate investigation. For an undertaking that is active in a market referred and which is potentially facing Article 81 proceedings, it is unclear which is most burdensome—facing both procedures at the same time or having to endure two consecutive investigations by different investigators.[118]

Agreements: obligation to reach a result that is compatible with EC law The **13.83** CC is bound by the general principle of supremacy of EC law and by the obligation of loyal cooperation in Article 10 EC. In the competition law field, this means that it cannot apply national competition law in a manner incompatible with EC law (see Chapter 3 for a discussion of what this entails). In addition, since 1 May 2004, Article 3(2) of Regulation 1/2003 applies to the CC, even though it is not a designated authority.[119] Under Article 3(2), the CC may not prohibit agreements affecting trade that either do not fall within Article 81(1) or that satisfy the conditions of Article 81(3). This obligation has

---

[118] See Chapter 11 for a consideration of the principle of *ne bis in idem* in such a context.

[119] Art 3(2) by its terms applies wherever national competition law is applied, irrespective of the authority applying it.

been recognised by the CC.[120] In practice, this obligation means that the CC is left disempowered vis-à-vis all agreements affecting trade that would not be prohibited under Article 81: objecting to part of an agreement or making the approval or continuance of an agreement subject to certain conditions amounts, in effect, to prohibiting the existence of the agreement in a certain format.

13.84 Article 3(2) of Regulation 1/2003 considerably broadened the scope of the obligation not to apply national competition law in a manner that is inconsistent with EC law. Now, the CC must ensure that its application of the market investigation provisions is neither more lenient or more strict, than Article 81 when analysing agreements affecting trade between Member States. This calls into question how much leeway for CC action has actually been preserved after modernisation.[121]

(ii) Article 82

13.85 With respect to Article 82, the guidance provides:

> It is possible that a reference could be made that included conduct which the CC investigation showed was in fact conduct that amounted to an abuse of a dominant position prohibited by Article 82. In such cases, the CC would complete its investigation and impose remedies under the Act. The OFT would then take these remedies into account when carrying out an Article 82 investigation.[122]

13.86 It appears from the guidance cited above that where the CC finds an abuse of Article 82 in the context of a market investigation, this issue will not be remitted back to the OFT. The CC will report on the market and impose any suitable remedies (including remedies addressing the Article 82 issue). The OFT will then initiate an investigation to apply Article 82 after the CC has completed its investigation, taking account in its decision of any remedies imposed by the Commission. An undertaking may therefore find that it is the subject of an OFT market study, a CC market investigation, and finally an OFT Article 82 investigation all relating to the same conduct.

13.87 From the authorities' point of view, this is the most efficient way to proceed:

---

[120] See *Store Cards, Statement of Issues*, 21 September 2004, para 3: 'In addition, pursuant to Article 10 of the EC Treaty and in the light of Council Regulation (EC) No 1/2003 on the implementation of the rules on competition laid down in Articles 81 and 82 of the EC (the Modernisation Regulation), the CC needs to consider the requirement that the application of national competition law must be consistent with, and must not prejudice, the full and uniform application of EC competition law.'

[121] S Dhana, 'Impact of Modernisation: have the UK competition authorities seen their power to issue remedies reduced?' (2005) Competition LJ 33.

[122] OFT511, *Market investigation references: Guidance about the making of references under Part 4 of the Enterprise Act* (March 2006) para 2.15.

under s 241(3) of the Enterprise Act 2002, the CC can provide the OFT with relevant information in its possession necessary for the OFT to discharge its functions. This saves resources and reduces duplication. In many cases, the CC will have comprehensively addressed the Article 82 issue in the context of a broader market investigation. After the CC has acted, there will therefore be no real need for the OFT to carry out extensive investigative or remedial work. It will be able to rely on information received from the CC under the gateway provided by s 241(3) of the Enterprise Act 2002 and make a decision 'applying' Article 82 and noting that remedies have been imposed by the CC.

However, there are great disadvantages to this approach for undertakings, as **13.88** consecutive investigations impose heavy burdens. As explained above at para 13.72, an undertaking in this situation is unlikely to prevent the multiplicity of proceedings on the grounds of the rule against double jeopardy, but broader arguments based on the right to a fair trial under Article 6 ECHR and undue delay may be of aid in such a situation. Although the OFT and CC may view the subsequent OFT finding applying Article 82 after a CC market investigation as a mere formality, such a finding is very detrimental for the undertakings concerned, even if no additional remedy is imposed, as the finding of abuse may be relied upon to found claims for damages. Undertakings will therefore retain every incentive to resist such a finding by the OFT, thereby further lengthening the investigatory process.

There may additionally be certain situations when it will not be possible for **13.89** the OFT to avoid concurrent Article 82 proceedings—for example, where an undertaking in the market referred complains directly to and/or seeks an interim remedy from the OFT to prevent an allegedly dominant undertaking in the market referred from abusing its dominant position. In such a situation, the OFT might find it difficult to refuse to proceed on the complaint or to reject an application for interim relief based on Article 82, on the ground that the issue is being dealt with by another authority acting under domestic law, without breaching its obligations of loyal cooperation under Article 10 EC.

The obligation to reach a result that is compatible with European law   Ensur- **13.90** ing consistency in market investigations with EC law in references involving Article 82 issues is simpler than ensuring consistency where there are Article 81 issues. Article 3(2) of Regulation 1/2003 expressly preserves the national authorities' ability to apply stricter national law to unilateral conduct. This gives the CC considerably more freedom to act in respect of unilateral conduct than it enjoys with respect to agreements that may affect trade between Member States. Where the CC makes a finding relating to unilateral conduct, it need only satisfy itself that its analysis of the conduct at issue is not more lenient than an Article 82 analysis—without having to consider whether it may be stricter. It can therefore impose remedies on unilateral conduct without fear of challenge, even where the conduct at issue is compatible with Article 82.

(e) Conclusion

13.91 The strict obligation to apply Articles 81 and 82 under Regulation 1/2003 is predicated on *ex post* national competition law systems, in which context it is relatively easy to comply with. However, the obligation has a more uneasy relationship with the *ex ante* market investigation regime.

13.92 The current approach to accommodating the obligation to apply Articles 81 and 82, which maintains separate roles for the OFT and the CC but does not (yet) provide any clear mechanism for their cooperation on these matters, is far from ideal. It entails a multiplication of investigatory burdens for both undertakings and authorities. Further, as it envisages the consecutive application of national law and European law (with European law being applied in second place), there is a risk (albeit minor) of inconsistent decisions.

E. The Discretion to Refer

13.93 The wording of s 131(1) ('may . . . make a reference') provides the OFT with a discretion to make a reference. This is to be contrasted with its duty to refer mergers provided in s 22 of the Enterprise Act 2002.[123] The Explanatory Notes to the Enterprise Act emphasise the breadth of the OFT's discretion to refer:

> The OFT is not obliged to make a reference where it has reasonable grounds for suspecting that the reference criteria are satisfied (unlike in the merger regime, where the provisions of Part 3 place it under a duty to refer in certain circumstances). Since potential market investigation cases will often raise many complex issues, the section sets no limits to the matters that may be taken into account in deciding whether or not to make a reference, once the OFT has reasonable grounds to suspect that the reference criteria are satisfied. For example, there could be circumstances in which the reference criteria were satisfied, but the competition problems in the market concerned were of a kind that it was more appropriate for the OFT to address using its powers under CA 1998. Or the OFT might take the view that the competition problems in a market that it had the power to refer were likely only to be temporary, or were too trivial for it to be likely that the costs and

---

[123] s 22(1) provides: 'The OFT shall, subject to subsections (2) and (3), make a reference to the Commission if the OFT believes that it is or may be the case that . . .'.

burdens of a CC investigation would be justified by any likely outcome of such an investigation.[124]

The OFT guidance sets out the factors that are relevant to the exercise of the **13.94** OFT's discretion. It provides that the OFT will only make references where each of the following criteria have been met:

- it would not be more appropriate to deal with the competition issues identified by applying the Competition Act or using other powers available to the OFT or, where appropriate, to sectoral regulators [**alternative powers**];
- it would not be more appropriate to address the problem identified by means of undertakings in lieu of a reference [**undertakings in lieu**];
- the scale of the suspected problem, in terms of its adverse effect on competition, is such that a reference would be an appropriate response to it [**proportionality**];
- there is a reasonable chance that appropriate remedies will be available [**availability of remedies**].[125]

Although not listed as a relevant factor in current OFT guidance, since 1 May **13.95** 2004 one important additional factor to be taken into consideration by the OFT in exercising its discretion to refer is what consequences making a reference would have in relation to the obligation to apply Articles 81 and 82 under Regulation 1/2003.

Each of the above factors will be considered in turn below. **13.96**

(a) Alternative powers

It is the OFT's policy always to consider first whether a matter may involve an **13.97** infringement of Chapter I, Chapter II, Article 81, and/or Article 82 before making a reference.[126] The OFT will, according to its guidance,[127] only consider a reference to the CC in one of two circumstances:

(i) The competition prohibitions do not apply

First, a reference may be appropriate when the OFT has reasonable grounds **13.98** to suspect that there are market features, which prevent, restrict, or distort

---

[124] Explanatory Notes to the Enterprise Act 2002, para 305.
[125] OFT511, *Market investigation references: Guidance about the making of references under Part 4 of the Enterprise Act* (March 2006) para 2.1.
[126] 'When dealing with a suspected competition problem, the OFT will consider first both whether it might involve an infringement of CA98 and whether it might involve any infringement of Article 81 and/or 82', ibid, para 2.13. Sectoral regulators will usually also consider whether it would be more appropriate to deal with a competition problem under any sector specific legislation or rules.
[127] ibid, para 2.3.

competition, but these do not establish a breach of the Competition Act 1998 prohibitions, Article 81, and/or Article 82. Issues traditionally identified as requiring a reference because they cannot be resolved by application of the Competition Act prohibitions, Article 81, or Article 82 include the following: uncoordinated parallel conduct by several firms,[128] industry-wide features of a market in cases where the OFT does not have reasonable grounds to suspect the existence of anti-competitive agreements or dominance,[129] anti-competitive conduct by a single firm which is associated with structural features of the market[130] (for example, barriers to entry or regulation and government policies),[131] and anti-competitive practices by undertakings that are not dominant.[132]

(ii) Procedural efficiency

13.99 Secondly, a reference may be appropriate when action under the Competition Act 1998 has been or is likely to be ineffective for dealing with the adverse effect on competition identified. It appears that the OFT envisages making a reference in cases where, although it has identified a breach of Chapter I, Chapter II, Article 81, and/or Article 82, it considers that action under the Competition Act is likely to be or has been ineffective.

13.100 The question arises whether the OFT is able to choose to make a reference to the CC and expect it to resolve the problems identified where these fall within Article 81 and Article 82. In *Domestic LPG*, it referred a market that possibly gave rise to Article 81 or Article 82 issues to the CC on the basis of procedural efficiency:

> Given the breadth of issues arising in relation to domestic bulk LPG, the OFT does not currently consider that action taken under the Competition Act, or under Articles 81 or 82 of the EC Treaty, as appropriate, if a breach of one or more of the relevant prohibitions were established, would be effective in resolving all the adverse effects on competition which it has identified.[133]

13.101 The OFT's assertion that it can refer cases otherwise falling under the Competition Act to the CC with a view to procedural and remedial efficacy should be

---

[128] eg OFT796, *Personal current account banking services in Northern Ireland: The OFT's reasons for making a reference to the Competition Commission* (May 2005).

[129] OFT511, *Market investigation references: Guidance about the making of references under Part 4 of the Enterprise Act* (March 2006) para 2.4.

[130] eg OFT787, *Classified directory advertising services: The OFT's reasons for making a reference to the Competition Commission* (April 2005) para 55.

[131] OFT511, *Market investigation references: Guidance about the making of references under Part 4 of the Enterprise Act* (March 2006) para 2.8.

[132] OFT845, *The grocery market: The OFT's reasons for making a reference to the Competition Commission* (May 2006) para 8.26.

[133] *The supply of liquefied petroleum gas to domestic bulk storage tanks: The OFT's reasons for making a reference to the Competition Commission* (July 2004) para 20.

read as subject to one caveat springing from its obligations under Regulation 1/2003: given that the CC is currently not designated to apply Articles 81 and 82, it would not be compatible with Article 3(1) of Regulation 1/2003[134] for the OFT to refer a market containing an Article 81 or Article 82 issue to the CC, with a view to that issue being resolved by the Commission solely by reference to the Enterprise Act 2002. This amounts to evading (albeit for reasons of procedural efficiency) national competition authorities' obligations to apply Article 81 and/or Article 82 wherever national law is applied to agreements within the meaning of Article 81 and conduct prohibited by Article 82 (see further para 13.119 below and Chapter 3 in relation to obligations under Article 3(1) more generally).

One area which may give rise to a reference for reasons of procedural efficiency **13.102** relates to the OFT's power, under Article 29 of Regulation 1/2003, to withdraw in any particular case the benefit of an EC block exemption regulation.[135] Paragraph 2.18 of the OFT guidance on market investigation references indicates that where it has reasonable grounds to suspect that the conditions for the withdrawal of a block exemption are met, it may refer the relevant markets to the CC. If the CC, after conducting a market investigation inquiry, recommends the withdrawal of the block exemption, the OFT would then initiate individual investigations under Article 81 and/or Article 82 against undertakings operating in the market concerned to remove the benefit of the block exemption regulation from those individual undertakings.[136]

(b) Accepting an undertaking in lieu of a reference

Section 154 of the Enterprise Act 2002 gives the OFT the power to accept **13.103** undertakings from one or more parties instead of making a reference to the CC.

(i) When appropriate

It is a pre-condition to the exercise of this power that the OFT must consider **13.104** that it has the power to make a reference under s 131 of the Enterprise Act 2002 and that it would otherwise intend to make such a reference.[137]

Where it considers that it could and would otherwise make a reference, the **13.105** OFT may, instead of making the reference, and for the purpose of remedying,

---

[134] On Art 3(1) see paras 3.49 et seq above.
[135] The OFT and concurrent regulators are designated to exercise the powers in Pt IX of Regulation 1/2003 by reg 3 of SI 2004/1261.
[136] See paras 4.72 et seq for the procedure that the OFT must follow to remove the benefit of a block exemption from an undertaking.
[137] Enterprise Act 2002, s 154(1).

mitigating, or preventing any adverse effect on competition identified and any detrimental effect on customers that results (or may be expected to result) therefrom, accept from such persons as it considers appropriate undertakings to take such action as it considers appropriate.[138] In so doing, it must have regard to the need to achieve as *comprehensive* a solution as is reasonable and practicable,[139] and it may have regard to the effect of any action on any relevant customer benefits (such as lower prices, higher quality, or greater choice of goods or services in any UK market, or greater innovation in relation to such goods or services) of the feature or features of the market concerned.[140]

13.106 To date, there have not been many cases in which an undertaking has been accepted in lieu of a reference.[141] Ofcom accepted a number of highly complex undertakings from BT in the context of its Strategic Review of Telecommunications.[142] In that case the factors considered by Ofcom in concluding that undertakings were appropriate were:

- whether the problem was sufficiently serious to merit regulatory intervention at all;
- whether it might otherwise proceed by means of the other powers available to it under the Competition Act 1998 and the Communications Act 2003;
- whether the undertakings were apt to address the features identified; and
- whether the undertakings satisfied the need to achieve as comprehensive a solution as is reasonable and practicable to the adverse effect on competition concerned and to any detrimental effects on customers which resulted from the adverse effect on competition.[143]

13.107 According to OFT guidance, undertakings in lieu of a reference are unlikely to be common as it will not have done a sufficiently detailed investigation of a competition problem to be able to judge with any certainty whether particular undertakings will achieve as comprehensive a solution as is reasonable and practicable.[144] In *Home Credit*, the OFT stated that this is particularly likely to be the case when the adverse effect on competition arises from market features involving several firms or industry-wide practices.[145] The OFT further

---

[138] ibid, s 154(2).   [139] ibid, s 154(3).   [140] ibid, s 154(4).

[141] The first time undertakings were accepted by the OFT was in 2005; see OFT press release 110/05, 'OFT accepts postal franking machines undertakings', 17 June 2005.

[142] Strategic Review of Telecommunications, *Final statements on the Strategic Review of Telecommunications, and undertakings in lieu of a reference under the Enterprise Act 2002*, 22 September 2005.

[143] Ofcom, *Notice under Section 155(1) of the Enterprise Act 2002*, 30 June 2005, para 5.1.

[144] OFT511, *Market investigation references: Guidance about the making of references under Part 4 of the Enterprise Act* (March 2006) para 2.21.

[145] OFT769, *Home Credit: The OFT's reasons for making a reference to the Competition Commission* (January 2005) para 87.

explained that although it had reasonable grounds to suspect that competition was restricted, it was not sufficiently certain that it was restricted (or of the extent to which it was restricted) to be able to judge either the extent to which an undertaking in lieu was necessary or the form that it should take.[146] In such cases, there is the additional difficulty of achieving consensus among the various parties concerned as to the undertakings that were necessary.[147] It is only where the adverse effect on competition is relatively simple, for example it arises from the conduct of a very few firms, that the OFT considers that there may be more scope for accepting undertakings given the difficulty of negotiating them with several parties. In the Ofcom and BT case mentioned above, this general rule did not hold true: the proposed reference sprang from Ofcom's consideration of fixed telecoms in the United Kingdom in the context of its Strategic Review of Telecommunications, so that its prior investigation was detailed, as is reflected in the nature of the undertakings that were accepted.

13.108 In many cases, undertakings in lieu will not arise, because they are not offered by the relevant parties. In others, the features of the market that the OFT has identified as leading to the reference are largely non-behavioural. In such cases, an undertaking in lieu may not address the issues comprehensively.

(ii) Consultation process

13.109 The OFT, prior to accepting an undertaking, is obliged under s 155 of the Enterprise Act 2002 to publish notice of the proposed undertaking which sets out, inter alia:

- the adverse effect on competition (and any detrimental effect on customers so far as resulting from the adverse effect on competition) which the OFT has identified;
- the terms of the reference which the OFT otherwise intends to make;
- the purpose and effect of the undertaking,
- the situation that the undertaking is seeking to deal with; and
- any other facts which the OFT considers justify the acceptance of the undertaking.

13.110 The OFT must allow interested parties at least 15 days from publication of the notice to make representations in relation to the proposed undertaking. In the Ofcom/BT case, Ofcom allowed approximately six weeks for consultation. There is a power for the Secretary of State to intervene at this stage if he/she believes that wider public interest matters are relevant to the case (see para 13.138 below).

13.111 Upon acceptance, the OFT is obliged under s 155(7) to serve a copy of

---

[146] ibid, para 89.   [147] ibid, para 89.

the undertaking on any person by whom it is given as well as publishing the undertaking. Undertakings are published on the OFT website.[148]

(iii) Effect of undertakings

13.112 Where an undertaking in lieu has been accepted, the OFT may not make a market investigation reference involving the same goods or services for a period of 12 months unless it considers the undertaking has been breached or it has been given false or misleading information by the person responsible for giving the undertaking. The OFT is obliged to monitor compliance with undertakings and report on them from time to time or where requested to do so by the Secretary of State.[149] In case of breach of an undertaking, it is empowered to enforce undertakings by civil proceedings for an injunction or for interdict or any other appropriate relief or remedy.[150] A breach of an undertaking is actionable in damages by any person who may be affected by a contravention of the undertaking.[151] Before releasing an undertaking, the OFT is obliged to publish a notice of the proposed release and to consider any representations made.[152]

(c) Scale of the problem

13.113 According to its guidance,[153] the OFT will only make a reference when it has reasonable grounds to suspect that the adverse effects on competition identified are significant. Where the adverse effect is not significant, considerations such as the burden on business and the public expenditure costs are likely to mean that the costs associated with a reference would be disproportionate in relation to any benefits flowing therefrom, so that the OFT would not make a reference.

13.114 The OFT will consider whether suspected adverse effects are likely to have a significant detrimental effect on customers through higher prices, lower quality, less choice, or less innovation. It will consider the question in the round, taking account also of whether the adverse effects are off-set by customer benefits, such as more innovation. It has highlighted[154] that the following factors are likely to be relevant in making its evaluation of the scale of the problem:

- **The size of the market.** It is interesting to note that the market size need not necessarily be very big to be significant. In *Domestic LPG*, the OFT found

---

[148] Enterprise Act 2002, s 166.   [149] ibid, s 163.   [150] ibid, s 167(6).
[151] ibid, s 167(2)–(4).   [152] ibid, s 155(10) and Sch 10, paras 6–8.
[153] OFT511, *Market investigation references: Guidance about the making of references under Part 4 of the Enterprise Act* (March 2006) para 2.27.
[154] ibid, para 2.28.

that: 'Firstly, the size of the market is significant: we estimate the supply of LPG and related services to be in excess of £100 million p.a.'[155]

- **The proportion of the market affected.** The OFT indicates in its guidance[156] that it will so far as possible approach this concept consistently with its approach to 'appreciability' under Chapter I of the Competition Act 1998. Currently, agreements will as, a matter of practice, generally not be considered to have an appreciable effect under the Competition Act where the combined aggregate market share of the parties does not exceed 10 per cent (if they are competitors) or 15 per cent of the markets affected by the agreement.[157] In *Domestic LPG*, the OFT found that evidence of low levels of switching between suppliers indicated that a significant proportion of the market was affected: 'Secondly, a significant proportion of the market is affected by the features that may prevent, restrict or distort competition, as is suggested by the low levels of switching and the nature of these features, which exist throughout the market.'[158]

- **The persistence of the feature giving rise to adverse effects on competition.** Where the concerns identified by the OFT are temporary and short lived, a reference is not appropriate

(d) Appropriate remedies

The OFT will take into account the availability of appropriate remedies for the suspected adverse effects should it make a reference to the CC. **13.115**

Given the broad range of the CC's remedial powers it is unlikely to be the case that no action or recommendation by the CC could remedy a problem. OFT guidance provides one example of where a reference may not be appropriate: where a particular market is global in scope, any remedy by the CC may have no discernible impact on the way the market operated. Even then however, the guidance requires the OFT to have regard to situations in which a CC investigation and report with recommendations for action (including recommendations for action by the European Commission or other bodies) is likely to make a useful contribution. **13.116**

Where the OFT is satisfied that adverse effects on competition arise primarily **13.117**

---

[155] *The supply of liquefied petroleum gas to domestic bulk storage tanks: The OFT's reasons for making a reference to the Competition Commission* (July 2004) para 25.

[156] OFT511, *Market investigation references: Guidance about the making of references under Part 4 of the Enterprise Act* (March 2006) para 2.28.

[157] See para 1.61 above for a more detailed discussion of appreciability under the Competition Act 1998.

[158] *The supply of liquefied petroleum gas to domestic bulk storage tanks: The OFT's reasons for making a reference to the Competition Commission* (July 2004) para 25.

from laws, regulations, or government policies which the CC cannot itself directly remedy, it may not make a reference, and choose instead to make the necessary recommendations for action itself after conducting a market study. However, given the prospective value of CC investigations and reports, it may nonetheless choose to make the reference when it considers a CC investigation and report would be more appropriate, for example because the CC has greater resources, stronger legal powers to require information, or more formal evidence gathering procedures.[159]

13.118 Another consideration to which the OFT should have regard with respect to remedies is that where the competition problem identified by the OFT relates to agreements that may affect trade between Member States, Article 3(2) of Regulation 1/2003 will prevent the CC from imposing conditions or any other type of remedy constraining agreements that do not fall foul of Article 81 (see paras 13.52, 13.83, and 13.90 above for a discussion of the effect of Article 3(2) on the CC's powers). In such cases, a reference would be deprived of effect in so far as the CC would not be able to remedy the problems identified.

(e) Interaction of the reference with Regulation 1/2003 obligations

13.119 The OFT's discretion to refer will, in addition to the factors above, carefully weigh the practical implications of making the reference with respect to any obligation to apply Articles 81 and 82 that may arise under Article 3(1) of Regulation 1/2003.

13.120 Article 3(1) of Regulation 1/2003 obliges national competition authorities, wherever they apply national competition law to agreements within the meaning of Article 81(1) or to conduct prohibited by Article 82, also to apply Article 81 and/or Article 82 as relevant. The obligation to apply Article 81 and Article 82 could therefore arise in the context of a market investigation. The CC has not been designated as a national competition authority, which means that it cannot apply Article 81 or Article 82 as required by Regulation 1/2003. Should the market referred possibly contain an Article 81 or an Article 82 issue, this could give rise to considerable difficulties (see paras 13.52 to 13.91 above for a discussion as to the difficulties that arise in such a situation and how the OFT and CC seek to accommodate the obligation to apply Articles 81 and 82 in the context of a market investigation regime).

13.121 In view of the difficulties to which references containing Article 81 and Article 82 issues give rise, the OFT has indicated that it will, in principle avoid referring to

---

[159] OFT511, *Market investigation references: Guidance about the making of references under Part 4 of the Enterprise Act* (March 2006) paras 2.30–2.31.

the CC matters that could possibly give rise to Article 81 issues in particular[160] (note however that its existing practice does not entirely reflect this concern, see para 13.55 above).

F. The Rights of Undertakings Active in the Market that may be Referred

Formally, undertakings active in the market potentially referred do not have a large role to play in the OFT process leading up to a market investigation reference. **13.122**

This is attributable to two factors. First, although it is presented as a reasoned published decision, the decision to make a market investigation reference is essentially a decision to begin to investigate, more akin to the OFT's decision to begin investigating under s 25 of the Competition Act 1998 where it has formed reasonable grounds to suspect that one of the prohibitions has been breached. Secondly, because no single undertaking is 'in the dock' and the OFT tends to rely on its informal powers to collect information, usually no formal investigation powers are exercised prior to making a reference. The procedure leading up to the reference does not usually have an adversarial flavour, nor does it give rise to any of the rights for undertakings that are associated with a more adversarial process, such as access to file. **13.123**

However, in view of the potentially far-reaching consequences a market investigation reference may have upon undertakings active in a market referred, it is generally to those undertakings' advantage to seek to become involved in the process as early as possible. In addition to the formal avenues of involvement described below, it is important to bear in mind that there is considerable room for informal dialogue with the OFT, particularly if an informal request for information has been made to an undertaking by the OFT. **13.124**

(a) Access to information

There are no statutory provisions addressing access to the OFT's file by undertakings active in a market that may be referred to the CC. Further, Pt 9 of the Enterprise Act 2002 forbids the disclosure of information obtained by a public authority such as the OFT in connection with the exercise of its functions under the relevant parts of the Act (these include those parts relating to market studies, super-complaints, and s 174) and under the Competition Act **13.125**

---

[160] OFT511, *Market investigation references: Guidance about the making of references under Part 4 of the Enterprise Act* (March 2006) para 2.14.

1998 unless it is permitted under Pt 9. It is a criminal offence to make a disclosure not permitted by Pt 9.[161] For these reasons, the OFT takes rather a cautious approach to providing access to the file on an informal basis. However, the OFT does have discretion under Pt 9 to disclose specified information where it considers that this facilitates the exercise of its statutory functions[162] (see generally, Chapter 8 above). This may be an avenue that undertakings may wish to explore with the OFT to obtain access to relevant documents.

13.126 In the absence of access to the file, it is worth considering whether a request for information under the Freedom of Information 2000 may yield relevant information. For discussion of the Freedom of Information Act and the OFT's approach to requests for information made there under, see Chapter 8.

(b) Consultation

(i) *Who will be consulted?*

13.127 Whenever the OFT decides whether or not to make a reference, to accept undertakings in lieu thereof, or to vary a reference, if it considers its decision is likely to have a substantial impact on the interests of any person, it is obliged, so far as is practicable, to consult with that person before making that decision.[163] The obligation to consult is not absolute but is subject *to what is practicable*. Section 169(4) of the Enterprise Act 2002 provides in particular that the OFT may have regard to timetable restrictions and confidentiality requirements in determining what is practicable. It is unlikely that the OFT would be able to justify dispensing with the consultation process altogether because of timetabling constraints. However, certain consultees may in practice be more difficult to consult and the OFT may therefore seek to rely on the caveat of practicability to avoid consulting undertakings that are not immediately identifiable or easy to locate.

13.128 The wording of s 169 entrusts the determination of whose interests are likely to be affected to the OFT's subjective assessment. It will accordingly be difficult to challenge that assessment by judicial review under s 179 of the Enterprise Act 2002.

13.129 Initial indications are that the OFT appears to be taking quite a generous view as to who may be affected. It appears that in cases where the OFT decides to make a reference, it will consult undertakings upon whom a remedy could eventually be imposed by the CC, for example in *Store Cards*, it consulted seven credit providers and ten retailers and in *Home Credit* it consulted large lenders as well as some smaller lenders. Possible complainants, competitors, and consumers may also be considered sufficiently affected so as to be consulted—for

---

[161] Enterprise Act 2002, s 245.   [162] ibid, s 241(1).
[163] ibid, s 169. This requirement is also imposed on the Secretary of State (s 169(6)).

example, in *Supermarkets: the code of practice and other competition issues*,[164] the OFT consulted the Association of Convenience Stores. In *Supermarkets*,[165] the OFT invited comments on its proposed decision, and received 1,250 responses, most of which were from consumers but a number of which were from affected undertakings (including supermarkets, other retailers, wholesalers, producers, and suppliers).

(ii) Content of consultation

In undertaking this consultation the OFT must, so far as practicable bearing in   **13.130**
mind time constraints and confidentiality issues,[166] give its reasons for the proposed reference.[167] According to OFT guidance, this statement of reasons will
generally include:

- a description of the goods or services concerned
- the identity of the main parties affected by the reference, whether as suppliers
  or as customers
- a view as to the possible definition of the market (or markets) affected
- a summary of the evidence that has led the OFT to have a reasonable suspicion that competition has been prevented, restricted or distorted, including
  the possible market features that may be relevant.[168]

It is clear from the *Store Cards*[169] market investigation reference that quite   **13.131**
detailed discussion took place with the consultees, for example on the issue of
market definition. In some cases, such as *Home Credit*,[170] and *Personal account
banking services in Northern Ireland*[171] the OFT was prepared to meet certain
consultees in person in addition to receiving written representations.

(iii) Timing of consultation

There is no statutory timetable for the consultation exercise. Usually, the OFT   **13.132**
will have liaised with the undertakings and held informal discussions with them
well before the formal consultation exercise. The formal consultation process
usually takes place immediately before the OFT makes its decision as to whether

---

[164] OFT807, subsequently quashed by the CAT in *Association of Convenience Stores v OFT* [2005] CAT 36.
[165] OFT845, *The grocery market: The OFT's reasons for making a reference to the Competition Commission* (May 2006).
[166] Enterprise Act 2002, s 169(4).   [167] ibid, s 169(3).
[168] OFT511, *Market investigation references: Guidance about the making of references under Part 4 of the Enterprise Act* (March 2006) para 3.7.
[169] OFT706, *Store Cards: Report of the OFT's inquiry* (March 2004).
[170] OFT747a, *Response to the super-complaint on home credit made by the National Consumer Council* (September 2004).
[171] OFT796, *Personal current account banking services in Northern Ireland: The OFT's reasons for making a reference to the Competition Commission* (May 2005).

or not to refer. The process is short. It is unlikely that parties consulted will get more than four to five weeks in which to provide their views.[172]

G. The Reference and the Information Related Thereto

13.133 The OFT is obliged, under s 172 of the Enterprise Act 2002, to publish market investigation references[173] as well as the reasons for making the reference, although the latter need not be provided at the same time as the reference. In *Association of Convenience Stores v OFT*,[174] the Association challenged the OFT's decision not to make a reference to the CC, inter alia, because the decision was insufficiently reasoned. The OFT withdrew its decision not to refer, re-investigated and subsequently produced a more thorough and comprehensive reasoned decision in *Groceries*.[175] In *OFT & others v IBA Health Ltd*[176] the Court of Appeal commented on the OFT's duty to give reasons in the context of merger references. The Court of Appeal disagreed with the CAT's criticisms of the OFT's decision in this respect. It emphasised that the statutory duty to give reasons is an important one, but is not the same as a duty to give a judgment. There was no general test for this, other than the requirement that the reasons must be intelligible and must adequately meet the substance of the arguments advanced. In a matter such as a merger reference, where the subject matter is complex and the supporting material voluminous, there was no obligation for the OFT's reference to set out all the evidence.[177]

13.134 Lastly, the OFT must under s 170(1)(b) give the CC any other assistance which the Commission may reasonably require for the purpose of assisting it in carrying out its functions and which it is in the power of the OFT to give. It is unclear whether this would entail exercising any powers it may have to investigate.

H. Ministerial Intervention

(a) The power to make a reference

13.135 The test for a reference by an appropriate Minister proceeds by way of two steps. The first step is similar to that provided for the OFT and sectoral regulators

---

[172] In OFT845, *The grocery market: The OFT's reasons for making a reference to the Competition Commission* (May 2006), the consultees had four weeks.

[173] Enterprise Act 2002, s 133 requires that a market investigation reference shall specify the enactment under which it is made, the date on which it is made, and the description of the goods or services to which the feature or combination of features concerned relates.

[174] [2005] CAT 36.   [175] OFT845, May 2006.

[176] [2004] EWCA Civ 142.   [177] Paras 102–106, LJ Cornwath.

acting under s 131 of the Enterprise Act 2002: the appropriate Minister (the Secretary of State, or the Secretary of State and one Minister (or more) of the Crown acting jointly)[178] must have reasonable grounds for suspecting that a feature or combination of features of a market are preventing, restricting, or distorting competition in the supply of specified goods or services before he or she can make a reference.[179]

The second step is solely applicable to references by the appropriate Minister. **13.136** The appropriate Minister must either be dissatisfied with the OFT's decision not to make a reference;[180] or must have both brought to the attention of the OFT information which the appropriate Minister considers to be relevant to the decision to refer (ie whatever evidence has led the Secretary of State to form a suspicion) and be satisfied that the OFT is not likely to reach a decision as to whether or not to make a reference within a reasonable period of time.[181] At the time of writing, no reference under s 132 has been made. In the authors' view it is unlikely that the power will be exercised.

(b) Intervention by the Minister

The Enterprise Act 2002 reserves a power for the Secretary of State to intervene **13.137** in a market investigation that he or she believes raises considerations of public interest.[182]

Where the OFT is considering accepting an undertaking in lieu of making a **13.138** market investigation reference under s 154 of the Enterprise Act 2002 instead of making a reference and has published a notice to that effect, the Secretary of State may intervene where he or she believes that a public interest consideration[183] is relevant to the case.[184] Where the Secretary of State has served such an intervention notice on the OFT, the OFT may not accept the proposed undertaking (or an undertaking which does not materially differ from it) without the consent of the Secretary of State.[185] The Secretary of State may withhold consent where he or she believes that the undertaking will, if accepted, operate against the public interest.[186]

Section 153 of the Enterprise Act 2002 currently only specifies one consider- **13.139** ation which may be considered to fall in the category of public interest, namely national security (the definition includes the notion of public security as defined in Article 21(4) of the EC Merger Regulation).[187]

---

[178] Enterprise Act 2002, s 132(5).
[179] For consideration of this test see paras 13.10 et seq above.
[180] Enterprise Act 2002, s 132(1).   [181] ibid, s 132(2) and (3).   [182] ibid, s 139.
[183] ibid, s 139(5).   [184] ibid, s 139(2).   [185] ibid, s 150(1).   [186] ibid, s 150(2).
[187] Council Regulation (EC) 139/2004 of 20 January 2004 on the control of concentrations between undertakings [2004] OJ L24/1.

13.140 However, the Secretary of State may specify further considerations of public interest by order, subject to affirmative resolution by Parliament.[188] To date, this power has not been used. Where the Secretary of State believes that a consideration ought to be specified as being in the public interest but no order to this effect has been approved by Parliament, it is possible for the Secretary of State to serve an intervention notice on the basis of this consideration, provided the Secretary of State takes action, as soon as practicable, for Parliament to approve the specification of the consideration.[189]

I. After the Reference

(a) Varying the reference

13.141 The OFT may at any time vary the terms of a reference.[190] A variation will not affect the timetable by which the CC has to report. A request for the OFT to vary its reference may come from the CC (as in *Store Cards*[191]) or from those affected by the reference (as in *Domestic LPG*).[192] Where the OFT proposes to vary the terms of a reference, it must consult before varying its reference[193] as it did in varying the references in *Store Cards*[194] and in *Domestic LPG*.[195] Where the request for variation does not come from the CC, the OFT is obliged also to consult the CC prior to varying the reference.[196]

(b) Appeal

13.142 Section 179(1) of the Enterprise Act 2002 provides that 'a decision of the OFT, the appropriate Minister, the Secretary of State or the Commission [CC] in connection with a reference or possible reference under this Part' may be challenged to the CAT by way of judicial review. See para 12.109 for a discussion of challenges under s 179(1).

---

[188] Enterprise Act 2002, ss 139(7), 153(3) and 181(6).
[189] ibid, s 139(5) and (6).　　　[190] ibid, s 135(1).
[191] Reference varied on 3 March 2005.　　　[192] Reference varied on 20 October 2004.
[193] Enterprise Act 2002, s 169.　　　[194] Reference varied on 3 March 2005.
[195] Reference varied on 20 October 2004.　　　[196] Enterprise Act 2002, s 135(2).

14

MARKET INVESTIGATIONS:
THE INQUIRY

A. Introduction

14.01 The Competition Commission (**CC**) is a specialist second stage competition and regulatory authority to which referrals are made by other competition or regulatory authorities where an in-depth inquiry is necessary. Although the CC carries out a number of different types of inquiries, including those into mergers, this book considers only one aspect of its work, namely market investigation inquiries. There is no intention to address the substantive aspects of market investigation inquiries: our interest lies exclusively in the process followed by the CC in conducting market inquiries.

14.02 CC market investigations 'focus upon the function of the market as a whole rather than the conduct of a single firm in a market'.[1] This is reflected in its procedure, which is, in the first instance, collaborative in nature and which does not give any undertaking the status of 'defendant'—even though in many cases CC inquiries can lead to extensive remedies as well as public relations damage for undertakings active in the market referred. CC procedure ensures fairness to undertakings affected by a market inquiry by emphasising transparency and consultation,[2] without granting these undertakings the formal rights of defence such as exist in relation to Competition Act proceedings. The CC's practice to date has demonstrated that it is very committed to consultation and transparency. This enthusiasm for consultation alleviates the procedural shortcomings in its procedure, without however altogether remedying them.

14.03 This chapter begins by way of background, with a brief account of the CC's general functions and the substantive evaluation undertaken by the CC in conducting a market investigation inquiry, before turning to CC market inquiry procedure. We provide an overview of CC market inquiry procedure, before addressing each of the stages of CC procedure in more detail. The starting point of this chapter's consideration of market inquiry procedure is the receipt of a market investigation reference by the CC. Turn to Chapter 13 for the procedure by which such market investigation references are made.

B. Statutory Background

(a) The Competition Commission

14.04 Section 45 of the Competition Act dissolved the Monopolies and Mergers Commission, the CC's predecessor, and established in its stead the CC, an

---

[1] CC4, *General Advice and Information* (March 2006) para 4.1.
[2] CC's Annual Review and Accounts 2004/2005. Enterprise Act 2002, Pt 4 introduced an obligation on the CC to consult those affected by its inquiries.

independent non-departmental public body. It came into being on 1 April 1999.

(i) Functions

The CC's functions are predominantly provided to it under the Enterprise Act **14.05** 2002, which introduced a new regime for the referral of mergers and markets to the CC in the United Kingdom in June 2003. In addition to the powers and obligations vested in the CC under the Enterprise Act 2002, various regulatory statutes such as the Water Industry Act 1991, the Telecommunications Act 1984, the Gas Act 1986, the Electricity Act 1989, the Postal Services Act 2000, the Financial Services and Markets Act 2000, and the Communications Act 2003 make provision for regulatory references to be made to the CC on specific issues.[3] None of the above legislation provides the CC with power to conduct inquiries on its own initiative, it is entirely dependent on receiving references from the Office of Fair Trading (**OFT**), sectoral regulators and (more rarely) the appropriate Minister. See para 13.135 for a definition of the appropriate Minister.

In broad terms, CC inquiries fall into three distinct categories: **14.06**

- **merger references**: these inquiries consider whether anticipated or completed mergers can be expected to result in a substantial lessening of competition and whether any appropriate remedial action can be taken in relation thereto by the CC or others;[4]
- **market investigation references**: these consider whether any feature, or combination of features, of the market referred prevents, restricts, or distorts competition and whether any appropriate remedial action can be taken in relation thereto by the CC or others;
- **regulatory references**: these inquiries address the specific questions posed by the referring regulatory authority. Questions referred cover issues such as licence modifications and price determinations in regulated markets.

This book exclusively addresses the second of the above categories of inquiries.

(ii) Structure

The CC is governed by a board known as the Council.[5] The Council consists of **14.07** the Chairman of the CC, any Deputy Chairmen that may be appointed at the

---

[3] For a complete list of the relevant legislation see the table at <http://www.competition-commission.org.uk/our_role/what_investigate/index.htm>.

[4] The CC can itself impose remedies and it may recommend remedial action should be taken by others, such as government, regulators, and public authorities; see paras 14.88 et seq.

[5] Competition Act 1998, Sch 7, para 5.

time, two non-executive members appointed to the Council by the Secretary of State for Trade and Industry, and the Chief Executive. The Council's duties include preparing an annual report, publishing general advice and information about the CC's approach to inquiries and its procedures, and discharging the CC's accounting and staffing responsibilities.[6]

14.08 The CC has approximately 50 members, who are appointed by the Secretary of State for Trade and Industry for an eight-year term following an open competition.[7] The members work part-time and come from diverse backgrounds and have differing expertise and skills, so as to ensure that the CC is well placed to determine references from across the spectrum of trade and industry. The members are supported by CC staff, who answer to the Chief Executive.

14.09 The CC discharges all its functions through groups of members selected for the purpose by the Chairman.[8] Market, merger, and special reference groups are appointed for individual inquiries. There are specialist panels of members from which one or more persons must be chosen for some regulatory inquiries, for example telecoms, water, electricity. CC Standing Groups conduct CC management: the Operations Board, the Analysis Group, Procedures and Practices Group, and the Remedies Standing Group.

14.10 The Secretary of State for Trade and Industry appoints the Chairman of the CC and any Deputy Chairmen.[9] The Chairman may attend meetings or otherwise take part in the proceedings of an inquiry group for the purpose of offering the group advice about the exercise of their functions.[10]

(b) Market investigation references: the test

14.11 The substantive analysis that the CC undertakes in market investigations inquiries can be divided into two stages.

14.12 At the first stage, it must decide whether any feature, or combination of features of the market(s) referred, restricts or distorts competition in connection with the supply or acquisition of any goods or services in the United Kingdom or a part of the United Kingdom.[11] To do so, the CC defines what market or markets exist in connection with the supply or acquisition of the goods or services described in the reference (the relevant market(s)). It then determines whether any feature or combination of features of the markets identified prevents, restricts, or distorts competition in connection with the supply or acquisition of

---

[6] ibid, Sch 7, para 5.   [7] ibid, Sch 7, para 2.
[8] ibid, Sch 7, para 15; CC1, *Competition Commission: Rules of Procedure* (2006) (**CC's Procedural Rules**) r 4.1.
[9] Competition Act 1998, Sch 7, para 3.   [10] CC's Procedural Rules, r 4.5.
[11] Enterprise Act 2002, s 134(1).

goods or services in the United Kingdom. Where the CC finds that a feature or combination of features on the markets identified prevents, restricts or distorts competition, there is an 'adverse effect on competition' (the evaluation the CC undertakes is referred to as the AEC test).[12]

The competition evaluation undertaken by the CC in considering whether **14.13** there is an adverse effect on competition is much broader than the scrutiny undertaken under the prohibitions in the Competition Act 1998 and Articles 81 and 82 EC.[13] This is primarily because a 'feature of the market' is a broad concept that embraces not only behavioural factors, but also non-behavioural factors such as barriers to entry, information asymmetries (inequality in the information available to the various participants in the market),[14] and regulation. This is consistent with the purpose of the market investigation regime, which is to look at markets as a whole. For a discussion of the AEC test more generally and the meaning of the terms 'feature or combination of features' and 'prevents, restricts or distorts competition in connection with the supply or acquisition of goods or services in the UK' see paras 13.13 et seq above.

At the second stage, where the CC identifies one or more adverse effects on **14.14** competition, s 134(4) of the Enterprise Act 2002 requires it to decide whether (and what) action should be taken by it or should be recommended to others, such as regulators, public authorities, and government, to remedy, mitigate, or prevent the adverse effects on competition or any 'detrimental effects on customers' resulting from any adverse effect on competition that it has identified. Detrimental effects on consumers can take the form of higher prices, lower quality or less choice of goods or services, or less innovation in relation to goods or services in any UK market.[15] The CC has a particularly sophisticated and extensive palette of remedies to choose from: these range from making non-binding recommendations to others (such as regulators or government), to exercising its own order-making powers, for example to compel undertakings to make a divestiture.[16]

(c) Relationship with Articles 81 and 82

Articles 81 and 82 are significant in the context of market inquiries in two **14.15** different ways.

---

[12] ibid, s 134(2).

[13] 'Regulation and Competition: Chalk and Cheese?' Speech by Peter Freeman, Chairman of the CC, 7 September 2006.

[14] eg, in *Domestic LPG* one of the features identified by the CC was the lack of information available to customers on the costs and benefits of switching and on the level of inconvenience involved in the switching process.

[15] Enterprise Act 2002, s 134(5).   [16] ibid, ss 138, 161, and Sch 8, para 13.

14.16   First, Article 3(1) of Regulation 1/2003[17] compels national competition authorities to apply Article 81 and Article 82 (as relevant) wherever national competition law is applied to agreements within the meaning of Article 81(1) or to
conduct prohibited by Article 82.[18] A market referred may contain agreements
that affect trade and/or undertakings that abuse a dominant position under
Article 82. The CC, however, has not been designated as a national competition
authority for the purposes of Regulation 1/2003 and cannot therefore apply
Article 81 and/or Article 82, even if the market(s) referred contain such issues.
Wherever an Article 81 and Article 82 issue arises in the context of a market that
is referred, this can therefore give rise to procedural difficulties.[19] See paras 13.52
et seq for an examination of the procedural consequences of an Article 81
and/or Article 82 issue arising in the context of a market that has been referred.

14.17   Secondly, although the CC is not a designated national competition authority
for the purposes of applying Articles 81 and 82, it is bound by general principles
of European law to ensure that it applies the market investigation regime in a
manner that is consistent with European law, in particular Articles 81 and 82.[20]
This means that agreements and conduct that are prohibited under EC law cannot be cleared under national law (including the market investigation regime).[21]
Further, Article 3(2) of Regulation 1/2003 has extended the obligation of consistency[22] so that the CC cannot apply *stricter* national competition law to
prohibit agreements that do not breach Article 81 or that satisfy Article 81(3).
In practice, therefore, in cases giving rise to Article 81 and Article 82 issues, the
CC has to undertake a shadow analysis of the issues under Articles 81 and 82 to
ensure that when it reports on markets containing relevant agreements/conduct
under the Enterprise Act 2002, it does so in a manner that would be consistent
with the application of Articles 81 and 82 to the same.[23] The market investigation inquiries that have been concluded to date reveal that the CC has given
careful thought to how its findings, most particularly the remedies it imposes,
interact with its obligations of consistency with respect to Articles 81 and 82 EC
and Regulation 1/2003.[24]

---

[17] Council Regulation (EC) 1/2003 of 16 December 2002 on the implementation of the rules
on competition laid down in Articles 81 and 82 of the Treaty [2003] OJ L1/1.
[18] See Chapter 3 for a discussion of this obligation more generally,
[19] These are considered by Peter Freeman, Chairman of the CC, in the Lord Fletcher Lecture,
'UK Competition Law after Modernisation', 15 March 2005.
[20] Case 14/68 *Wilhelm v Bundeskartellamt* [1969] ECR 1.
[21] See paras 3.03–3.06 above.
[22] Article 3(2), by its terms, is triggered by the application of national competition law,
irrespective of the body applying it.
[23] See paras 3.79–3.93 above for a fuller discussion of the obligation in Art 3(2).
[24] See *Store Cards*, para 10.9: 'Whilst it is the OFT that has been designated by the UK as the
national authority responsible for the applications of Articles 81 and 82 EC (by virtue of Article
35 of Regulation 1/2003), we have had regard to the relevant requirements of that Regulation in

C. An Overview of Market Investigation Procedure

Market inquiries are conducted by small groups of CC members supported **14.18** by CC professional staff. The procedure is fairly flexible, to allow the groups conducting the inquiries to tailor their approach to the demands of a particular inquiry. Certain basic procedural provisions are set out in the Enterprise Act 2002 and in Sch 7 to the Competition Act 1998. Further, clear procedural parameters that must be followed by groups in all cases are set out in the CC's Procedural Rules, published by the Chairman under para 19A(1) of Sch 7 to the Competition Act. Groups must also have regard to the *Chairman's Guidance to Groups*[25] issued pursuant to paras 19A(7) and (8) of Sch 7 to the Competition Act. Subject to these provisions, a certain margin of discretion allows each group to determine its own procedure relating to how it proposes to deal with a market investigation.[26] When the CC's predecessor, the Monopolies and Mergers Commission, conducted market inquiries under the Fair Trading Act 1973, it enjoyed a wide discretion to regulate its own procedure.[27] Part 4 of the Enterprise Act 2002 has reduced the procedural uncertainty in that it has codified many aspects of the informal procedures that existed under the Fair Trading Act and introduced the requirement on the CC to produce guidance.[28]

(a) Appointment of groups and group decision-making

When a reference has been made to the CC, the Chairman must appoint **14.19** members to form the group that will undertake the inquiry, as well as the chairman of the group.[29] The group must consist of at least three persons, but usually consists of four or five members including the chairman of the group. A group constituted in connection with a market investigation reference is known as a 'market reference group'. The group will take all decisions in relation to the market reference.

In addition to the group, CC professional staff play an important role in the **14.20** conduct of inquiries. Each group is allocated one Inquiry Director (**ID**) and one Inquiry Secretary (**IS**) (depending on the demands of the inquiry, it may appoint two ISs, as in *Groceries*). The ID and IS will take the lead in conducting the practicalities of the inquiry on a day-to-day basis. It is important to establish a good dialogue with the ID, the IS, and the professional staff

---

considering and adopting appropriate remedies in the context of our findings and conclusions.'
See also *Domestic LPG*, paras 7.112–7.114, *Home Credit*, para 9.7.

[25] CC6 (March 2006).　　[26] Competition Act 1998, Sch 7, para 19(6).
[27] *R v Monopolies and Mergers Commission, ex p Matthew Brown plc* [1987] 1 WLR 1235.
[28] Enterprise Act 2002, s 172(3).
[29] Competition Act 1998, Sch 7, para 15 and CC's Procedural Rules, r 4.1.

(lawyers, economists etc) that support the group. Effective dialogue with inquiry staff plays a very important role as the inquiry develops: for example, parties involved in the investigation can obtain meetings with the staff to explain particular issues[30]—such a meeting provides a valuable avenue for a party to make its case which would not otherwise be available.

14.21 Rule 4.5 of the CC's Procedural Rules of Procedure obliges the Chairman, in appointing members to the group, to have regard to the Commission Guidance on Conflicts of Interest[31] and to the Code of Practice for Reporting Panel Members and Specialist Panel Members.[32] Members are required by Commission Guidance to disclose any interest that might give rise to a conflict of interest when the prospect of their serving on a group is first raised.[33] Usually, if a potential conflict is identified, the member is not appointed, or is asked to dispose of the interest. The Chief Executive will take legal advice to determine appropriate action. Occasionally, where a member has an insignificant interest, and subject to the Chairman's approval, it may be sufficient simply to inform the parties involved in the investigations of the interest. Disclosures of interest are also posted on the Commission website, in the pages that relate to a particular reference. There is no formal provision for parties active in the market referred to be consulted or to make submissions on the issue of appointment of the members of the group but, as explained above, where there is a minor conflict, parties will be notified (usually by the ID or the IS) and will have an opportunity to express their views.

14.22 Different rules govern the way in which a decision is reached by the group, depending on the decision at issue. In the everyday conduct of the inquiry, a simple majority suffices, with the Chairman of the group having the casting vote.[34] However, in order to reach a decision of adverse effects on competition, two thirds of the members of the group must agree.[35] A simple majority suffices for decisions relating to remedies.

14.23 Groups are appointed until the statutory conclusion of the investigation, which is either the final report or the making or accepting of remedies. Where a group appointed to deal with a particular inquiry has been disbanded, and an issue arises requiring a decision to be made by the CC (for example, the variation or

---

[30] In *Store Cards* and *Home Credit*, for example, individual store card providers held meetings with the professional staff to explain their position on remedies (see para 10.2 of the *Store Cards* Final Report and para 9.2 of the *Home Credit* Final Report).
[31] <http://www.competition-commission.org.uk/our_peop/conflicts_of_interest.htm>.
[32] <http://www.competition-commission.org.uk/our_role/ms_and_fm/annex_b.htm>.
[33] Commission Guidance on Conflicts of Interest, para 4.
[34] CC's Procedural Rules, r 4.3. and Competition Act 1998, Sch 7, para 21.
[35] Competition Act 1998, Sch 7, para 20 as amended by Enterprise Act 2002, Sch 11, paras 5–7.

revocation of an order), the group's functions may be performed by a standing group appointed by the Chairman to deal with the general functions of the Commission.[36]

(b) Timetable

(i) Statutory deadline

Section 137 of the Enterprise Act 2002 provides that the CC shall publish its **14.24** report on a reference within the period of two years from the date of the market investigation reference. The Secretary of State has the power to shorten this period by order.[37] The government stated that this should be viewed very much as a long-stop date and that it would not expect an investigation to take much longer than 13 months (which was the average period of a monopoly reference under the Fair Trading Act 1973).[38] The CC indicated that it expects to complete certain inquiries within a shorter time, approximately within 12 to 15 months of the reference.[39]

To date, the CC has completed three market investigation inquiries, all of **14.25** which were concluded immediately before the statutory deadline. The first market investigation reference, *Store Cards*, was initially scheduled to be completed in July 2005. The CC's timetable was pushed back several times, so that in fact it was published on 7 March 2006, just before the statutory deadline on 16 March 2006. Similarly, in *Domestic Bulk Liquid Petroleum Gas* (*LPG*), the CC reported on 29 June 2006, just before the statutory deadline of 4 July 2006. In *Home Credit*, the CC published its report on 30 November 2006, before the statutory deadline of 19 December 2006. Administrative timetables for these and current inquiries such as *Classified directory advertising services* have been pushed back several times. When contrasted with the average time scale for such inquiries under the Fair Trading Act, the extra time that has been necessary can be attributed to the more demanding consultative element that is involved in market investigation references under the Enterprise Act 2002—the process of seeking interested parties' views as the inquiry is developing is extremely time consuming, particularly given the number of interested parties (for example, there were more than 450 in *Home Credit* and 375 in *Store Cards*).

---

[36] CC's Procedural Rules, r 5.6 and CC6, *Chairman's Guidance to Groups* (March 2006) para 6.

[37] Enterprise Act 2002, s 137(2).

[38] See *Hansard*, HC Standing Committee B (Pt 2) on the Enterprise Bill (7 May 2002) paras 129–456.

[39] CC4, *General Advice and Information* (March 2006) para 6.7.

(ii) Administrative timetable

14.26 Once a group has been appointed in connection with a market investigation reference, the group must, as soon as practicable, draw up an administrative timetable for the progression of the inquiry.[40] The timetable will fix a date for the key stages of the inquiry, such as the gathering of evidence, the hearings, and the publication of CC preliminary views for consultation. The timetable is notified to the public and to the parties, who must comply with the timetable.[41] There are no sanctions for non-compliance with the timetable (although see paras 14.57 et seq below for the sanctions that can apply where the CC exercises its compulsory powers), but the CC is free to disregard those submissions/evidence that it receives out of time, which in many cases is a very real incentive to ensure compliance with the timetable (see CC's Procedural Rules, r 9.3). Annex A to this chapter contains the administrative timetables that have been published by the CC in relation to the market investigations references undertaken to date.

14.27 The group is obliged, under para 6.4 of the CC's Procedural Rules, to have regard to the views of the 'main parties' on drawing up the timetable. Usually, at the outset of a case, the ID will write to the main parties in what is called the 'First Day Letter', giving them the proposed timetable and other relevant information relating to the progress of the inquiry and invite them to a meeting with the ID, the IS, and other staff dealing with the inquiry, but not the members. This initial 'case management' meeting is critical and provides an important opportunity to establish a good working relationship with the staff taking the inquiry forward.

14.28 Although the main parties are consulted on the timetable, it should not be assumed that this means that the main parties are in a position to dictate the pace of progression of the inquiry: all CC timetables have to date been tightly drawn, allowing the main parties little time in which to prepare and draw up their submissions and evidence. Because CC inquiries are into markets, and not into the behaviour of individual undertakings, there is no defendant whose rights have to be given particular consideration when drawing up the timetable. Further, the CC must bear in mind its statutory deadlines and the needs of the inquiry as a whole. Given that the CC has the intention of conducting its inquiries as efficiently and promptly as possible (in many cases before the two-year statutory time limit), there is not much flexibility for undertakings participating in the inquiry to seek extensions of time, although the CC has, in the few

---

[40] CC's Procedural Rules, r 6.2. See also CC6, *Chairman's Guidance to Groups* (March 2006) para 7.
[41] CC's Procedural Rules, r 6.6.

inquiries conducted to date, been willing to overlook minor delays in communicating submissions or evidence. The administrative timetable is not unalterable:
the group is free to change it at any point during the reference, should it consider
this to be necessary.[42] When the group changed the timetable in *Store Cards* it
was at its own initiative and it did not consult the interested parties.

To date, the rapidity with which the administrative timetable has been fixed is **14.29**
variable: in *Groceries* and in *Northern Ireland personal banking* the timetable was
published within one month of the reference, whereas in *Domestic LPG* the
timetable was fixed four and a half months after the reference.

Although it may take some time for the group to draw up the administrative **14.30**
timetable for the inquiry, it should not be assumed that the inquiry is inactive
pending publication of the administrative timetable. Quite the contrary, while
the administrative timetable is being drawn up, the CC embarks on various
information-gathering exercises.

(c) Key procedural steps

CC procedure is not intended to be adversarial, in contrast to proceedings **14.31**
conducted under the Competition Act 1998 (although this may not always be
fully appreciated by the main parties subject to the full rigours of a CC inquiry).
There is no statement of objections and no defence. The parties involved in the
procedure, apart from the CC itself, fall into two broad categories. CC guidance
indicates that it considers 'interested parties' to include the main parties
(defined as companies that form part of the market under investigation) and
third parties that may be affected by the reference, such as customers, suppliers,
government departments, trade, or consumer organisations.[43]

Rule 6.3 of the CC's Procedural Rules lists the typical stages of an investigation **14.32**
that may be provided for in the administrative timetable as follows:

a.   gathering information
b.   issuing questionnaires
c.   hearing of witnesses
d.   verifying information
e.   providing a statement of issues
f.   considering responses to the statement of issues
g.   notifying provisional findings
h.   notifying and considering possible remedies
i.   considering exclusions from disclosure
j.   publishing reports.

---

[42] ibid, para 6.7.   [43] CC4, *General Advice and Information* (March 2006) para 6.12.

14.33   As the six administrative timetables relating to market investigation references published to date reveal,[44] the above list of major stages of an inquiry is not entirely representative of the process that is followed by the CC in relation to a market investigation reference. This is recognised in CC guidance, which states that the stages listed above 'often overlap and do not necessarily take place in this order'.[45]

14.34   The procedure followed by the CC can be more easily understood if the ten stages identified above are divided into three distinct phases:

- Phase 1 of the inquiry is the information gathering stage: this comprises the stages listed at (a) to (e) above. Phase 1 culminates in the CC's publication of the Statement of Issues.
- Phase 2 of the inquiry is the analytical phase. The CC embarks on the main analytical work—it begins to formulate its views on the basis of the evidence submitted to it, culminating in the publication of its provisional findings. In practice, this phase comprises (in addition to stages (f) and (g) identified above) three additional elements. First, the CC holds an Issues Hearing with the parties following the publication of the Statement of Issues. Secondly, the CC publishes a document for consultation entitled the CC's Emerging Thinking. Thirdly, the CC considers the views and evidence submitted in response to the Emerging Thinking (if necessary holding further hearings). In order to assist its analysis of the views and evidence presented to it in response to the Emerging Thinking, and before the conclusion of this phase with the publication of its Provisional Findings, the CC may produce a series of working papers which it circulates to the relevant parties to solicit further views.
- Phase 3 is the remedies stage, during which the CC considers which, if any, remedies to apply, consults the affected parties, and holds a remedies hearing where necessary, before publishing its report.

A diagram by the CC setting out the main steps of the CC's procedure is appended at Annex B to this chapter.

14.35   Hearings are not confined to Phase 1: the administrative timetables published to date all envisage hearings taking place throughout the three stages of the procedure (in fact the main hearings of the parties are in Phase 2, as hearings in Phase 1 are usually confined to hearings of third parties).

---

[44] These have been reproduced in Annex A to this Chapter.
[45] CC4, *General Advice and Information* (March 2006) para 6.10.

D. Phase 1: Information Gathering

The CC does not begin its information gathering on a blank canvas: along with   **14.36**
the market investigation reference, the CC will have received from the OFT the
information held by the OFT that is relevant to the reference, to which the CC
is obliged to have regard[46] (see para 13.133 above). On receipt of a market
investigation reference (and while the Chairman is selecting the market reference group and the group is considering the administrative timetable for the
reference) the CC immediately begins to gather information on the market
investigation reference. It does so by several means, relying both on voluntary
cooperation and its compulsory powers. Whatever the basis on which information is provided to the CC, it should be noted at the outset that it is an offence
for individuals and bodies corporate knowingly or recklessly to provide the CC
with false or misleading material in connection with any of its functions under
Pt 4 of the Enterprise Act 2002.[47]

(a) Voluntary provision of information

(i) Generalised call for evidence

At the very outset of the inquiry, the CC publicly invites evidence from all parties   **14.37**
likely to have an interest in the market investigation reference. This is done by
announcement on its website, press notices, and advertisements, and is usually
very prompt: in *Home Credit*, the CC invited evidence from 'all interested parties'
by a press release published on its website on the very same day it received the
reference. In *Domestic LPG* and in *Store Cards* the general invitation was issued on
the day following receipt of the reference. Those wishing to respond are given
between three to four weeks in which to reply to the general invitation. This does
not leave much time to prepare and submit evidence and submissions in relation
to the matters referred. In view of the importance to each party potentially
affected by the market inquiry, of formulating their position persuasively at an
early stage in the inquiry, interested parties are well advised to begin to prepare
their submissions for this stage before the OFT makes its reference.

(ii) First day letter, individual letters, and questionnaires requesting evidence

In addition to a general invitation to interested parties to submit evidence, the   **14.38**
CC also writes, on an individual basis, to the main parties and certain other
undertakings or associations that it considers may have an interest in the reference, inviting evidence from them, and in some cases requesting them to reply
to questionnaires.

---

[46] Enterprise Act 2002, s 170.   [47] ibid, s 180.

14.39 At the very outset of an inquiry, the CC will send the main parties the 'First Day Letter' which outlines the scope and conduct of the inquiry, addresses administrative arrangements (document delivery and such like) and requests that the parties produce (within one or two weeks) certain basic 'off the shelf material' such as annual reports, board minutes, accounts etc. It will also request a structured submission covering issues such as market definition, market structure, and market behaviour.

14.40 Parties that have been selected for direct information requests are also given between three to four weeks to respond to questionnaires and individual letters. Responses to the initial call for evidence can influence the direction the inquiry will take.

(iii) Publicly available documents, commissioned research, visits

14.41 In addition to calling for evidence from interested parties, the CC, like the OFT before it, uses publicly available sources of information such as surveys that have been published by analysts or consultants on the markets under consideration.

14.42 Surveys such as consumer surveys or expert advice can also be especially commissioned by the CC to provide evidence about a particular market. For example, in *Store Cards* the CC commissioned several pieces of research to explore users' perceptions and experiences of store cards. It asked an independent market research company to conduct an initial qualitative survey that used in-depth interviews with members of the general public who had store cards and then commissioned the same company to undertake a quantitative survey, which included telephone interviews with 1,002 respondents. In *Home Credit*, the CC commissioned two pieces of market research, a qualitative survey of home credit customers, and a quantitative survey of home credit customers. In view of the importance of expert evidence, main parties must give serious consideration to commissioning similar research and evidence, should they not wish to be bound by the evidence adduced by the experts commissioned by the CC.

14.43 The CC may also undertake visits to the main parties. These site visits help the CC to gain a first-hand understanding of the workings of the company and industry in question.

(b) Hearings

(i) Hearings with third parties

14.44 The CC will also, in the first phase of the inquiry, invite third parties to hearings as a more interactive and dynamic means of collecting information. Parties that have received a questionnaire from the CC are likely to be invited to third party hearings. Usually the CC is most interested to hear from main suppliers and customers at this stage. Should a third party decline the CC's invitation to attend a hearing, the CC can, of course, resort to statutory powers,[48] but in practice attendance is voluntary.

14.45 The CC's Procedural Rules leave it for the group to determine whether the hearing will be in private or in public.[49] In so doing, it is obliged to have regard, inter alia, to the views of the main and third parties. In general, hearings held with third parties in Phase 1 tend to be held in private, in order to enable them to provide detailed and confidential information to the group in an uninhibited fashion.[50]

14.46 Under the CC's Procedural Rules, it is solely for the group to determine whether the hearings will be held with each party separately or whether it will hold joint hearings with one or more parties.[51] Usually hearings are held with one party to the inquiry at a time and in private. Although the group is not required to consult on this issue, there is generally room for third parties in Phase 1 to make suggestions/submissions on this issue, particularly given the voluntary nature of their attendance at the hearing. Occasionally, third parties such as statutory bodies or consumer groups may request a joint hearing, which the group will seek to accommodate. The group is also given a free hand to determine the modalities of the hearing, in particular, who will be able to attend, who will have a right to be heard, whether witnesses will be cross-examined. Although there is substantial room for the parties to suggest who should attend the hearing on their behalf (eg Marketing Manager, CEO, legal and economic advisers) the CC may require the evidence of one person (eg the person who negotiated an agreement).

14.47 In general, there is no 'cross-examination' as such—the hearings take the form of a discussion between the members of the group and representatives of the undertakings, assisted by their legal representatives. The CC may send out an agenda before the hearing setting out the areas in which it is interested. As the purpose of the hearing is for the CC to obtain information, the group actively questions those appearing before it and it will use questioning in an attempt to 'drill down' to the relevant issues and the particular party's interest in the matter. The group will often raise questions arising from the party's written submissions or questionnaire. It makes sense therefore, before attending the hearing, for those representatives of the undertakings that are to reply to the group's questions, to prepare thoroughly, and to be assisted by legal and economic advisers. The parties will usually be provided with a 'Topics'

---

[48] Enterprise Act 2002, s 99.   [49] CC's Procedural Rules, r 7.1.   [50] ibid, r 7.2(c).
[51] ibid, r 7.4.

letter to allow them to attend with the appropriate staff members and advisers.

14.48 The parties attending a hearing are given an opportunity to check the transcript, and they may also subsequently supplement or clarify points in the hearing by writing to the CC.[52] It appears that the practice of the CC has not been to transmit such transcripts of hearings to other parties involved in the inquiry. However, it is able to do so (under s 241(1) of the Enterprise Act 2002) where it makes the disclosure for the purpose of facilitating the performance of any of its functions. Should the CC decide to make such a disclosure, it will be bound by s 244 of the Enterprise Act to have regard, *inter alia*, to the need to exclude from disclosure commercial information whose disclosure might in the CC's opinion harm the legitimate business interests of the undertaking to which it relates.[53] It is therefore in the undertakings' interest to preface any submission containing confidential information appropriately for the purposes of the transcript.

(ii) Open hearings or 'open meetings'

14.49 The CC may also, during the first phase, decide to hold a voluntary open hearing at which it hears submissions from parties that it has specifically invited to the hearing. These open hearings are meant to facilitate transparency and access to the group, to stimulate the debate and to allow parties with differing positions an opportunity to hear each other's views as well as allowing those interested but not formally participating an opportunity to attend and voice questions from the floor. Such hearings are far less inquisitorial and function more like a talking shop (the group's main function is to listen and they do not generally pose questions). In *Store Cards*, the CC held an open hearing at which it invited presentations from several speakers representing a broad spectrum of interests affected by the inquiry: consumer associations, store card providers, the Department of Trade and Industry, a charity, and an independent market analysis company were amongst those making contributions.

14.50 For undertakings and organisations considering participation in such an open hearing, it should be noted that despite the emphasis on friendly cooperation and the 'talking shop' aspect of these hearings, they are transcribed (the transcripts are subsequently posted on the CC's website) and they are open to the press, who are able to pose questions from the floor to the participants. Parties may therefore find that a statement made at such a hearing may be relied upon against them at a subsequent stage of the inquiry.

---

[52] CC4, *General Advice and Information*, para 6.18.
[53] See paras 8.34 et seq above for a discussion of s 244.

(iii) Hearings with main parties

As with hearings of third parties, these are usually held on a voluntary basis with **14.51** each party in turn, although the CC may fall back on its statutory powers and compel attendance if necessary.[54]

CC hearings, in particular main party hearings, cannot be compared to OFT **14.52** hearings or European Commission hearings. They are not aimed at allowing the parties to be heard and to develop their arguments, but are geared instead at providing the CC with an opportunity to obtain information that it needs from the parties concerned. The proceedings may therefore have inquisitorial aspects, and attendees should come prepared to respond to a wide range of questions. CC guidance provides that: 'Companies or their representatives are expected to be able to answer the Commission's questions about matters arising in the inquiry including those raised in the statement of issues.'[55] These hearings are usually more inquisitorial in nature than the hearings of third parties, and there is, even more than in the case of third party hearings, an interest for undertakings to ensure that they have considered, and addressed areas that may be of concern to the CC, with the assistance of legal advisers and specialist economic advisers. If possible, the preparation of economic reports or other tangible evidence in support of the main parties' case will bolster their case as well as facilitating an appeal in the event that the CC should not take account of the evidence presented.

Although there is no express provision to this effect, should a party wish to make **14.53** a representation to the group at the hearing, it is advised they make such a request in advance. The group is unlikely to turn down such a request, provided it is made sufficiently in advance. The time allowed for such submissions is short (in the range of 20 minutes). Parties wishing to make more developed submissions should consider requesting a meeting with CC professional staff. As to whether, given that parties are potentially subjected to the CC's extensive remedial powers at the conclusion of the inquiry, they are given a sufficient opportunity to be heard for the purposes of Article 6 of the European Convention on Human Rights (**ECHR**) (see paras 14.67 et seq below).

It may be that an undertaking may not be able to respond to all the CC's **14.54** questions at a hearing—in such a case it should undertake to provide the answer in written form or it may receive a request for the information by the CC employing its compulsory powers under s 109 of the Enterprise Act.

---

[54] Enterprise Act 2002, s 109.
[55] CC4, *General Advice and Information* (March 2006) para 6.19.

(c) Compulsory requests for information

14.55 The Enterprise Act 2002 endows the CC with significant compulsory powers to obtain information. Although it prefers to rely on voluntary cooperation from the relevant undertakings, the CC appears to be increasingly relying on its compulsory powers.

14.56 Sections 109 and 176 of the Enterprise Act 2002 empower the CC to issue notices requiring a person to attend at a certain time or place, to produce documents, or to supply other estimates, forecasts, returns, or other specified information. The CC may also copy any document provided to it.[56] Sections 109 and 176 of the Enterprise Act 2002 empower the CC to issue notices requiring a person to attend at a certain time or place and to give evidence (if necessary, on oath). It is implicit that the CC is not able to compel production of evidence or replies to questions that are not relevant to the inquiry: the powers are expressly given 'for the purposes of any investigation on a reference' — a question that has no bearing on the investigation could not therefore be made pursuant to the notice. The powers are subject to the rules on legal and professional privilege and self-incrimination.[57]

(d) Non-compliance with compulsory requests

14.57 Severe consequences attach to non-compliance with CC requests made under s 109. First, the CC is not obliged to have regard to any information that it receives after the date reasonably specified for its receipt. Secondly, s 110 of the Enterprise Act 2002 provides a power for the CC to impose monetary penalties for non-compliance with requests made by the CC under s 109. The CC has a power to impose penalties where the CC considers that either:

- a person has, without reasonable excuse, failed to comply with any requirement of a notice under s 109;[58] or
- a person has intentionally obstructed or delayed another person in exercising the powers under s 109(6) (copying of documents).[59]

14.58 The CC may impose a monetary penalty (up to a maximum of £20,000) or set at a daily rate (up to a daily maximum of £5,000) or a combination of both.[60] These powers are not redundant: the CC is quite ready to use them and has on several occasions come quite close to doing so. Section 114 of the Enterprise Act 2002 provides for a full right of appeal on the merits to the Competition Appeal

---

[56] Enterprise Act 2002, s 109(6).
[57] ibid, s 109(7). See paras 7.09 and 7.30 et seq respectively.
[58] ibid, s 110(1).   [59] ibid, s 110(3).
[60] ibid, s 111 and the CC (Penalties) Order 2003, SI 2003/1371. See CC5, *Statement of Policy on Penalties* (June 2003) for further details.

Tribunal against any CC decision to impose a penalty, and the amount of a penalty (see generally, Chapter 12).

Thirdly, s 110(5) of the Enterprise Act 2002 provides that the intentional **14.59** alteration, suppression, or destruction of any documents a person is required to produce under s 109 constitutes a criminal offence punishable on summary conviction to a fine not exceeding the statutory maximum or, on indictment, to imprisonment for a term not exceeding two years or to a fine or both. The criminal offence and the CC's powers to impose a monetary penalty for failure to comply with a notice are mutually exclusive—a person is therefore not exposed, in relation to the same act, to both a CC penalty and a criminal prosecution.[61]

(e) The Statement of Issues

At the culmination of Phase 1 of the inquiry, once the CC has gathered and **14.60** considered sufficient evidence to form an initial view of the relevant market and the issues arising therein, it will publish a 'Statement of Issues'. This lists the main issues that the CC believes are relevant in deciding whether any feature of the market referred distorts, restricts, or prevents competition. The Statement of Issues will generally, on the basis of evidence received by the CC, highlight relevant issues that the CC wishes to explore relating to definition of the relevant market(s), the individual features of the markets, and possible detrimental effects. As the CC is at pains to emphasise, the Statement of Issues does not reflect the group's final view on any of the issues in the inquiry. This is borne out in its practice to date. For example, the Statement of Issues in *Domestic LPG* raises whether it may be possible for a LPG supplier to supply LPG to a customer despite not owning the customer's LPG tank. Its Final Report, however, chose not to disturb the arrangement that tied the supply of LPG to the ownership of the tank.

On publication of the Statement of Issues, the CC invites interested parties to **14.61** comment. It usually allows interested parties three weeks in which to respond and submit additional evidence on the issues raised.

The Statement of Issues serves several purposes. From the interested parties' **14.62** perspective, it informs them of what the CC considers are the issues and gives them an opportunity to comment. From the CC's perspective, it has the effect of prompting the submission of further relevant arguments and evidence for it to consider. Lastly, the Statement of Issues also provides the main parties with an indication of the main lines of inquiry the group is likely to pursue at the

---

[61] Enterprise Act 2002, s 110(6) and (8).

hearings with them, which it conducts at the second stage of the inquiry, the decision-making stage. From the main parties' perspective, this is a very useful document—given that there is no obligation on the CC to serve a 'statement of objections' on parties or anything resembling such a statement on the main parties, the Statement of Issues is the first tangible document setting out issues of concern in relation to which the parties who may potentially adversely be affected by the CC's report can begin to construct their 'defence'.

E. Phase 2: The Decision-Making Process

(a) Collection of further information

14.63 Phase 2 does not signal the end of information collection as such. The CC will continue to solicit and receive additional information right to the very end of its inquiry. Following the closure of Phase 1 with the publication of the Statement of Issues, interested and main parties submit further oral and written evidence to the CC in response to the Statement of Issues. In Phase 2, the CC will, in particular, solicit further evidence and submissions from interested and main parties following the publication of its Emerging Thinking and Provisional Findings (see paras 14.69 et seq below).

(b) Hearings

14.64 In Phase 2, the CC holds several types of hearings.

(i) The Issues Hearing

14.65 The Issues Hearing follows on from the Statement of Issues: as indicated above, the Statement of Issues provides all interested parties, at the conclusion of Phase 1, with an indication of what the CC considers to be the main issues arising in the inquiry. The opportunity to respond to the CC's Statement of Issues is then provided to the main parties at the Issues Hearing, which is held at the beginning of Phase 2.

14.66 The hearing is usually held on a voluntary basis. For a description of the form such hearings take, see the comments made in relation to hearings at paras 14.44 et seq, above.

14.67 Although there is no express provision to this effect, should a party wish to make a representation to the CC at the hearing, it is advised they make such a request in advance. The CC is unlikely to turn down such a request, provided it is made sufficiently in advance. The time allowed for such Opening Statements is short (in the range of 20 minutes). As to whether parties are given a sufficient opportunity to be heard see paras 14.77 et seq below.

(ii) Hearings with third parties and open hearings

In Phase 2, the CC may also hold further hearings with third parties or an open **14.68** hearing (see paras 14.49–14.50, above), as, for example, in *Home Credit*. In *Home Credit*, the CC sought, in particular, to encourage home credit customers to attend its open meeting, which it publicised widely (it even set up a free-phone line for potential attendees to contact for further information).

(c) The CC's Emerging Thinking

Given the volume of material that the CC receives in its response to the **14.69** Statement of Issues and in the course of the hearings with the main parties, the CC has developed the practice of publishing an interim document entitled 'the CC's Emerging Thinking' which sets out its thinking and summarises the evidence upon which its thinking is based, before going on to publish its provisional findings.

The Emerging Thinking is a useful intermediary step that bridges the publica- **14.70** tion of the Statement of Issues and that of the CC's provisional findings. It is more comprehensive and detailed than the Statement of Issues, and usually includes a summary of the evidence that is relied upon, as was provided in *Store Cards*.[62] This is where those potentially affected by a market inquiry get a real sense of the CC's thinking. The Emerging Thinking gives interested and main parties a valuable chance to comment and submit further evidence for the CC's consideration on a more informed basis, as well as allowing the CC a chance to develop its thinking before committing itself to provisional findings.

The practice of publishing the 'Emerging Thinking' document was introduced **14.71** following the introduction of Regulation 1/2003, with a view to serving some of the purposes that are served by the statement of objections in Article 81 and Article 82 competition procedure.[63] For reasons that are set out in more detail at paras 14.82 et seq below, one cannot equate the Emerging Thinking document with a Statement of Objections, mainly because the document does not afford the undertakings concerned the rights of response and access to the file that

---

[62] 'The CC has considered carefully the further written and oral evidence from parties that was submitted in response to the Issues Statement. In the light of this and other evidence submitted throughout the investigation, it has begun to focus its thinking on the central issues that appear to merit consideration . . . Its current thinking is set out below, together with summaries of support-ing evidence in the form of a number of annexes that address aspects of the store card sector. These summaries do not purport to be comprehensive or definitive, and will be supplemented as the inquiry progresses.' *Store Cards*, para 2 of *The CC's Emerging Thinking*.

[63] According to Prof Paul Geroski, then Chairman of the CC, 'Market Inquiries and Market Studies: the view from the Clapham Omnibus', 1 July 2005 <http://www.competition-commis-sion.org.uk/our_peop/members/chair_speeches/pdf/geroski_chatham_house_010705.pdf>.

would be associated with a statement of objections in Article 81 and Article 82 competition procedure.

(d) The CC's provisional findings

14.72 Article 169 of the Enterprise Act 2002 imposes a duty on the CC, where it considers that a proposed decision on questions under s 134 of the Enterprise Act is likely to have a substantial impact on the interests of any person, to consult that person in so far as is practicable.

14.73 The CC discharges this obligation by publishing the provisional findings on a reference.[64] The Provisional Findings must include the provisional decision in relation to each of the statutory questions arising and must also include an explanation of the group's reasons for reaching its findings. The *Chairman's Guidance to Groups*[65] specifies that the reasoning should be sufficient to enable a meaningful consideration of the provisional findings by the parties.

14.74 Provisional Findings may also contain proposals for remedies: if they do not do so, then remedies must be consulted on separately.[66] The CC is under an obligation[67] to have regard to the need to give as much notice as is practicable of remedial action. If the proposed remedial action is not notified in the Provisional Findings, it must be notified to the main parties as soon as possible thereafter.

14.75 The CC must notify the 'main parties' of the Provisional Findings and invite responses thereto, allowing the parties at least 21 days in which to submit a written response.[68] In *Store Cards*, the CC also provided the main parties with an opportunity to comment on the Provisional Findings prior to publication, on issues of confidentiality and factual accuracy only.

14.76 Following the publication of and consultation on the provisional findings, the group will meet to discuss responses that have been submitted, and consider whether or not, in the light of responses received, the provisional findings should be altered. The CC may at this stage consider that a further hearing with one or more of the parties is necessary. However, apart from their right to submit a written response to the Provisional Findings, main parties do not have a right to be heard and there is accordingly no obligation on the CC to hold a hearing.[69]

---

[64] CC's Procedural Rules, rr 10.1–10.8.   [65] CC6 (March 2006) para 12.
[66] CC4, *General Advice and Information* (March 2006) paras 6.20 and 6.22; CC's Procedural Rules, r 11.2.
[67] CC's Procedural Rules, r 11.1.   [68] ibid, r 10.5.   [69] ibid, r 10.6.

(e) Access to file and other rights of the defence

Market investigation inquiries are likely to meet the threshold of determining **14.77** civil rights and obligations for the purposes of Article 6 ECHR (this is discussed at paras 11.49 et seq above). Accordingly, the CC's decision-making procedure must meet the requirements of Article 6 ECHR.

As market investigations are concerned with the competition process in a mar- **14.78** ket as a whole and are not intended to place any undertaking 'in the dock', CC procedure has for obvious reasons not been developed with the classic adversarial rights associated with the right to a fair trial under Article 6 ECHR that can be found in the OFT's and the European Commission's procedure. As a result, parties will find that they do not have the full range of procedural rights that would be available to them were they investigated by the OFT or the European Commission in relation to a suspected breach of competition law.

An important aspect of the right to a fair trial is for a party to have knowledge **14.79** of, and comment on, the observations or evidence adduced by the other party (including any relevant evidence).[70] However, there are no formal procedures that deal with access to the CC's file for the main parties (or indeed any party). Although the ethos of CC procedure is one of transparency, with an emphasis on publication of relevant materials and consultation at each of the key stages of the inquiry, parties are reliant on the CC to determine what it chooses to disclose. This is to be contrasted with the (still imperfect, but more developed) right of access to the file in both OFT and European Commission procedure.[71]

The CC's commitment to transparency is not open to question: it publishes a **14.80** very significant amount of the documents relevant to an inquiry on its website for any interested party to consult. However, for the main parties, it is difficult to construct a case without knowledge of all the submissions and evidence that is submitted by third parties. Further, there is very little means for the main parties to ascertain what there is (if anything) that is not being disclosed to them. Although much of the relevant submissions and the evidence is published, a considerable amount of evidence is not disclosed. For example, the CC uses hearings as a way of gathering evidence and taking submissions from third parties. However, evidence gathered this way, although of some importance, is not usually accessible to main parties as the CC does not usually disclose the transcripts to other parties (although the CC summarises key transcripts and

---

[70] *Ruiz-Mateos v Spain* Series A No 262 (1993) 16 EHRR 505, para 63; *Brandstetter v Austria* [1991] ECHR 39, Application no 11/70/84, para 67.
[71] Commission Regulation (EC) 773/2004 of 7 April 2004 relating to the conduct of proceedings by the Commission pursuant to Articles 81 and 82 of the EC Treaty [2004] OJ L123/18, Art 15; OFT's Procedural Rules, r 5(3).

includes key pieces of evidence in provisional findings). The CC also enters into informal dialogue with interested parties—for example meetings can be arranged between CC staff and a party on a particular issue. The material it collects from this dialogue is not always accessible to others. Lastly, the CC, as it works, generates 'working papers' which set out its developing thinking and upon which it invites the views of certain interested parties. Whilst this dialogue is an important way of ensuring that certain parties are heard, for those not invited to comment, and who have no view of this correspondence, this can pose a problem. To some extent, therefore, undertakings may be obliged to formulate their case, if not entirely blind, then at least with only partial sight of the material against them.

14.81 Article 6 ECHR also entails allowing each party a reasonable opportunity to present its case (including the evidence in support thereof).[72] It is fundamental to both OFT and European Commission procedure that the parties have the right to be heard. This means that they have, inter alia, the following rights: they are entitled to be informed of each aspect of the case made against them;[73] they are then given an opportunity to make written representations on all the objections raised against them;[74] and they have the right to develop their arguments at an oral hearing.[75]

14.82 This is not the case in the CC inquiries. The CC's *General Advice and Information*[76] provides that: 'The Commission aims to keep parties to investigations well informed and seeks to ensure that all information and arguments which it may rely on in reaching its conclusions are put to the relevant parties for comment.' It is clear from the above (and from the absence of any procedural rules granting such rights to the undertakings that may be affected by a negative finding in the CC's report) that, while the CC will generally seek to inform parties of the arguments made against them (this is done by means of the Statement of Issues, the CC's Emerging Thinking, and its Provisional Findings), there is no obligation for it to inform parties of all arguments made against them. Further, although the CC is obliged to consult parties on certain decisions that may affect them, this does not amount to giving those parties a right to respond to arguments made against them. CC hearings are not aimed at (and cannot be viewed as) affording the parties an opportunity to make submissions as to their case: they are fact-finding measures conducted for the group's benefit. Although undertakings are given the opportunity to make an

---

[72] *Dombo Beheer BV v Netherlands* Series A No 274–A (1994) 18 EHRR 213.
[73] Regulation 773/2004, Art 10(1); OFT's Procedural Rules, rr 4 and 5.
[74] Regulation 773/2004, Art 10(2); OFT's Procedural Rules, r 5(2).
[75] Regulation 773/2004, Art 12; OFT's Procedural Rules, r 5(4).
[76] CC4 (March 2006) para 6.31.

opening statement, this cannot be equated to a full submission setting out the undertaking's position.

The CC's emphasis on cooperation, dialogue, and transparency does much to **14.83** assuage the above difficulties. For example, the CC consults parties more than it is obliged to under the Enterprise Act 2002, and parties are given ample opportunity to make written representations. Further, CC staff working on the inquiry are willing to hold meetings with parties to hear any views the parties wish to communicate. However, CC procedure is not without ambiguities for undertakings that are active in the relevant market: although they are potentially subject to extremely stringent remedies, they cannot take shield behind the formal procedural rights of the defence, nor will they wish to antagonise or alert the decision-maker by adopting an overly defensive or aggressive stance.

(f) Information disclosure

Information that the CC receives in connection with a market inquiry is **14.84** 'specified information' for the purposes of Part 9 of the Enterprise Act 2002.[77] Accordingly, whilst the CC is subject to a general prohibition on the disclosure of such information, it may, in certain circumstances, disclose information where this falls within the disclosure 'gateways' set out in Pt 9 (these are discussed at paras 8.18 et seq above). For example, the CC may disclose (and even publish) information where this would facilitate the exercise of any of its statutory functions (for example, disclosure to other parties in the inquiry may assist in conducting a market inquiry).[78] It may also pass information on to other authorities, such as the OFT, under s 241(3) of the Enterprise Act where this would facilitate the OFT's exercise of certain statutory functions (including its functions under the Competition Act 1998).

Should the CC decide to disclose information pursuant to the gateways in Pt 9 **14.85** of the Enterprise Act 2002, it will in all cases be bound by s 244 of the Act to have regard, inter alia, to the need to exclude from disclosure commercial information whose disclosure might in the CC's opinion harm the legitimate business interests of the undertaking to which it relates. Parties providing information to the CC should therefore always indicate whether any information submitted is confidential, and, if possible, identify the information that is confidential, so that the CC will take account of this in applying the balancing test[79] set out in Pt 9 of the Enterprise Act in deciding whether to disclose. A blanket assertion of confidentiality will not serve the purpose. CC guidance

---

[77] Enterprise Act 2002, s 238.
[78] ibid, s 241(1), subject to s 244. See paras 8.27 et seq above on the operation of these provisions.
[79] ibid, s 244, see paras 8.34 et seq.

provides 'the group should take the view that a party has failed to give sufficient explanation about the sensitivity of the information if the information is marked sensitive without further narrative'.[80] Another avenue that may be worth exploring with the CC (particularly where information is provided on a voluntary basis), is whether the CC would be prepared to agree to give prior notice of any disclosure. As is discussed at para 8.70 above, there are arguments to be made that notice of disclosure is required on ECHR grounds. See paras 8.18 et seq above for a detailed discussion of permitted disclosure under Pt 9 of the Enterprise Act 2002.

F. Remedies

14.86 The CC has extensive remedial powers. As the late, much-respected, Paul A Geroski, Chairman of the CC indicated: '[w]ith the power to impose remedies on parties (if necessary) comes the responsibility to act responsibly, and this, in turn, requires one to act with as full an appreciation of the consequences of one's actions as possible'.[81] The remedies stage (the third and final stage of a market investigation), is very far from an addendum to the main event. The choice of remedy to resolve competition issues identified is of central importance to the undertakings that are affected by the inquiry and commands much time and effort from all participants. The CC considers questions relating to remedies in painstaking detail.

(a) The statutory questions

14.87 Where the CC has decided that there is an adverse effect on competition, s 134(4) of the Enterprise Act 2002 obliges it to consider the following questions:

(a) whether action should be taken by it under s 138 of the Enterprise Act for the purpose of remedying, mitigating or preventing the adverse effect on competition concerned or any detrimental effect on customers so far as it has resulted from, or may be expected to result from the adverse effect on competition;

(b) whether it should recommend the taking of action by others for the purpose outlined in (a) above; and

---

[80] CC7, *Chairman's Guidance on Disclosure of Information in Merger and Market Inquiries* (July 2003) para 4.1.
[81] 'Market Inquiries and Market Studies: the view from the Clapham Omnibus', 1 July 2005 <http://www.competition-commission.org.uk/our_peop/members/chair_speeches/pdf/geroski_chatham_house_010705.pdf>.

(c) in either case, if action should be taken, what action should be taken and what is to be remedied, mitigated, or prevented.

(b) CC remedies

The CC can take extremely wide-ranging remedial action. Action can be taken **14.88** by the CC itself through exercising its own extensive remedial powers[82] and/or by accepting undertakings from the relevant parties.[83] Alternatively, it may make (non-binding) recommendations that remedial action should be taken by others,[84] such as government, regulators, and public authorities, to remedy the adverse effects on competition or any detrimental effect on customers resulting from the adverse effect on competition.

The CC's own remedial powers include behavioural remedies (such as impos- **14.89** ing contractual conditions,[85] but also extend to imposing significant struc- tural remedies, such as ordering divestiture.[86] The CC Guidelines on Market Investigations distinguish between the following categories of remedies it can impose:

(a) remedies designed to make a significant and direct change to the struc- ture of a market by a requirement, for example, to divest a business or assets to a newcomer to the market or to an existing, perhaps smaller, competitor;

(b) remedies designed to change the structure of a market less directly by reducing entry barriers or switching costs, for example, by requiring the licensing of know-how or intellectual property rights or by extending the compatibility of products through industry-wide technical standards;

(c) as a particular category of (b), recommendations for changes to regulations found to have adverse effects on competition or detrimental effects on customers, for example, by limiting entry to a market;

(d) remedies directing firms (whether sellers or buyers) to discontinue certain behaviour (for example, giving advance notice of price changes) or to adopt certain behaviour (for example, more prominently displaying prices and other terms and conditions of sale);

(e) remedies designed to restrain the way in which firms would otherwise behave, for example, the imposition of a price cap . . .[87]

---

[82] Enterprise Act 2002, ss 138(2), 161, and Sch 8.
[83] ibid, ss 138(2) and 159.   [84] ibid, s 134(b).
[85] Eg Domestic LPG   [86] Enterprise Act 2002, ss 138(2), 161, and Sch 8.
[87] CC3, *Market Investigation References: Competition Commission Guidelines* (June 2003) para 4.18.

(c) The CC's discretion

14.90 Section 138(2) of the Enterprise Act 2002 places a duty on the CC to take such remedial action as it considers to be reasonable and practical. Given the breadth of remedial choices available to the CC, and the specialist and expert nature of its decison-making, it is likely that it will be allowed a broad margin of discretion in respect of its remedial decisions. In *Somerfield plc v Competition Commission*[88] the CAT evaluated the CAT's choice of remedies in the context of a merger inquiry. After considering ss 35(3), 35(4), and s 138 the CAT concluded the CC had a clear margin of appreciation to decide what reasonable action was appropriate. The CC must have regard to several factors in determining what remedial action is appropriate.

(i) The remedy must be comprehensive, reasonable, and practicable

14.91 In considering remedies, the CC must, pursuant to s 134(6) of the Enterprise Act 2002, have regard to the need to achieve as comprehensive a remedy to the adverse effect on competition and to any detrimental effects on customers that have resulted so far from the adverse effect as is reasonable and practical. In practice, this has been interpreted to mean the remedies should be effective and proportionate.[89]

14.92 The Explanatory Notes to the Enterprise Act 2002 explain that:

> The requirement to have regard to reasonableness and practicability means, inter alia, that the CC must, in relation to each proposed remedy, consider what effect it will have on the future conduct of those operating in the market, how it will interact with any other proposed remedies, and whether the adverse effect(s) or customer detriment(s) that it was designed to address are sufficiently serious for their removal or mitigation to justify whatever costs and disruption to businesses and others will be involved in the implementation of that remedy.

14.93 **Comprehensive:** The Explanatory Notes indicate that the test should operate to favour remedies that address the adverse effect on competition as opposed to those that address the detrimental effects flowing therefrom:

> All other things being equal, a remedy that, for example, removes an adverse effect on competition will be considered more comprehensive than one that only removes detrimental effects on customers resulting from that adverse effect, since by removing the adverse effect, the CC will also (at least so far as is within its power) remove the detrimental effect on customers.

CC Guidelines on Market Investigation References take the same stance.[90]

---

[88] [2006] CAT 4, para 88.   [89] Enterprise Act 2002, s 134(6).
[90] CC3, *Market Investigation References: Competition Commission Guidelines* (June 2003) para 4.6.

Practicable: In *Store Cards*, the CC indicated that, in practice, this requirement **14.94** entails that: 'appropriate remedies should be effective in addressing, within a reasonable timescale, the feature or features giving rise to the AEC and/or the detrimental effects. Consideration of effectiveness includes considering the feasibility of implementation and the practicability of monitoring and enforcing compliance.' Similar comments were made in *Home Credit* (Final Report, para 9.5). See paras 4.13 et seq of CC3.

Reasonable: In seeking to achieve a solution that is reasonable, the Group 'will **14.95** aim to ensure that no remedy is disproportionate in relation to the adverse effect on competition and any adverse effects on customers' and in 'choosing between two remedies which it considers would be equally effective, it will choose the remedy that imposes the least cost or that is least restrictive'.[91] See paras 4.10 et seq of CC Guidelines on Market Investigation References (CC3 (June 2003)) for more information on proportionality of remedies.

(ii) The impact on customer benefit

The CC must, in formulating remedies, consider any customer benefits (in the **14.96** form of lower prices, or higher quality or greater choice of goods or services, or greater innovation in relation to goods or services in any UK market) arising from the relevant feature or features of the market that have given rise to adverse effects on competition.[92] To qualify for consideration, the benefit must in the CC's view be unlikely to accrue without the relevant feature or features.[93] In *Domestic LPG*, the CC indicated that what the Enterprise Act requires is that the CC consider the impact of the remedy on any relevant customer benefit. It does not require that the CC weigh the adverse effect of the feature or features in deciding whether remedies are appropriate.[94] In *Home Credit*, the CC was deterred from imposing a price cap on home credit loans, inter alia, because the price caps could contribute to a reduction in access to credit for riskier customers. It seemed unlikely to the CC that a general price cap in the home credit market could be implemented which achieved a significant reduction in customer detriment but did not at the same time have an adverse effect on a substantial number of customers which outweighed the benefits of the remedy.[95] However, the CC did not identify access to credit for riskier customers as a 'customer benefit' presumably because this benefit could not be attributed to the features identified.

---

[91] *Store Cards*, paras 10.5 and 10.6. See also, *Home Credit*, para 9.6.
[92] Enterprise Act 2002, s 134(7).   [93] *Store Cards*, para 10.7.
[94] *Domestic LPG*, para 7.119.   [95] *Home Credit*, para 9.140.

(iii) Sectoral powers

14.97 Section 168 of the Enterprise Act 2002 requires the CC to have regard to the sectoral regulators'[96] statutory functions when determining what remedial action would be reasonable and practicable. The Chairman of the CC has explained this as ensuring that remedies do not impinge on duties of sectoral regulators.[97]

(iv) European law

14.98 As explained at para 14.17, the CC is bound by general principles of EC law (and its obligation of loyal cooperation under Article 10 EC) to ensure that its decisions under Pt 4 of the Enterprise Act 2002 are consistent with Article 81 and Article 82 EC. The obligation to achieve consistency with respect to agreements falling within Article 81 EC is the more onerous:[98] Article 3(2) of Regulation 1/2003 prevents the application of stricter national law to agreements within the meaning of Article 81(1) EC. However, the CC is able to apply stricter national law to unilateral conduct, even if the conduct is not prohibited under Article 82 EC.[99]

14.99 Undertakings have already sought to rely on the 'protective effect' of Article 3(2) to preclude the CC from adopting particular remedies applicable to agreements. For example, in *Domestic LPG*, one of the suppliers queried whether the remedies relating to contracts for supply to metered estates would be compatible with the requirement that Member State competition authorities do not prohibit agreements that would be permitted under Article 81.[100] The CC's response was that the contracts at issue did not appreciably affect trade between Member States[101] (it is not clear whether it considered the network effect of these contracts).

(d) Process

14.100 The CC's procedure leading to its decision on remedies reflects the significance and importance of its decision on the undertakings affected. The CC devotes a considerable part of its two-year timetable to the determination of remedies. The average length of the remedies stage of investigations that have been completed to date exceeds six months.

14.101 Section 169 of the Enterprise Act 2002 requires that the CC shall, where it

---

[96] The sectoral regulators are identified in s 168(5) of the Enterprise Act 2002.

[97] 'Regulation and Competition: Chalk and Cheese?' Speech by Peter Freeman, Chairman of the CC, 7 September 2006, p 5.

[98] See paras 13.52 et seq for a discussion of this obligation in the context of market investigations.

[99] See para 3.79 for a detailed discussion of Art 3(2) of Regulation 1/2003.

[100] *Domestic LPG*, para 7.114.   [101] ibid.

proposes to take a 'relevant decision', consult those persons on whose interests it considers the decision is likely to have a substantial impact. A decision on remedies under s 134(4) of the Enterprise Act is one of the decisions giving rise to the obligation to consult.[102]

The basic framework for consultation is set out in the CC's Procedural Rules. **14.102** Rule 11(1) requires that the CC shall have regard to the need to give as much notice as is practicable of the actions which it considers it might take for the purpose of remedying the adverse effects of a market investigation. Rule 11(2) requires that a notice of remedies may be contained in the Provisional Findings, but, if not, the CC shall notify the main parties as soon as practicable after the Provisional Findings. Rule 11(5) requires that the CC shall consult the main parties and must have regard to the representations it receives from them.

In practice, the CC's consultation is more extensive than its rules provide. It **14.103** has adopted a practice of publishing, in addition to the Remedies Notice, a Statement of Provisional Decision on Remedies or a Proposed Remedies Paper. In addition to inviting written responses to both the Remedies Notice and the Statement of Provisional Decision on Remedies, it holds hearings and is also prepared to hold staff meetings with undertakings to discuss the theoretical and practical suitability of remedies.

The CC can, and does, change its position, having considered the views that **14.104** are expressed to it in the course of the extensive consultation. In *Home Credit*, for example, although the CC indicated in its Remedies Notice that it was minded to consider a price cap on home credit loans, it decided, after considering the mostly negative responses that were submitted from both lenders and interested third parties on a general price cap on home loans, that it was not an appropriate remedy given (amongst other factors) the product and the customer base.[103]

It is critical that undertakings voice every reservation and objection they may **14.105** have in respect of proposed remedies directly with the CC, as not to do so will in all likelihood preclude novel objections being raised at appeal stage. In *Somerfield plc v CC*,[104] the Competition Appeal Tribunal refused to entertain grounds of challenge in respect of the remedies that the applicant had failed to challenge before the CC.

---

[102] Enterprise Act 2002, s 169(6)(c).
[103] See paras 9.136–9.139 of the Final Report.
[104] *Somerfield plc v Competition Commission* [2006] CAT 4, para 71.

(e) Implementation

14.106 Where the CC publishes a report that identifies an adverse effect on competition, it is obliged under s 138(2) of the Enterprise Act 2002 to take action that it
considers reasonable and practicable to remedy, mitigate, or prevent the adverse
effect on competition and any detriment to consumers. The CC can implement
the measures it has identified as necessary on its part by making what is
known as an enforcement order[105] or by accepting enforcement undertakings.[106]
Schedule 10 to the Enterprise Act 2002 governs the procedure relating to undertakings and orders. Section 138(3) requires that the CC's remedial decision
should be consistent with its decisions as included in its report by virtue of s
134(4), unless there has been a material change of circumstances since the
preparation of the report, or the CC has a special reason for deciding differently.
The implementation process may be fairly lengthy. In *Store Cards*, for example,
it took in excess of one year from the publication of the CC's final report for the
CC's enforcement order to take effect.[107] The CC may, before it makes the final
enforcement order or undertaking, make an interim order[108] or accept an
interim undertaking.[109]

14.107 The CC begins the process by which it implements the report by publishing an
administrative timetable for the implementation process. The CC discusses the
terms of the draft order or undertakings with those that are most immediately
affected. In *Store Cards* the draft administrative timetable provided for two
months of discussions between the CC and store card providers. In *Domestic
LPG* the administrative timetable indicates that the relevant discussions took
place with 'suppliers and other relevant parties' (presumably because the orders
affected contractual relationships). After the discussions with the concerned
parties, the CC publishes the draft order. Paragraph 2(2)(f) of Sch 10 to the Act
requires consultation of a minimum of 30 days. Written representations are
invited from any interested persons. If there are significant changes to the draft
order arising from the public consultation, a further round of consultation is
required. However, where the changes are immaterial, the CC need not consult
again (as in *Store Cards*).

(f) Monitoring and enforcement of undertakings and orders

14.108 The OFT is obliged to monitor undertakings and orders. It must, from time to
time, consider whether the orders and undertakings are complied with and

---

[105] Enterprise Act 2002, ss 161 and 162(8).   [106] ibid, ss 159 and 161.
[107] *Store Cards*: Report, 7 March 2006; Notice of Intention to make an Order, 31 May 2006;
Order, 27 July 2006; Order to come into force on 1 May 2007.
[108] Enterprise Act 2002, s 158.   [109] ibid, s 157.

whether, by reasons of any change of circumstances, they are no longer appropriate and need to be varied or revoked.[110] The OFT is also required to keep under review the effectiveness of the orders and undertakings and report on this to the Secretary of State and the CC from time to time or where requested to do so by the Secretary of State.[111] In the case of breach of an undertaking or order, it is empowered to enforce undertakings by civil proceedings for an injunction or for interdict or any other appropriate relief or remedy.[112] A breach of an undertaking is actionable in damages by any person who may be affected by a contravention of the undertaking.[113]

G. Ministerial Intervention in the Public Interest

The Secretary of State has a reserve power to intervene in CC market investigation procedure. Where the Secretary of State believes that a public interest consideration[114] is relevant to a case, the Secretary of State may, no more than four months after a reference has been made to the CC by the OFT, give notice of intervention to the CC (provided that the reference has not been finally determined by the CC).[115] **14.109**

The effect of an intervention notice is that the CC continues with its investigation with a slightly altered focus. Although it addresses essentially the same questions that it is requested to consider under s 134 of the Enterprise Act 2002 in respect of normal references (see paras 114.11 et seq), the CC is required to advise the Secretary of State whether action should be taken by the Secretary of State under s 147 (and if so what action, etc), before deciding separately, on the assumption that it is dealing with the matter itself, whether it should itself take action under s 138 of the Act. **14.110**

When the CC has reported, the Secretary of State can within 90 days decide to take the case over, in which case taking such action as he or she considers appropriate to remedy the problem in light of the public interest consideration. **14.111**

H. Conclusion

CC procedure comprises significant collaborative and consultative elements, but investigations can also, at times, take on an inquisitorial nature, as is necessary for a body that is entrusted with an in-depth analysis of problematic **14.112**

---

[110] ibid, s 162(2).   [111] ibid, s 162(5), (6) and (7).   [112] ibid, s 167(6).
[113] ibid, s 167(2)–(4).   [114] See para 13.139 for a definition of public interest.
[115] ibid, s 139.

markets. The CC's emphasis on consultation is real, and the investigation process is quite organic—its views do change (sometimes significantly) along the way, as it gathers additional information and hears various views. The absence of formalised procedural 'rights of the defence' is both an advantage and a disadvantage: on the positive side, there is much to be said for resolving competition issues—many of which are not (or not exclusively) behavioural—by means of allowing experts such as the CC group members to engage in an in-depth dialogue with the main and interested parties in the relevant market/s, assisted by their staff and expert reports and other economic evidence. The absence of a marked adversarial procedure facilitates such a dialogue and encourages a more 'civilised' approach to resolving competition problems that is not punctuated by needless adversarial wrangles between the regulator and the undertakings active in the market referred. However, in view of its sweeping remedial powers, it may be that certain undertakings may find, depending on the outcome of the investigation, that the CC's current procedure is insufficiently formalised and developed to ensure that the rights of the parties are sufficiently protected.

Annex A

1. Store Cards administrative timetable (final version)

14.113

18 March 2004	Reference made by Office of Fair Trading
March to August	Gathering information, issuing questionnaires, hearing third parties, clarification hearings with main parties, open hearing
September	Statement of Issues published
October to December	Issues hearings with main parties
Early January	Publish CC's emerging thinking
January to March 2005	Verifying information from parties, moving to provisional findings
February to March	Further hearings with main parties
End June	Deadline for all parties' responses/submissions required before provisional findings
Early August	Finalise checking of draft provisional findings with parties
Early September	Notifying provisional findings and (if required) possible remedies
Early October	Responses due on provisional findings and possible remedies
October to December	Remedies hearings
December	Publish Statement of Provisional Decisions on Remedies
9 January 2005	Final deadline for responses to Statement of Provisional Decisions on Remedies
Late January	Final deadline for all parties' responses/submissions
February	Publish report
17 March 2006	Statutory deadline

2. Domestic bulk LPG administrative timetable (final version)

5 July 2004	Reference made by Office of Fair Trading
July / August	Request for off the shelf material; adverts; letters to third parties etc
September / October	Issue questionnaires, for reply early / mid November
September / October	Hearings with third parties
November	Visits
December	Statement of Issues published
Late January / February 2005	Issues hearings with parties
March to April	Verifying information, considering provisional findings
Late March / Early April	Publication on website of 'Emerging Thinking', Safety Working Paper, results of surveys carried out by ORC International and Mott Macdonalds
Mid April	Annexes of Emerging Thinking published. Parties comments on Emerging Thinking documents published
May	Further hearings with parties
Early June	Deadline for all parties' responses/submissions required before provisional findings
August	Notifying provisional findings
August	Notifying and considering possible remedies
October	Remedies hearings
March	Further consultation on remedies
March	Further consultation on draft report and appendices
Early April	Final deadline for all parties' responses/submissions
Mid / Late June	Publish report
4 July 2006	Statutory deadline

3. Home Credit administrative timetable (final version)

20 December 2004	Reference made by Office of Fair Trading
December 2004 / January 2005	Request for off the shelf material; adverts; letters to third parties etc
January 2005 / February	Issue questionnaires, for reply by end March
January / February	Hearings with third parties
February / March	Visits
April	Statement of Issues published
May / June	Issues hearings with parties
July	Verifying information
October	Notifying emerging thinking
November / December	Possible further hearings with parties

13 April 2006	Deadline for all parties' responses / submissions required before provisional findings
April	Notifying provisional findings
April / May / June / July	Notifying and considering possible remedies
May / June / July	Further hearings
31 October	Final deadline for all parties' responses / submissions
November	Publish report
19 December 2006	Statutory deadline

4. Classified directory advertising services administrative timetable
(version published on 6 November 2006)

5 April 2005	Reference made by Office of Fair Trading
April to July	Gathering information; issuing questionnaires; assessing evidence from parties
August	Statement of Issues published
September to October	Issues hearings
November to December	Assessing survey and other evidence; analysis
January 2006	Notifying emerging thinking
February to March	Further hearings with main parties
2 June 2006	Deadline for parties' responses / submissions required before provisional findings
June 2006	Notifying provisional findings
June 2006	Notifying and considering possible remedies
June to August 2006	Remedies hearings
10 November 2006	Deadline for responses on revised remedies proposals
End November 2006	Publish report
4 April 2007	Statutory deadline

5. Northern Irish personal banking administrative timetable (version published on 23 March 2006)

26 May 2005	Reference made by the Office of Fair Trading
June–September	Gathering information; issuing questionnaires; assessing evidence from parties
October–November	Statement of Issues published
October–November	Response to Issues statement
November–December	Issues hearings
January–March	Assessing survey and other evidence; analysis and verifying information
April 2006	Notifying emerging thinking
May–June	Emerging Thinking hearings

End July	Deadline for parties' responses/submissions required before provisional findings
September–early October	Notifying provisional findings and possible remedies
October–November	Remedies hearings (if required)
Mid December	Final deadline for all parties' responses/submissions
January–February	Publish report
25 May 2007	Statutory deadline

6. Supermarkets administrative timetable (version published on 7 June 2006)

9 May 2006	Reference made by Office of Fair Trading.
May / June 2006	Request for off the shelf material; adverts; letters to third parties, etc.
June 2006	Statement of Issues published.
June 2006	Issue questionnaires.
June to September 2006	Visits & hearings with main and third parties.
December 2006	Notifying emerging thinking.
February / March 2007	Possible further hearings with parties.
April 2007	Deadline for all parties responses/submissions required before provisional findings.
May 2007	Notifying provisional findings.
May / June 2007	Notifying and considering possible remedies (if required).
July / August 2007	Report if no adverse effect on competition; or remedies hearings (if required).
September 2007	Final deadline for all parties' responses/submissions.
October 2007	Publish report.
8 May 2008	Statutory deadline.

14.114   **Annex B: Typical Shape of a Market Investigation**

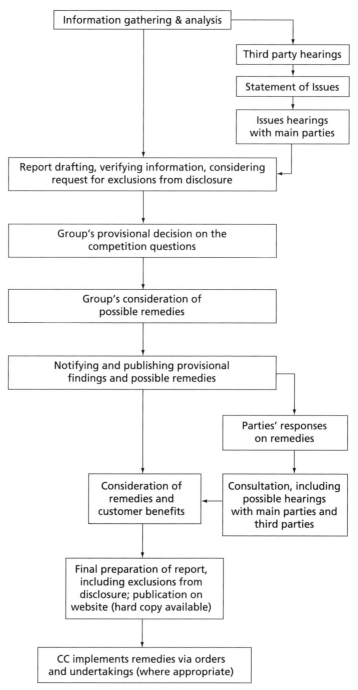

Document CC4, General Advice and Information <http://www.competition-commission.org.uk>

Council Regulation (EC) No 1/2003 of 16 December 2002 on the implementation of the rules on competition laid down in Articles 81 and 82 of the Treaty

(Text with EEA relevance)

THE COUNCIL OF THE EUROPEAN UNION,

Having regard to the Treaty establishing the European Community, and in particular Article 83 thereof,

Having regard to the proposal from the Commission[1],

Having regard to the opinion of the European Parliament[2],

Having regard to the opinion of the European Economic and Social Committee[3],

Whereas:

(1) In order to establish a system which ensures that competition in the common market is not distorted, Articles 81 and 82 of the Treaty must be applied effectively and uniformly in the Community. Council Regulation No 17 of 6 February 1962, First Regulation implementing Articles 81 and 82[4] of the Treaty[5], has allowed a Community competition policy to develop that has helped to disseminate a competition culture within the Community. In the light of experience, however, that Regulation should now be replaced by legislation designed to meet the challenges of an integrated market and a future enlargement of the Community.

(2) In particular, there is a need to rethink the arrangements for applying the exception from the prohibition on agreements, which restrict competition, laid down in Article 81(3) of the Treaty. Under Article 83(2)(b) of the Treaty, account must be taken in this regard of the need to ensure effective supervision, on the one hand, and to simplify administration to the greatest possible extent, on the other.

(3) The centralised scheme set up by Regulation No 17 no longer secures a balance between those two objectives. It hampers application of the Community competition rules by the courts and competition authorities of the Member States, and the system of notification it involves prevents the Commission from concentrating its resources on curbing the most serious infringements. It also imposes considerable costs on undertakings.

(4) The present system should therefore be replaced by a directly applicable exception system in which the competition authorities and courts of the Member States have the power to apply not only Article 81(1) and Article 82 of the Treaty, which have direct applicability by virtue of the case-law of the Court of Justice of the European Communities, but also Article 81(3) of the Treaty.

---

[1] OJ C 365 E, 19.12.2000, p. 284.   [2] OJ C 72 E, 21.3.2002, p. 305.

[3] OJ C 155, 29.5.2001, p. 73.

[4] The title of Regulation No 17 has been adjusted to take account of the renumbering of the Articles of the EC Treaty, in accordance with Article 12 of the Treaty of Amsterdam; the original reference was to Articles 85 and 86 of the Treaty.

[5] OJ 13, 21.2.1962, p. 204/62. Regulation as last amended by Regulation (EC) No 1216/1999 (OJ L 148, 15.6.1999, p. 5).

(5) In order to ensure an effective enforcement of the Community competition rules and at the same time the respect of fundamental rights of defence, this Regulation should regulate the burden of proof under Articles 81 and 82 of the Treaty. It should be for the party or the authority alleging an infringement of Article 81(1) and Article 82 of the Treaty to prove the existence thereof to the required legal standard. It should be for the undertaking or association of undertakings invoking the benefit of a defence against a finding of an infringement to demonstrate to the required legal standard that the conditions for applying such defence are satisfied. This Regulation affects neither national rules on the standard of proof nor obligations of competition authorities and courts of the Member States to ascertain the relevant facts of a case, provided that such rules and obligations are compatible with general principles of Community law.

(6) In order to ensure that the Community competition rules are applied effectively, the competition authorities of the Member States should be associated more closely with their application. To this end, they should be empowered to apply Community law.

(7) National courts have an essential part to play in applying the Community competition rules. When deciding disputes between private individuals, they protect the subjective rights under Community law, for example by awarding damages to the victims of infringements. The role of the national courts here complements that of the competition authorities of the Member States. They should therefore be allowed to apply Articles 81 and 82 of the Treaty in full.

(8) In order to ensure the effective enforcement of the Community competition rules and the proper functioning of the cooperation mechanisms contained in this Regulation, it is necessary to oblige the competition authorities and courts of the Member States to also apply Articles 81 and 82 of the Treaty where they apply national competition law to agreements and practices which may affect trade between Member States. In order to create a level playing field for agreements, decisions by associations of undertakings and concerted practices within the internal market, it is also necessary to determine pursuant to Article 83(2)(e) of the Treaty the relationship between national laws and Community competition law. To that effect it is necessary to provide that the application of national competition laws to agreements, decisions or concerted practices within the meaning of Article 81(1) of the Treaty may not lead to the prohibition of such agreements, decisions and concerted practices if they are not also prohibited under Community competition law. The notions of agreements, decisions and concerted practices are autonomous concepts of Community competition law covering the coordination of behaviour of undertakings on the market as interpreted by the Community Courts. Member States should not under this Regulation be precluded from adopting and applying on their territory stricter national competition laws which prohibit or impose sanctions on unilateral conduct engaged in by undertakings. These stricter national laws may include provisions which prohibit or impose sanctions on abusive behaviour toward economically dependent undertakings. Furthermore, this Regulation does not apply to national laws which impose criminal sanctions on natural persons except to the extent that such sanctions are the means whereby competition rules applying to undertakings are enforced.

(9) Articles 81 and 82 of the Treaty have as their objective the protection of competition on the market. This Regulation, which is adopted for the implementation of these Treaty provisions, does not preclude Member States from implementing on their territory national legislation, which protects other legitimate interests provided that such legislation is compatible with general principles and other provisions of Community law. In so far as such national legislation pursues predominantly an objective different from that of protecting competition on the market, the competition authorities and courts of the Member States may apply such legislation on their territory. Accordingly, Member States may under this Regulation implement on their territory national legislation that prohibits or imposes sanctions on acts of unfair trading practice, be they unilateral or contractual. Such legislation pursues a specific objective, irrespective of the actual or presumed effects of such acts on competition on the market. This is particularly the case of legislation which prohibits undertakings from imposing on their trading partners, obtaining or attempting to obtain from them terms and conditions that are unjustified, disproportionate or without consideration.

(10) Regulations such as 19/65/EEC[6], (EEC) No 2821/71[7], (EEC) No 3976/87[8], (EEC) No 1534/91[9], or (EEC) No 479/92[10] empower the Commission to apply Article 81(3) of the Treaty by Regulation to certain categories of agreements, decisions by associations of undertakings and concerted practices. In the areas defined by such Regulations, the Commission has adopted and may continue to adopt so called 'block' exemption Regulations by which it declares Article 81(1) of the Treaty inapplicable to categories of agreements, decisions and concerted practices. Where agreements, decisions and concerted practices to which such Regulations apply nonetheless have effects that are incompatible with Article 81(3) of the Treaty, the Commission and the competition authorities of the Member States should have the power to withdraw in a particular case the benefit of the block exemption Regulation.

(11) For it to ensure that the provisions of the Treaty are applied, the Commission should be able to address decisions to undertakings or associations of undertakings for the purpose of bringing to an end infringements of Articles 81 and 82 of the Treaty. Provided there is a legitimate interest in doing so, the Commission should also be able to adopt decisions which find that an infringement has been committed in the past even if it does not impose a fine. This Regulation should also make explicit provision for the Commission's power to adopt decisions ordering interim measures, which has been acknowledged by the Court of Justice.

(12) This Regulation should make explicit provision for the Commission's power to impose any remedy, whether behavioural or structural, which is necessary to bring the infringement effectively to an end, having regard to the principle of proportionality. Structural remedies should only be imposed either where there is no equally effective behavioural remedy or where any equally effective behavioural remedy would be more burdensome for the undertaking concerned than the structural remedy. Changes to the structure of an undertaking as it existed before the infringement was committed would only be proportionate where there is a substantial risk of a lasting or repeated infringement that derives from the very structure of the undertaking.

(13) Where, in the course of proceedings which might lead to an agreement or practice being prohibited, undertakings offer the Commission commitments such as to meet its concerns, the Commission should be able to adopt decisions which make those commitments binding on the undertakings concerned. Commitment decisions should find that there are no longer grounds for action by the Commission without concluding whether or not there has been or still is an

---

[6] Council Regulation No 19/65/EEC of 2 March 1965 on the application of Article 81(3) (The titles of the Regulations have been adjusted to take account of the renumbering of the Articles of the EC Treaty, in accordance with Article 12 of the Treaty of Amsterdam; the original reference was to Article 85(3) of the Treaty) of the Treaty to certain categories of agreements and concerted practices (OJ 36, 6.3.1965, p. 533). Regulation as last amended by Regulation (EC) No 1215/1999 (OJ L 148, 15.6.1999, p. 1).

[7] Council Regulation (EEC) No 2821/71 of 20 December 1971 on the application of Article 81(3) (The titles of the Regulations have been adjusted to take account of the renumbering of the Articles of the EC Treaty, in accordance with Article 12 of the Treaty of Amsterdam; the original reference was to Article 85(3) of the Treaty) of the Treaty to categories of agreements, decisions and concerted practices (OJ L 285, 29.12.1971, p. 46). Regulation as last amended by the Act of Accession of 1994.

[8] Council Regulation (EEC) No 3976/87 of 14 December 1987 on the application of Article 81(3) (The titles of the Regulations have been adjusted to take account of the renumbering of the Articles of the EC Treaty, in accordance with Article 12 of the Treaty of Amsterdam; the original reference was to Article 85(3) of the Treaty) of the Treaty to certain categories of agreements and concerted practices in the air transport sector (OJ L 374, 31.12.1987, p. 9). Regulation as last amended by the Act of Accession of 1994.

[9] Council Regulation (EEC) No 1534/91 of 31 May 1991 on the application of Article 81(3) (The titles of the Regulations have been adjusted to take account of the renumbering of the Articles of the EC Treaty, in accordance with Article 12 of the Treaty of Amsterdam; the original reference was to Article 85(3) of the Treaty) of the Treaty to certain categories of agreements, decisions and concerted practices in the insurance sector (OJ L 143, 7.6.1991, p. 1).

[10] Council Regulation (EEC) No 479/92 of 25 February 1992 on the application of Article 81(3) (The titles of the Regulations have been adjusted to take account of the renumbering of the Articles of the EC Treaty, in accordance with Article 12 of the Treaty of Amsterdam; the original reference was to Article 85(3) of the Treaty) of the Treaty to certain categories of agreements, decisions and concerted practices between liner shipping companies (Consortia) (OJ L 55, 29.2.1992, p. 3). Regulation amended by the Act of Accession of 1994.

infringement. Commitment decisions are without prejudice to the powers of competition authorities and courts of the Member States to make such a finding and decide upon the case. Commitment decisions are not appropriate in cases where the Commission intends to impose a fine.

(14) In exceptional cases where the public interest of the Community so requires, it may also be expedient for the Commission to adopt a decision of a declaratory nature finding that the prohibition in Article 81 or Article 82 of the Treaty does not apply, with a view to clarifying the law and ensuring its consistent application throughout the Community, in particular with regard to new types of agreements or practices that have not been settled in the existing case-law and administrative practice.

(15) The Commission and the competition authorities of the Member States should form together a network of public authorities applying the Community competition rules in close cooperation. For that purpose it is necessary to set up arrangements for information and consultation. Further modalities for the cooperation within the network will be laid down and revised by the Commission, in close cooperation with the Member States.

(16) Notwithstanding any national provision to the contrary, the exchange of information and the use of such information in evidence should be allowed between the members of the network even where the information is confidential. This information may be used for the application of Articles 81 and 82 of the Treaty as well as for the parallel application of national competition law, provided that the latter application relates to the same case and does not lead to a different outcome. When the information exchanged is used by the receiving authority to impose sanctions on undertakings, there should be no other limit to the use of the information than the obligation to use it for the purpose for which it was collected given the fact that the sanctions imposed on undertakings are of the same type in all systems. The rights of defence enjoyed by undertakings in the various systems can be considered as sufficiently equivalent. However, as regards natural persons, they may be subject to substantially different types of sanctions across the various systems. Where that is the case, it is necessary to ensure that information can only be used if it has been collected in a way which respects the same level of protection of the rights of defence of natural persons as provided for under the national rules of the receiving authority.

(17) If the competition rules are to be applied consistently and, at the same time, the network is to be managed in the best possible way, it is essential to retain the rule that the competition authorities of the Member States are automatically relieved of their competence if the Commission initiates its own proceedings. Where a competition authority of a Member State is already acting on a case and the Commission intends to initiate proceedings, it should endeavour to do so as soon as possible. Before initiating proceedings, the Commission should consult the national authority concerned.

(18) To ensure that cases are dealt with by the most appropriate authorities within the network, a general provision should be laid down allowing a competition authority to suspend or close a case on the ground that another authority is dealing with it or has already dealt with it, the objective being that each case should be handled by a single authority. This provision should not prevent the Commission from rejecting a complaint for lack of Community interest, as the case-law of the Court of Justice has acknowledged it may do, even if no other competition authority has indicated its intention of dealing with the case.

(19) The Advisory Committee on Restrictive Practices and Dominant Positions set up by Regulation No 17 has functioned in a very satisfactory manner. It will fit well into the new system of decentralised application. It is necessary, therefore, to build upon the rules laid down by Regulation No 17, while improving the effectiveness of the organisational arrangements. To this end, it would be expedient to allow opinions to be delivered by written procedure. The Advisory Committee should also be able to act as a forum for discussing cases that are being handled by the competition authorities of the Member States, so as to help safeguard the consistent application of the Community competition rules.

(20) The Advisory Committee should be composed of representatives of the competition authorities of the Member States. For meetings in which general issues are being discussed, Member States

should be able to appoint an additional representative. This is without prejudice to members of the Committee being assisted by other experts from the Member States.

(21) Consistency in the application of the competition rules also requires that arrangements be established for cooperation between the courts of the Member States and the Commission. This is relevant for all courts of the Member States that apply Articles 81 and 82 of the Treaty, whether applying these rules in lawsuits between private parties, acting as public enforcers or as review courts. In particular, national courts should be able to ask the Commission for information or for its opinion on points concerning the application of Community competition law. The Commission and the competition authorities of the Member States should also be able to submit written or oral observations to courts called upon to apply Article 81 or Article 82 of the Treaty. These observations should be submitted within the framework of national procedural rules and practices including those safeguarding the rights of the parties. Steps should therefore be taken to ensure that the Commission and the competition authorities of the Member States are kept sufficiently well informed of proceedings before national courts.

(22) In order to ensure compliance with the principles of legal certainty and the uniform application of the Community competition rules in a system of parallel powers, conflicting decisions must be avoided. It is therefore necessary to clarify, in accordance with the case-law of the Court of Justice, the effects of Commission decisions and proceedings on courts and competition authorities of the Member States. Commitment decisions adopted by the Commission do not affect the power of the courts and the competition authorities of the Member States to apply Articles 81 and 82 of the Treaty.

(23) The Commission should be empowered throughout the Community to require such information to be supplied as is necessary to detect any agreement, decision or concerted practice prohibited by Article 81 of the Treaty or any abuse of a dominant position prohibited by Article 82 of the Treaty. When complying with a decision of the Commission, undertakings cannot be forced to admit that they have committed an infringement, but they are in any event obliged to answer factual questions and to provide documents, even if this information may be used to establish against them or against another undertaking the existence of an infringement.

(24) The Commission should also be empowered to undertake such inspections as are necessary to detect any agreement, decision or concerted practice prohibited by Article 81 of the Treaty or any abuse of a dominant position prohibited by Article 82 of the Treaty. The competition authorities of the Member States should cooperate actively in the exercise of these powers.

(25) The detection of infringements of the competition rules is growing ever more difficult, and, in order to protect competition effectively, the Commission's powers of investigation need to be supplemented. The Commission should in particular be empowered to interview any persons who may be in possession of useful information and to record the statements made. In the course of an inspection, officials authorised by the Commission should be empowered to affix seals for the period of time necessary for the inspection. Seals should normally not be affixed for more than 72 hours. Officials authorised by the Commission should also be empowered to ask for any information relevant to the subject matter and purpose of the inspection.

(26) Experience has shown that there are cases where business records are kept in the homes of directors or other people working for an undertaking. In order to safeguard the effectiveness of inspections, therefore, officials and other persons authorised by the Commission should be empowered to enter any premises where business records may be kept, including private homes. However, the exercise of this latter power should be subject to the authorisation of the judicial authority.

(27) Without prejudice to the case-law of the Court of Justice, it is useful to set out the scope of the control that the national judicial authority may carry out when it authorises, as foreseen by national law including as a precautionary measure, assistance from law enforcement authorities in order to overcome possible opposition on the part of the undertaking or the execution of the decision to carry out inspections in non-business premises. It results from the case-law that the national judicial authority may in particular ask the Commission for further information which it needs to carry out its control and in the absence of which it could refuse the authorisation. The case-law

also confirms the competence of the national courts to control the application of national rules governing the implementation of coercive measures.

(28) In order to help the competition authorities of the Member States to apply Articles 81 and 82 of the Treaty effectively, it is expedient to enable them to assist one another by carrying out inspections and other fact-finding measures.

(29) Compliance with Articles 81 and 82 of the Treaty and the fulfilment of the obligations imposed on undertakings and associations of undertakings under this Regulation should be enforceable by means of fines and periodic penalty payments. To that end, appropriate levels of fine should also be laid down for infringements of the procedural rules.

(30) In order to ensure effective recovery of fines imposed on associations of undertakings for infringements that they have committed, it is necessary to lay down the conditions on which the Commission may require payment of the fine from the members of the association where the association is not solvent. In doing so, the Commission should have regard to the relative size of the undertakings belonging to the association and in particular to the situation of small and medium-sized enterprises. Payment of the fine by one or several members of an association is without prejudice to rules of national law that provide for recovery of the amount paid from other members of the association.

(31) The rules on periods of limitation for the imposition of fines and periodic penalty payments were laid down in Council Regulation (EEC) No 2988/74[11], which also concerns penalties in the field of transport. In a system of parallel powers, the acts, which may interrupt a limitation period, should include procedural steps taken independently by the competition authority of a Member State. To clarify the legal framework, Regulation (EEC) No 2988/74 should therefore be amended to prevent it applying to matters covered by this Regulation, and this Regulation should include provisions on periods of limitation.

(32) The undertakings concerned should be accorded the right to be heard by the Commission, third parties whose interests may be affected by a decision should be given the opportunity of submitting their observations beforehand, and the decisions taken should be widely publicised. While ensuring the rights of defence of the undertakings concerned, in particular, the right of access to the file, it is essential that business secrets be protected. The confidentiality of information exchanged in the network should likewise be safeguarded.

(33) Since all decisions taken by the Commission under this Regulation are subject to review by the Court of Justice in accordance with the Treaty, the Court of Justice should, in accordance with Article 229 thereof be given unlimited jurisdiction in respect of decisions by which the Commission imposes fines or periodic penalty payments.

(34) The principles laid down in Articles 81 and 82 of the Treaty, as they have been applied by Regulation No 17, have given a central role to the Community bodies. This central role should be retained, whilst associating the Member States more closely with the application of the Community competition rules. In accordance with the principles of subsidiarity and proportionality as set out in Article 5 of the Treaty, this Regulation does not go beyond what is necessary in order to achieve its objective, which is to allow the Community competition rules to be applied effectively.

(35) In order to attain a proper enforcement of Community competition law, Member States should designate and empower authorities to apply Articles 81 and 82 of the Treaty as public enforcers. They should be able to designate administrative as well as judicial authorities to carry out the various functions conferred upon competition authorities in this Regulation. This Regulation recognises the wide variation which exists in the public enforcement systems of Member States. The effects of Article 11(6) of this Regulation should apply to all competition authorities. As an exception to this general rule, where a prosecuting authority brings a case before a separate judicial

---

[11] Council Regulation (EEC) No 2988/74 of 26 November 1974 concerning limitation periods in proceedings and the enforcement of sanctions under the rules of the European Economic Community relating to transport and competition (OJ L 319, 29.11.1974, p. 1).

authority, Article 11(6) should apply to the prosecuting authority subject to the conditions in Article 35(4) of this Regulation. Where these conditions are not fulfilled, the general rule should apply. In any case, Article 11(6) should not apply to courts insofar as they are acting as review courts.

(36) As the case-law has made it clear that the competition rules apply to transport, that sector should be made subject to the procedural provisions of this Regulation. Council Regulation No 141 of 26 November 1962 exempting transport from the application of Regulation No 17[12] should therefore be repealed and Regulations (EEC) No 1017/68[13], (EEC) No 4056/86[14] and (EEC) No 3975/87[15] should be amended in order to delete the specific procedural provisions they contain.

(37) This Regulation respects the fundamental rights and observes the principles recognised in particular by the Charter of Fundamental Rights of the European Union. Accordingly, this Regulation should be interpreted and applied with respect to those rights and principles.

(38) Legal certainty for undertakings operating under the Community competition rules contributes to the promotion of innovation and investment. Where cases give rise to genuine uncertainty because they present novel or unresolved questions for the application of these rules, individual undertakings may wish to seek informal guidance from the Commission. This Regulation is without prejudice to the ability of the Commission to issue such informal guidance,

HAS ADOPTED THIS REGULATION:

CHAPTER I. PRINCIPLES

Article 1
Application of Articles 81 and 82 of the Treaty

1. Agreements, decisions and concerted practices caught by Article 81(1) of the Treaty which do not satisfy the conditions of Article 81(3) of the Treaty shall be prohibited, no prior decision to that effect being required.

2. Agreements, decisions and concerted practices caught by Article 81(1) of the Treaty which satisfy the conditions of Article 81(3) of the Treaty shall not be prohibited, no prior decision to that effect being required.

3. The abuse of a dominant position referred to in Article 82 of the Treaty shall be prohibited, no prior decision to that effect being required.

Article 2
Burden of proof

In any national or Community proceedings for the application of Articles 81 and 82 of the Treaty, the burden of proving an infringement of Article 81(1) or of Article 82 of the Treaty shall rest on the party or the authority alleging the infringement. The undertaking or association of undertakings claiming the benefit of Article 81(3) of the Treaty shall bear the burden of proving that the conditions of that paragraph are fulfilled.

---

[12] OJ 124, 28.11.1962, p. 2751/62; Regulation as last amended by Regulation No 1002/67/EEC (OJ 306, 16.12.1967, p. 1).

[13] Council Regulation (EEC) No 1017/68 of 19 July 1968 applying rules of competition to transport by rail, road and inland waterway (OJ L 175, 23.7.1968, p. 1). Regulation as last amended by the Act of Accession of 1994.

[14] Council Regulation (EEC) No 4056/86 of 22 December 1986 laying down detailed rules for the application of Articles 81 and 82 (The title of the Regulation has been adjusted to take account of the renumbering of the Articles of the EC Treaty, in accordance with Article 12 of the Treaty of Amsterdam; the original reference was to Articles 85 and 86 of the Treaty) of the Treaty to maritime transport (OJ L 378, 31.12.1986, p. 4). Regulation as last amended by the Act of Accession of 1994.

[15] Council Regulation (EEC) No 3975/87 of 14 December 1987 laying down the procedure for the application of the rules on competition to undertakings in the air transport sector (OJ L 374, 31.12.1987, p. 1). Regulation as last amended by Regulation (EEC) No 2410/92 (OJ L 240, 24.8.1992, p. 18).

Article 3

Relationship between Articles 81 and 82 of the Treaty and national competition Laws

1. Where the competition authorities of the Member States or national courts apply national competition law to agreements, decisions by associations of undertakings or concerted practices within the meaning of Article 81(1) of the Treaty which may affect trade between Member States within the meaning of that provision, they shall also apply Article 81 of the Treaty to such agreements, decisions or concerted practices. Where the competition authorities of the Member States or national courts apply national competition law to any abuse prohibited by Article 82 of the Treaty, they shall also apply Article 82 of the Treaty.

2. The application of national competition law may not lead to the prohibition of agreements, decisions by associations of undertakings or concerted practices which may affect trade between Member States but which do not restrict competition within the meaning of Article 81(1) of the Treaty, or which fulfil the conditions of Article 81(3) of the Treaty or which are covered by a Regulation for the application of Article 81(3) of the Treaty. Member States shall not under this Regulation be precluded from adopting and applying on their territory stricter national laws which prohibit or sanction unilateral conduct engaged in by undertakings.

3. Without prejudice to general principles and other provisions of Community law, paragraphs 1 and 2 do not apply when the competition authorities and the courts of the Member States apply national merger control laws nor do they preclude the application of provisions of national law that predominantly pursue an objective different from that pursued by Articles 81 and 82 of the Treaty.

CHAPTER II. POWERS

Article 4

Powers of the Commission

For the purpose of applying Articles 81 and 82 of the Treaty, the Commission shall have the powers provided for by this Regulation.

Article 5

Powers of the competition authorities of the Member States

The competition authorities of the Member States shall have the power to apply Articles 81 and 82 of the Treaty in individual cases. For this purpose, acting on their own initiative or on a complaint, they may take the following decisions:

— requiring that an infringement be brought to an end,
— ordering interim measures,
— accepting commitments,
— imposing fines, periodic penalty payments or any other penalty provided for in their national law.

Where on the basis of the information in their possession the conditions for prohibition are not met they may likewise decide that there are no grounds for action on their part.

Article 6

Powers of the national courts

National courts shall have the power to apply Articles 81 and 82 of the Treaty.

CHAPTER III. COMMISSION DECISIONS

Article 7

Finding and termination of infringement

1. Where the Commission, acting on a complaint or on its own initiative, finds that there is an infringement of Article 81 or of Article 82 of the Treaty, it may by decision require the undertakings

614

and associations of undertakings concerned to bring such infringement to an end. For this purpose, it may impose on them any behavioural or structural remedies which are proportionate to the infringement committed and necessary to bring the infringement effectively to an end. Structural remedies can only be imposed either where there is no equally effective behavioural remedy or where any equally effective behavioural remedy would be more burdensome for the undertaking concerned than the structural remedy. If the Commission has a legitimate interest in doing so, it may also find that an infringement has been committed in the past.

2. Those entitled to lodge a complaint for the purposes of paragraph 1 are natural or legal persons who can show a legitimate interest and Member States.

Article 8
Interim measures

1. In cases of urgency due to the risk of serious and irreparable damage to competition, the Commission, acting on its own initiative may by decision, on the basis of a prima facie finding of infringement, order interim measures.
2. A decision under paragraph 1 shall apply for a specified period of time and may be renewed in so far this is necessary and appropriate.

Article 9
Commitments

1. Where the Commission intends to adopt a decision requiring that an infringement be brought to an end and the undertakings concerned offer commitments to meet the concerns expressed to them by the Commission in its preliminary assessment, the Commission may by decision make those commitments binding on the undertakings. Such a decision may be adopted for a specified period and shall conclude that there are no longer grounds for action by the Commission.
2. The Commission may, upon request or on its own initiative, reopen the proceedings:
   (a) where there has been a material change in any of the facts on which the decision was based;
   (b) where the undertakings concerned act contrary to their commitments; or
   (c) where the decision was based on incomplete, incorrect or misleading information provided by the parties.

Article 10
Finding of inapplicability

Where the Community public interest relating to the application of Articles 81 and 82 of the Treaty so requires, the Commission, acting on its own initiative, may by decision find that Article 81 of the Treaty is not applicable to an agreement, a decision by an association of undertakings or a concerted practice, either because the conditions of Article 81(1) of the Treaty are not fulfilled, or because the conditions of Article 81(3) of the Treaty are satisfied.

The Commission may likewise make such a finding with reference to Article 82 of the Treaty.

CHAPTER IV. COOPERATION

Article 11
Cooperation between the Commission and the competition authorities of the Member States

1. The Commission and the competition authorities of the Member States shall apply the Community competition rules in close cooperation.
2. The Commission shall transmit to the competition authorities of the Member States copies of the most important documents it has collected with a view to applying Articles 7, 8, 9, 10 and Article 29(1). At the request of the competition authority of a Member State, the Commission shall provide it with a copy of other existing documents necessary for the assessment of the case.
3. The competition authorities of the Member States shall, when acting under Article 81 or Article 82 of the Treaty, inform the Commission in writing before or without delay after commencing the first

formal investigative measure. This information may also be made available to the competition authorities of the other Member States.

4. No later than 30 days before the adoption of a decision requiring that an infringement be brought to an end, accepting commitments or withdrawing the benefit of a block exemption Regulation, the competition authorities of the Member States shall inform the Commission. To that effect, they shall provide the Commission with a summary of the case, the envisaged decision or, in the absence thereof, any other document indicating the proposed course of action. This information may also be made available to the competition authorities of the other Member States. At the request of the Commission, the acting competition authority shall make available to the Commission other documents it holds which are necessary for the assessment of the case. The information supplied to the Commission may be made available to the competition authorities of the other Member States. National competition authorities may also exchange between themselves information necessary for the assessment of a case that they are dealing with under Article 81 or Article 82 of the Treaty.

5. The competition authorities of the Member States may consult the Commission on any case involving the application of Community law.

6. The initiation by the Commission of proceedings for the adoption of a decision under Chapter III shall relieve the competition authorities of the Member States of their competence to apply Articles 81 and 82 of the Treaty. If a competition authority of a Member State is already acting on a case, the Commission shall only initiate proceedings after consulting with that national competition authority.

Article 12
Exchange of information

1. For the purpose of applying Articles 81 and 82 of the Treaty the Commission and the competition authorities of the Member States shall have the power to provide one another with and use in evidence any matter of fact or of law, including confidential information.

2. Information exchanged shall only be used in evidence for the purpose of applying Article 81 or Article 82 of the Treaty and in respect of the subject-matter for which it was collected by the transmitting authority. However, where national competition law is applied in the same case and in parallel to Community competition law and does not lead to a different outcome, information exchanged under this Article may also be used for the application of national competition law.

3. Information exchanged pursuant to paragraph 1 can only be used in evidence to impose sanctions on natural persons where:
   — the law of the transmitting authority foresees sanctions of a similar kind in relation to an infringement of Article 81 or Article 82 of the Treaty or, in the absence thereof,
   — the information has been collected in a way which respects the same level of protection of the rights of defence of natural persons as provided for under the national rules of the receiving authority. However, in this case, the information exchanged cannot be used by the receiving authority to impose custodial sanctions.

Article 13
Suspension or termination of proceedings

1. Where competition authorities of two or more Member States have received a complaint or are acting on their own initiative under Article 81 or Article 82 of the Treaty against the same agreement, decision of an association or practice, the fact that one authority is dealing with the case shall be sufficient grounds for the others to suspend the proceedings before them or to reject the complaint. The Commission may likewise reject a complaint on the ground that a competition authority of a Member State is dealing with the case.

2. Where a competition authority of a Member State or the Commission has received a complaint against an agreement, decision of an association or practice which has already been dealt with by another competition authority, it may reject it.

Article 14
Advisory Committee

1. The Commission shall consult an Advisory Committee on Restrictive Practices and Dominant Positions prior to the taking of any decision under Articles 7, 8, 9, 10, 23, Article 24(2) and Article 29(1).

2. For the discussion of individual cases, the Advisory Committee shall be composed of representatives of the competition authorities of the Member States. For meetings in which issues other than individual cases are being discussed, an additional Member State representative competent in competition matters may be appointed. Representatives may, if unable to attend, be replaced by other representatives.

3. The consultation may take place at a meeting convened and chaired by the Commission, held not earlier than 14 days after dispatch of the notice convening it, together with a summary of the case, an indication of the most important documents and a preliminary draft decision. In respect of decisions pursuant to Article 8, the meeting may be held seven days after the dispatch of the operative part of a draft decision. Where the Commission dispatches a notice convening the meeting which gives a shorter period of notice than those specified above, the meeting may take place on the proposed date in the absence of an objection by any Member State. The Advisory Committee shall deliver a written opinion on the Commission's preliminary draft decision. It may deliver an opinion even if some members are absent and are not represented. At the request of one or several members, the positions stated in the opinion shall be reasoned.

4. Consultation may also take place by written procedure. However, if any Member State so requests, the Commission shall convene a meeting. In case of written procedure, the Commission shall determine a time-limit of not less than 14 days within which the Member States are to put forward their observations for circulation to all other Member States. In case of decisions to be taken pursuant to Article 8, the time-limit of 14 days is replaced by seven days. Where the Commission determines a time-limit for the written procedure which is shorter than those specified above, the proposed time-limit shall be applicable in the absence of an objection by any Member State.

5. The Commission shall take the utmost account of the opinion delivered by the Advisory Committee. It shall inform the Committee of the manner in which its opinion has been taken into account.

6. Where the Advisory Committee delivers a written opinion, this opinion shall be appended to the draft decision. If the Advisory Committee recommends publication of the opinion, the Commission shall carry out such publication taking into account the legitimate interest of undertakings in the protection of their business secrets.

7. At the request of a competition authority of a Member State, the Commission shall include on the agenda of the Advisory Committee cases that are being dealt with by a competition authority of a Member State under Article 81 or Article 82 of the Treaty. The Commission may also do so on its own initiative. In either case, the Commission shall inform the competition authority concerned.

A request may in particular be made by a competition authority of a Member State in respect of a case where the Commission intends to initiate proceedings with the effect of Article 11(6).

The Advisory Committee shall not issue opinions on cases dealt with by competition authorities of the Member States. The Advisory Committee may also discuss general issues of Community competition law.

Article 15
Cooperation with national courts

1. In proceedings for the application of Article 81 or Article 82 of the Treaty, courts of the Member States may ask the Commission to transmit to them information in its possession or its opinion on questions concerning the application of the Community competition rules.

2. Member States shall forward to the Commission a copy of any written judgment of national courts deciding on the application of Article 81 or Article 82 of the Treaty. Such copy shall be forwarded without delay after the full written judgment is notified to the parties.

3. Competition authorities of the Member States, acting on their own initiative, may submit written

observations to the national courts of their Member State on issues relating to the application of Article 81 or Article 82 of the Treaty. With the permission of the court in question, they may also submit oral observations to the national courts of their Member State. Where the coherent application of Article 81 or Article 82 of the Treaty so requires, the Commission, acting on its own initiative, may submit written observations to courts of the Member States. With the permission of the court in question, it may also make oral observations.

For the purpose of the preparation of their observations only, the competition authorities of the Member States and the Commission may request the relevant court of the Member State to transmit or ensure the transmission to them of any documents necessary for the assessment of the case.

4. This Article is without prejudice to wider powers to make observations before courts conferred on competition authorities of the Member States under the law of their Member State.

Article 16
Uniform application of Community competition law

1. When national courts rule on agreements, decisions or practices under Article 81 or Article 82 of the Treaty which are already the subject of a Commission decision, they cannot take decisions running counter to the decision adopted by the Commission. They must also avoid giving decisions which would conflict with a decision contemplated by the Commission in proceedings it has initiated. To that effect, the national court may assess whether it is necessary to stay its proceedings. This obligation is without prejudice to the rights and obligations under Article 234 of the Treaty.

2. When competition authorities of the Member States rule on agreements, decisions or practices under Article 81 or Article 82 of the Treaty which are already the subject of a Commission decision, they cannot take decisions which would run counter to the decision adopted by the Commission.

CHAPTER V. POWERS OF INVESTIGATION

Article 17
Investigations into sectors of the economy and into types of agreements

1. Where the trend of trade between Member States, the rigidity of prices or other circumstances suggest that competition may be restricted or distorted within the common market, the Commission may conduct its inquiry into a particular sector of the economy or into a particular type of agreements across various sectors. In the course of that inquiry, the Commission may request the undertakings or associations of undertakings concerned to supply the information necessary for giving effect to Articles 81 and 82 of the Treaty and may carry out any inspections necessary for that purpose.

The Commission may in particular request the undertakings or associations of undertakings concerned to communicate to it all agreements, decisions and concerted practices. The Commission may publish a report on the results of its inquiry into particular sectors of the economy or particular types of agreements across various sectors and invite comments from interested parties.

2. Articles 14, 18, 19, 20, 22, 23 and 24 shall apply mutatis mutandis.

Article 18
Requests for information

1. In order to carry out the duties assigned to it by this Regulation, the Commission may, by simple request or by decision, require undertakings and associations of undertakings to provide all necessary information.

2. When sending a simple request for information to an undertaking or association of undertakings, the Commission shall state the legal basis and the purpose of the request, specify what information is required and fix the time-limit within which the information is to be provided, and the penalties provided for in Article 23 for supplying incorrect or misleading information.

3. Where the Commission requires undertakings and associations of undertakings to supply information by decision, it shall state the legal basis and the purpose of the request, specify what information is required and fix the time-limit within which it is to be provided. It shall also indicate the penalties

provided for in Article 23 and indicate or impose the penalties provided for in Article 24. It shall further indicate the right to have the decision reviewed by the Court of Justice.

4. The owners of the undertakings or their representatives and, in the case of legal persons, companies or firms, or associations having no legal personality, the persons authorised to represent them by law or by their constitution shall supply the information requested on behalf of the undertaking or the association of undertakings concerned. Lawyers duly authorised to act may supply the information on behalf of their clients. The latter shall remain fully responsible if the information supplied is incomplete, incorrect or misleading.

5. The Commission shall without delay forward a copy of the simple request or of the decision to the competition authority of the Member State in whose territory the seat of the undertaking or association of undertakings is situated and the competition authority of the Member State whose territory is affected.

6. At the request of the Commission the governments and competition authorities of the Member States shall provide the Commission with all necessary information to carry out the duties assigned to it by this Regulation.

Article 19
Power to take statements

1. In order to carry out the duties assigned to it by this Regulation, the Commission may interview any natural or legal person who consents to be interviewed for the purpose of collecting information relating to the subject-matter of an investigation.

2. Where an interview pursuant to paragraph 1 is conducted in the premises of an undertaking, the Commission shall inform the competition authority of the Member State in whose territory the interview takes place. If so requested by the competition authority of that Member State, its officials may assist the officials and other accompanying persons authorised by the Commission to conduct the interview.

Article 20
The Commission's powers of inspection

1. In order to carry out the duties assigned to it by this Regulation, the Commission may conduct all necessary inspections of undertakings and associations of undertakings.

2. The officials and other accompanying persons authorised by the Commission to conduct an inspection are empowered:
   (a) to enter any premises, land and means of transport of undertakings and associations of undertakings;
   (b) to examine the books and other records related to the business, irrespective of the medium on which they are stored;
   (c) to take or obtain in any form copies of or extracts from such books or records;
   (d) to seal any business premises and books or records for the period and to the extent necessary for the inspection;
   (e) to ask any representative or member of staff of the undertaking or association of undertakings for explanations on facts or documents relating to the subject-matter and purpose of the inspection and to record the answers.

3. The officials and other accompanying persons authorised by the Commission to conduct an inspection shall exercise their powers upon production of a written authorisation specifying the subject matter and purpose of the inspection and the penalties provided for in Article 23 in case the production of the required books or other records related to the business is incomplete or where the answers to questions asked under paragraph 2 of the present Article are incorrect or misleading. In good time before the inspection, the Commission shall give notice of the inspection to the competition authority of the Member State in whose territory it is to be conducted.

4. Undertakings and associations of undertakings are required to submit to inspections ordered by decision of the Commission. The decision shall specify the subject matter and purpose of the

inspection, appoint the date on which it is to begin and indicate the penalties provided for in Articles 23 and 24 and the right to have the decision reviewed by the Court of Justice. The Commission shall take such decisions after consulting the competition authority of the Member State in whose territory the inspection is to be conducted.

5. Officials of as well as those authorised or appointed by the competition authority of the Member State in whose territory the inspection is to be conducted shall, at the request of that authority or of the Commission, actively assist the officials and other accompanying persons authorised by the Commission. To this end, they shall enjoy the powers specified in paragraph 2.

6. Where the officials and other accompanying persons authorised by the Commission find that an undertaking opposes an inspection ordered pursuant to this Article, the Member State concerned shall afford them the necessary assistance, requesting where appropriate the assistance of the police or of an equivalent enforcement authority, so as to enable them to conduct their inspection.

7. If the assistance provided for in paragraph 6 requires authorisation from a judicial authority according to national rules, such authorisation shall be applied for. Such authorisation may also be applied for as a precautionary measure.

8. Where authorisation as referred to in paragraph 7 is applied for, the national judicial authority shall control that the Commission decision is authentic and that the coercive measures envisaged are neither arbitrary nor excessive having regard to the subject matter of the inspection. In its control of the proportionality of the coercive measures, the national judicial authority may ask the Commission, directly or through the Member State competition authority, for detailed explanations in particular on the grounds the Commission has for suspecting infringement of Articles 81 and 82 of the Treaty, as well as on the seriousness of the suspected infringement and on the nature of the involvement of the undertaking concerned. However, the national judicial authority may not call into question the necessity for the inspection nor demand that it be provided with the information in the Commission's file. The lawfulness of the Commission decision shall be subject to review only by the Court of Justice.

Article 21
Inspection of other premises

1. If a reasonable suspicion exists that books or other records related to the business and to the subject-matter of the inspection, which may be relevant to prove a serious violation of Article 81 or Article 82 of the Treaty, are being kept in any other premises, land and means of transport, including the homes of directors, managers and other members of staff of the undertakings and associations of undertakings concerned, the Commission can by decision order an inspection to be conducted in such other premises, land and means of transport.

2. The decision shall specify the subject matter and purpose of the inspection, appoint the date on which it is to begin and indicate the right to have the decision reviewed by the Court of Justice. It shall in particular state the reasons that have led the Commission to conclude that a suspicion in the sense of paragraph 1 exists. The Commission shall take such decisions after consulting the competition authority of the Member State in whose territory the inspection is to be conducted.

3. A decision adopted pursuant to paragraph 1 cannot be executed without prior authorisation from the national judicial authority of the Member State concerned. The national judicial authority shall control that the Commission decision is authentic and that the coercive measures envisaged are neither arbitrary nor excessive having regard in particular to the seriousness of the suspected infringement, to the importance of the evidence sought, to the involvement of the undertaking concerned and to the reasonable likelihood that business books and records relating to the subject matter of the inspection are kept in the premises for which the authorisation is requested. The national judicial authority may ask the Commission, directly or through the Member State competition authority, for detailed explanations on those elements which are necessary to allow its control of the proportionality of the coercive measures envisaged.

However, the national judicial authority may not call into question the necessity for the inspection nor demand that it be provided with information in the Commission's file. The lawfulness of the Commission decision shall be subject to review only by the Court of Justice.

4. The officials and other accompanying persons authorised by the Commission to conduct an inspection ordered in accordance with paragraph 1 of this Article shall have the powers set out in Article 20(2)(a), (b) and (c). Article 20(5) and (6) shall apply mutatis mutandis.

Article 22
Investigations by competition authorities of Member States

1. The competition authority of a Member State may in its own territory carry out any inspection or other fact-finding measure under its national law on behalf and for the account of the competition authority of another Member State in order to establish whether there has been an infringement of Article 81 or Article 82 of the Treaty. Any exchange and use of the information collected shall be carried out in accordance with Article 12.
2. At the request of the Commission, the competition authorities of the Member States shall undertake the inspections which the Commission considers to be necessary under Article 20(1) or which it has ordered by decision pursuant to Article 20(4). The officials of the competition authorities of the Member States who are responsible for conducting these inspections as well as those authorised or appointed by them shall exercise their powers in accordance with their national law.

If so requested by the Commission or by the competition authority of the Member State in whose territory the inspection is to be conducted, officials and other accompanying persons authorised by the Commission may assist the officials of the authority concerned.

CHAPTER VI. PENALTIES

Article 23
Fines

1. The Commission may by decision impose on undertakings and associations of undertakings fines not exceeding 1 % of the total turnover in the preceding business year where, intentionally or negligently:
   (a) they supply incorrect or misleading information in response to a request made pursuant to Article 17 or Article 18(2);
   (b) in response to a request made by decision adopted pursuant to Article 17 or Article 18(3), they supply incorrect, incomplete or misleading information or do not supply information within the required time-limit;
   (c) they produce the required books or other records related to the business in incomplete form during inspections under Article 20 or refuse to submit to inspections ordered by a decision adopted pursuant to Article 20(4);
   (d) in response to a question asked in accordance with Article 20(2)(e),
      — they give an incorrect or misleading answer,
      — they fail to rectify within a time-limit set by the Commission an incorrect, incomplete or misleading answer given by a member of staff, or
      — they fail or refuse to provide a complete answer on facts relating to the subject-matter and purpose of an inspection ordered by a decision adopted pursuant to Article 20(4);
   (e) seals affixed in accordance with Article 20(2)(d) by officials or other accompanying persons authorised by the Commission have been broken.
2. The Commission may by decision impose fines on undertakings and associations of undertakings where, either intentionally or negligently:
   (a) they infringe Article 81 or Article 82 of the Treaty; or
   (b) they contravene a decision ordering interim measures under Article 8; or
   (c) they fail to comply with a commitment made binding by a decision pursuant to Article 9.
   For each undertaking and association of undertakings participating in the infringement, the fine shall not exceed 10 % of its total turnover in the preceding business year.

   Where the infringement of an association relates to the activities of its members, the fine shall not exceed 10 % of the sum of the total turnover of each member active on the market affected by the infringement of the association.

3. In fixing the amount of the fine, regard shall be had both to the gravity and to the duration of the infringement.
4. When a fine is imposed on an association of undertakings taking account of the turnover of its members and the association is not solvent, the association is obliged to call for contributions from its members to cover the amount of the fine.

Where such contributions have not been made to the association within a time-limit fixed by the Commission, the Commission may require payment of the fine directly by any of the undertakings whose representatives were members of the decision-making bodies concerned of the association.

After the Commission has required payment under the second subparagraph, where necessary to ensure full payment of the fine, the Commission may require payment of the balance by any of the members of the association which were active on the market on which the infringement occurred.

However, the Commission shall not require payment under the second or the third subparagraph from undertakings which show that they have not implemented the infringing decision of the association and either were not aware of its existence or have actively distanced themselves from it before the Commission started investigating the case.

The financial liability of each undertaking in respect of the payment of the fine shall not exceed 10 % of its total turnover in the preceding business year.
5. Decisions taken pursuant to paragraphs 1 and 2 shall not be of a criminal law nature.

Article 24
Periodic penalty payments

1. The Commission may, by decision, impose on undertakings or associations of undertakings periodic penalty payments not exceeding 5 % of the average daily turnover in the preceding business year per day and calculated from the date appointed by the decision, in order to compel them:
   (a) to put an end to an infringement of Article 81 or Article 82 of the Treaty, in accordance with a decision taken pursuant to Article 7;
   (b) to comply with a decision ordering interim measures taken pursuant to Article 8;
   (c) to comply with a commitment made binding by a decision pursuant to Article 9;
   (d) to supply complete and correct information which it has requested by decision taken pursuant to Article 17 or Article 18(3);
   (e) to submit to an inspection which it has ordered by decision taken pursuant to Article 20(4).
2. Where the undertakings or associations of undertakings have satisfied the obligation which the periodic penalty payment was intended to enforce, the Commission may fix the definitive amount of the periodic penalty payment at a figure lower than that which would arise under the original decision. Article 23(4) shall apply correspondingly.

CHAPTER VII. LIMITATION PERIODS

Article 25
Limitation periods for the imposition of penalties

1. The powers conferred on the Commission by Articles 23 and 24 shall be subject to the following limitation periods:
   (a) three years in the case of infringements of provisions concerning requests for information or the conduct of inspections;
   (b) five years in the case of all other infringements.
2. Time shall begin to run on the day on which the infringement is committed. However, in the case of continuing or repeated infringements, time shall begin to run on the day on which the infringement ceases.
3. Any action taken by the Commission or by the competition authority of a Member State for the purpose of the investigation or proceedings in respect of an infringement shall interrupt the limitation period for the imposition of fines or periodic penalty payments. The limitation period shall be

interrupted with effect from the date on which the action is notified to at least one undertaking or association of undertakings which has participated in the infringement. Actions which interrupt the running of the period shall include in particular the following:

(a) written requests for information by the Commission or by the competition authority of a Member State;

(b) written authorisations to conduct inspections issued to its officials by the Commission or by the competition authority of a Member State;

(c) the initiation of proceedings by the Commission or by the competition authority of a Member State;

(d) notification of the statement of objections of the Commission or of the competition authority of a Member State.

4. The interruption of the limitation period shall apply for all the undertakings or associations of undertakings which have participated in the infringement.

5. Each interruption shall start time running afresh. However, the limitation period shall expire at the latest on the day on which a period equal to twice the limitation period has elapsed without the Commission having imposed a fine or a periodic penalty payment. That period shall be extended by the time during which limitation is suspended pursuant to paragraph 6.

6. The limitation period for the imposition of fines or periodic penalty payments shall be suspended for as long as the decision of the Commission is the subject of proceedings pending before the Court of Justice.

Article 26
Limitation period for the enforcement of penalties

1. The power of the Commission to enforce decisions taken pursuant to Articles 23 and 24 shall be subject to a limitation period of five years.

2. Time shall begin to run on the day on which the decision becomes final.

3. The limitation period for the enforcement of penalties shall be interrupted:

(a) by notification of a decision varying the original amount of the fine or periodic penalty payment or refusing an application for variation;

(b) by any action of the Commission or of a Member State, acting at the request of the Commission, designed to enforce payment of the fine or periodic penalty payment.

4. Each interruption shall start time running afresh.

5. The limitation period for the enforcement of penalties shall be suspended for so long as:

(a) time to pay is allowed;

(b) enforcement of payment is suspended pursuant to a decision of the Court of Justice.

CHAPTER VIII. HEARINGS AND PROFESSIONAL SECRECY

Article 27
Hearing of the parties, complainants and others

1. Before taking decisions as provided for in Articles 7, 8, 23 and Article 24(2), the Commission shall give the undertakings or associations of undertakings which are the subject of the proceedings conducted by the Commission the opportunity of being heard on the matters to which the Commission has taken objection. The Commission shall base its decisions only on objections on which the parties concerned have been able to comment. Complainants shall be associated closely with the proceedings.

2. The rights of defence of the parties concerned shall be fully respected in the proceedings. They shall be entitled to have access to the Commission's file, subject to the legitimate interest of undertakings in the protection of their business secrets. The right of access to the file shall not extend to confidential information and internal documents of the Commission or the competition authorities of the Member States. In particular, the right of access shall not extend to correspondence between the Commission and the competition authorities of the Member States, or between the latter, including documents drawn up pursuant to Articles 11 and 14. Nothing in this paragraph

shall prevent the Commission from disclosing and using information necessary to prove an infringement.

3. If the Commission considers it necessary, it may also hear other natural or legal persons. Applications to be heard on the part of such persons shall, where they show a sufficient interest, be granted. The competition authorities of the Member States may also ask the Commission to hear other natural or legal persons.

4. Where the Commission intends to adopt a decision pursuant to Article 9 or Article 10, it shall publish a concise summary of the case and the main content of the commitments or of the proposed course of action. Interested third parties may submit their observations within a time limit which is fixed by the Commission in its publication and which may not be less than one month. Publication shall have regard to the legitimate interest of undertakings in the protection of their business secrets.

Article 28
Professional secrecy

1. Without prejudice to Articles 12 and 15, information collected pursuant to Articles 17 to 22 shall be used only for the purpose for which it was acquired.

2. Without prejudice to the exchange and to the use of information foreseen in Articles 11, 12, 14, 15 and 27, the Commission and the competition authorities of the Member States, their officials, servants and other persons working under the supervision of these authorities as well as officials and civil servants of other authorities of the Member States shall not disclose information acquired or exchanged by them pursuant to this Regulation and of the kind covered by the obligation of professional secrecy. This obligation also applies to all representatives and experts of Member States attending meetings of the Advisory Committee pursuant to Article 14.

CHAPTER IX. EXEMPTION REGULATIONS

Article 29
Withdrawal in individual cases

1. Where the Commission, empowered by a Council Regulation, such as Regulations 19/65/EEC, (EEC) No 2821/71, (EEC) No 3976/87, (EEC) No 1534/91 or (EEC) No 479/92, to apply Article 81(3) of the Treaty by regulation, has declared Article 81(1) of the Treaty inapplicable to certain categories of agreements, decisions by associations of undertakings or concerted practices, it may, acting on its own initiative or on a complaint, withdraw the benefit of such an exemption Regulation when it finds that in any particular case an agreement, decision or concerted practice to which the exemption Regulation applies has certain effects which are incompatible with Article 81(3) of the Treaty.

2. Where, in any particular case, agreements, decisions by associations of undertakings or concerted practices to which a Commission Regulation referred to in paragraph 1 applies have effects which are incompatible with Article 81(3) of the Treaty in the territory of a Member State, or in a part thereof, which has all the characteristics of a distinct geographic market, the competition authority of that Member State may withdraw the benefit of the Regulation in question in respect of that territory.

CHAPTER X. GENERAL PROVISIONS

Article 30
Publication of decisions

1. The Commission shall publish the decisions, which it takes pursuant to Articles 7 to 10, 23 and 24.

2. The publication shall state the names of the parties and the main content of the decision, including any penalties imposed. It shall have regard to the legitimate interest of undertakings in the protection of their business secrets.

Article 31
Review by the Court of Justice

The Court of Justice shall have unlimited jurisdiction to review decisions whereby the Commission has fixed a fine or periodic penalty payment. It may cancel, reduce or increase the fine or periodic penalty payment imposed.

Article 32
Exclusions

This Regulation shall not apply to:
(a) international tramp vessel services as defined in Article 1(3)(a) of Regulation (EEC) No 4056/86;
(b) a maritime transport service that takes place exclusively between ports in one and the same Member State as foreseen in Article 1(2) of Regulation (EEC) No 4056/86;
(c) air transport between Community airports and third countries.

Article 33
Implementing provisions

1. The Commission shall be authorised to take such measures as may be appropriate in order to apply this Regulation. The measures may concern, inter alia:
    (a) the form, content and other details of complaints lodged pursuant to Article 7 and the procedure for rejecting complaints;
    (b) the practical arrangements for the exchange of information and consultations provided for in Article 11;
    (c) the practical arrangements for the hearings provided for in Article 27.
2. Before the adoption of any measures pursuant to paragraph 1, the Commission shall publish a draft thereof and invite all interested parties to submit their comments within the time-limit it lays down, which may not be less than one month. Before publishing a draft measure and before adopting it, the Commission shall consult the Advisory Committee on Restrictive Practices and Dominant Positions.

Chapter XI. Transitional, Amending and Final Provisions

Article 34
Transitional provisions

1. Applications made to the Commission under Article 2 of Regulation No 17, notifications made under Articles 4 and 5 of that Regulation and the corresponding applications and notifications made under Regulations (EEC) No 1017/68, (EEC) No 4056/86 and (EEC) No 3975/87 shall lapse as from the date of application of this Regulation.
2. Procedural steps taken under Regulation No 17 and Regulations (EEC) No 1017/68, (EEC) No 4056/86 and (EEC) No 3975/87 shall continue to have effect for the purposes of applying this Regulation.

Article 35
Designation of competition authorities of Member States

1. The Member States shall designate the competition authority or authorities responsible for the application of Articles 81 and 82 of the Treaty in such a way that the provisions of this regulation are effectively complied with. The measures necessary to empower those authorities to apply those Articles shall be taken before 1 May 2004. The authorities designated may include courts.
2. When enforcement of Community competition law is entrusted to national administrative and judicial authorities, the Member States may allocate different powers and functions to those different national authorities, whether administrative or judicial.
3. The effects of Article 11(6) apply to the authorities designated by the Member States including courts

that exercise functions regarding the preparation and the adoption of the types of decisions foreseen in Article 5. The effects of Article 11(6) do not extend to courts insofar as they act as review courts in respect of the types of decisions foreseen in Article 5.

4. Notwithstanding paragraph 3, in the Member States where, for the adoption of certain types of decisions foreseen in Article 5, an authority brings an action before a judicial authority that is separate and different from the prosecuting authority and provided that the terms of this paragraph are complied with, the effects of Article 11(6) shall be limited to the authority prosecuting the case which shall withdraw its claim before the judicial authority when the Commission opens proceedings and this withdrawal shall bring the national proceedings effectively to an end.

Article 36
Amendment of Regulation (EEC) No 1017/68

Regulation (EEC) No 1017/68 is amended as follows:

1. Article 2 is repealed;
2. in Article 3(1), the words 'The prohibition laid down in Article 2' are replaced by the words 'The prohibition in Article 81(1) of the Treaty';
3. Article 4 is amended as follows:
   (a) In paragraph 1, the words 'The agreements, decisions and concerted practices referred to in Article 2' are replaced by the words 'Agreements, decisions and concerted practices pursuant to Article 81(1) of the Treaty';
   (b) Paragraph 2 is replaced by the following:
   '2. If the implementation of any agreement, decision or concerted practice covered by paragraph 1 has, in a given case, effects which are incompatible with the requirements of Article 81(3) of the Treaty, undertakings or associations of undertakings may be required to make such effects cease.'
4. Articles 5 to 29 are repealed with the exception of Article 13(3) which continues to apply to decisions adopted pursuant to Article 5 of Regulation (EEC) No 1017/68 prior to the date of application of this Regulation until the date of expiration of those decisions;
5. in Article 30, paragraphs 2, 3 and 4 are deleted.

Article 37
Amendment of Regulation (EEC) No 2988/74

In Regulation (EEC) No 2988/74, the following Article is inserted:

'Article 7a

Exclusion

This Regulation shall not apply to measures taken under Council Regulation (EC) No 1/2003 of 16 December 2002 on the implementation of the rules on competition laid down in Articles 81 and 82 of the Treaty[16].'

Article 38
Amendment of Regulation (EEC) No 4056/86

Regulation (EEC) No 4056/86 is amended as follows:

1. Article 7 is amended as follows:
   (a) Paragraph 1 is replaced by the following:
   '1. Breach of an obligation
   Where the persons concerned are in breach of an obligation which, pursuant to Article 5, attaches to the exemption provided for in Article 3, the Commission may, in order to put an end to such breach and under the conditions laid down in Council Regulation (EC) No 1/2003 of 16 December 2002 on the implementation of the rules on competition laid down in Articles 81

---

[16] OJ L 1, 4.1.2003, p. 1.

and 82 of the Treaty[17] adopt a decision that either prohibits them from carrying out or requires them to perform certain specific acts, or withdraws the benefit of the block exemption which they enjoyed.'

(b) Paragraph 2 is amended as follows:

    (i) In point (a), the words 'under the conditions laid down in Section II' are replaced by the words 'under the conditions laid down in Regulation (EC) No 1/2003';

    (ii) The second sentence of the second subparagraph of point (c)(i) is replaced by the following: 'At the same time it shall decide, in accordance with Article 9 of Regulation (EC) No 1/2003, whether to accept commitments offered by the undertakings concerned with a view, inter alia, to obtaining access to the market for non-conference lines.'

2. Article 8 is amended as follows:

(a) Paragraph 1 is deleted.

(b) In paragraph 2 the words 'pursuant to Article 10' are replaced by the words 'pursuant to Regulation (EC) No 1/2003'.

(c) Paragraph 3 is deleted;

3. Article 9 is amended as follows:

(a) In paragraph 1, the words 'Advisory Committee referred to in Article 15' are replaced by the words 'Advisory Committee referred to in Article 14 of Regulation (EC) No 1/2003';

(b) In paragraph 2, the words 'Advisory Committee as referred to in Article 15' are replaced by the words 'Advisory Committee referred to in Article 14 of Regulation (EC) No 1/2003';

4. Articles 10 to 25 are repealed with the exception of Article 13(3) which continues to apply to decisions adopted pursuant to Article 81(3) of the Treaty prior to the date of application of this Regulation until the date of expiration of those decisions;

5. in Article 26, the words 'the form, content and other details of complaints pursuant to Article 10, applications pursuant to Article 12 and the hearings provided for in Article 23(1) and (2)' are deleted.

Article 39
Amendment of Regulation (EEC) No 3975/87

Articles 3 to 19 of Regulation (EEC) No 3975/87 are repealed with the exception of Article 6(3) which continues to apply to decisions adopted pursuant to Article 81(3) of the Treaty prior to the date of application of this Regulation until the date of expiration of those decisions.

Article 40
Amendment of Regulations No 19/65/EEC, (EEC) No 2821/71 and (EEC) No 1534/91

Article 7 of Regulation No 19/65/EEC, Article 7 of Regulation (EEC) No 2821/71 and Article 7 of Regulation (EEC) No 1534/91 are repealed.

Article 41
Amendment of Regulation (EEC) No 3976/87

Regulation (EEC) No 3976/87 is amended as follows:

1. Article 6 is replaced by the following:

'Article 6

The Commission shall consult the Advisory Committee referred to in Article 14 of Council Regulation (EC) No 1/2003 of 16 December 2002 on the implementation of the rules on competition laid down in Articles 81 and 82 of the Treaty[18] before publishing a draft Regulation and before adopting a Regulation.'

2. Article 7 is repealed.

---

[17] OJ L 1, 4.1.2003, p. 1.   [18] OJ L 1, 4.1.2003, p. 1.

Article 42
Amendment of Regulation (EEC) No 479/92

Regulation (EEC) No 479/92 is amended as follows:

1. Article 5 is replaced by the following:

   'Article 5

   Before publishing the draft Regulation and before adopting the Regulation, the Commission shall consult the Advisory Committee referred to in Article 14 of Council Regulation (EC) No 1/2003 of 16 December 2002 on the implementation of the rules on competition laid down in Articles 81 and 82 of the Treaty[19] (19).'

2. Article 6 is repealed.

Article 43
Repeal of Regulations No 17 and No 141

1. Regulation No 17 is repealed with the exception of Article 8(3) which continues to apply to decisions adopted pursuant to Article 81(3) of the Treaty prior to the date of application of this Regulation until the date of expiration of those decisions.

2. Regulation No 141 is repealed.

3. References to the repealed Regulations shall be construed as references to this Regulation.

Article 44
Report on the application of the present Regulation

Five years from the date of application of this Regulation, the Commission shall report to the European Parliament and the Council on the functioning of this Regulation, in particular on the application of Article 11(6) and Article 17.

On the basis of this report, the Commission shall assess whether it is appropriate to propose to the Council a revision of this Regulation.

Article 45
Entry into force

This Regulation shall enter into force on the 20th day following that of its publication in the Official Journal of the European Communities.

It shall apply from 1 May 2004.

This Regulation shall be binding in its entirety and directly applicable in all Member States.

Done at Brussels, 16 December 2002.

For the Council
The President
M. Fischer Boel

---

[19] OJ L 1, 4.1.2003, p. 1.

APPENDIX 2

Competition Act 1998

[2006 consolidated version[1]]

An Act to make provision about competition and the abuse of a dominant position in the market; to confer powers in relation to investigations conducted in connection with Article 81 or 82 of the treaty establishing the European Community; to amend the Fair Trading Act 1973 in relation to information which may be required in connection with investigations under that Act; to make provision with respect to the meaning of 'supply of services' in the Fair Trading Act 1973; and for connected purposes.

[9th November 1998]

PART I

COMPETITION

CHAPTER I. AGREEMENTS

Introduction

1 Enactments replaced

The following shall cease to have effect—

(a) the Restrictive Practices Court Act 1976 (c 33),

(b) the Restrictive Trade Practices Act 1976 (c 34),

(c) the Resale Prices Act 1976 (c 53), and

(d) the Restrictive Trade Practices Act 1977 (c 19).

The prohibition

2 Agreements etc preventing, restricting or distorting competition

(1) Subject to section 3, agreements between undertakings, decisions by associations of undertakings or concerted practices which—

(a) may affect trade within the United Kingdom, and

(b) have as their object or effect the prevention, restriction or distortion of competition within the United Kingdom

are prohibited unless they are exempt in accordance with the provisions of this Part.

(2) Subsection (1) applies, in particular, to agreements, decisions or practices which—

(a) directly or indirectly fix purchase or selling prices or any other trading conditions;

(b) limit or control production, markets, technical development or investment;

(c) share markets or sources of supply;

(d) apply dissimilar conditions to equivalent transactions with other trading parties, thereby placing them at a competitive disadvantage;

---

[1] This consolidated version of the Competition Act 1998 takes into account changes made by the following enactments and statutory instruments: SI 2004/1261, Enterprise Act 2002, Criminal Justice and Police Act 2001, Constitutional Reform Act 2005, Communications Act 2003, Water Act 2003, Railways and Transport Safety Act 2003, Transport Act 2000, SI 2003/419, Financial Services and Markets Act 2000, Companies (Audit, Investigations and Community Enterprise) Act 2004, SI 2003/1592, Utilities Act 2000, SI 2002/1555, SI 2001/2916, SI 2003/1398, SI 2003/3180, SI 2000/311, SI 2000/2031. Legislative interpretation amendments (providing that the relevant section is to be read and applied in a particular way) have been included as if they were actual amendments.

(e) make the conclusion of contracts subject to acceptance by the other parties of supplementary obligations which, by their nature or according to commercial usage, have no connection with the subject of such contracts.

(3) Subsection (1) applies only if the agreement, decision or practice is, or is intended to be, implemented in the United Kingdom.

(4) Any agreement or decision which is prohibited by subsection (1) is void.

(5) A provision of this Part which is expressed to apply to, or in relation to, an agreement is to be read as applying equally to, or in relation to, a decision by an association of undertakings or a concerted practice (but with any necessary modifications).

(6) Subsection (5) does not apply where the context otherwise requires.

(7) In this section 'the United Kingdom' means, in relation to an agreement which operates or is intended to operate only in a part of the United Kingdom, that part.

(8) The prohibition imposed by subsection (1) is referred to in this Act as 'the Chapter I prohibition'.

Excluded agreements

3 Excluded agreements

(1) The Chapter I prohibition does not apply in any of the cases in which it is excluded by or as a result of—
  (a) Schedule 1 (mergers and concentrations);
  (b) Schedule 2 (competition scrutiny under other enactments);
  (c) Schedule 3 (planning obligations and other general exclusions).

(2) The Secretary of State may at any time by order amend Schedule 1, with respect to the Chapter I prohibition, by—
  (a) providing for one or more additional exclusions; or
  (b) amending or removing any provision (whether or not it has been added by an order under this subsection).

(3) The Secretary of State may at any time by order amend Schedule 3, with respect to the Chapter I prohibition, by—
  (a) providing for one or more additional exclusions; or
  (b) amending or removing any provision—
    (i) added by an order under this subsection; or
    (ii) included in paragraph 1, 2, 8 or 9 of Schedule 3.

(4) The power under subsection (3) to provide for an additional exclusion may be exercised only if it appears to the Secretary of State that agreements which fall within the additional exclusion—
  (a) do not in general have an adverse effect on competition, or
  (b) are, in general, best considered under Chapter II or the Enterprise Act 2002.

(5) An order under subsection (2)(a) or (3)(a) may include provision (similar to that made with respect to any other exclusion provided by the relevant Schedule) for the exclusion concerned to cease to apply to a particular agreement.

(6) Schedule 3 also gives the Secretary of State power to exclude agreements from the Chapter I prohibition in certain circumstances.

Exemptions

4 . . .

5 . . .

6 Block exemptions

(1) If agreements which fall within a particular category of agreement are, in the opinion of the OFT, likely to be exempt agreements, the OFT may recommend that the Secretary of State make an order specifying that category for the purposes of this section.

(2) The Secretary of State may make an order ('a block exemption order') giving effect to such a recommendation—

   (a) in the form in which the recommendation is made; or

   (b) subject to such modifications as he considers appropriate.

(3) An agreement which falls within a category specified in a block exemption order is exempt from the Chapter I prohibition.

(4) An exemption under this section is referred to in this Part as a block exemption.

(5) A block exemption order may impose conditions or obligations subject to which a block exemption is to have effect.

(6) A block exemption order may provide—

   (a) that breach of a condition imposed by the order has the effect of cancelling the block exemption in respect of an agreement;

   (b) that if there is a failure to comply with an obligation imposed by the order, the OFT may, by notice in writing, cancel the block exemption in respect of the agreement;

   (c) that if the OFT considers that a particular agreement is not an exempt agreement, it may cancel the block exemption in respect of that agreement.

(7) A block exemption order may provide that the order is to cease to have effect at the end of a specified period.

(8) In this section—

'exempt agreement' means an agreement which is exempt from the Chapter I prohibition as a result of section 9; and

'specified' means specified in a block exemption order.

7 . . .

8 Block exemptions: procedure

(1) Before making a recommendation under section 6(1), the OFT must—

   (a) publish details of its proposed recommendation in such a way as it thinks most suitable for bringing it to the attention of those likely to be affected; and

   (b) consider any representations about it which are made to it.

(2) If the Secretary of State proposes to give effect to such a recommendation subject to modifications, he must inform the OFT of the proposed modifications and take into account any comments made by the OFT.

(3) If, in the opinion of the OFT, it is appropriate to vary or revoke a block exemption order it may make a recommendation to that effect to the Secretary of State.

(4) Subsection (1) also applies to any proposed recommendation under subsection (3).

(5) Before exercising his power to vary or revoke a block exemption order (in a case where there has been no recommendation under subsection (3)), the Secretary of State must—

   (a) inform the OFT of the proposed variation or revocation; and

   (b) take into account any comments made by the OFT.

(6) A block exemption order may provide for a block exemption to have effect from a date earlier than that on which the order is made.

9 Exempt agreements

(1) An agreement is exempt from the Chapter I prohibition if it—

   (a) contributes to—

      (i) improving production or distribution, or

      (ii) promoting technical or economic progress,

   while allowing consumers a fair share of the resulting benefit; and

   (b) does not—

      (i) impose on the undertakings concerned restrictions which are not indispensable to the attainment of those objectives; or

(ii) afford the undertakings concerned the possibility of eliminating competition in respect of a substantial part of the products in question.

(2) In any proceedings in which it is alleged that the Chapter I prohibition is being or has been infringed by an agreement, any undertaking or association of undertakings claiming the benefit of subsection (1) shall bear the burden of proving that the conditions of that subsection are satisfied.

10 Parallel exemptions

(1) An agreement is exempt from the Chapter I prohibition if it is exempt from the Community prohibition—
   (a) by virtue of a Regulation, or
   (b) because of a decision of the Commission under Article 10 of the EC Competition Regulation.

(2) An agreement is exempt from the Chapter I prohibition if it does not affect trade between Member States but otherwise falls within a category of agreement which is exempt from the Community prohibition by virtue of a Regulation.

(3) An exemption from the Chapter I prohibition under this section is referred to in this Part as a parallel exemption.

(4) A parallel exemption—
   (a) takes effect on the date on which the relevant exemption from the Community prohibition takes effect or, in the case of a parallel exemption under subsection (2), would take effect if the agreement in question affected trade between Member States; and
   (b) ceases to have effect—
      (i) if the relevant exemption from the Community prohibition ceases to have effect; or
      (ii) on being cancelled by virtue of subsection (5) or (7).

(5) In such circumstances and manner as may be specified in rules made under section 51, the OFT may—
   (a) impose conditions or obligations subject to which a parallel exemption is to have effect;
   (b) vary or remove any such condition or obligation;
   (c) impose one or more additional conditions or obligations;
   (d) cancel the exemption.

(6) In such circumstances as may be specified in rules made under section 51, the date from which cancellation of an exemption is to take effect may be earlier than the date on which notice of cancellation is given.

(7) Breach of a condition imposed by the OFT has the effect of cancelling the exemption.

(8) In exercising its powers under this section, the OFT may require any person who is a party to the agreement in question to give it such information as it may require.

(9) For the purpose of this section references to an agreement being exempt from the Community prohibition are to be read as including references to the prohibition being inapplicable to the agreement by virtue of a Regulation other than the EC Competition Regulation or a decision by the Commission.

(10) In this section—
   'the Community prohibition' means the prohibition contained in—
   (a) Article 81(1);
   (b) any corresponding provision replacing, or otherwise derived from, that provision;
   (c) such other Regulation as the Secretary of State may by order specify; and
   'Regulation' means a Regulation adopted by the Commission or by the Council.

(11) This section has effect in relation to the prohibition contained in paragraph 1 of Article 53 of the EEA Agreement (and the EFTA Surveillance Authority) as it has effect in relation to the Community prohibition (and the Commission) subject to any modifications which the Secretary of State may by order prescribe.

11 Exemption for certain other agreements

(1) The fact that a ruling may be given by virtue of Article 84 of the Treaty on the question whether or not agreements of a particular kind are prohibited by Article 81(1) does not prevent such agreements from being subject to the Chapter I prohibition.

(2) But the Secretary of State may by regulations make such provision as he considers appropriate for the purpose of granting an exemption from the Chapter I prohibition, in prescribed circumstances, in respect of such agreements.

(3) An exemption from the Chapter I prohibition by virtue of regulations under this section is referred to in this Part as a section 11 exemption.

Notification

12 ...

13 ...

14 ...

15 ...

16 ...

Chapter II. Abuse of Dominant Position

Introduction

17 Enactments replaced

Sections 2 to 10 of the Competition Act 1980 (control of anti-competitive practices) shall cease to have effect.

The prohibition

18 Abuse of dominant position

(1) Subject to section 19, any conduct on the part of one or more undertakings which amounts to the abuse of a dominant position in a market is prohibited if it may affect trade within the United Kingdom.

(2) Conduct may, in particular, constitute such an abuse if it consists in—

    (a) directly or indirectly imposing unfair purchase or selling prices or other unfair trading conditions;

    (b) limiting production, markets or technical development to the prejudice of consumers;

    (c) applying dissimilar conditions to equivalent transactions with other trading parties, thereby placing them at a competitive disadvantage;

    (d) making the conclusion of contracts subject to acceptance by the other parties of supplementary obligations which, by their nature or according to commercial usage, have no connection with the subject of the contracts.

(3) In this section—

'dominant position' means a dominant position within the United Kingdom; and

'the United Kingdom' means the United Kingdom or any part of it.

(4) The prohibition imposed by subsection (1) is referred to in this Act as 'the Chapter II prohibition'.

Excluded cases

19 Excluded cases

(1) The Chapter II prohibition does not apply in any of the cases in which it is excluded by or as a result of—

    (a) Schedule 1 (mergers and concentrations); or

    (b) Schedule 3 (general exclusions).

(2) The Secretary of State may at any time by order amend Schedule 1, with respect to the Chapter II prohibition, by—

    (a) providing for one or more additional exclusions; or

    (b) amending or removing any provision (whether or not it has been added by an order under this subsection).

(3) The Secretary of State may at any time by order amend paragraph 8 of Schedule 3 with respect to the Chapter II prohibition.

(4) Schedule 3 also gives the Secretary of State power to provide that the Chapter II prohibition is not to apply in certain circumstances.

Notification

20 . . .

21 . . .

22 . . .

23 . . .

24 . . .

Chapter III. Investigation and Enforcement

Investigations

25 Power of OFT to investigate

(1) In any of the following cases, the OFT may conduct an investigation.

(2) The first case is where there are reasonable grounds for suspecting that there is an agreement which—

    (a) may affect trade within the United Kingdom; and

    (b) has as its object or effect the prevention, restriction or distortion of competition within the United Kingdom.

(3) The second case is where there are reasonable grounds for suspecting that there is an agreement—

    (a) which may affect trade between Member States; and

    (b) which has as its object or effect the prevention, restriction or distortion of competition within the Community.

(4) The third case is where there are reasonable grounds for suspecting that the Chapter II prohibition has been infringed.

(5) The fourth case is where there are reasonable grounds for suspecting that the prohibition in Article 82 has been infringed.

(6) The fifth case is where there are reasonable grounds for suspecting that, at some time in the past, there was an agreement which at that time—

    (a) may have affected trade within the United Kingdom; and

    (b) had as its object or effect the prevention, restriction or distortion of competition within the United Kingdom.

(7) The sixth case is where there are reasonable grounds for suspecting that, at some time in the past, there was an agreement which at that time—

    (a) may have affected trade between Member States; and

    (b) had as its object or effect the prevention, restriction or distortion of competition within the Community.

(8) Subsection (2) does not permit an investigation to be conducted in relation to an agreement if the OFT—

(a) considers that the agreement is exempt from the Chapter I prohibition as a result of a block exemption or a parallel exemption; and

(b) does not have reasonable grounds for suspecting that the circumstances may be such that it could exercise its power to cancel the exemption.

(9) Subsection (3) does not permit an investigation to be conducted if the OFT—

(a) considers that the agreement is an agreement to which the prohibition in Article 81(1) is inapplicable by virtue of a regulation of the Commission ('the relevant regulation'); and

(b) does not have reasonable grounds for suspecting that the conditions set out in Article 29(2) of the EC Competition Regulation for the withdrawal of the benefit of the relevant regulation may be satisfied in respect of that agreement.

(10) Subsection (6) does not permit an investigation to be conducted in relation to any agreement if the OFT considers that, at the time in question, the agreement was exempt from the Chapter I prohibition as a result of a block exemption or a parallel exemption.

(11) Subsection (7) does not permit an investigation to be conducted in relation to any agreement if the OFT considers that, at the time in question, the agreement was an agreement to which the prohibition in Article 81(1) was inapplicable by virtue of a regulation of the Commission.

(12) It is immaterial for the purposes of subsection (6) or (7) whether the agreement in question remains in existence.

26 Powers when conducting investigations

(1) For the purposes of an investigation, the OFT may require any person to produce to it a specified document, or to provide it with specified information, which it considers relates to any matter relevant to the investigation.

(2) The power conferred by subsection (1) is to be exercised by a notice in writing.

(3) A notice under subsection (2) must indicate—

(a) the subject matter and purpose of the investigation; and

(b) the nature of the offences created by sections 42 to 44.

(4) In subsection (1) 'specified' means—

(a) specified, or described, in the notice; or

(b) falling within a category which is specified, or described, in the notice.

(5) The OFT may also specify in the notice—

(a) the time and place at which any document is to be produced or any information is to be provided;

(b) the manner and form in which it is to be produced or provided.

(6) The power under this section to require a person to produce a document includes power—

(a) if the document is produced—

(i) to take copies of it or extracts from it;

(ii) to require him, or any person who is a present or past officer of his, or is or was at any time employed by him, to provide an explanation of the document;

(b) if the document is not produced, to require him to state, to the best of his knowledge and belief, where it is.

27 Power to enter business premises without a warrant

(1) Any officer of the OFT who is authorised in writing by the OFT to do so ('an investigating officer') may enter any business premises in connection with an investigation.

(2) No investigating officer is to enter any premises in the exercise of his powers under this section unless he has given to the occupier of the premises a written notice which—

(a) gives at least two working days' notice of the intended entry;

(b) indicates the subject matter and purpose of the investigation; and

(c) indicates the nature of the offences created by sections 42 to 44.

(3) Subsection (2) does not apply—

(a) if the OFT has a reasonable suspicion that the premises are, or have been, occupied by—

    (i)   a party to an agreement which it is investigating under section 25; or

    (ii) an undertaking the conduct of which it is investigating under section 25; or

  (b) if the investigating officer has taken all such steps as are reasonably practicable to give notice but has not been able to do so.

(4) In a case falling within subsection (3), the power of entry conferred by subsection (1) is to be exercised by the investigating officer on production of—

  (a) evidence of his authorisation; and

  (b) a document containing the information referred to in subsection (2)(b) and (c).

(5) An investigating officer entering any premises under this section may—

  (a) take with him such equipment as appears to him to be necessary;

  (b) require any person on the premises—

    (i)   to produce any document which he considers relates to any matter relevant to the investigation; and

    (ii) if the document is produced, to provide an explanation of it;

  (c) require any person to state, to the best of his knowledge and belief, where any such document is to be found;

  (d) take copies of, or extracts from, any document which is produced;

  (e) require any information which is stored in any electronic form and is accessible from the premises and which the investigating officer considers relates to any matter relevant to the investigation, to be produced in a form—

    (i)   in which it can be taken away, and

    (ii) in which it is visible and legible or from which it can readily be produced in a visible and legible form.

  (f) take any steps which appear to be necessary for the purpose of preserving or preventing interference with any document which he considers relates to any matter relevant to the investigation.

(6) In this section—

'business premises' means premises (or any part of premises) not used as a dwelling.

28 Power to enter business premises under a warrant

(1) On an application made by the OFT to the court in accordance with rules of court, a judge may issue a warrant if he is satisfied that—

  (a) there are reasonable grounds for suspecting that there are on any business premises documents—

    (i)   the production of which has been required under section 26 or 27; and

    (ii) which have not been produced as required;

  (b) there are reasonable grounds for suspecting that—

    (i)   there are on any business premises documents which the OFT has power under section 26 to require to be produced; and

    (ii) if the documents were required to be produced, they would not be produced but would be concealed, removed, tampered with or destroyed; or

  (c) an investigating officer has attempted to enter premises in the exercise of his powers under section 27 but has been unable to do so and that there are reasonable grounds for suspecting that there are on the premises documents the production of which could have been required under that section.

(2) A warrant under this section shall authorise a named officer of the OFT, and any other of the OFT's officers whom the OFT has authorised in writing to accompany the named officer—

  (a) to enter the premises specified in the warrant, using such force as is reasonably necessary for the purpose;

  (b) to search the premises and take copies of, or extracts from, any document appearing to be of a kind in respect of which the application under subsection (1) was granted ('the relevant kind');

  (c) to take possession of any documents appearing to be of the relevant kind if—

      (i)   such action appears to be necessary for preserving the documents or preventing interference with them; or

      (ii) it is not reasonably practicable to take copies of the documents on the premises;

  (d) to take any other steps which appear to be necessary for the purpose mentioned in paragraph (c)(i);

  (e) to require any person to provide an explanation of any document appearing to be of the relevant kind or to state, to the best of his knowledge and belief, where it may be found;

  (f) to require any information which is stored in any electronic form and is accessible from the premises and which the named officer considers relates to any matter relevant to the investigation, to be produced in a form—

      (i)   in which it can be taken away, and

      (ii) in which it is visible and legible or from which it can readily be produced in a visible and legible form.

(3) If, in the case of a warrant under subsection (1)(b), the judge is satisfied that it is reasonable to suspect that there are also on the premises other documents relating to the investigation concerned, the warrant shall also authorise action mentioned in subsection (2) to be taken in relation to any such document.

(3A) A warrant under this section may authorise persons specified in the warrant to accompany the named officer who is executing it.

(4) Any person entering premises by virtue of a warrant under this section may take with him such equipment as appears to him to be necessary.

(5) On leaving any premises which he has entered by virtue of a warrant under this section, the named officer must, if the premises are unoccupied or the occupier is temporarily absent, leave them as effectively secured as he found them.

(6) A warrant under this section continues in force until the end of the period of one month beginning with the day on which it is issued.

(7) Any document of which possession is taken under subsection (2)(c) may be retained for a period of three months.

(8) In this section 'business premises' has the same meaning as in section 27.

28A Power to enter domestic premises under a warrant

(1) On an application made by the OFT to the court in accordance with rules of court, a judge may issue a warrant if he is satisfied that—

  (a) there are reasonable grounds for suspecting that there are on any domestic premises documents—

      (i)   the production of which has been required under section 26; and

      (ii) which have not been produced as required; or

  (b) there are reasonable grounds for suspecting that—

      (i)   there are on any domestic premises documents which the OFT has power under section 26 to require to be produced; and

      (ii) if the documents were required to be produced, they would not be produced but would be concealed, removed, tampered with or destroyed.

(2) A warrant under this section shall authorise a named officer of the OFT, and any other of its officers whom the OFT has authorised in writing to accompany the named officer—

  (a) to enter the premises specified in the warrant, using such force as is reasonably necessary for the purpose;

  (b) to search the premises and take copies of, or extracts from, any document appearing to be of a kind in respect of which the application under subsection (1) was granted ('the relevant kind');

  (c) to take possession of any documents appearing to be of the relevant kind if—

      (i)   such action appears to be necessary for preserving the documents or preventing interference with them; or

      (ii) it is not reasonably practicable to take copies of the documents on the premises;

(d) to take any other steps which appear to be necessary for the purpose mentioned in paragraph (c)(i);

(e) to require any person to provide an explanation of any document appearing to be of the relevant kind or to state, to the best of his knowledge and belief, where it may be found;

(f) to require any information which is stored in any electronic form and is accessible from the premises and which the named officer considers relates to any matter relevant to the investigation, to be produced in a form—

    (i) in which it can be taken away, and

    (ii) in which it is visible and legible or from which it can readily be produced in a visible and legible form.

(3) If, in the case of a warrant under subsection (1)(b), the judge is satisfied that it is reasonable to suspect that there are also on the premises other documents relating to the investigation concerned, the warrant shall also authorise action mentioned in subsection (2) to be taken in relation to any such document.

(4) A warrant under this section may authorise persons specified in the warrant to accompany the named officer who is executing it.

(5) Any person entering premises by virtue of a warrant under this section may take with him such equipment as appears to him to be necessary.

(6) On leaving any premises which he has entered by virtue of a warrant under this section, the named officer must, if the premises are unoccupied or the occupier is temporarily absent, leave them as effectively secured as he found them.

(7) A warrant under this section continues in force until the end of the period of one month beginning with the day on which it is issued.

(8) Any document of which possession is taken under subsection (2)(c) may be retained for a period of three months.

(9) In this section, 'domestic premises' means premises (or any part of premises) that are used as a dwelling and are—

(a) premises also used in connection with the affairs of an undertaking or association of undertakings; or

(b) premises where documents relating to the affairs of an undertaking or association of undertakings are kept.

29 Entry of premises under warrant: supplementary

(1) A warrant issued under section 28 or 28A must indicate—

(a) the subject matter and purpose of the investigation;

(b) the nature of the offences created by sections 42 to 44.

(2) The powers conferred by section 28 or 28A are to be exercised on production of a warrant issued under that section.

(3) If there is no one at the premises when the named officer proposes to execute such a warrant he must, before executing it—

(a) take such steps as are reasonable in all the circumstances to inform the occupier of the intended entry; and

(b) if the occupier is informed, afford him or his legal or other representative a reasonable opportunity to be present when the warrant is executed.

(4) If the named officer is unable to inform the occupier of the intended entry he must, when executing the warrant, leave a copy of it in a prominent place on the premises.

(5) In this section—

'named officer' means the officer named in the warrant; and

'occupier', in relation to any premises, means a person whom the named officer reasonably believes is the occupier of those premises.

30 Privileged communications

(1) A person shall not be required, under any provision of this Part, to produce or disclose a privileged communication.
(2) 'Privileged communication' means a communication—
   (a) between a professional legal adviser and his client, or
   (b) made in connection with, or in contemplation of, legal proceedings and for the purposes of those proceedings,
   which in proceedings in the High Court would be protected from disclosure on grounds of legal professional privilege.
(3) In the application of this section to Scotland—
   (a) references to the High Court are to be read as references to the Court of Session; and
   (b) the reference to legal professional privilege is to be read as a reference to confidentiality of communications.

30A Use of statements in prosecution

A statement made by a person in response to a requirement imposed by virtue of any of sections 26 to 28A may not be used in evidence against him on a prosecution for an offence under section 188 of the Enterprise Act 2002 unless, in the proceedings—
(a) in giving evidence, he makes a statement inconsistent with it, and
(b) evidence relating to it is adduced, or a question relating to it is asked, by him or on his behalf.

31 Decisions following an investigation

(1) If as a result of an investigation the OFT proposes to make a decision, the OFT must—
   (a) give written notice to the person (or persons) likely to be affected by the proposed decision; and
   (b) give that person (or those persons) an opportunity to make representations.
(2) For the purposes of this section and sections 31A and 31B 'decision' means a decision of the OFT—
   (a) that the Chapter I prohibition has been infringed;
   (b) that the Chapter II prohibition has been infringed;
   (c) that the prohibition in Article 81(1) has been infringed; or
   (d) that the prohibition in Article 82 has been infringed.

31A Commitments

(1) Subsection (2) applies in a case where the OFT has begun an investigation under section 25 but has not made a decision (within the meaning given by section 31(2)).
(2) For the purposes of addressing the competition concerns it has identified, the OFT may accept from such person (or persons) concerned as it considers appropriate commitments to take such action (or refrain from taking such action) as it considers appropriate.
(3) At any time when commitments are in force the OFT may accept from the person (or persons) who gave the commitments—
   (a) a variation of them if it is satisfied that the commitments as varied will address its current competition concerns;
   (b) commitments in substitution for them if it is satisfied that the new commitments will address its current competition concerns.
(4) Commitments under this section—
   (a) shall come into force when accepted; and
   (b) may be released by the OFT where—
      (i) it is requested to do so by the person (or persons) who gave the commitments; or
      (ii) it has reasonable grounds for believing that the competition concerns referred to in subsection (2) or (3) no longer arise.
(5) The provisions of Schedule 6A to this Act shall have effect with respect to procedural requirements for the acceptance, variation and release of commitments under this section.

31B Effect of commitments under section 31A

(1) Subsection (2) applies if the OFT has accepted commitments under section 31A (and has not released them).

(2) In such a case, the OFT shall not—

    (a) continue the investigation,

    (b) make a decision (within the meaning of section 31(2)), or

    (c) give a direction under section 35,

    in relation to the agreement or conduct which was the subject of the investigation (but this subsection is subject to subsections (3) and (4)).

(3) Nothing in subsection (2) prevents the OFT from taking any action in relation to competition concerns which are not addressed by commitments accepted by it.

(4) Subsection (2) also does not prevent the OFT from continuing the investigation, making a decision, or giving a direction where—

    (a) it has reasonable grounds for believing that there has been a material change of circumstances since the commitments were accepted;

    (b) it has reasonable grounds for suspecting that a person has failed to adhere to one or more of the terms of the commitments; or

    (c) it has reasonable grounds for suspecting that information which led it to accept the commitments was incomplete, false or misleading in a material particular.

(5) If, pursuant to subsection (4), the OFT makes a decision or gives a direction the commitments are to be treated as released from the date of that decision or direction.

31C Review of commitments

(1) Where the OFT is reviewing or has reviewed the effectiveness of commitments accepted under section 31A it must, if requested to do so by the Secretary of State, prepare a report of its findings.

(2) The OFT must—

    (a) give any report prepared by it under subsection (1) to the Secretary of State; and

    (b) publish the report.

31D Guidance

(1) The OFT must prepare and publish guidance as to the circumstances in which it may be appropriate to accept commitments under section 31A.

(2) The OFT may at any time alter the guidance.

(3) If the guidance is altered, the OFT must publish it as altered.

(4) No guidance is to be published under this section without the approval of the Secretary of State.

(5) The OFT may, after consulting the Secretary of State, choose how it publishes its guidance.

(6) If the OFT is preparing or altering guidance under this section it must consult such persons as it considers appropriate.

(7) If the proposed guidance or alteration relates to a matter in respect of which a regulator exercises concurrent jurisdiction, those consulted must include that regulator.

(8) When exercising its discretion to accept commitments under section 31A, the OFT must have regard to the guidance for the time being in force under this section.

31E Enforcement of commitments

(1) If a person from whom the OFT has accepted commitments fails without reasonable excuse to adhere to the commitments (and has not been released from them), the OFT may apply to the court for an order—

    (a) requiring the defaulter to make good his default within a time specified in the order; or

    (b) if the commitments relate to anything to be done in the management or administration of an undertaking, requiring the undertaking or any of its officers to do it.

(2) An order of the court under subsection (1) may provide for all the costs of, or incidental to, the application for the order to be borne by—

(a) the person in default; or

(b) any officer of an undertaking who is responsible for the default.

(3) In the application of subsection (2) to Scotland, the reference to 'costs' is to be read as a reference to 'expenses'.

Enforcement

32 Directions in relation to agreements

(1) If the OFT has made a decision that an agreement infringes the Chapter I prohibition or that it infringes the prohibition in Article 81(1), it may give to such person or persons as it considers appropriate such directions as it considers appropriate to bring the infringement to an end.

(2) . . .

(3) A direction under this section may, in particular, include provision—

(a) requiring the parties to the agreement to modify the agreement; or

(b) requiring them to terminate the agreement.

(4) A direction under this section must be given in writing.

33 Directions in relation to conduct

(1) If the OFT has made a decision that conduct infringes the Chapter II prohibition or that it infringes the prohibition in Article 82, it may give to such person or persons as it considers appropriate such directions as it considers appropriate to bring the infringement to an end.

(2) . . .

(3) A direction under this section may, in particular, include provision—

(a) requiring the person concerned to modify the conduct in question; or

(b) requiring him to cease that conduct.

(4) A direction under this section must be given in writing.

34 Enforcement of directions

(1) If a person fails, without reasonable excuse, to comply with a direction under section 32 or 33, the OFT may apply to the court for an order—

(a) requiring the defaulter to make good his default within a time specified in the order; or

(b) if the direction related to anything to be done in the management or administration of an undertaking, requiring the undertaking or any of its officers to do it.

(2) An order of the court under subsection (1) may provide for all of the costs of, or incidental to, the application for the order to be borne by—

(a) the person in default; or

(b) any officer of an undertaking who is responsible for the default.

(3) In the application of subsection (2) to Scotland, the reference to 'costs' is to be read as a reference to 'expenses'.

35 Interim measures

(1) Subject to subsections (8) and (9), this section applies if the OFT has begun an investigation under section 25 and not completed it (but only applies so long as the OFT has power under section 25 to conduct that investigation).

(2) If the OFT considers that it is necessary for it to act under this section as a matter of urgency for the purpose—

(a) of preventing serious, irreparable damage to a particular person or category of person, or

(b) of protecting the public interest,

it may give such directions as it considers appropriate for that purpose.

(3) Before giving a direction under this section, the OFT must—

(a) give written notice to the person (or persons) to whom it proposes to give the direction; and

(b) give that person (or each of them) an opportunity to make representations.

(4) A notice under subsection (3) must indicate the nature of the direction which the OFT is proposing to give and its reasons for wishing to give it.

(5) A direction given under this section may if the circumstances permit be replaced by—

    (a) a direction under section 32 or (as appropriate) section 33, or

    (b) commitments accepted under section 31A,

    but, subject to that, has effect while this section applies.

(6) In the cases mentioned in section 25(2), (3), (6) and (7), sections 32(3) and 34 also apply to directions given under this section.

(7) In the cases mentioned in section 25(4) and (5), sections 33(3) and 34 also apply to directions given under this section.

(8) In the case of an investigation conducted by virtue of section 25(2) or (6), this section does not apply if a person has produced evidence to the OFT in connection with the investigation that satisfies it on the balance of probabilities that, in the event of it reaching the basic infringement conclusion, it would also reach the conclusion that the suspected agreement is exempt from the Chapter I prohibition as a result of section 9(1); and in this subsection 'the basic infringement conclusion' is the conclusion that there is an agreement which—

    (a) may affect trade within the United Kingdom, and

    (b) has as its object or effect the prevention, restriction or distortion of competition within the United Kingdom.

(9) In the case of an investigation conducted by virtue of section 25(3) or (7), this section does not apply if a person has produced evidence to the OFT in connection with the investigation that satisfies it on the balance of probabilities that, in the event of it reaching the basic infringement conclusion, it would also reach the conclusion that the suspected agreement is an agreement to which the prohibition in Article 81(1) is inapplicable because the agreement satisfies the conditions in Article 81(3); and in this subsection 'the basic infringement conclusion' is the conclusion that there is an agreement which—

    (a) may affect trade between Member States, and

    (b) has as its object or effect the prevention, restriction or distortion of competition within the Community.

36 Penalties

(1) On making a decision that an agreement has infringed the Chapter I prohibition or that it has infringed the prohibition in Article 81(1), the OFT may require an undertaking which is a party to the agreement to pay the OFT a penalty in respect of the infringement.

(2) On making a decision that conduct has infringed the Chapter II prohibition or that it has infringed the prohibition in Article 82, the OFT may require the undertaking concerned to pay the OFT a penalty in respect of the infringement.

(3) The OFT may impose a penalty on an undertaking under subsection (1) or (2) only if the OFT is satisfied that the infringement has been committed intentionally or negligently by the undertaking.

(4) Subsection (1) is subject to section 39 and does not apply in relation to a decision that an agreement has infringed the Chapter I prohibition if the OFT is satisfied that the undertaking acted on the reasonable assumption that that section gave it immunity in respect of the agreement.

(5) Subsection (2) is subject to section 40 and does not apply in relation to a decision that conduct has infringed the Chapter II prohibition if the OFT is satisfied that the undertaking acted on the reasonable assumption that that section gave it immunity in respect of the conduct.

(6) Notice of a penalty under this section must—

    (a) be in writing; and

    (b) specify the date before which the penalty is required to be paid.

(7) The date specified must not be earlier than the end of the period within which an appeal against the notice may be brought under section 46.

(8) No penalty fixed by the OFT under this section may exceed 10% of the turnover of the undertaking

(determined in accordance with such provisions as may be specified in an order made by the Secretary of State).

(9) Any sums received by the OFT under this section are to be paid into the Consolidated Fund.

37 Recovery of penalties

(1) If the specified date in a penalty notice has passed and—
  (a) the period during which an appeal against the imposition, or amount, of the penalty may be made has expired without an appeal having been made, or
  (b) such an appeal has been made and determined,
  the OFT may recover from the undertaking, as a civil debt due to the OFT, any amount payable under the penalty notice which remains outstanding.

(2) In this section—
  'penalty notice' means a notice given under section 36; and
  'specified date' means the date specified in the penalty notice.

38 The appropriate level of a penalty

(1) The OFT must prepare and publish guidance as to the appropriate amount of any penalty under this Part.

(1A) The guidance must include provision about the circumstances in which, in determining a penalty under this Part, the OFT may take into account effects in another Member State of the agreement or conduct concerned.

(2) The OFT may at any time alter the guidance.

(3) If the guidance is altered, the OFT must publish it as altered.

(4) No guidance is to be published under this section without the approval of the Secretary of State.

(5) The OFT may, after consulting the Secretary of State, choose how it publishes its guidance.

(6) If the OFT is preparing or altering guidance under this section it must consult such persons as it considers appropriate.

(7) If the proposed guidance or alteration relates to a matter in respect of which a regulator exercises concurrent jurisdiction, those consulted must include that regulator.

(8) When setting the amount of a penalty under this Part, the OFT must have regard to the guidance for the time being in force under this section.

(9) If a penalty or a fine has been imposed by the Commission, or by a court or other body in another Member State, in respect of an agreement or conduct, the OFT, an appeal tribunal or the appropriate court must take that penalty or fine into account when setting the amount of a penalty under this Part in relation to that agreement or conduct.

(10) In subsection (9) 'the appropriate court' means—
  (a) in relation to England and Wales, the Court of Appeal;
  (b) in relation to Scotland, the Court of Session;
  (c) in relation to Northern Ireland, the Court of Appeal in Northern Ireland;
  (d) the House of Lords.

39 Limited immunity in relation to the Chapter I prohibition

(1) In this section 'small agreement' means an agreement—
  (a) which falls within a category prescribed for the purposes of this section; but
  (b) is not a price fixing agreement.

(2) The criteria by reference to which a category of agreement is prescribed may, in particular, include—
  (a) the combined turnover of the parties to the agreement (determined in accordance with prescribed provisions);
  (b) the share of the market affected by the agreement (determined in that way).

(3) A party to a small agreement is immune from the effect of section 36(1) so far as that provision relates to decisions about infringement of the Chapter I prohibition; but the OFT may withdraw that immunity under subsection (4).

(4) If the OFT has investigated a small agreement, it may make a decision withdrawing the immunity given by subsection (3) if, as a result of its investigation, it considers that the agreement is likely to infringe the Chapter I prohibition.

(5) The OFT must give each of the parties in respect of which immunity is withdrawn written notice of its decision to withdraw the immunity.

(6) A decision under subsection (4) takes effect on such date ('the withdrawal date') as may be specified in the decision.

(7) The withdrawal date must be a date after the date on which the decision is made.

(8) In determining the withdrawal date, the OFT must have regard to the amount of time which the parties are likely to require in order to secure that there is no further infringement of the Chapter I prohibition with respect to the agreement.

(9) In subsection (1) 'price fixing agreement' means an agreement which has as its object or effect, or one of its objects or effects, restricting the freedom of a party to the agreement to determine the price to be charged (otherwise than as between that party and another party to the agreement) for the product, service or other matter to which the agreement relates.

40 Limited immunity in relation to the Chapter II prohibition

(1) In this section 'conduct of minor significance' means conduct which falls within a category prescribed for the purposes of this section.

(2) The criteria by reference to which a category is prescribed may, in particular, include—
   (a) the turnover of the person whose conduct it is (determined in accordance with prescribed provisions);
   (b) the share of the market affected by the conduct (determined in that way).

(3) A person is immune from the effect of section 36(2), so far as that provision relates to decisions about infringement of the Chapter II prohibition, if his conduct is conduct of minor significance; but the OFT may withdraw that immunity under subsection (4).

(4) If the OFT has investigated conduct of minor significance, it may make a decision withdrawing the immunity given by subsection (3) if, as a result of its investigation, it considers that the conduct is likely to infringe the Chapter II prohibition.

(5) The OFT must give the person, or persons, whose immunity has been withdrawn written notice of its decision to withdraw the immunity.

(6) A decision under subsection (4) takes effect on such date ('the withdrawal date') as may be specified in the decision.

(7) The withdrawal date must be a date after the date on which the decision is made.

(8) In determining the withdrawal date, the OFT must have regard to the amount of time which the person or persons affected are likely to require in order to secure that there is no further infringement of the Chapter II prohibition.

41 . . .

Offences

42 Offences

(1) A person is guilty of an offence if he fails to comply with a requirement imposed on him under section 26, 27, 28 or 28A.

(2) If a person is charged with an offence under subsection (1) in respect of a requirement to produce a document, it is a defence for him to prove—
   (a) that the document was not in his possession or under his control; and
   (b) that it was not reasonably practicable for him to comply with the requirement.

(3) If a person is charged with an offence under subsection (1) in respect of a requirement—
   (a) to provide information,
   (b) to provide an explanation of a document, or
   (c) to state where a document is to be found,

it is a defence for him to prove that he had a reasonable excuse for failing to comply with the requirement.

(4) Failure to comply with a requirement imposed under section 26 or 27 is not an offence if the person imposing the requirement has failed to act in accordance with that section.

(5) A person is guilty of an offence if he intentionally obstructs an officer acting in the exercise of his powers under section 27.

(6) A person guilty of an offence under subsection (1) or (5) is liable—
   (a) on summary conviction, to a fine not exceeding the statutory maximum;
   (b) on conviction on indictment, to a fine.

(7) A person who intentionally obstructs an officer in the exercise of his powers under a warrant issued under section 28 or 28A is guilty of an offence and liable—
   (a) on summary conviction, to a fine not exceeding the statutory maximum;
   (b) on conviction on indictment, to imprisonment for a term not exceeding two years or to a fine or to both.

43 Destroying or falsifying documents

(1) A person is guilty of an offence if, having been required to produce a document under section 26, 27, 28 or 28A—
   (a) he intentionally or recklessly destroys or otherwise disposes of it, falsifies it or conceals it, or
   (b) he causes or permits its destruction, disposal, falsification or concealment.

(2) A person guilty of an offence under subsection (1) is liable—
   (a) on summary conviction, to a fine not exceeding the statutory maximum;
   (b) on conviction on indictment, to imprisonment for a term not exceeding two years or to a fine or to both.

44 False or misleading information

(1) If information is provided by a person to the OFT in connection with any function of the OFT under this Part, that person is guilty of an offence if—
   (a) the information is false or misleading in a material particular, and
   (b) he knows that it is or is reckless as to whether it is.

(2) A person who—
   (a) provides any information to another person, knowing the information to be false or misleading in a material particular, or
   (b) recklessly provides any information to another person which is false or misleading in a material particular,
knowing that the information is to be used for the purpose of providing information to the OFT in connection with any of its functions under this Part, is guilty of an offence.

(3) A person guilty of an offence under this section is liable—
   (a) on summary conviction, to a fine not exceeding the statutory maximum;
   (b) on conviction on indictment, to imprisonment for a term not exceeding two years or to a fine or to both.

CHAPTER IV. THE COMPETITION COMMISSION AND APPEALS

The Commission

45 The Competition Commission

(1) There is to be a body corporate known as the Competition Commission.

(2) The Commission is to have such functions as are conferred on it by or as a result of this Act.

(3) The Monopolies and Mergers Commission is dissolved and its functions are transferred to the Competition Commission.

(4) In any enactment, instrument or other document, any reference to the Monopolies and Mergers Commission which has continuing effect is to be read as a reference to the Competition Commission.

(5) The Secretary of State may by order make such consequential, supplemental and incidental provision as he considers appropriate in connection with—
  (a) the dissolution of the Monopolies and Mergers Commission; and
  (b) the transfer of functions effected by subsection (3).

(6) An order made under subsection (5) may, in particular, include provision—
  (a) for the transfer of property, rights, obligations and liabilities and the continuation of proceedings, investigations and other matters; or
  (b) amending any enactment which makes provision with respect to the Monopolies and Mergers Commission or any of its functions.

(7) Schedules 7 and 7A make further provision about the Competition Commission.

(8) The Secretary of State may by order make such modifications in Part 2 of Schedule 7 and in Schedule 7A (performance of the Competition Commission's general functions) as he considers appropriate for improving the performance by the Competition Commission of its functions.

Appeals

46 Appealable decisions

(1) Any party to an agreement in respect of which the OFT has made a decision may appeal to the Tribunal against, or with respect to, the decision.

(2) Any person in respect of whose conduct the OFT has made a decision may appeal to the Tribunal against, or with respect to, the decision.

(3) In this section 'decision' means a decision of the OFT—
  (a) as to whether the Chapter I prohibition has been infringed,
  (b) as to whether the prohibition in Article 81(1) has been infringed,
  (c) as to whether the Chapter II prohibition has been infringed,
  (d) as to whether the prohibition in Article 82 has been infringed,
  (e) cancelling a block or parallel exemption,
  (f) withdrawing the benefit of a regulation of the Commission pursuant to Article 29(2) of the EC Competition Regulation,
  (g) not releasing commitments pursuant to a request made under section 31A(4)(b)(i),
  (h) releasing commitments under section 31A(4)(b)(ii),
  (i) as to the imposition of any penalty under section 36 or as to the amount of any such penalty,
  and includes a direction under section 32, 33 or 35 and such other decisions under this Part as may be prescribed.

(4) Except in the case of an appeal against the imposition, or the amount, of a penalty, the making of an appeal under this section does not suspend the effect of the decision to which the appeal relates.

(5) Part I of Schedule 8 makes further provision about appeals.

47 Third party appeals

(1) A person who does not fall within section 46(1) or (2) may appeal to the Tribunal with respect to—
  (a) a decision falling within paragraphs (a) to (f) of section 46(3);
  (b) a decision falling within paragraph (g) of section 46(3);
  (c) a decision of the OFT to accept or release commitments under section 31A, or to accept a variation of such commitments other than a variation which is not material in any respect;
  (d) a decision of the OFT to make directions under section 35;
  (e) a decision of the OFT not to make directions under section 35; or
  (f) such other decision of the OFT under this Part as may be prescribed.

(2) A person may make an appeal under subsection (1) only if the Tribunal considers that he has a sufficient interest in the decision with respect to which the appeal is made, or that he represents persons who have such an interest.

(3) The making of an appeal under this section does not suspend the effect of the decision to which the appeal relates.

47A Monetary claims before Tribunal

(1) This section applies to—
  (a) any claim for damages, or
  (b) any other claim for a sum of money,
  which a person who has suffered loss or damage as a result of the infringement of a relevant prohibition may make in civil proceedings brought in any part of the United Kingdom.
(2) In this section 'relevant prohibition' means any of the following—
  (a) the Chapter I prohibition;
  (b) the Chapter II prohibition;
  (c) the prohibition in Article 81(1) of the Treaty;
  (d) the prohibition in Article 82 of the Treaty;
  (e) the prohibition in Article 65(1) of the Treaty establishing the European Coal and Steel Community;
  (f) the prohibition in Article 66(7) of that Treaty.
(3) For the purpose of identifying claims which may be made in civil proceedings, any limitation rules that would apply in such proceedings are to be disregarded.
(4) A claim to which this section applies may (subject to the provisions of this Act and Tribunal rules) be made in proceedings brought before the Tribunal.
(5) But no claim may be made in such proceedings—
  (a) until a decision mentioned in subsection (6) has established that the relevant prohibition in question has been infringed; and
  (b) otherwise than with the permission of the Tribunal, during any period specified in subsection (7) or (8) which relates to that decision.
(6) The decisions which may be relied on for the purposes of proceedings under this section are—
  (a) a decision of the OFT that the Chapter I prohibition or the Chapter II prohibition has been infringed;
  (b) a decision of the OFT that the prohibition in Article 81(1) or Article 82 of the Treaty has been infringed;
  (c) a decision of the Tribunal (on an appeal from a decision of the OFT) that the Chapter I prohibition, the Chapter II prohibition or the prohibition in Article 81(1) or Article 82 of the Treaty has been infringed;
  (d) a decision of the European Commission that the prohibition in Article 81(1) or Article 82 of the Treaty has been infringed; or
  (e) a decision of the European Commission that the prohibition in Article 65(1) of the Treaty establishing the European Coal and Steel Community has been infringed, or a finding made by the European Commission under Article 66(7) of that Treaty.
(7) The periods during which proceedings in respect of a claim made in reliance on a decision mentioned in subsection (6)(a), (b) or (c) may not be brought without permission are—
  (a) in the case of a decision of the OFT, the period during which an appeal may be made to the Tribunal under section 46, section 47 or the EC Competition Law (Articles 84 and 85) Enforcement Regulations 2001 (SI 2001/2916);
  (b) in the case of a decision of the OFT which is the subject of an appeal mentioned in paragraph (a), the period following the decision of the Tribunal on the appeal during which a further appeal may be made under section 49 or under those Regulations;
  (c) in the case of a decision of the Tribunal mentioned in subsection (6)(c), the period during which a further appeal may be made under section 49 or under those Regulations;
  (d) in the case of any decision which is the subject of a further appeal, the period during which an appeal may be made to the House of Lords from a decision on the further appeal;

and, where any appeal mentioned in paragraph (a), (b), (c) or (d) is made, the period specified in that paragraph includes the period before the appeal is determined.

(8) The periods during which proceedings in respect of a claim made in reliance on a decision or finding of the European Commission may not be brought without permission are—

(a) the period during which proceedings against the decision or finding may be instituted in the European Court; and

(b) if any such proceedings are instituted, the period before those proceedings are determined.

(9) In determining a claim to which this section applies the Tribunal is bound by any decision mentioned in subsection (6) which establishes that the prohibition in question has been infringed.

(10) The right to make a claim to which this section applies in proceedings before the Tribunal does not affect the right to bring any other proceedings in respect of the claim.

47B Claims brought on behalf of consumers

(1) A specified body may (subject to the provisions of this Act and Tribunal rules) bring proceedings before the Tribunal which comprise consumer claims made or continued on behalf of at least two individuals.

(2) In this section 'consumer claim' means a claim to which section 47A applies which an individual has in respect of an infringement affecting (directly or indirectly) goods or services to which subsection (7) applies.

(3) A consumer claim may be included in proceedings under this section if it is—

(a) a claim made in the proceedings on behalf of the individual concerned by the specified body; or

(b) a claim made by the individual concerned under section 47A which is continued in the proceedings on his behalf by the specified body;

and such a claim may only be made or continued in the proceedings with the consent of the individual concerned.

(4) The consumer claims included in proceedings under this section must all relate to the same infringement.

(5) The provisions of section 47A(5) to (10) apply to a consumer claim included in proceedings under this section as they apply to a claim made in proceedings under that section.

(6) Any damages or other sum (not being costs or expenses) awarded in respect of a consumer claim included in proceedings under this section must be awarded to the individual concerned; but the Tribunal may, with the consent of the specified body and the individual, order that the sum awarded must be paid to the specified body (acting on behalf of the individual).

(7) This subsection applies to goods or services which—

(a) the individual received, or sought to receive, otherwise than in the course of a business carried on by him (notwithstanding that he received or sought to receive them with a view to carrying on a business); and

(b) were, or would have been, supplied to the individual (in the case of goods whether by way of sale or otherwise) in the course of a business carried on by the person who supplied or would have supplied them.

(8) A business includes—

(a) a professional practice;

(b) any other undertaking carried on for gain or reward;

(c) any undertaking in the course of which goods or services are supplied otherwise than free of charge.

(9) 'Specified' means specified in an order made by the Secretary of State, in accordance with criteria to be published by the Secretary of State for the purposes of this section.

(10) An application by a body to be specified in an order under this section is to be made in a form approved by the Secretary of State for the purpose.

48 ...

49 Further appeals

(1) An appeal lies to the appropriate court—
   (a) from a decision of the Tribunal as to the amount of a penalty under section 36;
   (b) from a decision of the Tribunal as to the award of damages or other sum in respect of a claim made in proceedings under section 47A or included in proceedings under section 47B (other than a decision on costs or expenses) or as to the amount of any such damages or other sum; and
   (c) on a point of law arising from any other decision of the Tribunal on an appeal under section 46 or 47.

(2) An appeal under this section—
   (a) may be brought by a party to the proceedings before the Tribunal or by a person who has a sufficient interest in the matter; and
   (b) requires the permission of the Tribunal or the appropriate court.

(3) In this section 'the appropriate court' means the Court of Appeal or, in the case of an appeal from Tribunal proceedings in Scotland, the Court of Session.

Chapter V. Miscellaneous

Vertical agreements and land agreements

50 Vertical agreements and land agreements

(1) The Secretary of State may by order provide for any provision of this Part to apply in relation to—
   (a) vertical agreements, or
   (b) land agreements,
   with such modifications as may be prescribed.

(2) An order may, in particular, provide for exclusions or exemptions, or otherwise provide for prescribed provisions not to apply, in relation to—
   (a) vertical agreements, or land agreements, in general; or
   (b) vertical agreements, or land agreements, of any prescribed description.

(3) An order may empower the OFT to give directions to the effect that in prescribed circumstances an exclusion, exemption or modification is not to apply (or is to apply in a particular way) in relation to an individual agreement.

(4) Subsections (2) and (3) are not to be read as limiting the powers conferred by section 71.

(5) In this section—
   'land agreement' and 'vertical agreement' have such meaning as may be prescribed; and
   'prescribed' means prescribed by an order.

OFT's rules, guidance and fees

51 Rules

(1) The OFT may make such rules about procedural and other matters in connection with the carrying into effect of the provisions of this Part as it considers appropriate.

(2) Schedule 9 makes further provision about rules made under this section but is not to be taken as restricting the OFT's powers under this section.

(3) If the OFT is preparing rules under this section it must consult such persons as it considers appropriate.

(4) If the proposed rules relate to a matter in respect of which a regulator exercises concurrent jurisdiction, those consulted must include that regulator.

(5) No rule made by the OFT is to come into operation until it has been approved by an order made by the Secretary of State.

(6) The Secretary of State may approve any rule made by the OFT—
    (a) in the form in which it is submitted; or
    (b) subject to such modifications as he considers appropriate.
(7) If the Secretary of State proposes to approve a rule subject to modifications he must inform the OFT of the proposed modifications and take into account any comments made by the OFT.
(8) Subsections (5) to (7) apply also to any alteration of the rules made by the OFT.
(9) The Secretary of State may, after consulting the OFT, by order vary or revoke any rules made under this section.
(10) If the Secretary of State considers that rules should be made under this section with respect to a particular matter he may direct the OFT to exercise its powers under this section and make rules about that matter.

52 Advice and information

(1) As soon as is reasonably practicable after the passing of this Act, the Director must prepare and publish general advice and information about—
    (a) the application of the Chapter I prohibition and the Chapter II prohibition, and
    (b) the enforcement of those prohibitions.
(1A) As soon as is reasonably practicable after 1st May 2004, the OFT must prepare and publish general advice and information about—
    (a) the application of the prohibitions in Article 81(1) and Article 82; and
    (b) the enforcement by it of those prohibitions.
(2) The OFT may at any time publish revised, or new, advice or information.
(3) Advice and information published under this section must be prepared with a view to—
    (a) explaining provisions of this Part to persons who are likely to be affected by them; and
    (b) indicating how the OFT expects such provisions to operate.
(4) Advice (or information) published by virtue of subsection (3)(b) may include advice (or information) about the factors which the OFT may take into account in considering whether, and if so how, to exercise a power conferred on it by Chapter I, II or III.
(5) Any advice or information published by the OFT under this section is to be published in such form and in such manner as it considers appropriate.
(6) If the OFT is preparing any advice or information under this section it must consult such persons as it considers appropriate.
(7) If the proposed advice or information relates to a matter in respect of which a regulator exercises concurrent jurisdiction, those consulted must include that regulator.
(8) In preparing any advice or information under this section about a matter in respect of which he may exercise functions under this Part, a regulator must consult—
    (a) the OFT;
    (b) the other regulators; and
    (c) such other persons as he considers appropriate.

53 . . .

Regulators

54 Regulators

(1) In this Part 'regulator' means—
    (a) the Office of Communications;
    (b) the Gas and Electricity Markets Authority;
    (c) the Director General of Electricity Supply for Northern Ireland;
    (d) the Water Services Regulation Authority;
    (e) the Office of Rail Regulation;
    (f) the Director General of Gas for Northern Ireland; and
    (g) the Civil Aviation Authority.

(2) Parts II and III of Schedule 10 provide for functions of the OFT under this Part to be exercisable concurrently by regulators.

(3) Parts IV and V of Schedule 10 make minor and consequential amendments in connection with the regulators' competition functions.

(4) The Secretary of State may make regulations for the purpose of co-ordinating the performance of functions under this Part ('Part I functions') which are exercisable concurrently by two or more competent persons as a result of any enactment (including any subordinate legislation) whenever passed or made.

(5) The regulations may, in particular, make provision—

    (a) as to the procedure to be followed by competent persons when determining who is to exercise Part I functions in a particular case;

    (b) as to the steps which must be taken before a competent person exercises, in a particular case, such Part I functions as may be prescribed;

    (c) as to the procedure for determining, in a particular case, questions arising as to which competent person is to exercise Part I functions in respect of the case;

    (d) for Part I functions in a particular case to be exercised jointly—

        (i) by the OFT and one or more regulators, or

        (ii) by two or more regulators,

    and as to the procedure to be followed in such cases;

    (e) as to the circumstances in which the exercise by a competent person of such Part I functions as may be prescribed is to preclude the exercise of such functions by another such person;

    (f) for cases in respect of which Part I functions are being, or have been, exercised by a competent person to be transferred to another such person;

    (g) for the person ('A') exercising Part I functions in a particular case—

        (i) to appoint another competent person ('B') to exercise Part I functions on A's behalf in relation to the case; or

        (ii) to appoint officers of B (with B's consent) to act as officers of A in relation to the case;

    (h) for notification as to who is exercising Part I functions in respect of a particular case.

(6) Provision made by virtue of subsection (5)(c) may provide for questions to be referred to and determined by the Secretary of State or by such other person as may be prescribed.

(7) 'Competent person' means the OFT or any of the regulators.

(8) In this section, 'subordinate legislation' has the same meaning as in section 21(1) of the Interpretation Act 1978 (c 30) and includes an instrument made under—

    (a) any Act of the Scottish Parliament;

    (b) Northern Ireland legislation.

Confidentiality and immunity from defamation

55 . . .

56 . . .

57 Defamation

For the purposes of the law relating to defamation, absolute privilege attaches to any advice, guidance, notice or direction given, or decision made, by the OFT in the exercise of any of its functions under this Part.

Findings of fact by OFT

58 Findings of fact by OFT

(1) Unless the court directs otherwise, an OFT's finding which is relevant to an issue arising in Part I proceedings is binding on the parties if—

(a) the time for bringing an appeal under section 46 or 47 in respect of the finding has expired and the relevant party has not brought such an appeal; or

(b) the decision of the Tribunal on such an appeal has confirmed the finding.

(2) In this section—

'an OFT's finding' means a finding of fact made by the OFT in the course of conducting an investigation;

'Part 1 proceedings' means proceedings brought otherwise than by the OFT—

(a) in respect of an alleged infringement of the Chapter I prohibition or of the Chapter II prohibition; or

(b) in respect of an alleged infringement of the prohibitions in Article 81(1) or Article 82;

'relevant party' means—

(a) in relation to the Chapter I prohibition or the prohibition in Article 81(1), a party to the agreement which is alleged to have infringed the prohibition; and

(b) in relation to the Chapter II prohibition or the prohibition in Article 82, the undertaking whose conduct is alleged to have infringed the prohibition.

(3) Rules of court may make provision in respect of assistance to be given by the OFT to the court in Part I proceedings.

Findings of infringements

58A Findings of infringements

(1) This section applies to proceedings before the court in which damages or any other sum of money is claimed in respect of an infringement of—

(a) the Chapter I prohibition;

(b) the Chapter II prohibition;

(c) the prohibition in Article 81(1) of the Treaty;

(d) the prohibition in Article 82 of the Treaty.

(2) In such proceedings, the court is bound by a decision mentioned in subsection (3) once any period specified in subsection (4) which relates to the decision has elapsed.

(3) The decisions are—

(a) a decision of the OFT that the Chapter I prohibition or the Chapter II prohibition has been infringed;

(b) a decision of the OFT that the prohibition in Article 81(1) or Article 82 of the Treaty has been infringed;

(c) a decision of the Tribunal (on an appeal from a decision of the OFT) that the Chapter I prohibition or the Chapter II prohibition has been infringed, or that the prohibition in Article 81(1) or Article 82 of the Treaty has been infringed.

(4) The periods mentioned in subsection (2) are—

(a) in the case of a decision of the OFT, the period during which an appeal may be made to the Tribunal under section 46 or 47 or the EC Competition Law (Articles 84 and 85) Enforcement Regulations 2001 (SI 2001/2916);

(b) in the case of a decision of the Tribunal mentioned in subsection (3)(c), the period during which a further appeal may be made under section 49 or under those Regulations;

(c) in the case of any decision which is the subject of a further appeal, the period during which an appeal may be made to the House of Lords from a decision on the further appeal;

and, where any appeal mentioned in paragraph (a), (b) or (c) is made, the period specified in that paragraph includes the period before the appeal is determined.

Interpretation and governing principles

59 Interpretation of Part I

(1) In this Part—

'agreement' is to be read with section 2(5) and (6);

'Article 81(1)' means Article 81 of the Treaty;

'Article 81(3)' means Article 81(3) of the Treaty;

'Article 82' means Article 82 of the Treaty;

'block exemption' has the meaning given in section 6(4);

'block exemption order' has the meaning given in section 6(2);

'the Chapter I prohibition' has the meaning given in section 2(8);

'the Chapter II prohibition' has the meaning given in section 18(4);

'the Commission' (except in relation to the Competition Commission) means the European Commission;

'the Council' means the Council of the European Union;

'the court', except in sections 58, 58A and 60 and the expression 'European Court', means—

(a) in England and Wales, the High Court;

(b) in Scotland, the Court of Session; and

(c) in Northern Ireland, the High Court;

'document' includes information recorded in any form;

'the EEA Agreement' means the Agreement on the European Economic Area signed at Oporto on 2nd May 1992 as it has effect for the time being;

'the European Court' means the Court of Justice of the European Communities and includes the Court of First Instance;

'the EC Competition Regulation' means Council Regulation (EC) No. 1/2003 of 16th December 2002 on the implementation of the rules on competition laid down in Articles 81 and 82 of the Treaty;

'information' includes estimates and forecasts;

'investigating officer' has the meaning given in section 27(1);

'investigation' means an investigation under section 25;

'Minister of the Crown' has the same meaning as in the Ministers of the Crown Act 1975;

'OFCOM' means the Office of Communications;

'officer', in relation to a body corporate, includes a director, manager or secretary and, in relation to a partnership in Scotland, includes a partner;

'the OFT' means the Office of Fair Trading;

'parallel exemption' has the meaning given in section 10(3);

'person', in addition to the meaning given by the Interpretation Act 1978, includes any undertaking;

'premises' includes any land or means of transport;

'prescribed' means prescribed by regulations made by the Secretary of State;

'regulator' has the meaning given by section 54;

'section 11 exemption' has the meaning given in section 11(3); and

'the Treaty' means the treaty establishing the European Community;

'the Tribunal' means the Competition Appeal Tribunal;

'Tribunal rules' means rules under section 15 of the Enterprise Act 2002;

'working day' means a day which is not—

(a) Saturday,

(b) Sunday,

(c) Christmas Day,

(d) Good Friday, or

(e) a day which is a bank holiday under the Banking and Financial Dealings Act 1971 (c.80) in any part of the United Kingdom.

(2) The fact that to a limited extent the Chapter I prohibition does not apply to an agreement, because of an exclusion provided by or under this Part or any other enactment, does not require those provisions of the agreement to which the exclusion relates to be disregarded when considering whether the agreement infringes the prohibition for other reasons.

(3) For the purposes of this Part, the power to require information, in relation to information recorded otherwise than in a legible form, includes power to require a copy of it in a legible form.

(4) Any power conferred on the OFT by this Part to require information includes power to require any document which it believes may contain that information.

60 Principles to be applied in determining questions

(1) The purpose of this section is to ensure that so far as is possible (having regard to any relevant differences between the provisions concerned), questions arising under this Part in relation to competition within the United Kingdom are dealt with in a manner which is consistent with the treatment of corresponding questions arising in Community law in relation to competition within the Community.

(2) At any time when the court determines a question arising under this Part, it must act (so far as is compatible with the provisions of this Part and whether or not it would otherwise be required to do so) with a view to securing that there is no inconsistency between—

(a) the principles applied, and decision reached, by the court in determining that question; and

(b) the principles laid down by the Treaty and the European Court, and any relevant decision of that Court, as applicable at that time in determining any corresponding question arising in Community law.

(3) The court must, in addition, have regard to any relevant decision or statement of the Commission.

(4) Subsections (2) and (3) also apply to—

(a) the OFT; and

(b) any person acting on behalf of the OFT, in connection with any matter arising under this Part.

(5) In subsections (2) and (3), 'court' means any court or tribunal.

(6) In subsections (2)(b) and (3), 'decision' includes a decision as to—

(a) the interpretation of any provision of Community law;

(b) the civil liability of an undertaking for harm caused by its infringement of Community law.

PART 2

INSPECTIONS UNDER ARTICLES 20, 21 AND 22(2)

61 Interpretation of Part 2

In this Part—

'Article 20 inspection' means an inspection ordered by a decision of the Commission under Article 20(4) of the EC Competition Regulation which is not an Article 22(2) inspection;

'Article 21 inspection' means an inspection ordered by a decision of the Commission under Article 21 of the EC Competition Regulation;

'Article 22(2) inspection' means an inspection requested by the Commission under Article 22(2) of the EC Competition Regulation;

'books and records' includes books and records stored on any medium;

'the Commission' means the European Commission;

'the EC Competition Regulation' means Council Regulation (EC) No. 1/2003 of 16th December 2002 on the implementation of the rules on competition laid down in Articles 81 and 82 of the Treaty;

'the OFT' means the Office of Fair Trading;

'premises' includes any land or means of transport;

'the Treaty' means the treaty establishing the European Community.

62 Power to enter business premises under a warrant: Article 20 inspections

(1) A judge of the High Court shall issue a warrant if satisfied, on an application made to the High Court in accordance with rules of court by the OFT, that—

(a) the Commission has ordered an Article 20 inspection;

(b) the Article 20 inspection is being, or is likely to be, obstructed; and

(c) the measures that would be authorised by the warrant are neither arbitrary nor excessive having regard to the subject matter of the Article 20 inspection.

(2) An Article 20 inspection is being obstructed if—

(a) a Commission official exercising his power in accordance with Article 20(3) of the EC Competition Regulation, has attempted to enter any business premises but has been unable to do so; and

(b) there are reasonable grounds for suspecting that there are on any business premises books or records which the Commission official has power to examine.

(3) An Article 20 inspection is also being obstructed if there are reasonable grounds for suspecting that there are on any business premises books or records—

(a) the production of which has been required by a Commission official exercising his power in accordance with Article 20(3) of the EC Competition Regulation; and

(b) which have not been produced as required.

(4) An Article 20 inspection is likely to be obstructed if—

(a) . . .

(b) there are reasonable grounds for suspecting that there are on any business premises books or records which a Commission official has power to examine; and

(c) there are also reasonable grounds for suspecting that, if the Commission official attempted to exercise his power to examine any of the books or records, they would not be produced but would be concealed, removed, tampered with or destroyed.

(5) A warrant under this section shall authorise a named officer of the OFT and any other OFT officer, or Commission official, accompanying the named officer—

(a) to enter any business premises specified in the warrant using such force as is reasonably necessary for the purpose;

(b) to search for books and records which a Commission official has power to examine, using such force as is reasonably necessary for the purpose;

(c) to take or obtain copies of or extracts from such books and records; and

(d) to seal the premises, any part of the premises or any books or records which a Commission official has power to seal, for the period and to the extent necessary for the inspection.

(5A) A warrant under this section may authorise persons specified in the warrant to accompany the named officer who is executing it.

(6) Any person entering any premises by virtue of a warrant under this section may take with him such equipment as appears to him to be necessary.

(7) On leaving any premises entered by virtue of the warrant the named officer must, if the premises are unoccupied or the occupier is temporarily absent, leave them as effectively secured as he found them.

(8) A warrant under this section continues in force until the end of the period of one month beginning with the day on which it is issued.

(9) In the application of this section to Scotland, references to the High Court are to be read as references to the Court of Session.

(10) In this section—

'business premises' means any premises of an undertaking or association of undertakings which a Commission official has under Article 20 of the EC Competition Regulation power to enter in the course of the Article 20 inspection;

'Commission official' means any of the persons authorised by the Commission to conduct the Article 20 inspection; and

'OFT officer' means any officer of the OFT whom the OFT has authorised in writing to accompany the named officer.

(11) In subsection (10), the reference in the definition of 'business premises' to Article 20 of the EC Competition Regulation does not include a reference to that Article as applied by Article 21 of that Regulation.

62A Power to enter non-business premises under a warrant: Article 21 inspections

(1)   A judge of the High Court shall issue a warrant if satisfied, on an application made to the High Court in accordance with the rules of court by the OFT, that—
    (a) the Commission has ordered an Article 21 inspection; and
    (b) the measures that would be authorised by the warrant are neither arbitrary nor excessive having regard in particular to the matters mentioned in subsection (2).

(2)   Those matters are—
    (a) the seriousness of the suspected infringement of Article 81(1) or 82 of the Treaty;
    (b) the importance of the evidence sought;
    (c) the involvement of the undertaking or association of undertakings concerned; and
    (d) whether it is reasonably likely that business books and records relating to the subject matter of the Article 21 inspection are kept on the non-business premises that would be specified in the warrant.

(3)   A warrant under this section shall authorise a named officer of the OFT and any other OFT officer, or Commission official, accompanying the named officer to enter any non-business premises specified in the warrant.

(4)   A warrant under this section may authorise a named officer of the OFT and any other OFT officer, or Commission official, accompanying the named officer to search for books or records which a Commission official has power to examine.

(5)   A warrant under this section may authorise a named officer of the OFT and any other OFT officer, or Commission official, accompanying the named officer to take or obtain copies of books or records of which a Commission official has power to take or obtain copies.

(6)   A warrant granted under this section may authorise the use, for either or both of the purposes mentioned in subsections (3) and (4), of such force as is reasonably necessary.

(7)   A warrant under this section may authorise persons specified in the warrant to accompany the named officer who is executing it.

(8)   Any person entering any premises by virtue of a warrant under this section may take with him such equipment as appears to him to be necessary.

(9)   On leaving any premises entered by virtue of a warrant the named officer must, if the premises are unoccupied or the occupier is temporarily absent, leave them as effectively secured as he found them.

(10) A warrant under this section continues in force until the end of the period of one month beginning with the day on which it is issued.

(11) In the application of this section to Scotland, references to the High Court are to be read as references to the Court of Session.

(12) In this section—
    'non-business premises' means any premises to which a decision of the Commission ordering the Article 21 inspection relates;
    'Commission official' means any of the persons authorised by the Commission to conduct the Article 21 inspection; and
    'OFT officer' means any officer of the OFT whom the OFT has authorised in writing to accompany the named officer.

62B Powers when conducting an Article 22(2) inspection

(1)   For the purposes of an Article 22(2) inspection, an authorised officer of the OFT has the powers specified in Article 20(2) of the EC Competition Regulation.

(2)   For the purposes of this section and section 63—
    'authorised officer of the OFT' means any officer of the OFT to whom an authorisation has been given; and
    'authorisation' means an authorisation given in writing by the OFT for the purposes of the Article 22(2) inspection which—
        (i) identifies the officer;

(ii) indicates the subject matter and purpose of the inspection; and

(iii) draws attention to any penalties which a person may incur under the EC Competition Regulation in connection with the inspection.

63 Power to enter business premises under a warrant: Article 22(2) inspections

(1) A judge of the High Court shall issue a warrant if satisfied, on an application made to the High Court in accordance with rules of court by the OFT, that—

(a) the Commission has requested the OFT to conduct an Article 22(2) inspection which the Commission has ordered by a decision under Article 20(4) of the EC Competition Regulation;

(b) the Article 22(2) inspection is being, or is likely to be, obstructed; and

(c) the measures that would be authorised by the warrant are neither arbitrary nor excessive having regard to the subject matter of the Article 22(2) inspection.

(2) An Article 22(2) inspection is being obstructed if—

(a) an authorised officer of the OFT has attempted to enter any business premises but has been unable to do so;

(b) the officer has produced his authorisation to the undertaking, or association of undertakings, concerned; and

(c) there are reasonable grounds for suspecting that there are on any business premises books or records which the officer has power to examine.

(3) An Article 22(2) inspection is also being obstructed if—

(a) there are reasonable grounds for suspecting that there are on any business premises books or records which an authorised officer of the OFT has power to examine;

(b) the officer has produced his authorisation to the undertaking, or association of undertakings, and has required production of the books or records; and

(c) the books and records have not been produced as required.

(4) An Article 22(2) inspection is likely to be obstructed if—

(a) there are reasonable grounds for suspecting that there are on any business premises books or records which an authorised officer of the OFT has power to examine; and

(b) there are also reasonable grounds for suspecting that, if the officer attempted to exercise his power to examine any of the books or records, they would not be produced but would be concealed, removed, tampered with or destroyed.

(5) A warrant under this section shall authorise a named authorised officer of the OFT and any other authorised officer of the OFT, or Commission official, accompanying the named authorised officer—

(a) to enter any business premises specified in the warrant using such force as is reasonably necessary for the purpose;

(b) to search for books and records which an authorised officer of the OFT has power to examine, using such force as is reasonably necessary for the purpose;

(c) to take or obtain copies of or extracts from such books and records; and

(d) to seal the premises, any part of the premises or any books or records which an authorised officer of the OFT has power to seal, for the period and to the extent necessary for the inspection.

(5A) A warrant under this section may authorise persons specified in the warrant to accompany the named authorised officer who is executing it.

(6) Any person entering any premises by virtue of a warrant under this section may take with him such equipment as appears to him to be necessary.

(7) On leaving any premises which he has entered by virtue of the warrant the named authorised officer must, if the premises are unoccupied or the occupier is temporarily absent, leave them as effectively secured as he found them.

(8) A warrant under this section continues in force until the end of the period of one month beginning with the day on which it is issued.

(9)   In the application of this section to Scotland, references to the High Court are to be read as references to the Court of Session.

(10) In this section—

'business premises' means any premises of an undertaking or association of undertakings which an authorised officer of the OFT has power to enter in the course of the Article 22(2) inspection;

'Commission official' means any person authorised by the Commission to assist with the Article 22(2) inspection.

64 Entry of premises under sections 62, 62A and 63: supplementary

(1)   A warrant issued under section 62, 62A or 63 must indicate—

(a) the subject matter and purpose of the inspection;

(b) the nature of the offence created by section 65.

(2)   The powers conferred by section 62, 62A or 63 are to be exercised on production of a warrant issued under that section.

(3)   If there is no one at the premises when the named officer proposes to execute such a warrant he must, before executing it—

(a) take such steps as are reasonable in all the circumstances to inform the occupier of the intended entry; and

(b) if the occupier is informed, afford him or his legal or other representative a reasonable opportunity to be present when the warrant is executed.

(4)   If the named officer is unable to inform the occupier of the intended entry he must, when executing the warrant, leave a copy of it in a prominent place on the premises.

(5)   In this section—

'named officer' means—

(a) for the purposes of a warrant issued under section 62 or 62A, the officer named in the warrant; and

(b) for the purposes of a warrant issued under section 63, the authorised officer named in the warrant; and

'occupier', in relation to any premises, means a person whom the named officer reasonably believes is the occupier of those premises.

65 Offences

(1)   A person is guilty of an offence if he intentionally obstructs any person in the exercise of his powers under a warrant issued under section 62, 62A or 63.

(2)   A person guilty of an offence under subsection (1) is liable—

(a) on summary conviction, to a fine not exceeding the statutory maximum;

(b) on conviction on indictment, to imprisonment for a term not exceeding two years or to a fine or to both.

65A Privileged communications: Article 22(2) inspections

(1)   A person shall not be required, by virtue of any provision of section 62B or 63, to produce or disclose a privileged communication.

(2)   'Privileged communication' means a communication—

(a) between a professional legal adviser and his client, or

(b) made in connection with, or in contemplation of, legal proceedings and for the purposes of those proceedings,

which in proceedings in the High Court would be protected from disclosure on grounds of legal professional privilege.

(3)   In the application of this section to Scotland—

(a) the reference to the High Court is to be read as a reference to the Court of Session; and

(b) the reference to legal professional privilege is to be read as a reference to confidentiality of communications.

65B Use of statements in prosecution: Article 22(2) inspections

A statement made by a person in response to a requirement imposed by virtue of section 62B or 63 may not be used in evidence against him on a prosecution for an offence under section 188 of the Enterprise Act 2002 unless, in the proceedings—

(a) in giving evidence, he makes a statement inconsistent with it, and

(b) evidence relating to it is adduced, or a question relating to it is asked, by him or on his behalf.

PART 2A

ARTICLE 22(1) INVESTIGATIONS

65C Interpretation of Part 2A

(1) In this Part—

'Article 22(1) investigation' means an investigation conducted by the OFT on behalf and for the account of a competition authority of another Member State pursuant to Article 22(1) of the EC Competition Regulation;

'the Commission' means the European Commission;

'competition authority of another Member State' means a competition authority designated as such under Article 35 of the EC Competition Regulation by a Member State other than the United Kingdom;

'the EC Competition Regulation' means Council Regulation (EC) No. 1/2003 of 16th December 2002 on the implementation of the rules on competition laid down in Articles 81 and 82 of the Treaty; and

'investigating officer' has the meaning given in section 65F(1).

(2) In this Part, the following expressions have the same meanings as in Part 1—

'Article 81(1)';

'Article 82';

'the court';

'document';

'information';

'officer';

'the OFT';

'person';

'premises'

'the Treaty'; and

'working day'.

(3) For the purposes of this Part, the power to require information, in relation to information recorded otherwise than in a legible form, includes power to require a copy of it in a legible form.

(4) Any power conferred on the OFT by this Part to require information includes power to require any document which it believes may contain that information.

65D Power to conduct an Article 22(1) investigation

(1) In any of the following cases, the OFT may conduct an Article 22(1) investigation.

(2) The first case is where there are reasonable grounds for suspecting that there is an agreement which—

(a) may affect trade between Member States; and

(b) has as its object or effect the prevention, restriction or distortion of competition within the Community.

(3) The second case is where there are reasonable grounds for suspecting that the prohibition in Article 82 has been infringed.

(4) The third case is where there are reasonable grounds for suspecting that, at some time in the past, there was an agreement which at that time—

(a) may have affected trade between Member States; and

(b) had as its object or effect the prevention, restriction or distortion of competition within the Community.

(5) It is immaterial for the purposes of subsection (4) whether the agreement in question remains in existence.

(6) A provision of this Part which is expressed to apply to, or in relation to, an agreement is to be read as applying equally to, or in relation to, a decision by an association of undertakings or a concerted practice.

65E Powers when conducting Article 22(1) investigations

(1) For the purposes of an Article 22(1) investigation, the OFT may require any person to produce to it a specified document, or to provide it with specified information, which it considers relates to any matter relevant to the investigation.

(2) The power conferred by subsection (1) is to be exercised by a notice in writing.

(3) A notice under subsection (2) must indicate—
    (a) the subject matter and purpose of the Article 22(1) investigation; and
    (b) the nature of the offences created by sections 65L to 65N.

(4) In subsection (1) 'specified' means—
    (a) specified, or described, in the notice; or
    (b) falling within a category which is specified, or described, in the notice.

(5) The OFT may also specify in the notice—
    (a) the time and place at which any document is to be produced or any information is to be provided;
    (b) the manner and form in which it is to be produced or provided.

(6) The power under this section to require a person to produce a document includes power—
    (a) if the document is produced—
        (i) to take copies of it or extracts from it;
        (ii) to require him, or any person who is a present or past officer of his, or is or was at any time employed by him, to provide an explanation of the document;
    (b) if the document is not produced, to require him to state, to the best of his knowledge and belief, where it is.

65F Power to enter business premises without a warrant

(1) Any officer of the OFT who is authorised in writing by the OFT to do so ('an investigating officer') may enter any business premises in connection with an Article 22(1) investigation.

(2) No investigating officer is to enter any premises in the exercise of his powers under this section unless he has given to the occupier of the premises a written notice which—
    (a) gives at least two working days' notice of the intended entry;
    (b) indicates the subject matter and purpose of the Article 22(1) investigation; and
    (c) indicates the nature of the offences created by sections 65L to 65N.

(3) Subsection (2) does not apply—
    (a) if the OFT has a reasonable suspicion that the premises are, or have been, occupied by—
        (i) a party to an agreement which it is investigating under section 65D; or
        (ii) an undertaking the conduct of which it is investigating under section 65D; or
    (b) if the investigating officer has taken all such steps as are reasonably practicable to give notice but has not been able to do so.

(4) In a case falling within subsection (3), the power of entry conferred by subsection (1) is to be exercised by the investigating officer on production of—
    (a) evidence of his authorisation; and
    (b) a document containing the information referred to in subsection (2)(b) and (c).

(5) An investigating officer entering any premises under this section may—
    (a) take with him such equipment as appears to him to be necessary;
    (b) require any person on the premises—

     (i)   to produce any document which he considers relates to any matter relevant to the investigation; and

     (ii) if the document is produced, to provide an explanation of it;

 (c) require any person to state, to the best of his knowledge and belief, where any such document is to be found;

 (d) take copies of, or extracts from, any document which is produced;

 (e) require any information which is stored in any electronic form and is accessible from the premises and which the investigating officer considers relates to any matter relevant to the investigation, to be produced in a form—

     (i)   in which it can be taken away, and

     (ii) in which it is visible and legible or from which it can readily be produced in a visible and legible form;

 (f) take any steps which appear to be necessary for the purpose of preserving or preventing interference with any document which he considers relates to any matter relevant to the investigation.

(6) In this section—

'business premises' means premises (or any part of premises) not used as a dwelling.

65G Power to enter business premises under a warrant

(1) On an application made by the OFT to the court in accordance with rules of court, a judge may issue a warrant if he is satisfied that—

 (a) there are reasonable grounds for suspecting that there are on any business premises documents—

     (i)   the production of which has been required under section 65E or 65F; and

     (ii) which have not been produced as required;

 (b) there are reasonable grounds for suspecting that—

     (i)   there are on any business premises documents which the OFT has power under section 65E to require to be produced; and

     (ii) if the documents were required to be produced, they would not be produced but would be concealed, removed, tampered with or destroyed; or

 (c) an investigating officer has attempted to enter premises in the exercise of his powers under section 65F but has been unable to do so and that there are reasonable grounds for suspecting that there are on the premises documents the production of which could have been required under that section.

(2) A warrant under this section shall authorise a named officer of the OFT and any other of its officers whom the OFT has authorised in writing to accompany the named officer—

 (a) to enter the premises specified in the warrant, using such force as is reasonably necessary for the purpose;

 (b) to search the premises and take copies of, or extracts from, any document appearing to be of a kind in respect of which the application under subsection (1) was granted ('the relevant kind');

 (c) to take possession of any documents appearing to be of the relevant kind if—

     (i)   such action appears to be necessary for preserving the documents or preventing interference with them; or

     (ii) it is not reasonably practicable to take copies of the documents on the premises;

 (d) to take any other steps which appear to be necessary for the purpose mentioned in paragraph (c)(i);

 (e) to require any person to provide an explanation of any document appearing to be of the relevant kind or to state, to the best of his knowledge and belief, where it may be found;

 (f) to require any information which is stored in any electronic form and is accessible from the premises and which the named officer considers relates to any matter relevant to the Article 22(1) investigation, to be produced in a form—

     (i)   in which it can be taken away, and

    (ii) in which it is visible and legible or from which it can readily be produced in a visible and legible form.

(3) If, in the case of a warrant under subsection (1)(b), the judge is satisfied that it is reasonable to suspect that there are also on the premises other documents relating to the Article 22(1) investigation concerned, the warrant shall also authorise action mentioned in subsection (2) to be taken in relation to any such document.

(4) A warrant under this section may authorise persons specified in the warrant to accompany the named officer who is executing it.

(5) Any person entering premises by virtue of a warrant under this section may take with him such equipment as appears to him to be necessary.

(6) On leaving any premises which he has entered by virtue of a warrant under this section, the named officer must, if the premises are unoccupied or the occupier is temporarily absent, leave them as effectively secured as he found them.

(7) A warrant under this section continues in force until the end of the period of one month beginning with the day on which it is issued.

(8) Any document of which possession is taken under subsection (2)(c) may be retained for a period of three months.

(9) In this section 'business premises' has the same meaning as in section 65F.

65H Power to enter domestic premises under a warrant

(1) On an application made by the OFT to the court in accordance with rules of court, a judge may issue a warrant if he is satisfied that—

    (a) there are reasonable grounds for suspecting that there are on any domestic premises documents—

        (i) the production of which has been required under section 65E; and

        (ii) which have not been produced as required; or

    (b) there are reasonable grounds for suspecting that—

        (i) there are on any domestic premises documents which the OFT has power under section 65E to require to be produced; and

        (ii) if the documents were required to be produced, they would not be produced but would be concealed, removed, tampered with or destroyed.

(2) A warrant under this section shall authorise a named officer of the OFT, and any other of its officers whom the OFT has authorised in writing to accompany the named officer—

    (a) to enter the premises specified in the warrant, using such force as is reasonably necessary for the purpose;

    (b) to search the premises and take copies of, or extracts from, any document appearing to be of a kind in respect of which the application under subsection (1) was granted ('the relevant kind');

    (c) to take possession of any documents appearing to be of the relevant kind if—

        (i) such action appears to be necessary for preserving the documents or preventing interference with them; or

        (ii) it is not reasonably practicable to take copies of the documents on the premises;

    (d) to take any other steps which appear to be necessary for the purpose mentioned in paragraph (c)(i);

    (e) to require any person to provide an explanation of any document appearing to be of the relevant kind or to state, to the best of his knowledge or belief, where it may be found;

    (f) to require any information which is stored in any electronic form and is accessible from the premises and which the named officer considers relates to any matter relevant to the investigation, to be produced in a form—

        (i) in which it can be taken away; and

        (ii) in which it is visible and legible or from which it can readily be produced in a visible and legible form.

(3) If, in the case of a warrant under subsection (1)(b), the judge is satisfied that it is reasonable to suspect that there are also on the premises other documents relating to the investigation concerned, the warrant shall also authorise action mentioned in subsection (2) to be taken in relation to any such document.

(4) A warrant under this section may authorise persons specified in the warrant to accompany the named officer who is executing it.

(5) Any person entering premises by virtue of a warrant under this section may take with him such equipment as appears to him to be necessary.

(6) On leaving any premises which he has entered by virtue of a warrant under this section, the named officer must, if the premises are unoccupied or the occupier is temporarily absent, leave them as effectively secured as he found them.

(7) A warrant under this section continues in force until the end of the period of one month beginning with the day on which it is issued.

(8) Any document of which possession is taken under subsection (2)(c) may be retained for a period of three months.

(9) In this section, 'domestic premises' means premises (or any part of premises) that are used as a dwelling and are—
   (a) premises also used in connection with the affairs of an undertaking or association of undertakings; or
   (b) premises where documents relating to the affairs of an undertaking or association of undertakings are kept.

65I Entry of premises under a warrant: supplementary

(1) A warrant issued under section 65G or 65H must indicate—
   (a) the subject matter of the Article 22(1) investigation;
   (b) the nature of the offences created by sections 65L to 65N.

(2) The powers conferred by section 65G or 65H are to be exercised on production of a warrant issued under that section.

(3) If there is no one at the premises when the named officer proposes to execute such a warrant he must, before executing it—
   (a) take such steps as are reasonable in all the circumstances to inform the occupier of the intended entry; and
   (b) if the occupier is informed, afford him or his legal or other representative a reasonable opportunity to be present when the warrant is executed.

(4) If the named officer is unable to inform the occupier of the intended entry he must, when executing the warrant, leave a copy of it in a prominent place on the premises.

(5) In this section—
   'named officer' means the officer named in the warrant; and
   'occupier', in relation to any premises, means a person whom the named officer reasonably believes is the occupier of those premises.

65J Privileged communications

(1) A person shall not be required, under any provision of this Part, to produce or disclose a privileged communication.

(2) 'Privileged communication' means a communication—
   (a) between a professional legal adviser and his client, or
   (b) made in connection with, or in contemplation of, legal proceedings and for the purposes of those proceedings,
   which in proceedings in the High Court would be protected from disclosure on grounds of legal professional privilege.

(3) In the application of this section to Scotland—
   (a) the reference to the High Court is to be read as a reference to the Court of Session; and

(b) the reference to legal professional privilege is to be read as a reference to confidentiality of communications.

65K Use of statements in prosecution

A statement made by a person in response to a requirement imposed by virtue of any of sections 65E to 65H may not be used in evidence against him on a prosecution for an offence under section 188 of the Enterprise Act 2002 unless, in the proceedings—
(a) in giving evidence, he makes a statement inconsistent with it, and
(b) evidence relating to it is adduced, or a question relating to it is asked, by him or on his behalf.

65L Offences

(1) A person is guilty of an offence if he fails to comply with a requirement imposed on him under section 65E, 65F, 65G or 65H.
(2) If a person is charged with an offence under subsection (1) in respect of a requirement to produce a document, it is a defence for him to prove—
    (a) that the document was not in his possession or under his control; and
    (b) that it was not reasonably practicable for him to comply with the requirement.
(3) If a person is charged with an offence under subsection (1) in respect of a requirement—
    (a) to provide information,
    (b) to provide an explanation of a document, or
    (c) to state where a document is to be found,
    it is a defence for him to prove that he had a reasonable excuse for failing to comply with the requirement.
(4) Failure to comply with a requirement imposed under section 65E or 65F is not an offence if the person imposing the requirement has failed to act in accordance with that section.
(5) A person is guilty of an offence if he intentionally obstructs an officer acting in the exercise of his powers under section 65F.
(6) A person guilty of an offence under subsection (1) or (5) is liable—
    (a) on summary conviction, to a fine not exceeding the statutory maximum;
    (b) on conviction on indictment, to a fine.
(7) A person who intentionally obstructs an officer in the exercise of his powers under a warrant issued under section 65G or 65H is guilty of an offence and liable—
    (a) on summary conviction, to a fine not exceeding the statutory maximum;
    (b) on conviction on indictment, to imprisonment for a term not exceeding two years or to a fine or to both.

65M Destroying or falsifying documents

(1) A person is guilty of an offence if, having been required to produce a document under section 65E, 65F, 65G or 65H—
    (a) he intentionally or recklessly destroys or otherwise disposes of it, falsifies it or conceals it, or
    (b) he causes or permits its destruction, disposal, falsification or concealment.
(2) A person guilty of an offence under subsection (1) is liable—
    (a) on summary conviction, to a fine not exceeding the statutory maximum;
    (b) on conviction on indictment, to imprisonment for a term not exceeding two years or to a fine or to both.

65N False or misleading information

(1) If information is provided by a person to the OFT in connection with any function of the OFT under this Part, that person is guilty of an offence if—
    (a) the information is false or misleading in a material particular; and
    (b) he knows that it is or is reckless as to whether it is.
(2) A person who—

(a) provides any information to another person, knowing the information to be false or misleading in a material particular, or

(b) recklessly provides any information to another person which is false or misleading in a material particular,

knowing that the information is to be used for the purpose of providing information to the OFT in connection with any of its functions under this Part, is guilty of an offence.

(3) A person guilty of an offence under this section is liable—

(a) on summary conviction, to a fine not exceeding the statutory maximum;

(b) on conviction on indictment, to imprisonment for a term not exceeding two years or to a fine or to both.

Part III
Monopolies

66 . . .

67 . . .

68 Services relating to use of land

In section 137 of the Fair Trading Act 1973, after subsection (3) insert—

'(3A) The Secretary of State may by order made by statutory instrument—

(a) provide that "the supply of services" in the provisions of this Act is to include, or to cease to include, any activity specified in the order which consists in, or in making arrangements in connection with, permitting the use of land; and

(b) for that purpose, amend or repeal any of paragraphs (c), (d), (e) or (g) of subsection (3) above.

(3B) No order under subsection (3A) above is to be made unless a draft of the order has been laid before Parliament and approved by a resolution of each House of Parliament.

(3C) The provisions of Schedule 9 to this Act apply in the case of a draft of any such order as they apply in the case of a draft of an order to which section 91(1) above applies.'

69 Reports: monopoly references

In section 83 of the Fair Trading Act 1973—

(a) in subsection (1), omit 'Subject to subsection (1A) below'; and

(b) omit subsection (1A) (reports on monopoly references to be transmitted to certain persons at least twenty-four hours before laying before Parliament).

Part IV
Supplemental and Transitional

70 Contracts as to patented products etc

Sections 44 and 45 of the Patents Act 1977 shall cease to have effect.

71 Regulations, orders and rules

(1) Any power to make regulations or orders which is conferred by this Act is exercisable by statutory instrument.

(2) The power to make rules which is conferred by section 48 is exercisable by statutory instrument.

(3) Any statutory instrument made under this Act may—

(a) contain such incidental, supplemental, consequential and transitional provision as the Secretary of State considers appropriate; and

(b) make different provision for different cases.

(4) No order is to be made under—

(a) section 3,

(b) section 19,

(c) section 36(8),

(ca) section 45(8),

(d) section 50, or

(e) paragraph 6(3) of Schedule 4,

unless a draft of the order has been laid before Parliament and approved by a resolution of each House.

(5) Any statutory instrument made under this Act, apart from one made—

(a) under any of the provisions mentioned in subsection (4), or

(b) under section 76(3),

shall be subject to annulment by a resolution of either House of Parliament.

72 Offences by bodies corporate etc

(1) This section applies to an offence under any of sections 42 to 44, 65 or 65L to 65N.

(2) If an offence committed by a body corporate is proved—

(a) to have been committed with the consent or connivance of an officer, or

(b) to be attributable to any neglect on his part,

the officer as well as the body corporate is guilty of the offence and liable to be proceeded against and punished accordingly.

(3) In subsection (2) 'officer', in relation to a body corporate, means a director, manager, secretary or other similar officer of the body, or a person purporting to act in any such capacity.

(4) If the affairs of a body corporate are managed by its members, subsection (2) applies in relation to the acts and defaults of a member in connection with his functions of management as if he were a director of the body corporate.

(5) If an offence committed by a partnership in Scotland is proved—

(a) to have been committed with the consent or connivance of a partner, or

(b) to be attributable to any neglect on his part,

the partner as well as the partnership is guilty of the offence and liable to be proceeded against and punished accordingly.

(6) In subsection (5) 'partner' includes a person purporting to act as a partner.

73 Crown application

(1) Any provision made by or under this Act binds the Crown except that—

(a) the Crown is not criminally liable as a result of any such provision;

(b) the Crown is not liable for any penalty under any such provision; and

(c) nothing in this Act affects Her Majesty in her private capacity.

(2) Subsection (1)(a) does not affect the application of any provision of this Act in relation to persons in the public service of the Crown.

(3) Subsection (1)(c) is to be interpreted as if section 38(3) of the Crown Proceedings Act 1947 (interpretation of references in that Act to Her Majesty in her private capacity) were contained in this Act.

(4) If an investigation is conducted under section 25 or 65D in respect of an agreement where none of the parties is the Crown or a person in the public service of the Crown, or in respect of conduct otherwise than by the Crown or such a person—

(a) the power conferred by section 27 or (as the case may be) section 65F may not be exercised in relation to land which is occupied by a government department, or otherwise for purposes of the Crown, without the written consent of the appropriate person; and

(b) none of sections 28, 28A, 65G and 65H applies in relation to land so occupied.

(5) In any case in which consent is required under subsection (4), the person who is the appropriate person in relation to that case is to be determined in accordance with regulations made by the Secretary of State.

(6) Sections 62, 62A and 63 do not apply in relation to land which is occupied by a government department, or otherwise for purposes of the Crown, unless the matter being investigated is an

agreement to which the Crown or a person in the service of the Crown is a party, or conduct by the Crown or such a person.

(6A) In subsections (4) and (6) 'agreement' includes a suspected agreement and is to be read as applying equally to, or in relation to, a decision by an association of undertakings or a concerted practice; and 'conduct' includes suspected conduct.

(7) . . .

(8) If the Secretary of State certifies that it appears to him to be in the interests of national security that the powers of entry—

(a) conferred by section 27 or 65F, or

(b) that may be conferred by a warrant under section 28, 28A, 62, 62A, 63, 65G or 65H,

should not be exercisable in relation to premises held or used by or on behalf of the Crown and which are specified in the certificate, those powers are not exercisable in relation to those premises.

(9) Any amendment, repeal or revocation made by this Act binds the Crown to the extent that the enactment amended, repealed or revoked binds the Crown.

74 Amendments, transitional provisions, savings and repeals

(1) The minor and consequential amendments set out in Schedule 12 are to have effect.

(2) The transitional provisions and savings set out in Schedule 13 are to have effect.

(3) The enactments set out in Schedule 14 are repealed.

75 Consequential and supplementary provision

(1) The Secretary of State may by order make such incidental, consequential, transitional or supplemental provision as he thinks necessary or expedient for the general purposes, or any particular purpose, of this Act or in consequence of any of its provisions or for giving full effect to it.

(2) An order under subsection (1) may, in particular, make provision—

(a) for enabling any person by whom any powers will become exercisable, on a date specified by or under this Act, by virtue of any provision made by or under this Act to take before that date any steps which are necessary as a preliminary to the exercise of those powers;

(b) for making savings, or additional savings, from the effect of any repeal made by or under this Act.

(3) Amendments made under this section shall be in addition, and without prejudice, to those made by or under any other provision of this Act.

(4) No other provision of this Act restricts the powers conferred by this section.

75A Rules in relation to Part 2 and Part 2A

(1) The OFT may make such rules about procedural and other matters in connection with the carrying into effect of the provisions of Parts 2 and 2A as it considers appropriate.

(2) If the OFT is preparing rules under this section it must consult such persons as it considers appropriate.

(3) No rule made by the OFT is to come into operation until it has been approved by an order made by the Secretary of State.

(4) The Secretary of State may approve any rule made by the OFT—

(a) in the form in which it is submitted; or

(b) subject to such modifications as he considers appropriate.

(5) If the Secretary of State proposes to approve a rule subject to modifications he must inform the OFT of the proposed modifications and take into account any comments made by the OFT.

(6) Subsections (3) to (5) apply also to any alteration of the rules made by the OFT.

(7) The Secretary of State may, after consulting the OFT, by order vary or revoke any rules made under this section.

(8) If the Secretary of State considers that rules should be made under this section with respect to a particular matter he may direct the OFT to exercise its powers under this section and make rules about that matter.

76 Short title, commencement and extent

(1) This Act may be cited as the Competition Act 1998.

(2) Sections 71 and 75 and this section and paragraphs 1 to 7 and 35 of Schedule 13 come into force on the passing of this Act.

(3) The other provisions of this Act come into force on such day as the Secretary of State may by order appoint; and different days may be appointed for different purposes.

(4) This Act extends to Northern Ireland.

SCHEDULE I

EXCLUSIONS: MERGERS AND CONCENTRATIONS

Sections 3(1)(a) and 19(1)(a)

PART I

MERGERS

1 Enterprises ceasing to be distinct: the Chapter I prohibition

(1) To the extent to which an agreement (either on its own or when taken together with another agreement) results, or if carried out would result, in any two enterprises ceasing to be distinct enterprises for the purposes of Part 3 of the Enterprise Act 2002 ('the 2002 Act'), the Chapter I prohibition does not apply to the agreement.

(2) The exclusion provided by sub-paragraph (1) extends to any provision directly related and necessary to the implementation of the merger provisions.

(3) . . .

(4) Section 26 of the 2002 Act applies for the purposes of this paragraph as if—

    (a) in subsection (3) (circumstances in which a person or group of persons may be treated as having control of an enterprise), and

    (b) in subsection (4) (circumstances in which a person or group of persons may be treated as bringing an enterprise under their control),

    for 'may' there were substituted 'must'.

2 Enterprises ceasing to be distinct: the Chapter II prohibition

(1) To the extent to which conduct (either on its own or when taken together with other conduct)—

    (a) results in any two enterprises ceasing to be distinct enterprises for the purposes of Part 3 of the 2002 Act), or

    (b) is directly related and necessary to the attainment of the result mentioned in paragraph (a),

    the Chapter II prohibition does not apply to that conduct.

(2) Section 26 of the 2002 Act applies for the purposes of this paragraph as it applies for the purposes of paragraph 1.

3 . . .

4 Withdrawal of the paragraph 1 exclusion

(1) The exclusion provided by paragraph 1 does not apply to a particular agreement if the OFT gives a direction under this paragraph to that effect.

(2) If the OFT is considering whether to give a direction under this paragraph, it may by notice in writing require any party to the agreement in question to give the OFT such information in connection with the agreement as it may require.

(3) The OFT may give a direction under this paragraph only as provided in sub-paragraph (4) or (5).

(4) If at the end of such period as may be specified in rules under section 51 a person has failed, without reasonable excuse, to comply with a requirement imposed under sub-paragraph (2), the OFT may give a direction under this paragraph.

(5) The OFT may also give a direction under this paragraph if—

(a) it considers that the agreement will, if not excluded, infringe the Chapter I prohibition; and

(b) the agreement is not a protected agreement.

(6) . . .

(7) A direction under this paragraph—

(a) must be in writing;

(b) may be made so as to have effect from a date specified in the direction (which may not be earlier than the date on which it is given).

5 Protected agreements

An agreement is a protected agreement for the purposes of paragraph 4 if—

(a) the OFT or (as the case may be) the Secretary of State has published its or his decision not to make a reference to the Competition Commission under section 22, 33, 45 or 62 of the 2002 Act in connection with the agreement;

(b) the OFT or (as the case may be) the Secretary of State has made a reference to the Competition Commission under section 22, 33, 45 or 62 of the 2002 Act in connection with the agreement and the Commission has found that the agreement has given rise to, or would if carried out give rise to, a relevant merger situation or (as the case may be) a special merger situation;

(c) the agreement does not fall within paragraph (a) or (b) but has given rise to, or would if carried out give rise to, enterprises to which it relates being regarded under section 26 of the 2002 Act as ceasing to be distinct enterprises (otherwise than as the result of subsection (3) or (4)(b) of that section); or

(d) the OFT has made a reference to the Competition Commission under section 32 of the Water Industry Act 1991 in connection with the agreement and the Commission has found that the agreement has given rise to, or would if carried out give rise to, a merger of any two or more water enterprises of the kind to which that section applies.

PART II
CONCENTRATIONS SUBJECT TO EC CONTROLS

6

(1) To the extent to which an agreement (either on its own or when taken together with another agreement) gives rise to, or would if carried out give rise to, a concentration, the Chapter I prohibition does not apply to the agreement if the Merger Regulation gives the Commission exclusive jurisdiction in the matter.

(2) To the extent to which conduct (either on its own or when taken together with other conduct) gives rise to, or would if pursued give rise to, a concentration, the Chapter II prohibition does not apply to the conduct if the Merger Regulation gives the Commission exclusive jurisdiction in the matter.

(3) In this paragraph—

'concentration' means a concentration with a Community dimension within the meaning of Articles 1 and 3 of the Merger Regulation; and

'Merger Regulation' means Council Regulation (EEC) No 4064/89 of 21st December 1989 on the control of concentrations between undertakings as amended by Council Regulation (EC) No 1310/97 of 30th June 1997.

SCHEDULE 2
EXCLUSIONS: OTHER COMPETITION SCRUTINY

Section 3(1)(b)

PART I
FINANCIAL SERVICES

1 The Financial Services Act 1986 (c 60)

(1) The Financial Services Act 1986 is amended as follows.

(2) For section 125 (effect of the Restrictive Trade Practices Act 1976), substitute—

'125 The Competition Act 1998: Chapter I prohibition

(1) The Chapter I prohibition does not apply to an agreement for the constitution of—

(a) a recognised self-regulating organisation,

(b) a recognised investment exchange, or

(c) a recognised clearing house,

to the extent to which the agreement relates to the regulating provisions of the body concerned.

(2) Subject to subsection (3) below, the Chapter I prohibition does not apply to an agreement for the constitution of—

(a) a self-regulating organisation,

(b) an investment exchange, or

(c) a clearing house,

to the extent to which the agreement relates to the regulating provisions of the body concerned.

(3) The exclusion provided by subsection (2) above applies only if—

(a) the body has applied for a recognition order in accordance with the provisions of this Act; and

(b) the application has not been determined.

(4) The Chapter I prohibition does not apply to a decision made by—

(a) a recognised self-regulating organisation,

(b) a recognised investment exchange, or

(c) a recognised clearing house,

to the extent to which the decision relates to any of that body's regulating provisions or specified practices.

(5) The Chapter I prohibition does not apply to the specified practices of—

(a) a recognised self-regulating organisation, a recognised investment exchange or a recognised clearing house; or

(b) a person who is subject to—

(i) the rules of one of those bodies, or

(ii) the statements of principle, rules, regulations or codes of practice made by a designated agency in the exercise of functions transferred to it by a delegation order.

(6) The Chapter I prohibition does not apply to any agreement the parties to which consist of or include—

(a) a recognised self-regulating organisation, a recognised investment exchange or a recognised clearing house; or

(b) a person who is subject to—

(i) the rules of one of those bodies, or

(ii) the statements of principle, rules, regulations or codes of practice made by a designated agency in the exercise of functions transferred to it by a delegation order,

to the extent to which the agreement consists of provisions the inclusion of which is required or contemplated by any of the body's regulating provisions or specified practices or by the statements of principle, rules, regulations or codes of practice of the agency.

(7) The Chapter I prohibition does not apply to—

    (a) any clearing arrangements; or

    (b) any agreement between a recognised investment exchange and a recognised clearing house, to the extent to which the agreement consists of provisions the inclusion of which in the agreement is required or contemplated by any clearing arrangements.

(8) If the recognition order in respect of a body of the kind mentioned in subsection (1)(a), (b) or (c) above is revoked, subsections (1) and (4) to (7) above are to have effect as if that body had continued to be recognised until the end of the period of six months beginning with the day on which the revocation took effect.

(9) In this section—

'the Chapter I prohibition' means the prohibition imposed by section 2(1) of the Competition Act 1998;

'regulating provisions' means—

    (a) in relation to a self-regulating organisation, any rules made, or guidance issued, by the organisation;

    (b) in relation to an investment exchange, any rules made, or guidance issued, by the exchange;

    (c) in relation to a clearing house, any rules made, or guidance issued, by the clearing house;

'specified practices' means—

    (a) in the case of a recognised self-regulating organisation, the practices mentioned in section 119(2)(a)(ii) and (iii) above (read with section 119(5) and (6)(a));

    (b) in the case of a recognised investment exchange, the practices mentioned in section 119(2)(b)(ii) and (iii) above (read with section 119(5) and (6)(b));

    (c) in the case of a recognised clearing house, the practices mentioned in section 119(2)(c)(ii) and (iii) above (read with section 119(5) and (6)(b));

    (d) in the case of a person who is subject to the statements of principle, rules, regulations or codes of practice issued or made by a designated agency in the exercise of functions transferred to it by a delegation order, the practices mentioned in section 121(2)(c) above (read with section 121(4));

and expressions used in this section which are also used in Part I of the Competition Act 1998 are to be interpreted in the same way as for the purposes of that Part of that Act.'

(3) Omit section 126 (certain practices not to constitute anti-competitive practices for the purposes of the Competition Act 1980).

(4) For section 127 (modification of statutory provisions in relation to recognised professional bodies), substitute—

'127 Application of Competition Act 1998 in relation to recognised professional bodies: Chapter I prohibition

(1) This section applies to—

    (a) any agreement for the constitution of a recognised professional body to the extent to which it relates to the rules or guidance of that body relating to the carrying on of investment business by persons certified by it ('investment business rules'); and

    (b) any other agreement, the parties to which consist of or include—

        (i) a recognised professional body,

        (ii) a person certified by such a body, or

        (iii) a member of such a body,

and which contains a provision required or contemplated by that body's investment business rules.

(2) If it appears to the Treasury, in relation to some or all of the provisions of an agreement to which this section applies—

    (a) that the provisions in question do not have, and are not intended or likely to have, to any significant extent the effect of restricting, distorting or preventing competition; or

(b) that the effect of restricting, distorting or preventing competition which the provisions in question do have, or are intended or are likely to have, is not greater than is necessary for the protection of investors,

the Treasury may make a declaration to that effect.

(3) If the Treasury make a declaration under this section, the Chapter I prohibition does not apply to the agreement to the extent to which the agreement consists of provisions to which the declaration relates.

(4) If the Treasury are satisfied that there has been a material change of circumstances, they may—

(a) revoke a declaration made under this section, if they consider that the grounds on which it was made no longer exist;

(b) vary such a declaration, if they consider that there are grounds for making a different declaration; or

(c) make a declaration even though they have notified the Director of their intention not to do so.

(5) If the Treasury make, vary or revoke a declaration under this section they must notify the Director of their decision.

(6) If the Director proposes to exercise any Chapter III powers in respect of any provisions of an agreement to which this section applies, he must—

(a) notify the Treasury of his intention to do so; and

(b) give the Treasury particulars of the agreement and such other information—

(i) as he considers will assist the Treasury to decide whether to exercise their powers under this section; or

(ii) as the Treasury may request.

(7) The Director may not exercise his Chapter III powers in respect of any provisions of an agreement to which this section applies, unless the Treasury—

(a) have notified him that they have not made a declaration in respect of those provisions under this section and that they do not intend to make such a declaration; or

(b) have revoked a declaration under this section and a period of six months beginning with the date on which the revocation took effect has expired.

(8) A declaration under this section ceases to have effect if the agreement to which it relates ceases to be one to which this section applies.

(9) In this section—

'the Chapter I prohibition' means the prohibition imposed by section 2(1) of the Competition Act 1998,

'Chapter III powers' means the powers given to the Director by Chapter III of Part I of that Act so far as they relate to the Chapter I prohibition, and expressions used in this section which are also used in Part I of the Competition Act 1998 are to be interpreted in the same way as for the purposes of that Part of that Act.

(10) In this section references to an agreement are to be read as applying equally to, or in relation to, a decision or concerted practice.

(11) In the application of this section to decisions and concerted practices, references to provisions of an agreement are to be read as references to elements of a decision or concerted practice.'

Part II

Companies

2 . . .

3 . . .

Part III

Broadcasting

4 The Broadcasting Act 1990 (c 42)

(1) The Broadcasting Act 1990 is amended as follows.

(2) In section 194A (which modifies the Restrictive Trade Practices Act 1976 in its application to agreements relating to Channel 3 news provision), for subsections (2) to (6), substitute—

'(2) If, having sought the advice of the Director, it appears to the Secretary of State, in relation to some or all of the provisions of a relevant agreement, that the conditions mentioned in subsection (3) are satisfied, he may make a declaration to that effect.

(3) The conditions are that—

    (a) the provisions in question do not have, and are not intended or likely to have, to any significant extent the effect of restricting, distorting or preventing competition; or

    (b) the effect of restricting, distorting or preventing competition which the provisions in question do have or are intended or are likely to have, is not greater than is necessary—

        (i) in the case of a relevant agreement falling within subsection (1)(a), for securing the appointment by holders of regional Channel 3 licences of a single body corporate to be the appointed news provider for the purposes of section 31(2), or

        (ii) in the case of a relevant agreement falling within subsection (1)(b), for compliance by them with conditions included in their licences by virtue of section 31(1) and (2).

(4) If the Secretary of State makes a declaration under this section, the Chapter I prohibition does not apply to the agreement to the extent to which the agreement consists of provisions to which the declaration relates.

(5) If the Secretary of State is satisfied that there has been a material change of circumstances, he may—

    (a) revoke a declaration made under this section, if he considers that the grounds on which it was made no longer exist;

    (b) vary such a declaration, if he considers that there are grounds for making a different declaration; or

    (c) make a declaration, even though he has notified the Director of his intention not to do so.

(6) If the Secretary of State makes, varies or revokes a declaration under this section, he must notify the Director of his decision.

(7) The Director may not exercise any Chapter III powers in respect of a relevant agreement, unless—

    (a) he has notified the Secretary of State of his intention to do so; and

    (b) the Secretary of State—

        (i) has notified the Director that he has not made a declaration in respect of the agreement, or provisions of the agreement, under this section and that he does not intend to make such a declaration; or

        (ii) has revoked a declaration under this section and a period of six months beginning with the date on which the revocation took effect has expired.

(8) If the Director proposes to exercise any Chapter III powers in respect of a relevant agreement, he must give the Secretary of State particulars of the agreement and such other information—

673

(a) as he considers will assist the Secretary of State to decide whether to exercise his powers under this section; or

(b) as the Secretary of State may request.

(9) In this section—

'the Chapter I prohibition' means the prohibition imposed by section 2(1) of the Competition Act 1998;

'Chapter III powers' means the powers given to the Director by Chapter III of Part I of that Act so far as they relate to the Chapter I prohibition;

'Director' means the Director General of Fair Trading;

'regional Channel 3 licence' has the same meaning as in Part I; and expressions used in this section which are also used in Part I of the Competition Act 1998 are to be interpreted in the same way as for the purposes of that Part of that Act.

(10) In this section references to an agreement are to be read as applying equally to, or in relation to, a decision or concerted practice.

(11) In the application of this section to decisions and concerted practices, references to provisions of an agreement are to be read as references to elements of a decision or concerted practice.'

5 Networking arrangements under the Broadcasting Act 1990 (c 42)

(1) The Chapter I prohibition does not apply in respect of any networking arrangements to the extent that they—

(a) have been approved for the purposes of licence conditions imposed under section 291 of the Communications Act 2003; or

(b) are arrangements that have been considered under Schedule 4 to the Broadcasting Act 1990 and fall to be treated as so approved;

nor does that prohibition apply in respect of things done with a view to arrangements being entered into or approved to the extent that those things have effect for purposes that are directly related to, and necessary for compliance with, conditions so imposed.

(2) OFCOM must publish a list of the networking arrangements which in their opinion are excluded from the Chapter I prohibition by virtue of sub-paragraph (1).

(3) OFCOM must—

(a) consult the Director before publishing the list, and

(b) publish the list in such a way as they think most suitable for bringing it to the attention of persons who, in their opinion, would be affected by, or likely to have an interest in, it.

(4) In this paragraph 'networking arrangements' has the same meaning as in Part 3 of the Communications Act 2003.

SCHEDULE 3
GENERAL EXCLUSIONS

Sections 3(1)(c) and 19(1)(b)

1 Planning obligations

(1) The Chapter I prohibition does not apply to an agreement—

(a) to the extent to which it is a planning obligation;

(b) which is made under section 75 (agreements regulating development or use of land) or 246 (agreements relating to Crown land) of the Town and Country Planning (Scotland) Act 1997; or

(c) which is made under Article 40 of the Planning (Northern Ireland) Order 1991.

(2) In sub-paragraph (1)(a), 'planning obligation' means—

(a) a planning obligation for the purposes of section 106 of the Town and Country Planning Act 1990; or

(b) a planning obligation for the purposes of section 299A of that Act.

2 . . .

3 EEA Regulated Markets

(1) The Chapter I prohibition does not apply to an agreement for the constitution of an EEA regulated market to the extent to which the agreement relates to any of the rules made, or guidance issued, by that market.

(2) The Chapter I prohibition does not apply to a decision made by an EEA regulated market, to the extent to which the decision relates to any of the market's regulating provisions.

(3) The Chapter I prohibition does not apply to—
   (a) any practices of an EEA regulated market; or
   (b) any practices which are trading practices in relation to an EEA regulated market.

(4) The Chapter I prohibition does not apply to an agreement the parties to which are or include—
   (a) an EEA regulated market, or
   (b) a person who is subject to the rules of that market,

   to the extent to which the agreement consists of provisions the inclusion of which is required or contemplated by the regulating provisions of that market.

(5) In this paragraph—

   'EEA regulated market' is a market which—
   (a) is listed by an EEA State other than the United Kingdom pursuant to article 16 of Council Directive No 93/22/EEC of 10th May 1993 on investment services in the securities field; and
   (b) operates without any requirement that a person dealing on the market should have a physical presence in the EEA State from which any trading facilities are provided or on any trading floor that the market may have;

   'EEA State' means a State which is a contracting party to the EEA Agreement;

   'regulating provisions', in relation to an EEA regulated market, means—
   (a) rules made, or guidance issued, by that market,
   (b) practices of that market, or
   (c) practices which, in relation to that market, are trading practices;

   'trading practices', in relation to an EEA regulated market, means practices of persons who are subject to the rules made by that market, and—
   (a) which relate to business in respect of which those persons are subject to the rules of that market, and which are required or contemplated by those rules or by guidance issued by that market; or
   (b) which are otherwise attributable to the conduct of that market as such.

4 Services of general economic interest etc

Neither the Chapter I prohibition nor the Chapter II prohibition applies to an undertaking entrusted with the operation of services of general economic interest or having the character of a revenue-producing monopoly in so far as the prohibition would obstruct the performance, in law or in fact, of the particular tasks assigned to that undertaking.

5 Compliance with legal requirements

(1) The Chapter I prohibition does not apply to an agreement to the extent to which it is made in order to comply with a legal requirement.

(2) The Chapter II prohibition does not apply to conduct to the extent to which it is engaged in an order to comply with a legal requirement.

(3) In this paragraph 'legal requirement' means a requirement—
   (a) imposed by or under any enactment in force in the United Kingdom;
   (b) imposed by or under the Treaty or the EEA Agreement and having legal effect in the United Kingdom without further enactment; or

(c) imposed by or under the law in force in another Member State and having legal effect in the United Kingdom.

6 Avoidance of conflict with international obligations

(1) If the Secretary of State is satisfied that, in order to avoid a conflict between provisions of this Part and an international obligation of the United Kingdom, it would be appropriate for the Chapter I prohibition not to apply to—
   (a) a particular agreement, or
   (b) any agreement of a particular description,
   he may by order exclude the agreement, or agreements of that description, from the Chapter I prohibition.
(2) An order under sub-paragraph (1) may make provision for the exclusion of the agreement or agreements to which the order applies, or of such of them as may be specified, only in specified circumstances.
(3) An order under sub-paragraph (1) may also provide that the Chapter I prohibition is to be deemed never to have applied in relation to the agreement or agreements, or in relation to such of them as may be specified.
(4) If the Secretary of State is satisfied that, in order to avoid a conflict between provisions of this Part and an international obligation of the United Kingdom, it would be appropriate for the Chapter II prohibition not to apply in particular circumstances, he may by order provide for it not to apply in such circumstances as may be specified.
(5) An order under sub-paragraph (4) may provide that the Chapter II prohibition is to be deemed never to have applied in relation to specified conduct.
(6) An international arrangement relating to civil aviation and designated by an order made by the Secretary of State is to be treated as an international obligation for the purposes of this paragraph.
(7) In this paragraph and paragraph 7 'specified' means specified in the order.

7 Public policy

(1) If the Secretary of State is satisfied that there are exceptional and compelling reasons of public policy why the Chapter I prohibition ought not to apply to—
   (a) a particular agreement, or
   (b) any agreement of a particular description,
   he may by order exclude the agreement, or agreements of that description, from the Chapter I prohibition.
(2) An order under sub-paragraph (1) may make provision for the exclusion of the agreement or agreements to which the order applies, or of such of them as may be specified, only in specified circumstances.
(3) An order under sub-paragraph (1) may also provide that the Chapter I prohibition is to be deemed never to have applied in relation to the agreement or agreements, or in relation to such of them as may be specified.
(4) If the Secretary of State is satisfied that there are exceptional and compelling reasons of public policy why the Chapter II prohibition ought not to apply in particular circumstances, he may by order provide for it not to apply in such circumstances as may be specified.
(5) An order under sub-paragraph (4) may provide that the Chapter II prohibition is to be deemed never to have applied in relation to specified conduct.

8 Coal and steel

(1) The Chapter I prohibition does not apply to an agreement which relates to a coal or steel product to the extent to which the ECSC Treaty gives the Commission exclusive jurisdiction in the matter.
(2) Sub-paragraph (1) ceases to have effect on the date on which the ECSC Treaty expires ('the expiry date').

(3) The Chapter II prohibition does not apply to conduct which relates to a coal or steel product to the extent to which the ECSC Treaty gives the Commission exclusive jurisdiction in the matter.

(4) Sub-paragraph (3) ceases to have effect on the expiry date.

(5) In this paragraph—

'coal or steel product' means any product of a kind listed in Annex I to the ECSC Treaty; and

'ECSC Treaty' means the Treaty establishing the European Coal and Steel Community.

9 Agricultural products

(1) The Chapter I prohibition does not apply to an agreement to the extent to which it relates to production of or trade in an agricultural product and—

  (a) forms an integral part of a national market organisation;

  (b) is necessary for the attainment of the objectives set out in Article 33 of the Treaty; or

  (c) is an agreement of farmers or farmers' associations (or associations of such associations) belonging to a single member State which concerns—

    (i) the production or sale of agricultural products, or

    (ii) the use of joint facilities for the storage, treatment or processing of agricultural products,

and under which there is no obligation to charge identical prices.

(2) If the Commission determines that an agreement does not fulfil the conditions specified by the provision for agricultural products for exclusion from Article 81(1), the exclusion provided by this paragraph ('the agriculture exclusion') is to be treated as ceasing to apply to the agreement on the date of the decision.

(3) The agriculture exclusion does not apply to a particular agreement if the OFT gives a direction under this paragraph to that effect.

(4) If the OFT is considering whether to give a direction under this paragraph, it may by notice in writing require any party to the agreement in question to give the OFT such information in connection with the agreement as it may require.

(5) The OFT may give a direction under this paragraph only as provided in sub-paragraph (6) or (7).

(6) If at the end of such period as may be specified in rules under section 51 a person has failed, without reasonable excuse, to comply with a requirement imposed under sub-paragraph (4), the OFT may give a direction under this paragraph.

(7) The OFT may also give a direction under this paragraph if it considers that an agreement (whether or not it considers that it infringes the Chapter I prohibition) is likely, or is intended, substantially and unjustifiably to prevent, restrict or distort competition in relation to an agricultural product.

(8) A direction under this paragraph—

  (a) must be in writing;

  (b) may be made so as to have effect from a date specified in the direction (which may not be earlier than the date on which it is given).

(9) In this paragraph—

'agricultural product' means any product of a kind listed in Annex I to the Treaty; and

'provision for agricultural products' means Council Regulation (EEC) No 26/62 of 4th April 1962 applying certain rules of competition to production of and trade in agricultural products.

SCHEDULE 4

. . .

SCHEDULE 5

. . .

SCHEDULE 6

. . .

SCHEDULE 6A
COMMITMENTS

Section 31A

PART I
PROCEDURAL REQUIREMENTS FOR THE ACCEPTANCE AND VARIATION
OF COMMITMENTS

1

Paragraph 2 applies where the OFT proposes to—
(a) accept any commitments under section 31A; or
(b) accept any variation of such commitments other than a variation which is not material in any respect.

2

(1) Before accepting the commitments or variation, the OFT must—
  (a) give notice under this paragraph; and
  (b) consider any representations made in accordance with the notice and not withdrawn.
(2) A notice under this paragraph must state—
  (a) that the OFT proposes to accept the commitments or variation;
  (b) the purpose of the commitments or variation and the way in which the commitments or variation would meet the OFT's competition concerns;
  (c) any other facts which the OFT considers are relevant to the acceptance or variation of the commitments; and
  (d) the period within which representations may be made in relation to the proposed commitments or variation.
(3) The period stated for the purposes of sub-paragraph (2)(d) must be at least 11 working days starting with the date the notice is given or, if that date is not a working day, with the date of the first working day after that date.

3

(1) The OFT must not accept the commitments or variation of which notice has been given under paragraph 2(1) with modifications unless it—
  (a) gives notice under this paragraph of the proposed modifications; and
  (b) considers any representations made in accordance with the notice and not withdrawn.
(2) A notice under this paragraph must state—
  (a) the proposed modifications;
  (b) the reasons for them; and
  (c) the period within which representations may be made in relation to the proposed modifications.
(3) The period stated for the purposes of sub-paragraph (2)(c) must be at least 6 working days starting

with the date the notice is given or, if that date is not a working day, with the date of the first working day after that date.

4

If, after giving notice under paragraph 2 or 3 the OFT decides—
(a) not to accept the commitments or variation concerned, and
(b) not to proceed by virtue of paragraph 5 or 6,
the OFT must give notice that it has so decided.

5

The requirements of paragraph 3 shall not apply if the OFT—
(a) has already given notice under paragraph 2 but not under paragraph 3; and
(b) considers that the modifications which are now being proposed are not material in any respect.

6

The requirements of paragraph 3 shall not apply if the OFT—
(a) has already given notices under paragraphs 2 and 3; and
(b) considers that the further modifications which are now being proposed are not material in any respect or do not differ in any material respect from the modifications in relation to which notice was last given under paragraph 3.

7

As soon as practicable after accepting commitments or a variation under section 31A the OFT must publish the commitments or the variation in such manner as the OFT considers appropriate.

8

A notice under paragraph 2 or 3 shall be given by—
(a) sending a copy of the notice to such person or persons as the OFT considers appropriate for the purpose of bringing the matter to which it relates to the attention of those likely to be affected by it; or
(b) publishing the notice in such manner as the OFT considers appropriate for the purpose of bringing the matter to which it relates to the attention of those likely to be affected by it.

PART II
PROCEDURAL REQUIREMENTS FOR THE RELEASE OF COMMITMENTS

10

Paragraph 11 applies where the OFT proposes to release any commitments under section 31A.

11

(1) Before releasing the commitments, the OFT must—
    (a) give notice under this paragraph;
    (b) send a copy of the notice to the person (or persons) who gave the commitments; and
    (c) consider any representations made in accordance with the notice and not withdrawn.
(2) A notice under this paragraph must state—
    (a) the fact that a release is proposed;
    (b) the reasons for it; and
    (c) the period within which representations may be made in relation to the proposed release.
(3) The period stated for the purposes of sub-paragraph (2)(c) must be at least 11 working days starting with the date the notice is given or, if that date is not a working day, with the date of the first working day after that date.

12

If after giving notice under paragraph 11 the OFT decides not to proceed with the release, it must—

(a) give notice that it has so decided; and

(b) send a copy of the notice to the person (or persons) who gave the commitments.

13

As soon as practicable after releasing the commitments, the OFT must—

(a) publish the release in such manner as it considers appropriate; and

(b) send a copy of the release to the person (or persons) who gave the commitments.

14

A notice under paragraph 11 or 12 shall be given by—

(a) sending a copy of the notice to such other person or persons as the OFT considers appropriate for the purpose of bringing the matter to which it relates to the attention of those likely to be affected by it; or

(b) publishing the notice in such manner as the OFT considers appropriate for the purpose of bringing the matter to which it relates to the attention of those likely to be affected by it.

SCHEDULE 7

THE COMPETITION COMMISSION

Section 45(7)

PART I

GENERAL

1 Interpretation

In this Schedule—

'the 1973 Act' means the Fair Trading Act 1973;

'Chairman' means the chairman of the Commission;

'the Commission' means the Competition Commission;

'Council' has the meaning given in paragraph 5;

'general functions.' means any functions of the Commission other than functions—

(a) . . .

(b) which are to be discharged by the Council;

'member' means a member of the Commission;

'newspaper merger reference' means a newspaper merger reference under section 45 of the Enterprise Act 2002 which specifies a newspaper public interest consideration (within the meaning of paragraph 20A of Schedule 8 to that Act) or a reference under section 62 of that Act which specifies a consideration specified in section 58(2A) or (2B) of that Act;

'newspaper panel member' means a member of the panel maintained under paragraph 22;

'reporting panel member' means a member appointed under paragraph 2(1)(b);

'secretary' means the secretary of the Commission appointed under paragraph 9; and

'specialist panel member' means a member appointed under any of the provisions mentioned in paragraph 2(1)(d).

2 Membership of the Commission

(1) The Commission is to consist of—

(a) . . .

(b) members appointed by the Secretary of State to form a panel for the purposes of the Commission's general functions;

(c) the members of the panel maintained under paragraph 22;

(d) members appointed by the Secretary of State under or by virtue of—

    (i) ...

    (ii) section 104 of the Utilities Act 2000;

    (iii) section 194(1) of the Communications Act 2003;

    (iv) Article 15(9) of the Electricity (Northern Ireland) Order 1992;

  (e) one or more members appointed by the Secretary of State to serve on the Council.

(1A) A person may not be, at the same time, a member of the Commission and a member of the Tribunal.

(2) A person who is appointed as a member of a kind mentioned in one of paragraphs (aa) to (c) of sub-paragraph (3) may also be appointed as a member of either or both of the other kinds mentioned in those paragraphs.

(3) The kinds of member are—

  (a) ...

  (aa) a newspaper panel member;

  (b) a reporting panel member;

  (c) a specialist panel member.

(4) ...

(5) The validity of the Commission's proceedings is not affected by a defect in the appointment of a member.

3 Chairman and deputy chairmen

(1) The Commission is to have a chairman appointed by the Secretary of State from among the reporting panel members.

(2) The Secretary of State may appoint one or more of the reporting panel members to act as deputy chairman.

(3) The Chairman, and any deputy chairman, may resign that office at any time by notice in writing addressed to the Secretary of State.

(4) If the Chairman (or a deputy chairman) ceases to be a member he also ceases to be Chairman (or a deputy chairman).

(5) If the Chairman is absent or otherwise unable to act, or there is no chairman, any of his functions may be performed—

  (a) if there is one deputy chairman, by him;

  (b) if there is more than one—

    (i) by the deputy chairman designated by the Secretary of State; or

    (ii) if no such designation has been made, by the deputy chairman designated by the deputy chairmen;

  (c) if there is no deputy chairman able to act-

    (i) by the member designated by the Secretary of State; or

    (ii) if no such designation has been made, by the member designated by the Commission.

4. ...

5 The Council

(1) The Commission is to have a . . . board to be known as the Competition Commission Council (but referred to in this Schedule as 'the Council').

(2) The Council is to consist of—

  (a) the Chairman and any deputy chairmen of the Commission;

  (b) ...

  (bb) the member or members appointed under paragraph 2(1)(e);

  (c) such other members as the Secretary of State may appoint; and

  (d) the secretary.

(3) In exercising its functions under paragraphs 3 and 7 to 12, the Commission is to act through the Council.

(3A) Without prejudice to the question whether any other functions of the Commission are to be so discharged, the functions of the Commission under sections 106, 116, and 171 of the Enterprise Act 2002 (and under section 116 as applied for the purposes of references under Part 4 of that Act by section 176 of that Act) are to be discharged by the Council.

(4) The Council may determine its own procedure including, in particular, its quorum.

(5) The Chairman (and any person acting as Chairman) is to have a casting vote on any question being decided by the Council.

6 Term of office

(1) Subject to the provisions of this Schedule, each member is to hold and vacate office in accordance with the terms of his appointment.

(2) A person is not to be appointed as a member for more than eight years (but this does not prevent a re-appointment for the purpose only of continuing to act as a member of a group selected under paragraph 15 before the end of his term of office).

(3) Any member may at any time resign by notice in writing addressed to the Secretary of State.

(4) The Secretary of State may remove a member on the ground of incapacity or misbehaviour.

(5) . . .

7 Expenses, remuneration and pensions

(1) The Secretary of State shall pay to the Commission such sums as he considers appropriate to enable it to perform its functions.

(2) The Commission may pay, or make provision for paying, to or in respect of each member such salaries or other remuneration and such pensions, allowances, fees, expenses or gratuities as the Secretary of State may determine.

(3) If a person ceases to be a member otherwise than on the expiry of his term of office and it appears to the Secretary of State that there are special circumstances which make it right for him to receive compensation, the Commission may make a payment to him of such amount as the Secretary of State may determine.

(4) . . .

7A

The Commission may publish advice and information in relation to any matter connected with the exercise of its functions.

8 The Commission's powers

Subject to the provisions of this Schedule, the Commission has power to do anything (except borrow money)—

(a) calculated to facilitate the discharge of its functions; or

(b) incidental or conducive to the discharge of its functions.

9 Staff

(1) The Commission is to have a secretary, appointed by the Secretary of State on such terms and conditions of service as he considers appropriate.

(2) . . .

(3) Before appointing a person to be secretary, the Secretary of State must consult the Chairman.

(4) Subject to obtaining the approval of the Secretary of State as to numbers and terms and conditions of service the Commission may appoint such staff as it thinks appropriate.

10 . . .

11 Application of seal and proof of instruments

(1) The application of the seal of the Commission must be authenticated by the signature of the secretary or of some other person authorised for the purpose.

(2) Sub-paragraph (1) does not apply in relation to any document which is or is to be signed in accordance with the law of Scotland.

(3) A document purporting to be duly executed under the seal of the Commission—

(a) is to be received in evidence; and

(b) is to be taken to have been so executed unless the contrary is proved.

12 Accounts

(1) The Commission must—

(a) keep proper accounts and proper records in relation to its accounts;

(b) prepare a statement of accounts in respect of each of its financial years; and

(c) send copies of the statement to the Secretary of State and to the Comptroller and Auditor General before the end of the month of August next following the financial year to which the statement relates.

(2) The statement of accounts must comply with any directions given by the Secretary of State with the approval of the Treasury as to—

(a) the information to be contained in it,

(b) the manner in which the information contained in it is to be presented, or

(c) the methods and principles according to which the statement is to be prepared,

and must contain such additional information as the Secretary of State may with the approval of the Treasury require to be provided for informing Parliament.

(3) The Comptroller and Auditor General must—

(a) examine, certify and report on each statement received by him as a result of this paragraph; and

(b) lay copies of each statement and of his report before each House of Parliament.

(4) In this paragraph 'financial year' means the period beginning with the date on which the Commission is established and ending with March 31st next, and each successive period of twelve months.

12A Annual reports

(1) The Commission shall make to the Secretary of State a report for each financial year on its activities during the year.

(2) The annual report must be made before the end of August next following the financial year to which it relates.

(3) The Secretary of State shall lay a copy of the annual report before Parliament and arrange for the report to be published.

13 Status

(1) The Commission is not to be regarded as the servant or agent of the Crown or as enjoying any status, privilege or immunity of the Crown.

(2) The Commission's property is not to be regarded as property of, or held on behalf of, the Crown.

Part II
Performance of the Commission's General Functions

14 Interpretation

In this Part of this Schedule 'group' means a group selected under paragraph 15.

15 Discharge of certain functions by groups

(1) Except where sub-paragraph (7) or (8) gives the Chairman power to act on his own, any general function of the Commission must be performed through a group selected for the purpose by the Chairman.

(2) The group must consist of at least three persons one of whom may be the Chairman.

(3) In selecting the members of the group, the Chairman must comply with any requirement as to its constitution imposed by any enactment applying to specialist panel members.

(4) If the functions to be performed through the group relate to a newspaper merger reference, the group must, subject to sub-paragraph (5), consist of such reporting panel members as the Chairman may select.

(5) The Chairman must select one or more newspaper panel members to be members of the group dealing with functions relating to a newspaper merger reference and, if he selects at least three such members, the group may consist entirely of those members.

(6) Subject to sub-paragraphs (2) to (5), a group must consist of reporting panel members or specialist panel members selected by the Chairman.

(7) While a group is being constituted to perform a particular general function of the Commission, the Chairman may—

(a) take such steps (falling within that general function) as he considers appropriate to facilitate the work of the group when it has been constituted; or

(aa) in the case of an investigation under section 162 of the Financial Services and Markets Act 2000, decide not to make a report in accordance with subsection (2) of that section (decision not to make a report where no useful purpose would be served).

(b) . . .

(8) The Chairman may exercise the power conferred by section 37(1), 48(1) or 64(1) of the Enterprise Act 2002 while a group is being constituted to perform a relevant general function of the Commission or, when it has been so constituted, before it has held its first meeting.

16 Chairmen of groups

The Chairman must appoint one of the members of a group to act as the chairman of the group.

17 Replacement of member of group

(1) If, during the proceedings of a group—

(a) a member of the group ceases to be a member of the Commission,

(b) the Chairman is satisfied that a member of the group will be unable for a substantial period to perform his duties as a member of the group, or

(c) it appears to the Chairman that because of a particular interest of a member of the group it is inappropriate for him to remain in the group,

the Chairman may appoint a replacement.

(2) The Chairman may also at any time appoint any reporting panel member to be an additional member of a group.

18 Attendance of other members

(1) At the invitation of the chairman of a group, any reporting panel member who is not a member of the group may attend meetings or otherwise take part in the proceedings of the group.

(2) But any person attending in response to such an invitation may not—

(a) vote in any proceedings of the group; or

(b) have a statement of his dissent from a conclusion of the group included in a report made by them.

(3) Nothing in sub-paragraph (1) is to be taken to prevent a group, or a member of a group, from consulting any member of the Commission with respect to any matter or question with which the group is concerned.

19 Procedure

(1) Subject to any special or general directions given by the Secretary of State, each group may determine its own procedure.

(2) Each group may, in particular, determine its quorum and determine—

(a) the extent, if any, to which persons interested or claiming to be interested in the subject-matter of the reference are allowed—

(i) to be present or to be heard, either by themselves or by their representatives;

(ii) to cross-examine witnesses; or

(iii) otherwise to take part; and

(b) the extent, if any, to which sittings of the group are to be held in public.

(3) In determining its procedure a group must have regard to any guidance issued by the Chairman.

(4) Before issuing any guidance for the purposes of this paragraph the Chairman must consult the members of the Commission.

(5) This paragraph does not apply to groups for which rules must be made under paragraph 19A.

19A

(1) The Chairman must make rules of procedure in relation to merger reference groups, market reference groups and special reference groups.

(2) Schedule 7A makes further provision about rules made under this paragraph but is not to be taken as restricting the Chairman's powers under this paragraph.

(3) The Chairman must publish rules made under this paragraph in such manner as he considers appropriate for the purpose of bringing them to the attention of those likely to be affected by them.

(4) The Chairman must consult the members of the Commission and such other persons as he considers appropriate before making rules under this paragraph.

(5) Rules under this paragraph may—
  (a) make different provision for different cases or different purposes;
  (b) be varied or revoked by subsequent rules made under this paragraph.

(6) Subject to rules made under this paragraph, each merger reference group, market reference group and special reference group may determine its own procedure.

(7) In determining how to proceed in accordance with rules made under this paragraph and in determining its procedure under sub-paragraph (6), a group must have regard to any guidance issued by the Chairman.

(8) Before issuing any guidance for the purposes of this paragraph the Chairman shall consult the members of the Commission and such other persons as he considers appropriate.

(9) In this paragraph and in Schedule 7A—
  'market reference group' means any group constituted in connection with a reference under section 131 or 132 of the Enterprise Act 2002 (including that section as it has effect by virtue of another enactment);
  'merger reference group' means any group constituted in connection with a reference under section 32 of the Water Industry Act 1991 (c 56) or section 22, 33, 45 or 62 of the Enterprise Act 2002; and
  'special reference group' means any group constituted in connection with a reference or (in the case of the Financial Services and Markets Act 2000 (c 8)) an investigation under—
    (a) section 11 of the Competition Act 1980 (c 21);
    (b) . . .
    (c) section 43 of the Airports Act 1986 (c 31);
    (d) section 24 or 41E of the Gas Act 1986 (c 44);
    (e) section 12 or 56C of the Electricity Act 1989 (c 29);
    (f) . . .
    (g) section 12 or 14 of the Water Industry Act 1991 (c 56);
    (h) article 15 of the Electricity (Northern Ireland) Order 1992 (SI 1992/231 (NI 1));
    (i) section 13 of, or Schedule 4A to, the Railways Act 1993 (c 43);
    (j) article 34 of the Airports (Northern Ireland) Order 1994 (SI 1994/426 (NI 1));
    (k) article 15 of the Gas (Northern Ireland) Order 1996 (SI 1996/275 (NI 2));
    (l) section 15 of the Postal Services Act 2000 (c 26);
    (m) section 162 or 306 of the Financial Services and Markets Act 2000 (c 8);
    (n) section 12 of the Transport Act 2000 (c 38); or
    (o) section 193 of the Communications Act 2003.

20 Effect of exercise of functions by group

(1) Subject to sub-paragraphs (2) to (9), anything done by or in relation to a group in, or in connection

with, the performance of functions to be performed by the group is to have the same effect as if done by or in relation to the Commission.

(2) For the purposes of Part 3 of the Enterprise Act 2002 (mergers) any decision of a group under section 35(1) or 36(1) of that Act (questions to be decided on non-public interest merger references) that there is an anti-competitive outcome is to be treated as a decision under that section that there is not an anti-competitive outcome if the decision is not that of at least two-thirds of the members of the group.

(3) For the purposes of Part 3 of the Act of 2002, if the decision is not that of at least two-thirds of the members of the group—

(a) any decision of a group under section 47 of that Act (questions to be decided on public interest merger references) that a relevant merger situation has been created is to be treated as a decision under that section that no such situation has been created;

(b) any decision of a group under section 47 of that Act that the creation of a relevant merger situation has resulted, or may be expected to result, in a substantial lessening of competition within any market or markets in the United Kingdom for goods or services is to be treated as a decision under that section that the creation of that situation has not resulted, or may be expected not to result, in such a substantial lessening of competition;

(c) any decision of a group under section 47 of that Act that arrangements are in progress or in contemplation which, if carried into effect, will result in the creation of a relevant merger situation is to be treated as a decision under that section that no such arrangements are in progress or in contemplation; and

(d) any decision of a group under section 47 of that Act that the creation of such a situation as is mentioned in paragraph (c) may be expected to result in a substantial lessening of competition within any market or markets in the United Kingdom for goods or services is to be treated as a decision under that section that the creation of that situation may be expected not to result in such a substantial lessening of competition.

(4) For the purposes of Part 3 of the Act of 2002, if the decision is not that of at least two-thirds of the members of the group—

(a) any decision of a group under section 63 of that Act (questions to be decided on special public interest merger references) that a special merger situation has been created is to be treated as a decision under that section that no such situation has been created; and

(b) any decision of a group under section 63 of that Act that arrangements are in progress or in contemplation which, if carried into effect, will result in the creation of a special merger situation is to be treated as a decision under that section that no such arrangements are in progress or in contemplation.

(5) For the purposes of Part 4 of the Act of 2002 (market investigations), if the decision is not that of at least two-thirds of the members of the group, any decision of a group under section 134 or 141 (questions to be decided on market investigation references) that a feature, or combination of features, of a relevant market prevents, restricts or distorts competition in connection with the supply or acquisition of any goods or services in the United Kingdom or a part of the United Kingdom is to be treated as a decision that the feature or (as the case may be) combination of features does not prevent, restrict or distort such competition.

(6) Accordingly, for the purposes of Part 4 of the Act of 2002, a group is to be treated as having decided under section 134 or 141 that there is no adverse effect on competition if—

(a) one or more than one decision of the group is to be treated as mentioned in sub-paragraph (5); and

(b) there is no other relevant decision of the group.

(7) In sub-paragraph (6) 'relevant decision' means a decision which is not to be treated as mentioned in sub-paragraph (5) and which is that a feature, or combination of features, of a relevant market prevents, restricts or distorts competition in connection with the supply or acquisition of any goods or services in the United Kingdom or a part of the United Kingdom.

(8) Expressions used in sub-paragraphs (2) to (7) shall be construed in accordance with Part 3 or (as the case may be) 4 of the Act of 2002.

(9) Sub-paragraph (1) is also subject to specific provision made by or under other enactments about decisions which are not decisions of at least two-thirds of the members of a group.

21 Casting votes

The chairman of a group is to have a casting vote on any question to be decided by the group.

22 Newspaper merger references

There are to be members of the Commission appointed by the Secretary of State to form a panel of persons available for selection as members of a group constituted in connection with a newspaper merger reference.

PART III

. . .

PART IV
MISCELLANEOUS

28 Disqualification of members for House of Commons

In Part II of Schedule 1 to the House of Commons Disqualification Act 1975 (bodies of which all members are disqualified) insert at the appropriate place—
'The Competition Commission'.

29 Disqualification of members for Northern Ireland Assembly

In Part II of Schedule 1 to the Northern Ireland Assembly Disqualification Act 1975 (bodies of which all members are disqualified) insert at the appropriate place—
'The Competition Commission'.

PART V
TRANSITIONAL PROVISIONS

30 Interpretation

In this Part of this Schedule—
'commencement date' means the date on which section 45 comes into force; and
'MMC' means the Monopolies and Mergers Commission.

31 Chairman

(1) The person who is Chairman of the MMC immediately before the commencement date is on that date to become both a member of the Commission and its chairman as if he had been duly appointed under paragraphs 2(1)(b) and 3.

(2) He is to hold office as Chairman of the Commission for the remainder of the period for which he was appointed as Chairman of the MMC and on the terms on which he was so appointed.

32 Deputy chairmen

The persons who are deputy chairmen of the MMC immediately before the commencement date are on that date to become deputy chairmen of the Commission as if they had been duly appointed under paragraph 3(2).

33 Reporting panel members

(1) The persons who are members of the MMC immediately before the commencement date are on that

date to become members of the Commission as if they had been duly appointed under paragraph 2(1)(b).

(2) Each of them is to hold office as a member for the remainder of the period for which he was appointed as a member of the MMC and on the terms on which he was so appointed.

34 Specialist panel members

(1) The persons who are members of the MMC immediately before the commencement date by virtue of appointments made under any of the enactments mentioned in paragraph 2(1)(d) are on that date to become members of the Commission as if they had been duly appointed to the Commission under the enactment in question.

(2) Each of them is to hold office as a member for such period and on such terms as the Secretary of State may determine.

35 Secretary

The person who is the secretary of the MMC immediately before the commencement date is on that date to become the secretary of the Commission as if duly appointed under paragraph 9, on the same terms and conditions.

36 Council

(1) The members who become deputy chairmen of the Commission under paragraph 32 are also to become members of the Council as if they had been duly appointed under paragraph 5(2)(c).

(2) Each of them is to hold office as a member of the Council for such period as the Secretary of State determines.

SCHEDULE 7A

THE COMPETITION COMMISSION:
PROCEDURAL RULES FOR MERGERS AND MARKET REFERENCES ETC

Section 45(7)

1

In this Schedule—

'market investigation' means an investigation carried out by a market reference group in connection with a reference under section 131 or 132 of the Enterprise Act 2002 (including that section as it has effect by virtue of another enactment);

'market reference group' has the meaning given by paragraph 19A(9) of Schedule 7 to this Act;

'merger investigation' means an investigation carried out by a merger reference group in connection with a reference under section 32 of the Water Industry Act 1991 (c 56) or section 22, 33, 45 or 62 of the Act of 2002;

'merger reference group' has the meaning given by paragraph 19A(9) of Schedule 7 to this Act;

'relevant group' means a market reference group, merger reference group or special reference group;

'special investigation' means an investigation carried out by a special reference group—

(a) in connection with a reference under a provision mentioned in any of paragraphs (a) to (l), (n) and (o) of the definition of 'special reference group' in paragraph 19A(9) of Schedule 7 to this Act; or

(b) under a provision mentioned in paragraph (m) of that definition; and

'special reference group' has the meaning given by paragraph 19A(9) of Schedule 7 to this Act.

2

Rules may make provision—

(a) for particular stages of a merger investigation, a market investigation or a special investigation to be dealt with in accordance with a timetable and for the revision of that timetable;

(b) as to the documents and information which must be given to a relevant group in connection with a merger investigation, a market investigation or a special investigation;

(c) as to the documents or information which a relevant group must give to other persons in connection with such an investigation.

3

Rules made by virtue of paragraph 2(a) and (b) may, in particular, enable or require a relevant group to disregard documents or information given after a particular date.

4

Rules made by virtue of paragraph 2(c) may, in particular, make provision for the notification or publication of, and for consultation about, provisional findings of a relevant group.

5

Rules may make provision as to the quorum of relevant groups.

6

Rules may make provision—

(a) as to the extent (if any) to which persons interested or claiming to be interested in a matter under consideration which is specified or described in the rules are allowed—

   (i) to be (either by themselves or by their representatives) present before a relevant group or heard by that group;

   (ii) to cross-examine witnesses; or

   (iii) otherwise to take part;

(b) as to the extent (if any) to which sittings of a relevant group are to be held in public; and

(c) generally in connection with any matters permitted by rules made under paragraph (a) or (b) (including, in particular, provision for a record of any hearings).

7

Rules may make provision for—

(a) the notification or publication of information in relation to merger investigations, market investigations or special investigations;

(b) consultation about such investigations.

SCHEDULE 8
APPEALS

Sections 46(5) and 48(4)

PART I
GENERAL

1 ...

2 General procedure

(1) An appeal to the Tribunal under section 46 or 47 must be made by sending a notice of appeal to it within the specified period.

(2) The notice of appeal must set out the grounds of appeal in sufficient detail to indicate—

   (a) under which provision of this Act the appeal is brought;

   (b) to what extent (if any) the appellant contends that the decision against, or with respect to which, the appeal is brought was based on an error of fact or was wrong in law; and

   (c) to what extent (if any) the appellant is appealing against the OFT's exercise of its discretion in making the disputed decision.

(3) The Tribunal may give an appellant leave to amend the grounds of appeal identified in the notice of appeal.

(4) In this paragraph references to the Tribunal are to the Tribunal as constituted (in accordance with section 14 of the Enterprise Act 2002) for the purposes of the proceedings in question.

(5) Nothing in this paragraph restricts the power under section 15 of the Enterprise Act 2002 (Tribunal rules) to make provision as to the manner of instituting proceedings before the Tribunal.

3 Decisions of the Tribunal

(A1) This paragraph applies to any appeal under section 46 or 47 other than—
- (a) an appeal under section 46 against, or with respect to, a decision of the kind specified in subsection (3)(g) or (h) of that section, and
- (b) an appeal under section 47(1)(b) or (c).

(1) The Tribunal must determine the appeal on the merits by reference to the grounds of appeal set out in the notice of appeal.

(2) The Tribunal may confirm or set aside the decision which is the subject of the appeal, or any part of it, and may—
- (a) remit the matter to the OFT,
- (b) impose or revoke, or vary the amount of, a penalty,
- (c) . . .
- (d) give such directions, or take such other steps, as the OFT could itself have given or taken, or
- (e) make any other decision which the OFT could itself have made.

(3) Any decision of the Tribunal on an appeal has the same effect, and may be enforced in the same manner, as a decision of the OFT.

(4) If the Tribunal confirms the decision which is the subject of the appeal it may nevertheless set aside any finding of fact on which the decision was based.

3A

(1) This paragraph applies to—
- (a) any appeal under section 46 against, or with respect to, a decision of the kind specified in subsection (3)(g) or (h) of that section, and
- (b) any appeal under section 47(1)(b) or (c).

(2) The Tribunal must, by reference to the grounds of appeal set out in the notice of appeal, determine the appeal by applying the same principles as would be applied by a court on an application for judicial review.

(3) The Tribunal may—
- (a) dismiss the appeal or quash the whole or part of the decision to which it relates; and
- (b) where it quashes the whole or part of that decision, remit the matter back to the OFT with a direction to reconsider and make a new decision in accordance with the ruling of the Tribunal.

4 . . .

Part II

. . .

Schedule 9
Oft's Rules

Section 51(2)

1 General

In this Schedule 'rules' means rules made by the OFT under section 51.

2 . . .

3 ...

4 ...

5 Decisions

(1) Rules may make provision as to—
  (a) the form and manner in which notice of any decision is to be given;
  (b) the person or persons to whom the notice is to be given;
  (c) the manner in which the OFT is to publish a decision;
  (d) the procedure to be followed if—
    (i) the OFT takes further action with respect to an agreement after having decided that it does not infringe the Chapter I prohibition;
    (ii) the OFT takes further action with respect to an agreement after having decided that it does not infringe the prohibition in Article 81(1);
    (iii) the OFT takes further action with respect to conduct after having decided that it does not infringe the Chapter II prohibition; or
    (iv) the OFT takes further action with respect to conduct after having decided that it does not infringe the prohibition in Article 82.
(2) In this paragraph 'decision' means a decision of the OFT—
  (a) as to whether or not an agreement has infringed the Chapter I prohibition;
  (b) as to whether or not an agreement has infringed the prohibition in Article 81(1);
  (c) as to whether or not conduct has infringed the Chapter II prohibition; or
  (d) as to whether or not conduct has infringed the prohibition in Article 82.

6 ...

7 ...

8 Block exemptions

Rules may make provision as to—
(a) the procedure to be followed by the OFT if it cancels a block exemption;
(b) the procedure to be followed by the OFT if it withdraws the benefit of a regulation of the Commission pursuant to Article 29(2) of the EC Competition Regulation.

9 Parallel exemptions

Rules may make provision as to—
(a) the circumstances in which the OFT may—
    (i) impose conditions or obligations in relation to a parallel exemption,
    (ii) vary or remove any such conditions or obligations,
    (iii) impose additional conditions or obligations, or
    (iv) cancel the exemption;
(b) as to the procedure to be followed by the OFT if it is acting under section 10(5);
(c) the form and manner in which notice of a decision to take any of the steps in sub-paragraph (a) is to be given;
(d) the circumstances in which an exemption may be cancelled with retrospective effect.

10 Section 11 exemptions

Rules may, with respect to any exemption provided by regulations made under section 11, make provision similar to that made with respect to parallel exemptions by section 10 or by rules under paragraph 9.

11 Directions withdrawing exclusions

Rules may make provision as to the factors which the OFT may take into account when it is determining the date on which a direction given under paragraph 4(1) of Schedule 1 or paragraph 9(3) of Schedule 3 is to have effect.

12 Disclosure of information

(1) Rules may make provision as to the circumstances in which the OFT is to be required, before disclosing information given to it by a third party in connection with the exercise of any of the OFT's functions under Part I, to give notice, and an opportunity to make representations, to the third party.

(2) In relation to the agreement (or conduct) concerned, 'third party' means a person who is not a party to the agreement (or who has not engaged in the conduct).

13 Applications under section 47

Rules may make provision as to—
(a) the period within which an application under section 47(1) must be made;
(b) the procedure to be followed by the OFT in dealing with the application;
(c) the person or persons to whom notice of the OFT's response to the application is to be given.

14 Enforcement

Rules may make provision as to the procedure to be followed when the OFT takes action under any of sections 32 to 40 with respect to the enforcement of the provisions of this Part.

SCHEDULE 10
REGULATORS

Sections 54 and 66(5)

PART I

. . .

PART II
THE PROHIBITIONS

2 . . .

3 Gas

(1) In consequence of the repeal by this Act of provisions of the Competition Act 1980, the functions transferred by subsection (3) of section 36A of the Gas Act 1986 (functions with respect to competition) are no longer exercisable by the Director General of Gas Supply.

(2) Accordingly, that Act is amended as follows.

(3) . . .

(4) Section 36A is amended as follows.

(5) For subsection (3) substitute—

'(3) The Director shall be entitled to exercise, concurrently with the Director General of Fair Trading, the functions of that Director under the provisions of Part I of the Competition Act 1998 (other than sections 38(1) to (6) and 51), so far as relating to—

(a) agreements, decisions or concerted practices of the kind mentioned in section 2(1) of that Act, or

(b) conduct of the kind mentioned in section 18(1) of that Act,

which relate to the carrying on of activities to which this subsection applies.

(3A) So far as necessary for the purposes of, or in connection with, the provisions of subsection (3) above, references in Part I of the Competition Act 1998 to the Director General of Fair Trading are to be read as including a reference to the Director (except in sections 38(1) to (6), 51, 52(6) and (8) and 54 of that Act and in any other provision of that Act where the context otherwise requires).'

(6) . . .

(7) In subsection (6), omit 'or (3)'.

(8) In subsection (7), for paragraph (b) substitute—

'(b) Part I of the Competition Act 1998 (other than sections 38(1) to (6) and 51),'.

(9) . . .

(10). . .

(11). . .

4 Electricity

(1) In consequence of the repeal by this Act of provisions of the Competition Act 1980, the functions transferred by subsection (3) of section 43 of the Electricity Act 1989 (functions with respect to competition) are no longer exercisable by the Director General of Electricity Supply.

(2) Accordingly, that Act is amended as follows.

(3) . . .

(4) Section 43 is amended as follows.

(5) For subsection (3) substitute—

'(3) The Director shall be entitled to exercise, concurrently with the Director General of Fair Trading, the functions of that Director under the provisions of Part I of the Competition Act 1998 (other than sections 38(1) to (6) and 51), so far as relating to—

(a) agreements, decisions or concerted practices of the kind mentioned in section 2(1) of that Act, or

(b) conduct of the kind mentioned in section 18(1) of that Act,

which relate to commercial activities connected with the generation, transmission or supply of electricity.

(3A) So far as necessary for the purposes of, or in connection with, the provisions of subsection (3) above, references in Part I of the Competition Act 1998 to the Director General of Fair Trading are to be read as including a reference to the Director (except in sections 38(1) to (6), 51, 52(6) and (8) and 54 of that Act and in any other provision of that Act where the context otherwise requires).'

(6) . . .

(7) In subsection (5), omit 'or (3)'.

(8) In subsection (6), for paragraph (b) substitute—

'(b) Part I of the Competition Act 1998 (other than sections 38(1) to (6) and 51),'.

(9) . . .

5 Water

(1) In consequence of the repeal by this Act of provisions of the Competition Act 1980, the functions exercisable by virtue of subsection (3) of section 31 of the Water Industry Act 1991 (functions of Director with respect to competition) are no longer exercisable by the Director General of Water Services.

(2) Accordingly, that Act is amended as follows.

(3) In section 2 (general duties with respect to water industry), in subsection (6)(a), at the beginning, insert 'subject to subsection (6A) below'.

(4) In section 2, after subsection (6), insert—

'(6A) Subsections (2) to (4) above do not apply in relation to anything done by the Director in the exercise of functions assigned to him by section 31(3) below ('Competition Act functions').

(6B) The Director may nevertheless, when exercising any Competition Act function, have regard to any matter in respect of which a duty is imposed by any of subsections (2) to (4) above, if it is a matter to which the Director General of Fair Trading could have regard when exercising that function.'

(5) Section 31 is amended as follows.

(6) For subsection (3) substitute—

'(3) The Director shall be entitled to exercise, concurrently with the Director General of Fair

Trading, the functions of that Director under the provisions of Part I of the Competition Act 1998 (other than sections 38(1) to (6) and 51), so far as relating to—

(a) agreements, decisions or concerted practices of the kind mentioned in section 2(1) of that Act, or

(b) conduct of the kind mentioned in section 18(1) of that Act,

which relate to commercial activities connected with the supply of water or securing a supply of water or with the provision or securing of sewerage services.'

(7) ...

(8) After subsection (4), insert—

'(4A) So far as necessary for the purposes of, or in connection with, the provisions of subsection (3) above, references in Part I of the Competition Act 1998 to the Director General of Fair Trading are to be read as including a reference to the Director (except in sections 38(1) to (6), 51, 52(6) and (8) and 54 of that Act and in any other provision of that Act where the context otherwise requires).'

(9) ...

(10) ...

(11) In subsection (7), omit 'or (3)'.

(12) In subsection (8), for paragraph (b) substitute—

'(b) Part I of the Competition Act 1998 (other than sections 38(1) to (6) and 51),'.

(13) ...

6 Railways

(1) In consequence of the repeal by this Act of provisions of the Competition Act 1980, the functions transferred by subsection (3) of section 67 of the Railways Act 1993 (respective functions of the Regulator and the Director etc) are no longer exercisable by the Office of Rail Regulation.

(2) Accordingly, that Act is amended as follows.

(3) In section 4 (general duties of the Secretary of State and the Regulator), after subsection (7), insert—

'(7A) Subsections (1) to (6) above do not apply in relation to anything done by the Regulator in the exercise of functions assigned to him by section 67(3) below ('Competition Act functions').

(7B) The Regulator may nevertheless, when exercising any Competition Act function, have regard to any matter in respect of which a duty is imposed by any of subsections (1) to (6) above, if it is a matter to which the Director General of Fair Trading could have regard when exercising that function.'

(4) Section 67 is amended as follows.

(5) For subsection (3) substitute—

'(3) The Regulator shall be entitled to exercise, concurrently with the Director, the functions of the Director under the provisions of Part I of the Competition Act 1998 (other than sections 38(1) to (6) and 51), so far as relating to—

(a) agreements, decisions or concerted practices of the kind mentioned in section 2(1) of that Act, or

(b) conduct of the kind mentioned in section 18(1) of that Act,

which relate to the supply of railway services.

(3A) So far as necessary for the purposes of, or in connection with, the provisions of subsection (3) above, references in Part I of the Competition Act 1998 to the Director are to be read as including a reference to the Regulator (except in sections 38(1) to (6), 51, 52(6) and (8) and 54 of that Act and in any other provision of that Act where the context otherwise requires).'

(6) ...

(7) In subsection (6)(a), omit 'or (3)'.

(8) In subsection (8), for paragraph (b) substitute—

'(b) Part I of the Competition Act 1998 (other than sections 38(1) to (6) and 51),'.

(9) ...

Part III
The Prohibitions: Northern Ireland

7 Electricity

(1) In consequence of the repeal by this Act of provisions of the Competition Act 1980, the functions transferred by paragraph (3) of Article 46 of the Electricity (Northern Ireland) Order 1992 (functions with respect to competition) are no longer exercisable by the Director General of Electricity Supply for Northern Ireland.

(2) Accordingly, that Order is amended as follows.

(3) . . .

(4) Article 46 is amended as follows.

(5) For paragraph (3) substitute—

'(3) The Director shall be entitled to exercise, concurrently with the Director General of Fair Trading, the functions of that Director under the provisions of Part I of the Competition Act 1998 (other than sections 38(1) to (6) and 51), so far as relating to—

(a) agreements, decisions or concerted practices of the kind mentioned in section 2(1) of that Act, or

(b) conduct of the kind mentioned in section 18(1) of that Act,

which relate to commercial activities connected with the generation, transmission or supply of electricity.

(3A) So far as necessary for the purposes of, or in connection with, the provisions of paragraph (3), references in Part I of the Competition Act 1998 to the Director General of Fair Trading are to be read as including a reference to the Director (except in sections 38(1) to (6), 51, 52(6) and (8) and 54 of that Act and in any other provision of that Act where the context otherwise requires).'

(6) . . .

(7) In paragraph (5), omit 'or (3)'.

(8) In paragraph (6), for sub-paragraph (b) substitute—

'(b) Part I of the Competition Act 1998 (other than sections 38(1) to (6) and 51),'.

(9) . . .

8 Gas

(1) In consequence of the repeal by this Act of provisions of the Competition Act 1980, the functions transferred by paragraph (3) of Article 23 of the Gas (Northern Ireland) Order 1996 (functions with respect to competition) are no longer exercisable by the Director General of Gas for Northern Ireland.

(2) Accordingly, that Order is amended as follows.

(3) . . .

(4) Article 23 is amended as follows.

(5) For paragraph (3) substitute—

'(3) The Director shall be entitled to exercise, concurrently with the Director General of Fair Trading, the functions of that Director under the provisions of Part I of the Competition Act 1998 (other than sections 38(1) to (6) and 51), so far as relating to—

(a) agreements, decisions or concerted practices of the kind mentioned in section 2(1) of that Act, or

(b) conduct of the kind mentioned in section 18(1) of that Act, connected with the conveyance, storage or supply of gas.

(3A) So far as necessary for the purposes of, or in connection with, the provisions of paragraph (3), references in Part I of the Competition Act 1998 to the Director General of Fair Trading are to be read as including a reference to the Director (except in sections 38(1) to (6), 51, 52(6) and (8) and 54 of that Act and in any other provision of that Act where the context otherwise requires).'

(6) ...

(7) In paragraph (5), omit 'or (3)'.

(8) In paragraph (6), for sub-paragraph (b) substitute—

'(b) Part I of the Competition Act 1998 (other than sections 38(1) to (6) and 51),'.

(9) ...

(10) ...

(11) ...

PART IV
UTILITIES: MINOR AND CONSEQUENTIAL AMENDMENTS

9 The Telecommunications Act 1984 (c 12)

(1) The Telecommunications Act 1984 is amended as follows.

(2) ...

(3) ...

(4) ...

(5) ...

(6) ...

(7) In section 101(3) (general restrictions on disclosure of information)—

(a) omit paragraphs (d) and (e) (which refer to the Restrictive Trade Practices Act 1976 and the Resale Prices Act 1976);

(b) after paragraph (m), insert—

'(n) the Competition Act 1998'.

(8) At the end of section 101, insert—

'(6) Information obtained by the Director in the exercise of functions which are exercisable concurrently with the Director General of Fair Trading under Part I of the Competition Act 1998 is subject to sections 55 and 56 of that Act (disclosure) and not to subsections (1) to (5) of this section.'

10 The Gas Act 1986 (c 44)

(1) The Gas Act 1986 is amended as follows.

(2) ...

(3) In section 25, omit subsection (2) (which falls with the repeal of the Restrictive Trade Practices Act 1976).

(4) ...

(5) In section 28 (orders for securing compliance with certain provisions), in subsection (5), after paragraph (aa), omit 'or' and after paragraph (b), insert 'or (c) that the most appropriate way of proceeding is under the Competition Act 1998.'

(6) In section 42(3) (general restrictions on disclosure of information)—

(a) omit paragraphs (e) and (f) (which refer to the Restrictive Trade Practices Act 1976 and the Resale Prices Act 1976);

(b) after paragraph (n), insert—

'(o) the Competition Act 1998'.

(7) At the end of section 42, insert—

'(7) Information obtained by the Director in the exercise of functions which are exercisable concurrently with the Director General of Fair Trading under Part I of the Competition Act 1998 is subject to sections 55 and 56 of that Act (disclosure) and not to subsections (1) to (6) of this section.'

11 The Water Act 1989 (c 15)

In section 174(3) of the Water Act 1989 (general restrictions on disclosure of information)—

(a) omit paragraphs (d) and (e) (which refer to the Restrictive Trade Practices Act 1976 and the Resale Prices Act 1976);

(b) after paragraph (l), insert—

'(ll) the Competition Act 1998'.

12 The Electricity Act 1989 (c 29)

(1) The Electricity Act 1989 is amended as follows.

(2) In section 12 (modification references to Competition Commission), for subsections (8) and (9) substitute—

'(8) The provisions mentioned in subsection (8A) are to apply in relation to references under this section as if—

(a) the functions of the Competition Commission in relation to those references were functions under the 1973 Act;

(b) the expression 'merger reference' included a reference under this section;

(c) in section 70 of the 1973 Act—

(i) references to the Secretary of State were references to the Director, and

(ii) the reference to three months were a reference to six months.

(8A) The provisions are—

(a) sections 70 (time limit for report on merger) and 85 (attendance of witnesses and production of documents) of the 1973 Act;

(b) Part II of Schedule 7 to the Competition Act 1998 (performance of the Competition Commission's general functions); and

(c) section 24 of the 1980 Act (modification of provisions about performance of such functions).

(9) For the purposes of references under this section, the Secretary of State is to appoint not less than eight members of the Competition Commission.

(9A) In selecting a group to perform the Commission's functions in relation to any such reference, the chairman of the Commission must select up to three of the members appointed under subsection (9) to be members of the group.'

(3) In section 13, omit subsection (2) (which falls with the repeal of the Restrictive Trade Practices Act 1976).

(4) . . .

(5) In section 25 (orders for securing compliance), in subsection (5), after paragraph (b), omit 'or' and after paragraph (c), insert 'or (d) that the most appropriate way of proceeding is under the Competition Act 1998.'

(6) . . .

(7) In section 57(3) (general restrictions on disclosure of information)—

(a) omit paragraphs (d) and (e) (which refer to the Restrictive Trade Practices Act 1976 and the Resale Prices Act 1976);

(b) after paragraph (no), insert—

'(nop) the Competition Act 1998'.

(8) At the end of section 57, insert—

'(7) Information obtained by the Director in the exercise of functions which are exercisable concurrently with the Director General of Fair Trading under Part I of the Competition Act 1998 is subject to sections 55 and 56 of that Act (disclosure) and not to subsections (1) to (6) of this section.'

13 The Water Industry Act 1991 (c 56)

(1) The Water Industry Act 1991 is amended as follows.

(2) . . .

(3) . . .

(4) In section 15, omit subsection (2) (which falls with the repeal of the Restrictive Trade Practices Act 1976).

(5) In section 17 (modification by order under other enactments)—

    (a) in subsection (1), omit paragraph (b) and the 'or' immediately before it;

    (b) in subsection (2)—

        (i) after paragraph (a), insert 'or';

        (ii) omit paragraph (c) and the 'or' immediately before it;

    (c) in subsection (4), omit 'or the 1980 Act'.

(6) In section 19 (exceptions to duty to enforce), after subsection (1), insert—

    '(1A) The Director shall not be required to make an enforcement order, or to confirm a provisional enforcement order, if he is satisfied that the most appropriate way of proceeding is under the Competition Act 1998.'

(7) In section 19(3), after 'subsection (1) above', insert 'or, in the case of the Director, is satisfied as mentioned in subsection (1A) above,'.

(8) . . .

(9) After section 206(9) (restriction on disclosure of information), insert—

    '(9A) Information obtained by the Director in the exercise of functions which are exercisable concurrently with the Director General of Fair Trading under Part I of the Competition Act 1998 is subject to sections 55 and 56 of that Act (disclosure) and not to subsections (1) to (9) of this section.'

(10) In Schedule 15 (disclosure of information), in Part II (enactments in respect of which disclosure may be made)—

    (a) omit the entries relating to the Restrictive Trade Practices Act 1976 and the Resale Prices Act 1976;

    (b) after the entry relating to the Railways Act 1993, insert the entry—

    'The Competition Act 1998'.

14 The Water Resources Act 1991 (c 57)

In Schedule 24 to the Water Resources Act 1991 (disclosure of information), in Part II (enactments in respect of which disclosure may be made)—

(a) omit the entries relating to the Restrictive Trade Practices Act 1976 and the Resale Prices Act 1976;

(b) after the entry relating to the Coal Industry Act 1994, insert the entry—

    'The Competition Act 1998'.

15 The Railways Act 1993 (c 43)

(1) The Railways Act 1993 is amended as follows.

(2) . . .

(3) In section 14, omit subsection (2) (which falls with the repeal of the Restrictive Trade Practices Act 1976).

(4) . . .

(5) In section 22, after subsection (6), insert—

    '(6A) Neither the Director General of Fair Trading nor the Regulator may exercise, in respect of an access agreement, the powers given by section 32 (enforcement directions) or section 35(2) (interim directions) of the Competition Act 1998.

    (6B) Subsection (6A) does not apply to the exercise of the powers given by section 35(2) in respect of conduct—

    (a) which is connected with an access agreement; and

    (b) in respect of which section 35(1)(b) of that Act applies.'

(6) In section 55 (orders for securing compliance), after subsection (5), insert—

    '(5A) The Regulator shall not make a final order, or make or confirm a provisional order, in relation to a licence holder or person under closure restrictions if he is satisfied that the most appropriate way of proceeding is under the Competition Act 1998.'

(7) In section 55—

    (a) . . .

    (b) in subsection (11), for 'subsection (10)' substitute 'subsections (5A) and (10)'.

(8) Omit section 131 (modification of Restrictive Trade Practices Act 1976).

(9) In section 145(3) (general restrictions on disclosure of information)—

    (a) omit paragraphs (d) and (e) (which refer to the Restrictive Trade Practices Act 1976 and the Resale Prices Act 1976);

    (b) after paragraph (q), insert—

       '(qq) the Competition Act 1998.'

(10) After section 145(6), insert—

    '(6A) Information obtained by the Regulator in the exercise of functions which are exercisable concurrently with the Director General of Fair Trading under Part I of the Competition Act 1998 is subject to sections 55 and 56 of that Act (disclosure) and not to subsections (1) to (6) of this section.'

16 The Channel Tunnel Rail Link Act 1996 (c 61)

(1) The Channel Tunnel Rail Link Act 1996 is amended as follows.

(2) In section 21 (duties as to exercise of regulatory functions), in subsection (6), at the end of the paragraph about regulatory functions, insert—

    'other than any functions assigned to him by virtue of section 67(3) of that Act ('Competition Act functions').

    (7) The Regulator may, when exercising any Competition Act function, have regard to any matter to which he would have regard if—

    (a) he were under the duty imposed by subsection (1) or (2) above in relation to that function; and

    (b) the matter is one to which the Director General of Fair Trading could have regard if he were exercising that function.'

(3) In section 22 (restriction of functions in relation to competition etc), for subsection (3) substitute—

    '(3) The Rail Regulator shall not be entitled to exercise any functions assigned to him by section 67(3) of the Railways Act 1993 (by virtue of which he exercises concurrently with the Director General of Fair Trading certain functions under Part I of the Competition Act 1998 so far as relating to matters connected with the supply of railway services) in relation to—

    (a) any agreements, decisions or concerted practices of the kind mentioned in section 2(1) of that Act that have been entered into or taken by, or

    (b) any conduct of the kind mentioned in section 18(1) of that Act that has been engaged in by,

    a rail link undertaker in connection with the supply of railway services, so far as relating to the rail link.'

PART V

MINOR AND CONSEQUENTIAL AMENDMENTS: NORTHERN IRELAND

17 The Electricity (Northern Ireland) Order 1992

(1) The Electricity (Northern Ireland) Order 1992 is amended as follows.

(2) In Article 15 (modification references to Competition Commission), for paragraphs (8) and (9) substitute—

    '(8) The provisions mentioned in paragraph (8A) are to apply in relation to references under this Article as if—

    (a) the functions of the Competition Commission in relation to those references were functions under the 1973 Act;

    (b) 'merger reference' included a reference under this Article;

    (c) in section 70 of the 1973 Act—

        (i)   references to the Secretary of State were references to the Director, and

        (ii) the reference to three months were a reference to six months.

    (8A) The provisions are—

    (a) sections 70 (time limit for report on merger) and 85 (attendance of witnesses and production of documents) of the 1973 Act;

    (b) Part II of Schedule 7 to the Competition Act 1998 (performance of the Competition Commission's general functions); and

    (c) section 24 of the 1980 Act (modification of provisions about performance of such functions).

    (9) The Secretary of State may appoint members of the Competition Commission for the purposes of references under this Article.

    (9A) In selecting a group to perform the Commission's functions in relation to any such reference, the chairman of the Commission must select up to three of the members appointed under paragraph (9) to be members of the group.'

(3) In Article 16, omit paragraph (2) (which falls with the repeal of the Restrictive Trade Practices Act 1976).

(4) In Article 18 (modification by order under other statutory provisions)—

    (a) in paragraph (1), omit sub-paragraph (b) and the 'or' immediately before it;

    (b) in paragraph (2)—

        (i)   after sub-paragraph (a), insert 'or';

        (ii) omit sub-paragraph (c) and the 'or' immediately before it;

    (c) in paragraph (3), omit 'or the 1980 Act'.

(5) . . .

(6) . . .

(7) . . .

(8) . . .

(9) In Schedule 12, omit paragraph 16 (which amends the Restrictive Trade Practices Act 1976).

18 The Gas (Northern Ireland) Order 1996

(1) The Gas (Northern Ireland) Order 1996 is amended as follows.

(2) . . .

(3) In Article 16, omit paragraph (2) (which falls with the repeal of the Restrictive Trade Practices Act 1976).

(4) In Article 18 (modification by order under other statutory provisions)—

    (a) in paragraph (1), omit sub-paragraph (b) and the 'or' immediately before it;

    (b) in paragraph (3)—

        (i)   after sub-paragraph (a), insert 'or';

        (ii) omit sub-paragraph (c) and the 'or' immediately before it;

    (c) in paragraph (5), omit 'or the 1980 Act'.

(5) . . .

(6) . . .

(7) . . .

SCHEDULE II

. . .

SCHEDULE 12
MINOR AND CONSEQUENTIAL AMENDMENTS

Section 74(1)

1 The Fair Trading Act 1973 (c 41)

(1) The Fair Trading Act 1973 is amended as follows.

(2) Omit section 4 and Schedule 3 (which make provision in respect of the Monopolies and Mergers Commission).

(3) Omit—

    (a) section 10(2),

    (b) section 54(5),

    (c) section 78(3),

    (d) paragraph 3(1) and (2) of Schedule 8,

    (which fall with the repeal of the Restrictive Trade Practices Act 1976).

(4) . . .

(5) . . .

(6) . . .

(7) . . .

(8) Omit section 45 (power of the Director to require information about complex monopoly situations).

(9) . . .

(10) . . .

(11) . . .

(12) . . .

(13) . . .

(14) . . .

(15) In section 135(1) (financial provisions)—

    (a) in the words before paragraph (a) and in paragraph (b), omit 'or the Commission'; and

    (b) omit paragraph (a).

2 The Energy Act 1976 (c 76)

In the Energy Act 1976, omit section 5 (temporary relief from restrictive practices law in relation to certain agreements connected with petroleum).

3 . . .

4 The Competition Act 1980 (c 21)

(1) The Competition Act 1980 is amended as follows.

(2) In section 11(8) (public bodies and other persons referred to the Commission), omit paragraph (b) and the 'and' immediately before it.

(3) . . .

(4) . . .

(5) In section 15 (special provisions for agricultural schemes) omit subsections (2)(b), (3) and (4).

(6) In section 16 (reports), omit subsection (3).

(7) In section 17 (publication etc of reports)—

    (a) in subsections (1) and (3) to (5), omit '8(1)';

    (b) in subsection (2), omit '8(1) or'; and

    (c) in subsection (6), for 'sections 9, 10 or' substitute 'section'.

701

(8) In section 19(3) (restriction on disclosure of information), omit paragraphs (d) and (e).

(9) . . .

(10) . . .

(11) Omit section 22 (which amends the Fair Trading Act 1973).

(12) . . .

(13) Omit sections 25 to 30 (amendments of the Restrictive Trade Practices Act 1976).

(14) In section 31 (orders and regulations)—

    (a) omit subsection (2); and

    (b) in subsection (3), omit '10'.

(15) In section 33 (short title etc)—

    (a) . . .

    (b) omit subsections (3) and (4).

5 Magistrates' Courts (Northern Ireland) Order 1981 (SI 1981/1675 (NI 26))

In Schedule 6 to the Magistrates' Courts (Northern Ireland) Order 1981, omit paragraphs 42 and 43 (which amend the Restrictive Trade Practices Act 1976).

6 Agricultural Marketing (Northern Ireland) Order 1982 (SI 1982/1080 (NI 12))

In Schedule 8 to the Agricultural Marketing (Northern Ireland) Order 1982—

(a) omit the entry relating to paragraph 16(2) of Schedule 3 to the Fair Trading Act 1973; and

(b) in the entry relating to the Competition Act 1980—

    (i) for 'sections' substitute 'section';

    (ii) omit 'and 15(3)'.

7 . . .

8 The Financial Services Act 1986 (c 60)

In Schedule 11 to the Financial Services Act 1986, in paragraph 12—

(a) in sub-paragraph (1), omit '126';

(b) omit sub-paragraph (2).

9 The Companies Consolidation (Consequential Provisions) (Northern Ireland) Order 1986 (SI 1986/1035 (NI 9))

In Part II of Schedule 1 to the Companies Consolidation (Consequential Provisions)(Northern Ireland) Order 1986, omit the entries relating to the Restrictive Trade Practices Act 1976 and the Resale Prices Act 1976.

10 . . .

11 . . .

12 The Road Traffic (Consequential Provisions) Act 1988 (c 54)

In Schedule 3 to the Road Traffic (Consequential Provisions) Act 1988 (consequential amendments), omit paragraph 19.

13 The Companies Act 1989 (c 40)

In Schedule 20 to the Companies Act 1989 (amendments about mergers and related matters), omit paragraphs 21 to 24.

14 . . .

15 The Tribunals and Inquiries Act 1992 (c 53)

In Schedule 1 to the Tribunals and Inquiries Act 1992 (tribunals under the supervision of the Council on Tribunals), after paragraph 9, insert—

'Competition 9A An appeal tribunal established under section 48 of the Competition Act 1998.'

16 ...

17 ...

18 The Coal Industry Act 1994 (c 21)

In section 59(4) of the Coal Industry Act 1994 (information to be kept confidential by the Coal Authority)—

(a) omit paragraphs (e) and (f); and

(b) after paragraph (m), insert—

'(n) the Competition Act 1998.'

19 The Deregulation and Contracting Out Act 1994 (c 40)

(1) The Deregulation and Contracting Out Act 1994 is amended as follows.

(2) Omit—

    (a) section 10 (restrictive trade practices: non-notifiable agreements); and

    (b) section 11 (registration of commercially sensitive information).

(3) In section 12 (anti-competitive practices: competition references), omit subsections (1) to (6).

(4) In Schedule 4, omit paragraph 1.

(5) In Schedule 11 (miscellaneous deregulatory provisions: consequential amendments), in paragraph 4, omit sub-paragraphs (3) to (7).

20 ...

21 The Broadcasting Act 1996 (c 55)

In section 77 of the Broadcasting Act 1996 (which modifies the Restrictive Trade Practices Act 1976 in its application to agreements relating to Channel 3 news provision), omit subsection (2).

SCHEDULE 13

TRANSITIONAL PROVISIONS AND SAVINGS

Section 74(2)

PART I

GENERAL

1 Interpretation

(1) In this Schedule—

    'RPA' means the Resale Prices Act 1976;

    'RTPA' means the Restrictive Trade Practices Act 1976;

    'continuing proceedings' has the meaning given by paragraph 15;

    'the Court' means the Restrictive Practices Court;

    'Director' means the Director General of Fair Trading;

    'document' includes information recorded in any form;

    'enactment date' means the date on which this Act is passed;

    'information' includes estimates and forecasts;

    'interim period' means the period beginning on the enactment date and ending immediately before the starting date;

    'prescribed' means prescribed by an order made by the Secretary of State;

'regulator' means any person mentioned in paragraphs (a) to (g) of paragraph 1 of Schedule 10 and the Civil Aviation Authority;

'starting date' means the date on which section 2 comes into force;

'transitional period' means the transitional period provided for in Chapters III and IV of Part IV of this Schedule.

(2) Sections 30, 44, 51, 53, 55, 56, 57 and 59(3) and (4) and paragraph 12 of Schedule 9 ('the applied provisions') apply for the purposes of this Schedule as they apply for the purposes of Part I of this Act.

(3) Section 2(5) applies for the purposes of any provisions of this Schedule which are concerned with the operation of the Chapter I prohibition as it applies for the purposes of Part I of this Act.

(4) In relation to any of the matters in respect of which a regulator may exercise powers as a result of paragraph 35(1), the applied provisions are to have effect as if references to the Director included references to the regulator.

(5) The fact that to a limited extent the Chapter I prohibition does not apply to an agreement, because a transitional period is provided by virtue of this Schedule, does not require those provisions of the agreement in respect of which there is a transitional period to be disregarded when considering whether the agreement infringes the prohibition for other reasons.

2 General power to make transitional provision and savings

(1) Nothing in this Schedule affects the power of the Secretary of State under section 75 to make transitional provisions or savings.

(2) An order under that section may modify any provision made by this Schedule.

3 Advice and information

(1) The Director may publish advice and information explaining provisions of this Schedule to persons who are likely to be affected by them.

(2) Any advice or information published by the Director under this paragraph is to be published in such form and manner as he considers appropriate.

Part II

During the Interim Period

4 Block exemptions

(1) The Secretary of State may, at any time during the interim period, make one or more orders for the purpose of providing block exemptions which are effective on the starting date.

(2) An order under this paragraph has effect as if properly made under section 6.

5 Certain agreements to be non-notifiable agreements

An agreement which—

(a) is made during the interim period, and

(b) satisfies the conditions set out in paragraphs (a), (c) and (d) of section 27A(1) of the RTPA,

is to be treated as a non-notifiable agreement for the purposes of RTPA.

6 Application of RTPA during the interim period

In relation to agreements made during the interim period—

(a) the Director is no longer under the duty to take proceedings imposed by section 1(2)(c) of the RTPA but may continue to do so;

(b) section 21 of that Act has effect as if subsections (1) and (2) were omitted; and

(c) section 35(1) of that Act has effect as if the words 'or within such further time as the Director may, upon application made within that time, allow' were omitted.

7 Guidance

(1) Sub-paragraphs (2) to (4) apply in relation to agreements made during the interim period.

(2) An application may be made to the Director in anticipation of the coming into force of section 13 in accordance with directions given by the Director and such an application is to have effect on and after the starting date as if properly made under section 13.

(3) The Director may, in response to such an application—

(a) give guidance in anticipation of the coming into force of section 2; or

(b) on and after the starting date, give guidance under section 15 as if the application had been properly made under section 13.

(4) Any guidance so given is to have effect on and after the starting date as if properly given under section 15.

PART III
ON THE STARTING DATE

8 Applications which fall

(1) Proceedings in respect of an application which is made to the Court under any of the provisions mentioned in sub-paragraph (2), but which is not determined before the starting date, cease on that date.

(2) The provisions are—

(a) sections 2(2), 35(3), 37(1) and 40(1) of the RTPA and paragraph 5 of Schedule 4 to that Act;

(b) section 4(1) of the RTPA so far as the application relates to an order under section 2(2) of that Act; and

(c) section 25(2) of the RPA.

(3) The power of the Court to make an order for costs in relation to any proceedings is not affected by anything in this paragraph or by the repeals made by section 1.

9 Orders and approvals which fall

(1) An order in force immediately before the starting date under—

(a) section 2(2), 29(1), 30(1), 33(4), 35(3) or 37(1) of the RTPA; or

(b) section 25(2) of the RPA,

ceases to have effect on that date.

(2) An approval in force immediately before the starting date under section 32 of the RTPA ceases to have effect on that date.

PART IV
ON AND AFTER THE STARTING DATE

CHAPTER I. GENERAL

10 Duty of Director to maintain register etc

(1) This paragraph applies even though the relevant provisions of the RTPA are repealed by this Act.

(2) The Director is to continue on and after the starting date to be under the duty imposed by section 1(2)(a) of the RTPA to maintain a register in respect of agreements—

(a) particulars of which are, on the starting date, entered or filed on the register;

(b) which fall within sub-paragraph (4);

(c) which immediately before the starting date are the subject of proceedings under the RTPA which do not cease on that date by virtue of this Schedule; or

(d) in relation to which a court gives directions to the Director after the starting date in the course of proceedings in which a question arises as to whether an agreement was, before that date—

(i) one to which the RTPA applied;

(ii) subject to registration under that Act;

(iii) a non-notifiable agreement for the purposes of that Act.

(3) The Director is to continue on and after the starting date to be under the duties imposed by section 1(2)(a) and (b) of the RTPA of compiling a register of agreements and entering or filing certain particulars in the register, but only in respect of agreements of a kind referred to in paragraph (b), (c) or (d) of sub-paragraph (2).

(4) An agreement falls within this sub-paragraph if—

    (a) it is subject to registration under the RTPA but—

        (i) is not a non-notifiable agreement within the meaning of section 27A of the RTPA, or

        (ii) is not one to which paragraph 5 applies;

    (b) particulars of the agreement have been provided to the Director before the starting date; and

    (c) as at the starting date no entry or filing has been made in the register in respect of the agreement.

(5) Sections 23 and 27 of the RTPA are to apply after the starting date in respect of the register subject to such modifications, if any, as may be prescribed.

(6) In sub-paragraph (2)(d) 'court' means—

    (a) the High Court;

    (b) the Court of Appeal;

    (c) the Court of Session;

    (d) the High Court or Court of Appeal in Northern Ireland; or

    (e) the House of Lords.

11 RTPA section 3 applications

(1) Even though section 3 of the RTPA is repealed by this Act, its provisions (and so far as necessary that Act) are to continue to apply, with such modifications (if any) as may be prescribed—

    (a) in relation to a continuing application under that section; or

    (b) so as to allow an application to be made under that section on or after the starting date in respect of a continuing application under section 1(3) of the RTPA.

(2) 'Continuing application' means an application made, but not determined, before the starting date.

12 RTPA section 26 applications

(1) Even though section 26 of the RTPA is repealed by this Act, its provisions (and so far as necessary that Act) are to continue to apply, with such modifications (if any) as may be prescribed, in relation to an application which is made under that section, but not determined, before the starting date.

(2) If an application under section 26 is determined on or after the starting date, this Schedule has effect in relation to the agreement concerned as if the application had been determined immediately before that date.

13 Right to bring civil proceedings

(1) Even though section 35 of the RTPA is repealed by this Act, its provisions (and so far as necessary that Act) are to continue to apply in respect of a person who, immediately before the starting date, has a right by virtue of section 27ZA or 35(2) of that Act to bring civil proceedings in respect of an agreement (but only so far as that right relates to any period before the starting date or, where there are continuing proceedings, the determination of the proceedings).

(2) Even though section 25 of the RPA is repealed by this Act, the provisions of that section (and so far as necessary that Act) are to continue to apply in respect of a person who, immediately before the starting date, has a right by virtue of subsection (3) of that section to bring civil proceedings (but only so far as that right relates to any period before the starting date or, where there are continuing proceedings, the determination of the proceedings).

Chapter II. Continuing Proceedings

14 The general rule

(1) The Chapter I prohibition does not apply to an agreement at any time when the agreement is the subject of continuing proceedings under the RTPA.

(2) The Chapter I prohibition does not apply to an agreement relating to goods which are the subject of

continuing proceedings under section 16 or 17 of the RPA to the extent to which the agreement consists of exempt provisions.

(3) In sub-paragraph (2) 'exempt provisions' means those provisions of the agreement which would, disregarding section 14 of the RPA, be—

    (a) void as a result of section 9(1) of the RPA; or

    (b) unlawful as a result of section 9(2) or II of the RPA.

(4) If the Chapter I prohibition does not apply to an agreement because of this paragraph, the provisions of, or made under, the RTPA or the RPA are to continue to have effect in relation to the agreement.

(5) The repeals made by section 1 do not affect—

    (a) continuing proceedings; or

    (b) proceedings of the kind referred to in paragraph 11 or 12 of this Schedule which are continuing after the starting date.

15 Meaning of 'continuing proceedings'

(1) For the purposes of this Schedule 'continuing proceedings' means proceedings in respect of an application made to the Court under the RTPA or the RPA, but not determined, before the starting date.

(2) But proceedings under section 3 or 26 of the RTPA to which paragraph 11 or 12 applies are not continuing proceedings.

(3) The question whether (for the purposes of Part III, or this Part, of this Schedule) an application has been determined is to be decided in accordance with sub-paragraphs (4) and (5).

(4) If an appeal against the decision on the application is brought, the application is not determined until—

    (a) the appeal is disposed of or withdrawn; or

    (b) if as a result of the appeal the case is referred back to the Court—

        (i) the expiry of the period within which an appeal ('the further appeal') in respect of the Court's decision on that reference could have been brought had this Act not been passed; or

        (ii) if later, the date on which the further appeal is disposed of or withdrawn.

(5) Otherwise, the application is not determined until the expiry of the period within which any party to the application would have been able to bring an appeal against the decision on the application had this Act not been passed.

16 RTPA section 4 proceedings

Proceedings on an application for an order under section 4 of the RTPA are also continuing proceedings if—

(a) leave to make the application is applied for before the starting date but the proceedings in respect of that application for leave are not determined before that date; or

(b) leave to make an application for an order under that section is granted before the starting date but the application itself is not made before that date.

17 RPA section 16 or 17 proceedings

Proceedings on an application for an order under section 16 or 17 of the RPA are also continuing proceedings if—

(a) leave to make the application is applied for before the starting date but the proceedings in respect of that application for leave are not determined before that date; or

(b) leave to make an application for an order under section 16 or 17 of the RPA is granted before the starting date, but the application itself is not made before that date.

18 Continuing proceedings which are discontinued

(1) On an application made jointly to the Court by all the parties to any continuing proceedings, the Court must, if it is satisfied that the parties wish it to do so, discontinue the proceedings.

(2) If, on an application under sub-paragraph (1) or for any other reason, the Court orders the

proceedings to be discontinued, this Schedule has effect (subject to paragraphs 21 and 22) from the date on which the proceedings are discontinued as if they had never been instituted.

Chapter III. The Transitional Period

19 The general rule

(1) Except where this Chapter or Chapter IV provides otherwise, there is a transitional period, beginning on the starting date and lasting for one year, for any agreement made before the starting date.

(2) The Chapter I prohibition does not apply to an agreement to the extent to which there is a transitional period for the agreement.

(3) The Secretary of State may by regulations provide for sections 13 to 16 and Schedule 5 to apply with such modifications (if any) as may be specified in the regulations, in respect of applications to the Director about agreements for which there is a transitional period.

20 Cases for which there is no transitional period

(1) There is no transitional period for an agreement to the extent to which, immediately before the starting date, it is—
  (a) void under section 2(1) or 35(1)(a) of the RTPA;
  (b) the subject of an order under section 2(2) or 35(3) of the RTPA; or
  (c) unlawful under section 1, 2 or 11 of the RPA or void under section 9 of that Act.

(2) There is no transitional period for an agreement to the extent to which, before the starting date, a person has acted unlawfully for the purposes of section 27ZA(2) or (3) of the RTPA in respect of the agreement.

(3) There is no transitional period for an agreement to which paragraph 25(4) applies.

(4) There is no transitional period for—
  (a) an agreement in respect of which there are continuing proceedings, or
  (b) an agreement relating to goods in respect of which there are continuing proceedings,
  to the extent to which the agreement is, when the proceedings are determined, void or unlawful.

21 Continuing proceedings under the RTPA

In the case of an agreement which is the subject of continuing proceedings under the RTPA, the transitional period begins—
(a) if the proceedings are discontinued, on the date of discontinuance;
(b) otherwise, when the proceedings are determined.

22 Continuing proceedings under the RPA

(1) In the case of an agreement relating to goods which are the subject of continuing proceedings under the RPA, the transitional period for the exempt provisions of the agreement begins—
  (a) if the proceedings are discontinued, on the date of discontinuance;
  (b) otherwise, when the proceedings are determined.

(2) In sub-paragraph (1) 'exempt provisions' has the meaning given by paragraph 14(3).

23 Provisions not contrary to public interest

(1) To the extent to which an agreement contains provisions which, immediately before the starting date, are provisions which the Court has found not to be contrary to the public interest, the transitional period lasts for five years.

(2) Sub-paragraph (1) is subject to paragraph 20(4).

(3) To the extent to which an agreement which on the starting date is the subject of continuing proceedings is, when the proceedings are determined, found by the Court not to be contrary to the public interest, the transitional period lasts for five years.

24 Goods

(1) In the case of an agreement relating to goods which, immediately before the starting date, are exempt under section 14 of the RPA, there is a transitional period for the agreement to the extent to which it consists of exempt provisions.

(2) Sub-paragraph (1) is subject to paragraph 20(4).

(3) In the case of an agreement relating to goods—
   (a) which on the starting date are the subject of continuing proceedings, and
   (b) which, when the proceedings are determined, are found to be exempt under section 14 of the RPA,
   there is a transitional period for the agreement, to the extent to which it consists of exempt provisions.

(4) In each case, the transitional period lasts for five years.

(5) In sub-paragraphs (1) and (3) 'exempt provisions' means those provisions of the agreement which would, disregarding section 14 of the RPA, be—
   (a) void as a result of section 9(1) of the RPA; or
   (b) unlawful as a result of section 9(2) or 11 of the RPA.

25 Transitional period for certain agreements

(1) This paragraph applies to agreements—
   (a) which are subject to registration under the RTPA but which—
       (i) are not non-notifiable agreements within the meaning of section 27A of the RTPA, or
       (ii) are not agreements to which paragraph 5 applies; and
   (b) in respect of which the time for furnishing relevant particulars as required by or under the RTPA expires on or after the starting date.

(2) 'Relevant particulars' means—
   (a) particulars which are required to be furnished by virtue of section 24 of the RTPA; or
   (b) particulars of any variation of an agreement which are required to be furnished by virtue of sections 24 and 27 of the RTPA.

(3) There is a transitional period of one year for an agreement to which this paragraph applies if—
   (a) relevant particulars are furnished before the starting date; and
   (b) no person has acted unlawfully (for the purposes of section 27ZA(2) or (3) of the RTPA) in respect of the agreement.

(4) If relevant particulars are not furnished by the starting date, section 35(1)(a) of the RTPA does not apply in relation to the agreement (unless sub-paragraph (5) applies).

(5) This sub-paragraph applies if a person falling within section 27ZA(2) or (3) of the RTPA has acted unlawfully for the purposes of those subsections in respect of the agreement.

26 Special cases

(1) In the case of an agreement in respect of which—
   (a) a direction under section 127(2) of the Financial Services Act 1986 ('the 1986 Act') is in force immediately before the starting date, or
   (b) a direction under section 194A(3) of the Broadcasting Act 1990 ('the 1990 Act') is in force immediately before the starting date,
   the transitional period lasts for five years.

(2) To the extent to which an agreement is the subject of a declaration—
   (a) made by the Treasury under section 127(3) of the 1986 Act, and
   (b) in force immediately before the starting date,
   the transitional period lasts for five years.

(3) Sub-paragraphs (1) and (2) do not affect the power of—
   (a) the Treasury to make a declaration under section 127(2) of the 1986 Act (as amended by Schedule 2 to this Act),

(b) the Secretary of State to make a declaration under section 194A of the 1990 Act (as amended by Schedule 2 to this Act),

in respect of an agreement for which there is a transitional period.

Chapter IV. The Utilities

27 General

In this Chapter 'the relevant period' means the period beginning with the starting date and ending immediately before the fifth anniversary of that date.

28 Electricity

(1) For an agreement to which, immediately before the starting date, the RTPA does not apply by virtue of a section 100 order, there is a transitional period—
   (a) beginning on the starting date; and
   (b) ending at the end of the relevant period.

(2) For an agreement which is made at any time after the starting date and to which, had the RTPA not been repealed, that Act would not at the time at which the agreement is made have applied by virtue of a section 100 order, there is a transitional period—
   (a) beginning on the date on which the agreement is made; and
   (b) ending at the end of the relevant period.

(3) For an agreement (whether made before or after the starting date) which, during the relevant period, is varied at any time in such a way that it becomes an agreement which, had the RTPA not been repealed, would at that time have been one to which that Act did not apply by virtue of a section 100 order, there is a transitional period—
   (a) beginning on the date on which the variation is made; and
   (b) ending at the end of the relevant period.

(4) If an agreement for which there is a transitional period as a result of sub-paragraph (1), (2) or (3) is varied during the relevant period, the transitional period for the agreement continues if, had the RTPA not been repealed, the agreement would have continued to be one to which that Act did not apply by virtue of a section 100 order.

(5) But if an agreement for which there is a transitional period as a result of sub-paragraph (1), (2) or (3) ceases to be one to which, had it not been repealed, the RTPA would not have applied by virtue of a section 100 order, the transitional period ends on the date on which the agreement so ceases.

(6) Sub-paragraph (3) is subject to paragraph 20.

(7) In this paragraph and paragraph 29—
   'section 100 order' means an order made under section 100 of the Electricity Act 1989; and
   expressions which are also used in Part I of the Electricity Act 1989 have the same meaning as in that Part.

29 Electricity: power to make transitional orders

(1) There is a transitional period for an agreement (whether made before or after the starting date) relating to the generation, transmission or supply of electricity which—
   (a) is specified, or is of a description specified, in an order ('a transitional order') made by the Secretary of State (whether before or after the making of the agreement but before the end of the relevant period); and
   (b) satisfies such conditions as may be specified in the order.

(2) A transitional order may make provision as to when the transitional period in respect of such an agreement is to start or to be deemed to have started.

(3) The transitional period for such an agreement ends at the end of the relevant period.

(4) But if the agreement—
   (a) ceases to be one to which a transitional order applies, or

(b) ceases to satisfy one or more of the conditions specified in the transitional order,

the transitional period ends on the date on which the agreement so ceases.

(5) Before making a transitional order, the Secretary of State must consult the Gas and Electricity Markets Authority and the Director.

(6) The conditions specified in a transitional order may include conditions which refer any matter to the Secretary of State for determination after such consultation as may be so specified.

(7) In the application of this paragraph to Northern Ireland, the reference in sub-paragraph (5) to the Gas and Electricity Markets Authority is to be read as a reference to the Director General of Electricity Supply for Northern Ireland.

30 Gas

(1) For an agreement to which, immediately before the starting date, the RTPA does not apply by virtue of section 62 or a section 62 order, there is a transitional period—
   (a) beginning on the starting date; and
   (b) ending at the end of the relevant period.

(2) For an agreement which is made at any time after the starting date and to which, had the RTPA not been repealed, that Act would not at the time at which the agreement is made have applied by virtue of section 62 or a section 62 order, there is a transitional period—
   (a) beginning on the date on which the agreement is made; and
   (b) ending at the end of the relevant period.

(3) For an agreement (whether made before or after the starting date) which, during the relevant period, is varied at any time in such a way that it becomes an agreement which, had the RTPA not been repealed, would at that time have been one to which that Act did not apply by virtue of section 62 or a section 62 order, there is a transitional period—
   (a) beginning on the date on which the variation is made; and
   (b) ending at the end of the relevant period.

(4) If an agreement for which there is a transitional period as a result of sub-paragraph (1), (2) or (3) is varied during the relevant period, the transitional period for the agreement continues if, had the RTPA not been repealed, the agreement would have continued to be one to which that Act did not apply by virtue of section 62 or a section 62 order.

(5) But if an agreement for which there is a transitional period as a result of sub-paragraph (1), (2) or (3) ceases to be one to which, had it not been repealed, the RTPA would not have applied by virtue of section 62 or a section 62 order, the transitional period ends on the date on which the agreement so ceases.

(6) Sub-paragraph (3) also applies in relation to a modification which is treated as an agreement made on or after 28th November 1985 by virtue of section 62(4).

(7) Sub-paragraph (3) is subject to paragraph 20.

(8) In this paragraph and paragraph 31—

'section 62' means section 62 of the Gas Act 1986;

'section 62 order' means an order made under section 62.

31 Gas: power to make transitional orders

(1) There is a transitional period for an agreement of a description falling within section 62(2)(a) and (b) or section 62(2A)(a) and (b) which—
   (a) is specified, or is of a description specified, in an order ('a transitional order') made by the Secretary of State (whether before or after the making of the agreement but before the end of the relevant period); and
   (b) satisfies such conditions as may be specified in the order.

(2) A transitional order may make provision as to when the transitional period in respect of such an agreement is to start or to be deemed to have started.

(3) The transitional period for such an agreement ends at the end of the relevant period.

(4) But if the agreement—

(a) ceases to be one to which a transitional order applies, or

(b) ceases to satisfy one or more of the conditions specified in the transitional order,

the transitional period ends on the date when the agreement so ceases.

(5) Before making a transitional order, the Secretary of State must consult the Gas and Electricity Markets Authority and the Director.

(6) The conditions specified in a transitional order may include—

(a) conditions which are to be satisfied in relation to a time before the coming into force of this paragraph;

(b) conditions which refer any matter (which may be the general question whether the Chapter I prohibition should apply to a particular agreement) to the Secretary of State, the Director or the Gas and Electricity Markets Authority for determination after such consultation as may be so specified.

32 Gas: Northern Ireland

(1) For an agreement to which, immediately before the starting date, the RTPA does not apply by virtue of an Article 41 order, there is a transitional period—

(a) beginning on the starting date; and

(b) ending at the end of the relevant period.

(2) For an agreement which is made at any time after the starting date and to which, had the RTPA not been repealed, that Act would not at the time at which the agreement is made have applied by virtue of an Article 41 order, there is a transitional period—

(a) beginning on the date on which the agreement is made; and

(b) ending at the end of the relevant period.

(3) For an agreement (whether made before or after the starting date) which, during the relevant period, is varied at any time in such a way that it becomes an agreement which, had the RTPA not been repealed, would at that time have been one to which that Act did not apply by virtue of an Article 41 order, there is a transitional period—

(a) beginning on the date on which the variation is made; and

(b) ending at the end of the relevant period.

(4) If an agreement for which there is a transitional period as a result of sub-paragraph (1), (2) or (3) is varied during the relevant period, the transitional period for the agreement continues if, had the RTPA not been repealed, the agreement would have continued to be one to which that Act did not apply by virtue of an Article 41 order.

(5) But if an agreement for which there is a transitional period as a result of sub-paragraph (1), (2) or (3) ceases to be one to which, had it not been repealed, the RTPA would not have applied by virtue of an Article 41 order, the transitional period ends on the date on which the agreement so ceases.

(6) Sub-paragraph (3) is subject to paragraph 20.

(7) In this paragraph and paragraph 33—

'Article 41 order' means an order under Article 41 of the Gas (Northern Ireland) Order 1996;

'Department' means the Department of Economic Development.

33 Gas: Northern Ireland—power to make transitional orders

(1) There is a transitional period for an agreement of a description falling within Article 41(1) which—

(a) is specified, or is of a description specified, in an order ('a transitional order') made by the Department (whether before or after the making of the agreement but before the end of the relevant period); and

(b) satisfies such conditions as may be specified in the order.

(2) A transitional order may make provision as to when the transitional period in respect of such an agreement is to start or to be deemed to have started.

(3) The transitional period for such an agreement ends at the end of the relevant period.

(4) But if the agreement—

(a) ceases to be one to which a transitional order applies, or

(b) ceases to satisfy one or more of the conditions specified in the transitional order,

the transitional period ends on the date when the agreement so ceases.

(5) Before making a transitional order, the Department must consult the Director General of Gas for Northern Ireland and the Director.

(6) The conditions specified in a transitional order may include conditions which refer any matter (which may be the general question whether the Chapter I prohibition should apply to a particular agreement) to the Department for determination after such consultation as may be so specified.

34 Railways

(1) In this paragraph—

'section 131' means section 131 of the Railways Act 1993 ('the 1993 Act');

'section 131 agreement' means an agreement—

    (a) to which the RTPA does not apply immediately before the starting date by virtue of section 131(1); or

    (b) in respect of which a direction under section 131(3) is in force immediately before that date;

'non-exempt agreement' means an agreement relating to the provision of railway services (whether made before or after the starting date) which is not a section 131 agreement; and

'railway services' has the meaning given by section 82 of the 1993 Act.

(2) For a section 131 agreement there is a transitional period of five years.

(3) There is a transitional period for a non-exempt agreement to the extent to which the agreement is at any time before the end of the relevant period required or approved—

    (a) by the Secretary of State or the Office of Rail Regulation in pursuance of any function assigned or transferred to him under or by virtue of any provision of the 1993 Act;

    (b) by or under any agreement the making of which is required or approved by the Secretary of State or the Office of Rail Regulation in the exercise of any such function; or

    (c) by or under a licence granted under Part I of the 1993 Act.

(4) The transitional period conferred by sub-paragraph (3)—

    (a) is to be taken to have begun on the starting date; and

    (b) ends at the end of the relevant period.

(5) Sub-paragraph (3) is subject to paragraph 20.

(6) Any variation of a section 131 agreement on or after the starting date is to be treated, for the purposes of this paragraph, as a separate non-exempt agreement.

35 The regulators

(1) Subject to sub-paragraph (3), each of the regulators may exercise, in respect of sectoral matters and concurrently with the Director, the functions of the Director under paragraph 3, 7, 19(3), 36, 37, 38 or 39.

(2) In sub-paragraph (1) 'sectoral matters' means—

    (a) . . .

    (b) in the case of the Gas and Electricity Markets Authority, the matters referred to in section 36A(3) and (4) of the Gas Act 1986;

    (c) in the case of the Gas and Electricity Markets Authority, the matters referred to in section 43(3) of the Electricity Act 1989;

    (d) in the case of the Director General of Electricity Supply for Northern Ireland, the matters referred to in Article 46(3) of the Electricity (Northern Ireland) Order 1992;

    (e) in the case of the Water Services Regulation Authority, the matters referred to in section 31(3) of the Water Industry Act 1991;

    (f) in the case of the Office of Rail Regulation, the matters referred to in section 67(3) of the Railways Act 1993;

    (g) in the case of the Director General of Gas for Northern Ireland, the matters referred to in Article 23(3) of the Gas (Northern Ireland) Order 1996;

(h) in the case of the Civil Aviation Authority, the supply of air traffic services within the meaning given by section 98 of the Transport Act 2000.

(3) The power to give directions in paragraph 7(2) is exercisable by the Director only but if the Director is preparing directions which relate to a matter in respect of which a regulator exercises concurrent jurisdiction, he must consult that regulator.

(4) Consultations conducted by the Director before the enactment date, with a view to preparing directions which have effect on or after that date, are to be taken to satisfy sub-paragraph (3).

(5) References to enactments in sub-paragraph (2) are to the enactments as amended by or under this Act.

Chapter V. Extending the Transitional Period

36

(1) A party to an agreement for which there is a transitional period may apply to the Director, not less than three months before the end of the period, for the period to be extended.

(2) The Director may (on his own initiative or on an application under sub-paragraph (1))—
   (a) extend a one-year transitional period by not more than twelve months;
   (b) extend a transitional period of any period other than one year by not more than six months.

(3) An application under sub-paragraph (1) must—
   (a) be in such form as may be specified; and
   (b) include such documents and information as may be specified.

(4) If the Director extends the transitional period under this paragraph, he must give notice in such form, and to such persons, as may be specified.

(5) The Director may not extend a transitional period more than once.

(6) In this paragraph—
   'person' has the same meaning as in Part I; and
   'specified' means specified in rules made by the Director under section 51.

Chapter VI. Terminating the Transitional Period

37 General

(1) Subject to sub-paragraph (2), the Director may by a direction in writing terminate the transitional period for an agreement, but only in accordance with paragraph 38.

(2) The Director may not terminate the transitional period, nor exercise any of the powers in paragraph 38, in respect of an agreement which is excluded from the Chapter I prohibition by virtue of any of the provisions of Part I of this Act other than paragraph 1 of Schedule 1 or paragraph 2 or 9 of Schedule 3 or the Competition Act 1998 (Land and Vertical Agreements Exclusion) Order 2000.

38 Circumstances in which the Director may terminate the transitional period

(1) If the Director is considering whether to give a direction under paragraph 37 ('a direction'), he may in writing require any party to the agreement concerned to give him such information in connection with that agreement as he may require.

(2) If at the end of such period as may be specified in rules made under section 51, a person has failed, without reasonable excuse, to comply with a requirement imposed under sub-paragraph (1), the Director may give a direction.

(3) The Director may also give a direction if he considers—
   (a) that the agreement would, but for the transitional period or a relevant exclusion, infringe the Chapter I prohibition; and
   (b) that he would not be likely to grant the agreement an unconditional individual exemption.

(4) For the purposes of sub-paragraph (3) an individual exemption is unconditional if no conditions or obligations are imposed in respect of it under section 4(3)(a).

(5) In this paragraph—

'person' has the same meaning as in Part I;

'relevant exclusion' means an exclusion under paragraph 1 of Schedule 1 or paragraph 2 or 9 of Schedule 3 or the Competition Act 1998 (Land and Vertical Agreements Exclusion) Order 2000.

39 Procedural requirements on giving a paragraph 37 direction

(1) The Director must specify in a direction under paragraph 37 ('a direction') the date on which it is to have effect (which must not be less than 28 days after the direction is given).

(2) Copies of the direction must be given to—

    (a) each of the parties concerned, and

    (b) the Secretary of State,

not less than 28 days before the date on which the direction is to have effect.

(3) In relation to an agreement to which a direction applies, the transitional period (if it has not already ended) ends on the date specified in the direction unless, before that date, the direction is revoked by the Director or the Secretary of State.

(4) If a direction is revoked, the Director may give a further direction in respect of the same agreement only if he is satisfied that there has been a material change of circumstance since the revocation.

(5) If, as a result of paragraph 24(1) or (3), there is a transitional period in respect of provisions of an agreement relating to goods—

    (a) which immediately before the starting date are exempt under section 14 of the RPA, or

    (b) which, when continuing proceedings are determined, are found to be exempt under section 14 of the RPA,

the period is not affected by paragraph 37 or 38.

PART V

THE FAIR TRADING ACT 1973

40 References to the Monopolies and Mergers Commission

(1) If, on the date on which the repeal by this Act of a provision mentioned in sub-paragraph (2) comes into force, the Monopolies and Mergers Commission has not completed a reference which was made to it before that date, continued consideration of the reference may include consideration of a question which could not have been considered if the provision had not been repealed.

(2) The provisions are—

    (a) sections 10(2), 54(5) and 78(3) and paragraph 3(1) and (2) of Schedule 8 to the Fair Trading Act 1973 (c 41);

    (b) section 11(8)(b) of the Competition Act 1980 (c 21);

    (c) section 14(2) of the Telecommunications Act 1984 (c 12);

    (d) section 45(3) of the Airports Act 1986 (c 31);

    (e) section 25(2) of the Gas Act 1986 (c 44);

    (f) section 13(2) of the Electricity Act 1989 (c 29);

    (g) section 15(2) of the Water Industry Act 1991 (c 56);

    (h) article 16(2) of the Electricity (Northern Ireland) Order 1992;

    (i) section 14(2) of the Railways Act 1993 (c 43);

    (j) article 36(3) of the Airports (Northern Ireland) Order 1994;

    (k) article 16(2) of the Gas (Northern Ireland) Order 1996.

41 Orders under Schedule 8

(1) In this paragraph—

'the 1973 Act' means the Fair Trading Act 1973;

'agreement' means an agreement entered into before the date on which the repeal of the limiting provisions comes into force;

'the order' means an order under section 56 or 73 of the 1973 Act;

715

'the limiting provisions' means sub-paragraph (1) or (2) of paragraph 3 of Schedule 8 to the 1973 Act (limit on power to make orders under paragraph 1 or 2 of that Schedule) and includes any provision of the order included because of either of those sub-paragraphs; and

'transitional period' means the period which—

> (a) begins on the day on which the repeal of the limiting provisions comes into force; and
> (b) ends on the first anniversary of the starting date.

(2) Sub-paragraph (3) applies to any agreement to the extent to which it would have been unlawful (in accordance with the provisions of the order) but for the limiting provisions.

(3) As from the end of the transitional period, the order is to have effect in relation to the agreement as if the limiting provisions had never had effect.

42 Part III of the Act

(1) The repeals made by section 1 do not affect any proceedings in respect of an application which is made to the Court under Part III of the Fair Trading Act 1973, but is not determined, before the starting date.

(2) The question whether (for the purposes of sub-paragraph (1)) an application has been determined is to be decided in accordance with sub-paragraphs (3) and (4).

(3) If an appeal against the decision on the application is brought, the application is not determined until—

> (a) the appeal is disposed of or withdrawn; or
> (b) if as a result of the appeal the case is referred back to the Court—
>> (i) the expiry of the period within which an appeal ('the further appeal') in respect of the Court's decision on that reference could have been brought had this Act not been passed; or
>> (ii) if later, the date on which the further appeal is disposed of or withdrawn.

(4) Otherwise, the application is not determined until the expiry of the period within which any party to the application would have been able to bring an appeal against the decision on the application had this Act not been passed.

(5) Any amendment made by Schedule 12 to this Act which substitutes references to a relevant Court for references to the Court is not to affect proceedings of the kind referred to in sub-paragraph (1).

PART VI

THE COMPETITION ACT 1980

43 Undertakings

(1) Subject to sub-paragraph (2), an undertaking accepted by the Director under section 4 or 9 of the Competition Act 1980 ceases to have effect on the coming into force of the repeal by this Act of that section.

(2) If the undertaking relates to an agreement which on the starting date is the subject of continuing proceedings, the undertaking continues to have effect for the purposes of section 29 of the Competition Act 1980 until the proceedings are determined.

44 Application of sections 25 and 26

The repeals made by section 1 do not affect—

(a) the operation of section 25 of the Competition Act 1980 in relation to an application under section 1(3) of the RTPA which is made before the starting date;

(b) an application under section 26 of the Competition Act 1980 which is made before the starting date.

Part VII
Miscellaneous

45 Disclosure of information

(1) Section 55 of this Act applies in relation to information which, immediately before the starting date, is subject to section 41 of the RTPA as it applies in relation to information obtained under or as a result of Part I.

(2) But section 55 does not apply to any disclosure of information of the kind referred to in sub-paragraph (1) if the disclosure is made—
   (a) for the purpose of facilitating the performance of functions of a designated person under the Control of Misleading Advertisements Regulations 1988; or
   (b) for the purposes of any proceedings before the Court or of any other legal proceedings under the RTPA or the Fair Trading Act 1973 or the Control of Misleading Advertisements Regulations 1988.

(3) Section 56 applies in relation to information of the kind referred to in sub-paragraph (1) if particulars containing the information have been entered or filed on the special section of the register maintained by the Director under, or as a result of, section 27 of the RTPA or paragraph 10 of this Schedule.

(4) Section 55 has effect, in relation to the matters as to which section 41(2) of the RTPA had effect, as if it contained a provision similar to section 41(2).

46 The Court

If it appears to the Lord Chancellor that a person who ceases to be a non-judicial member of the Court as a result of this Act should receive compensation for loss of office, he may pay to him out of moneys provided by Parliament such sum as he may with the approval of the Treasury determine.

Schedule 14
Repeals and Revocations

Section 74(3)

Part I
Repeals

Chapter	Short title	Extent of repeal
1973 c 41.	The Fair Trading Act 1973.	Section 4. Section 10(2). Section 45. Section 54(5). Section 78(3). In section 81(1), in the words before paragraph (a), from 'and the Commission' to 'of this Act)'; in paragraph (b), 'or the Commission, as the case may be' and 'or of the Commission'; in subsection (2), 'or the Commission' and 'or of the Commission' and in subsection (3), from 'and, in the case,' to '85 of this Act', and 'or the Commission, as the case may be,'. In section 83, in subsection (1) 'Subject to subsection (1A) below' and subsection (1A).

Continued overleaf

Chapter	Short title	Extent of repeal
		In section 135(1), in the words before paragraph (a) and in paragraph (b), 'or the Commission', and paragraph (a).
		Schedule 3.
		In Schedule 8, paragraph 3(1) and (2).
1976 c 33.	The Restrictive Practices Court Act 1976.	The whole Act.
1976 c 34.	The Restrictive Trade Practices Act 1976.	The whole Act.
1976 c 53.	The Resale Prices Act 1976.	The whole Act.
1976 c 76.	The Energy Act 1976.	Section 5.
1977 c 19.	The Restrictive Trade Practices Act 1977.	The whole Act.
1977 c 37.	The Patents Act 1977.	Sections 44 and 45.
1979 c 38.	The Estate Agents Act 1979.	In section 10(3), 'or the Restrictive Trade Practices Act 1976.'
1980 c 21.	The Competition Act 1980.	Sections 2 to 10.
		In section 11(8), paragraph (b) and the 'and' immediately before it.
		In section 13(1), from 'but the giving' to the end.
		In section 15, subsections (2)(b), (3) and (4).
		Section 16(3).
		In section 17, '8(1)' in subsections (1) and (3) to (5) and in subsection (2) '8(1) or'.
		In section 19(3), paragraph (d).
		In section 19(5)(a), 'or in anything published under section 4(2)(a) above'.
		Section 22.
		Sections 25 to 30.
		In section 31, subsection (2) and '10' in subsection (3).
		Section 33(3) and (4).
1984 c 12.	The Telecommunications Act 1984.	Section 14(2).
		In section 16(5), the 'or' immediately after paragraph (a).
		In section 50(4), paragraph (c) and the 'and' immediately after it.
		In section 50(5), 'or (3)'.
		In section 50(7), 'or the 1980 Act'.
		In section 95(1), 'or section 10(2)(a) of the 1980 Act'.
		In section 95(2), paragraph (c) and the 'or' immediately before it.
		In section 95(3), 'or the 1980 Act'.
		In section 101(3), paragraphs (d) and (e).
1986 c 31.	The Airports Act 1986.	Section 45(3).
		In section 54(1), 'or section 10(2)(a) of the 1980 Act'.
		In section 54(3), paragraph (c) and the 'or' immediately before it.
		In section 54(4), 'or the 1980 Act'.
		In section 56(a)(ii), 'or the 1980 Act'.
1986 c 44.	The Gas Act 1986.	Section 25(2).
		In section 27(1), 'or section 10(2)(a) of the Competition Act 1980'.

		In section 27(3)(a), from 'or' to 'competition reference'.
		In section 27(6), 'or the said Act of 1980'.
		In section 28(5), the 'or' immediately after paragraph (aa).
		In section 36A(5), paragraph (d) and the 'and' immediately before it.
		In section 36A(6), 'or (3)'.
		In section 36A(8), 'or under the 1980 Act'.
		In section 36A(9), 'or the 1980 Act'.
		In section 42(3), paragraphs (e) and (f).
1986 c 60.	The Financial Services Act 1986.	Section 126.
1987 c 43.	The Consumer Protection Act 1987.	In section 38(3), paragraphs (e) and (f).
1987 c 53.	The Channel Tunnel Act 1987.	In section 33(2), paragraph (c) and the 'and' immediately before it.
		In section 33(5), paragraphs (b) and (c).
1988 c 54.	The Road Traffic (Consequential Provisions) Act 1988.	In Schedule 3, paragraph 19.
1989 c 15.	The Water Act 1989.	In section 174(3), paragraphs (d) and (e).
1989 c 29.	The Electricity Act 1989.	Section 13(2).
		In section 15(1), paragraph (b) and the 'or' immediately before it.
		In section 15(2), paragraph (c) and the 'or' immediately before it.
		In section 15(3), 'or the 1980 Act'.
		In section 25(5), the 'or' immediately after paragraph (b).
		In section 43(4), paragraph (c) and the 'and' immediately after it.
		In section 43(5), 'or (3)'.
		In section 43(7), 'or the 1980 Act'.
		In section 57(3), paragraphs (d) and (e).
1989 c 40.	The Companies Act 1989.	In Schedule 20, paragraphs 21 to 24.
1990 c 42.	The Broadcasting Act 1990.	In section 193(2), paragraph (c) and the 'and' immediately before it.
		In section 193(4), 'or the Competition Act 1980'.
1991 c 56.	The Water Industry Act 1991.	In section 12(5), 'or the 1980 Act'.
		Section 15(2).
		In section 17(1), paragraph (b) and the 'or' immediately before it.
		In section 17(2), paragraph (c) and the 'or' immediately before it.
		In section 17(4), 'or the 1980 Act'.
		In section 31(4), paragraph (c) and the 'and' immediately before it.
		In section 31(5), 'or in subsection (3) above'.
		In section 31(6), 'or in subsection (3) above'.
		In section 31(7), 'or (3)'.
		In section 31(9), 'or the 1980 Act'.
		In Part II of Schedule 15, the entries relating to the Restrictive Trade Practices Act 1976 and the Resale Prices Act 1976.
1991 c 57.	The Water Resources Act 1991.	In Part II of Schedule 24, the entries relating to the Restrictive Trade Practices Act 1976 and the Resale Prices Act 1976.

Continued overleaf

Chapter	Short title	Extent of repeal
1993 c 21.	The Osteopaths Act 1993.	In section 33(4), paragraph (b) and the 'or' immediately before it. In section 33(5), 'or section 10 of the Act of 1980'.
1993 c 43.	The Railways Act 1993.	Section 14(2). In section 16(1), paragraph (b) and the 'or' immediately before it. In section 16(2), paragraph (c) and the 'or' immediately before it. In section 16(5), 'or the 1980 Act'. In section 67(4), paragraph (c) and the 'and' immediately after it. In section 67(6)(a), 'or (3)'. In section 67(9), 'or under the 1980 Act'. Section 131. In section 145(3), paragraphs (d) and (e).
1994 c 17.	The Chiropractors Act 1994.	In section 33(4), paragraph (b) and the 'or' immediately before it. In section 33(5), 'or section 10 of the Act of 1980'.
1994 c 21.	The Coal Industry Act 1994.	In section 59(4), paragraphs (e) and (f).
1994 c 40.	The Deregulation and Contracting Out Act 1994.	Sections 10 and 11. In section 12, subsections (1) to (6). In Schedule 4, paragraph 1. In Schedule 11, in paragraph 4, sub-paragraphs (3) to (6).
1996 c 55.	The Broadcasting Act 1996.	Section 77(2).

PART II
REVOCATIONS

Reference	Title	Extent of revocation
SI 1981/1675 (NI 26).	The Magistrates' Courts (Northern Ireland) Order 1981.	In Schedule 6, paragraphs 42 and 43.
SI 1982/1080 (NI 12).	The Agricultural Marketing (Northern Ireland) Order 1982.	In Schedule 8, the entry relating to paragraph 16(2) of Schedule 3 to the Fair Trading Act 1973 and in the entry relating to the Competition Act 1980, 'and 15(3)'.
SI 1986/1035 (NI 9).	The Companies Consolidation (Consequential Provisions) (Northern Ireland) Order 1986.	In Part II of Schedule 1, the entries relating to the Restrictive Trade Practices Act 1976 and the Resale Prices Act 1976.
SI 1992/231 (NI 1).	The Electricity (Northern Ireland) Order 1992.	Article 16(2). In Article 18— (a) in paragraph (1), sub-paragraph (b) and the 'or' immediately before it; (b) in paragraph (2), sub-paragraph (c) and the 'or' immediately before it; (c) in paragraph (3) 'or the 1980 Act'. In Article 28(5), the 'or' immediately after sub-paragraph (b).

In Article 46—
(a) in paragraph (4), sub-paragraph (c) and the 'and' immediately after it;
(b) in paragraph (5), 'or (3)';
(c) in paragraph (7), 'or the 1980 Act'.
Article 61(3)(f) and (g).
In Schedule 12, paragraph 16.

SI 1994/426 (NI 1).	The Airports (Northern Ireland) Order 1994.	Article 36(3).

In Article 45—
(a) in paragraph (1), 'or section 10(2)(a) of the 1980 Act';
(b) in paragraph (3), sub-paragraph (c) and the 'or' immediately before it;
(c) in paragraph (4), 'or the 1980 Act'.

In Article 47(a)(ii), 'or the 1980 Act'.
In Schedule 9, paragraph 5.

SI 1996/275 (NI 2).	The Gas (Northern Ireland) Order 1996.	Article 16(2).

In Article 18—
(a) in paragraph (1), sub-paragraph (b) and the 'or' immediately before it;
(b) in paragraph (3), sub-paragraph (c) and the 'or' immediately before it;
(c) in paragraph (5), 'or the 1980 Act'.

In Article 19(5), the 'or' immediately after sub-paragraph (b).

In Article 23—
(a) in paragraph (4), sub-paragraph (d) and the 'and' immediately before it;
(b) in paragraph (5), 'or (3)';
(c) in paragraph (7), 'or under the 1980 Act';
(d) in paragraph (8), 'or the 1980 Act'.

Article 44(4)(f) and (g).

The Competition Act 1998 (Office of Fair Trading's Rules) Order 2004

SI 2004/2751

Made	20th October 2004
Laid before Parliament	25th October 2004
Coming into force	17th November 2004

Whereas the Office of Fair Trading ('the OFT') has, in exercise of the powers conferred upon it by sections 51(1) and 75A(1) of and Schedule 9 to the Competition Act 1998 ('the Act')[1], made rules about procedural and other matters in connection with the carrying into effect of the provisions of Parts 1, 2 and 2A of the Act ('the Rules');

And whereas the OFT has, in accordance with sections 51(3) and 75A(2) of the Act, consulted such persons as it considered appropriate in preparing the Rules;

And whereas the OFT has, in accordance with section 51(4) of the Act, also consulted the regulators mentioned in section 54(1) of the Act ('the regulators') in preparing the Rules insofar as they relate to matters in respect of which the regulators exercise concurrent jurisdiction;

And whereas following its consultation the OFT has, in accordance with sections 51(5) and 75A(3) of the Act, submitted the Rules to the Secretary of State for approval;

Now, therefore, the Secretary of State, in exercise of the powers conferred upon her by sections 51(5) and (6), 71, and 75A(3) and (4) of the Act, hereby makes the following Order:

Citation and Commencement

1. This Order may be cited as the Competition Act 1998 (Office of Fair Trading's Rules) Order 2004 and shall come into force on 17th November 2004.

Approval of the Office of Fair Trading's Rules

2. The Secretary of State hereby approves without modification the Rules made by the OFT which are set out in the Schedule hereto.

Revocation

3. The Competition Act 1998 (Director's rules) Order 2000[2] is hereby revoked.

Gerry Sutcliffe,
Parliamentary Under Secretary of State for Employment
Relations, Postal Services and Consumers,
Department of Trade and Industry

20th October 2004

---

[1] 1998 c.41.   [2] S.I. 2000/293.

SCHEDULE   Article 2

OFFICE OF FAIR TRADING'S RULES

The OFT, in exercise of the powers conferred upon it by sections 51(1) and 75A(1) of and Schedule 9 to the Competition Act 1998[3], hereby makes the following Rules:

Interpretation

1.—(1) In these Rules—

'the Act' means the Competition Act 1998;

'confidential information' means—

(a) commercial information whose disclosure the OFT or a regulator thinks might significantly harm the legitimate business interests of the undertaking to which it relates, or

(b) information relating to the private affairs of an individual whose disclosure the OFT or a regulator thinks might significantly harm the individual's interests, or

(c) information whose disclosure the OFT or a regulator thinks is contrary to the public interest;

'infringement decision' means a decision that one or more of the Chapter I prohibition, the Chapter II prohibition, the prohibition in Article 81(1) and the prohibition in Article 82 has been infringed;

'internal document' means—

(a) a document produced by, or exchanged between, any of the OFT, a regulator or another public authority, or

(b) a document produced by any person from time to time retained under a contract for services by any of the OFT, a regulator or another public authority in connection with such a contract;

'public authority' includes—

(a) in the United Kingdom, a court or tribunal and any person exercising functions of a public nature, and

(b) in any country or territory outside the United Kingdom, a court or tribunal and any person or body which appears to the OFT or a regulator to be exercising functions of a public nature;

'writing' includes text that is—

(a) transmitted by electronic means,

(b) received in legible form, and

(c) capable of being used for subsequent reference.

(2) In these Rules, any reference to:

(a) a numbered rule is to the rule in these Rules which is so numbered;

(b) a numbered paragraph or sub-paragraph is to the paragraph or sub-paragraph which is so numbered in the rule where the reference occurs.

(3) Except where these Rules otherwise provide, expressions used in the Act which are also used in these Rules have the same meaning in these Rules as they have in section 59 of the Act.

(4) Except in this rule and rule 20, any reference in these Rules to the OFT means the OFT or a regulator.

Application of the Rules

2.—(1) Subject to paragraphs (2) and (3), these Rules apply when the OFT takes investigation or enforcement action under the Act in relation to any one or more of the Chapter I prohibition, the Chapter II prohibition, the prohibition in Article 81(1) and the prohibition in Article 82.

(2) Rule 11 on the cancellation etc. of an individual exemption, rule 12 on the cancellation etc. of a parallel exemption, rule 14 on the withdrawal of an exclusion, rule 15 on the termination of the

---

[3] 1998 c. 41.

transitional period and rule 16 on the application for extension of the transitional period apply only when the OFT takes investigation or enforcement action in relation to the Chapter I prohibition or the Chapter II prohibition.

(3) Rule 13 on the withdrawal of the benefit of a regulation of the Commission pursuant to Article 29(2) of the EC Competition Regulation applies only when the OFT takes investigation or enforcement action in relation to the prohibition in Article 81(1).

Legal advice during investigations and inspections

3.—(1) An officer shall grant a request of the occupier of premises entered by the officer to allow a reasonable time for the occupier's legal adviser to arrive at the premises before the investigation continues, if the officer considers it reasonable in the circumstances to do so and if the officer is satisfied that such conditions as he considers it appropriate to impose in granting the occupier's request are, or will be, complied with.

(2) For the purposes of paragraph (1), 'a reasonable time' means such period of time as the officer considers is reasonable in the circumstances.

(3) A person required by the OFT under section 26(6)(a)(ii) or (b) or section 65E(6)(a)(ii) or (b) of the Act to provide an explanation of a document in person may be accompanied by a legal adviser.

(4) In this rule, 'officer' means an investigating officer within the meaning of section 27(1) or 65F(1) of the Act or a named officer of the OFT authorised by a warrant issued under section 28, 28A, 65G or 65H of the Act.

Statement of objections

4.—(1) If the OFT proposes to make an infringement decision—

    (a) the OFT shall give notice of this stating which one or more of the Chapter I prohibition, the Chapter II prohibition, the prohibition in Article 81(1) and the prohibition in Article 82 the OFT considers has been infringed; and

    (b) the provisions of rule 5 shall apply.

(2) Subject to rules 17 and 18, the notice referred to in paragraph (1)(a) must be given to each person who the OFT considers is a party to the agreement, or is engaged in conduct, which the OFT considers infringes one or more of the prohibitions mentioned in paragraph (1)(a).

Notices, access to file and representations

5.—(1) In this rule—

    (a) 'notice' means a notice that the OFT is required to give under rule 4, 12(3) or 13(1); and

    (b) 'relevant person' means a person to whom notice is required to be given under the rules mentioned in sub-paragraph (a).

(2) A notice shall state:

    (a) the facts on which the OFT relies, the objections raised by the OFT, the action the OFT proposes and its reasons for the proposed action;

    (b) the period within which a relevant person may make written representations to the OFT identifying the information contained in the notice which that relevant person considers the OFT should treat as confidential information and explaining why he considers the OFT should treat such information as confidential information; and

    (c) the period within which a relevant person may make written representations to the OFT on the matters referred to in the notice.

(3) The OFT shall give a relevant person a reasonable opportunity to inspect the documents in the OFT's file that relate to the matters referred to in a notice given to that relevant person, except that the OFT may withhold any document—

    (a) to the extent that it contains confidential information; or

    (b) which is an internal document.

(4) Where, in written representations on the matters referred to in a notice given to a relevant person, that relevant person states that he wishes to make oral representations to the OFT on such matters, the OFT shall give that relevant person a reasonable opportunity to make such oral representations.

(5) Where, upon the expiry of the period mentioned in paragraph (2)(c), no written representations on the matters referred to in a notice given to a relevant person have been made by that relevant person, the OFT may proceed with the case in the absence of such representations.

(6) Where the OFT has given a relevant person a reasonable opportunity to make oral representations under paragraph (4) but no oral representations have been made, the OFT may proceed with the case in the absence of such representations.

(7) Paragraph (2)(b) is not to be construed as restricting the application of rule 6(1) and (2).

Confidential information

6.—(1) Where a person who has supplied information to the OFT has made representations to the OFT identifying such information as being information that the OFT should treat as confidential information and the OFT proposes to disclose such information under these Rules, the OFT shall take all reasonable steps to—

(a) inform that person of the OFT's proposed action; and

(b) give that person a reasonable opportunity to make representations to the OFT on the OFT's proposed action.

(2) The OFT may at any time request a person who has supplied information to the OFT to make written representations to the OFT in respect of the information supplied—

(a) identifying the information which that person considers the OFT should treat as confidential information; or

(b) explaining why that person considers the OFT should treat the information as confidential information; or

(c) on the matters referred to in both sub-paragraphs (a) and (b).

(3) If a person who has supplied information to the OFT makes written representations to the OFT in respect of the information supplied identifying the information which that person considers the OFT should treat as confidential information or explaining why he considers the OFT should treat the information as confidential information, whether or not such representations are made under this rule, the OFT may seek from that person such further clarification as the OFT considers is needed.

(4) If the OFT requests any person to make representations or to give further clarification under this rule, the OFT may specify the period within which such representations or further clarification should be made.

(5) For the purposes of this rule, where, in the OFT's opinion, information supplied to the OFT by any person relates to or originates from another person, that other person may be treated as a person who has supplied the information to the OFT.

Notice of decision

7.—(1) Where the OFT has made an infringement decision, it shall without delay—

(a) subject to rules 17 and 18, give notice of the infringement decision to each person who the OFT considers is or was a party to the agreement, or is or was engaged in conduct, stating the facts on which the OFT bases the infringement decision and the OFT's reasons for making the infringement decision; and

(b) publish the infringement decision.

(2) Where the OFT has made a decision that there are no grounds for action in respect of—

(a) an agreement either because the conditions of the Chapter I prohibition are not met or because the agreement is excluded from the Chapter I prohibition or satisfies the conditions in section 9(1) of the Act; or

(b) an agreement either because the conditions of the prohibition in Article 81(1) are not met or because the agreement satisfies the conditions of Article 81(3); or

(c) conduct because the conditions of the Chapter II prohibition or the prohibition in Article 82 are not met;

the OFT shall without delay, subject to rules 17 and 18, give notice of the decision, to any person whom it has undertaken to inform of the decision and to any person in respect of whom the OFT or an officer has exercised any of the powers of investigation in the Act, stating the facts on which the OFT bases the decision and the OFT's reasons for making the decision.

(3) Where the OFT is required to give notice of a decision under paragraph (2), it may publish the decision.

(4) In this rule, 'officer' has the same meaning as in rule 3.

Directions and penalties

8.—(1) Where the OFT gives a direction to a person under section 32 or 33 of the Act, it shall at the same time inform that person in writing of the facts on which it bases the direction and its reasons for giving the direction.

(2) Where the OFT requires an undertaking to pay a penalty under section 36 of the Act, it shall at the same time inform that undertaking in writing of the facts on which it bases the penalty and its reasons for requiring that undertaking to pay the penalty.

(3) The OFT shall publish directions given under section 32 or 33 of the Act.

(4) The OFT shall publish penalties imposed under section 36 of the Act.

Interim measures

9.—(1) Subject to paragraph (2), if the OFT proposes to give a direction under section 35 of the Act, it shall give each person to whom it proposes to give the direction a reasonable opportunity to inspect the documents in the OFT's file relating to the proposed direction.

(2) The OFT may withhold any document—

(a) to the extent that it contains confidential information; or

(b) which is an internal document.

(3) When giving a person an opportunity to make representations under section 35(3)(b) of the Act, the OFT shall specify the period within which that person may make such representations.

(4) Where the OFT gives a direction to a person under section 35 of the Act, it shall at the same time inform that person in writing of the facts on which it bases the direction and its reasons for giving the direction, and it shall publish the direction.

Election to apply a relevant prohibition to a case

10.—(1) The OFT may, at any time prior to making an infringement decision, elect to apply to a case one or more of the Chapter I prohibition, the Chapter II prohibition, the prohibition in Article 81(1) and the prohibition in Article 82 (whether or not any such election has previously been made by the OFT in that case).

(2) If the OFT proposes—

(a) to make a decision that one or both of the prohibition in Article 81(1) and the prohibition in Article 82 has been infringed, but in any notice given under rule 4 the OFT has stated that it considers that only one or both of the Chapter I prohibition and the Chapter II prohibition has been infringed; or

(b) to make a decision that one or both of the Chapter I prohibition and the Chapter II prohibition has been infringed but in any notice given under rule 4 the OFT has stated that it considers that only one or both of the prohibition in Article 81(1) and the prohibition in Article 82 has been infringed,

the provisions of rules 4 and 5 shall apply to the extent that they have not already been applied.

(3) In paragraph (2), 'any notice given under rule 4' means any notice given under rule 4 that has not been superseded by a subsequent notice given under rule 4.

Cancellation etc. of an individual exemption

11.—(1) If the OFT proposes to take any of the steps mentioned in section 5(1) of the Act[4], it shall consult the public, the applicant and, subject to rules 17 and 18, the other parties to the agreement.

(2) If the OFT decides to take any of the steps mentioned in section 5(1) of the Act, it shall—

    (a) give notice of its decision to do so—

        (i) to the applicant; and

        (ii) subject to rules 17 and 18, to the other parties to the agreement, stating the facts on which the OFT bases the decision and the OFT's reasons for the decision; and

    (b) publish the decision.

(3) In this rule—

    (a) 'applicant' means the person who applied for the exemption; and

    (b) 'the other parties to the agreement' means those persons who the applicant identified in his application as being the other parties to the agreement to which the exemption relates.

Cancellation etc. of a parallel exemption

12.—(1) The circumstances in which the OFT may exercise the powers in section 10(5)(a), 10(5)(c) and 10(5)(d) of the Act are where it finds that an agreement which benefits from a parallel exemption nevertheless has effects in the United Kingdom, or a part of it, which are incompatible with the conditions laid down in section 9(1) of the Act.

(2) The circumstances in which the OFT may exercise the powers in section 10(5)(b) of the Act are where, having previously exercised the powers in section 10(5)(a) or 10(5)(c) of the Act in respect of an agreement, the OFT finds that—

    (a) as a result of a material change in circumstances since the exercise of those powers, any condition or obligation it has imposed in exercise of those powers is no longer necessary to ensure that the effects of the agreement in the United Kingdom, or a part of it, are compatible with the conditions laid down in section 9(1) of the Act; or

    (b) as a result of a material change in circumstances since the exercise of those powers, or as a result of information supplied in response to a notice given under paragraph (3) being incomplete, false or misleading in a material particular, the agreement has effects in the United Kingdom, or a part of it, which are incompatible with the conditions laid down in section 9(1) of the Act.

(3) Subject to rules 17 and 18, if (other than in the circumstances referred to in paragraph (2)(a)) the OFT proposes to exercise any of the powers in section 10(5) of the Act it shall give notice to each person who it considers is a party to the agreement and the provisions of rule 5 shall apply.

(4) Subject to rules 17 and 18, if the OFT proposes to exercise any of the powers in section 10(5)(b) of the Act in the circumstances referred to in paragraph (2)(a) it shall consult each person who it considers is a party to the agreement.

(5) If the OFT proposes to exercise any of the powers in section 10(5) of the Act it may consult the public.

(6) If the OFT has made a decision in exercise of any of its powers in section 10(5) of the Act it shall—

    (a) subject to rules 17 and 18, give notice of the decision to each person who the OFT considers is a party to the agreement, stating the facts on which it bases the decision and its reasons for the decision; and

    (b) publish the decision.

---

[4] Section 5 of the Act has been repealed by article 4 of the Competition Act 1998 and Other Enactments (Amendment) Regulations 2004 (S.I. 2004/1261) with effect from 1st May 2004 but by virtue of article 6(3) of those Regulations it will continue in effect while any individual exemption has effect.

Withdrawal of the benefit of a Commission Regulation pursuant to Article 29(2) of the EC Competition Regulation

13.—(1) Subject to rules 17 and 18, if the OFT proposes, in any particular case, to withdraw in the whole or any part of the United Kingdom the benefit of a Commission Regulation pursuant to Article 29(2) of the EC Competition Regulation, it shall give notice to each person who the OFT considers is a party to the agreement, and the provisions of rule 5 shall apply.

(2) If the OFT proposes to exercise its powers under Article 29(2) of the EC Competition Regulation it may consult the public.

(3) If the OFT has made a decision withdrawing in the whole or any part of the United Kingdom the benefit of a Commission Regulation pursuant to Article 29(2) of the EC Competition Regulation it shall—

(a) subject to rules 17 and 18, give notice of the decision to each person who the OFT considers is a party to the agreement, stating the facts on which it bases the decision and its reasons for the decision; and

(b) publish the decision.

Withdrawal of an exclusion

14.—(1) Subject to rules 17 and 18, if the OFT proposes to give a direction under paragraph 4 of Schedule 1 to the Act or paragraph 2 or 9 of Schedule 3 to the Act, or in accordance with an order made under section 50 of the Act, to the effect that an exclusion made by a provision specified in paragraph (2) does not apply to an agreement, it shall consult each person who it considers is a party to the agreement.

(2) The provisions specified for the purposes of paragraph (1) are—

(a) paragraph 1 of Schedule 1 to the Act (enterprises ceasing to be distinct: the Chapter I prohibition);

(b) paragraph 2(1) of Schedule 3 to the Act (section 21(2) agreements);

(c) paragraph 9(1) of Schedule 3 to the Act (agricultural products); and

(d) an order made under section 50 of the Act (vertical agreements and land agreements).

(3) The period specified for the purposes of paragraph 4(4) of Schedule 1 to the Act and paragraphs 2(6) and 9(6) of Schedule 3 to the Act is ten working days starting with the date the notice is given.

(4) If the OFT has given a direction referred to in paragraph (1), it shall publish the direction.

Termination of the transitional period

15.—(1) Subject to rules 17 and 18, if the OFT proposes to give a direction under paragraph 37 of Schedule 13 to the Act terminating the transitional period for an agreement, it shall consult each person who it considers is a party to the agreement.

(2) For the purposes of paragraph 38(2) of Schedule 13 to the Act, the period is ten working days starting with the date on which the person in question receives the requirement to give information to the OFT.

(3) The OFT shall publish a direction given under paragraph 37 of Schedule 13 to the Act after the date on which the direction takes effect; if the direction is revoked, it shall publish a notice of that fact.

Application for extension of the transitional period

16.—(1) An application under paragraph 36 of Schedule 13 to the Act for the extension of the transitional period shall—

(a) be submitted in writing to the OFT;

(b) comply with paragraph (2); and

(c) include the documents specified in paragraph (3).

(2) An application submitted under paragraph (1) shall—

(a) be signed by the applicant or by a duly authorised representative of the applicant;

(b) contain an explanation of—

       (i)   the purpose of the agreement;

       (ii) the basis for the applicant's belief that there is a transitional period;

       (iii) the need for an extension of the transitional period; and

       (iv) the likely application of the Chapter I prohibition to the agreement at the end of the transitional period, including any grounds for believing that the agreement is likely to satisfy the conditions in section 9(1) of the Act; and

   (c) specify the length of the transitional period, the date of its expiry and the period of extension applied for.

(3)   The documents specified for the purposes of paragraph (1) are the following—

   (a) two copies of the application;

   (b) three copies of the agreement, each copy certified by the applicant to be a true copy of the original; and

   (c) where the application is signed by a representative of an applicant, proof in writing of that representative's authority to act on that applicant's behalf.

(4)   If the OFT—

   (a) refuses an application submitted to it under paragraph (1);

   (b) grants the application; or

   (c) grants an extension which is of shorter duration than that applied for,

   it shall give notice of its decision to the applicant not less than one month before the date of expiry of the transitional period, specifying, if appropriate, the period of extension granted.

(5)   Subject to rules 17 and 18, if the OFT extends the transitional period on its own initiative, it shall give notice of its decision to each person who it considers is a party to the agreement, specifying the period of extension granted.

(6)   Where a joint application is submitted, the application shall be submitted by or on behalf of all of the applicants, and a joint representative may be appointed as authorised to act on behalf of some or all of the applicants for the purposes of this rule.

(7)   Subject to paragraph (8), the application shall be correct and complete.

(8)   The OFT may, by giving notice to the applicant, dispense with the obligation to submit any particular information, including any supporting document required by this rule for an application under paragraph 36 of Schedule 13 to the Act, if it considers that such information or document is unnecessary for the examination of the application.

(9)   Where the applicant knows of material changes in the information contained in the application he shall without delay communicate those changes to the OFT.

(10) An application is made on the date on which the application is received by the OFT.

(11) The OFT shall acknowledge receipt of an application by giving notice to the applicant without delay.

(12) If the OFT extends the transitional period, it shall publish a notice of that fact, specifying the period of extension granted.

Associations of undertakings

17.—(1) Where a rule requires the OFT to give notice of any matter to an association of undertakings the OFT shall give such notice to the director, secretary, manager or other similar officer of the association on its behalf.

(2) Where a rule requires the OFT to give notice of any matter to each of more than twenty members of an association of undertakings, the OFT may, instead of giving such notice to any such member, give such notice to the director, secretary, manager or other similar officer of the association on that member's behalf.

Time limits and giving notice

18.—(1) Where—

   (a) the OFT has taken all reasonable steps to give notice to the persons mentioned in paragraph (3) but has been unable to give such notice or in the OFT's opinion there is doubt that it has been able to give such notice; or

   (b) there are no reasonable steps that can be taken by the OFT to give notice to the persons mentioned in paragraph (3),

the OFT may, instead, take all the steps mentioned in paragraph (2).

(2) The steps mentioned for the purposes of paragraph (1) are the following—

   (a) publish a summary of the notice by means of entry in the register maintained by the OFT under rule 20; and

   (b) cause a reference to the summary of the notice published in that register to be published in—

      (i) the London, Edinburgh and Belfast Gazettes;

      (ii) at least one national daily newspaper; and

      (iii) if there is in circulation an appropriate trade journal which is published at intervals not exceeding one month, in such trade journal.

(3) The persons mentioned for the purposes of paragraph (1) are the following—

   (a) a person under rule 4, 7(1)(a), 7(2), 11(2)(a)(ii), 12(3), 12(6)(a), 13(1), 13(3)(a), 16(5) or 19(8)(b);

   (b) the other parties to the agreement in order to consult them under rule 11(1); or

   (c) a person in order to consult him under rule 12(4), 14(1), 15(1) or 19(7).

(4) Except where paragraph (1) is applied, where these Rules allow or require notice to be given to a person, such notice shall be treated as having been given on the date on which that person receives it.

(5) Where paragraph (1) is applied, the notice shall be treated as having been given on the date of its publication in accordance with paragraph (2).

(6) Any notice given under these Rules must be in writing.

(7) Where the time prescribed by these Rules for doing any act expires on a day which is not a working day, the act is in time if done at or before 5.30 p.m. on the next following working day.

(8) Where an act done in accordance with these Rules is done on a day which is not a working day, or after 5.30 p.m. on a working day, the act shall be treated as done on the next following working day.

(9) In this rule, 'the other parties to the agreement' has the same meaning as in rule 11.

Third party appeals

19.—(1) An application in relation to a decision made before 20 June 2003 under section 47(1) of the Act, asking the OFT to withdraw or vary a decision shall—

   (a) be submitted in writing to the OFT within one month from the date of publication of that decision;

   (b) comply with paragraph (2); and

   (c) include the documents specified in paragraph (3).

(2) An application submitted under paragraph (1) shall be signed by the applicant, or by a duly authorised representative of the applicant, and shall state the applicant's reasons—

   (a) for considering that he has a sufficient interest in the decision referred to in paragraph (1); or

   (b) where he claims to represent persons who have sufficient interest in that decision—

      (i) for claiming that he represents those persons; and

      (ii) for claiming that those persons have a sufficient interest in that decision.

(3) The documents specified for the purposes of paragraph (1) are the following—

   (a) three copies of the application; and

   (b) where the application is signed by a representative of an applicant, proof in writing of that representative's authority to act on that applicant's behalf.

(4) An application is made on the date on which it is received by the OFT.

(5) The OFT shall acknowledge receipt of an application by giving notice to the applicant without delay.

(6) Where the applicant knows of any material change in the information contained in the application he shall without delay communicate that change to the OFT.

(7) Subject to rules 17 and 18, if the OFT proposes to grant the application it shall consult all persons whom it was required to notify of the decision referred to in paragraph (1).

(8) If the OFT grants the application, it shall give notice of its decision—
  (a) to the applicant; and
  (b) subject to rules 17 and 18, to all persons whom it was required to notify of the decision referred to in paragraph (1),
  stating in the notice the facts on which it bases the decision and its reasons for the decision.

(9) Where the OFT is required to give notice of a decision under paragraph (8) it shall publish the decision.

(10) For the purpose of this rule, the reference in paragraph (1) to section 47(1) of the Act is to be construed as a reference to section 47(1) of the Act as preserved by article 5 of the Enterprise Act 2002 (Commencement No 3, Transitional and Transitory Provisions and Savings) Order 2003[5].

Public register

20.—(1) The OFT shall maintain a register in which there shall be entered—
  (a) all decisions that the OFT is required to publish under these Rules;
  (b) all decisions published under rule 7(3);
  (c) all directions that the OFT is required to publish under these Rules;
  (d) all notices that the OFT is required to publish under rules 15(3), 16(12) and 21(2);
  (e) all summaries of notices published under rule 18(2)(a); and
  (f) all penalties that the OFT is required to publish under rule 8(4).

(2) The register shall be open to public inspection—
  (a) at the OFT's offices at Fleetbank House, 2–6 Salisbury Square, London EC4Y 8JX, or such other address as may be notified, between 10.00 a.m. and 4.30 p.m. on every working day; and
  (b) on the OFT's website at http://www.oft.gov.uk.

Consultation

21.—(1) Where the OFT, if it proposes to take action, is required to consult a person under these Rules, it shall—
  (a) subject to rules 17 and 18, give notice to that person; and
  (b) state in that notice the action the OFT proposes to take, its reasons for proposing such action and the period within which that person may make written representations to the OFT on these matters.

(2) Where the OFT, if it proposes to take action—
  (a) is required to consult the public under these Rules; or
  (b) proposes to consult the public in exercise of its discretion to do so under these Rules,
  it shall publish a notice stating the action it proposes to take, its reasons for proposing such action and the period within which written representations may be made to the OFT on these matters.

EXPLANATORY NOTE

(This note is not part of the Order)

By article 2 of this Order, the Secretary of State approves the Rules made by the Office of Fair Trading ('the OFT') pursuant to section 51 of the Competition Act 1998 (c. 41) ('the Act').

Article 3 of this Order revokes the Competition Act 1998 (Director's rules) Order 2000 (S.I. 2000/293) ('the 2000 Order'). By the 2000 Order, the Secretary of State approved the rules made by the Director General of Fair Trading (the exercise of whose functions were transferred to the OFT by section 2(1) of

---

[5] S.I. 2003/1397.

the Enterprise Act 2002 (c. 40)) pursuant to sections 51 and 53 of the Act. The rules approved by the 2000 Order are superseded by the Rules approved by this Order as a consequence of amendments made to the Act by the Competition Act 1998 and Other Enactments (Amendment) Regulations 2004 (S.I. 2004/1261).

The Schedule to this Order specifies the Rules that are approved by article 2.

A regulatory impact assessment has been prepared. A copy can be obtained from the Modernisation Project Team, Consumer and Competition Policy Directorate, Bay 606, 1 Victoria Street, London SW1H 0ET, telephone 020 7215 2174. A copy can also be found at http://www.dti.gov.uk/ccp/consultations.htm.

List of European Competition Network Members

Member State	National authorities that have signed the Statement regarding the Commission Notice on Cooperation within the Network of Competition Authorities[1]	Is there a leniency programme[2] in operation?	
Austria	Bundeswettbewerbsbehörde (Austrian National Competition Authority)	No	*A leniency programme is expected to be introduced by 1 January 2006 when the Cartel Act 2005 (Kartellgesetz 2005) comes into force.[3]*
Belgium	Conseil de la Concurrence/ Raad voor de Mededinging (Competition Council) Corps des rapporteurs / Korps Verslaggevers Ministre de l'Economie, de l'Energie, du Commerce extérieur et de la Politique Scientifique / Minister van Economie, Energie, Buitenlandse Handel en Wetenschapsbeleid (Belgian Federal Minister of Economy, Energy, Foreign Trade and Science Policy)	Yes	Adopted 2004
Cyprus	Επιτροπής Προστασίας Ανταγωνισμού (Ε.Π.Α.) (Commission for the Protection of Competition)	Yes	Adopted 2003
Czech Republic	Úřad pro ochranu hospodářské soutěže (Office for the Protection of Competition)	Yes	Adopted 2002
Denmark	Konkurrencestyrelsen (Danish Competition Authority)	No	
Estonia	Konkurentsiamet (Estonian Competition Board)	Yes	Adopted 2004
Finland	Kilpailuvirasto (Finnish Competition Authority)	Yes	Adopted 2004
France	Conseil de la concurrence (Competition Council) Ministère de l'Economie (Ministry of Economy)	Yes	Adopted 2001
Germany	Bundeskartellamt (Federal Cartel Office)	Yes	Adopted 2001

Greece	ΕΠΙΤΠΟΠΗ ΑΝΤΑΓΩΝΙΣΜΟΥ (Hellenic Competition Commission)	Yes	Adopted 2005
Hungary	Gazdasági Versenyhivatal (GVH—Hungarian Office of Economic Competition)	Yes	Adopted 2004
Ireland	The Competition Authority	Yes	Adopted 2001
Italy	Autorità Garante della Concorrenza e del Mercato (AGCM) (Italian Antitrust Authority) Banca d'Italia	No	
Latvia	Konkurences padome (Competition Council Republic of Latvia)	Yes	Adopted 2003
Lithuania	Lietuvos Respublikos konkurencijos taryba (Competition Council of the Republic of Lithuania)	Yes	Adopted 1999
Luxembourg	Ministère de l'Economie et du Commerce extérieur (Ministry of Economics and Foreign Trade)	Yes	Adopted 2004
Malta	Ministry of Finance and Economic Affairs	No	
Poland	Urząd Ochrony Konkurencji I Konsumentów (Office for Competition and Consumer Protection)	Yes	Adopted 2001 Reviewed 2004
Portugal	National Competition Authority	No	
Slovakia	Protimonopolný úrad Slovenskej republiky (AMO—Antimonopoly Office of the Slovak Republic)	Yes	Adopted 2002
Slovenia	Urad RS za varstvo konkurence (Competition Protection Office)	No	
Spain	Ministerio de Economía Servicio de Defensa de la Competencia (SDC)	No	*On 20 January 2005, the Spanish Government published a White Paper[4] on reform of competition which proposes, inter alia, the introduction of a leniency programme for whistleblowers in Spanish cartels. It is intended that this will be along the lines of the European Commission's Notice.*
Sweden	Konkurrensverket (Swedish Competition Authority)	Yes	Adopted 2002
The Netherlands	Nederlandse Mededingingsautoriteit (NMa—Netherlands Competition Authority)	Yes	Adopted 2002

United Kingdom	Office of Fair Trading (OFT) Office of Communications (Ofcom) Gas and Electricity Markets Authority (Ofgem) Northern Ireland Authority for Energy Regulation (Ofreg NI) Office of Water Services (Ofwat) Office of Rail Regulation (ORR) The Civil Aviation Authority (CAA)	Yes	Corporate Leniency adopted 2000 Reviewed 2004 (Individual Immunity adopted 2003)

---

[1] ibid, paras 42 and 72. See also <http://europa.eu.int/comm/competition/antitrust/legislation/list_of_authorities_joint_statement.pdf>.

[2] The term 'leniency programme' is used to describe 'all programmes (including the Commission's programme) which offer either full immunity or a significant reduction in penalties which would otherwise have been imposed on a participant in a cartel, in exchange for the freely volunteered disclosure of information on the cartel which satisfies specific criteria prior to or during the investigative stage of the case. The term does not cover reductions in the penalty granted for other reasons.' (ibid, fn 14). See also <http://europa.eu.int/comm/competition/antitrust/legislation/authorities_with_leniency_programme.pdf>.

[3] R Roniger and A Ablasser-Neuhuber, 'Austria—a brief summary of the main rules and principles of Austrian competition law', *The European Antitrust Review 2005* (Global Competition Review special report, S 99).

[4] *Libro Blanco para la reforma del sistema español de Defensa de la Competencia.* The White Book is available at <http://documentacion.meh.es/doc/C18/C6/SEE/Presentación%20Libro%20Blanco%20SEE%20final%2020%20enero%2005.pdf >.